FAIRNESS AND EFFECTIVENESS IN
POLICING
THE EVIDENCE

Committee to Review Research on Police Policy and Practices
Wesley Skogan and Kathleen Frydl, editors

Committee on Law and Justice
Division of Behavioral and Social Sciences and Education

NATIONAL RESEARCH COUNCIL
OF THE NATIONAL ACADEMIES

THE NATIONAL ACADEMIES PRESS
Washington, D.C.
www.nap.edu

THE NATIONAL ACADEMIES PRESS • 500 Fifth Street, N.W. • Washington, DC 20001

NOTICE: The project that is the subject of this report was approved by the Governing Board of the National Research Council, whose members are drawn from the councils of the National Academy of Sciences, the National Academy of Engineering, and the Institute of Medicine. The members of the committee responsible for the report were chosen for their special competences and with regard for appropriate balance.

This project was supported by Grant No. 2000-IJ-CX-0014 awarded by the National Institute of Justice, Office of Justice Programs, U.S. Department of Justice. Points of view in this document are those of the author and do not necessarily represent the official position or policies of the U.S. Department of Justice.

Library of Congress Cataloging-in-Publication Data

Fairness and effectiveness in policing : the evidence / Wesley Skogan and Kathleen Frydl, editors.
    p. cm.
Includes bibliographical references and index.
  ISBN 0-309-08433-4 (hc) — ISBN 0-309-52557-8 (PDF)
  1. Police—United States. 2. Police administration—United States. 3. Law enforcement—United States. I. Skogan, Wesley G. II. Frydl, Kathleen.
  HV8138.F35 2003
  363.2'3'0973—dc21

                                    2003014400

Additional copies of this report are available from the National Academies Press, 500 Fifth Street, N.W., Lockbox 285, Washington, DC 20055; (800) 624-6242 or (202) 334-3313 (in the Washington metropolitan area); Internet, http://www.nap.edu.

Printed in the United States of America.

Suggested citation: National Research Council. (2004). *Fairness and Effectiveness in Policing: The Evidence*. Committee to Review Research on Police Policy and Practices. Wesley Skogan and Kathleen Frydl, editors. Committee on Law and Justice, Division of Behavioral and Social Sciences and Education. Washington, DC: The National Academies Press.

THE NATIONAL ACADEMIES
Advisers to the Nation on Science, Engineering, and Medicine

The **National Academy of Sciences** is a private, nonprofit, self-perpetuating society of distinguished scholars engaged in scientific and engineering research, dedicated to the furtherance of science and technology and to their use for the general welfare. Upon the authority of the charter granted to it by the Congress in 1863, the Academy has a mandate that requires it to advise the federal government on scientific and technical matters. Dr. Bruce M. Alberts is president of the National Academy of Sciences.

The **National Academy of Engineering** was established in 1964, under the charter of the National Academy of Sciences, as a parallel organization of outstanding engineers. It is autonomous in its administration and in the selection of its members, sharing with the National Academy of Sciences the responsibility for advising the federal government. The National Academy of Engineering also sponsors engineering programs aimed at meeting national needs, encourages education and research, and recognizes the superior achievements of engineers. Dr. Wm. A. Wulf is president of the National Academy of Engineering.

The **Institute of Medicine** was established in 1970 by the National Academy of Sciences to secure the services of eminent members of appropriate professions in the examination of policy matters pertaining to the health of the public. The Institute acts under the responsibility given to the National Academy of Sciences by its congressional charter to be an adviser to the federal government and, upon its own initiative, to identify issues of medical care, research, and education. Dr. Harvey V. Fineberg is president of the Institute of Medicine.

The **National Research Council** was organized by the National Academy of Sciences in 1916 to associate the broad community of science and technology with the Academy's purposes of furthering knowledge and advising the federal government. Functioning in accordance with general policies determined by the Academy, the Council has become the principal operating agency of both the National Academy of Sciences and the National Academy of Engineering in providing services to the government, the public, and the scientific and engineering communities. The Council is administered jointly by both Academies and the Institute of Medicine. Dr. Bruce M. Alberts and Dr. Wm. A. Wulf are chair and vice chair, respectively, of the National Research Council.

www.national-academies.org

Preface

When the Committee to Review Research on Police Policies and Practice began its deliberations, crime rates were plunging, and the role of the police in this startling phenomenon was the subject of vigorous public debate. At the same time, well-known police scandals linked to major U.S. police departments—including the Diallo and Louima cases in New York City and the Rampart scandal in Los Angeles—were shaping the nation's dialogue on policing. By the time the committee concluded its deliberations, terrorists had attacked the nation.

The committee attended to its charge to review policing research with these developments in mind. Consistent with the policies of the National Research Council (NRC), the committee confined its attention to social science research. When evidence was lacking concerning critical questions—such as solutions to the challenges facing local law enforcement agencies in responding to terrorism—the committee includes them in its recommendations for future research. On other subjects, such as the police role in preventing crime, there is a substantial body of cumulative research, and the committee makes recommendations for police policy and practice, as well as for research. In its deliberations, the committee returned again and again to the twin issues of fairness and effectiveness in policing. Many of the controversies and challenges facing today's police reflect a perception that these may be to a certain extent antithetical goals, but the committee concluded otherwise. These important concepts became the cornerstones of our report.

Many people made generous contributions to the report's success. We thank the authors of the papers presented—Geoffrey Alpert, University of South Carolina; Ian Ayres, Yale Law School; Ron DeLord, Combined Law Enforcement Associations of Texas; Edward A. Flynn, Chief, Arlington County Police Department; Lorie Fridell, Police Executive Research Forum; James Fyfe, John Jay College of Criminal Justice; William King, Bowling Green University; Robert Langworthy, University of Alaska, Anchorage; James Lynch, American University; Gary Miller, Washington University in St. Louis; Joel Miller, Vera Institute of Justice; Craig Uchida, 21st Century Solutions; Carole Willis and Stella Yarrow, Producing and Reducing Crime Unit, Home Office, London, England.

The committee would also like to acknowledge the hard work of the consultants for this report—Edward Maguire, George Mason University; Tom Tyler, New York University; and Alexander Weiss, Center for Public Safety.

A special thank you goes to Joan Weiss, Executive Director of the Justice Research and Statistics Association (JRSA), for agreeing to publish a thematic volume of the JRSA journal featuring the papers from our workshop on improving data.

This report has been reviewed in draft form by individuals chosen for their diverse perspectives and technical expertise, in accordance with procedures approved by the NRC's Report Review Committee. The purpose of this independent review is to provide candid and critical comments that will assist the institution in making its published report as sound as possible and to ensure that the report meets institutional standards for objectivity, evidence, and responsiveness to the study charge. The review comments and draft manuscript remain confidential to protect the integrity of the deliberative process.

We thank the following individuals for their participation in the review of this report: Richard Berk, Department of Statistics, University of California, Los Angeles; Brian Forst, Department of Justice, Law, and Society, American University; James J. Fyfe, Commission on Training, New York City Police Department; George L. Kelling, School of Criminal Justice, Rutgers University-Newark; David Kennedy, Kennedy School of Government, Harvard University; Gil Kerlikowske, Chief of Police, Seattle Police Department; Jerome H. Skolnick, School of Law, New York University; James Wilson, Anderson School, University of California, Los Angeles.

Although the reviewers listed above have provided many constructive comments and suggestions, they were not asked to endorse the conclusions or recommendations nor did they see the final draft of the report before its release. The review of this report was overseen by Philip J. Cook, Department of Public Policy, Duke University, and Alfred Blumstein, H. John Heinz III School of Public Policy and Management, Carnegie Mellon University. Appointed by the National Research Council, they were responsible for making certain that an independent examination of this report was carried out in accordance with institutional procedures and that all review comments were carefully considered. Responsibility for the final content of this report rests entirely with the authoring committee and the institution.

Wesley G. Skogan, *Chair*
Committee to Review Research on Police Policy and Practices

Contents

EXECUTIVE SUMMARY   1
    The Nature of Policing in America, 2
    Explaining Police Behavior, 3
    Crime Control Effectiveness, 4
    Lawfulness and Legitimacy, 5
    Recommendations, 6

1   INTRODUCTION   11
    Scope and Themes of the Report, 12
    Plan of the Report, 13

2   CRIMINAL JUSTICE RESEARCH ON POLICE   20
    Scale of Police Research, 21
    Subject Matter of Police Research, 22
    Police Research Methodologies, 27
    Auspices of Police Research, 29
    Research Impact of the 1994 Crime Act, 30
    Conclusion, 34
    Appendix 2A: Methodology of Keyword Search, 36

3   THE NATURE OF POLICING IN THE UNITED STATES   47
    Organizational Structure of American Policing, 48
    Activities of the Police, 57
    Staffing the Police, 79
    Recent Innovations in Policing, 82

The Process of Adapting to Change, 93
Research Recommendations, 106

4 EXPLAINING POLICE BEHAVIOR:
   PEOPLE AND SITUATIONS   109
   Nature of the Evidence, 111
   Situational Influences on Police Behavior, 114
   Legal Factors, 115
   Officers' Outlooks and Characteristics, 128
   Knowledge, Skills, and Ability, 137
   Experiences of Officers, 139
   Equal Employment Opportunity, Affirmative Action, and the
      Effects of Officer Race and Sex, 147
   Implications, 152

5 EXPLAINING POLICE BEHAVIOR:
   ORGANIZATIONS AND CONTEXT   155
   Measures of Organization Activities and Outputs, 157
   Neglected Dimensions of Police Behavior, 162
   Influence of Police Organization, 168
   Influence of External Forces, 189
   Conclusion, 214

6 THE EFFECTIVENESS OF POLICE ACTIVITIES IN
   REDUCING CRIME, DISORDER, AND FEAR   217
   Strength of the Evidence, 219
   Standard Model of Police Practices, 223
   Community-Oriented Policing, 232
   Focused Policing Efforts, 235
   Problem-Oriented Policing, 243
   Conclusion, 246

7 LAWFUL POLICING   252
   Police Compliance with the Law and the Constitution, 253
   Promoting Compliance with Legal and Constitutional Rules, 275
   External Accountability Mechanisms, 288

8 POLICE FAIRNESS: LEGITIMACY AS THE
   CONSENT OF THE PUBLIC   291
   Legitimacy and Policing, 293
   Creating Legitimacy, 298
   Building Legitimacy Through Organizational Reform, 308
   Conclusion, 326

9   THE FUTURE OF POLICING RESEARCH   327
    Enhancing Crime Control Effectiveness, 328
    Enhancing the Lawfulness of Police Actions, 328
    Enhancing the Legitimacy of Policing, 329
    Improving Personnel Practices, 329
    Fostering Innovation, 329
    Assessing Problem-Oriented and Community Policing, 330
    Respondng to Terrorism, 330
    Organizing Research, 330

REFERENCES   332

APPENDIX: Biographical Sketches   393

INDEX   401

FAIRNESS AND EFFECTIVENESS IN
POLICING
THE EVIDENCE

Executive Summary

Across the United States, thousands of local, state, and federal police agencies work to safeguard communities and ensure justice. Police are perhaps the most visible face of government, one that most people recognize and encounter with frequency. They also have special and awesome powers, as they are authorized to use force in their dealings with the public. Policing is primarily shaped by two public expectations. First, the police are called on to deal with crime and disorder, preventing them when possible, and to bring to account those who disobey the law. Second, the public expects their police to be impartial, producing justice through the fair, effective, and restrained use of their authority. The standards by which the public judges police success in meeting these expectations have become more exacting and challenging, and police agencies today must find ways to respond in an effective, affordable, and legitimate way.

In 1968 and 1994, landmark legislation increased the federal government's involvement in policing. The Omnibus Crime Control and Safe Streets Act of 1968 created what became the National Institute of Justice, which has sponsored a substantial body of research on police practice. The Violent Crime Control and Law Enforcement Act of 1994 encouraged the adoption of community policing, as well as fostering the hiring of many new police officers and the adoption of modern information technology. The 1994 crime act included a mandate to evaluate policing programs already under way or to be sponsored by funds from the legislation itself.

Because of this investment in law enforcement practice and research under the 1994 crime act, the National Institute of Justice and the Community Oriented Policing Services Office, both in the Department of Justice, asked the National Research Council to convene the Committee to Review Research on Police Policy and Practices. The committee was asked to assess police research and its influence on policing, as well as the influence and operation of the community policing philosophy.

In responding to this charge, the committee examined police research done primarily since 1968, including that sponsored by the 1994 crime act. The committee developed an analytic framework that embodies the mandate of the police to effectively control crime and ensure justice. The dual mandate with regard to effectiveness and fairness forms the cornerstone of this report. Much of our analysis focuses on the evaluation of police operations in light of these two dimensions. Evidence from policing research contradicts any concern that an emphasis on policing that is fair and restrained will necessarily undermine their crime control effectiveness, and vice versa, for fairness and effectiveness are not mutually exclusive, but mutually reinforcing. The work of this committee suggests that policing that is perceived as just is more effective in fostering a law-abiding society, and that success in reducing crime enhances police legitimacy.

THE NATURE OF POLICING IN AMERICA

The report traces major themes in the development of American policing. It describes a policing "industry" that is highly diverse and decentralized, as well as locally controlled and financed. While this is consistent with America's political tradition, it limits the ability of the federal government to spark innovation or encourage uniform and progressive police policies. Instead, such factors as crime, demographic change, local political culture, the courts, and state legislation play important roles in stimulating reactive change in this decentralized system. On one hand, fragmentation of the police industry may hinder the development of coordinated responses to national threats such as domestic antiterrorism efforts, although there is almost no research on this topic at present. On the other hand, a highly decentralized system avoids the risk of nationwide adoption of programs that have little utility for a given locale. There is no systematic evidence on what industry structure best promotes effectiveness, innovation, and experimentation.

At the street level, policing is highly discretionary, and individual officers work virtually without direct supervision. The discretionary nature of routine police work increases the difficulty of ensuring the fairness and lawfulness in everyday policing. Police are authorized to exercise their authority in encounters with the public by issuing citations, making arrests, and using force. While most encounters are trouble-free, the sheer volume of police-citizen contact means that a significant number of individual citizens come away dissatisfied with how they were treated. There is also evidence of racial and ethnic disparities in these assessments, as well as in public opinion about the police generally. These disparities contribute to a lowered sense of police legitimacy among minority groups.

In addition to their enforcement duties, the police provide a broad range of services to the public, and more recently they have expanded their range of crime prevention efforts, but there has been little research on these matters. Most research on detectives is dated, but the committee's review of it seriously challenges the idea that the capacity of the police to solve individual crimes can be substantially improved. Traffic enforcement commands significant police resources, but it too has escaped the attention of researchers. The emergence of racial profiling on the nation's public agenda is changing that, but the committee concludes that most current data collection efforts in this area are unlikely to speak to any of the policy issues involved. One of our recommendations calls for more attention to the measurement and research design issues involved in the study of traffic enforcement.

EXPLAINING POLICE BEHAVIOR

The committee assessed research on the causes of police behavior. Among them are studies that address the central issue of the report: how to ensure the effectiveness and lawfulness of policing. Research in this area includes observational studies of police operations, analyses of administrative records, and surveys of the public and the police. Almost all of this research focuses on patrol officers, thus excluding many important elements of police work.

The committee divided research on the determinants of police behavior into analytic categories. The first chapter on this topic examines the impact of situational factors and officer characteristics on police work. Situational factors include features of the incident itself, the background and demeanor of suspects, and their immediate context. Many studies of officers engaged in encounters with citizens contrast the impact of legally relevant factors with the influence of extralegal factors in shaping their on-street decisions and actions. The outcomes that have been examined range from making an arrest to using force, negotiating dispute settlements, or choosing to do nothing at all. This research finds that the impact of legally relevant factors is strong. Taking these into account, the class and gender of suspects play a small role. However, more research is needed on the complex interplay of race, ethnicity, and other social factors in police-citizen interactions.

Among officer characteristics, neither race nor gender has a direct influence on the outcome of routine police-citizen encounters, and there is no clear effect of officer's attitudes, job satisfaction, or personality. The committee found that research on factors linked to officer recruitment and training is surprisingly limited. There are few studies of the link between officer's knowledge, skill, ability, or intelligence and actual police practice. There is no strong research support for police educational requirements, and research on the effects of training on officer effectiveness is unconvincing. Recruitment and training are among the most important activities of police organizations, and more needs to be known about their role in ensuring effective and lawful police conduct; the committee therefore offers a strong research recommendation along these lines.

The committee also examined the impact of organizational and community factors on policing. The decisions and actions of officers are situated within these larger contexts, and they affect the quality of policing. Organizations exist in order to define the roles of their members and regularize the activities of individuals who fill them. Research indicates, for example, that the policies and practices of police departments directly affect the rate at which officers use lethal force. Arrests, citation rates, and measures of their success in solving cases vary greatly across police organizations, reflecting differences in their policies, performance standards, and characteristic styles of operation. The committee notes the limited research on police leadership and the role of leadership in affecting organizational change.

Likewise, neighborhood and city-level factors affect both the decisions of individual police officers and features of their departments. Police-citizen encounters are situated in a neighborhood context that seems to independently affect how they are conducted, and community factors affect police resource allocation decisions and patrol activities. At the city level, issues like how many officers the taxpayers are willing to support are locally determined matters that are affected by a range of political, economic, and crime factors. Local political cultures and the priorities of political leaders affect policies and spending levels as well.

CRIME CONTROL EFFECTIVENESS

The committee examined research on police effectiveness at reducing crime, disorder, and fear. There has been a great deal of research on these topics, and the committee was able to distinguish between studies that employed adequate methods for studying them and others about which there is less confidence. The committee assessed all work along two tracks: to what extent are strategies effective, and to what extent do they utilize a broad range of tools, including traditional law enforcement powers.

The committee concludes that contemporary policing has relied on an operating model emphasizing reactive strategies to suppress crime. The committee's assessment of several decades of research is that there is weak or, at best, mixed evidence regarding the effectiveness of what we have defined as the "standard model" of policing. A large body of carefully conducted research has found much evidence of the effectiveness of what we have called the "focused model" of policing.

The standard model is defined by the more or less across-the-board reliance on random patrol, rapid response to calls for service, follow-up investigations by detectives, and unfocused enforcement efforts. Debates over the proper size of a city's police department also usually hinge on the standard assumption that larger is better when it comes to crime control.

There is strong research evidence that the more focused and specific the strategies of the police, the more they are tailored to the problems they seek to address, the more effective police will be in controlling crime and disorder. Research on police effectiveness in attacking chronic concentrations of crime, widely known as "hot spots," has found that well-managed investigations and crackdowns can suppress crime, deter its future reappearance, and avoid simply displacing a similar number of crimes elsewhere. Discovering hot spots and tracking the effectiveness of policing efforts against them has been facilitated by the widespread adoption of new computer mapping and crime analysis technologies by the police, another new development awaiting careful evaluation and analysis.

The committee reviewed evidence of the effectiveness of two widely discussed alternatives to the standard model of policing: community and problem-oriented policing. Problem-oriented policing stands in sharp contrast to the standard model because of its focus on developing highly localized responses to the diverse problems that plague different communities. Community policing always involves some form of public involvement, frequently in the identification of priority problems and often with some role for the community and for city service agencies in helping solve them. This approach also adopts a problem-oriented stance that emphasizes developing local solutions to locally identified problems. Both are examples of what the report dubs "tailored" responses to crime and disorder. In addition, both seek to look beyond the traditional exercise of the law enforcement powers of the police to reduce crime, disorder, and fear. Our review suggests that such approaches have promise and should be the subject of more systematic investigation.

LAWFULNESS AND LEGITIMACY

The committee also reviewed research on the criteria by which people make judgments about the police: their *lawfulness*, that is, their compliance with constitutional, statutory, and professional norms, and their *legitimacy*, defined by the public's beliefs about the police and their willingness to recognize police authority. These beliefs transcend mere popularity, which can vacillate quite a bit. Rather, legitimacy as it used in this report means the degree to which citizens recognize the police as appropriate and justified representatives of government. Many controversies regarding policing fall under these broad criteria of lawfulness and legitimacy; the current crisis of racial profiling is only the most recent example of the challenge police agencies face in balancing the demands of effective crime control, lawfulness, and legitimacy. Research in this area includes studies of the implementation and impact of court decisions and administrative policies on police behavior in the field, and survey studies of the public that examine their attitudes and experiences with police in their community.

Research has examined police compliance with the rules governing police interrogations, searches and seizures, and the use of excessive and lethal force. Compliance has been found to be variable, but it can be enhanced by the actions of determined police administrators. Research on corruption finds that, like other forms of misconduct, police corruption can be traced in part to lax administrative arrangements and a supportive informal peer culture. The solutions to both problems are generally the same: determined leadership, enforcement of department policies and rules, and the creation of new mechanisms for monitoring problem behavior. There is only limited research on the impact of formal legal efforts to control misconduct, through criminal prosecution and civil suits against individual officers and federal "pattern and practice" actions against police departments. Another area about which more needs to be known is the effectiveness of civilian oversight bodies and review commissions that have been created to bring external accountability to the police.

The committee concludes that the more lawful police are, the more likely the outcomes produced by their actions will be accepted and embraced by the public. Lawful policing increases the stature of the police in the eyes of citizens, creates a reservoir of support for police work, and expedites the production of community safety by enhancing cooperation with the police. In the end, policing in a democracy must be accomplished by consent; that is, citizens must agree to the exercise of police power. Research has found that people obey the law not just because they are afraid of being punished or because they believe the law is morally right, but also because they believe that the law and its enforcement are fairly administered. The public's judgment can be heavily influenced by the conduct of the police, one of the most visible representatives of law and government in most citizens' lives. This suggests the need to extend theories of police effectiveness beyond the communication of a deterrent threat of punishment to encompass police engagement with communities.

RECOMMENDATIONS

A scientific knowledge base exists for helping communities to decide what strategies to use to reduce crime and disorder while increasing police legitimacy. Relative to other institutions of criminal justice, the police are very open to innovations and evaluations in collaboration with universities and other research institutions. This is a remarkable transformation, and it creates the potential for creating an even more effective, fair, efficient, and accountable police in the 21st century. Our specific recommendations build on these findings to provide specific guidance to communities, to state and national lawmakers, and to police themselves.

Recommendation 1: Enhancing crime control effectiveness. The committee recommends that police continue to turn their attention from providing standardized levels of police resources and activities to achieving measurable results related to focused effectiveness and fairness issues that reflect community goals. Research demonstrates that the more police focus on achieving localized and specific results, the more effective they will be in controlling crime and disorder. Because one-size-fits-all requirements restrict the police's ability to match resources to priorities, communities will be safer holding police accountable for results rather than resources. This new management philosophy, coupled with advances in information systems that support more rigorous monitoring and evaluation of the effectiveness of policing strategies, promises to stimulate further innovation in policing in the United States.

Recommendation 2: Enhancing the lawfulness of police actions. The committee recommends research on the fairness and lawfulness of police practices and a coordinated research emphasis on the effectiveness of organizational mechanisms that foster police rectitude. In its review of police research, the committee noted that early research focused to a significant degree on lawfulness. That research examined the exercise of police discretion, the use of police authority, violence and corruption by police, and the use of lethal force. More recently, a new emphasis on crime control effectiveness has emerged. While this is important, one of the findings of this report is the importance of police fairness and restraint in the use of force and of equity in the allocation of police resources. Research on the contrasting roles played by legally relevant and extralegal factors in shaping on-street police behavior has continued and plays an important role in this discussion. We note some new approaches to the study of police integrity and the processes that promote an environment less tolerant of police corruption, and this line of research should be encouraged.

The committee also recommends legislation requiring agencies to file annual reports to the public on the number of persons shot at, wounded, or killed by police officers in the line of duty. Few communities are prepared to understand fully the causal context and mechanisms for minimizing the rate of lethal and nonlethal shootings by police. A reporting system, comparable to that created for reporting crime statistics, would help local agencies monitor their own levels of weapon use, in relation to such risk factors as community violence, gun carrying, and arrest rates. Such benchmarking may further contribute to the declining frequency of legally justifiable homicide by police, which has proven to be greatly affected by organizational controls.

Recommendation 3: Enhancing the legitimacy of policing. Research on public opinion documents the profound gulf between the races in the United States in people's views of the legitimacy of the police. The committee calls for more research on the experiences of crime victims, individuals stopped by the police, and the public, focusing on practices in policing that support or undermine public confidence. To support this, the committee recommends conducting a regular national survey to gauge the extent and nature of police-citizen contacts, including items that address public assessments of the quality of police service in their community.

Current efforts to collect data on public encounters with police that are intended to inform judgments on whether police agencies engage in racial profiling are not very effective. The committee calls for more research on the collection of reliable and valid encounter data under field conditions that can then be analyzed in ways that point unambiguously to policy recommendations and personnel decisions.

The committee also recommends research on mechanisms for ensuring lawfulness. A number of programs have emerged for collecting data on officer performance for the purpose of identifying problem behavior and providing a basis for corrective action. Some early intervention or early warning programs collect data on a broad range of officer performance measures. They have been adopted voluntarily by many law enforcement agencies and have been imposed by consent decrees in other agencies. Rigorous evaluations are required to determine if these programs effectively produce police accountability.

Recommendation 4: Improving personnel practices. The committee recommends research on personnel practices that will help them ensure the crime control effectiveness and legitimacy in the eyes of the public. This includes strategies for police recruitment, personnel development, and job assignment; and research on police performance monitoring, officer assessment, and incentive systems. The committee found research inadequate to address two key personnel questions: the utility of requiring college credits for new applicants and what training is most effective in promoting good performance. Recruitment and training are among the most important activities of police organizations, and more needs to be known about their role in ensuring effective and lawful police conduct.

Recommendation 5: Fostering innovation. The committee recommends research on police organization, innovation processes, and organizational change. Although several federal agencies are charged with encouraging innovation in law enforcement, the committee found little research about the innovation process or how it can be facilitated. There is likewise little systematic, cross-agency research on the extent and effectiveness of organizational change strategies in policing, or on the role of police leadership in securing lawful policing. To support this research, the committee recommends that the Bureau of Justice Statistics regularly conduct an enhanced version of its current Law Enforcement Management and Administrative Statistics survey. The report makes several suggestions to increase the utility of the data for research and policy analysis, as well as for potentially fruitful research topics. These include the need to monitor the broad range of nonenforcement activities performed by the police, many of which fall under the rubric of community and problem-oriented policing.

Recommendation 6: Assessing problem-oriented and community policing. These are two of the most widely discussed innovations in policing today. Each involves complex packages of programs and organizational adaptations, and each calls for indicators of efficiency and effectiveness that currently are not well measured by most police information systems. The organizational structures and practices that comprise these innovations are highly varied, making it difficult to form general conclusions about their effectiveness on the basis of existing research. Police employ tactics under each of these strategies that can be rigorously evaluated, but the committee found generally that there was not yet enough evidence to document their successes or failures. Future research should do more to advance knowledge about the effectiveness of these innovations by focusing on their key elements. The organizational arrangements that foster effective community and problem-oriented policing and the effectiveness of police training in this area are also not well understood.

Recommendation 7: Responding to terrorism. The committee recommends research on the demands of responding to terrorism, a topic of urgent national interest. There is little research on this topic in the domestic context of the United States, but what exists suggests that responding to terrorism places new demands on municipal police agencies. It requires them to coordinate their efforts with multiple levels of government; to plan in coordination with public health and medical organizations and with the military; and to learn to safeguard their own employees from new chemical and biological risks. They must continue to maintain open communication with the communities they serve and their commitment to lawful conduct, while they are faced with new information and intelligence needs. From the perspective of local departments, more research is needed on how to respond to these organizational challenges.

Recommendation 8: Organizing research. The committee recommends that the National Institute of Justice take the steps necessary to ensure the growth and stability of its policing research portfolio. In reviewing past research, the committee was impressed by the record of growing police openness to investigations of all aspects of their work. They serve as an example for all the institutions responsible for public safety. However, despite this support by practitioners, the committee identified significant gaps in what is known about contemporary policing. There are many important subjects about which there is virtually no scientific research. By any metric—whether lives lost to crime, the costs and benefits of government expenditures on law enforcement, or the moral obligation embedded in the use of coercive authority—police research deserves more serious attention than it has received. Local communities and the states bear the costs of law enforcement, but the federal government is particularly well situated to provide them the findings of research on police and the communities they serve.

A major impediment to advancing policing through research is the need for consistent funding and research planning and administration. Support for police research has been episodic and historically low, given the importance of the institution itself and the vast gaps in knowledge of what works in this area. Organizational changes in the National Institute of Justice providing for an office devoted to research on policing and communities might well resolve the problems of erratic funding and noncumulative development of research. Whether or not a separate office is formed, the police research portfolio requires stable, long-term research funding managed by a professional staff, which could implement broad strategies of knowledge development. The development of the policing portfolio should be under the direction of an official recruited from senior ranks of the scientific community.

Finally, funding for the policing portfolio should be balanced between questions of police lawfulness, legitimacy, and crime control effectiveness, to support a research program that reflects the highest standards of science applied to empirical questions of great national concern.

1

Introduction

I n 1968 and 1994, landmark legislation increased the federal government's involvement in policing. The Omnibus Crime Control and Safe Streets Act of 1968 created what became the National Institute of Justice, which has sponsored a substantial body of research on police practices. The Violent Crime Control and Law Enforcement Act of 1994 encouraged the adoption of community policing, as well as fostering the hiring of many new police officers and the adoption of modern information technology. The 1994 crime act also included a mandate to evaluate policing programs already under way or to be sponsored by funds from the legislation itself.

As part of the U.S. Department of Justice's considerable investment in law enforcement practice and research under the 1994 crime act, the National Institute of Justice (NIJ) and the Community Oriented Policing Services Office (COPS), both within the Department of Justice, asked the National Research Council to establish the Committee to Review Research on Police Policy and Practices. The committee was asked to assess police research and its influence on policing, as well as the influence and operation of the community policing philosophy.

The committee was charged with four specific tasks:

- Develop an analytic framework for reviewing existing research on police operations and practices, to identify factors that contribute to crime prevention or reduction, public safety, and police service quality.
- Identify other factors influencing crime, public safety and community satisfaction with policing services, and how they interact with policing practices to influence the impact of policing on the community.

• Identify mechanisms for accelerating the diffusion and institutional-ization of innovation in police organizations, to facilitate the adoption of scientifically supported policing strategies, tactics and technologies.

• Describe shortcomings or gaps in research on the topics identified in these reviews, and summarize them in a detailed agenda for future research.

In the course of our two-year study, the committee considered many aspects of police research and how to best organize our review and conclusions. We also set some boundaries. The committee examined police research done primarily since 1968, including that sponsored by the 1994 crime act. Since the vast bulk of research is devoted to local law enforcement agencies serving communities located in metropolitan areas, the committee made an early decision to focus its attention on these departments. Research on foreign police is reviewed only to the extent that it informs specific topics in U.S. policing. Since the influence of technology on law enforcement practice has not been the subject of much social science research—which is the focus of this report—the committee could only trace the increasing technological capacities of the police, rather than draw conclusions about the nature of its effects. The committee also wrote this report with multiple audiences in mind: policy makers, police practitioners, scholars, and other interested readers. Thus in addition to operating under constraints of existing research, we have attempted to address the combined interests of these communities without elevating one over the other. No single audience, therefore, will find all the answers to all of their most immediate questions. The committee compensates for whatever is lost by this multiple service by the insights derived from drawing connections among these communities.

SCOPE AND THEMES OF THE REPORT

The committee developed an analytic framework for organizing policing research that embodies the mandate to effectively control crime and ensure justice. The police are called to prevent crime and disorder and to bring to account those who do not comply, and these goals have shaped their organization and activities. But the public also expects the police to conduct themselves in an impartial manner, producing justice through the fair, effective, and restrained use of their authority. The standards by which police success in meeting these dual expectations is judged have become more exacting and challenging, and police agencies today must find ways to respond in an effective, affordable, and legitimate way. This dual mandate forms the cornerstone of this report. Much of the committee's analysis focuses on the evaluation of police operations in light of these two dimensions.

In reviewing this body of research, the committee was impressed by the record of growing police openness to research on all aspects of their work. This can serve as an example for all institutions responsible for public safety. Police have been far more willing to accept the use of advanced scientific methods in program evaluation, such as randomized controlled trials, than have other parts of the criminal justice system. Agencies have also been willing to allow systematic observation studies of how police interact with citizens in various situations. They have been remarkably willing to let scholars investigate highly sensitive issues, such as use of force and even police misconduct. The community is vitally interested in the quality of policing, and there has been an impressive amount of research on citizen involvement in policing and public safety issues. However, despite this support by practitioners and the community, the committee identified significant gaps in what is known about contemporary policing. There are many important subjects about which there is virtually no scientific research whatsoever. Each chapter of the report identifies research priorities, and among our recommendations we call for greater willingness by federal research agencies to take advantage of the research opportunities presented by police departments across the country.

PLAN OF THE REPORT

State of Research on Policing

Following this introduction, Chapter 2 provides a broad overview of the development of police research. It focuses on studies that examine how American policing actually works, most of which have appeared since 1967. Early police studies arose out of concern with the fairness and lawfulness of police actions. They documented the enormous discretion enjoyed by officers on the street and the racially discriminatory way in which many decisions were made. The next generation of studies began the tradition of contrasting the impact of legal and extralegal factors on officer behavior, reflecting a growing understanding of the complexities of street-level policing. More recent work in this tradition has focused on a narrower topic, the use of deadly force by the police. It has demonstrated the important influence of department policies and leadership on the rate at which citizens are killed. More recently, the issue of racial profiling sparked new interest by the public in the implications of this research. New research examines the effectiveness of civilian review and other administrative mechanisms for dealing with abuse of police authority.

While fairness and lawfulness remained key issues in policing, many researchers turned their attention to other issues during the late 1970s and 1980s. Work in the field increasingly focused on the effectiveness of the standard strategies of policing, ranging from random patrol to criminal investigations, at reducing crime. The conclusions of this research were also critical, for it appeared that many elements of the standard policing repertoire—including random motorized patrol, rapid response to calls for service, follow-up investigations by detectives, and unfocused enforcement efforts—were of limited effectiveness. A notable feature of this work is the surprisingly limited role for replication studies: many of the most important lessons of research on police effectiveness depend to this day on the conclusions of one or a few now-dated studies.

The end of the 1980s brought a new focus on the intersection between police and communities. The advent of problem-oriented and community policing heralded new attention to community-based crime prevention. Earlier, the concept of "co-production" had been coined to describe the dependence of the police on public support and involvement in their efforts to secure neighborhood safety, and this became the focus of new research. The committee notes, however, that research on the police has contributed little to the understanding of their role in the precipitous drop in crime that took place during the 1990s, despite the many claims that are made about it.

Chapter 2 also describes the growing methodological sophistication of police research. Individual ethnographic research has been overshadowed by larger scale systematic observational studies; statistical studies now typically employ sophisticated econometric techniques; experimental designs are used whenever possible, to increase the ability to make causal inferences in field settings; and large-scale surveys are routinely used to collect data about individuals and organizations.

Organization of American Policing

Chapter 3 traces major themes in the development of American policing. It describes a policing "industry" that is highly diverse and decentralized, as well as locally controlled and financed. There is a substantial, and growing, private policing component as well. While all of this is consistent with America's democratic tradition, it limits the ability of the federal government to spark innovation or encourage uniform and progressive police policies. Instead, such factors as crime, demographic change, local political culture, the courts, and state legislation play important roles in stimulating reactive change within this decentralized system. And fragmentation of the police industry may hinder the development of coordinated responses to domestic antiterrorism efforts, although there is almost no research on this topic at present.

At the street level, policing is highly discretionary, and individual officers work virtually without direct supervision. As a result, police departments are highly dependent on personnel arrangements—how they recruit, train, motivate and promote officers—to achieve their goals. The committee found that research on the effectiveness of all of these practices is quite limited.

The highly discretionary nature of police work increases the difficulty of ensuring the fairness and lawfulness of everyday policing. Police are authorized to exercise their authority in encounters with the public, by issuing citations, making arrests, using physical force, and sometimes employing lethal force. While most encounters are trouble-free, the sheer volume of police-citizen contact means that a large number of individual citizens come away dissatisfied with how they were treated. There is also evidence of racial and ethnic disparities in these assessments, as well as in public opinion about the police generally. These disparities contribute to a lowered sense of police legitimacy among minority groups.

In addition to their enforcement duties, the police provide a broad range of services to the public, and more recently they have expanded their range of crime prevention efforts, but little research has been conducted on these matters. Most research on detectives is dated, but the committee's review of it seriously challenges the idea that one can substantially improve the capacity of the police to solve individual crimes. Traffic enforcement commands significant police resources, but it too has escaped the attention of researchers. The emergence of racial profiling on the nation's public agenda is changing that, but the committee concluded that most current data collection efforts in this area are unlikely to speak to any of the policy issues involved. One of our recommendations calls for more attention to the measurement and research design issues involved in the study of traffic enforcement.

Explaining Police Behavior

Chapters 4 and 5 assess research on the causes of police behavior. Among them are studies that address the central issue of the report: how to ensure the effectiveness and lawfulness of policing. Research in this area includes observational studies of police operations, analyses of administrative records, and surveys of the public and the police. Almost all of this research focuses on the work of patrol officers, thus excluding many important elements of police work.

The committee divided research on the determinants of police behavior into analytic categories. Chapter 4 examines the impact of situational factors, the background of citizens they encounter, and officers' characteristics on police work. Situational factors include features of the incident itself, the demeanor of suspects, and their immediate context. Many studies of officers engaged in encounters with citizens contrast the impact of "legally relevant" factors with the influence of extralegal factors in shaping their on-street decisions and actions. The outcomes that have been examined range from making an arrest to using force, negotiating dispute settlements, or choosing to do nothing at all. Research finds that the impact of legally relevant factors is strong. Taking these into account, the evidence is mixed that the social class and gender of suspects play a role, and their effect may be small. The evidence is also mixed about the impact of suspects' demeanor on their eventual treatment. There is widespread concern about the differential treatment of citizens based on their race, and more research is needed on the complex interplay of race, demeanor, context, and other social factors in police-citizen interactions. Police handling of the mentally ill has been the subject of some research, but more is needed.

Among the officer characteristics, neither race nor gender has a direct influence on the outcome of routine police-citizen encounters, and there is no clear effect of officer's attitudes, job satisfaction, or personality. While there has been much discussion of the impact of police culture on officer behavior, there is no rigorous evidence regarding its influence. The committee found that research on factors linked to officer recruitment and training is surprisingly limited. There are few studies of the link between an officer's knowledge, skill, ability, or intelligence and actual police practice. There is no strong research support for police education requirements, and research on the effects of training on officer effectiveness is unconvincing. Recruitment and training are among the most important activities of police organizations, and more needs to be known about their role in ensuring effective and lawful police conduct.

Chapter 5 examines the impact of organizational, community, and governmental factors on the police. The decisions and actions of officers are situated within these larger contexts, and they affect the quality of policing. Organizations exist in order to define the roles of their members and regularize the activities of the individuals who fill them. Research indicates, for example, that the policies and practices of police departments directly affect the rate at which both deadly and nonlethal force is used by officers. Arrests, citation rates, and measures of success in solving cases vary greatly across police organizations, as do the rate at which citizen's complaints are filed. Research demonstrates that these reflect in part differences in the size, centralization, specialization, and hierarchical structure of agencies, the formality of their policies regarding the use of force and other key aspects of police work, and the extent to which they have taken a geographic focus. We review the limited systematic research on "CompStat" style accountability systems, and call for further investigation of this new management philosophy.

Likewise, neighborhood and city-level factors affect both the decisions of individual police officers and the features of their departments. Police-citizen encounters occur in a neighborhood context that seems to independently affect how they are conducted, and community factors affect police resource allocation decisions and patrol activities. At the city level, issues like how many officers the taxpayers will support are locally determined matters that are affected by a range of political, economic, and crime factors. Local political cultures and the priorities of political leaders affect policies and spending levels as well. The police are importantly affected by the policies and practices of other parts of the criminal justice system, as well as by state and local legislation. The chapter also examines the influence of the federal government in two key police areas, the handling of civil protests and responding to terrorism.

Chapter 5 notes that important aspects of police work, indeed activities that often consume the majority of their time, are not captured by current data systems. It calls for the development of measures of informal applications of police authority, service and assistance delivered to citizens, mobilizing and working with the community, and problem solving. This could be accomplished as part of the tremendous expansion of the technological capacity of police to gather, analyze, and disseminate information, which also requires careful evaluation.

Crime Control Effectiveness

Chapter 6 addresses research on police effectiveness at reducing crime, disorder, and fear. There has been a great deal of research on these topics, and the committee has distinguished between studies that employed adequate methods for studying them and others about which there is less confidence.

The committee concludes that contemporary policing has relied on an operating model emphasizing reactive strategies to suppress crime. Many aspects of the "standard model" of policing are not particularly effective, despite their prominence. The standard model is defined by the more or less across-the-board reliance on random patrol, rapid response to calls for service, follow-up investigations by detectives, and unfocused enforcement efforts. Debates over the proper size of a city's police department also usually hinge on the standard assumption that larger is better when it comes to crime control.

In contrast, there is strong research evidence that the more focused and specific the strategies of the police, and the more they are tailored to the problems they seek to address, the more effective the police will be in controlling crime and disorder. Research on police effectiveness in attacking chronic concentrations of crime—widely known as "hot spots"—has found that well-managed investigations and crackdowns can suppress crime, deter its future reappearance, and avoid simply displacing a similar number of crimes elsewhere. Discovering hot spots and tracking the effectiveness of policing efforts against them have been facilitated by the widespread adoption of new computer mapping and crime analysis technologies by the police, another new development awaiting careful evaluation and analysis.

The committee reviewed evidence of the effectiveness of two widely discussed alternatives to the standard model of policing: problem-oriented policing and community policing. Problem-oriented policing stands in sharp contrast to the standard model because of its focus on developing highly localized responses to the diverse problems that plague different communities. Community policing always involves some form of public involvement, frequently in the identification of priority problems and often with some role for the community and for city service agencies in helping solve them. It also involves adopting a problem-solving stance that emphasizes developing local solutions to locally identified problems. Both are examples of what the report dubs "tailored" responses to crime and disorder. Both seek to look beyond the traditional exercise of the law enforcement powers of the police to reduce crime, disorder, and fear. Our review suggests that such approaches have promise and should be the subject of more systematic investigation.

Lawfulness and Legitimacy

Chapters 7 and 8 turn to research on the criteria by which society makes judgments about the police: their *lawfulness*—that is, police compliance with constitutional, statutory, and professional norms—and their *legitimacy*—defined by the public's beliefs about the police and their willingness to recognize police authority. Many controversies in policing reflect these broad concerns; the recent crisis regarding racial profiling is only the most recent example of the challenge police agencies face in balancing the demands of effective crime control, lawfulness, and legitimacy. Research in this area includes studies of the implementation and impact of court decisions and administrative policies on police behavior in the field, as well as survey studies of the public that examine their attitudes and experiences with police in their community.

Research has examined police compliance with the rules governing police interrogations, searches and seizures, and the use off excessive and deadly force. Their compliance has been found to be variable, but it can be enhanced by determined police administrators. Research on corruption finds that, like other forms of misconduct, police corruption can be traced in part to lax administrative arrangements and a supportive informal peer culture. The solutions to both problems are generally the same: determined leadership, enforcement of department policies and rules, and the creation of new mechanisms for monitoring problem behavior. Research is limited on the impact of formal legal efforts to control misconduct, through criminal prosecution and civil suits against individual officers, and federal "pattern and practice" actions against police departments. Another area about which more needs to be known is the effectiveness of civilian oversight bodies and review commissions that have been created to impose external accountability on the police.

Evidence from policing research contradicts any concern that an emphasis on policing that is fair and restrained will necessarily undermine their crime control effectiveness, and vice versa, for fairness and effectiveness are not mutually exclusive, but mutually reinforcing. The work of this committee suggests that policing that is perceived as fair is more effective in fostering a law-abiding society, and success in reducing crime enhances police legitimacy. In the committee's view, the more lawful the police are, the more likely the public is to embrace their actions and their outcomes. Lawful policing increases the stature of the police in the eyes of citizens, creates a reservoir of support for police work, and expedites community safety by enhancing cooperation with the police. In the end, policing in a democracy must be accomplished by consent; that is, citizens must agree to the exercise of police power. Research has found that people obey the law not just because they are afraid of being punished or because they believe the law is morally right, but also because they believe that the law and its enforcement is impartial and being fairly administered. The conduct of the police, the most visible representative of law and government in most citizens' lives, can heavily influence the strength of that judgment. This suggests the need to extend theories of police effectiveness beyond the communication of a deterrent threat of punishment to encompass police engagement with communities.

Future of Police Research

Chapter 9 discusses the future of police research, places it in the context of emerging federal policy that can be expected to guide it, and summarizes the committee's major recommendations. The real test of any program of research is what it accomplishes. This report identifies many lines of research aimed at enhancing the effectiveness of police in pursuing their dual mandate to control crime and ensure justice. Police chiefs, communities, police, and crime victims all need to know more about these issues. What has been accomplished thus far demonstrates the importance of research on policing. What will be accomplished in the future depends heavily on the priority the federal government places on fair and effective policing.

2

Criminal Justice Research on Police

The research evaluated in this report was generated during a relatively short but extraordinarily productive period of intellectual effort. Before publication of the report of the President's Commission on Law Enforcement and the Administration of Justice, *The Challenge of Crime in a Free Society* (Black and Reiss, 1967a), there was hardly any scientific research on the police. Today there is so much that scholars and police find it difficult to keep up, let alone to evaluate its qualitative merits and practical utility.

This chapter describes the scientific enterprise of police research that has developed since 1967—its scale, substantive coverage, methods, and the auspices under which it has been conducted. Special attention is paid to the body of research funded by the 1994 crime act in the final section. It is not an intellectual history of the field or a detailed portrait of its development, but rather a description of its scale and scope.[1]

The research described here does not exhaust all that has been written about the police. We focused on studies that follow the scientific method, were subjected to peer review, and were publicly disseminated. Our assess-

---

[1]Important examples of this kind of intellectual history include L.W. Sherman (1973) "Sociology and Social Reform of the American Police 1950-1973" in *Journal of Police Science and Administration*; Bittner and Rumbaut (1979) "Changing Conceptions of the Police Role-A Sociological Review" in *Crime and Justice: An Annual Review*,Volume 1, edited by M. Tonry and N. Morris (Chicago: University of Chicago Press); R. Reiner (1994) "Policing and the Police" in M. Maguire, R. Morgan, and R. Reiner (eds.), *The Oxford Handbook of Criminology*. London and New York: Oxford University Press, 705-772.

ment does not include studies done by police departments for in-house purposes, by management consultants on contract, by investigating commissions, or by experts involved in civil and criminal proceedings.

SCALE OF POLICE RESEARCH

The publication of the President's Commission on Law Enforcement and the Administration of Justice was a watershed in the development of research on the police. Before 1967 only a handful of scholarly books had been published, notably *American Police Systems* by Raymond Fosdick (1920), *Police Systems in the United States* by Bruce Smith (1949), and *Violence and the Police* by William Westley (1953).[2] Today, one of the most complete collections of books on the police in the United States, Northwestern University's Transportation Library, lists 2,934 books on the police published since 1967. In the history of *Dissertation Abstracts International*, which lists Ph.D. dissertations going back to 1861, over 1,300 with the word "police" in the title have been written: 69 before 1967 and just over 1,250 after 1967.

Today the National Criminal Justice Reference Service of the U.S. Department of Justice lists approximately 31,000 references under the heading "police and law enforcement." These documents, which constitute 20 percent of its total holdings, include federal, state, and local government reports, books, journal articles, and published and unpublished research reports.

The cascade of peer-reviewed research on the police since 1967 has been part of the development of criminal justice studies generally. Of the 12 most highly regarded journals in criminology and police studies published today, only 3 existed before 1967.[3] Altogether these journals have published over 6,900 articles dealing with the police and law enforcement, the larger part after 1967.[4] *Sociological Abstracts*, which covers 2,500 journals and periodicals, lists 6,929 citations to material published between 1963 and 2001.

---

[2]Westley's book was originally entitled *The Police: A Sociological Study of Law, Custom, and Morality*. It was republished by M.I.T. Press as *Violence and the Police* in 1970.

[3]These are *Crime and Delinquency* (1960), *Criminology* (1963, known before 1970 as *Criminologica*), and the *Journal of Research on Crime and Delinquency* (1964). Those published after 1967 are *Criminal Justice History* (1980), the *Journal of Crime and Justice* (1981), the *Journal of Criminal Justice* (1973), *Justice Quarterly* (1984), the *Journal of Quantitative Criminology* (1985), the *Journal of Police Science and Administration* (1973-1990), *Police and Society* (1990), *Police Studies* (1978), and the *American Journal of Police* (1981).

[4]The figure is actually somewhat larger because indexes of titles available for a keyword search are not available for all the journals for the entire post-1967 period.

Police research is now published overwhelmingly in specialty criminal justice journals rather than the mainline social science journals. For example, in the 33 years before 1967, the *American Sociological Review*, the *American Journal of Sociology*, and the *American Political Science Review* published 12 articles having to do with "police." In the 33 years following, they published 18. During their entire publishing histories, these journals have published only 33 articles with "police" in the title.

In addition to criminal justice journals, police research is also reported in three periodicals intended for police professionals: the *FBI Law Enforcement Bulletin*, *Police Chief Magazine*, and *Law Enforcement News*. All but the latter predate the creation of the academic journals. Their articles frequently summarize reports of peer-reviewed research.

Assuming that most of the people who do scientific research on the police probably belong to either the American Society of Criminology or the Academy of Criminal Justice Sciences, they are estimated to number somewhere between 300 and 400. In 2000, 307 members of the American Society of Criminology (11 percent of the membership) belonged to its special-interest police section, while 187 members of the Academy of Criminal Justice Sciences identified themselves as police researchers (5 percent of the membership) (personal communications with these associations). Although the Academy of Criminal Justice Sciences is generally regarded as the more practitioner-oriented of the two, a larger proportion of members of the American Society of Criminology identified themselves as police researchers.

In sum, police research has become a substantial industry in 35 years, with a dedicated core of scholars, a large body of published work, several specialized journals, many publicly accessible data sets, and regular professional meetings.

SUBJECT MATTER OF POLICE RESEARCH

The scientific study of the police in the United States arose out of concern with the fairness of police actions, especially discriminatory treatment of black Americans. It reflected growing sensitivity to the unequal treatment of minorities generally, whether formally through discriminatory laws—voting, education, employment, and housing—or informally through the pervasive exercise of prejudice, especially by government officials.

Beginning in the late 1950s, the American Bar Foundation undertook a series of studies designed to describe the way in which the institutions of criminal justice actually worked, going beyond the traditional descriptions of their formal organization or legal empowerment. The key discovery was that officials, among them the police, possessed enormous discretion in the way they applied the law (LaFave, 1965; Davis, 1969). Two classic studies confirmed this insight: *Justice Without Trial* by Jerome Skolnick (1966), about criminal investigations, and *The Functions of the Police in Modern Society* by Egon Bittner (1970), about police patrolling. This discovery also led to the first attempt to describe police behavior through systematic observation of police encounters with the public (Reiss, 1971). The data, which were collected in Boston, MA; Washington, DC; and Chicago, IL, were used to explore several hypotheses about factors shaping police actions. Systematic observation was extended by the Police Services Study in 1976 to Rochester, NY; St. Louis, MO; St. Petersburg and Dade County, FL.

Research on police behavior and its determinants declined after the 1970s. With the exception of two smaller scale studies in Denver and New York, writing about the determinants of police behavior relied on information collected in the 1960s and 1970s (Bayley and Bittner, 1984; Bayley and Garofalo, 1989). This situation persisted until the early 1990s, when the National Institute of Justice (NIJ) sponsored a major new effort at systematic observation in Indianapolis, IN, and St. Petersburg, FL (the Policing Neighborhoods Project).

The 1960s also saw the beginning of scientific surveys of public as well as police opinion about police matters (Biderman et al., 1967; Bayley and Mendelson, 1969; Kerner Commission, 1968; Jacob, 1971; Smith and Hawkins, 1973). These studies have remained a staple of police research ever since. They also provided a tool for broadening the criteria used to judge police performance, from a narrow focus on crime and arrest rates to consideration of public satisfaction, respect, legitimacy, and perceptions of bias. These criteria are now explicitly included in lists of police performance indicators.

Neglecting the precedent set by Skolnick, studies of the exercise of police discretion have focused almost exclusively on patrol. Only a handful of scholars have studied criminal investigation, and most of that has been, like the work on patrol, during the 1970s (Greenwood et al., 1977; Wilson, 1977; Manning, 1977; Eck, 1983). Another precedent of the 1960s that has been neglected was James Q. Wilson's attempt to account for variations in police behavior at the organizational level (1968). In *Varieties of Police Behavior*, he described three styles of police interaction with communities and explored their contextual determinants. Although scholars continually deplore the absence of research about the behavior of police agencies as a whole, most analysis continues to focus on the behavior of individual police officers.

In addition to discretion and its determinants, police research focused initially on evaluating the effectiveness of the standard strategies of policing, notably motorized and foot patrolling and rapid response to calls for service (Kelling et al., 1974; Trojanowicz, 1986). In general, this research found that police were not getting the results expected in terms of crime prevention and public satisfaction. Curiously, although these evaluations cast serious doubt on the efficacy of contemporary police practices and were, as a result, hotly contested by the police, very few replications were undertaken. The research findings were accepted as true, despite methodological criticisms by other scholars, and became the basis for a profound rethinking of the police role in crime control and prevention in the 1980s.

The new strategy of policing that emerged in the 1980s is called community-oriented policing. Very closely related to it is problem-oriented policing. Although there are important philosophical differences between the two, their operational practices tend to overlap. The lesson that the proponents of community-oriented policing drew from the research on the efficacy of customary police practices was that the police were unable to control crime on their own without the cooperation and support of the public. This could involve reporting crime, identifying criminal suspects, calling attention to conditions that breed disorder and crime, and taking self-protecting actions. The other major intellectual inputs to the reform movement were Herman Goldstein's (1979) insight that police needed to involve communities in cooperative problem solving and James Q. Wilson's and George Kelling's (1982) proposal, captured in the metaphor of broken windows, that police should help communities create a crime-deterrent environment by minimizing public disorder.

With the advent of community policing in the 1980s, police scholarship underwent a dramatic change and became explicitly prescriptive. Scholars became advocates as well as analysts. In the 1960s, by contrast, police scholars undertook research on police behavior, notably the exercise of discretion, in order to serve the implicit agenda of providing information about its fairness, but they were reluctant to prescribe programs of remedy. Furthermore, the advocacy of the 1980s focused on issues of community safety, not on the exercise of police powers in individual encounters with the public. A vast literature grew up that outlined, elaborated, and encouraged the philosophy of community policing. Training seminars were held and instructional manuals prepared. Although a few pilot projects were undertaken, only a few systematic attempts were made to test the efficacy of community policing. Indeed, police as well as scholars lamented throughout the 1990s that both the extent and the effectiveness of community policing remained largely unknown (Rosenbaum, 1994; Roth et al., 2000).

The community policing movement reflected not only the willingness of scholars to work with, rather than simply on, the police, but also the acceptance by police of the value of such collaboration. Viewed with intense suspicion and often outright rejection in the 1960s, research by professional scholars was now viewed as a tool of progressive management and innovation.

Along with efforts to reform the core strategies of policing in the 1980s, empirical research continued but was more narrowly focused than previously. Descriptive studies of the use of deadly force, reminiscent of research about police discretion in the 1960s, prompted police agencies to adopt general policies about its use. Research showed that police behavior could successfully be changed through this mechanism. Larry Sherman and his colleagues undertook a series of studies that evaluated the deterrent effect of arrest on men accused of spouse assault (Sherman, 1992). The findings of the Minneapolis Spouse Assault Project, which was the initial study, were almost immediately incorporated into legislation and police practice. Although its findings were significantly modified by later research, the Minneapolis Spouse Assault Project is probably the single most influential research undertaken since 1967.

During the 1990s, evaluations of the impact of police strategies on community safety expanded without a dominant focus—drug crackdowns, community crime prevention, DARE, beat patrols, crime prevention education, and coordinated interagency crime prevention. While community policing dominated the headlines, due largely to the federal government's investment of $8.8 billion in the Community Oriented Policing Program in 1994, researchers pursued a more diverse agenda. The record suggests, in fact, that during the 1990s researchers recognized that in order to be evaluated successfully, police strategies, including community-oriented policing, had to be disaggregated, broken down into specific crime and disorder programs.

By the end of the decade, the evaluation literature about crime control and prevention was so extensive, as well as contradictory, that the University of Maryland, supported by the National Institute of Justice, attempted to summarize what research evidence had shown to work, not to work, and to have promise (Sherman et al., 1997). In the process, the Maryland team developed a scale for judging the scientific rigor of evaluation research based on the control of variables, measurement error, and statistical power.

Although the range and sophistication of evaluative research increased during the 1990s, the contribution of the police to the decade's remarkable decline in crime was undetermined and controversial. This may have been due to the unexpectedness of the decline, which prevented data about police activities, as well as contextual social correlates, from being collected early enough so that a connection could be explored. Also during the 1990s, a research theme from the 1960s emerged with renewed force—the unequal and sometimes abusive treatment of blacks at the hands of the police. It began with concern about police brutality (Skolnick and Fyfe, 1993; Toch and Geller, 1996) and grew to encompass racial profiling by the police (Fridell et al., 2001). Although interest in police misbehavior had never entirely died out, the events of the 1990s rekindled interest in police accountability and discipline (Walker, 2001).

Taking the period as a whole (1967 to 2000), the 10 most important topics that police researchers studied were:

1. Organization and management.
2. Crime.
3. Strategies, including community-oriented policing.
4. Drugs.
5. Women.
6. Discrimination.
7. Evaluation.
8. Ethics/accountability/discipline.
9. International/comparative policing.
10. Patrol.

This finding is based on a keyword search of four citation indexes: *Criminal Justice Abstracts*, *Sociological Abstracts*, the 12 leading criminology/criminal justice journals (listed earlier), and the three professional police periodicals (mentioned above). The 10 topics were most frequently coupled with the words "police," "policing," and "law enforcement" in the titles, identifiers, or abstracts of articles that appeared in the serials covered by these indexes. Details about this study and its methodology appear in the chapter appendix.

There was remarkable agreement across the three social science indexes with respect to these topics, even to the rank order. At the same time, the popularity of the topics, indicated by the frequency of their citation, varied enormously from the top to the bottom of the list. For example, articles about organization and management, depending on the index, were from 8 to 18 times more likely to be written about than patrol.

The most popular topics selected for discussion in the three police-oriented journals also appeared at the top of the social science lists: crime, organization and management, drugs, and strategies, including community-oriented policing. Only two topics were unique to the practitioner list: traffic and criminal investigation. Interestingly, practitioners were as interested in ethics/accountability/discipline as scholars. And international/comparative articles about police occurred more frequently in the practitioner journals.

From negligible beginnings, scientific research on the police has become a large and diverse enterprise by the beginning of the 21st century. It has sought both to explain police activity—the social science perspective—and to evaluate its effects—the public policy perspective. Although the topics studied have varied in popularity over time, no intellectual thread disappears entirely in any period. Police research has consistently described police behavior, analyzed its determinants, evaluated its efficacy, and judged its rectitude. Police research is more diverse than any particular set of substantive fashions.

POLICE RESEARCH METHODOLOGIES

The early police researchers studied the police by "walking around" (Bittner, 1970). Their research was qualitative and ethnographic, providing subtle understanding of the working life of police officers (Skolnick, 1966; Van Maanen, 1974; Manning, 1977; Muir, 1977; Brown, 1981). Descriptive research by scholars working alone remained fashionable through the 1970s, but it tended to die out during the 1980s and 1990s.

Qualitative research by individuals was quickly overtaken by controlled observations by multiple observers recording the behavior of large samples of police officers. Both sorts of studies focused almost exclusively on the behavior of patrol officers. Selective and often impressionistic observation by one person is referred to as participant observation; observation by many people using a predesigned protocol is called systematic social observation (Skolnick, 1965; Reiss, 1979). Participant observation is somewhat of a misnomer. On one hand, participant-observers are carefully instructed not to become actively involved in what they witness—indeed, not to participate. On the other hand, ethnographic observers participate in the same sense as participant-observers, in that they accompany police officers at work. It is not participation that distinguishes the two observational methodologies, but the systematization of observations, which reflects differences in the scale of research.

Systematic social observation is costly and requires considerable organizational skill, and for these reasons it has been rare: Black and Reiss (1967a, b), Bayley and Garofalo (1987), and Mastrofski et al., 1998). The data collected by these efforts have been analyzed and reanalyzed as scholars explore hypotheses about the determinants of police behavior (Sherman, 1983; Chermak and Riksheim, 1993).

Descriptive studies of the police have also utilized two sorts of surveys: (1) surveys of the attitudes and behaviors of individual police officers, often stratified by rank, and of the public (Flanagan and Longmire, 1996; Bureau of Justice Statistics, 1998; Weisburd, 2000) and (2) "establishment surveys" of police organizations to determine structures and practices (Law Enforcement Management and Administrative Survey or LEMAS).

With respect to evaluation studies that assess the social consequences of police activity, especially their contribution to public safety, the major methodological distinction is between experiments and quasi-experiments. Both, it should be noted, may employ ethnographic as well as systemic observation. In the well-known Kansas City Preventive Patrol Experiment (Kelling et al., 1974), for example, researchers varied the strength of patrol deployment in demographically similar areas. Despite the difficulties in controlling police behavior and the reluctance of police forces to adhere to experimental requirements, this methodology has been employed extensively: in Newark, NJ, to study foot patrol (Brown, 1981); in Flint, MI, for community policing (Trojanowicz, 1986); in Oakland, CA, for "beat health" (Green-Mazerolle, 1999); in Jersey City, NJ, for drug market interdiction (Weisburd and Green, 1995); and in Detroit, MI, for drug crackdowns (Bynum and Worden, 1996).

In a quasi-experimental research design, the researchers monitor naturally occurring changes in police practices and the social factors that they are assumed to affect. Little is required of the police beyond supplying information. The problem with such designs is that it is extraordinarily difficult to infer causal impact due to the multiplicity of variables that generally need to be controlled. For this reason, studies undertaken to determine so fundamental a matter as whether increasing or decreasing the number of police hired or deployed affects crime, while of enduring interest, continue to be problematic and controversial (Loftin and McDowall, 1982; Levitt, 1997; Marvel and Moody, 1996).

The emphasis on careful evaluation of the impact of police strategies led to the making of a theoretical distinction with important methodological consequences. In order to judge the effectiveness of any police practice, it is critical to describe accurately the practice itself, especially its quality and quantity. In the parlance of research, evaluation of social outcomes from police activity requires careful delineation of the outputs that constitute that activity. Evaluation requires the study of both process and result. This distinction has informed the recent movement in policing to develop performance indicators to measure what police do. Police find it easier to report outputs than outcomes, while people outside the police want evaluation of outcomes. Both, it turns out, are essential to sound evaluation. And both are essential to public accountability.

Although ethnographic research is probably less popular today than it was in the 1960s and 1970s, the methodologies adopted by police researchers have been relatively stable over time. More attention is given today to random assignment in experiments, as well as to problems of displacement. Understanding of the difficulties of causal inference from statistical correlations has also increased. As a result, the requirements of statistical analysis have become more demanding. These developments represent changes in the sophistication with which methods are used and not the development of new methods. Police research has profited from the fact that it has developed along with the social sciences. It has not had to invent new methods, but rather has been able to employ appropriate research practices from all the social sciences.

At the same time, it would be naive to expect that all police research, even all research that is responsive to the canons of scientific method, has produced equally valid and conclusive results. The scientific quality of research varies widely. The University Maryland team developed a scale for rating the scientific merit of research studies evaluating the effectiveness of crime prevention initiatives, including many undertaken by police (Sherman et al., 1997). The scale takes into consideration the control of other variables, measurement error, and statistical power (Sherman et al., 1998). The average score on a 5-point scale was 3.0, with 5 being the highest score. Only 13.4 percent of the studies could be considered to have no serious threats to internal validity. The rest had some defect, mostly commonly failing to control for causal direction and context.

AUSPICES OF POLICE RESEARCH

Scientific, peer-reviewed research on the police in the United States is currently carried out by and large by people who are not employed by either the police or the government. They are professional researchers working in colleges and universities, nonprofit think tanks, or nongovernmental organizations.[5] The police themselves do very little genuine scientific research, although since 1967 they have become more accessible to it and more understanding of it. The research and development units of most police agencies serve instead as all-purpose staff for senior executives.

Although few people who do scientific research on the police are government employees, the bulk of funding for police research comes from government. This was not always so. The American Bar Foundation's pioneering descriptions of criminal justice practices in the late 1950s and early 1960s were supported by private foundations. So, too, was the Reiss and Black systematic observation of patrol behavior for the President's Commission on Law Enforcement and the Administration of Justice (1967). In 1970 the Ford Foundation created the Police Foundation with a grant of $30 million for the purpose of inducing progressive change through the scientific description and analysis of police activities (Lewis and Kelling, 1979). The Police Foundation later created the Police Executive Research Forum, whose purpose was to study policy issues important to the country's largest municipal police departments.

Despite the precedent set by Ford and a handful of other foundations, the dominant source of financial support for research on the police has been

---

[5]Scholars working for state universities are technically government employees, but the standards of academic freedom with respect to research are so well developed that they should be considered independent of government.

government. Moreover, government funding has also become increasingly concentrated. First, the federal government substantially outspends state and local governments for peer-reviewed research—by the Law Enforcement Assistance Administration from the late 1960s to 1978 and by the National Institute of Justice after 1978. Second, the U.S. Department of Justice accounts for most of the federal government's investment in scientific police research, through the National Institute of Justice, the Office of Justice Programs, and the Office of Community Oriented Police Services. Over the past two decades, other federal research agencies, for example the National Science Foundation, have increasingly deferred to the Department of Justice with respect to criminal justice research.

It is very difficult to estimate changes in financial support for police research since the 1967 crime commission, even the proportion of investment coming from the federal government. The federal government does not maintain a central register of the cost of programs supporting criminal justice, nor is it possible to isolate the research component of such investments without examining each program separately. The report of the University of Maryland team concluded that federal investment across the board for crime prevention was small, in the range of $8 million in 1996, and probably had not changed much since the beginning of federal funding for this purpose in 1969 (Sherman et al., 1997). This impression is supported by figures from the National Research Council (1993) that showed that in the early 1990s, the U.S. government spent approximately $800 per year of potential life lost to cancer, almost $700 per life from AIDS, $40 per life from heart, lung, and blood diseases, but only $31 for potential lives lost due to interpersonal violence (cited in Travis, 1995). Paradoxically, then, police research in the United States today is independent of government in its practice but dependent on it for funding.

RESEARCH IMPACT OF THE 1994 CRIME ACT

The committee is well aware of a federally funded body of research that resulted from the Violent Crime Control and Law Enforcement Act of 1994, which mandated evaluation of existing police programs as well as new ones funded directly by the act itself. The Department of Justice implemented this mandate by transferring money internally from the Community Oriented Policing Services (COPS) Office to the National Institute of Justice. The COPS-funded research allocation to the National Institute of Justice totaled $46,639,165, the largest single investment in police research undertaken by this, or any other, government (Figure 2-1 shows yearly expenditures).

In managing this enormous investment in police research, the National Institute of Justice set as its overarching goal: "to explore practices that will

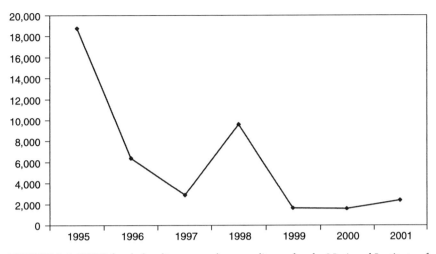

FIGURE 2-1 COPS-funded police research expenditures by the National Institute of Justice.

improve the quality of police services." It specified several strategies to achieve this goal: "one, identifying effective tactics and technologies; two, highlighting efficient organizational processes and structures; three, improving mechanisms by which police identify public needs or expectations; and, four, informing the public debate regarding what the police do on the job" (Samuels, 2000).

From 1995 through 2001, 177 grants were given by the National Institute of Justice using COPS money. Half (88) were in the range of $150,000 to $399,999; 38 percent (67) were $150,000 and under. Only 12 percent (22) were $400,000 and over, and only 4 of those were over $900,000 (see Figure 2-1).

The largest research grant from 1994 crime act monies was awarded to the Urban Institute—$3,356,156—to evaluate the success of the COPS office in encouraging the adoption of community policing. Using nationwide phone surveys, site visits, and case studies, the report (Roth et al., 2000) found:

1. High crime areas applied for and received 31 percent of all funds awarded by the COPS office.

2. COPS grants increased the number of police officers working on the street.

3. COPS initiatives lead to the spread of community policing practices throughout the country, although the content and quality of those initiatives varied considerably.

4. The impact of technology purchased with COPS money was also uneven across the country.

The Urban Institute did not evaluate the link between COPS investments and crime rates, although others have attempted to do so (Eck and Maguire, 2000; Zhao and Thurman, 2001; Muhlhausen, 2002).

With COPS funds the National Institute of Justice also sponsored the largest study of police patrol activity since the 1970s—the Project on Policing Neighborhoods in Indianapolis and St. Petersburg, 1996-1997—at a cost of $1,969,701. The study produced five major findings with respect to patrol activity and community police:

1. Patrol officers specializing in community policing spend more time problem solving than do patrol generalists (Parks et al., 1999).
2. Community police officers tend to interact more with people of higher socioeconomic status and less with those with severe problems than do police generalists.
3. Police officers' views toward community policing bear little relationship to their behavior, suggesting that imbuing officers with the philosophy of community policing will do little to advance its implementation.
4. Officers' views about community policing have no effect on their success in getting citizens to comply with police commands (McCluskey et al., 1999), the amount of coercion used against suspects (Terrill, 1997), or the amount of time engaged in problem-solving activities (DeJong et al., 2001).
5. Officers with a positive predisposition toward community policing were more likely to comply with requests to control other citizens (Mastrofski et al., 2000).

Within the COPS portfolio, the National Institute of Justice has also devoted significant resources to research on firearm violence, especially firearm violence by young people. The largest of these grants was for the National Evaluation of Youth Firearms Violence Initiative ($1,314,787). The COPS office itself created the Youth Firearms Violence Initiative in 1995, which involved spending approximately $1 million to assist 10 police departments to develop and implement programs to reduce youth gun violence. Evaluations of these efforts showed that traditional police practices are not effective in achieving this goal. Instead, success was achieved when departments worked cooperatively with other government and community organizations, initiated aggressive arrest policies for gun crime, and created special units to target gun crime (Dunworth, 2000). The studies also showed that when federal money for such programs was no longer available, departments returned to traditional practices.

Although it is important to assess the quality of COPS-funded research through NIJ, the committee decided not to do so for two reasons. First, many committee members have been recipients of these grants and have worked at universities or research organizations that have financially benefited from them, creating a potential conflict of interest. Second, by summer 2002, when this report was written, only 50 percent of COPS-supported research projects had produced written results that appeared in the National Criminal Justice Research Service data base. A total of 40 projects, representing 27 percent of the NIJ portfolio, were officially closed without a publication of any kind, while 41 grants (23 percent) were still active but have not produced a publication (see Figure 2-2).

It should be noted that a significant proportion of COPS-supported research was not designed to produce peer-reviewed publications, although some nonetheless did. These constitute the Locally Initiated Research Project, which represented 23 percent of the COPS-supported grants awarded (41 of 177) and 11.4 percent of the money awarded. The purpose of these grants was to create partnerships between police agencies and research groups for the development and evaluation of new strategies for the delivery of police services.

Despite the large investment in research on community policing, outcome evaluations and other research still cannot comprehensively and definitively provide a guide to the usefulness of this strategy. Therefore, the committee recommends more research on problem-oriented and community policing. These are two of the most widely discussed innovations in

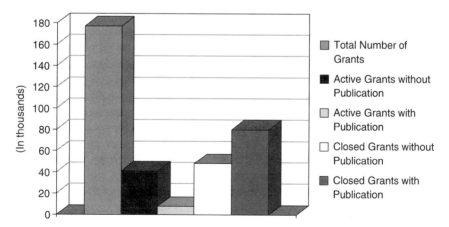

FIGURE 2-2 Total number of COPS-funded police research expenditures by grant and publication status.

policing today, each involving complex packages of programs and organizational adaptations, and each calling for efficiency and effectiveness measures that currently are not well captured by most police information systems. The organizational structures and practices that comprise these innovations are highly varied, making it difficult to form general conclusions about their effectiveness. Police employ tactics under each of these strategies that can be rigorously evaluated, but we found that there generally was not yet enough evidence to document their successes or failures. Future research should do more to advance knowledge about the effectiveness of these innovations by focusing on their key elements. The organizational arrangements that foster effective community and problem-oriented policing, and the effectiveness of police training in this area, are also not well understood.

CONCLUSION

The enterprise of police research that has developed in the United States since 1967 is unique in the world in several respects.

First, no other country has made a more concerted effort to harness the rigor of social science to the study of policing. The scale of this effort is greater than that of any other country, perhaps of the rest of the world put together.

Second, police research in the United States is behavioral rather than jurisprudential. It is based more on accurate description of the police in action, whether by individuals or agencies, and less on its legal authorization. Police researchers in the United States are trained primarily in social science rather than law.

Third, rigorous police research is done mostly by people who are employed outside of government. In the United States there is a division of labor between those who do policing and those who study it. This is often deplored, because it deprives police of in-house research capacity, but it has helped to ensure more independent inquiry.

Fourth, over the past 35 years, private philanthropy has largely withdrawn from the support of police research. Today, government dominates the funding of police research.

In this connection, one must ask whether the growing dependence of police research on the financial support of government has affected what has been studied or how studies are conducted. In our view, it undoubtedly has. Governments are more interested in evaluation that helps to reform police activity than in description that can be used to explain it. Furthermore, governments are more inclined to accept what police do (outputs) as a measure of effectiveness than what they achieve (outcomes). Police are, after all, part of government, and therefore they share an interest in shaping appearances. It is also easier and cheaper to document output activity than outcome accomplishments. Ironically, the emphasis on developing "performance indicators" in the Western democracies in recent years has encouraged this tendency. Although the impulse to demonstrate usefulness to the public is laudable, outcome evaluations, which take years to complete, do not satisfy the political need for instantaneous accountability.

Governments are also more likely to support research that evaluates the effectiveness of the police in terms of instrumental goals, such as crime control, drug interdiction, and traffic safety, than research documenting the normative and legal rectitude of police in achieving these objectives. Although governments generally embrace performance assessment for the police more than they did a generation ago, they are still reluctant to monitor normative performance. This accounts in part for the rapid development of civilian review in the United States over the last decade (Walker, 2001). As a general rule, governments fund research on the normative aspects of police conduct only when driven to it by public outrage over revelations of alleged misbehavior.

Since the President's Commission on Law Enforcement and the Administration of Justice (1967), the United States has developed a research enterprise that is substantial, empirical, expert, and independent of direct governmental, including police, control. But police research in the United States is distinctive in more than its generation of knowledge, extensive though that has been. Research has become part of the institutional practice of American policing. State and local police agencies, which account for the bulk of American policing, are the most open bureaucracies in the land, second only, perhaps, to schools. Few other American institutions, public or private, allow outsiders to observe routine operations or share in-house information as freely as the police do.

Understanding research and incorporating its insights into policy have become hallmarks of police management in the United States. Facts matter in a way that they didn't a generation ago. Research—along with higher educational standards for recruits, encouragement of postgraduate degrees for promotion, and specialized in-service courses for managers—has made American policing considerably more intelligent and less insular than it was when the president's crime commission reported in 1967.

Police research has also made American police more accountable by opening them to outside opinions, by creating partnerships with independent observers, and by helping the public and its representatives to judge whether the police are fulfilling their mandate to provide security in accordance with the principles of a democratic society. These indirect benefits from police research, which arise as much out of the conduct as the findings of research, may be even more important than its substantive contributions to police policy.

APPENDIX 2A: METHODOLOGY OF KEYWORD SEARCH

The data used to document the popularity of topics that have been studied by police researchers since 1967 are based on a keyword search of the following four bibliographic indexes:

1. *Sociological Abstracts*, covering 2,500 periodicals.
2. *Criminal Justice Abstracts*, covering 549 periodicals.
3. Twelve criminal justice journals:
    American Journal of Police (1981)
    Crime and Delinquency (1960)
    Criminal Justice History (1980)
    Criminology (1963)
    Journal of Crime and Justice (1981)
    Journal of Criminal Justice (1973)
    Journal of Quantitative Criminology (1985)
    Journal of Research on Crime and Delinquency (1964)
    Justice Quarterly (1984)
    Police and Society (1990)
    Police Science and Administration (1973)
    Police Studies (1978).
4. Three professional police journals:
    FBI Law Enforcement Bulletin
    Police Chief Magazine
    Law Enforcement News.

The titles, abstracts, and delimiters were searched to determine how frequently the keywords listed below were found with "police," "policing," and "law enforcement." The search determines the number of separate citations in which words are associated and not the number of times these associations appear in titles, abstracts, and delimiters. Because the indexes do not cover the life of all the journals indexed, the number of citations for particular keywords found understates slightly the number actually published.

A total of 68 keywords were searched for their association with "police," "policing," and "law enforcement." Tables 2A-1 through 2A-6 display the results.

Accountability
Affirmative action
Battered women
Broken windows
Brutality
Budget(s)
Civil rights
Community policing
Comparative
Corruption
Cost(s)
Crime
Crime prevention
Criminal investigation
Criminal justice
Criminal proceedings
Crowd control
Deadly force
Discipline
Discretion
Discrimination
Disorder
Diversity
Domestic violence

Drug(s)
Effectiveness
Ethics
Evaluation
Fear of crime
Firearm(s)
Gender
Gender bias
Grievance
Homosexuality
Human rights
Inequality
Information technology
Integrity
International
Leadership
Management
Morale
Narcotics
Order maintenance
Organization
Patrol
Penology

Police community
  relations
Prejudice
Problem-oriented
  policing
Public opinion
Quality of life
Race
Rank(s)
Recruitment
Riot(s)
Road safety
Spouse abuse
Spouse assault
Strategy
Structure
Supervision
Tactic(s)
Technology
Traffic
Training
Victimology
Women

TABLE 2A-1 Keyword Frequency by Index

Keyword	Sociology Abstracts Data Base	Criminal Justice Abstracts Data Base	12 Research Journals	3 Professional Journals
Accountability	102	396	21	6
Affirmative action	25	57	7	9
Battered women	129	92	8	3
Broken windows	3	17	1	2
Brutality	52	163	24	178
Budget or budgets	34	152	6	38
Civil rights	98	138	27	110
Community policing	177	570	68	75
Comparative	149	356	86	11
Corruption	124	463	70	192
Cost or costs	157	821	80	77
Crime	1,503	5,998	1,384	1,790
Crime prevention	101	1,133	182	677
Criminal investigation	29	80	61	375
Criminal justice	512	2,588	695	639
Criminal proceedings	55	45	7	0
Crowd control	7	22	10	45
Deadly force	17	170	19	54
Discipline	119	398	60	124
Discretion	107	468	96	42
Discrimination	169	353	100	296
Disorder	87	300	35	4
Diversity	54	119	10	8
Domestic violence	163	440	81	82
Drug(s)	409	1,433	254	726
Effectiveness	217	925	85	32
Ethics	63	283	82	106
Evaluation	234	1,055	221	207
Fear of crime	80	321	43	18
Firearm(s)	56	367	29	248
Gender	230	257	133	1
Gender bias	5	8	8	0
Grievance	29	79	10	2
Homosexuality	53	73	6	31

TABLE 2A-1 Continued

Keyword	Sociology Abstracts Data Base	Criminal Justice Abstracts Data Base	12 Research Journals	3 Professional Journals
Human rights	74	111	5	5
Inequality	94	78	46	3
Information technology	30	21	1	6
Integrity	16	108	13	18
International	167	593	35	556
Leadership	91	282	23	45
Management	213	1,146	118	351
Morale	20	104	6	19
Narcotics	40	349	65	597
Order maintenance	31	64	8	0
Organization	850	2,091	236	134
Patrol	138	1,449	108	550
Penology	15	27	34	9
Police community relations	455	600	282	890
Prejudice	49	108	13	4
Problem-oriented policing	10	76	6	4
Public opinion	85	208	115	46
Quality of life	24	87	6	4
Race	371	651	151	19
Rank or ranks	84	336	13	19
Recruitment	79	338	15	18
Riot(s)	142	266	28	60
Road safety	1	8	3	0
Highway safety	2	14	0	22
Traffic safety	7	25	2	124
Spouse abuse	23	77	13	14
Spouse assault	4	16	3	0
Strategy	159	440	53	23
Structure	670	1,343	137	13
Supervision	54	377	66	25
Tactic(s)	98	379	15	89
Technology	92	283	24	321
Traffic	73	497	28	468
Training	294	2,053	190	959
Victimology	8	34	11	5
Women or woman	505	1,003	244	149

TABLE 2A-2 Citation Frequency by Topics

Topic	Sociology Abstracts Data Base	Criminal Justice Abstracts Data Base	12 Research Journals	3 Professional Journals
Crime	1,503	5,998	1,384	1,790
Disorder	87	300	35	4
Broken windows	3	17	1	6
Fear of crime	80	321	43	18
	1,673	**6,636**	**1,463**	**1,808**

(If drugs, domestic violence, and crime prevention are added the totals are as follow)

	(2,519)	(10,099)	(2,056)	(3,239)
Drugs	409	1,433	254	732
Narcotics	40	349	65	597
	449	**1,782**	**319**	**1,379**
Domestic violence	163	440	81	82
Spouse assault	4	16	3	0
Battered women	129	92	8	3
	296	**548**	**92**	**85**
Women	505	1,003	244	149
Gender	230	257	133	1
	735	**1,260**	**377**	**150**
Police community relations	455	600	282	890
Public opinion	85	208	115	46
	540	**808**	**397**	**936**
Evaluation	234	1,055	221	207
Effectiveness	217	925	85	32
	451	**1,980**	**306**	**239**
Organization	850	2,091	236	134
Structure	670	1,343	137	13
Management	213	1,146	118	351
Leadership	91	282	23	35
Supervision	54	377	66	25
Budget(s)	34	152	6	38
Cost(s)	157	821	80	77
Grievance	29	79	10	2
Morale	20	104	6	19
Rank(s)	84	336	13	19
Recruitment	79	338	15	18
Training	294	2,053	190	959
	2,383	**11,505**	**690**	**1,709**

TABLE 2A-2 Continued

Topic	Sociology Abstracts Data Base	Criminal Justice Abstracts Data Base	12 Research Journals	3 Professional Journals
(If accountability/discipline are added, then)				
	(2,605)	(12,299)	(771)	(1,839)
International	167	593	35	556
Comparative	149	356	86	11
	316	**628**	**121**	**566**
Community policing	177	570	68	75
POP	10	76	6	4
Order maintenance	31	64	8	0
Quality of life	24	87	6	4
	242	**797**	**88**	**83**
(If police-community relations are added, then)				
	(782)	(1,605)	(485)	(973)
Patrol	138	1,449	108	550
Discrimination	169	353	100	296
Prejudice	49	108	13	4
Race	371	651	151	19
Diversity	54	119	10	8
Gender bias	5	8	9	0
Inequality	94	78	46	3
Homosexuality	53	73	6	31
Affirmative action	25	57	7	9
	820	**1,447**	**342**	**370**
Strategy	159	440	53	23
Tactics	98	379	15	89
	257	**819**	**68**	**112**
Traffic	73	497	28	468
Road safety	1	8	3	0
Highway safety	2	14	0	22
Traffic safety	7	25	2	124
	83	**544**	**33**	**614**
Technology	92	283	24	321
Information	30	21	1	6
technology	**122**	**304**	**25**	**327**

continued

TABLE 2A-2 Continued

Keyword	Sociology Abstracts Data Base	Criminal Justice Abstracts Data Base	12 Research Journals	3 Professional Journals
Crime prevention	101	1,133	182	677
Disorder	87	300	35	4
Broken Windows	3	17	1	2
	90	317	36	6
Ethics	63	283	82	102
Integrity	16	108	13	18
Corruption	124	463	70	192
Brutality	52	163	24	178
	255	1,017	189	490
Human rights	74	111	5	5
Civil rights	98	138	27	110
	172	249	33	115
Riot	142	266	28	60
Crowd control	7	22	10	45
	149	288	38	105
Accountability	102	396	21	6
Discipline	119	398	60	124
	221	794	81	130
Discretion	107	468	96	42
Firearms	56	367	29	248
Deadly force	17	170	19	54
	73	537	48	302
Criminal investigation	29	80	61	375

NOTE: Keywords have been grouped into topics—subject matter that involves more than one keyword.

TABLE 2A-3 Topics Rank-Ordered in *Sociology Abstracts*

Topics	Citations
1 Organization	2,383
(with accountability/discipline)	(2,605)
2 Crime	1,673
(with drugs, domestic violence, and crime prevention)	(2,519)
2a See strategies	(1,382)
3 Discrimination	820
4 Women	735
5 Police community relations	540
6 Strategies, including COP	499
(with COP at	242
COP with c-p rels	782
Crime prevention 101)	(1,382)
6a See ethics/acct/discipline	(477)
7 Evaluation	451
8 Narcotics	449
9 International/comparative	316
10 Domestic violence	296
11 Ethics	255
12 Accountability/discipline	222
(with ethics)	(477)
13 Human rights	172
14 Riots	149
15 Patrol	138
16 Technology	122
17 Discretion	107
18 Crime prevention	101
19 Disorder	90
20 Traffic	83
21 Firearms	73
22 Criminal investigation	29

TABLE 2A-4 Topics Rank-Ordered in *Criminal Justice Abstracts*

Topics	Citations
1 Organization	11,505
(with accountability/discipline)	(12,299)
2 Crime	6,636
(with drugs, domestic	(10,099)
violence, and crime prevention)	
3 Evaluation	1,980
4 Drugs	1,782
4a Strategy with COP	(1,616)
4b COP with community relations	(1,605)
5 Patrol	1,449
6 Discrimination	1,447
7 Women	1,260
8 Crime prevention	1,133
9 Ethics	1,017
(with acct/discipline)	(1,239)
10 Strategy	819
11 Police-community relations	808
12 COP	797
13 Accountability/discipline	794
14 International/comparative	628
15 Domestic violence	548
16 Traffic	544
17 Firearms	537
18 Discretion	468
19 Technology	304
20 Riots	288
21 Human rights	249
22 Criminal investigation	80

TABLE 2A-5 Topics Rank-Ordered in 12 Criminal Justice Journals

Topics	Citations
1 Crime	1,463
(with drugs, domestic violence, and crime prevention)	(2,056)
2 Organization	690
(with accountability/discipline)	(771)
2a COP with police-community relations	(485)
3 Police community relations	397
4 Women	377
5 Discrimination	342
6 Drugs	319
7 Evaluation	306
8 Ethics	189
9 Crime prevention	182
(with strategy and COP)	(156)
10 International/comparative	121
11 Patrol	108
12 Discretion	96
13 Domestic violence	82
14 COP	88
15 Accountability/discipline	81
16 Strategy	68
17 Criminal investigation	61
18 Firearms	48
19 Riots	38
20 Traffic	33
21 Human rights	33
22 Technology	25

TABLE 2A-6 Topics Rank-Ordered in Three Professional Police Journals

Topics	Citations
1 Crime	1,808
(With drugs, domestic violence, and crime prevention	(3,239)
2 Organization	1,709
(With accountability/discipline)	(1,839)
3 Drugs	1,379
(3a Community policing with police-community relations	973)
4 Police community relations	936
5 Crime prevention	677
6 Traffic	614
7 International/comparative	566
8 Patrol	550
9 Ethics	490
10 Criminal investigation	375
11 Discrimination	370
12 Technology	327
13 Firearms	302
14 Evaluation	239
15 Women	150
16 Accountability/discipline	130
17 Human rights	115
18 Strategy	112
19 Riots	105
20 Domestic violence	85
21 Community policing	83
22 Discretion	42

3

The Nature of Policing in the United States

The public view of policing—police officers patrolling streets and responding to emergency crime calls; police detectives interviewing witnesses, examining forensic clues, checking records and interrogating suspects; police chiefs and officers struggling to escape from the threat of political interference—is not entirely inaccurate. But it owes far too much to a particular view of policing that is presented on television and in movies for dramatic effect, and far too little to statistics and research. In this chapter we rely on the latter to more accurately describe the landscape of policing—in the United States, a varied and complex structure that we call the "police industry." Especially noteworthy characteristics of this industry include the wide variety of functions that law enforcement organizations are asked to perform and the role of individual police officer discretion, and we give both special attention. Within these two broad themes we focus on issues of importance to the rest of the committee's work: the complexity of police-public encounters and the special question of what determines when, why, and how individual police officers exercise authority and force. Finally, the chapter describes recent major innovations in policing that are referred to and evaluated throughout this report. These include new policing strategies and the changing profile of rank-and-file police officers. Like much of this report, most of this discussion is limited to the findings of research on big-city police, because rural and small-town policing has been so underevaluated.

Because governments at all levels are concerned with fostering further efficiency, effectiveness, and fairness, this chapter also includes an examination of the innovation process itself. The decentralized nature of policing in the United States presents special assets, but it also complicates the process by which police innovate and learn. The locally funded and locally controlled world of policing challenges the ability of federal and state governments to promote systematic and directed change.

Efforts to increase the efficiency, effectiveness, and fairness of policing are also limited by what is known. As this report makes clear, there is a tremendous imbalance in what is known about certain aspects of policing and about "what works." Some aspects of policing have been heavily studied, and others have been neglected. This limits our ability to recommend specific programs or policies in many areas. The report calls for further research more often than one might hope, because the knowledge base for policing is so limited on many key topics.

ORGANIZATIONAL STRUCTURE OF AMERICAN POLICING

It is useful to describe American policing as an industry because, as is the case with other goods and services, services are delivered by a number of different providers (Ostrom, Whitaker, and Parks, 1978:3). Unlike police in most other industrialized countries, the structure of the American police industry is highly fragmented, in the sense that there is a multiplicity of loosely coordinated agencies at different levels of government. In recent years, the relationships between public agencies at different levels of government have been further complicated by the existence of multijurisdictional task forces directed toward particular problems, such as drug trafficking (Geller and Scott, 1992; Jeffries et al., 1998). Estimates vary, depending on the definition that is used, but the most expansive estimate is that there are as many as 21,143 federal, state, and local law enforcement agencies (Roth et al., 2000). The Bureau of Justice Statistics (BJS), however, estimates that in 1997 there were approximately 19,160 public law enforcement agencies (Reeves and Goldberg, 2000). For many years, experts in the field believed there were 40,000 agencies (President's Commission, 1967). The number of employees similarly varies from the 608,540 police officers and civilian employees counted by the Urban Institute in 1996 (Roth et al., 2000) to the Bureau of Justice Statistics survey, which found over 1,000,000 employees, about 775,000 of whom were police officers with arrest powers (Reeves and Goldberg, 2000).

The main focus of this report is on local police departments. In 1999, BJS counted 13,500 agencies at this level of government, with about 557,000 employees overall, and about 436,000 sworn police officers (Hickman and Reeves, 2001).

Public law enforcement agencies vary considerably in size, as measured by the number of sworn officers (Hickman and Reeves, 2001). A relatively small number of large (1,000 or more officers) agencies (62) provide policing services for 17.2 percent of the U.S. population (Brown and Langan, 2001). Large cities also have a disproportionate share of violent crime: in 2000, cities with over 1 million population accounted for 18.6 percent of all violent crime reported to the police (Federal Bureau of Investigation, 2001; Langan et al., 2001). At the same time, thousands of the smallest agencies, many with one or two officers, respond to very small numbers of violent crimes. Agency size is an extremely important factor in policing: Not only do the largest police departments face the most complex responsibilities, in large part because they are in urban environments with the most serious social problems, but they are also intricate bureaucracies and as a consequence extremely difficult to manage and to change. Because of these variations, it is virtually impossible to talk about policing as a homogenous institution.

Law enforcement agencies at different levels of government have substantially different formal responsibilities, as prescribed by law, and therefore engage in different kinds of activities. Local police (municipal police departments, county police departments, and county sheriffs) have the broadest mandate: nearly all municipal and county police agencies enforce criminal laws, maintain order, and provide miscellaneous services to the public on a day-to-day basis. Because these agencies engage in routine patrol throughout the communities they serve and respond to requests for service, they are the agencies most visible to the public and also have the most direct contact with them.

At the local level, municipal law enforcement agencies provide the lion's share of police services in the United States, with a few sheriffs providing general policing services. The 1999 BJS agency survey (Brown and Langan, 2001) indicates that there were approximately 13,524 municipal police forces in the United States. Only 46 of these departments employed more than 1,000 sworn officers, yet these same agencies constituted 34.1 percent of all local sworn officers in the country. Meanwhile, 771 local police departments employ just one sworn officer.

Local law enforcement is also organized at the county level, primarily around the office of county sheriff. Fewer than 100 of the 3,100 or so county law enforcement agencies go by the designation "police department," while the rest are titled "sheriff's office" (or "department") (Reaves and Goldberg, 2000). The 1997 BJS survey indicates that there were nearly 175,000 sworn officers employed by the approximately 3,000 sheriff's offices throughout the nation (Bureau of Justice Statistics, 2000). One of the major distinctions between sheriff's offices and county and municipal police departments is that the head of the agency (i.e., the sheriff) is nearly always an elected official, while both city and county police chiefs generally are appointed executive branch employees. Sheriff's departments are also unique in that they serve all three branches of the criminal justice system:

law enforcement, courts, and corrections. About 98 percent of all sheriff's departments also provide bailiff and other services to the county courts, including serving summonses and other civil law matters, and about 80 percent also operate the primary jail in their counties (Brown and Langan, 2001).

State law enforcement agencies fall into two basic categories. About half are primarily responsible for traffic enforcement on highways, while the other half have general law enforcement responsibilities throughout the state. In addition, many states maintain state-level bureaus of criminal investigation with broad law enforcement responsibilities. In 1996 state police agencies employed about 85,000 people, 56,000 of whom were sworn officers (Hickman and Reaves, 2001). Most states also maintain other organizations with special and limited law enforcement powers, such as fish and game police, harbor police, and units that guard state buildings. There were an estimated 575 such agencies in 1993 employing 14,300 people (Roth et al., 2000). In addition, state agencies often cover jurisdiction anomalies or unincorporated areas and small towns that do not have their own police forces. Basic police services are provided to these areas by state law enforcement or county sheriff's departments, often under a formal contractual arrangement.

At the federal level, there are an estimated 69 law enforcement agencies employing a total of about 88,000 officers "with arrest and firearm authority" (Reaves and Hart, 2000). The responsibilities of federal agencies are generally very specific and defined by federal law—for example, the Customs Bureau enforces import and export laws. While the largest federal agencies—the Immigration and Naturalization Service, the Federal Bureau of Investigation (FBI)—are well known to the public, there are also many very small agencies, for example the Library of Congress police, which employs only 147 law enforcement officers.

Law enforcement services are also provided by a number of special district police, which are independent or semi-independent of other units of government. Of these, the most important are American Indian tribal law enforcement police. As a result of the historic and unique legal status of American Indian tribes, many tribal authorities operate their own police departments (and in some cases entire criminal justice systems) (Feinman, 1986; Luna, 1998; Wakeling et al., 1999). These agencies are not subject to many of the state and federal laws (e.g., equal employment opportunity requirements). Little research has been conducted on tribal policing; however, a recent federal report found very high rates of criminal victimization and inadequate law enforcement protection in tribal areas (U.S. Attorney General, 1997; Bureau of Justice Statistics, 1999).

Apart from tribal police, there are an estimated 1,316 other special district police departments, including 117 public school system police and

28 transportation system police agencies. (Bureau of Justice Statistics, 1998). There are between 581 and 1,316 campus law enforcement agencies; the varying estimates illustrate the difficulties in determining even how many law enforcement agencies there are in the country (Bromley and Reaves, 1998; Bureau of Justice Statistics, 1998).

Law enforcement and the criminal justice system more generally are an expensive item in the national budget. Most of the cost of policing is borne locally. Overall, local government spending on policing totaled about $41 billion during 1996-1997, the most recent figures available. This represented a near tripling in spending since 1981-1982, when local policing cost about $14 billion. In 2000, the nation's largest local police departments almost equaled the entire allocation of 1981-1982: the 62 local agencies that serve cities with 250,000 or more population spent $13.1 billion operating their departments. In 1996-1997, local government spent just over three times as much on education, the largest function of local government, as it did on policing (U.S. Census Bureau, 1997). Estimates of the cost of policing must consider the important role that overtime pay plays in certain police programs. Many departments pay police officers overtime to staff special events, extend the shifts of special units, and respond to emergencies, as well as to compensate for recurring understaffing. During the 1990s, federal support for overtime in order to provide personnel for projects of national interest played a growing role in agency finances (Bayley and Worden, 1998). As a result, spending, rather than personnel totals, best reflects the overall magnitude of police operations.

Governance of Public Police Agencies

As public-sector organizations, police agencies in the United States are subject to direct public control and influence. The bulk of these agencies serve municipalities and other local jurisdictions, and they are locally financed and locally controlled. The tradition of local control, which also prevails with respect to public education in the United States, generates both unique strengths and special problems for policing.

On one hand, local political control represents a fundamental aspect of democratic self-government: the principle that public agencies are subject to control by officials elected by and responsible to the taxpayers. Because of this preference, the decentralized nature of policing has been remarkably resistant to long-standing recommendations for consolidation into larger units serving several communities (Ostrom, Parks, and Whitaker, 1978). Local political control is a vital aspect of the legitimacy of the police. By providing a means by which residents can control the law enforcement agencies that serve their communities, the policies and priorities of these agencies are responsive to public concerns.

On the other hand, public control and influence—or what is often labeled "politics"—has historically resulted in problems for law enforcement in the United States, including inefficiency, corruption, and abuse of powerless groups, especially minorities (Fogelson, 1977; Walker, 1977). At various times in history, these problems have led to efforts to reform the governance of policing. One approach popular in the 19th century involved shifting control of big city agencies to state government. With only a few exceptions, control later returned to the municipalities. More often reformers attempted to insulate police departments from politics by protecting employees through civil service regulations or guaranteeing the chief executive long or lifetime tenure in office.

Consequences of Fragmentation

The fragmentation of law enforcement agencies has long raised concerns about the lack of coordination of effort among agencies in the same geographical jurisdiction and a consequent loss of effectiveness and efficiency. These concerns were part of a larger concern about a "nonsystem" of criminal justice and lack of coordination among all components of the criminal justice system (Law Enforcement Assistance Administration, 1973). In response to the coordination, effectiveness, and efficiency concerns, public administration experts have for decades advocated the consolidation of law enforcement agencies in certain geographic areas. Little consolidation has occurred, in large part because of opposition from entrenched political and bureaucratic interests. In addition, research by Ostrom, Whitaker, and Parks (1978:321) found that small law enforcement agencies were not as inefficient as they had traditionally been portrayed.

Apart from formal consolidation, considerable coordination and sharing of services exists along the lines described by Ostrom et al. (1978), and there is some reason to believe that such efforts have increased in the past 25 years. The International City Management Association (Fyfe, 1983) estimates that police communications and jail services are among the government services most commonly shared through contracting or joint agreements between local governments. New concerns about regional, national, and international criminal activity have led to the creation of regional task forces or strike forces related to specific forms of criminal activity, notably drugs (Jeffries et al., 1998).

The heightened national concern about terrorism following the events of September 11, 2001, has increased public interest in coordinated law enforcement efforts and new roles for local police in combating a previously faraway problem. While a number of new antiterrorism measures have been launched since September 11, as yet there is little systematic research to serve as a guide for these new ventures. Little is known, for example, about the factors related to successful interagency coordination or successful antiterrorist strategies and tactics in a domestic U.S. context.

As a result of the decentralized police industry, different levels of government exert different degrees and forms of influence on law enforcement.

Role of the Federal Government

Contrary to popular belief, the federal role in shaping the character of policing is relatively small. Federal influence or control over policing is expressed through each of the three branches of the federal government. For the most part, and especially in comparison to the organization of policing in many other industrial nations, the federal government has had little to do with the conduct of American policing. In the United Kingdom, for example, local agencies receive half of their annual budget from the national government, and senior police managers receive extensive training at a national police academy. The budgetary process and national training are used there used to ensure conformance with national standards for local policing.

Presidents of the United States have the power to influence law enforcement in very limited ways. Most directly, the president appoints the U.S. attorney general and the director of the FBI, thereby shaping federal law enforcement policy. The president also appoints the directors of the Office of Justice Programs and the National Institute of Justice, both charged with providing assistance to state and local criminal justice agencies, thereby influencing the policies and spending of these agencies. The U.S. Department of Justice (DOJ) can also take action to protect the rights of citizens. Most recently, the 1994 Violent Crime Control and Law Enforcement Act authorized the DOJ to sue police departments for a "pattern or practice" of violating the rights of citizens; before 1994, such broad powers were limited to police agencies receiving certain government funds or to individual complaints filed with the DOJ Civil Rights Division. To date about eight departments have resolved such suits with consent decrees requiring a variety of organizational reforms. These legal powers are a potentially important instrument of police reform (Chapter 7 considers them, and lawsuits more generally, in more detail). The president also sponsors federal legislation that may impact law enforcement. Finally, presidents appoint justices to the Supreme Court, which ultimately shapes constitutional law as it affects policing.

Federal financial support for state and local law enforcement funds represents less than 10 percent of all law enforcement spending. This percentage closely parallels the role of federal spending with regard to public education in the United States (8.5 percent of all spending in 1996) (U.S. Census Bureau, 1999:166). Through its research arm, the National Institute of Justice (and its predecessor the Law Enforcement Assistance Administration), the federal government funds research on various aspects of the criminal justice system, including policing. Under the 1994 Violent Crime Control Act, the Office of Community Oriented Policing Services had spent $7.6 billion by November 2000 to support community policing (Ramirez et al., 2001b). The Office of Justice Programs, meanwhile, has supported demonstration projects designed to spur innovation and promote police effectiveness. In the end, however, the typical local law enforcement agency could carry out its core functions without federal support.

Aside from financial support, the principal federal legislation affecting police departments are the various equal employment opportunity laws. The most important is Title VII of the 1964 Civil Rights Act, which outlaws employment discrimination on the basis of race, ethnicity, national origins, religion, and gender. Other federal laws, such as the Americans with Disabilities Act and the Pregnancy Discrimination Act, also affect the employment practices of law enforcement agencies. It is important to note, however, that these laws are negative in orientation, prohibiting various practices. They are not affirmative in the sense of creating federal standards of employment for law enforcement.

Decisions by the federal courts have significant implications for police policies and practices. The most important involve constitutional aspects of criminal procedure and cover such areas as searches and seizures (Fourth Amendment to the Constitution) and interrogations (Fifth Amendment). Some of the most important decisions have had important ancillary consequences in terms of prodding police departments to improve recruitment, training, and supervision (Walker, 1993). The federal courts are also currently involved in handling Justice Department "pattern or practice" suits and enforcing consent decrees that require major organizational reforms on the departments in question (Davis et al., 2002).

Role of State Governments

State governments also have a less limited but still relatively small role in shaping the overall character of public law enforcement in the United States. Historically, there has been almost no state financial support for municipal policing. Beginning in the late 1960s, the states set minimum standards for the training and certification of police officers. States have long had certification or licensing standards for other professions, but requirements for the police actually were developed later than those for many other jobs. State certification requirements (e.g., length of preservice training) are typically lower than those required by many large urban police agencies. A number of states have instituted procedures for decertifying officers guilty of misconduct, thereby denying them the right to be police officers in that state—but not other states (Puro, Goldman, and Smith, 1997).

More than federal law, state statutes impact police operations. State statutes define which employees have the official status of "peace officer" and describe the authority of police to arrest and to use force. Many states also have laws governing specific police actions, such as high-speed pursuits and handling domestic violence incidents. State laws also regulate the collective bargaining rights of organizations representing police employees. State laws regarding the appeal or arbitration of police officer discipline cases have an impact on accountability in local departments. States also codify the criminal statutes that the police enforce, setting procedural standards for apprehending and prosecuting those who violate them. State courts play a significant role, partly because they make operational the general principles of police conduct enunciated by federal appellate courts.

Role of Local Governments

Local governments exercise the greatest control over American law enforcement. This control is manifested in terms of budgetary support and the appointment or election of chief executives. Through the appointment process, local officials have a strong voice in shaping the general policies of police departments. For example, a mayor might dismiss a police chief because the chief is perceived to be insufficiently aggressive about fighting crime or has been unable to eliminate corruption in the department. Local governments in over 100 cities and counties (representing at least one-third of the U.S. population) have also created civilian oversight agencies, which have various roles and responsibilities with respect to complaints by the public against police officers and, as a consequence, have become significant factors with respect to regulating police behavior (Walker, 2001).

Private agencies provide a wide range of law enforcement services in the United States (Kakalik and Wildhorn, 1977). This already large and still rapidly growing private security sector can variously work to supplement, complement, and conflict with the activities of public police. The division of labor between public and private agencies is increasingly ambiguous (Bayley and Shearing, 2001).

The exact size of the private security industry is not known, in part because of the difficulty in measuring an enterprise that consists of many small firms employing a large number of part-time and short-term employees. One study estimated more than 400,000 employees in the private security industry in 1972, with just under 75 percent of these individuals being primarily employed in the industry (Kakalik and Wildhorn, 1977:18).

Some private security employees are uniformed and easily recognizable. They provide a broad spectrum of security services, such as guarding buildings or business districts, protecting shipments of valuable goods, patrolling neighborhoods, and responding to home security alarms. Other "white-collar" security workers conduct investigations, audits, and computer security projects that parallel to a certain extent the functions of public-sector police. Not only is the so-called private security industry large and complex, but also there are many arrangements whereby public agencies contract with private security providers and private groups contract with public agencies for services. Some police departments contract out a few of their activities to these firms, including prisoner services, training, court security, dispatching, and traffic and parking control. As Forst and Manning (1999:15) note, "The police no longer monopolize public safety."

Other Forms of Policing

Public and even private police represent only a part of the law enforcement and security apparatus of the United States. Because of its focus on larger municipal police departments—a focus imposed by the body of research open for review—a great deal of "law enforcement" in the United States falls outside the purview of this report. A broad range of organizations exist at least in part to protect the public from criminal attack, doing so at least in part by enforcing criminal laws. They include, for example, the Occupational Safety and Health Administration. It enforces a body of law that is both civil and criminal. Its goal is to protect workers from the negligent or malicious acts of employers. Yet it does not think of itself as a police organization. Neither do state-level alcoholic beverage control commissions, even though they, too, enforce laws with an eye to protecting the safety of the public. Viewed from this perspective, the police are a subset of the broader class of security and law enforcement agencies. These activities are carried out by a wide range of public agencies at the federal, state, and local levels of government.

It is also important to note (but this report does not further consider) that perhaps the most important source of community security is generated by individuals acting in their own self-defense, by exercising caution and good judgment, buying locks or dogs, and sometimes banding together with other community members in collective security efforts. Even the debate over civilians carrying licensed concealed weapons has taken on "policing" overtones, through their possible crime prevention effects (Kleck, 1991). Indeed, both self-help and private security came long before public policing. Public policing as we know it was invented only about a century and a half ago, and prior to that time, enforcement of criminal laws lay in the hands of private parties.

An important issue for the future is the extent to which state and local police, private security forces, and even neighborhood watch groups and citizen patrols should or could be more effectively integrated into a larger national security apparatus. Concerns about terrorism, drugs, and so on seem to push in this direction. By the same token, strong traditions that favor localism and instinctively distrust powerful central governments advise us to resist the temptation. Because we are focusing on American policing—understood to be primarily public agencies controlled at the local level—we have not addressed ourselves to these larger structural issues, but they will doubtless become increasingly important in the future.

ACTIVITIES OF THE POLICE

The police have many different responsibilities. Many of these are framed in very vague terms. It is not precisely clear, for example, what maintaining order might encompass. Interpreting these vague mandates and selecting priorities from among them requires a high level of discretion on the part of police executives and policy makers. In addition, there are potential conflicts between many of the various responsibilities. One of the core dilemmas of policing, for example, is that public demands for effective law enforcement may seem to conflict with the responsibility to protect individual civil liberties. Growing recognition of the complexity of police roles and responsibilities has led members of the profession (which includes both law enforcement officials and policy-oriented members of the academic community) to reconceptualize the police role and redirect police department activities in ways that are more in accord with the realities of policing and the needs of the American people (Goldstein, 1977; Sparrow, Moore, and Kennedy, 1990).

This section examines a number of police activities; these activities serve as the context in which police execute their many responsibilities. First, police encounter the public in a number of ways, including, especially, uniformed patrol. Under this broad rubric, the police work to maintain order, provide service, control traffic, prevent or investigate crimes, and process information. Occasionally, the police provide what can be called specialized services—wherein discrete organizational units, like SWAT (Special Weapons and Tactics) teams, perform unique functions. This section examines what is known about all of these activities.

Engagement with Citizens and the Community

Uniformed Patrol

The bulk of police work is conducted by uniformed officers assigned to patrol specific geographic areas (beats). Typically, roughly 60 percent of all sworn officers in city police departments are assigned to the patrol bureau, and these officers have the vast majority of police officer contacts with the general public. More than 90 percent of the local police agencies that employ 100 or more sworn officers assign at least three-fourths of their patrol force to automobile patrol (Reaves and Hart, 2000). A substantial proportion of agencies employing 100 or more officers (and nearly all of the big-city agencies) assign officers to walk foot beats, with some devoting more than a third of their patrol force to such duty (Reaves and Hart, 2000). Most agencies also conduct some patrol on motorcycles, although the vast majority of agencies assign fewer than 10 percent of their patrol officers to motorcycle duty, and none assigns more than 40 percent (Reaves and Hart, 2000). In the last decade or so, many agencies have added bicycles to the list of conveyances via which their officers patrol. Today, substantially more than half of the agencies employing 100 or more sworn officers conduct routine bicycle patrol, with some assigning more than a quarter of their patrol units to this task (Reaves and Hart, 2000). For example, big-city departments have almost universally (98 percent, in one federal study) added bicycles to their inventory of patrol vehicles (Brown and Langan, 2001).

The bulk of patrol officer contacts with the public involve responding to calls for service. Overall, 65 percent of all local police officers worked by responding to calls for service in 1999. In less specialized, smaller agencies, as many at 90 percent did so (Bureau of Justice Statistics, 2001d). Historically, one of the most important changes in policing has been the growth of publicly initiated, as opposed to police-initiated, interactions between police and community residents. This has been driven by the development and widespread adoption of communication systems designed to allow individuals to quickly contact the police and, in turn, for law enforcement agencies to quickly dispatch officers in response. Most important among these was the widespread adoption of a three-digit emergency number—911. People also initiate encounters by walking into their local police station, by flagging down patrol officers in the streets, and by requesting assistance via the telephone. Widespread use of cell phones has made contacting police departments or even individual officers even easier. On the police-to-resident side of the coin, the most important advancement has been the use of computer-aided dispatch (CAD) systems that allow dispatchers to track the status and whereabouts of patrol officers and direct them to the person who is requesting assistance in an efficient fashion. By 1999, virtually all police agencies serving cities of 50,000 residents or more relied on computer-aided dispatching systems (Brown and Langan, 2001).

About half of all calls to the police result in the dispatch of a police officer. Perhaps contrary to expectation, most of these calls do not involve either serious crimes or pressing emergencies. Officers are dispatched in a variety of situations. Research indicates that between 70 and 80 percent of dispatches are based on requests for order maintenance and service, rather than criminal activities (Scott, 1981:28-30). Moreover, when officers appear on the scene, they often find a somewhat different situation from what they expected on the basis of the initial call; many calls that initially appear to involve criminal activity in fact involve no actionable offense (Klinger and Bridges, 1995).

The ability to easily telephone the police has affected the allocation of police personnel and the nature of patrol work itself (Reiss, 1971; Sparrow, Moore, and Kennedy, 1990). In the absence of a formal program to actively screen calls and make decisions on whether or not to dispatch a car in response (McEwen, Connors, and Owen, 1986), what the general public defines as worthy of police attention dominates police patrol work. On the positive side, this ensures that, to no small degree, the police will be highly responsive to what local residents think they need from their local police department. On the negative side, the "you call, we come" system reduces the capacity of both police chiefs and the elected officials who represent the *collectively* defined goals and purposes of the police to achieve those goals. Too many of their resources may be committed to responding to individuals' insistent calls.

Recent thinking on policing, which has been driven by community policing and increased interest in crime prevention, has placed a high priority on increasing proactive activities initiated by uniformed patrol officers. Consequently, attention has turned to the larger management process through which police agencies engage in strategic planning, set clear priorities, and mobilize their resources. Proactive or officer-initiated police work involves a number of different activities: field interrogations of pedestrians, traffic stops, checks of buildings or other areas for possible criminal activity, and informal contacts with the public. There is substantial variation in the level of officer-initiated activity in different departments (Mastrofski et al., 1998), although there is no research on the factors that shape these differences. While these variations appear to be a consequence of department priorities (as communicated through management styles) and local organizational cultures, direct research of this issue would be particularly valuable, since community policing and problem-oriented policing programs have placed much emphasis on increasing proactive, officer-initiated activity.

Even though reacting to calls for service constitutes the bulk of police officer encounters with the public, patrol officers retain a certain degree of autonomous control over portions of their working hours. Officers spend considerable amounts of time handling routine paperwork and other administrative duties (Kelling et al., 1974; Parks et al., 1999). Moreover, they have some limited capacity to manipulate their availability for calls for service.

Patrol officers also spend a significant part of their unassigned time conducting what is known as "preventive patrol" (Kelling et al., 1974).

Since the advent of modern police forces in the 19th century, preventive patrol has been the core police activity, designed to prevent crime by deterring potential offenders through a visible police presence, to create feelings of public safety, and to make officers available for service in local communities with uniformed patrol forces.

One important idea animating interest in problem-solving and community policing (which are discussed in detail below) is that both call for less reactive and more proactive uses of the uniformed patrol force. Of course, the idea that the police patrol operations ought to be proactive is hardly a new idea. One goal of patrol was always to spot and investigate suspicious activity as well as respond to calls for service. Such activities were justified by a strong interest in *preventing* crime as well as responding after crime had occurred. Indeed, in the late 1960s, some police departments were relying on a police tactic described as "aggressive preventive patrol" (which bears a close resemblance to what is often described as "zero tolerance policing" today). The aim was to make the police a credible presence on the street by using their powers to stop people and ask questions. The hope was that, by doing so, the police could discourage offenders from committing offenses and interrupt situations that were leading to crimes.

To create time for such activities to occur, police administrators had to find some way to protect some of their patrol resources from nonemergency demands of the public. To accomplish this goal, they developed "differential response systems." This included efforts to distinguish among the calls for which an immediate response was very valuable (e.g., a crime in progress), from those for which an immediate response was not needed (e.g., a call about a burglary that had happened several days before, or a request for a kind of assistance that was relatively low priority compared with either responding to an urgent crime call or remaining available to respond to such a call). It also included efforts to sequester certain parts of the patrol force from the calls for service so that they could concentrate on proactive efforts. These "special operations units" often engaged in "directed patrol" tactics. Some of these directed patrol operations were described as "location-oriented patrol" (which focused on locations that were thought particularly likely to be the site of crimes). Others were "person-oriented patrols," which focused on individuals who were thought to be particularly likely to commit offenses.

Research on these proactive patrol methods tended to produce ambiguous results in terms of their crime control effectiveness. On one hand, Wilson and Boland (1980) found that one of the most powerful variables in explaining which police departments seemed to be more effective at reducing crime was the frequency of police traffic stops. They interpreted the traffic stops as an indicator of how proactive police departments were in searching for crime and trying to prevent it rather than simply waiting for it to occur. On the other hand, studies of location-oriented and perpetrator-oriented enforcement strategies carried out by the Police Foundation found little evidence of crime control effectiveness (Martin and Sherman, 1986). These issues are examined in detail in Chapter 6.

Regardless of their crime control effectiveness, these proactive police tactics generated a great deal of resentment among those who found themselves the objects of this special police attention. The methods also drew the ire of political figures representing the interests of the minorities and the poor who were overpoliced by these methods. The Kerner Commission, established to understand the causes of civil disorder in U.S. society, also found the abrasive encounters between police and citizens fostered by these tactics to be one of the important causes of the urban disorder of the late 1960s.

An important question is whether the new forms of proactive policing are any different from the old forms, especially in what is done about a wide variety of calls that are "in the middle" in terms of urgency. Today, police agencies have reasons to focus on both less serious offenses and on noncrime calls. The theory of order maintenance or "broken windows policing" has made minor offenses an important focus of police patrol operations. Such activities have been shown both to reduce serious crime and to enhance feelings of security. The theory of community policing also makes a virtue of providing service that is responsive to public priorities. Such efforts can be considered valuable in themselves ("service to the customers of policing"). But they can also be viewed as important ways of building both the legitimacy of the police and engaging the public in efforts to help the police accomplish their law enforcement objectives.

It also remains true that some police departments, under the rubric of community and problem-oriented policing, have embraced strategies that look a great deal like some of the old proactive strategies of policing. Aggressive preventive patrol has been resurrected as zero tolerance policing. Directed patrol operations, in which the police simply dispatch police officers to places and times where crimes are likely to occur, have reemerged as a limited form of problem solving policing. Location oriented patrol has reemerged as "hot spot policing" in which the police identify particular locations in which crimes are likely to occur, and dispatch patrol officers to watch over the hot spot.

Yet what seems most importantly new about the proactive forms of policing recommended under the rubric of community policing has less to do with proactivity than with the creation of the "warrant" for the proactive police activity. A crucial difference between reactive and proactive policing is that individuals calling the police for help provide legitimacy for the police in reactive policing, while in proactive policing legitimacy comes from the professionalism of the police themselves, as they identify crime and other community problems. One key concept of community policing is that communities should have a role in shaping police priorities with respect to the policing of their neighborhoods. Citizen guidance emanates not just from city hall and not just from individuals calling the police. Instead, formal and informal consultations with the community give the police some guidance about priorities, allowing them to be responsive not only to individual demands or city wide mandates, but also to local neighborhood concerns. This consultation, in turn, could be expected to warrant police actions through a political agreement as well as their legal authority and professional commitments. What might be new about the way that community policing approaches the idea of proactivity, then, is not only to agree that it is important, but also to take some pains to limit and justify the form that proactive policing takes. Community policing urges community consultation to create a political warrant for proactive policing.

Interacting with the Public

Police patrol work involves face-to-face contacts between the public and police officers. The nature and outcomes of these encounters are occasionally the subject of public attention and controversy. Understanding these common but complex and potentially volatile interactions has therefore been a major focus of police research. Yet studying this subject is a daunting research task, since police-public contacts take place episodically, in the field, 24 hours a day (Mastrofski et al., 1998). Official police data (e.g., 911 calls) do not provide meaningful information on police-public encounters, either in terms of the nature of the incident or the behaviors of civilians and police officers. Consequently, the bulk of knowledge comes from researcher-initiated, observational studies.

One approach to investigating the frequency and type of police-public interactions is through surveys of the public, asking them about their recent experiences, if any, with the police. A national survey conducted by Langan et al. (2001) found that about 21 percent of people age 16 and older (or almost 44 million people) had face-to-face contact with a police officer during 1999. One-third of them reported having more than one encounter. More than half of all contacts were motor vehicle stops, highlighting the importance of how police conduct these encounters. Only about 3 percent reported that they were stopped because police suspected them of involvement in any sort of nontraffic crime. More—about 8 percent—were involved in a traffic accident. About one-third of those interviewed recalled coming into contact with police because they reported or witnessed a crime or a traffic accident, and 12 percent because they asked police for some sort of assistance.

While such surveys provide useful context, they do not fully divulge the nature of police-public contact. An alternative method of assessing encounters is direct observation, usually by riding with officers on patrol or walking with them on foot (Teplin, 1986). This is a very powerful way of obtaining accurate information about the character and the dynamics of police encounters with the public, but it is also an extremely difficult and expensive type of research (Mastrofski et al., 1998). The first systematic observation of police patrols generating quantifiable data occurred in 1966, when a team of researchers accompanied officers from the Boston, Chicago, and Washington, DC, police departments on patrol, systematically recording what transpired during each shift (Reiss, 1971; Black, 1980). Reiss (1971) found that patrol work is organized around discrete interactions with the public, the vast majority of which are initiated by the publics' requests for police assistance. He labeled these public-initiated interactions "reactive" encounters to distinguish them from interactions that were initiated by the officers themselves, which he called "proactive" encounters.

Subsequent studies have explored the various contours of police-public encounters (Bayley, 1986; Teplin, 1986; Bayley and Garofalo, 1989; Mastrofski, Snipes, and Supina, 1996; Mastrofski et al., 1998). Earlier studies, focusing on police actions, characterized those with whom they came into contact using demographic categories. More recently, researchers have attended to the behavior of individuals who encounter the police, attempting to analyze how the actions of one party affect the actions of the other (Mastrofski, Snipes, and Supina, 1996).

Exercise of Authority

The core element of the police role in society is the use of their authority (Bittner, 1970). This authority consists of the capacity, at one extreme, to deprive people of their liberty (e.g., arrest), use physical force, or even to take human life. But lesser uses of force and authority include observations of conduct in public spaces, interrupting ordinary activities to ask questions, and the development of records that help shape individual reputations. A police officer's authority is implicit in the role and is understood by members of the public even when it is not overtly exercised in a particular incident. In a classic essay, Bittner (1970) argues that the capacity to use force lends "thematic unity" to all the police contacts with the public. Even when officers do not use force, the knowledge that they have the authority to use it shapes the behavior of both the public and police officers. In this context, use of authority involves different dimensions and levels of coercion. Because police authority includes degrees of coercion, police departments increasingly train officers to use the least amount of coercion or force appropriate to resolve any given situation (Garner and Maxwell, 1999).

The exercise of authority represents only one of several kinds of responses available to a police officer. Black (1976:5; 1980:130-131) conceptualized the range of responses in terms of four styles: penal (e.g., arrest), conciliatory (e.g., mediation), compensatory, and therapeutic (e.g., counseling, referral). His research found that police utilized the penal and conciliatory styles far more often than others, and that they frequently employed more than one style in the course of an encounter. He also found that, in 4 percent of cases, police declined to take any action at all. Other studies of how they handle disputes confirmed that police occasionally refuse to get involved. Klinger (1996) developed a measure that rank-orders officers' actions according to the amount of authority they exerted to resolve encounters. He reported that officers typically used low levels of authority, taking such actions as offering advice and resolving points of contention via discussion in 60 percent of the cases they handled. Worden (1989) developed a 16-category measure that captured the combinations of actions that officers might undertake to resolve disputes. He found that officers used tactics that involved some form of counseling, coercion (exclusive of arrest), or both in about two-thirds of the disputes they handled.

Arrest as an Exercise of Authority

The arrest of an individual represents a major exercise of coercive authority, a deprivation of liberty. The exercise of discretion in arrest has been a major focus of research, with particular attention to the question of whether there are patterns of discrimination against racial and ethnic minority groups (LaFave, 1965; Reiss, 1971; Black, 1980). The first study of the arrest decision confirmed that officers exercised broad discretion in making arrests, but they often made arrests for purposes other than criminal prosecution and in some cases used their powers illegally (LaFave, 1965). The first large-scale quantitative study of arrest discretion found that officers systematically underenforce the law, making arrests in only about half of all situations in which there was legal grounds for an arrest (Black, 1980:85-108). This study concluded that the arrest decision was largely shaped by situational factors, including primarily the seriousness of the alleged offense, the strength of the evidence, the preference of the victim or complainant, the relationship between the victim and offender, and the demeanor of the suspect. This study did not find a clear pattern of race discrimination in arrest.

Because of public concern about domestic violence in the past 30 years, police handling of domestic disputes has been the subject of considerable research and experimentation. One highly publicized reform effort in the early 1970s sought to train police in nonarrest dispositions of domestic disputes (Bard, 1970). As a result of lawsuits and concern that battered women were placed in jeopardy because of police failure to arrest male batterers in domestic violence situations, public policy shifted to an emphasis on mandating arrest in such situations (Loving, 1980). The first observational study of domestic violence incidents (Worden and Pollitz, 1984) found that officer decisions were affected by the same situational factors that affect arrests generally, concluding that police do not treat domestic and other disputes differently. This conclusion was supported by Klinger's (1995) finding that the odds of arrest were no lower in spousal assault than in other assault cases. Observational studies of police responses to intimate partner (or domestic) disturbances or violence also found that encounters involve far more than a simple arrest/no arrest decision. However, more recently, some scholars have raised the possibility that police do treat intimate partner violence differently (Fyfe et al., 1997; Avakame et al., 1999; Avakame and Fyfe, 2001). Confirming this differential would once again raise important questions regarding police discretion and the factors that most influence officers in situations that require relatively quick and important decisions.

Another line of research has investigated the deterrent effect of arrest, including the assertion that failure to arrest in domestic violence situations contributes to violence against women. The first study of this subject—one of the most highly publicized studies in all police research—found that arrest deterred future domestic violence more effectively than either counseling or separating the disputing parties (Sherman 1992). Replications of the original Minneapolis Domestic Violence Experiment have not supported its findings, however (Maxwell et al., 2001).

Some evidence suggests that, in recent years, the police have generally been responsive to concerns about the need to strike a sound balance between the individual citizen's rights and the need for social order. This responsiveness (like much in policing today) grew out of social conflicts that came to a head during the 1960s. Social protest against segregation, America's involvement in the Vietnam War, and other concerns led to numerous mass demonstrations (which sometimes led to rioting) in many major cities in the 1960s and into the 1970s. The way that the police typically responded to the mass demonstrations during that era was to use force (e.g., nightsticks, water from fire hoses, and so on) to disperse the protestors. This approach, dubbed "escalated force" by scholars who study the policing of protest (e.g., McPhail, Schweingruber, and McCarthy, 1998), was often ineffective in dealing with mass demonstrations and led to a concern in many quarters that the police were using excessive force. In the late 1980s, these concerns led many police departments to move away from the escalated force model to one that relies instead on meeting with protest leaders before demonstrations take place in order to set the parameters for demonstrator behavior and police action. Some large police departments, for example New York City, had been communicating with demonstration leaders since the late 1960s, pioneering this model. With this new negotiated management model of dealing with protest (e.g., McPhail, Schweingruber, and McCarthy, 1998), the police agree to protect the First Amendment rights of protestors so long as they do not blatantly violate the law (and sometimes even negotiate where and when arrests will be made when protest leaders indicate that the planned demonstration will include civil disobedience).

Use of Lethal Force

Reflecting intense public concern over fatal shootings, a substantial body of research has accumulated over the past 30 years on police use of deadly force. Following some initial research in the 1960s (Robin, 1963), the most influential work began to appear in the late 1970s. Milton et al. (1977) examined shooting incidents in seven large U.S. cities during 1973-1974 and found that shootings were relatively infrequent compared with other police actions (e.g., arrest). They recorded 320 incidents across the seven cities during the two study years and noted that over two-thirds of civilians shot by the police survived their wounds and that blacks were shot at higher rate than whites, but at a rate consistent with arrests of blacks for serious crimes. Finally, the researchers found that the seven cities had markedly different rates of police shootings, ranging from 1.6 to 8.5 shootings per 100,000 population.

Such variability in the use of lethal force has been a consistent finding. Fyfe (1978) reported on shootings by police in New York City during 1971-1975, expanding the scope of research from situations in which individuals were struck by police gunfire to all situations in which officers fired shots. He found that, in fact, the vast majority of shots fired by police did not hit anyone. Fyfe also reported that the rate at which shootings occurred varied substantially across the city; that shootings were more likely to occur in areas with higher crime rates; and that area of assignment was associated with individual officer shooting rates. The race of the officer did not explain variations in shooting rates. In Fyfe's study, black officers fired their weapons more often than white officers, and this was explained largely by their low seniority, which resulted in more assignments to high-crime areas and also because these officers were more likely to live in such neighborhoods. In addition, it should be noted that New York's highest crime neighborhoods at the time were largely nonwhite, and the assignment of nonwhite officers to these neighborhoods was largely a result of the department's attempts to make officers on the street representative of the neighborhoods they policed. Fyfe also found that the number of shootings decreased substantially following the promulgation of a new, more restrictive department policy regarding the use of firearms by officers.

Subsequent studies have confirmed such matters as variability in shooting rates both between and within police agencies, and they have offered fresh insights into the use of deadly force by police officers (Skolnick and Fyfe, 1993). One line of research has focused on the effects of a U.S. Supreme Court decision (*Tennessee* v. *Garner*, 1985) limiting the use of deadly force to the situations in which it is necessary for the defense of life or to effect the arrest of fleeing suspects who committed violent crimes. The use of deadly force by police officers decreased markedly following the Garner ruling, falling from about 400 in 1983 to approximately 300 in 1987 (Geller and Scott, 1992). Brown and Langan (2001) noted that the immediate post-Garner decrease was a continuation of a trend in fatal shootings that began in the late 1970s. However, the number of fatal police shootings increased again during the late 1980s, then began to decline again during the second half of the 1990s.

Use of Physical Force

Public attention has also focused on police use of physical force (Langan et al., 2001; Alpert and Dunham, 1999; Geller and Toch, 1995). Studies have consistently found that police officer use of force is statistically rare. Observational studies have found force to be used in about 1 percent of all police-public encounters, with the rate rising to about 4 percent for encounters involving criminal suspects. The most comprehensive national survey of police use of force is the victimization-style survey conducted by Langan et al. (2001). As reported earlier, this national study found that an estimated 21 percent of all adults in America had any contact with the police during the previous year, that more than half of those contacts were the result of a traffic stop, and that officers used force in slightly less than 1 percent of all encounters.

Studying police use of force raises a number of extremely difficult methodological issues. There is no universal definition of what constitutes force. Policies requiring officers to report use of force incidents vary from department to department. The extent of officer compliance with reporting requirements is not known and probably varies from department to department. Finally, judgments as to what constitutes excessive force are difficult, whether they are made by department administrators or researchers (Adams, 1995; Alpert and Dunham, 1999).

The BJS national survey, examining police use of force during encounters of all kinds, found that most respondents who were subject to force felt police had acted improperly. Subtracting the 20 percent who were subjected only to a *threat* to use force unless they complied, about 0.8 percent of Americans age 16 and older (about 340,000 individuals) were pushed, grabbed, kicked, hit, or sprayed by police or bitten by police dogs during 1999. More than half reported that they had themselves been drinking or were obstreperous at the time, and half had charges filed against them. However, three-quarters of those interviewed characterized police use of force as excessive, and more than 90 percent felt police had acted improperly during the incident. About 15 percent reported they were injured in some way as a result of these police actions (Langan et al., 2001). The BJS estimate that police use force in approximately 1 percent of all encounters with the general public is consistent with previous estimates using different methodologies (Adams, 1995).

Beginning in the 1980s, a smaller body of literature has developed on police use of nonlethal force—actions ranging from mild physical restraint, punches and kicks, and baton blows. Officers use this type of force far more frequently than firearms. Friedrich (1980) found police used some form of nonlethal physical force in about 5 percent of their encounters with suspects. Nine years later, Bayley and Garofalo (1989) reported that the New York City officers they observed used some form of nonlethal force against civilians in 8 percent of the encounters that the researchers classified as "potentially violent." In 1996 Worden reported a nonlethal force rate of 4 percent among the police-public encounters observed in many neighborhoods in three metropolitan areas during the 1970s. In sum, observational research conducted during the 1960s, 1970s, and 1980s indicates that while officers use nonlethal force far more often than they use deadly force, they use it in a small minority of their interactions with the public.

Research on nonlethal force during the 1990s considered the techniques that officers use when applying force. McLaughlin (1992) examined use of force reports filed by the Savannah, Georgia, police department. He developed a use of force continuum, based on police training that directed officers to use force proportionate to the degree of resistance offered by their protagonists. This and similar taxonomies rank-order specific actions that officers might take, from high physical force (e.g., shootings, baton strikes) to low force (e.g., grabbing someone) (Alpert and Dunham, 1999). Klinger (1995) utilized this continuum to assess the amount of force officers in the Miami area used when handling disputes between civilians. He reported that more than half of the time officers used physical force they merely grabbed them; that officers rarely struck members of the public with their batons; and that when officers used force more substantial than simply grabbing someone, they used more than one type of force (e.g., punching and grabbing, baton strikes and kicks). Klinger's force continuum included voice commands, and he found that verbal directives were used more often than physical force.

Research using a variety of methods has confirmed the key findings of Garner et al. (1996), Klinger (1995), McLaughlin (1992), and others that officers use physical force infrequently or that, when they do, it typically consists of minor forms of force (also see Garner and Maxfield, 1999; Alpert and Dunham, 1999; Terrill, 2001). It is important to note that changes in police technology have had some effect on patterns of use of force. In part because of public controversy over police use of deadly force, nonlethal technologies have been developed and adopted by police departments. These technologies include chemical agents, electronic stun guns, and various other tools designed to subdue the combative without killing or seriously injuring them. During the 1990s, more police agencies began to deploy "impact munitions," that is, firearm-delivered projectiles, such as beanbags and plastic batons that are designed to minimize serious bodily injury or death when they are deployed. Klinger and Hubbs (2000) examined 373 cases in which officers fired impact munitions that struck an individual and found that injuries were limited to bruises, abrasions, and lacerations in most of the cases, but that several targets of impact munitions suffered more serious wounds, and 8 died. While impact munitions often work as intended, the police have yet to find a technological fix for the consequences of their elemental task, the application of lawful force to protect society.

Other Means of Exercising Authority

Relatively little attention has focused on the other less serious forms of the use of authority, although academic research and a number of police department policies recognize a continuum ranging from the least to the most serious forms. Officers frequently gain compliance through their mere physical presence. Officers can increase their level of control over a situation through different forms of body language and where and how they place themselves. Verbal statements can also be authoritative, ranging from asking questions, making suggestions, and giving orders (Bayley and Garofalo, 1987). An officer's tone of voice can radically affect the level of coerciveness of a statement or a question. Misunderstandings related to verbal expressions and nonverbal behavior, including use of force, are often the source of conflict between police and racial and ethnic minority groups.

Maintaining Order

Recent thinking on policing has placed a high priority on increasing proactive or police-initiated activities. A major part of the proactive workload of police has historically been what is called order maintenance or peacekeeping policing. The idea that policing consisted primarily of enforcing laws dominated scholarly thinking about the police until the late 1950s, when the results of the American Bar Foundation study (1957) of policing emerged and, as noted earlier, demonstrated that police officers exercised considerable discretion and frequently did not arrest individuals whose actions clearly violated criminal statutes (Goldstein, 1960; LaFave, 1962, 1965:61-143). A second key finding was that officers often arrested people with no intention of preferring criminal charges against them; for example, in order to protect inebriates whose drunken state renders them vulnerable to criminal attack (see especially LaFave, 1965:437-489). Taken together, these findings indicate that the police are not automatons who merely enforce legal codes, but rather, they exercise great discretion in enforcing the law selectively to accomplish a variety of purposes.

Research conducted in the 1960s disclosed additional insights into the nature of police work vis-à-vis the criminal law. Bittner (1970), LaFave (1965), Reiss (1971), and Wilson (1968), among others, found that officers often invoke their powers to take individuals into custody for the purpose of maintaining control over the immediate situation or controlling social problems for purposes of maintaining public order, as opposed to arresting them for the purpose of punishment. Officers, for example, often jail individuals as a means to prevent potentially volatile situations from spinning out of control and to restore order when it had already been breeched. The research also disclosed that police officers exercise their authority through a variety of means other than arrest to control situations and to maintain order. This includes using their physical presence (body language), verbal expressions (questioning, suggesting, ordering), and the use of physical force (LaFave, 1965; Mastrofski, Snipes, and Supina, 1996; Terrill, 2001).

The early research on police activity (President's Commission on Law Enforcement and the Administration of Justice, 1967b:13-41) led to a new consensus that the police were generally peacekeepers rather than law enforcement agents, and that the central goal of the police was to maintain social order with criminal law enforcement as simply one of a number of means of achieving this goal. Goldstein (1977:33) characterized the police as "an agency of municipal government housing a variety of functions." As Wilson (1968:31) put it, officers deal with many incidents "not in terms of enforcing the law, but in terms of 'handling the situation.'"

Many order maintenance activities of the police are relatively mundane. Traffic control, for instance, can be seen as a form of order maintenance to the extent that it facilitates people going about the routines of their daily lives without interruption. Special events, such as sporting events or parades, also call on the police to maintain order. The policing of overtly political events is far more complicated, however. As noted earlier, in events in which there is an element of political protest, the police must balance their responsibility to maintain order with the equally important responsibility to protect individual civil and political liberties, such as freedom of speech and assembly. The changing face of disorder, however, militates against simplified and universal strategies in dealing with protests or disturbances. For instance, during recent World Trade Organization meetings, a minority of protesters deliberately attempted to create disturbances; interference reached such an extent during one meeting held in Seattle that it was dubbed the "battle for Seattle." Needless to say, the police represent the front line in these "battles" and often confront difficult situations, and these new strategies of the minority jeopardize any accord reached between the majority of demonstrators and the police. It must also be noted that some disturbances—such as rioting after athletic events—feature the impaired judgment of a number of inebriated participants; this can also create difficulty for police trying to maintain order without relying on broad use of law enforcement powers.

Providing Service

Another core feature of police activity involves the provision of miscellaneous services that are divorced from the law enforcement and order maintenance or peacekeeping functions (Goldstein, 1977). Research indicates that service activities constitute a major portion of what patrol officers do day in and day out, making up between one-third (Cumming et al., 1965) and one-half (Wilson, 1968) of all calls for service to police departments. These services include but are not limited to giving directions, answering questions from the public, monitoring crowds at public events, finding lost children, assisting motorists who have locked themselves out of their vehicles, escorting merchants to late night depositories, and ensuring that a drunk person makes it safely home.

Much police research over the past three decades has been directed toward enhancing understanding of how police officers ration their time among these three groupings—law enforcement, order maintenance, service provision—on a daily basis. Studies of patrol work focusing on contacts with the public, for example, indicate that patrol officers devote between 15 and 30 percent of their time to criminal law enforcement, with the remaining time devoted to order maintenance and service responsibilities (Reiss, 1971:96; Scott, 1981:28-30). Kelling et al. (1974:40-43) examined officers' use of time through full 8-hour shifts and found that about 14 percent was allocated to mobile police-related patrol, with an almost equal amount related to nonenforcement activities. These studies focus exclusively on patrol officers, however, and there are no estimates of the distribution of department-wide resources. Studies of criminal investigation, for instance, have focused only on the factors that correlated with the successful apprehension of criminal suspects (Eck, 1983a) and not on the allocation of investigators' time.

Controlling Traffic

In most large agencies, traffic enforcement is conducted primarily by officers assigned to a specialized traffic unit (although general patrol officers also make traffic stops). Traffic stops comprise the most common form of contact between police officers and the public (Langan et al., 2001). Recently, traffic enforcement has found itself at the center of great interest because of the controversy over racial profiling (Ramirez et al., 2000a; Fridell et al., 2001; Harris, 2002).

During 1999 police stopped about 10 percent of all licensed drivers and gave more than half of those a traffic ticket. They searched about 7 percent of those they stopped (for a total of about 1.3 million searches) and handcuffed and arrested about half of those they searched (Langan et al., 2001). It is hard to establish the context behind these numbers, since no detailed study of traffic enforcement has been undertaken since 1969 (Gardiner, 1969).

The current national controversy over racial profiling has provoked changes in legislation, administrative policies, and record-keeping practices (Ramirez et al., 2000b; Harris, 2002). A large number of data collection efforts at both the local and state levels are under way; some, which came as the result of lawsuits against the police, are already complete or have been ongoing for some time (e.g., in New Jersey, Maryland). Because of this massive new investment in data collection, one might expect that knowledge about traffic enforcement patterns will increase dramatically in the near future. Yet one major unresolved issue behind understanding these numbers involves the proper baseline to be used to determine whether or not enforcement patterns represent impermissible patterns of racial and ethnic discrimination (General Accounting Office, 2000a, b; Walker, 2001). Racial profiling is discussed in more detail in Chapter 8.

Preventing Crime

Developments in policing over the past 20 years have blurred the distinction between the traditional categories of law enforcement, service provision, and order maintenance. There has also been a new interest in expanding the traditional notions of the police role in crime prevention, creating a fourth general category of police activity. While many crime prevention programs include activities that have been defined along with more traditional categories, emergent ideas of crime prevention also include opportunity reduction strategies, such as target hardening, situational crime prevention, and reduction of repeat victimization. In addition, expanded crime prevention strategies often involve police mobilization of third parties to exert informal social control (Clarke, 1997).

Crime prevention embraces many of the police activities that have traditionally been conceptualized as order maintenance and law enforcement, but attention to it has recently been bolstered by community policing. Crime prevention relies on both punitive and positive models of deterrence: The arrest of criminal suspects, for example, is a law enforcement activity, but insofar as it deters future criminal behavior, it also has the effect of preventing crime. By the same token, the successful deescalation of a domestic disturbance by a patrol officer has traditionally been thought of as order maintenance but has the effect of preventing crime. (On the traditional false dichotomy between crime prevention and law enforcement, see Sherman et al., 1997).

The old (pre-1980s) crime prevention activities primarily involved public education efforts. Typically, officers assigned to a special unit would seek to educate people about how they could prevent residential burglaries ("target hardening") and avoid behaviors that would increase their risk of violent victimization. The new crime prevention model tends to involve a wider range of officers, to be more closely integrated into basic police operations and to be more proactive. Many, if not most, of these activities are closely related to community policing and problem-oriented policing activities and involve neighborhood residents and partner agencies in the community (Rosenbaum, 1989).

Investigating Crimes

The investigation of alleged criminal incidents is a basic police function, but probably one more significant in the popular mind than in the context of everyday policing. While investigation has been emphasized in entertainment media, in practice, criminal investigation plays a relatively small role in the day-to-day activities of police departments. In large departments, investigations are generally conducted by specialized units, such as homicide, robbery, sexual assault, property crimes, and so on. In small agencies, there is little specialization of function of any sort. Criminal investigation units typically involve only about 10 percent of all sworn officers in an agency.

Criminal investigative activities fall into two broad categories: reactive and proactive. Reactive activities involve attempting to identify and arrest the perpetrator(s) of reported crimes. Among the most important functions in this regard are the collection and official cataloging of the criminal evidence required to successfully prosecute individual offenders. Proactive activities involve attempting to expose criminal events or behavior and only then to identify and arrest the perpetrators. Among the targets of proactive efforts are so-called victimless crimes, including narcotics, gambling, and prostitution (Greenwood et al., 1977; Eck, 1983b).

The portrayal of detectives in the entertainment media is not a reliable guide to actual criminal investigative work. In 2000, the police "cleared by arrest"—meaning officers arrested, charged, and turned over to the courts for prosecution a person or group of people—only about 20.4 percent of all violent and property crime (Federal Bureau of Investigation, 2001). In the majority of these cases, an arrest is made by the first officers responding to the reported crime. Among crimes that are solved, success in making an arrest is largely owed to a victim or a witness who names the suspect even before detectives arrive on the scene (Eck, 1983a). In these cases, criminal investigators "begin with an identification, then collect evidence; they rarely collect evidence and then make an identification" (Bayley, 1994:27). Much detective work is therefore done retroactively and begins with an arrestee in hand or readily accessible. Detectives have the job of gathering the evidence to convict the offender, most notably a confession, and do the bulk of their work after the suspect is in custody (Ericson, 1981; Brandl, 1993).

Cases in which no suspect is initially identified typically go unsolved; the RAND Corporation estimated that only 3 percent of arrests were the result of the activities of detectives (Greenwood et al., 1977). Low clearance is particularly true for property crime (Bynum et al., 1982), but Wellford and Cronin (2000) also attribute declining clearance rates for homicide to the increasing proportion that are perpetrated by strangers, who leave fewer clues to their identity. Research on the factors that are linked to "solvability" have been used by most police agencies to establish guidelines for determining which cases will actually be investigated, with the remainder being administratively closed (Eck, 1983b). Factors included in assessments of the ability to "clear" a crime are related to the nature of the crimes themselves, in particular whether or not the officers initially responding to the crime were able to obtain good information about a specific suspect. The quality of the investigations and the witness interviews conducted by uniformed officers who are first on the scene seems to be the primary determinant of their eventual solution (Greenberg and Hantz, 1975; Eck, 1983b; Skogan, 1985; Wellford and Cronin, 2000). As a result of this research, some have questioned the need for elaborate detective units (Bayley, 1998); similarly, Greenwood et al. (1977:141) concluded that most detective work could be performed by clerical personnel. During the 1970s there was some interest in delegating responsibility for conducting follow-up investigations to responding officers on the scene, in light of findings about the importance of their role in actually clearing cases. Others are more sanguine about the role of detectives, especially when their work is disciplined by priority-setting and careful case selection and management (Eck, 1983b; Brandl and Frank, 1994).

Proactive police investigations raise troubling questions about police behavior. First, gambling and narcotics units have historically been the center of the worst forms of police corruption (Knapp, 1973; Sherman, 1978a, b). Second, proactive police work often involves the use of wiretaps or other intrusive measures that raise civil liberties concerns (Marx, 1988). Finally, undercover work necessarily involves the use of deception by police officers, a practice that potentially compromises their moral integrity (Marx, 1988).

In response to the terrorist attacks on the United States on September 11, 2001, there is increased interest in the role of state and local law enforcement agencies in both the prevention of terrorist crimes and the response to any such crimes as occur. At present, however, little is known about these capacities. It is generally believed that most law enforcement agencies have some formal plans for responding to large-scale disasters, such as civil disorders, earthquakes, tornados, and the accidental release of hazardous materials. There are neither survey data on the prevalence and nature of such plans, nor social science research evaluating the effectiveness of these plans or special units dedicated to these purposes. The periodic reports from the Law Enforcement Management and Administrative Survey (LEMAS), for example, report data on various special units but include no data on disaster planning (Reaves and Hart, 2000).

Processing Information

In a broad sense, one of the most important roles of the police is to process information (Erickson and Haggerty, 1997). That is to say, law enforcement agencies collect information, process it, act on it, and in some cases provide it to other agencies including the public; some of the information collected by the police is unique to their organization—for example, police reports—and plays an important role in the larger systems—for example, processing insurance claims.

Police data have important organizational and political consequences, and improving the systems by which they are collected and processed remains a top priority for many agencies. The 1994 federal crime law provided support for efforts to advance the information-processing capacities of local police, a capability that promises to become even more important in a post-September 11 world.

Calls for service represent the most common form of data "input" to police agencies, and these calls are the source of most reported crimes. Patrol officer encounters with the public also involve an important element of information processing. In addition, the investigation of crimes also involves information processing (Eck, 1983b). Typically, investigators take statements from crime victims and witnesses. Officers routinely make judgments about the credibility of these individuals and process the information accordingly. These judgments have been found to be particularly problematic with regard to the processing of alleged sexual assault cases (LaFree et al., 1983). Similarly, in the handling of complaints about police service, investigators receive and process information from complainants and witnesses, making judgments about the credibility of those individuals (Walker, 2001). Proactive investigations of such crimes as drug trafficking or other victimless crimes often involve the use of informants, who are themselves frequently involved in criminal activity (Marx, 1988).

Bolstered by the 1994 federal funds, important innovations of recent years involve police department efforts to engage in systematic data collection and analysis, for purposes of both crime fighting and accountability. First among them is the technical ability to engage in sophisticated crime mapping, that is, the collection and analysis of official crime data for the purpose of identifying patterns in the distribution of crime and in particular for identifying hot spots with high rates of criminal activity that need special police attention (Sherman, Gartin, and Buerger, 1989; Weisburd, 2002).

Modern management accountability systems are also built on the timely analysis of accurate small-area data about both crime and police operations. The best known of these is New York City's CompStat process: a layered system of information and oversight that focuses patrol activity on clearly defined and strategically important problems, rigorously monitors data concerning the implementation of crime reduction tactics by local commanders, and evaluates their impact on crime (Silverman, 1999; McDonald, 2001; Karmen, 2000). Although CompStat was originally developed by the New York City Police Department, it has been adopted by a number of other departments (Weisburd et al., 2003).

Finally, police early warning systems involve the systematic collection and analysis of performance data on individual officers, particularly with regard to indicators of problems in dealing effectively with the public. Typically, data are collected on use of force incidents, complaints, resisting arrest charges filed by officers, involvement in civil suits, use of sick leave, and so on. Early warning systems were originally developed for the purpose of identifying potential problem officers who would then be subject to some form of intervention (counseling or retraining) designed to correct their performance problems (Walker, Alpert, and Kenney, 2001).

All of these developments illustrate the increasing importance of police collection of systematic data, the use of advanced computer technology, and the analysis of data for the purpose of identifying problems that need departmental attention. At the national level, the FBI and the Bureau of Alcohol, Tobacco and Firearms (BATF) maintain data bases that federal, state and local agencies can access for information about individuals. Perhaps the most important of these is the National Crime Information Center (NCIC), which was launched in 1967 (Manning, 1992). The NCIC maintains data on criminal histories, fingerprints, mug shots, and the names of people under correctional supervision. It includes a separate data base of missing and unidentified persons. Also, following enactment of the 1993 Brady Act, the FBI has maintained the National Instant Criminal Background Check System (NICS), designed to identify persons who are ineligible to purchase a handgun.

Investigations by the U.S. General Accounting Office (GAO) and congressional hearings (General Accounting Office, 1996) have brought several problems in these systems to light. Many local law enforcement agencies do not fully cooperate with the NCIC system, and certain data are missing, incomplete, inaccurate, or not entered in a timely fashion. The BATF system for recording serial numbers of guns seized in conjunction with police investigations is also extremely incomplete. Nevertheless, data collection by law enforcement is increasing in its scope and sophistication.

Specialized Services

Since the Progressive Era at the turn of the 20th century, professional police administration has emphasized the development of specialized units to carry out particular police responsibilities (Walker, 1977). The most common specialized units are those related to criminal investigation, traffic enforcement (Gardiner, 1969), juvenile delinquency (IACP, 1973), police community relations (Law Enforcement Assistance Administration, 1973), crimes of vice, domestic violence (Sherman et al., 1992), gangs (Katz, 2001), and hate crimes (Garofalo and Martin, 1992). Specialized bomb and arson squads and SWAT units, or specially designated and trained officers are found in most law enforcement agencies. Some community policing programs have been carried out by specialized units, while others are department-wide efforts (Rosenbaum 1994).

The rationale for the formation of these units is both strategic and managerial. Specialization enables officers to focus their efforts on problems important to their organization and to gain special knowledge and expertise. In this respect, specialized unit officers stand in contrast to the generalist function of patrol officers. The existence of a specialized unit also signals to the wider community that police are taking a particular problem seriously (Crank and Langworthy, 1992).

SWAT teams are a good example. Prior to the late 1960s, police departments responded to special threat situations—such as those involving barricaded gunmen and hostages—on an ad hoc basis, simply handling the situation in whatever way seemed appropriate at the time. When several notorious incidents during the 1960s—one example is Charles Whitman's 1966 murderous sniping rampage in Austin, Texas—showed that the ad hoc approach was wanting in many regards, many police departments developed cadres of specially trained and equipped officers who could handle crisis situations in a systematic fashion. Over the years, SWAT teams have handled a myriad of assignments besides the aforementioned hostage and barricaded subject situations. These tasks include dignitary protection, responding to civil disturbances, stakeouts, and the service of search and arrest warrants that pose a greater than normal risk of injury to police officers and the public. Thus SWAT teams give police managers the ability to deal with a variety of problems that require specialized knowledge and equipment without having to go to the expense of training and equipping all of their officers (e.g., Mijares, McCarthy, and Perkins, 2000).

At the same time, specialized units have often been beset by serious management problems. Overspecialization can result in inefficiencies by diverting too many officers from other core functions (especially patrol) and the development of overly complex bureaucratic structures (Sparrow et al., 1990). Specialized units also create potential problems of control and accountability. Vice units, for example, have historically been the loci of some of the worst forms of corruption (Knapp, 1973; Rampart Independent Review Panel, 2000). Intelligence units engaged in illegal spying on legitimate political activities (Donner, 1990). Police-community relations units created in the 1960s were often detached from the mainstream of police operations and deemed largely irrelevant to the problem they were created to solve (Law Enforcement Assistance Administration, 1973). Some current gang units have become detached from the official channels of supervision, thereby raising serious issues related to effectiveness or accountability (Katz, 2001).

The dilemmas surrounding specialized units affect the implementation of community policing (Rosenbaum, 1994). As noted above, some community policing programs involve specialized units, while others are department-wide efforts. Supporters of the former note that assigning community-oriented work to units that often are composed of volunteers and run outside the management structure of the department enables them to get started quickly and forestall resistance from mid-level managers dubious about the concept and officers who do not want to participate. Others emphasize that making community policing a "specialized" function can marginalize it within the department, and it may signal that community policing is not "real policing" as it is defined by police culture (Skogan and Hartnett, 1997). The new concerns about terrorism and the appropriate response of state and local law enforcement agencies to that problem are likely to raise anew the issues surrounding specialized units. Police administrators will face the dilemma of responding appropriately to public concerns without diverting excessive resources from other core police functions.

STAFFING THE POLICE

The changing face of American policing is another important and fairly recent innovation. As of the mid-1960s, police officers were overwhelmingly white males from blue-collar backgrounds with little more than a high school education (President's Commission, 1967). Historically, policing was an all-male and virtually all-white occupation. Women were not employed until early in the 20th century, and even then in a severely limited role (Schulz, 1995). Racial and ethnic minorities were employed after the Civil War in some police departments, but until the 1960s only in a limited and largely token fashion (Dulaney, 1996). The dominant male and white composition of police forces had a significant impact on the norms of the police subculture and on the perception of the police by racial and ethnic minority communities. Today, the rank and file includes a growing number of racial and ethnic minority group members and women. Levels of educational achievement have also risen substantially, with the typical recruit having about two years of college (Carter, Sapp, and Stephens, 1983).

Employment of Women

Through the early 20th century, American police departments employed women only as matrons who handled only female arrestees. Female officers were assigned almost exclusively to juvenile operations and, in fact, the advent of women officers often accompanied the creation of the first juvenile units. This, in turn, was part of the specialization and development of complex police bureaucracies spurred by the professionalization movement in the early years of the 20th century. Female officers were not assigned to routine patrol but generally kept watch in areas where juveniles congregated. They did not wear traditional uniforms and did not carry weapons.

The status of women in policing began to change in the early 1960s as a part of the larger women's rights movement, and barriers to the full employment of women in policing finally began to fall in the late 1960s. The major turning point was the assignment of two female officers to routine patrol duty by the Indianapolis police department in 1968 (Schulz, 1995:131). This is generally believed to be the first such assignment in the history of American policing. Within a few years, virtually all departments eliminated formal barriers to employment and assignment, although informal barriers remain.

The advent of women as patrol officers provoked a national policy debate over their suitability for such duty. This debate prompted several studies of the effectiveness of women as patrol officers. The first and most influential was a comparative study of new male and female recruits in the Washington, DC, police department by the Police Foundation. This study and others that followed found that female patrol officers performed as effectively as male officers, with only slight differences in activity levels, for example in arrest practices (Bloch and Anderson, 1974). The research not only failed to confirm antifemale stereotypes that women were too physically weak to perform effectively, but also did not confirm the profemale stereotypes that women would be more effective than male officers in dealing with the public and in particular defusing conflict (but see discussion below).

There is considerable evidence of continuing resistance to women in police work, including a "glass ceiling" with respect to promotion. In 1998 only 7 percent of law enforcement agencies reported that more than 20 percent of their sworn officers were female, with no departments reporting as many as 30 percent female (National Center on Women and Policing, 1998). In contrast, an estimated 46 percent of the total U.S. workforce is female (U.S. Census Bureau, 1999). Affirmative action plans, including court-approved quota systems for recruitment, while they have increased the number of female officers in many departments (Martin, 1990), have not raised the level of female employment in any single agency to a level equal to the general labor force participation for women. In the nation's largest police agencies, which serve cities with populations of at least 250,000, women constitute 16.3 percent of the full-time sworn personnel. It is not known whether this continued underemployment is the result of a lack of recruiting effort on the part of police agencies or a lingering perception on the part of potential female applicants that policing is a male occupation and that police departments are likely to be hostile workplaces.

The advent of women had a significant impact on the norms of the police officer subculture. Academic research and popular accounts indicate that the very first female patrol officers encountered significant resistance from male officers. This resistance took the form of overt verbal hostility, attempts to embarrass or humiliate female officers, sexual harassment, and exclusion from choice assignments (Martin, 1980). Susan Martin's (1980: 102-108) research, however, found considerable variation in the attitudes of male officers. Those she characterized as "moderns" had little difficulty accepting female officers as equals (unlike the "traditionals" and to a lesser extent the "moderates"). This important finding suggested that traditional characterizations of the police subculture have been overly broad and do not take into account variations among even white male officers. With the advent of more female, black, Hispanic, Asian, and gay officers by the early 21st century, the officer rank and file has become steadily more heterogeneous.

Employment of Racial and Ethnic Minorities

Historically, blacks have been significantly underrepresented in police departments in the United States. In the 19th century, departments outside the Southeast often hired a token number of black officers but confined them to patrolling black neighborhoods. Discriminatory patrol assignment patterns in such cities as Chicago and Los Angeles were not ended until the early 1960s. During the era of segregation, most police departments in the old South did not employ any black officers. Some cities hired a few black officers but assigned them to black neighborhoods only and did not permit them to arrest whites (Dulaney, 1996).

The underemployment of black officers has been a major civil rights issue since the 1960s. The urban riots of that decade, for example, were explained in part by the lack of minority officers. The President's Crime Commission (1967) and the Kerner Commission (1968) found serious underrepresentation in big-city police departments. The civil rights movement and the 1964 Civil Rights Act ended de jure and other blatant but informal forms of employment discrimination in police departments in the Southeast. Insofar as covert employment discrimination persisted into the 1970s, departments in the South were essentially no different from departments in other parts of the country in this regard. By the 1980s, some of the most racially and ethnically integrated police departments were found in the Southeast, notably in Atlanta, New Orleans, and Miami (Walker and Turner, 1992). One of the reasons that Southeastern departments were so integrated by the early 1980s was that the Sunbelt was booming (and able to hire officers to deal with growing populations) while much of the Rust Belt was broke and had not engaged in significant police hiring since before the important Equal Employment Opportunity legislation and litigation of the 1970s (Fyfe, 1983).

Employment patterns outside the South followed an inconsistent pattern from the 1970s to the present. The generally accepted standard is that the racial composition of a police department should reflect the composition of the local population (CALEA, 1994:31-2), defined as the agency's official jurisdiction and not, for example, the larger metropolitan area. Only a few police departments met this standard by the 1990s. While big-city police departments are more representative today than they were even 10 years ago, minorities represent 38 percent of the police force, a percentage that does not equal the minority presence in the communities that these police agencies serve (Brown and Langan, 2001). Underrepresentation continues in most departments, and a few departments made little progress in minority employment.

Civil rights leaders have demanded increased employment of black officers in the belief that such officers will be better able to relate to black citizens and, consequently, that they will be less likely to use unjustified deadly force or excessive physical force and will be less likely to engage in discriminatory arrests (Kerner Commission, 1968). The social science evidence on police behavior does not support this view, however. Studies of police work have failed to find significant or consistent differences in the behavior of white and black officers. The use of deadly force, for example, is primarily a product of assignment, with officers assigned to high-crime areas more likely to fire their weapons (Fyfe, 1981). Official data on complaints by the public indicate that officers of different races and ethnicities receive complaints at rates equal to their presence in a police department (Walker, 2001).

In contrast to black police officers, there is very little research on Hispanic police officers (Carter, 1986). Yet this group made the largest gains in representation on big-city police forces throughout the 1990s; only 9.2 percent of large police departments were Hispanic in 1990, but by 2000, Hispanics constituted 14.1 percent of the full-time sworn personnel in these agencies. The lack of research in this area is a function of the general lack of research on Hispanics in the criminal justice system compared with research on blacks (Walker, Spohn, and Delone, 2000). This is true even as employment data indicate that Hispanics are generally underrepresented as police officers, in a pattern that parallels the underemployment of blacks. Exceptions to this rule include a few cities where the local population is predominantly Hispanic.

Employment of Gay and Lesbian Officers

A number of departments currently employ gay and lesbian officers without official prejudice. Some departments, particularly in cities with large homosexual communities, actively recruit gay and lesbian officers. In important respects, this change in police employment practices represents an even greater transformation of the traditional police subculture than the employment of female officers as equals in the 1970s (Leinen, 1993). None of these innovations has been complete or comprehensive, however, in part because police organizations change slowly even under the best of circumstances. The fragmented world of policing therefore prompts closer examination of the process of innovation itself.

RECENT INNOVATIONS IN POLICING

The past three decades have witnessed a remarkable degree of innovation in policing. The innovation has been occurring at several different levels (Moore, Sparrow, and Spelman, 1996). At the operational level, police have experimented (both formally and informally) with new programs and tactics for dealing with recurrent operational tasks. The police have, for example, experimented with the use of mandatory arrest policies to reduce domestic violence, with the use of decoys to reduce armed robbery, with the use of various tactics for disrupting street level drug markets, and with enforcement tactics focusing special attention on those adults and kids who seem to commit both frequent and serious criminal offenses, among others. They have also experimented with a variety of methods for managing calls for service to help ensure that their patrol force was being most effectively used both to reduce crime and to provide callers with something they could recognize as high-quality service. These operational innovations use existing resources better to accomplish the important substantive purposes of the police.

At an administrative level, the police have experimented with new ideas about how to structure and manage their organizations. They have sought to decentralize operations to give mid-level managers in the police department real responsibility—and to hold them accountable—for controlling crime in their areas, as well as to recognize and encourage the initiative and innovation of officers. As noted above, they have made special efforts to recruit members of the community who were not traditionally represented in police forces. They have also experimented with new methods of selecting and training police officers and with new methods of identifying those officers who seem to be particularly prone to abuse. They have also experimented with different ways of making themselves accountable to the public for their use of force and authority and to more effectively control corruption. And they have sought to find new ways of developing working partnerships with other law enforcement agencies, with other civilian agencies in government, and with groups of various kinds. These administrative innovations structure and lead departments differently while engaging in a wide variety of tasks.

At a still different level, the police have experimented with new uses of technology. For example, in the domain of information technology and processing, they have made extensive investments in improved computer-aided dispatching and record-keeping systems. In the domain of offender identification, they have invested in automated fingerprint identification systems and developed capacities for DNA testing. In the domain of training, they have developed computer-supported "shoot don't shoot" training programs to help officers practice making the split second decisions involved in the use of deadly force. In the domain of officer safety, they have developed lightweight, comfortable, bullet-proof vests. In the domain of offender safety, they have developed and deployed nonlethal weapons of various kinds.

It is worth noting that these technological innovations can be further classified into those that support police programs and operations (e.g., DNA testing, nonlethal weapons, records systems that can support the unbiased targeting of frequent offenders) and those that support the administrative operations of the police department (e.g., the training of officers, the improved ability to report on the aggregate performance of the police to the public). These are likely to evaluated on entirely different sets of criteria.

At another level, innovations can be described as strategic. A strategic innovation seeks to redefine and reprioritize the purposes that the police are trying to achieve, their most important methods for achieving the desired results, and the key working and reporting relationships that exist within the police on one hand, and between the police and other agencies of government and the community on the other. Strategic innovations in policing may entail or require a great many other innovations of the programmatic, administrative, and technical type in order to be implemented successfully. But what distinguishes them as strategic innovations is the radical challenge they pose to traditional definitions of police purposes and operations. Two contemporary strategic innovations are community policing and problem-oriented policing.

Community and Problem-Oriented Policing as Strategic Innovations

The ideas of community policing and problem-oriented policing have emerged as among the most important innovations in policing over the last few decades. There has been uncertainty about whether these ideas represent programmatic innovations, administrative innovations, or genuinely strategic innovations that seek to redefine, or at least prioritize, the *ends* of policing, to call for dramatically new *means* of accomplishing those ends, and to propose importantly new *working relationships* both within the police department and between the police department and other government agencies and the communities in which they operate. To many, the idea of community policing, for example, seems to consist of certain kinds of programmatic ideas (e.g., that the police should shift from patrolling in cars to patrolling on foot or on bicycles), or administrative ideas (e.g., that the police should create administrative positions with special responsibilities for liaisons with community groups) rather than a new strategic view of policing as a whole. Similarly, to many, the idea of problem-oriented policing represents nothing more than a shift to a more proactive approach to crime prevention that draws much of its inspiration from the ideas of location-directed patrol and hot spot policing. To create room for the analysis that guides proactive policing, departments must introduce administrative changes that will either protect time for problem solving or create a special unit to do it. But this is an administrative strategy that is very familiar to the police—the creation of another specialized unit.

While it is possible to view both community and problem-solving policing as small programmatic and administrative innovations that claimed a small portion of police resources and personnel to operate in a slightly new way, the supporters of community and problem-solving policing see these innovations in much larger and grander terms—as a set of ideas that can transform the structure, activities, operations, and even the culture of police departments. Those changes reflect a different mix of operational activities, a different set of administrative relationships, and (most importantly) a different set of results measured in terms of the police to reduce crime, enhance security, provide service, and enjoy legitimacy in the communities in which they operate.

Community Policing

Community policing, arguably the most important development in policing in the past quarter century, is described and presented by its advocates not as a programmatic innovation but as a strategic innovation. (Moore et al., 1992) It is characterized as something that transforms the "professional" model of policing, dominant since the end of World War II, to one that is "more focused, proactive, and community sensitive" and "portends significant changes in the social and formal organization of policing" (Greene, 2000:301). Community policing has been described as both a philosophy of policing and an organizational strategy. Greene (2000:301) describes it as a "plastic" concept, because the range and complexity of programs associated with it are large and continually evolving. When asked if they practice community policing, many agencies can point to a long list of projects as evidence that they are doing so. These activities range from bike and foot patrols to storefront offices and advisory committees. At root, however, community policing is not defined by a list of particular activities but rather as an organizational adaptation to a changing environment. Police departments embracing the philosophy of practicing community policing tend to adopt at least four new, interrelated organizational stances.

Police Functions

First, community policing departments tend to embrace a larger vision of the police function. Skogan and Hartnett (1997) describe this as "an expansion of the police mandate." Controlling serious crime remains the first priority of policing, and enforcing the criminal law remains the primary and distinctive method of the police in accomplishing that important objective. But instead of seeing the police exclusively in these terms and viewing any activities that depart from direct efforts to control serious crime by threatening and making arrests of offenders as a distraction from the fundamental mission of the police and a waste of police resources, those who embrace community policing recognize that the police have other additional important functions to perform and other ways than making arrests of controlling crime and enhancing security. Indeed, they argue that the overall crime control and security enhancing effectiveness of the police might actually be strengthened by recognizing the importance of different police functions rather than focusing solely on reducing crime by threatening and making arrests.

An example of this is fear reduction. One of the important reasons the police should be interested in reducing crime is not only to reduce injuries and economic losses to victims, but also more generally to reduce fear. Indeed, we could easily cast reducing fear or enhancing safety and security as ideas that would be high on the list of the ultimate goals of policing. One means of accomplishing this, of course, is reducing criminal victimization. However, research reveals that the relationship between criminal victimization and fear is far from perfect and that there are other things that can be done to reduce fear. For example, one reason that advocates of community policing encouraged the police to take minor disorder offenses more seriously than they tended to do under the dominant professional model of policing was because these offenses were generating fear. They were concerned that fear was discouraging people from acting as though they owned the streets, thus undermining many forms of informal social control that could help to keep communities both safe and feeling safe. These observations made the reduction of fear an important and somewhat different goal than the reduction of crime.

New thinking about the ends of policing also includes the idea that police should provide quality service to the taxpayers who employ them. Traditionally, quality service meant fast, courteous response to calls for service. Now, for example, it has grown to encompass the role of police in providing information, practical advice, and counseling and referring callers to public and private agencies that are able to assist them further with their problems. Research summarized in Chapter 8 documents the wide range of positive benefits for the police themselves that this generates among victims and even suspects.

Goals such as reducing fear and providing quality service can be seen as important in their own right, regardless of the effect of such activities on the crime reduction mission of the police. But these goals are also seen as important ways for the police to enhance their ability to reduce crime, by promoting the reclamation of public spaces and the exercise of more effective informal social control, as well as by fostering public cooperation, crime reporting, and willingness to step forward as witnesses. In short, the idea of community policing called for a wider engagement with the community in the interests of more effective crime control.

Community policing also involves an expansion of the means of policing. The professional model of policing implied that police use of their enforcement powers to threaten or make arrests of those who committed crimes ensured both a just result (offenders would be called to account for their crimes) and an effective result (offenders would either be discouraged from committing crimes or prevented from committing them via arrest, prosecution, and imprisonment). To threaten and produce arrests, the police organized themselves to patrol the streets looking for crimes (random and directed patrol), to be able to hear and respond to emergency crime calls from witnesses and victims (rapid response to calls for service), and to find guilty offenders (criminal investigation). The first two activities are carried out by patrol units; the third is carried out primarily by detective units. To this, community policing introduces the idea that the police can enlarge and widen their efforts to prevent as well as respond to crimes.

The ideas of prevention focused on at least two different concepts. One was intervening earlier with individuals who seemed on a trajectory to sustained, serious, criminal offending. Of course, much of the work of preventing the development of sustained offenders lay with agencies outside the police, including family courts, child protection agencies, and schools. But the police often found themselves involved with young people who were headed in the wrong direction and sought to use their resources and their commitment to controlling crime to prevent this from happening. In the past, this idea of preventing crime by preventing the development of offenders justified such activities as Police Athletic Leagues and specialized juvenile bureaus. More recently, preventive efforts focused on emergent offenders have included the DARE program, which sought to discourage drug use among children; special efforts to reduce violence in families as a crime problem in itself and as something that was likely to lead to the emergence of offenders in the future; the Serious Habitual Offender/Drug Involved (SHO/DI) Program which sought to focus police attention on serious youthful offenders; and various antigang initiatives that focused particular attention on the recruitment of kids into gangs.

Another idea focused less on offenders and more on the circumstances or situations that seemed to encourage or allow offenses to occur. Several scholars noted that crimes emerged from "routine activities" that could be understood in advance and disrupted. Others argued for a "situational approach to crime prevention," which sought to alter conditions in ways that reduced the likelihood of an offense being committed. These situational approaches to crime prevention are often very similar to ideas generated by problem-solving policing. The reason is that problem solving urges a close analysis of the circumstances leading to offenses or other community problems, as well as a search for an economical intervention that would solve the problem, not by arresting the offender, but by altering the social conditions so that there is less reason or opportunity to commit an offense.

These two ideas about crime prevention shift the focus of the police from people who are already committing offenses to people who are not yet committing serious offenses, and to situations that tend to produce or allow criminal offenses to occur. Once a police department begins thinking about crime prevention of this type, they quickly discover that their ability to interrupt offender trajectories or alter situations often depends on agencies and actors outside the boundary of the police department. To deal with youth trajectories, the police have to deal with social work agencies, schools, parents, community groups, and even gangs. To alter criminogenic circumstances, the police often have to work with community groups, with landlords, and with merchants. In effect, the operational capacity they need to pursue these preventive ideas often lies outside the boundaries of the police organizations. Thus, an additional idea that comes with the idea of prevention is the idea that the police need partners and coproducers to fully exploit the potential for crime prevention activities. This, in turn, means altering the operational style of the police from less autonomous action to more cooperative action with other government agencies and groups of various kinds.

It is these things that begin to transform the means of policing and the key working relationships within the departments and between the departments, the other agencies of government, and the communities they try to police. And it is these ideas about which goals are important to achieve and how they might best be accomplished that lead to the three other principles of community policing.

Decentralization

Decentralization is an organizational strategy that is closely linked to the implementation of community policing in law enforcement agencies. Decentralization happens at two levels. First, more responsibility for identifying and responding to crime conditions and other community problems is delegated to mid-level precinct and district commanders in police departments. Second, more responsibility for identifying and responding thoughtfully to community problems is delegated to individual patrol officers, who are encouraged to take the initiative in finding ways to deal with the problems of the communities in which they are operating. The consequence of this kind of decentralization is not only that the organization can become more proactive and more preventive, but also that it can respond to different sized problems. In the professional model of policing, the police are set up to respond to two different kinds of demands: calls from the public (which typically identify individual problems) and city-wide initiatives and programs that represent the initiative of the mayor or the city council. They cannot hear from residents formed in groups that are larger than individual citizens, but smaller than the kind of groups that can command a city-wide agenda. The decentralization of initiative in police departments, paired with a commitment to consultation and engagement with local communities and conditions, allows the police to respond to problems that are important to specific communities.

Community policing often leads departments to assign officers to fixed geographical areas and to keep them there during the course of their day. Usually they attempt to devolve authority and responsibility further down their agency's organizational hierarchy, to facilitate decision making that responds rapidly and effectively to local conditions, thus assisting the development of local solutions to neighborhood problems. It is also intended to encourage communication between officers and neighborhood residents and enables them to engage in community-oriented projects. Often there are moves to flatten the structure of the organization by compressing the rank structure, to shed layers of bureaucracy and speed communication and decision making.

Community Engagement

Another key feature of community policing is community engagement. Community policing encourages agencies to develop partnerships with community groups, designed to help the police to better listen to the community, enhance constructive information sharing, and discuss with residents their concerns and priorities. To this end, departments hold community meetings and form advisory committees, establish store front offices, survey the public, and create information web sites. In some places, police share information with residents through educational programs or by enrolling them in citizen-police academies that give them in-depth knowledge of law enforcement. Civic engagement usually extends to involving the public in some way in efforts to enhance community safety. Residents are asked to assist the police by reporting crimes promptly when they occur and cooperating as witnesses. Community policing often promises to strengthen the capacity of communities to fight and prevent crime on their own. Residents sometimes get involved in the coordinated or collaborative projects, such as when they participate in crime prevention projects or walk in officially sanctioned neighborhood patrol groups. Even where these ideas are well established, moving them to center stage as part of a larger strategic plan showcases the commitment of police departments to resident involvement.

An important set of partnerships involves relationships with other government organizations that have some direct responsibility for neighborhood quality of life. These agencies include those responsible for sanitation, housing inspection, street repair, and so forth. Following Wilson and Kelling's broken windows theory (1982), these partnerships are designed to complement and enhance traditional police activities (Eck and Spelman, 1987; Green, 1995; Braga et al., 1999).

Problem Orientation

Finally, as a predominant means of doing their work, community police organizations typically try to shift away from traditional reactive patrol and investigative activities designed to threaten and arrest offenders toward the embrace of the kind of problem-solving methods of policing that are advocated by the concept of problem-oriented policing. As noted above, problem-oriented policing is an analytic method for developing crime reduction strategies. The key difference between problem solving and community policing is that the latter stresses civic engagement in identifying and prioritizing a broad range of neighborhood problems, while the former frequently focuses on patterns of traditionally defined crimes that are identified on the basis of police information systems. As Eck (2003) notes, in problem-oriented policing, working with communities is a means to address problems, whereas in community policing, working with communities is an end in itself insofar as it enhances police legitimacy and public support, improves other police services (e.g., investigating crimes), and improves community functioning (Eck and Spelman, 1987; Goldstein, 1990; Eck and Rosenbaum, 1994). Problem-oriented policing, by contrast, can be assigned to specialized teams that have little intersection with the public and range widely, rather than focusing on particular service areas (Eck and Spelman, 1987). Since community policing frequently involves a broad definition of neighborhood problems, including many items that lie outside the traditional competence of the police, it can involve an expansion of the police role. In turn, this requires that police form partnerships with other public and private agencies that can join them in responding effectively to residents' priorities (Eck and Spelman, 1987; Green, 1995; Braga et al., 1999). It also requires extensive training, for traditional policing rarely equips officers for analyzing problems or crafting innovative solutions to them.

Problem-Oriented Policing

Problem-oriented policing is another important innovation gaining currency in the United States. As indicated above, there is significant overlap between it and community policing, particularly when one is examining the ways in which these ideas challenge the prevailing means of policing. Both make a virtue of proactive as opposed to reactive responses to crime, disorder, and other community problems. Both community and problem-oriented policing focus on preventing as well as reacting to crime. Both call for solutions tailored to the particular problems and circumstances at hand rather than rely on more generalized techniques of patrol and investigation. Both community and problem-oriented policing view deterring and incapacitating offenders as only one of many different kinds of interventions that might be mounted by the police. Both community and problem-oriented policing contemplate the police organizing problem interventions that depend on cooperation with agencies and other actors beyond the boundaries of the police organization.

What community and problem-oriented policing have in common is an idea about how the police should respond to problems they have taken as their responsibility. The heart of problem-oriented policing is that this concept calls on police to analyze problems, which can include learning more about victims as well as offenders, and to consider carefully why they came together where they did. The interconnectedness of person, place, and seemingly unrelated events needs to be examined and documented. Then police are to craft responses that may go beyond traditional police practices. Solutions to problems might, for example, require the help of other city service agencies, or using the civil courts or the health department, or turning to residents to help them "take back the night." Today, well-organized departments identify and promote "best practices" that draw from previous experience in solving problems. Finally, problem-oriented policing calls for police to assess how well they are doing. Did it work? *What* worked, exactly? Did the project fail because they had the wrong idea, or did they have a good idea but fail to implement it properly?

Together, these steps define what is known as "the SARA process." SARA is an acronym, developed by the Newport News Police Department and the Police Executive Research Forum, which stands for Scanning, Analysis, Response, and Assessment (Eck and Spelman, 1987). It is a policing philosophy that enjoys widespread popularity and has adherents throughout North America and Great Britain. Sherman and Eck (2002) reviewed problem-oriented policing evaluation findings and methods, including the recent rigorous evaluations of Braga et al. (1999) and Mazerolle et al. (2000). The evidence to date suggests that problem-oriented policing consistently shows effectiveness at preventing crime relative to common alternatives. In the same volume, Eck (2002) points to a body of evaluations of place-based prevention schemes implemented by police agencies that also provide evidence for the effectiveness of problem-oriented policing. Thus, there is a growing body of empirical evidence supporting the assertion that problem-oriented policing can deliver what it promises.

If community and problem-solving policing differ in any important way, it may have to do with how each regards the *ends* of policing and the *key working relationships* that must be established to ensure that the police can succeed in achieving their goals. Recall that community policing explicitly acknowledges that the important ends of policing include not only reducing crime, but also reducing fear, resolving disorder, and providing high-quality services to callers. Recall also that community policing views the community as a particularly important partner not only in nominating problems that they consider important for the police to solve, but also in taking the actions that are necessary to resolve the problem. Problem-solving policing is less explicit about the important ends of policing and less focused on the importance of relationships with the community.

As described by Eck (2003), problem-oriented policing is about putting problems first in all police decision making. Problems are defined as chronic conditions or clusters of events that have become the responsibility of the police, either because they have been reported to them, or they have been discovered by proactive police investigation, or because the problems have been found in an investigation of police records. In a seminal article, Herman Goldstein (1979) proposed this as an alternative to the "one incident at a time" approach that characterized policing of the day. Goldstein raised the point that clusters of calls, often from the same address, might have a common cause. He reasoned that if police came to understand these clusters of calls—he dubbed them "problems"—they could reduce the volume of future calls by resolving their common cause. In this model, policing would become problem-oriented rather than response-oriented. Subsequent research on 911 calls indicated that they were indeed heavily clustered. For example, a study in Minneapolis found that more than 50 percent of calls came from just 3.3 percent of the city's addresses (Sherman et al., 1989).

It is important that the idea of problems that become the responsibility of the police include more than crimes. Of course, many of the problems for which the police become responsible are, in fact, crime problems; for example, a rash of armed robberies of convenience stores, the sudden appearance of street level drug dealers in a residential neighborhood, an upsurge in drunken assaults in bars. But Goldstein understood that because the responsibilities of the police went well beyond the effective control of crime, the problems they would be expected to handle could also go beyond the issue of crime. They could be expected to find ways to reduce fear, control disorder, and provide certain kinds of service and assistance that would allow the public to use public space more securely and more easily than they otherwise could. So while the focus on problems seems to admit a wider set of purposes than the idea of crime control, problem-solving policing does not usually take an explicit stance on whether the police could or should take responsibility for problems in the community that are not, strictly speaking, crime problems, but to which the police can make important contributions.

Similarly, with respect to key working relationships, problem-solving policing acknowledges the potentially important role of the community in nominating problems for police attention, but it does not emphasize this as the best or only basis to rely on to nominate or prioritize problems the police should try to solve. In problem-solving policing, the police are often encouraged to use their own sources of information and professional judgment to decide what is an important problem to solve. They are urged to examine their own records of calls to find the hot spots. Whether it is important for the police to have their ideas about important community problems vetted and discussed by community, so that the views of the community about what is important can be added to the views of the police themselves, is not much discussed or emphasized as a desirable characteristic of problem-solving policing. Similarly, while community and neighborhood groups are viewed by problem-solving policing as potentially valuable in dealing with the problems the police have identified as important (with or without community guidance), they tend to be viewed as less important and less reliable than other law enforcement agencies or other government agencies. In all these respects, problem-solving policing, to the extent that it differs from community policing, relies a bit more on police autonomy and professionalism and gives less influence over police operations to community groups than does community policing. In these respects, problem-oriented policing represents a more incremental step away from the professional model of policing than does community policing.

THE PROCESS OF ADAPTING TO CHANGE

There is a powerful element of geographic consistency and temporal stability in policing. To a remarkable degree, the overall philosophy and strategy of the police (understood as both the important goals of the police as well as the primary theory of how they will operate to achieve their goal) has remained constant. While the initial mission of the public police (circa 1880) was to deal with any issue in society that would concern the public, for the past 50 years or so, the overriding goal of the police has narrowed to a sharp focus on reducing serious crime. The primary theory of how to accomplish that result has been to make (or threaten) an arrest. Arrests (both the threat and the reality) are deemed important not only because they produce a certain kind of justice (offenders can be called to account for their crimes), but also, more practically, because arrests can be expected to reduce crime through the mechanisms of general and specific deterrence, incapacitation, and (ideally) the rehabilitation of the offender while under state control.

The organizational structure of police has also been remarkably consistent. Most police departments think of themselves as centralized in a paramilitary structure. They also have divided themselves functionally by dividing the patrol force from the investigative units; both of these operational units are separated from the administrative units that produce the infrastructure that prepares the police to act effectively operational, and to be accountable to the broader public for the way that police resources are used.

Finally, the core operational procedures of the police have not much changed since the advent of the patrol car and the modern communications system: individuals call for service, a patrol car is dispatched, and a police officer handles the situation with a high degree of discretion (Mastrofski, 1990). Crimes that are not solved at the scene by the arrest of a suspect are referred to detectives for subsequent investigation. This basic process still accounts for the bulk of police contacts with the public and the majority of police department activities.

Recognizing Innovation

Despite this basic consistency, Bayley (1994) argues that the last two decades of the 20th century have witnessed the greatest period of change in all of police history. It is important to understand that this is an empirical claim that needs to be verified. In order to verify such a claim, we would have to have some way of recognizing important changes in the ways that police have thought about themselves, organized themselves, and (most importantly) acted. To a degree, we might use the discussion of the ways in which the police seem to have remained constant as a way of investigating the extent to which they have innovated. Viewed from this perspective, important innovations in policing would show up as some important changes in any of these relatively constant features: the conception of the overall mission and strategy of police (or at least, the relative importance of various elements of the police mission); the organizational structure of police departments; or the core operational procedures. Of particular importance would be large changes at the operational level, that is, the extent to which the police have expanded their range of activities beyond this core process (i.e., in the extent to which they have sequestered resources to engage in different activities), or in the particular ways in which the police are now performing these standard functions of patrolling, responding to calls for service, or investigating completed offenses.

As noted above, the concepts of community and problem-oriented policing could be seen as ideas that call for innovation at the strategic level of policing. They seek to widen the focus of police attention to include minor offenses, disorder, fear, and other community problems beyond serious crime. They seek to change the structure of police departments by encouraging operational initiative and creativity at lower levels of the organization and by encouraging the police to abandon their habitual autonomy and seek close working relationships with other government agencies and community groups. They seek to create room for the police to step away from the insistent demands of the 911 system so they have time to think about the important problems they were asked to solve and to find the means for solving the problems. These all mark a significant change in policing and justify Bayley's claim.

But one of the most important things to understand about these ideas of community and problem-oriented policing is that they are not designed to make only a one-time change in the way police departments operate. The fundamental idea of both these ideas is that police departments should not only engage in this one important strategic innovation, but also that the point of each of these strategic innovations is to create police organizations that are *continually innovative*.

Often when we think about the process of innovation, we imagine that some new policy or program has been tested and found to be effective. Consequently, that new policy or program ought to be incorporated into the operational routines of all police departments. We are satisfied when the innovation has diffused to all police departments.

But the ideas of community and problem-oriented policing are not simply programmatic ideas that are implemented and, once implemented, remain constant. The ideas of community and problem-solving policing are that effective policing requires continuing innovation, not the consistent use of a single operational method.

Continuing innovation is needed in part to deal with the highly varied and heterogeneous tasks that the police confront. Street-level drug dealing might be usefully controlled by regular "sweeps" of known drug markets. But sweeps are a bit hard to visualize and are not likely to work in dealing with either domestic violence or shoplifting. As Herman Goldstein reminded us, the police confront varied problems, and the problems require different solutions. The police have to be innovative to adapt successfully to the wide variety of problems they face.

Continuing innovation may also be necessary to search for more effective policies, programs, and tactics to deal with problems that loom large in the world of policing and are relatively homogeneous. For example, it is important for the police to find better ways of dealing with the big, constant problems they face, such as dealing with cold homicide investigations, or stopping strong-armed muggings, or taming street-level drug markets, or weakening and controlling criminally active youth gangs. So the police need innovation not only to deal with heterogeneous, unique problems, but also to learn how to deal with larger and more constant problems that continue to frustrate them.

Indeed, one of the important findings of this committee has been that tailored approaches seem to be much more effective than more general enforcement approaches in achieving crime control objectives. This means that if the police wish to be effective in controlling crime, they must find ways to make themselves into continuously innovative organizations, not just organizations that can adopt an important strategic, programmatic, or administrative innovation every now and then.

There is not much police-specific research on any of the following subjects that would be important to understand: (1) what causes or allows organizations to embrace a strategic change, (2) what has caused or allowed police departments in particular to embrace a strategy of community or problem-oriented policing, or (3) what causes or allows the police to become the kind of continuously innovative organization that seems necessary for them to achieve their full potential. What we offer here, then, are some ideas about innovation in policing drawn partly from more general studies of innovation and partly from some specific examinations of innovation in policing. We also seek to identify points at which additional research would be particularly valuable.

Serious limits exist in the diffusion of innovation literature on policing. First, there have been surprisingly few studies of the diffusion process among law enforcement agencies. This is an important research area for two reasons. First, economic analysis of private business has demonstrated that large firms adopt innovations more quickly but diffuse the innovation internally at a much slower rate (Meisel and Levin, 1985). The extent of successful implementation is therefore presumably open to question even after an organization reports that it has "adopted" the innovation. This seems particularly pertinent, since many diffusion studies use reported answers in the Law Enforcement Management and Administrative Survey (LEMAS) as their measure, yet Walker (bias crime) has shown that agencies occasionally misreport their status on adopting a certain policy or practice.

Second, and perhaps most important, there is no systematic analysis, either in the policing or other literatures, of discontinuation of an innovation. Some researchers have speculated that both nonadoption and discontinuation are remarkably "unconscious" processes: that is, an organization does not engage in conscious review or decision making in either case. However at least one researcher in the field of health care has speculated that discontinuation can be correlated to, among other things, the degree of agency involvement in the adoption of the innovation itself and the degree to which the innovation itself can be successfully integrated into established policies and procedures (Scheirer, 1990). While at least some attention has been paid to the institutional and sociological factors that inhibit or obstruct innovation among law enforcement in general (Sandler and Mintz, 1974), more analysis of the actual process of discontinuation would identify and highlight key levers in the adoption and implementation process.

Studying Innovation

In studying innovation, one can focus on three somewhat different phenomena. One is the process that produces an idea that is wholly new to the world—the original innovation. This can happen inside an operating organization as it tries to deal with a problem that has been frustrating it for a long time, or as it discovers a new and unexpected use of its capabilities. Or it can happen as the result of a planned research and development effort that is focused on coming up with either new products and activities for the organization or new processes for producing new products or delivering new services.

A second process is the one that causes an innovation to diffuse across an organizational field; in effect, the process that allows an innovation created in a lab, or in one organization, to jump organizational boundaries and be embraced by other organizations. This can happen as a result of professional learning as each organization in the field, committed to achieving its mission, discovers the superiority of some new method for accomplishing its goals. It can happen as a result of a process that Powell and DiMaggio (1991) labeled "institutional mimesis" as each organization in a particular field tries to bolster its reputation and legitimacy by looking like other organizations or quickly adopting innovations that are thought to be at the cutting edge. It can happen as a result of legal action that makes organizations vulnerable to civil suits or government regulatory enforcement if they fail to embrace the new innovation. It can happen as a result of spending by the federal government. It can happen as a result of a political movement (often spearheaded by an advocacy organization of some kind) that can operate nationally (and even internationally) to press a new idea on a field.

There are two important distinctions between these distinct processes of original organizational innovation on one hand, and the diffusion of that innovation across organizations on the other. The first is the difference between developing an idea that is new to the world versus copying that idea in other organizations. The second is the difference between the characteristics of a process that produces a new idea within a lab or within an organization, and the process that helps diffuse that idea across the organizational field. It is worth noting, however, that while a social analyst looking at the development and diffusion of an innovation might be interested in where the idea first came from and the mechanisms that spread the idea, those who are operating organizations and facing decisions about whether and how to adopt (or adapt) a new innovation look at the world very differently. From their point of view, they may think that they are inventing a new idea, or at least adapting an idea for their particular purposes. Thus, they do not think of themselves as merely embracing a standard idea; they think of themselves as developing a new idea for themselves. They also face the problem of gaining acceptance for the idea in their own organization. This means that they have to innovate inside their own organizations in order to embrace the new idea, and that process may not be all that different from developing the idea from scratch in the first organization that developed the concept.

One implication of these observations is that organizations might be considered more or less innovative based on three somewhat different ideas. First, how likely they are to come up with the wholly original new idea. Second, how likely they are to embrace ideas that are not "globally new" but are "locally new" (in the sense that their organization has not ever done this before). Third, how likely in embracing the idea are they to make significant changes in the idea in ways that improve the idea for future use in their own and other organizations. An organizational field could be considered more or less innovative depending on the representation of these different kinds of organizations in the field. The more creative originators, the more rapid adopters, and the more imaginative adapters in the organizational field, the more innovative the organizational field is likely to be.

Factors Shaping Innovativeness

The broad decentralization of American policing creates both opportunities and problems for the development and dissemination of innovations. On one hand, precisely because the system is very decentralized, and because, as a consequence, police organizations face somewhat different task environments and respond to different political aspirations, one might expect there to be lots of variability in what police departments do, and that that variability would be a reflection of a high degree of innovation and variety in the field as a whole. On the other hand, precisely because the field is decentralized, it is difficult to find a central point of leverage to move the field. There is not enough coherent authority over the field, nor enough centralized control of funding to be able to push a specific model of policing through the field as a whole.

Given these observations, it is surprising, then, to see how much consistency exists in the field of policing, how stable those patterns have been over time, and how, when strategies, programs, or administrative systems change in these organizations, they seem to change very rapidly and all at once. Apparently, there are some forces acting on thousands of local police departments that push them toward conformity with some kind of professional norm. Furthermore, these pressures produce a high degree of inertia most of the time. But finally, when these norms change, they seem to change widely and fairly quickly—say within a decade.

What these forces might be that produce consistency and stability within the field in some periods, and rapid change in the embrace of new strategic, programmatic, technological, or technological innovations on the other are hard to discern for the field of policing. Recently, police researchers have differed in their theories for explaining the factors that lead to innovation within individual police departments and across the field: Zhao (1996) argues that environmental factors stimulate innovations. Mullen (1996), sees internal, agency-specific decisions and factors as key. Given that there is as much consistency as there is in the field, and that the field seems to change all at once, one would be tempted to conclude that it must be environmental factors operating across the nation that cause the changes to occur. Yet one could save the idea that internal, agency-specific decisions and factors were the key if one considered as an important environmental factor the number of other police departments that seemed to be embracing or resisting a new innovation. If the individual choices of departments to embrace or reject an innovation are based in part on what the other organizations around them or known to them have done, then one could conclude that the distinction between the environmental hypothesis on one hand and the organizational decision-making process on the other were not so different. Indeed, one could say that the way the environmental factors work on policing is only through the choices made by organizational leaders and their skill in leading their organizations, and what makes it seem as if organizational factors are producing the results is that organizational leaders are all acting similarly in response to the changed environment.

As King (1998) points out, many researchers have formally or informally studied the adoption of a single innovation, from community policing (Zhao, 1996), to police technology (Seaskate, Inc., 1998), to even police uniforms (Monkonnen, 1981). However, only a smaller body of literature is devoted to the process of diffusion itself (Weiss, 1998; King, 1998; Weisburd, 2002). The lack of convergence among these studies (King, 1998) reflects the instability of the larger diffusion literature (Damanpour, 1991) and limits the ability of the committee to draw comprehensive conclusions that are sure to be useful to policy makers.

Drivers of Innovation in Policing

There needs to be more research on the sources of innovation in policing. Of particular importance would be findings about particular institutions and processes that give leverage on shaping the field of policing. We summarize this literature in terms of particular institutions and processes that have been investigated as important drivers of change in policing.

1. Innovation by Edict: Supreme Court Decisions and Civil Suits. Courts are obviously important drivers of change in the field of policing. Court

decisions can invalidate existing practices and define new minimum legal standards (e.g., the Miranda and Garner decisions). In many instances, court decisions defining minimum constitutional standards compel police departments to undertake various collateral changes (e.g., changes in recruitment standards to comply with equal employment opportunity requirements). More recently, consent decrees arising from Department of Justice suits over a pattern or practice of abuse have imposed major organizational reforms on some police departments. These consent decrees have, in effect, ratified and promoted a short list of best practices related to accountability and integrity (Klockars et al., 2000).

2. Innovation Through Research. As noted, academic research has been another important source of innovation. The creation of the Police Foundation in 1970, with funding from the Ford Foundation, introduced a new era of research and demonstration projects in policing. Published research on innovations has questioned many traditional assumptions about police work and validated and popularized certain innovations. The Kansas City Preventive Patrol Experiment (Kelling et al., 1974), for example, played a major role in undermining the traditional assumptions about preventive patrol and forced the search for alternative modes of service that culminated in the development of community policing and problem-oriented policing. The Minneapolis Domestic Violence Experiment (Sherman, 1992) and the controls over police use of deadly force (Milton et al., 1977; Fyfe, 1979) were particularly influential in the development of new police policies.

There is considerable concern in the field, however, about basing reforms on only one or perhaps a handful of scientific studies (Lempert, 1984, 1989; Sherman, 1992). Compared with other areas in which science and public policy intersect—such as the health impact of tobacco or global warming—and there are literally thousands of studies, the scientific literature on major police issues is scant.

3. Innovation as a Confluence of Problems and Solutions. One of the reasons that innovations of the programmatic and technological means tend to take off quickly in policing before adequate research has been completed is that one of the important drivers of innovation in policing are those occasions on which research findings, police practices, and technology suddenly come together in a powerful way. A detailed case study by Weisburd illustrates the point. After years of results that demonstrated the ineffectiveness of core policing practices, such as generalized patrol and decreased response time, research began to focus on the spatial concentration of crime and police. Some who are aware of this research, and some who are not, initiated hot-spot policing, a strategy designed to target specific crime areas. Crime-mapping software, a highly refined version of older police pin maps, demonstrated its usefulness in geographically tracking crime trends at the

very time when hot-spot policing seemed to promise the best results (Weisburd, 2002).

Thus the coincidence of strategy with technology led to the diffusion of crime-mapping. It seems likely that the cues to innovate differ based on the type of innovation, whether technological, as was the case in crime-mapping, administrative, or as a matter of policy. Finally, the perceived advantage of the innovation over and above the practice or item that it seeks to replace—what economists call the relative advantage—plays an important role behind the selection of any given innovation.

4. Innovation Stimulated by Local Governance. It is important to note a distinctive difference between private-sector innovation and that in the policing domain: the relative openness or permeability of police agencies to change is a function of the democratic structure of the governance of policing. In private organizations, profit or competitive advantage motivates most innovations. In policing, the external social and political environment penetrates police organizations and leads to change. The professionalization movement at the turn of the 20th century, for example, was part of the larger Progressive Era reform ethos that sought to make government agencies more efficient and at the same time promote social justice. The civil rights movement of the 1960s stimulated a wide range of changes designed to achieve greater racial equality in policing, through greater employment of minority officers, the creation of specialized police-community relations units and civilian oversight agencies, and the development of policies designed to curb police misconduct. As discussed earlier, the changing composition of police forces has occurred in response to larger trends related to the employment of women and racial and ethnic minorities. The community policing movement was driven by increased public demands for both more effective crime control and more positive relations between police and the public (Walker, 1977, 1998).

5. Innovation Through Professional, Accrediting, and Auditing Organizations. A third potentially important driver of change in policing are the influences that are brought to bear by professional organizations such as the International Association of Chiefs of Police (IACP), the Police Executive Research Forum (PERF), the National Sheriffs Association (NSA), and others. These organizations are important influences on innovation through two mechanisms. On one hand, they convene police professionals and encourage open-ended discussion through formal and informal means. This creates a sort of free market in ideas and a chance for the widely decentralized police field to come together to discuss their work. On the other, these organizations sometimes work to develop and disseminate new ideas and issue recommended policies on various issues in a manner similar to professional associations in other fields.

Accreditation is another source of change, if not innovation. The Commission on Accreditation for Law Enforcement Agencies (CALEA) was established in 1979 and published its first set of standards in 1983. The process of becoming accredited often forces departments to undertake significant organizational change in order to comply with required standards. The CALEA standards tend to codify innovations that have gained recognition as important minimum requirements. However, accreditation is entirely voluntary, and only a few hundred agencies have been accredited to date.

Similarly, auditing agencies, often called in by mayors or city councils to review the efficiency and effectiveness of police organizations, have a powerful effect on innovations in the field. To be able to audit an organization on some objective basis, there has to some agreement about the standards to be used. Those standards, in turn, tend to be set by past traditions and understandings rather than emergent ideas. As a result, many innovative ideas in policing are viewed by conventional auditing agencies as problems rather than advantages for police departments, and it takes a while for new ideas about what is valuable, efficient, and effective to work their way into existing audit standards.

6. Innovation as a Process of Social Learning. Closely related to the idea that innovation might be spread by professional associations is the idea that innovation is spread by a more generalized, informal process of social learning that animated, led, and legitimated by the action of particular organizations that are known to be particularly innovative. The importance of these particular organizations is suggested by research that shows that the process by which an innovation is spread is far from random across organizations. Indeed, organizational research has found that if one were to track the rate of any successfully adopted innovation, it would follow an S-curve pattern. The early adopters grouped at the lower end initiate the pattern and seem to set the stage for the adoption by others. The process of diffusion continues more rapidly in a distinctive spike in the rate of adoption and then settles into a plateau, indicating that adoption has spread to, and through, a community of potential adopters and is now at equilibrium. Importantly, the early, adopters are more "cosmopolitan" than their peers (Rogers, 1983)—that is, they participate in forums that mediate the exchange of ideas. Studies have confirmed this in the policing field (Moore, Spelman, and Young, 1992; Weiss, 2001; Weisburd, 2002).

One finding that has emerged from research is that police agencies, left to their own devices, follow a pattern of social learning (Kapur, 1995) in deciding whether or when to adopt an innovation (Weiss, 2001, 1998). Social learning describes an unstructured but effective process whereby an organization, in this case a police agency, judges whether to adopt an innovation based on the experience of a similarly situated police department. In most medium or large-size agencies, police planners function as the conduits of social learning: they identify, contact, and communicate the experiences of other departments to their own (Klockars and Harver, 1993). Weiss (1997) conducted a survey of 400 state and local police planners and found three key factors that determine which agencies police planners contact: the agency is in the same state or region; the agency faces the same problems and issues; and, finally, the agency has a good reputation. The first two criteria might be thought of as different kinds of peer agencies—regional or situational—whereas the last judgment seems to be based on subjective police professional knowledge. This "good reputation" category may also in part be determined, in the minds of practitioners, by selecting policing agencies that hosted well-publicized research projects germane to the innovation in question (Weiss, 2001).

Since early adoption among cosmopolitan agencies sets off the diffusion process, identification of these agencies becomes a priority for those who wish to spread desirable practices or technology. In drawing these distinctions among police agencies, Weiss's finding that networks of communication vary based on the type of innovation must be considered. For instance, Weiss found that on administrative topics, police planners contacted their "regional dyad or clique," yet on substantive strategies or issues, such as domestic violence or community policing, police agencies contacted the cosmopolitan "opinion leaders" (Weiss, 2001:12). Again, it is significant that publicized research projects played a role in the identification of this latter group.

7. Innovations Stimulated by the Federal Government. Of particular current interest is the role played by the federal government in encouraging innovation in policing. Much less is known of the role of federal executive branch agencies in stimulating innovation in policing. In an earlier period, special blue ribbon commissions, such as the President's Crime Commission in the 1960s (President's Commission, 1967), promulgated new ideas and minimum standards (Walker, 1985). The federal government continues to sponsor research and demonstration projects through the National Institute of Justice and the Bureau of Justice Assistance, but only a few follow-up studies have been made of their impact on police practices generally. A rare exception to this rule was a study carried out by the Urban Institute that evaluated the impact of the federal Community Oriented Policing Services (COPS) program on the spread of community and problem-solving policing across the field of policing. This study is sufficiently important in its own right as a source of information about how much the field of policing has changed, and the ways in which the federal government can make change, that it is worth exploring in some detail.

Adoption of Community Policing: A Case Study

The adoption of community policing over the past 20 years represents an important case study of the change process in policing. Hickman and Reaves (2001) report that the development of strategic plans incorporating community policing is common in most departments, especially among those serving communities over 50,000. By 1999, local departments employing about 80 percent of the nation's police officers had adopted some form of geographical responsibility for patrol personnel, and about half worked for agencies that were giving detectives turf-based assignments. In addition, by the same time, half of all officers worked for agencies engaging in problem-oriented policing in a systematic way, and one-third of these incorporated problem-oriented policing successes in performance evaluations. Most people lived in places where police had formalized problem-oriented policing partnerships with other agencies and groups, virtually all (96 percent) lived in places where police reported meeting regularly with residents, and over 90 percent of Americans live in cities providing residents with routine access to crime statistics.

Other estimates are available of the shape of American policing in the wake of the Violent Crime Control and Law Enforcement Act of 1994. The Law Enforcement Management and Administrative Statistics program conducted by the Bureau of Justice Statistics found that, by 1999, almost two-thirds of local police departments reported they had officers serving in full-time community policing roles. More than 91,000 officers reportedly were serving in that capacity, or 21 percent of all sworn personnel (Hickman and Reaves, 2001).

In terms of agencies, the Urban Institute's evaluation found that about 55 percent of the 19,175 law enforcement agencies that were eligible for federal grants (which includes many agencies that are not municipal police departments) requested and received at least one by the end of 1999 (Roth et al., 2000). Hickman and Reaves (2001) found that 34 percent of local police departments reported having officers with full-time assignments to community policing in 1997, a figure that rose to 64 percent by 1999. Full-time assignments to community policing were more common with increasing city size in 1999, ranging from 54 percent in towns under 2,500 to 100 percent in cities of 1 million or more. However, between 1997 and 1999, there were increases in the proportion of cities reporting assigning officers to community-oriented jobs in every size category. The largest percentage of new adoptions of community policing could be found in cities below 50,000 in population, and smaller towns were among those committing the largest fraction of their officers to these assignments.

What do agencies practice under community policing that is new? Zhao, Lovrich, and Thurman (1999) examined its adoption in cities of 25,000 and larger by surveying police agencies. They found that by 1996, 90 percent or more reported adopting activities implementing the kinds of core organizational strategies reviewed earlier: decentralization, community engagement, and problem solving. Roth et al. (2000) report substantial increases in partnership building by police between the mid-1990s and 1998. This included holding regular community meetings, surveying the public, and forming advisory committees. Over this same period, agencies were more likely to adopt new mission statements as well.

Federal Role in Community Policing

The federal government has played a large role in promoting community policing. Federal agencies funded demonstration programs and research projects that explored its possibilities, and they promoted it in a series of national conferences and through their publication channels. The Violent Crime Control and Law Enforcement Act of 1994 funded new positions for officers with community assignments, supported community policing training academies in every region of the country, and facilitated the purchase and utilization of new technologies that promised to support neighborhood-oriented policing and return sworn officers from desk jobs to the street. These responsibilities were assigned to a new agency in the Justice Department, the Office of Community Oriented Policing Services.

Federal funding did increase the number of officers with community-oriented assignments, although the magnitude of its effect is uncertain. An evaluation of the 1994 act by the Urban Institute concluded that, by the end of 1998, it had led to a net increase of 36,000 to 37,000 police officers. By the end of 1999 that number had risen to almost 61,000, and the federal government had awarded a total of about $4.3 billion for officer hiring. Many agencies also applied for technology support grants from the COPS Office. Their stated goal was to release sworn officers from office jobs by acquiring efficiency-enhancing equipment and hiring civilian technical staff. By the end of 1999, just over $1 billion had been allocated through this part of the program, resulting in claims of a projected yield of about 40,000 officer full-time equivalents for community policing (Roth et al., 2000).

Community policing requires more than hiring and assigning officers; police officers must also acquire new skills and perspectives. Major new innovations such as community policing highlight the importance of training for officers. The 1994 crime law also funded the creation of regional community policing centers around the country. By 1999, 88 percent of all new recruits and 85 percent of serving officers worked in departments that were providing some community policing training. Smaller agencies with fewer officers were less likely to provide specialized training, especially in cities of less than 50,000. Because those agencies are numerous, in 1999 only about 41 percent of all departments reported providing community policing training for all of their new recruits, and only 28 percent provided it for all of their serving officers (Hickman and Reaves, 2001).

There are a number of unanswered questions about the adoption and staffing of community policing programs around the country. Whether police departments will continue to expand and staff these projects in the absence of federal support remains an open question, as is whether local governments will continue to invest in new technologies for policing. Even where there is such a commitment, implementing an effective program also can prove difficult, for adopting community policing can involve significant structural changes in departments and a reorientation of their basic mission, as well as asking officers and their supervisors to think and act in new and unaccustomed ways. Roth et al. (1999) and others have observed that many agencies continue to define community policing only by the list of projects or programs that they have under way. In an earlier study, Wycoff and Skogan (1993) found that only about one-third of departments thought that structural changes were necessary to do community policing.

Assessments of the adoption of policing innovations of all kinds are limited by the inadequate measurement of the structure and functioning of American departments. All of the studies cited above made extensive use of data from questionnaires distributed to police departments by mail or conducted by telephone. As such, a single informant who completed the survey served to represent events and processes affecting an entire organization. Studies of the reliability and validity of such studies indicate that the results can be highly contingent on who is given responsibility for representing the agency and where they are positioned in the organization. For example, multiple informants answering questions about the same police department have been demonstrated to disagree significantly on such questions as whether and when their agency adopted a policy on domestic violence and about their stock of equipment (Weiss, 1997).

Finally, many are uncertain whether community policing can live up to its promises. Like many new programs, its adoption in many instances preceded careful evaluation of its consequences. The effectiveness of community policing has been the subject of some research, ranging from its impact on crime to how openly it is embraced by the officers charged with carrying it out. The findings of this research are evaluated along with other policing strategies in Chapter 6.

RESEARCH RECOMMENDATIONS

Policing is a highly complex enterprise in terms of the structure and governance of police agencies, the roles and responsibilities of the police, and the factors that influence policing. Because of this complexity, policy makers should not expect dramatic changes in policing from any single policy or innovation. Given the decentralized structure of policing, whereby control is exercised by local units of government, there is no central controlling authority capable of implementing any single policy change. Nor would a policy change in one area of police responsibilities necessarily affect performance in other areas.

In a time of rapid innovation in the fragmented and complex world of the policing industry, it is invaluable to monitor the pulse of policing in the United States. **The committee recommends that the Bureau of Justice Statistics continue to conduct an enhanced, yearly version of its current Law Enforcement Management and Administrative Statistics (LEMAS) survey.** Ongoing support for the survey, which began in 1987, has recently been supplemented by the Office of Community Oriented Policing Services, and the committee recommends that this extensive and now yearly survey be continued. The research utility of the survey would be enhanced by ensuring that a panel of consistently surveyed agencies be maintained within the framework of the survey sample. **The committee notes that other research projects have come to rely on the results of the BJS Agency Directory Survey of the Bureau of Justice Statistics, which forms the basis for the LEMAS sample, and recommends that they improve and update its coverage on a regular basis.** After reviewing methodological research on agency surveys like LEMAS, **the committee recommends that the Bureau of Justice Statistics conduct a special study of the validity of responses to the survey and experiment with methods to ensure accurate reporting of agency characteristics.**

Although several federal agencies are charged with encouraging innovation in law enforcement, the committee finds that little is known about the innovation process or how it can be facilitated. **The committee recommends a special study of innovation processes in policing, one that is designed to include factors that can be influenced by federal and state governments.**

There appears to have been tremendous growth in the private security sector in America, but the committee was unable to identify any reliable indicators of its size or operating characteristics. **The committee recommends a special study of the dimensions of the private security industry, and that the Current Population Survey be used to secure an estimate of the size and characteristics of the labor force in this sector.**

The committee recommends the launching of a periodic national survey to gauge the extent and nature of police-public contacts and public assessments of the quality of police service in their community. Methodological testing should be conducted to maximize the accuracy with which public encounters with the police can be recalled and profiles of those encounters can be drawn. The survey should be large enough to account for both traffic and other kinds of encounters, including pedestrian stops. The survey should include measures of subjective assessments of the quality of those encounters. In addition, the survey should be the vehicle for gathering attitudinal data from a general sample of adults (including young adults) concerning the performance of police serving their immediate communities.

4

Explaining Police Behavior:
People and Situations

C hapter 3 outlines the many things that police do. This chapter examines the forces that influence how, and how much, these things are done. Knowledge about these influences is essential for implementing policies that contribute to the fulfillment of the two public expectations expressed as core themes of this volume: crime control effectiveness and fairness. Achieving greater effectiveness and fairness depends in large part on the capacity of a society to get its police to carry out legitimate policies designed to further these ends. For example, knowing which practices will reduce domestic violence tells us nothing of how to ensure that officers engage in these practices at the appropriate times and places. Do the background characteristics of officers affect their enforcement practices? Can officers be trained to behave in certain ways, and what sort of training is most effective? Are certain work incentives and disciplinary practices necessary? Or to consider an example about police fairness, it is one thing to suggest that police who behave in a disrespectful manner toward citizens are perceived as less fair and less legitimate than those who avoid disrespectful behavior. But it is quite another thing to determine what causes police to behave disrespectfully toward some citizens and how to devise ways of preventing disrespectful officer behavior. Can officers be trained or disciplined not to be disrespectful? Can citizens be educated to behave in ways that avoid precipitating police disrespect while maintaining their own sense of self-respect? The first step toward answering questions such as these is to appreciate the state of knowledge about the causes of police practice.

Although most of the research in this review addresses academic questions about the causes of police practice, this literature has important implications for the central policy question of how to *control* police practice. "Control" is probably a misnomer if it is interpreted as "ruling" or "determining" what police do—as in the "command and control" model of police administration that became popular as an ideal by the mid-20th century (Wilson, 1963). Most current analysts and reformers accept some degree of police autonomy in decision making as a good thing, or at least an inevitable one (see, for example, Kelling, 1999; Moore and Stephens, 1991). Thus the term, as it used here, is intended to connote a significant degree of influence on police practice, but one that does not necessarily meet the command and control ideal of determining it. Whenever possible, we attempt to draw the implications of extant research for the control of what police do and how they do it. Ultimately, the findings of Chapters 4 and 5 speak to the governability of policing as communities experience it. Accountability of the police assumes a capacity to shape, if not determine, what they do.

This review covers a wide range of police activities and policies—from how police treat citizens they encounter on the street to the kinds of policies and organizational structures implemented by police departments. The substantial literature involved in this broad range has been divided into four general categories, beginning with the explanatory factors closest to everyday police work, namely, the characteristics of the situations in which officers make decisions, such as whether to make an arrest, use force, or engage in community policing. Such situational characteristics include, for example, the strength of evidence available to an officer about a suspect's guilt, the personal characteristics of the suspect, and the characteristics of the victim. This chapter then examines the characteristics and outlooks of the police officers who make those decisions—such things as their age, race, sex, education, and training. We examine these two proximate elements: the degree and the ways in which characteristics of people (both officer and citizen) and situations influence police actions.

In the next chapter, we consider less proximate but presumably influential factors that affect police behavior. For instance, policies and other characteristics of the police organization that may influence police behavior, such as policies on deadly force, structures and styles of supervision, performance incentive systems, and the nature of department leadership. The committee also examines forces external to police organizations, such as the social and economic makeup of the neighborhoods or jurisdiction served by the police, the political culture of the community, and political processes and decisions made in the jurisdiction, including the law.

In order to distill the considerable research on each of the above types of influences, the committee considers a series of commonly expressed views about the causes of police practice that have received publicity or consideration in the research literature. In many instances, there has not been enough research from which to generalize, but whenever possible the committee states a proposition about these influences based on its evaluation of the research literature. When the evidence is inadequate, the committee indicates the sort of research that would help to fill this knowledge gap. Before turning to these propositions, each chapter considers the nature of the evidence available in the research literature.

NATURE OF THE EVIDENCE

The studies reviewed for both this chapter and the next draw on a wide range of measurement and data collection methods and employ a similarly diverse set of designs. However, the preponderance of the literature is concentrated in certain areas; therefore this discussion is limited to the strengths and limitations of those methods. By far the largest proportion of empirical research on police practice has concentrated on patrol officers, who constitute the largest portion of the nation's police force. There are a handful of relevant studies on criminal investigators, juvenile officers, other sworn specialists, and telephone complaint operators and dispatchers. There are even fewer systematic studies of the behavior of police executives and middle management, constituting a major gap in knowledge about the causes of police behavior outside the realm of the rank-and-file patrol officer. Thus, most of the committee's analysis, especially when addressing the literature on the influences on individual officers, is in effect a discussion of what is known about police patrol.

Research on the forces that influence police behavior has been based on: (1) police records, such as incident reports or firearms discharge reports; (2) direct observation of police in the field; (3) surveys of the public about their contacts with the police; and (4) surveys of police officers. Most of the research on individual officer decision making draws on field observations of police, and much of that can be characterized as systematic social observation (Reiss, 1971; Mastrofski et al., 1998). Such studies employ trained observers who are assigned to accompany officers in selected beats on selected work shifts. Observers take brief field notes on officers' activities and behaviors and on the citizens with whom they interact, and later code data about police actions and other variables according to a standardized form. Measures based on observational data are more valid than those based on police records, which serve organizational purposes and hence may be biased or incomplete. Some observational studies have linked observations to surveys of officers, so that observations of individual officers can be combined with the same officers' survey responses.

Several systematic observation studies of police patrol, conducted since the 1960s, have produced a significant number of publications.[1] Three of these warrant more detailed description, due to their scale and the extent to which analyses of the data collected for these studies have been used by police researchers. The first large-scale observational study of police was undertaken by Albert J. Reiss, Jr., for the President's Commission on Law Enforcement and Administration of Justice (Black and Reiss, 1967). Conducted during summer 1966 in Boston, MA; Chicago, IL; and Washington, DC, observers accompanied patrol officers on sampled shifts in selected high-crime precincts. "In the data collection, emphasis was placed upon gaining detailed descriptions of police and citizen *behavior*.... The social and demographic characteristics of the participants as well as a detailed description of the settings and qualities of the encounters were also obtained" (Black and Reiss 1967:15; emphasis in original).

The Police Services Study (PSS), which was funded by the National Science Foundation, was designed to examine the effects of institutional arrangements on the delivery of police services. The second phase of the study provided for the collection of various kinds of data about 24 police departments in 3 metropolitan areas (Rochester, NY; St. Louis, MO; and Tampa-St. Petersburg, FL), with attention focused particularly on 60 neighborhoods served by those departments. During summer 1977, trained observers accompanied patrol officers on 900 patrol shifts, 15 in each of the 60 neighborhoods. Observers recorded information about 5,688 police-citizen encounters. In addition, the observed officers (and samples of other officers) were surveyed. The departments studied for this phase of the PSS ranged in size from 1 with only 13 officers to 1 with over 2,000, serving municipalities whose populations ranged from 6,000 to almost 500,000. Within jurisdictions, neighborhoods were selected with explicit reference to racial composition and wealth to ensure that different types of neighborhoods were represented. The departments and neighborhoods provide a rough cross-section of organizational arrangements and residential service conditions for urban policing in the United States, and thus the PSS data provide a much firmer basis for generalizing about police practices in U.S. metropolitan areas (and not only in urban, high-crime areas).

Finally, the Project on Policing Neighborhoods (POPN), which was funded by the National Institute of Justice, provided for direct observation

---

[1]See the following for details on the methodology of the more widely published of these studies (Bayley and Garofalo, 1989; Black and Reiss, 1967; Frank, 1996; Frank and Travis, 1998; Klinger, 1994; Mastrofski and Parks, 1990; Mastrofski et al., 1995; Mastrofski et al., 1998; Sykes and Brent, 1980; Worden, 1989). See Riksheim and Chermak, 1993, and Sherman, 1980, for reviews of the publications that drew on some of these projects.

of police in two cities, Indianapolis and St. Petersburg, during 1996 and 1997, respectively. Observation focused on 12 selected police beats in each city and over 5,700 hours of observation (approximately 30 shifts per beat), yielding information on approximately 11,000 police-citizen contacts. Beats were selected from each of three strata of socioeconomic distress, with selection biased toward the more distressed beats, in order to maximize the number of police-citizen encounters subject to observation. In addition, patrol officers and field supervisors in each department were surveyed.

Because of the rigor of the methodological design and the scale of systematic observation studies, they comprise the strongest data from which to draw conclusions regarding police behavior. Yet observational data are not without shortcomings. They may be tainted by officers' "reactivity" to observation, that is, officers might refrain from some actions (such as the use of force, running personal errands) or engage in other actions (such as stopping cars) due to the presence of observers. Efforts to assess the bias introduced by reactivity suggest that the validity of observational data, in general, is quite high (Mastrofski and Parks, 1990; Spano, 2002); moreover, evidence shows that the relationships between some forms of police behavior and other variables (such as characteristics of the situation) are unaffected by reactivity (Worden, 1989). As Reiss (1971:24) observes, "it is sociologically naive to assume that for many events the presence or participation of the observer is more controlling than other factors in the situation."

Observational data have other limitations. Direct observation of police is labor-intensive, making observational studies very costly; only three large-scale observational studies have been conducted. Furthermore, observational studies can be conducted only with the express permission and cooperation of the police departments, and as Fyfe et al. (1997) suggest, the findings from research in such police departments may not be generalizable to other U.S. police agencies.

Observational studies are best suited to inform judgments regarding the proximate and immediate influences at work during a police-citizen encounter. In the next chapter, data and research methodologies that examine police as organizations or look outside the police force—to the community, for instance—to explain police behavior are examined.

Finally, it must be noted that the vast majority of studies in this area rely on correlational designs. A smaller number are case studies, and a *very* small number use quasi-experiments or experimental designs. Since all studies are subject to error, the committee has rated these studies differently based on the strength of their design—that is, their ability to discount other variables that might explain the behavior under examination. Throughout we committee disclose our judgments regarding the strength and rigor of research design.

SITUATIONAL INFLUENCES ON POLICE BEHAVIOR

Situational influences represent forces that operate at what is sometimes called the tactical level of police decision making. These represent circumstances that vary from situation to situation and are expected to play a central role in shaping how officers act. Situational influences that have received considerable empirical evaluation include: the social class, race, gender, and demeanor of complainants and their dispositional preferences (e.g., whether they want offenders arrested or prefer that offenders not be arrested); the social class, race, age, gender, sobriety, and demeanor of suspects; the seriousness of the offense or problem and evidence available (if any); the nature of the relationships between complainants and suspects; the visibility of the encounters (whether they transpire in public or private locations, whether bystanders are present); the numbers of officers at the scene; and the character of the neighborhoods in which encounters take place.

Which situational factors are studied and how they are interpreted depends on the researcher's theoretical perspective. For example, Donald Black and Albert Reiss (1967:8-9) posited that police action is influenced by a citizen's "sanctioning capacity," which is, in turn, a function of the citizen's status—both social (gender, age, race, class) and situational (as complainant, suspect, witness, etc.)—and by the citizen's "subversive capability," that is, the "capability to undermine the means the police use to attain their goals." From this perspective, situational factors (Sherman, 1980a) are the cues on which officers form judgments about how incidents should be handled (Wilson, 1968; Berk and Loseke, 1981). Perhaps the most comprehensive statement of situational factors was that of Bittner, who posited that "the role of the police is best understood as a mechanism for the distribution of non-negotiably coercive force *employed in accordance with the dictates of an intuitive grasp of situational exigencies*" (Bittner 1970:46; emphasis added). The situational framework has been applied most frequently to the use of coercion by patrol officers, but also to the decisions of juvenile detectives and other investigators (e.g., Bynum, Cordner, and Green, 1982; Brandl, 1993; Terry, 1967).

To the extent that Bittner's is a valid and comprehensive description of police work, it suggests that the greatest part of the variation in police officer behavior will be accounted for by establishing those situational exigencies that most powerfully shape police action. Other influences, such as the officer's personal characteristics and attitudes, or department policy, would manifest more subtle effects. That is, in fact, the finding of virtually all studies that compare situational influences to officer and organization characteristics (see Riksheim and Chermak, 1993, and Worden, 1989, for reviews).

One objective in much of the research on situational influences is to determine whether patterns of police behavior are affected by factors that should, in a moral or legal sense, have no bearing on police dispositions, such as race and gender (see Bernard and Engel, 2001). The analytic strategy of such research has been to control statistically for the effects of legal factors—particularly the strength of evidence, the seriousness of the offense, and the preferences and cooperation of complainants—which are unambiguously legitimate criteria for police decision making and to estimate how much if any of the remaining variation in police behavior is attributable to extralegal factors, such as race. Research of this genre has found that most extralegal, situational factors have weak and inconsistent effects.

LEGAL FACTORS

Proposition 1: There is considerable public concern that police officer decision making ignores the constraints of the law. The evidence reviewed by the committee indicates that the exercise of police authority to control citizens is most heavily influenced by legal factors associated with each situation, particularly the seriousness of the reported incident, the evidence of wrongdoing, and the willingness of a complainant to request a controlling intervention.

Public opinion surveys show that a significant minority of the American public regards police as unfair and untrustworthy, and some fear being arrested when innocent (Gallagher et al., 2001; LaFree, 1998). However, evidence reviewed by the committee indicates that officers' use of coercion—their decisions to arrest or not and their use of physical force or verbal control—is most heavily influenced by legal factors (Black and Reiss, 1970; Black, 1971; Lundman, 1974; Freidrich, 1977; Lundman et al., 1978; Smith and Visher, 1981; Bayley, 1986; Mastrofski et al., 1995; Mastrofski et al., 2000; Worden and Myers, 1999; Terrill, 2001). In their encounters with suspected offenders, the likelihood that police will invoke their authority by making arrests, using physical force, or verbal methods of control rises directly with the strength of the evidence of criminal wrongdoing. So too does the likelihood of coercive action rise with the seriousness of the offense: thus police are more likely to make arrests or use force when the offense is a felony than when it is a lesser offense. But, as noted in Chapter 1, police frequently do not invoke the law, even when they have the authority to do so; when they have evidence of offending; or even sometimes when the alleged or suspected offense is a serious one. Important evidence on the influence of legal factors comes from major observational studies. Black (1971), for example, found that police were less likely to arrest when they did not observe the offense themselves and had to rely on citizen testimony instead; he also reports, however, that officers arrested only slightly more than half of the felony suspects against whom they had testimonial evidence. Most recently, Mastrofski et al. (1995), using a more comprehensive measure of evidence, found that the likelihood of arrest rose directly, and fairly steeply, with the strength of the evidence, a finding reproduced in a later observational study that examined only those cases in which a complainant requested that officers do something to control another citizen (Mastrofski et al., 2000).

Officers' decisions to arrest are also strongly influenced by the preferences of complainants, especially (but not only) when the offense is a less serious one and especially when the preference is for leniency. Complainants do not always articulate a clear preference for or against legal action, but when they do, police tend to comply. Smith and Visher (1981), for example, found that police made an arrest in almost half (46.6 percent) of the encounters in which the victim requested that an arrest be made, in only one-fifth (18.8 percent) of the cases in which the victim expressed no preference, and in less than one-tenth (6.6 percent) of the cases in which the victim requested that an arrest not be made. Black (1971) observes that this tendency "gives police work a radically democratic character" and also that the standard of justice that police apply is not uniform but rather varies with the moral standards of complainants. This is a pattern that has been observed in domestic incidents (Berk and Loseke, 1981), and it is one that recent pro-arrest statutory and policy changes have sought to alter, under the assumption that victims of abuse are not always in a position to request legal action against their abuser (see Ferraro, 1989; Jones and Belknap, 1999).

Researchers have observed that the preference of the complainant is most influential when they request levels of police control lower than making an arrest: advice and persuasion, warnings and threats, and banishment from the scene (Mastrofski et al., 2000). Furthermore, the success of a complainant's arrest request was highly sensitive to the strength of evidence available; the likelihood that police officers would fulfill a request for an arrest was found to be much higher in situations in which evidence was strong compared to those in which it was weak. Complainants requesting lesser forms of control experienced high levels of police compliance, regardless of evidence strength, although even here, stronger evidence produced a significantly higher chance of having the request fulfilled.

One dispositional factor, juvenile status, does not appear to affect police practice, in that patterns of decision making are based on the same criteria and weighed in the same ways (Worden and Myers, 2000). Riksheim and Chermak (1993) note that in the 1970s age was inversely related to the likelihood of arrest, but in the 1980s, controlling for other factors, suspects' age did not affect the likelihood of arrest (e.g., Smith and Visher, 1981; but compare Mastrofski et al., 1995). This shift may reflect the last decade's well-documented trend in public attitudes and justice system practices toward treating juveniles more like adults, especially those suspected of serious offenses (Triplett, 1996; National Research Council, 2001:Ch. 5).

One 1970 observational study of drunk-driving arrests in a Midwestern city did produce results somewhat at odds with others reviewed above (Lundman, 1998). It found that, although some legal variables showed significant effects (whether the officers had to chase the suspect and the degree of intoxication), they were less powerful than several extralegal influences, such as the suspect's social class and demeanor.

Before turning to the extralegal considerations in police practice, two caveats are in order. First, being influenced by the law is not the same as being governed by it. Studies of arrest show that as evidence of wrongdoing increases, so does the probability of arrest, but these studies do not judge how often the police ignore the specific standard of legal evidence that applies to the case, such as probable cause. Indeed, because we know that police often overlook minor violations, even when the evidence is strong, we must be careful not to interpret these findings as suggesting that police serve as legal automatons. Second, the available research suggests that officers tend to be constrained by law, but there are occasions when they clearly act outside it. However infrequent such incidents might be, they have a large impact on the perceived legitimacy of the police, in part because when they become known to the press, they are highly publicized, an issue considered in Chapter 8.

Extralegal Factors

Although most research shows that many police actions constrained by law (e.g., arrest) are most strongly influenced by legal considerations, it is still possible for extralegal influences to exert a significant effect. Indeed the available research shows that police behavior is also influenced by extralegal factors, but, for the most part, findings have not been consistent as to the nature and strength of those effects.

Citizens' Demeanor Toward the Police

Proposition 2: It is widely believed that officers punish citizens based on the citizen's untoward demeanor toward the police, even when that demeanor is itself not a legal violation. The committee finds conflicting evidence regarding the impact of suspects' demeanor on police actions toward suspects and victim-complainants.

The proposition that police officers respond punitively to suspects who fail to accord them deference emerged from some of the earliest systematic inquiry into police behavior. Westley (1953, 1970) found that the maintenance of respect is an important norm among police. Disrespect for the police, he reports, is symbolized by "the 'wise guy,' the fellow who thinks he knows more than they do, the fellow who talks back, the fellow who insults the policeman" (1970:123; see also Van Maanen, 1978) and, furthermore, such disrespect legitimates the use of force to compel deference.

Analyses of data collected in the 1960s and 1970s consistently found that the demeanor of suspects toward police affects the likelihood that they will be arrested and the likelihood that officers will use physical force against them (Black and Reiss, 1970; Black, 1971; Lundman, 1974, 1994, 1996, 1998; Sykes et al., 1974; Smith and Visher, 1981; Worden, 1989, 1995a; Worden and Shepard, 1996; Worden and Myers, 2000; compare Mastrofski et al., 1995; also see Van Maanen, 1978). Given the tendency of the police to underenforce the law (Wilson, 1968; also see Black, 1971; LaFave, 1965), this means that suspects who fail to show deference to police authority are less likely to get a break—to avoid justifiable arrest or to receive the benefit of an evidentiary doubt. Moreover, the magnitude of the estimated effect was substantial: one analysis of data collected in 1977 indicated that a disrespectful demeanor raised the estimated likelihood of arrest from .11 to .28 (Worden and Shepard, 1996), and the results of another analysis of the same data (Engel et al., 2000) indicated that police were 5.8 times more likely to use force against disrespectful suspects than against more deferential suspects.

Analyses of more recent data, however, are mixed. Two studies using data on police intervention into disputes, collected in 1986, yielded mixed findings on the effect of demeanor on arrest (Klinger, 1994, 1996). An analysis of data collected in 1992 showed that the likelihood of arrest was greater when the suspect resisted police authority—if, for example, they refused to comply with an explicit police command, acted threateningly, or offered physical resistance (Mastrofski et al., 1995). The effect of resistance on arrest was limited to citizens' actions that were illegal; resistance that did not take the form of illegal action did not affect the likelihood of arrest. Data collected for the Project on Policing Neighborhoods in 1996-1997 shows that disrespect by suspects raises the probability of arrest (Worden and Myers, 2000), and it is by far the most powerful situational influence on whether the officer will act disrespectfully toward the suspect (Mastrofski et al., 2002a). Importantly, however, it has no detectable effect on officers' use of coercion more generally (Terrill and Mastrofski, 2002). However, another study, based on officer self-report data on custody arrests in six jurisdictions, found that an antagonistic demeanor, as well as physical resistance, substantially increased the likelihood of police use of physical force

(Garner et al., 2002). Thus it appears that the effect of demeanor on police behavior may be quite complex, perhaps contingent on other factors: the era (contemporary police may be less prone to apply the "attitude test"),[2] the police department, and even the nature of the encounters in which police and suspects interact.

The demeanor of complainants and victims toward police has also demonstrated mixed effects on how police treat them. In one study, disrespectful demeanor from complainants was found to influence the likelihood that police will exert the degree of control on another citizen requested by the complainant, but this effect was evident in only one of the two cities studied (Mastrofski et al., 2000). Another study of a single department found that a complainant's display of disrespect toward the police did significantly reduce the likelihood that police would try to control the targeted offender (Snipes, 2001). A disrespectful demeanor by the offender had no bearing on the police response in the two-city study (Mastrofski et al., 2000), but an uncooperative demeanor toward the police did produce a significantly reduced likelihood that the police would try to control the offender in the single-city study (Snipes, 2001). When citizens asked the police for assistance that did not require controlling another person (e.g., help with a flat tire), the citizen's demeanor was found to exert no influence on the outcome of the request (Snipes, 2001). However, this study found that disrespectful citizens requesting *any* form of assistance were generally less likely to be treated by police in a friendly or comforting manner. This contrasts with the finding of the two-city study, in which the likelihood that police comforted citizens experiencing some form of distress was shown to be unrelated to the citizen's demeanor toward the officer (Mastrofski et al., 1998).

What can be taken from the studies on citizen demeanor that produce such a mixed pattern of findings? First, some of the diversity of the findings may be attributable to variations in how researchers have defined and measured citizens' demeanor (Worden et al., 1996). Some consider it to be anything that police might interpret negatively; others emphasize failure to show deference (involving both verbal and physical acts); and others distinguish verbal acts of disrespect from acts of resistance (some defining it as physical only, and others including both physical and verbal resistance). In general, physical acts of resistance fairly consistently increase the risk of a punitive police response. Second, effects of citizen demeanor may vary according to the particular feature of police behavior under consideration: arrest, use of force, granting citizens requests, and affective displays toward the citizen.

---

[2]However, a recent survey of police (Weisburd et al., 2000) revealed that nearly half agreed with the statement "A police officer is more likely to arrest a person who displays what he or she considers to be a bad attitude."

Despite the variability in how citizen demeanor is defined, there does seem to be a high level of consensus among multivariate studies of police use of force that the suspect's demeanor is a powerful influence on whether the police will resort to force (7 of 8 studies; see Garner et al., 2002). Most of the debate about the impact of a suspect's demeanor on arrest centers around how to control for and interpret the aspects of that demeanor that may be considered legally relevant to an arrest. This debate remains unresolved. The resolution of this issue is not merely of academic importance, since there is no legal justification for punishing a citizen whose demeanor is unpleasant but not illegal.

Citizens' Social Class

Proposition 3: Some members of the public are concerned that the police distribute coercion and assistance based on the citizen's social class. The evidence on the effects of social class on police behavior is scarce and the findings are mixed, precluding a judgment about its effects.

Research on policing in the 1960s and early 1970s noted that officers were more likely to invoke their authority against lower-class suspects (see, e.g., Lundman, 1994, 1998; Reiss, 1968, 1971; compare Friedrich, 1980) and more generally to treat lower-class parties in a coercive fashion (Black, 1980:Ch.5). More recent studies have yielded mixed findings on this issue. Some show that the likelihood of arrest is unaffected by suspects' social class (Mastrofski et al., 1995), while others demonstrate that class has a substantial effect on the use of force (Terrill and Mastrofski, 2002). One possible explanation for this discrepancy is that force as defined in the Terrill and Mastrofski study included coercion as minimal as verbal commands and threats, whereas the first study calculated the effect of social class only on arrest. Arrest must be documented and therefore, as a behavior, it is subject to more scrutiny, possibly leading to a more scrupulous behavior on the part of the officer. One recent study that did find a significant, though small, social class effect examined the likelihood that officers would comfort distressed citizens (Mastrofski et al., 1998); middle-class citizens were more likely to be comforted than lower-class citizens.

One might expect that if officers are influenced by citizens' social class, they would be affected by the social class not only of a suspect but also of a complainant: while police might be more likely to invoke the law against a lower-class suspect, they might be less likely to take action on an allegation by a lower-class complainant (Black, 1976). Such complex causal dynamics require social scientists to estimate correspondingly complex causal models, and null findings could be artifacts of oversimplified modeling. But when analyses have taken such potential interactions into account, they have not revealed class effects ostensibly hidden by simpler models (Mastrofski et al., 1995, 2000; Snipes 2001).

Finally, the pattern of mixed results with social class effects may be due to inconsistencies in or problems with measuring social class. Studies vary in how social class is conceptualized and measured. More fundamental are problems with reliable measurement. Survey researchers may solicit from respondents information about their wealth, education, and occupation—all of which can be challenging to determine from direct observation during a brief field encounter. Field observers must nearly always rely on inferences made from the circumstances, usually without detailed background information about the citizens observed. These inferences rely on the citizen's physical state, dress, speech patterns, home, vehicle, or other property at hand, as well as the neighborhood of the police-citizen encounter. Balancing this complex web of indicators, which sometimes produces conflicting signals, increases the risks that different observers would judge the social class of the same citizen differently. Furthermore, if the observed officer's knowledge and assumptions about these appearances differ radically from those of the observer, the likelihood of an erroneous inference increases greatly, assuming that the observer's task is to code how the citizen appeared to the officer. Research that tested the extent to which police officers' perceptions of social class match those of field researchers would help to establish the nature and scope of reliability problems with the measurement of social class.

Citizens' Sex

Proposition 4: Some are concerned that police officers are biased in favor of or against female suspects and victims. There is mixed evidence concerning whether and how citizen gender influences police behavior; the committee is unable to draw firm conclusions about the existence of widespread bias in police practices linked to gender bias.

The "chivalry hypothesis" holds that female offenders receive preferential treatment from the police (Visher, 1983). While the results of some early research were consistent with this expectation (i.e., women were less likely to be arrested than men), later research produced mixed results (e.g., Friedrich, 1980; Smith and Visher, 1981; see Riksheim and Chermak, 1993, for a review). Visher (1983) points out that preferential treatment may be extended by police only to women who fulfill sex role expectations. She found a complex pattern of interactions: for example, women were more likely than men to be arrested for property offenses, but less likely to be arrested for violent offenses. The more recent research finds support for the chivalry hypothesis (lower likelihood of arrest) even when only the main effect is estimated (Mastrofski et al., 1995; Worden, 1995b; Terrill and Mastrofski, 2002).

The "leniency hypothesis" holds that police are less likely to invoke their authority on behalf of female victims (Fyfe et al., 1997). Many advocates for victims of domestic violence have supposed that the police are reluctant to take legal action against their (often male) assailants. They have advanced—and many states have adopted—statutory changes that promote arrest. They have also advanced—and many departments have adopted—pro-arrest policies. The underlying assumption is that police treat incidents of domestic assault differently from other assaults, and thus that the protection of the law is less likely to be extended to (predominantly female) victims. The evidence on this hypothesis is also equivocal. Some research has found, in analyzing police responses to incidents of domestic conflict, that the pattern of police decision making follows the same patterns that have been observed in police encounters with suspected offenders generally (Berk and Loseke, 1981; Worden and Pollitz, 1984), with the implication that police handle domestic conflicts in much the same way that they handle other incidents. Other research that has examined more directly the proposition that police are less likely to invoke the law in incidents of domestic assault than in other cases of assault (Klinger, 1995; Fyfe et al., 1997) has generated mixed results.

Looking at a broader range of disputes, one study found that when a citizen asked police to control another person, the gender of the requester had no significant effect on the probability that the police would exert the requested control (Mastrofski et al., 2000). However, the gender of the targeted citizen did make a difference in one of the two cities studied. There police were less likely to control males than females. However, a similar study conducted in another city found that females there typically received a *less* compliant response from officers than did males (Snipes, 2001).

Another pair of analyses focused on the treatment of distressed citizens. One found that females were more likely to receive comfort or reassurance from police than males (Mastrofski et al., 1998), but the other found no significant difference between the sexes (Snipes, 2001).

One possible source of the mixed results reported on the influence of the citizen's sex is that these studies varied in jurisdiction and time. Taking into account the legal and community context of these effects should be an important element of future research that attempts to test hypotheses about the impact of citizens' sex on police practice.

Citizens' Race

Proposition 5: There is a widespread perception of systematic police bias against racial and ethnic minority groups. The evidence is mixed, ranging from findings that indicate bias against racial minorities, findings of bias in favor of racial minorities, and findings of no race effect. The results appear to be highly contingent on the measure of police practice, other influences that are taken into account, and the time and location context of the study.

Studies of police behavior have routinely examined the degree to which officers' treatment of citizens varies with their race. Some of the earliest inquiries reported disparities in the treatment of white and black suspects, to the expected disadvantage of the latter, but these disparities were attributed to causal factors other than race itself: to the more frequently disrespectful demeanor of black or other minority suspects (Black, 1971) or to the more frequently pro-arrest preferences of black complainants (Black and Reiss, 1970). One scholar reconsidered his earlier findings in later work (Black, 1980:107-108). Some later, more technically sophisticated analyses (Smith and Visher, 1981; Worden, 1995a) showed that race has an effect on the arrest decision independent of other factors. Lundman (1998) found in a Midwestern city in the early 1970s that blacks stopped on suspicion of drunk driving had a significantly higher likelihood of being arrested than did whites. Some studies of the use of deadly force also provide support for this hypothesis (Meyer, 1980; Geller and Karales, 1981:123-125; Fyfe, 1982), as have some studies of less-than-lethal force (Smith, 1986; Worden, 1995a; Terrill and Mastrofski, 2002). Even so, research has not consistently supported the proposition that minorities are treated more harshly than whites. Null findings have been reported in many studies of arrest (e.g., Mastrofski et al., 1995), the use of nonlethal force (Friedrich, 1980; Kavanagh, 1994; Garner et al., 1995, 2002; Engel et al., 2000), and the use of lethal force (Milton et al., 1977; Fyfe, 1980, 1981b; Blumberg, 1982; Geller and Karales, 1981; Alpert, 1989). Some studies find that blacks are significantly more likely to be arrested at one time period and set of locales, but they fail to find that effect at other time periods and locales (as did Engel and Silver, 2001, in their analysis of nontraffic misdemeanor suspects). And a few studies even find that whites are in some communities targeted for more harsh police demeanor than blacks (Reiss, 1971; Mastrofski et al., 2002a).

Smith, Visher, and Davidson (1984) conducted one of the more thorough analyses of race effects on police arrest decisions, using the PSS observation data from the late 1970s. They report that the effect of citizens' race depends on other factors. When only suspects are present at the encounter scene, the suspect's race shows no effect for males, but black women are much more likely to be arrested than white women. When both suspects and victims are present, an arrest is more likely if the victim is white and the crime is a property offense. The police are also more likely to comply with the preference of a white victim for arrest. These "interaction effects" between race and other features of the encounter must be interpreted cautiously, because when researchers test a large number of them, some may be significant only by chance. Indeed, these results were not replicated in subsequent research at later times and other places (Mastrofski et al., 1995, 1998).

More recently, hypothesized racial biases have concerned officers' decisions to stop suspected violators or to conduct searches incident to stops. Charges of racial profiling by the police have occasioned scores of data collection efforts, although the knowledge that has been gained has not been commensurate with the effort because the results are ambiguous and difficult to interpret; many have not been guided by the logic of scientific inquiry (see Chapter 5 for more discussion of racial profiling).

Social science research has focused on untangling the *causes* of police actions that are highly constrained by law (arrests, citations, and use of force), but by doing so, researchers have failed to produce results that are as useful as they might be to courts charged with reviewing police practices for potential racial bias. For example, much of the field research suggests that when other extralegal factors, such as the citizen's demeanor, are taken into account along with the citizen's race, no race effects are found. It may be that racial minorities have a more negative demeanor toward police (Anderson, 1990, 1999), and it may be that demeanor, not minority racial status, increases the likelihood of arrest. Nonetheless, it must be noted that a citizen cannot be arrested on demeanor evidence alone. Under the constitution, the Supreme Court has ruled that an officer cannot arrest without probable cause that an individual has committed a crime or is about to commit a crime (*Illinois* v. *Gates*, 462 U.S. 213 (1983)).[3] Officers who make a decision based only on demeanor evidence, regardless of whether the officer ties this behavior to race or not, remain outside the bounds of the law. Even if demeanor increases the likelihood of arrest, the reasons for this consistently more disrespectful demeanor may in fact be anchored in a larger race-based story.

For purposes of making a legal judgment about whether police arrest practices are racially biased, researchers should estimate the effects of citizens' race, controlling *only* for those factors that the law says should be taken into account. An analysis conducted by a member of the committee, built on an earlier analysis of POPN data (Mastrofski et al., 1998), found no race effects when a number of legal and other extralegal factors were taken into account. Similarly, additional analysis was also conducted on data in Richmond, Virginia, in the early 1990s (Mastrofski et al., 1995).

---

[3]The probable standard long predates Gates, which changed the standard by which applications for warrants based on anonymous tips should be assessed.

When *only* race and two legally relevant variables (seriousness of offense and strength of evidence) were used to account for patterns of arrest, race still showed no significant effects in all three cities covered by these two data sets.[4]

Only a few studies have explored the effects of race on the order maintenance and assistance aspects of police practice. One study examined how police responded to citizens' requests to control other citizens present at the scene (Mastrofski et al., 2000). In St. Petersburg, when a white citizen requested control of a minority citizen, the probability that police would comply was substantially greater than that with other racial pairings, but this did not achieve statistical significance at the conventional .05 level used by social scientists. A replication of this analysis in Richmond, Virginia, showed no race effect (Snipes, 2001). Three studies have examined the effects of race on the officer's demeanor toward citizens (whether the officer is friendly or offers comfort or reassurance), and none found a race effect (DeJong, 2000; Mastrofski et al., 1998; Snipes, 2001). An analysis of the police response to citizens' requests for assistance not involving the control of another citizen also found no race effect (Snipes, 2001).

In general, research on police behavior suggests that race effects are highly contingent. Some studies find effects—and those effects differ in direction—and others find no effects. Differences in how variables are measured, what other influences are taken into account, sampling, and the setting (both time and place) make it impossible to discern meaningful patterns at present. In the committee's view, the most fruitful research strategy for the future will be to systematically take into account the organizational and environmental context in which police-citizen interactions transpire. This, of course, requires some theory or logic about the aspects of the larger context in which they occur. One possibility is to consider the political power wielded by minority groups in the community and their representation in the police force itself, as well as the history of race relations (Mastrofski et al., 1998). One of the few studies showing black citizens with more positive evaluations of the police than whites was conducted in a city where local government was dominated by black elected officials and the majority of the police force was staffed by blacks (Frank et al., 1996).

Given the regular recurrence of allegations of racial injustice by the police and the inconclusive nature of the available findings, the committee judges it a high research priority to establish the nature and extent to which

---

[4]In one of the cities, St. Petersburg, the effects of race were significant at a probability of .09, which is above the .05 standard characteristically used by social scientists. In St. Petersburg, the odds of a minority suspect's being arrested, controlling for the seriousness of the offense and the strength of evidence, was about half again as great as the odds for white suspects.

race and ethnicity affect police practice, independent of other legal and extralegal considerations. Because of the contingent nature of race effects demonstrated in extant research, public policy would most benefit by a well-organized program of research that provides for the systematic testing of race effects across the most relevant contingencies. Such a program should consider a variety of contexts under which race effects might vary. Variation over time and place in legal sanctions for racial bias (e.g., changes in state and federal civil rights laws) should be evaluated. Researchers should carefully scrutinize the effects of variation in the community context in which policing occurs, such as the political power of racial and ethnic minorities in local government and their representation in police agencies. A wide array of police practices should be considered, including both those that are punitive and controlling and those that render some service. It will be especially important to consider the cumulative impact of police decision making. Most of the extant research considers each type of decision as if it were unconnected to prior choices made by police and others who mobilize them. For example, the racial distribution of arrests is dependent on prior decisions about whether and when to mobilize police to engage suspects. An analysis of police disrespect toward suspects showed that, although minority citizens were not more likely than whites to be treated disrespectfully, they were far more likely (than their representation in the neighborhood residential population) to have contact with the police, making minority citizens about twice as likely as whites to experience police disrespect (Mastrofski et al., 2002a:543). Research that incorporates the contingent nature of police decision making will better untangle the sources of racial disparity that may be uncovered.

Mental Illness

Proposition 6: Police have been accused of arresting mentally disordered citizens without legal justification. Although some initial studies supported this claim, later studies found that, other things being equal, mentally disordered suspects are no more likely or even less likely than other suspects to be arrested. Given the small number of rigorous studies on this topic, the committee recommends further research.

Urban police frequently encounter mentally disordered persons (Bittner, 1967; Teplin, 1984, 1986, 1994; Teplin et al., 1996), and the frequency of these contacts has increased considerably since the 1960s because of the deinstitutionalization of the mentally ill, more demanding standards for civil commitment, and the limited availability of community treatment programs (Engel and Silver, 2001:225-227). Recently urban police have been encouraged to initiate more interventions in dealing with the sorts of public disorders in which mentally disordered people may engage (Reiss, 1985; Wilson and Kelling, 1982; Kelling and Coles, 1996). Police may arrest and jail mentally disordered persons because (a) they have violated the law; (b) they wish to punish or control them, even though they may not have violated the law; or (c) no suitable alternative is readily available to care for the person, a complaint frequently voiced by officers. There is no dispute that mentally disordered persons are overrepresented among the incarcerated population of the nation, but the key question is whether that reflects a misapplication of the police authority to arrest, one that "criminalizes" mental illness (Engel and Silver, 2001:228).

Perhaps the most influential study offering support for the criminalization hypothesis—based on systematic field observations of police interactions with 506 Chicago suspects—found that mentally disordered suspects were arrested at 1.67 times the rate of those not judged to be mentally disordered, and this relationship held at different levels of incident seriousness (Teplin, 1984). Subsequently, some researchers have questioned the validity of the claim that the police had criminalized mental illness, noting that the Chicago study had not controlled for a variety of legal factors shown by prior research to exert considerable influence on police arrest practice (see earlier section on legal factors) (Engel and Silver, 2001). They conducted a separate analysis of systematic field observations drawn from the Police Services Study and the Project on Policing Neighborhoods. Their analyses drew on much larger samples of suspects drawn from 26 urban police agencies of varying sizes. Using multivariate regression, the researchers controlled for a large number of legal and extralegal variables (including evidence of the suspect's prior illegal behavior and the suspects' behavior toward police and others during the encounter that constitutes legal violations). From the POPN data they found that mentally disordered suspects were almost three times *less* likely to be arrested as those not judged to be mentally disordered. From the PSS data they found that mentally disordered suspects were not significantly different from other suspects in their chances of being arrested. The researchers suggested two possible reasons that their findings differed from the Chicago studies: the inability of the Chicago study to control for legally justifiable reasons to arrest suspects and different methods used to measure mental disorder. The Chicago study used clinical criteria, while the POPN and PSS studies used observers' perceptions, thought to more accurately reflect police officers' perceptions. If observers (or police) consistently failed to classify as mentally ill suspects who deserved that classification and who were arrested, this would understate the effects of the criminalization process. Whether officers have the knowledge and skill to make these determinations is not well established. Officers typically receive little training on handling mental health problems (Police Executive Research Forum, 1989), but one study found that officers are able to make reasonable judgments about the risk of violence and make judgments about mental health fairly consistent with the clinical diagnoses of mental health professionals (Menzies, 1987; Steadman, 1986). Another reason for the divergent findings is simply that police practices may change over time and differ from jurisdiction to jurisdiction—or even from neighborhood to neighborhood—factors not taken into account. Finally, the small number of mentally disordered suspects available for study in all of the field observations sums to only 133, hardly constituting a basis for a stable estimation of effects.

Given the limitations of the available research, the Committee is unable to draw a conclusion about the independent influence of a suspect's mental illness on the police arrest decision. For policy purposes, a more meaningful analysis would go beyond the mere determination of whether there was sufficient legal justification for an arrest. Future research should take into account certain contextual factors that may influence an officer's choices, especially the availability of adequate treatment alternatives (e.g., a medical or mental health facility willing to accept such cases). Without such alternatives, officers faced with severely disordered persons must usually choose between the least-worst alternatives of doing nothing, encouraging friends and family to exert control, or making an arrest.

OFFICERS' OUTLOOKS AND CHARACTERISTICS

Over the last 150 years, reformers in America have focused much effort on shaping the practices of police by shaping the characteristics and outlooks of police officers (Fogelson, 1977; Walker, 1977). A long line of reformers has made this the focal point of their efforts, including Theodore Roosevelt (Berman, 1987), August Vollmer (Douthit, 1975), O.W. Wilson (1963), and Herman Goldstein (1990). These and other reformers have concerned themselves with hiring, developing, and retaining officers who have high moral character (e.g., absence of a serious criminal record or abuse of drugs), who have an acceptable personality (e.g., that avoid certain psychological deficiencies), who embrace certain ideals (e.g., a commitment to public service, to observing legal constraints on police powers, to crime fighting, to working in partnership with the community), who have certain predispositions and not others (e.g., regarding the treatment of minority groups), whose personal characteristics represent certain underrepresented groups in policing (e.g., according to race, ethnicity, and gender), who have higher levels of education and training, and who have (or have the capacity to develop) a set of skills valuable to police work (communication, persuasion, mediation, physical adeptness). Police policies designed to shape the characteristics of *who does police work* typically take form in the following areas: recruitment and hiring policies; policies regarding performance review, promotion, and career advancement; disciplinary policies; job descriptions and personnel assignment practices; training policies; and approaches to and priorities of supervision and management.

These policies are expected to affect officers' behavior through two types of intervening mechanisms: officer attitudes and beliefs ("outlooks") and officer knowledge, skills, or ability. Policies may influence police practice through other mechanisms, such as organizationally provided incentives and disincentives to engage in certain behaviors. The following chapter is reserved for discussing the organization-level influences on police practice. In this part of the chapter we first consider a variety of propositions about officers' outlooks (both general and specific) before turning to the effects of knowledge, skill, and ability and closely associated characteristics, such as training, education, race, and gender.

General Police Outlooks

Researchers have been conducting surveys of police officers for over five decades, and there is no consensus about whether outlooks are important to examine and, if so, how they can be best measured. Studies have examined a number of general aspects of police personality, including authoritarianism, cynicism, and job satisfaction. The influence of these broad personality measures on police practice has not been extensively or rigorously tested. Relevant research on these general constructs is reviewed below.

Authoritarian Personalities

Proposition 7: A popular stereotype about police holds that officers embrace attitudes that are more authoritarian than the average person and that these attitudes influence police behavior in undesirable ways. The available evidence on the existence of an "authoritarian personality" among the police that distinguishes them from the general public is inconclusive, and there is very little research on the extent to which variation in authoritarianism among police accounts for differences in police behavior. The committee judges research on this issue to be insufficient to offer an assessment.

Some research in the 1960s and 1970s was based on the premise that police use and misuse of their authority stems from their authoritarian personalities, which predispose them to use force (Balch, 1972, and more generally, Frankel-Brunswik, Levinson, and Adorno, 1993). Authoritarianism is a cluster of beliefs that includes a strong adherence to conventional, middle-class values, a tendency to think in terms of rigid categories, identification with powerful figures, and a concern with displays of strength and toughness. Research on the police has little to say about the extent to which these personality traits vary among officers. Rather, it has been concerned mostly with whether the degree of authoritarianism among police as an occupational group differs from that of citizens. This research has turned on the question of a modal (and pathological) "police personality" that has all the earmarks of an authoritarian personality. Results have been inconclusive (Balch, 1972; compare Lefkowitz, 1975), in terms of whether police are more authoritarian than the population as a whole. But this research did not examine whether these personality attributes might account for variations in behavioral propensities among police.

Elements of authoritarianism might contribute to the issue of some "problem officers." Hans Toch has described the "violence-prone" officer, whose reactions to catalytic events are different from those of other officers and whose reactions might be attributed to personality characteristics. In a survey of police psychologists, Scrivner (1994) found some evidence of such an effect: respondents reported that among the officers referred to them because of their use of excessive force, one group had personality disorders that placed them at chronic risk. "These officers have pervasive and enduring personality traits (in contrast to characteristics acquired on the job) that are manifested in antisocial, narcissistic, paranoid, or abusive tendencies. These conditions interfere with judgment and interactions with others, particularly when officers perceive challenges or threats to their authority. Such officers generally lack empathy for others.... Individuals who exhibit these personality patterns generally do not learn from experience or accept responsibility for their behavior, so they are at greater risk for repeated citizen complaints"(1994:3).

It remains to be seen whether such personality traits are disproportionately characteristic of officers who use force improperly or excessively, and as Scrivner pointed out, "the number who fit this profile is the smallest of all the high-risk groups."

Police Culture

Proposition 8: Many patterns in officer behavior are attributed to the existence of a police culture that pressures police to share a similar view about their work, involving such things as being suspicious, being isolated from outsiders, and extreme loyalty to fellow officers. There is insufficient evidence to establish whether these or any other "cultural" perspectives distinguish police officers from the citizenry generally or from other occupations. There is no rigorous evidence that measures the influence of the police culture on actual police practice.

While the authoritarian police personality faded into intellectual obscurity, the police culture remains a widely accepted analytic construct, despite having some similar shortcomings. The police culture is a social psychological construct, rather than a psychological one, although it rests on similar presumptions about the degree of homogeneity among police officers. The police culture is a set of widely shared outlooks that are formed as adaptations to a working environment characterized by uncertainty, danger, and coercive authority and that serves to manage the strains that originate in this work environment (see Bittner, 1974; Brown, 1981; McNamara, 1967; Reuss-Ianni, 1983; Skolnick, 1966; Sparrow et al., 1990; Van Maanen, 1974; Westley, 1970).

Officers characterize how they cope with the danger and uncertainty of their interactions with the public as being "suspicious" and "maintaining the edge." Officers read people and situations in terms of the potential danger that they pose, and they maintain the edge in an authoritative, take-charge approach to citizen interactions (Sykes and Brent, 1980; Manning, 1994). Officers characterize how they cope with bureaucratic risks as adopting a "lie-low" attitude and a "crime-fighter" or "law enforcement" orientation. They minimize their risk of exposure and sanction. They also describe law enforcement as "real" police work compared with the more ambiguous order maintenance or service roles, and the inner-directed, aggressive street cop is seen as the cultural ideal.

The problems that officers confront in their working environment, as well as the coping mechanisms prescribed by the police culture, produce other defining characteristics of the police culture: social isolation and group loyalty. Officers' coercive authority distances them from society, and they further distance themselves in coping with the danger of their jobs. Some analysts hold that the professionalization of the police (i.e., taking the politics out of policing, focusing on scientific crime-fighting, and using motorized patrol, along with anticorruption measures) has further isolated police and strengthened the police culture (Brown, 1981; Sparrow et al., 1990). In this context, officers develop an "us versus them" attitude toward citizens (Sparrow et al., 1990) and strong norms of group loyalty. New recruits are tested before being accepted as one of the group, and officers are expected to provide mutual support vis-à-vis a hostile citizenry and a punitive bureaucracy.

To the extent that it exists and holds sway, police culture is important because, first, it is thought to represent a major obstacle to holding officers accountable, and second, it is an impediment to organizational change. The culture buffers officers from organizational sanctions and also serves to promulgate views about how police work should be performed.

Yet several studies, which were based on fieldwork conducted in the 1970s, cast some doubt on the extent to which officers subscribed to cultural views. These studies (White, 1972; Muir, 1977; Broderick, 1977; Brown, 1981) formed typologies of police officers based on two or three attitudinal dimensions. While research on the police culture has stressed what appeared to be the central tendencies in the occupational group, the typologies highlighted the variance. Although these studies were based on field research conducted in different places and at different times, and although they use different attitudinal dimensions to define the types, their descriptions of the types suggest that five composite types can be identified (Worden, 1995b). Their findings contrast with conventional views of the police culture, particularly with respect to the predominance of a role orientation defined by law enforcement, the idealization of an aggressive approach to policing, and an us versus them attitude toward citizens.

More recent developments in policing presumably have further attenuated the cohesiveness of the police culture. The increasing social diversity of the police, with the recruitment of women and racial minorities (Walker, 1985), and the rising education level of police might be expected to weaken the social bonds among officers (see Haar, 1997). The adoption of community policing as an operational philosophy might further challenge traditional cultural tenets. One study of a department that was trying to imbue a "community policing culture (proactive community building) in its patrol officers in the early 1990s found that the department had achieved modest success in getting its officers to share its vision of community policing, but there was tremendous variation in the styles of patrol that officers exhibited, suggesting that the police culture of that department was more fragmented than the "monoculture" literature would have predicted (Mastrofski et al., 2002b). Wood and colleagues (2003) also found that increasing gender, racial, and educational diversity had fragmented what was reputedly a monolithic police culture, and that various elements of these new police cultures either supported or opposed what was ultimately not a very successful attempt to institute community policing. While these studies cast some doubt on the claim that the police culture is an overwhelming influence on police practice, they do not preclude the possibility that it nonetheless exerts a powerful and significant influence.

Despite its popularity as a reputed cause of officer behavior, there have been no rigorous tests of the impact of a modal police culture containing all or most of the elements described above, whether it is a culture that promotes traditional or community policing perspectives. This flows in large part from the problem that most of the literature on the police culture views it as more or less uniform over time and place. Without variation in police culture, it is difficult to demonstrate its impact on police practice. At a minimum, such a study would require comparison of different police cultures (varying across place or over time). To the extent that police cultures co-vary with patterns of police practice, and to the extent that alternative causes of variation in those practices can be discounted, police culture will have been shown to have an impact. However, the measurement of police culture remains an obstacle to such a test. The theoretical framework for establishing the locus or font of the police culture has not been articulated. Police culture is a characteristic of an occupation, or at least a police organization, not an individual officer. To measure a culture's effects, it must exist independent of the outlooks of the individual officers it presumably affects, because we must be able to entertain the possibility that some, perhaps many, officers will not embrace the dominant cultural outlook, even though they may feel its pressure. But it is not clear where researchers should look to measure the police culture. Researchers might look to the formal or informal leadership of the entire occupation or a given department (e.g., high-visibility leaders, professional associations, unions). They might also consider the presumed structural sources of culture (e.g., size and degree of bureaucratization) (Herbert, 1998).

Cynicism

Proposition 9: Some researchers have hypothesized that the onset of cynicism among police officers leads them to use their authority abusively. Very little empirical research is available to test this claim, making it impossible to offer a judgment as to its validity.

Cynicism among police is the subject of numerous empirical inquiries, much of it based on the application of Arthur Niederhoffer's (1967) cynicism questionnaire or some modification of it. Indeed, few research instruments have enjoyed more widespread use in criminal justice research than has the Niederhoffer questionnaire. But in a review of this research, Robert Langworthy concludes that "we are left with both an elegant theory of the development of police officer attitudes and ample evidence that the measure Niederhoffer developed to test the theory is inadequate" (1987:33). Much of the research is implicitly predicated on a misconception of police cynicism, and, as a consequence, this research has produced inconsistent results. Cynicism entails a loss of faith in people, an unwillingness to attribute to them any but self-interested motives, a derisive skepticism of the efficacy of social institutions, and a posture of indifference. Niederhoffer's 20-item questionnaire, which he administered to samples of New York City policemen, has been administered (in its original or modified forms) to other samples in other police departments, and it has been subjected to more intensive scrutiny. These analyses show that the number and nature of the attitudinal dimensions tapped by Niederhoffer's questionnaire vary from department to department (Lefkowitz, 1975; Weiner, 1974; Regoli, 1975, 1976; Poole and Regoli, 1979).

One treatment of police cynicism, that of William Muir (1977), suggests that officers vary in their degree of cynicism, and also that it shapes how they use (and misuse) their authority. Cynicism is one dimension that serves as the basis of Muir's four-fold typology of police officers (the other dimension being the officer's comfort in using force). Muir's study was based on 28 officers in one department. Other scholars who have devised typologies of police have also described cynicism, even though it is not an explicit component of their typologies. More importantly, perhaps, this research forms the basis for—but does not systematically test—the hypothesis that officers' cynicism drives their behavior in important ways. An effort to replicate Muir's study to determine the strength of the relationship between his typology and patterns of behavior showed virtually no relationship between an officer's place in the typology (based on interview comments) and his observed behavior on the job (Snipes and Mastrofski, 1990).

Job Satisfaction

Proposition 10: Much of the police management literature argues that maintaining adequate levels of job satisfaction is essential for sustaining good or satisfactory police performance. No research is available to validate this claim.

Police research has borrowed concepts and methods from industrial psychology to examine the job satisfaction of police officers. Job satisfaction is a multidimensional construct: an officer may be satisfied with some elements of her job while she is dissatisfied with other elements. Police officers tend to be satisfied with the intrinsic elements of their jobs: the variety of tasks and the challenge and significance of the work (see, e.g., Zhao et al., 1999). They tend to be less satisfied with supervision and management. One might hypothesize that officers who are more satisfied with their jobs also tend to perform better—that is, that happy workers are productive workers—yet there is no research that could speak to this issue. It is especially challenging to determine how much job satisfaction influences work performance and how much work performance influences job satisfaction. This requires measuring both job satisfaction and work performance over time to link job satisfaction at an earlier time with work performance at a later one. Research is also needed on the factors that affect job satisfaction, especially those that can be promoted by police administrators. Furthermore, researchers should monitor the sources of satisfaction and dissatisfaction associated with new and experimental policing programs. Knowing what irks and pleases officers will prove valuable in designing more effective methods of implementing innovations in the future.

Effects of Specific Attitudes on Behavior

Proposition 11: Attitudes toward specific aspects of police officers' work and work environment are expected to affect how officers perform that work. However, a small body of quantitative research attempting to validate this linkage has with few exceptions found only weak relationships between specific officer attitudes and behavior.

The proposition that police officers' patterns of behavior correspond to their outlooks is certainly plausible, given the latitude that officers have in performing police work on the street. One might expect that officers' occupational attitudes would manifest themselves especially in the more discretionary forms of behavior, those that are not regulated by law or standard operating procedure, or that are difficult to subject to supervisory oversight or other review. Decisions to stop or other actions that officers initiate on their own authority (e.g., public relations contacts), might particularly be affected by their attitudes.

However, the few efforts to test such propositions systematically have produced, in the main, little or no support. One of the earliest and most striking findings from systematic observational research on police was that, while many officers professed to be prejudiced against blacks, they did not act on that prejudice in their encounters with citizens (Reiss, 1971). Freidrich confirmed that the use of force is unrelated to either officers' job satisfaction or (among white officers) their attitudes toward blacks (1980), and he also found that these outlooks bore weak relationships to other forms of behavior (1977). Worden (1989, 1995a) found that officers' occupational attitudes—for example, their conceptions of the police role, attitudes toward citizens, attitudes toward legal restrictions—are only weakly related to their patterns of behavior on the street in general and to their use of force in particular. Mastrofski et al. (1994) found that officers' attitudes, including their individual enforcement priorities, bore weak relationships to their patterns of enforcement of drunk-driving laws (also see Heeren et al., 1989). Terrill and Mastrofski (2002) found that officers' use of coercion was unrelated to their attitudes. Only two studies have reported relationships of a noteworthy magnitude. Mastrofski et al. (1995) found that officers who had more positive attitudes toward community policing were less likely to make arrests than their more negative colleagues. Brehm and Gates (1993) reported that officers' rates of "shirking" or time spent "goofing off" or "loafing" were influenced by their professionalism, their attitudes toward their jobs, and their satisfaction with their supervisors.[5] The

---

[5] "Professionalism" was measured in terms of summary characterizations by observers of how officers conducted themselves across a work shift; it is probably better interpreted as behavioral than attitudinal in nature.

results of this research are hardly definitive, and propositions that officers' outlooks or personality traits affect their behavior remain plausible but are not established scientific facts.

This small body of quantitative research is consistent with a much larger body of social psychological research on attitude-behavior consistency, which has shown that the estimated relationships between attitudes and behavior are counterintuitively small (Weinstein, 1972; Ajzen and Fishbein, 1977). Innumerable studies have analyzed various forms of behavior and their relationships to attitudes. In their review of this research, Schuman and Johnson (1976:167-168) reported that "few plausible studies fail to find significant relationships," however, "in most cases investigated, attitudes and behaviors are related to an extent that ranges from small to moderate in degree." This body of research also offers some clues about why the associations between attitudes and behavior are not stronger: it is attenuated by "situational cross-pressures," including the norms of reference groups. In policing, such cross-pressures might include the expectations of coworkers and the limitations imposed by bureaucratic controls. Another source of the weak attitude-behavior linkage is invalid and an unreliable measurement of both attitudes and behaviors. Often, the attitudes measured are not the ones most theoretically relevant to the behavior in question. Also, attitudes are frequently measured using responses to a single question, rather than the more reliable scales derived from combining responses to many questions that tap into the same attitude dimension. It is fair to say that some of the research on police attitudes is subject to these methodological limitations.

Finally, the whole point of creating police organizations is to attenuate the link between the views of individual officers and how they practice policing. Chiefs might prefer that their officers not hold racially prejudicial views, but what counts is whether officers act on those views. A department that structures police work and the consequences of police work to inhibit acting on prejudicial attitudes has accomplished its goal precisely by cutting the link between attitude and behavior. Thus, the failure to find substantial links between personal attitudes and behaviors is not necessarily bad news for control of police discretion, if that means that officers are behaving consistent with the organization's goals instead of their own beliefs. One study that explored this possibility in making drunk-driving arrests found that officers' personal beliefs about the importance of drunk-driving enforcement had far less influence on their arrest productivity than their capability (experience and training) and opportunity (work shift) to engage in this kind of enforcement activity (Mastrofski et al., 1994).

KNOWLEDGE, SKILLS, AND ABILITY

Proposition 12: It is widely believed that officers with greater knowledge, skills, and abilities will perform better than those with less of those traits. Research indicates that knowledge, skills, and ability do tend to predict better scores on performance tests, but these tests are of unknown value in predicting actual behavior and performance on the job. Consequently, the committee is unable to offer propositions about what forms of knowledge, skill, and ability are most useful for various aspects of actual job performance.

Police officer knowledge, skills, and abilities appear to have a moderately strong influence on the measures of their performance that researchers have used, but those measures bear a weak or unknown relationship to actual police practice. We are therefore unable to draw conclusions about the influence of knowledge skills and abilities on officer behavior. It is widely assumed in American society that those who have greater knowledge and more developed skills will generally perform better than those who do not. Reformers have made this a fundamental precept of professionalizing police, although police officers may be more inclined to adhere to the notion that knowledge derived from classroom instruction is of limited value, while learning by doing (or watching one's fellow officers) is how the most valuable knowledge and skills are obtained (Rubinstein, 1973; Van Maanen, 1978; Bayley and Bittner, 1984). Furthermore, police and outside experts may differ in what knowledge, skills, and abilities they believe are most valuable for police or police in a specific job assignment.

Police knowledge, skills, and abilities are typically measured by test scores—for example, reflecting the officer's grasp of search and seizure law or the ability to pass a physical fitness test. Most of what is known about the relationship of knowledge, skills, and abilities and job performance comes from research on the validity of various psychological tests. A recent extensive review provides some insight into this literature (Hogg and Wilson, 1995:42-52).[6]

Ability tests fall into four groups: cognitive aptitude (the capacity to learn the job with sufficient training), basic achievement (the extent to which an individual has knowledge or skills after training), specific ability (current performance ability for specific tasks), and intelligence tests (general capacity for problem solving, abstract thought, and understanding complexity). These abilities tend to be highly correlated, although different types of tests work better at predicting different sorts of things. An important caveat is

---

[6]The literature review in this section draws heavily on this comprehensive review.

that most of the evaluations of these tests rely on measures of officer perfor-mance that are very general in nature and far removed from the sorts of specific police actions toward which most of the commentary in this chap-ter has been directed. For example, "performance" might be defined as not being fired or not resigning, getting positive supervisor evaluations, or suc-cess in police training (higher test scores). These measures reflect outcomes, subjective rater judgments, or proxy measures of behavior (test scores) and must therefore be regarded with considerable caution for the purpose of predicting specific types of behavior, such as making an arrest, using force, or engaging in some form of community policing.

While many people believe that, other things being equal, more intelli-gent police officers will perform better, some have postulated that people of both low and high intelligence will not perform policing as competently as those in the middle range (Kenney and Watson, 1990). The explanation is that more intelligent officers may be understimulated by the routine aspects of police work. There is some research to support this curvilinear relation-ship as well as other research that produces mixed results (Hogg and Wil-son, 1995:44). Results are undoubtedly dependent on the type of job under consideration, and one might arguably expect a direct relationship between intelligence and job performance for officers assigned to a problem-solving specialty. However, level of educational attainment showed no such effect in predicting the amount of time officers spent on problem solving in one field study (DeJong et al., 2001:54).

In general, research tends to show that ability measures are predictors of police training performance, but it is less clear that training performance is itself a good predictor of performance in the field (Hogg and Wilson, 1995:45-46). It is assumed that testing during recruit academy training may successfully weed out those with the least ability, but this has not been demonstrated because of the lack of follow-up on those who were weeded out. One meta-analysis of 40 law enforcement studies showed that cogni-tive ability tests were fairly strong predictors of academy success, but only about one-third as effective in predicting actual job performance (Hirsh et al., 1986).

Police agencies use a variety of specific task assessment methods to evaluate ability: in-basket exercises, teamwork tests, and job simulations in assessment centers (Hogg and Wilson, 1995:51-52). Assessment center ex-ercises have been shown to do a better job of predicting job performance than ability tests, but they are much more costly to run. Structured inter-views are less valid in predicting job performance than ability tests, but they have achieved respectable levels of validity, especially when based on a job analysis, use multiple interviewers, are situation- and job-focused, and are standardized. All of this suggests that knowledge, skills, and abilities do influence performance, and that ability tests in policing (as well as most occupations) are better at predicting job performance than are personality tests (which concentrate on attitudes, perceptions, and predispositions). However, because most of the measures of performance used in these studies have a weak or unknown relationship to actual officer practice, we are unable to draw firm conclusions about the degree of influence that knowledge, skills, and abilities exert on officer practice.

EXPERIENCES OF OFFICERS

Thus far this chapter has considered what is known about the impact of outlooks and capabilities on police officer practice. Police organizations and government generally attempt to manipulate outlooks and develop capabilities by promoting such things as education and training and recruiting officers with certain characteristics. In recent years, equal opportunity and affirmative action policies have promoted the recruitment of a more racially and sexually diverse police force nationwide. By focusing on these considerations, police agencies are in effect attempting to manipulate the experiences that officers bring to bear on their work. They do this by selecting officers who have certain characteristics (and presumably certain types of experiences before becoming officers) and by socializing and training those selected to serve as police. In this section we consider what is known about the influence of these factors on police practice.

Education

Proposition 13: It is widely believed that higher education improves officer behavior, and, as a consequence, much effort has been invested over the years in raising education levels. The evidence reviewed by the committee does not permit conclusions regarding the impact of education on officer decision making. Prior research has not employed strong measures of police behavior and performance; it has not taken into account the content of the education; and it has not controlled for the effects of many other influences on behavior and performance.

There is widespread enthusiasm for college education as a valuable developer of knowledge, skill, and ethics for policing generally and community policing in particular (Shernock, 1992; Baro and Burlingame, 1999; Smith and Flanagan, 2000). The proportion of departments serving large cities that require new officers to have at least some college climbed from 19 to 37 percent between 1990 and 2000; the proportion requiring at least a 2-year degree increased from 6 to 14 percent during that period (Bureau of Justice Statistics, 2002). Much of the impetus for this trend can be credited to the desire to increase the regard in which others hold the police, but many advocates also expect that a college education improves the capacity of police to analyze and communicate, as well as to develop greater sensitivity to democratic values they are sworn to uphold in their work. Community policing, especially those approaches that emphasize problem solving and working closely with citizen organizations, is thought to call for the greater knowledge and skill that college is supposed to develop (Goldstein, 1990). The available evidence is limited in both quantity and quality, and the results are, at best, mixed—failing to show the sorts of dramatic differences reformers had hoped to see.

Much of the research on the effects of education focuses on attitudes or aspects of performance that are only indirectly related to community policing (Smith and Ostrom, 1974; Cascio, 1977; Weirman, 1978; Sherman and Blumberg, 1981; Worden, 1989). Several reviews of the literature have concluded that evidence on the effects of higher education on police performance is weak and mixed (Hayeslip, 1989; Buckley, 1991). A number of early studies indicated that college-educated officers are less dogmatic, authoritarian, cynical, prejudiced, intolerant, and punitive, but these studies measured attitudes, not performance (Shernock, 1992:73). Some studies found college education to be associated with fewer civilian complaints, quicker response times, and higher levels of enforcement activity (arrests, citations, stops, and checking businesses) (Finckenauer, 1975; Cascio, 1977; Hudzik, 1978; Sherman, 1980; Carter and Sapp, 1990). One study found that officers with a four-year college degree were substantially less likely to say they would arrest a mentally disordered person than were officers without the degree (LaGrange, 2000). An attempt to measure actual officer performance rather than attitude was based on department records. Controlling for age, length of service, and father's occupation, the researchers found that education had no significant relationship to the use of lethal force (Sherman and Blumberg, 1981). This and virtually all other studies have serious methodological flaws: weak measures of performance, inadequate measurement of the quality of college education, limited capacity to control for the effects of other variables (many of which are presumably correlated with a college degree), and lack of consensus on what constitutes good performance (Mastrofski, 1990:17; Shernock, 1992:74).

A few systematic observation studies have focused on actual police practices. Worden (1995a) identified three types of police behavior in handling suspects: no force, reasonable force, and improper force. He found that officers with a bachelor's degree were significantly more likely to use reasonable levels of force, but that they were indistinguishable from officers without a college degree in the use of improper force. Data from the POPN study found that college education had no significant effect on the amount of time officers spent on problem solving (DeJong et al., 2001), and no effect on officers' responsiveness to citizens' request to control other citizens in encounters (Mastrofski et al., 2000). However, college education was found to have a negative effect on providing comfort to citizens (DeJong, 2000). In the latter case, the negative effect of a college degree was concentrated among male officers. Similar results demonstrating no effect of a college education were found in a study in Cincinnati that used the same observation protocols as the POPN study (Novak et al., 1999:171).

Given the methodological limitations of past research on the effects of higher education on police practice, it is not surprising that the results are mixed and the effects generally weak. Even when relationships are found, researchers have not been able to distinguish how much of the effects of higher education are due to changes imparted by the educational experience and how much are due to the selection and screening involved in getting accepted into a college program (such as intelligence, initiative, wealth, family background, and knowledge, skills, and abilities acquired before college). Other limitations of existing research on the effects of college education are numerous. Almost all studies measure the quantity of higher education that officers receive but ignore the content of that education. Does the student's curriculum make a difference (e.g., majoring in criminal justice versus other majors, a theory-focused curriculum versus an applied, experiential one)?

Controlling for age, is there a difference in the behavior of a person with a college education acquired *before* becoming a police officer compared with the behavior of a person who obtained a college education while on the job? To what extent does the trend toward more college education produce a police force with less understanding and empathy for society's disadvantaged persons, and what are the consequences for street-level police practice? **The committee finds the available evidence inadequate to make recommendations regarding the desirability of higher education for improving police practice and strongly recommends rigorous research on the effects of higher education on job performance.**

Training

Proposition 14: For many decades it has been assumed that more and better police training leads to improved officer performance. The committee finds that past research on this topic has not addressed the complexities of the subject. Few studies evaluate the impact of training programs on actual performance on the job. Prior research has not taken into account the substantive content of training programs, modes of instruction, the abilities of the instructors, the timing of training, or the organizational support for reinforcing the objectives of the training program.

There is limited evidence available, scarcely more than a handful of studies, on the effects of training. Some research suggests that the influence of training depends on the extent to which training lessons are reinforced in the larger organizational environment, through top leadership, supervision, performance monitoring, and incentive systems. Most of the research on training suffers from one or more serious methodological limitations: poor measures of the actual performance that training is designed to improve, an inability to distinguish training effects from those of other influences, and failure to take the characteristics of the organizational environment into account. Research on the effects of training content, timing, instructor quali-fications, pedagogical methods, dosage, and long-term effects is virtually nonexistent.

Police training has been a growth industry since 1967 (Mastrofski, 1990:14). Between 1990 and 2000, median classroom training hours re-quired of recruits grew from 760 to 880, and field training requirements similarly grew from 520 to 600 hours during the past decade (Bureau of Justice Statistics, 2002). In addition, states require that minimum levels of in-service training be completed annually. Finally, when something goes wrong in a police department, additional training is usually at the top of the list of remedies proposed and undertaken.

Knowledge of the effects of police training is limited primarily to whether more training produces the desired change in police practice. This is typically acquired by conducting a controlled experiment (comparing police who have received training with those who have not) or by a study that measures the correlation between the amount of training officers have received and some police practice, while statistically controlling for the ef-fects of other influences, such as years of experience. There are too few of either type of study available to shed light on the effects of training.

Often evaluations of police training are embedded in assessments of larger organizational change interventions. An assessment of San Diego's Community Profile Development project in the early 1970s is an example (Boydstun and Sherry, 1975). This program attempted to implement many of the features that would later be incorporated into Goldstein's (1990) notion of problem-oriented policing. The program was intended to increase officers' knowledge and empathy for the people they served, and to get officers to focus on initiating innovative patrol strategies to deal with tar-geted problems in their assigned areas after carefully observing and analyz-ing those problems. It was evaluated using an experimental design that ran-domly assigned officers to treatment and control groups, taking pre- and post-treatment measures of a wide range of police behaviors, practices, atti-tudes, and perceptions. This program included not only training (60 hours), but also supervision and management direction given in support of these objectives. The evaluators found that the program had several encouraging outcomes: officers in the treatment group had a more developed sense of beat responsibility, more knowledge about their beats, and a greater involvement with community leaders. However, the evaluators were unable to distinguish the specific contribution that training made to produce these effects.

A randomized experimental evaluation that focused exclusively on the effects of training was conducted in Detroit in the 1980s (Rosenbaum, 1987). The 3-day training program, delivered to police officers undergoing a 16-week basic training curriculum, was designed to sensitize officers to the needs of victims. Surveys administered immediately before and after the training showed that the officers receiving the training showed much more favorable attitudes, perceptions, and intentions regarding victims than did officers in the control group. However, victims served by the treatment and control groups reported no differences in the way that officers treated them, suggesting that training may have affected officers' views and inclinations, but that it had no effect once they were actually at work.

These two studies illustrate a dilemma for understanding what effects training has on police practice and how to improve its effectiveness. The San Diego study evaluated an entire organizational change program, of which training was a significant part, but it was not the only organizational change strategy employed. It found generally positive results, but the researchers were unable to identify the specific contribution that training made, or whether it made any contribution at all. The Detroit study was able to isolate the effects of training, but it was unable to determine why its effects were limited. Future experimental evaluations should attempt to do both by increasing the number of training programs that are evaluated and varying the nature of the training and the context in which it occurs.

More numerous than experimental evaluations are studies that attempt to establish the relative contribution of police training and compare it with the effects of other possible influences, such as supervision and various incentives for performance. Typically, these studies examine the amount of training officers have received at a given point in time and then correlate it with some measure of officer performance (e.g., number of arrests), while controlling for the effects of other possible influences. The results of this research are mixed. The amount of training in community policing had no influence on the amount of time officers spent on problem solving (DeJong et al., 2001) and no effect on whether officers comforted citizens (Mastrofski, 1998). However, officers who had high levels of community policing training *and* who had a broad conception of their role (treating minor disorders as a priority) were significantly more likely to respond positively to citizens' requests to control other citizens who were troubling them (Mastrofski et al., 2000).

The contingent nature of training's effects appears to depend not only on what kind of officer receives it, but also on the kind of organizational environment in which the officer is operating. For example, training to deal with drunk-driving violations (driving under the influence or DUI) was found to be related to the number of arrests patrol officers made and that the effects of this training depended on the organizational environment in which the officers worked (Mastrofksi et al., 1996; Mastrofski and Ritti, 1996). When training was supported by ongoing supervisory and management practices that favored DUI arrest (leading by example, having officers work closely with victims' groups, closely monitoring arrest statistics, and supporting and protecting from internal criticism officers whose DUI arrest rates were exceptionally high). In departments that failed to provide a nurturing environment to sustain the DUI training, the amount of training received had no effect on the officers' DUI arrest rate.

A study of community policing training produced similar conclusions to the DUI study, in that academy training that was not reinforced in the field usually failed to produce lasting changes in officers' attitudes and beliefs (Haarr, 2001). This study of Arizona police recruits found that at the end of a 16-week program of training, recruits tended to show a more positive outlook toward community policing, problem solving, and traditional policing than when they began the training. However, these effects dissipated during the 12-week field training experience (except for views on the need for good police-public relations), and by the end of their 1-year probationary period, they tended to hold more negative attitudes toward community policing than they did at the end of academy training (except for police-public relations). Overall, with the exceptions of views on the need for good police-public relations and self-assessed capabilities in problemsolving, recruits entered the academy with more positive views than they held after one year on the job. During field training, the most powerful predictors of attitude were department policies supporting community policing. The change in attitude from pre-academy to the end of the one-year probationary period was strongly influenced by the officers' perceived view of coworkers' attitude toward community policing and the assigned work shift (presumably representing opportunities to spend time doing community policing on less busy shifts). Although this study focused on attitude changes and not performance, it underscores the notion that to sustain training's effects, it must be reinforced. A survey of training for community policing in over 500 police agencies indicated that few police agencies were even going so far as to require that their field training officers have knowledge of community policing (McEwen, 1997).

There are numerous limitations to the correlational research on training, including measurement of training itself. Most of this research is limited to measuring the amount of training but does not consider that the character, quality, and timing of the training can vary, even within the same department.[7] For example, some observers have criticized much police training for attempting to change officers' belief systems, while paying little or no attention to giving them the skills and incentives to change their practices, a common approach in the areas of domestic violence, cultural sensitivity, and community policing (Buerger, 1998; Haar, 2001). According to critics, such training is doomed to fail because it attempts to overcome strongly embedded habits and norms using a relatively light dose (at most, a few days of training), offers no really useful tools that officers can use, and fails to reinforce the training on the job. Nonetheless, much contemporary police training does attempt to imbue officers with a different set of outlooks about their work, so it would behoove researchers to take the content of the training into account. Another important unresolved issue about training content is determining what sort of curriculum is most effective in promoting the practice of various aspects of community policing. Minimum training standards are established by each state's police officer standards and training council, but there is virtually no rigorous research to guide them on how to structure recruit training curricula most effectively (for example, whether to integrate community policing training seamlessly throughout the curriculum or whether to highlight it in special segments).[8] Similarly, evidence is lacking on what sort of curriculum will best promote effective problem-solving projects. Should it be academic in nature (teaching recruits the rudiments of social science evaluation research), or should it be more inductive and experiential?

Correlational research has also failed to look for different patterns of training effects according to the type of officer who receives it. For example, it is conceivable that training on a given topic (such as handling domestic disputes) will be most effective when introduced in discrete segments over time, rather than all at once. Officers may need an opportunity to learn basic skills and try them out before moving on to more advanced techniques. The notion that training should be designed to build on past skill acquisition is different from the more common approach of simply retraining officers with the same material periodically. Until studies get more detailed information on when training of a given type was received in an officer's career, little will be known about the most effective way to develop a long-term training program for police.

What is known about the effects of training on police performance and

---

[7]Officers are typically asked to indicate how many hours of training on a given topic they have received in the last *x* time period.

[8]One analysis suggests that even after more than a decade in which community policing became very popular among police, training for officers has not changed much from its traditional focus on reactive activities (Bradford and Pynes, 1999).

practice is very limited, making the need for a systematic and rigorous research program in this area quite compelling. For example, recommendations about what constitutes desirable training to control police abuse of force *do* exist, but there is virtually no empirical validation of these claims (Geller and Toch, 1995:318). A number of issues that in the committee's view require attention:

- What should the content of training be? Should it focus on changing attitudes, developing skills, or both? How generalized can training be, and to what extent must it be tailored to the needs of the locale (Fyfe, 1995:171)?
- What training methods work best? Is realistic training that attempts to simulate conditions on the job the most effective (Fyfe, 1995:167)? For what kinds of training topics is "roll-call" training effective, and for what types of topics is more training immersion required?
- Who make the most effective instructors, those who are experts in training or those who are experts in the content area of interest?[9] Does the sworn versus civilian status of the instructor affect the willingness of officers to accept and implement the training?
- At what point in their career should officers receive training of a given type, what kind of follow-up training is effective, and when and how should it be given?
- What is the appropriate duration, intensity, or dosage of a given type of training?
- For a given type of training, what kind of on-the-job reinforcement is required to produce the desired change in officer behavior? How important are departmental rewards and sanctions for performing according to training compared with an individual officer's sense that the skills learned in training are useful? Is training an effective way to initiate change in an organization, or to be effective must it follow other organizational changes in such areas as supervision, incentive and disciplinary systems, and performance accountability?
- How long do the effects of training last? That is, how quickly do any effects decay over time? The received wisdom is that police academy training is quickly undercut by what officers learn from their more experienced colleagues on the job (Bayley and Bittner, 1984; Haar, 2001). Is this necessarily so for all training? What kinds of recruit training, if any, do officers find useful and follow as they gain experience?
- What kinds of control groups are appropriate?

---

[9]Experts may vary considerably in their ability to teach, but they will generally be far more knowledgeable about their topic, motivated to "sell" the training, and have higher credibility with the trainees (Buerger, 1998).

Given that departments invest extraordinary resources in training every year, **the committee strongly recommends more research on police training.** Perhaps the ultimate question for future research is to determine the limits of the effects of training. That is, just how much can training influence officers' attitudes, beliefs, knowledge, and skills? Much can undoubtedly be learned by studies of the effects of training in the military, the clergy, medicine, and the law. Ultimately, however, training competes with many other forces that come into play, so it is especially important to gain a realistic sense of what sorts of transformations can be expected. The committee anticipates that research on this issue will benefit from a careful consideration of two things: what skills and values police trainees bring to their experiences and the organizational context to which they return when they have been trained. Specifically, it is important for training evaluations to go beyond a narrow focus on the training program itself; they need to incorporate the entire package of management decisions made for monitoring, supervising, and rewarding desired behaviors.

EQUAL EMPLOYMENT OPPORTUNITY, AFFIRMATIVE ACTION, AND THE EFFECTS OF OFFICER RACE AND SEX

As discussed in Chapter 1, the trend in federal and state laws over the last 35 years has been to force police agencies to open their doors wider to racial and ethnic minorities and women. Although the principal legal justification for these laws has been to end and rectify employment discrimination, reformers have also argued that minority and female officers (a) will perform better (at least in certain situations or with certain groups of people) than white and male officers and (b) that their presence on the force will help to change the predispositions of the police subculture (Walker, 1998:232). Equal employment opportunity and affirmative action have served as principles that appear to have increased the representation of racial minorities and females on America's police forces (Walker, 1985; Martin, 1990), but does the race and gender of the officer have a significant effect on the way that officers exercise discretion?

The short answer to this question is that the limited research available provides little support for the notion that race and gender have a significant influence on officer behavior. Some recent research shows that female police officers are more inclined to engage in community policing and caregiving behavior, but the pattern is mixed and the number of studies limited. Indeed, the received wisdom from the research community is that whatever influence race and gender may exert on behavior is overwhelmed by the unifying effects of occupational socialization (see Donohue and Levitt, 2001, for a review). This may be disappointing to some reformers, who expected improved performance, but it may also be interpreted as good news, inasmuch as it discredits past discriminatory practices that equal employment policies attempted to rectify, and it shows that no appreciable differences in policing practice by officer race or sex should be anticipated.

Officer's Race

Proposition 15: Many reformers have argued that increasing the number of racial and ethnic minority group officers will lead to improved policing and better police-community relations. This proposition is based on the assumption that, for example, black officers will be less likely to shoot, arrest, or stop black citizens than white officers. The committee finds that in the small body of relevant studies there is no credible evidence that officers of different racial or ethnic backgrounds perform differently during interactions with citizens simply because of race or ethnicity.

Reformers of American police have for some time couched their criticisms and claims as if the race of the police officer has a significant influence on how the officer behaves (Kerner Commission, 1968:315). Many have argued that police forces will be more caring and service-oriented when the racial makeup of the police force approximates that of the department's jurisdiction, and for most center-city urban areas, that has meant increasing the number of minority officers on the force. Underlying this notion is that people with the same racial background will be more solicitous of each other. A contrary hypothesis is offered by Black (1976, 1980:9), who argues that citizens of high or dominant status are more likely to receive favorable police response when the lawgiver (i.e., police officer) is of a lower or nondominant status. Conversely, when the citizen is of a lower status than the officer, the probability of a favorable police action is lowest. Like-status individuals fall between these two poles, according to Black. Virtually all of the available studies compare whites and blacks.

Some research has found that officers of different races do tend to have different occupational outlooks (Alex, 1969; Rossi, 1974; Jacobs and Cohen, 1978; Decker and Smith, 1981; Leinen, 1984; Paoline et al., 2000; Weisburd et al., 2000) and knowledge about their neighborhoods (Mastrofski, 1983), but these differences do not seem to translate into significantly different patterns of behavior. Virtually all multivariate analyses that have tested for the effects of an officer's race on the use of coercion (arrest or force) show no appreciable difference between races (Reiss, 1968; Fyfe, 1981a; Smith and Klein, 1983; Worden, 1989, 1995a; Mastrofski et al., 1998; Engel, 2000; Terrill, 2001). A study of police disrespect toward suspects found that, in one of two cities studied, white officers were more inclined to be disrespectful to white suspects than minority suspects, an effect that the researchers suggested might have been due to the minority chief's strenuous efforts to reduce both police incivility and racial discrimination (Mastrofski et al., 2002a).

As with the punitive aspects of police work, little evidence in support of officer race effects has been found when researchers have attempted to predict various forms of order maintenance, police assistance, and engagement in community policing. Novak et al. (1999:176) found no effects of officer's race on the probability that officers would initiate order maintenance activity with suspects and disputants. DeJong (2000) found that the officer's race had no significant effect on the likelihood that a citizen would be comforted. Mastrofski (1998) found the same result when looking at officer-citizen race dyads. Two analyses of the effects of officer-citizen racial pairings found no effect on the likelihood that officers would grant citizens' requests to control another citizen (Mastrofski et al., 2000; Snipes, 2001). Only one of the reviewed studies found an officer race effect (Engel et al., 2000). White officers spent more time on problem-solving activities than did black officers.

In contrast to the above studies, all of which are based on field observations of individual officers' encounters with the public, is an analysis of arrest rates in 122 U.S. cities with populations greater than 100,000 for a time period spanning 1977-1993 (Donohue and Levitt, 2001). This study found that increases in the number of minority officers were associated with increases in arrests of whites (but not minority citizens), while more white police produced increases in the arrest rate of nonwhites (but not white citizens). These effects were particularly strong for minor offenses, such as public order offenses, prostitution, drunk driving, and other minor crimes. Extrapolating their results, the researchers estimated that "moving from random assignment of officers by race to a scenario in which same-race policing is maximized would lead arrests to decrease by over 15 percent" (Donohue and Levitt, 2001:390). It is important to note that this research does not allow us to make valid predictions about the effects of race on *individual* officers' behaviors, because the unit of analysis in this study is at an aggregated level—the entire municipal department. Arrest rates by officers' race may be affected by a number of factors not taken into account in this study (beat and shift assignment patterns), as well as other policies and practices that are associated with both the racial distribution of the police force and the distribution of arrests across citizens of different races. Moreover, arrest rates are calculated on the basis of people in a given population rather than on the number of incidents that could have resulted in an arrest. Inasmuch as quantitative analyses of individual officers' arrest practices have not produced similar cross-race effects as found in this aggregate study, it should be interpreted with great caution.[10]

One possible race effect is that the distribution of officers by race in a department affects the way that individual officers (by race) behave (Walker, 1985; Mastrofski et al., 1998). The vast majority of officers in most American police agencies are white, but possibly in those few departments in which the majority of officers are black, both black and white officers may behave differently, because there are a sufficient number of minority officers to sustain an alternative culture to that which has been found repeatedly in white-dominated departments. Underlying this notion is that a police force that is well integrated provides a context for developing greater mutual respect and understanding, as officers come to know each other as individuals. That is, the process may also change police officers' stereotypical views about people of a race other than their own. It also seems reasonable to hypothesize that when there is substantial racial heterogeneity in a police force, and that force also experiences substantial race-based tensions, officers' race may have an effect on how they practice policing, although the nature of the effects could well differ from situations in which there is racial heterogeneity and no such tension.

Although nearly all of the available multivariate research suggests that an officer's race is not a significant influence on police behavior, this issue should be explored more fully by considering different contexts in which the officer's race might matter. Researchers could test more fully the possibility that the effects of the officer's race depend on that of the citizens with whom they interact. More importantly, researchers should compare officer race effects in departments in which officers of a minority race constitute the majority of the sworn force, thus considering the possibility that these effects differ from departments in which minority race officers also comprise a minority of the sworn force.

---

[10]Indeed, a field observation study of Richmond, Virginia, in the early 1990s found that white officers dealing with minority citizens were the most likely to receive a compliant response when ordering a citizen not to engage in undesired behavior, and minority officers dealing with white citizens were the least likely (Mastrofski et al., 1996). Like-race pairings of officer and citizen were indistinguishable from each other in their success at securing citizen compliance and fell between the two racially heterogeneous pairings. Assuming that citizen compliance mitigates the need for arrest, these findings would predict that minority officers would have fewer enforcement alternatives to arrest when dealing with white citizens, while white officers dealing with minority citizens would have less need for arrest, given their higher rate of compliance success with that racial group.

Officer's Sex

Proposition 16: Many argue that the employment of more female officers will lead to changes in policing. This assumption is based on the belief that women are less aggressive and more nurturing than men and therefore more likely to use less coercion, relying instead on persuasion and assistance in dealing with citizens who cause problems or need help. The committee finds that the body of available research is too small and the findings too variable to draw firm conclusions about the effects of officer sex on police practice.

Relatively little work has been done on the differences in how men and women practice policing. A number of studies fail to find differences between male and female officers' beliefs and perceptions (Worden, 1993; Lasley, 1994; Finn and Stalans, 1997; Stewart and Maddren, 1997), and early evaluations of female officers indicated no sex-based differences in officer performance (see Feinman, 1994, for a review), focusing on the "masculine" or enforcement-oriented aspects of police work. Some of the early empirical work on police behavior suggested that female officers are less aggressive, less inclined to make arrests and citations, and less inclined to misbehave (see Sherman, 1980; Mastrofski, 1990; Riksheim and Chermak, 1993, for reviews). But this research suffers a number of methodological limitations, such as inadequate control for such confounding factors as age, experience, and duty assignment. Recent studies that control for many of these potentially confounding effects also fail to show significant differences between male and female officers in making arrests, issuing citations, and using force (Worden, 1989, 1995a; Engel, 2000; Terrill, 2001).

Some work has focused on specific community policing and order maintenance practices. Two of six systematic observation studies of patrol indicated that women were more inclined to engage in assistance or community policing; one study indicated that females were less inclined to do so; and three showed no difference. Engel et al. (2000) found that female officers spent more time on problem solving than male officers. Snipes (2001) found no difference between male and female officers in the amount of time they spent on encounters in which a citizen requested some form of assistance, and DeJong (2000) found that females were significantly more likely to comfort female citizens than males were to comfort male citizens. Cross-gender pairings of officer and citizen were not significantly different from the female officer-female citizen pairing. But Mastrofski et al. (2000) found that female officers were less likely to grant citizens' requests to control others who were causing trouble, regardless of the degree of control requested (ranging from advice to arrest). Snipes (2001) found a similar relationship in another city, but the sample of cases was much smaller and the results not significant. Finally, Novak (1999) found no difference between men and women in their proclivity to initiate order maintenance activities on their own. Thus, two of the studies do suggest that female officers are more likely to engage in the caregiving sorts of community building and problem-solving aspects of community policing, while the evidence is less clear on the kinds of behaviors that constitute a projection of the more intrusive and coercive aspects of police authority.

Future research exploring the possibility that officers' gender influences practice would benefit from a number of improvements. First, more refined measures of police practice should be considered. For example, whether or not an officer makes an arrest may not be linked to an officer's gender, but *how* that officer treats the people involved (whether or not an arrest was made) might be influenced by the officer's gender. Whether female officers tend to listen more to both sides of the story in a dispute is a question worth answering. Second, an examination of how officers spend their time that is free from assignments from the dispatcher and supervisors might reveal sex-linked differences. That is, there are few formal constraints determining when and where officers choose to mobilize, so any sex-linked inclinations would be most likely to be revealed in these patterns of behavior.

IMPLICATIONS

The committee explored research relevant to a number of propositions about the proximate influences of police behavior; both characteristics of the situation and of the officers. Virtually all of the literature reviewed focused on patrol officers. We found that the evidence available to test most of these propositions was inadequate to draw firm conclusions. Some implications are nonetheless possible.

That police practices, especially those tied to the enforcement function, are influenced far more by legal than extralegal considerations is encouraging news for those wishing to assess the state of policing in America. This is not necessarily cause for celebration, however, since there are a sufficient number of studies finding that race, sex, and social class influence police practice to be cause for concern. And even if these effects are much smaller than those of legal considerations, this says nothing about how much tolerance a society should have for these influences. Indeed the mixed evidence calls for more rigorous research to determine the circumstances under which the personal characteristics of the citizen do affect police practice. The situation with regard to the effects of citizen demeanor is different, inasmuch as a great deal of research *has* found this to be a relatively strong influence on whether a suspect is arrested. There is still debate about how much the extralegal aspects of citizen demeanor influence police enforcement practices, once the legally relevant aspects of that demeanor (constituting violations of the law) are taken into account, an issue that future research should resolve. More important for policy purposes, however, is determining what interventions, such as training, supervision, and discipline, prove most effective in reducing the scope of the extralegal aspects of citizen demeanor.

Researchers still have plenty to learn about the effects of legal and extralegal situational influences on police practices, but future research will make especially valuable contributions to improving policing if it can determine the *sources* of variation in these effects. For example, when legal considerations are not as influential as desired, is this due to a lack of police knowledge about legal requirements? Difficulties in applying the law to specific situations? A negative attitude about the law? The impact of competing priorities, such as the need to husband resources or deliver substantive justice? Are extralegal factors, such as revealed in race effects, less likely in departments with more active systems for detecting, correcting, or punishing racially biased officer practices?

Despite the considerable effort police leaders have devoted to winning the hearts and minds of police officers, the available evidence is not encouraging about the prospects of changing officer behavior by changing their outlook. Research on general outlooks (authoritarian personality, police culture, cynicism, and job satisfaction) has for the most part not tested the effects of these constructs, due in part to formidable measurement difficulties. The small body of research that has tested the influence of specific attitudes has shown at most only weak linkages between attitude and behavior, a finding that is consistent with findings in the field of social psychology generally. One implication is that attitudes and attitudinal change are poor proxies for actual practice when evaluating the impact of policy interventions on actual police practices. A second implication is that policies and management practices designed to shape officers' philosophies about their work appear to be unfruitful. However, an encouraging feature of this pattern of results is that police agencies may be fairly effective in breaking the link between individual beliefs and preferences on one hand and practice on the other. What remains to be shown is how successful organizations are—and through what mechanisms—in getting officers to pattern their practices consistent with the goals of the organization.

While the improvement of knowledge, skills, and abilities of police officers seems an unassailable objective, available research leaves largely untested the degree of influence these things exert on *actual police practice*, so policy makers and the public remain uninformed on the actual return received from these investments. This is also the case for two specific strategies that have been the mainstays of professional reform: increasing the quality and quantity of education and training for police. The small number of studies and the methodological limitations of most studies mean that particular programs to enhance police training and education are developed and offered *without* scientific evidence of their likely effects. Given the importance of these tools to those striving to improve policing, **the committee cannot overstate the importance of developing a comprehensive and scientifically rigorous program to learn what is and is not effective in the education and training of police officers.** Such evaluations should measure outcomes in terms of actual policing practices rather than tests and other proxies.

The absence of effects on police behavior related to the officer's race suggests that it may be irrelevant to actual practice on the street, although it leaves untested the impact of a more racially diverse police workforce on the legitimacy of the police (a topic for Chapter 8).

Because the available evidence on the effects of an officer's gender is inadequate to draw conclusions, it is difficult to draw specific implications in this area. Certainly there is a need for research that looks with greater care for areas of police practice in which differences between the sexes are most likely. Such studies will prove of limited practical value, however, unless they are able to determine the source of those differences. To what extent are they based on physiology, sex-role expectations, work environment differences, and so on?

Ultimately, the search for the causes and control of police behavior must extend beyond the limited domains of the situations and individual officers who handle them. Policing is shaped by the organizational and community contexts in which these events occur. These are the focus of the following chapter.

5

Explaining Police Behavior: Organizations and Context

P olice behavior is affected by broad forces, including features of the organizations that hire, train, and supervise police, as well as the environment within which they work. Organizational influences are important to understand because factors reflecting police organization and policies present possible points of leverage in shaping police practice. Those seeking to change police, whether they are inside or outside the agency, often pursue organizational changes, including instituting new policies, forming new units, changing supervisory practices, instituting performance quotas, or even hiring a new chief.

In contrast, many features of the environment are often beyond "easy human contrivance" (Bayley, 2002), and indeed, police practice is often *constrained by* the environment. The police may not be able to do much about the personal characteristics of residents, the economy, the distribution of wealth, the influx of immigrants, and the cultural habits of the people who live and work in their jurisdiction. Yet these characteristics do powerfully shape the workload of the police, so understanding the influence of these factors and the boundaries they may set on police practice is therefore an important component of police research. Because the effectiveness of a given policy in promoting a desired practice may vary across different environments, police leaders may find it especially useful to know when and where those policies are most and least effective.

Under some circumstances, environmental conditions can also be an object of policy manipulation by police. For instance, a department faced with an indifferent or hostile community may attempt to change the community's willingness to cooperate with the police in order to engage in more effective crime-control strategies. Or the department may wish to promote the community's capacity for collective action in partnership with the police. Organizing neighborhood groups, working with churches and religious organizations, and educating the public through citizen-police academies are all ways in which the police attempt to change outcomes, such as the crime rate, by changing the environment of policing (Mastrosfki and Ritti, 2000:191-192). When they engage in such environment-changing strategies, they may also change the way in which the department practices. For example, a police force that works closely with community groups may find that it can engage in more intrusive actions in that community without raising the distrust of community leaders. Thus some environmental factors will interest police precisely because they want to try to change them.

Research on these questions is not well developed. In order to understand the influence that organizational and environmental factors exert, the committee again presents its conclusions in the form of propositions that summarize large bodies of work. In terms of police organization, the committee reviews research on important law enforcement actions that administrative policy or structure might be expected to affect, such as the use of force, both lethal and nonlethal; citizen complaints and legal actions against the organization; arrest and clearance rates; and traffic citations. Each of these represents an important output in its own right, and each might also speak to and help depict a larger organizational style.

The environment in which police organizations operate is challenging to parse into meaningful categories. Many external forces can influence how the police act: their immediate surroundings, the historical relationship between a neighborhood and the police, the political tenor of the community, and even the regional culture in which they are situated. The committee organized this research in concentric circles: first the neighborhood that an agency serves, then the city or metropolitan area in which it is located, the politicians and civilians that oversee the department, and political forces—such as federal legislation—that address police operations. Of course, one important external force, the magnitude of which is not yet fully manifest, could not be ignored: as part of its review, the committee examined the effect of the terrorist attacks of September 11, 2001. While little systematic social science data exists on this topic for obvious reasons, the committee reviews what is known and culls from other research literatures in order to deepen its analysis of this vital issue.

We first consider some of the dependent variables used in this research. They reflect the activities and practices of policing that researchers have attempted to explain. Unlike research reviewed in the previous chapter, which concentrated on the behavior of individual officers, most of the research covered in this chapter focuses on police practices in the aggregate—that is, at the organization level. The committee makes some recommendations regarding measurement issues raised by this research; in addition, recommendations have been made about some of them in other chapters of the report. We then turn to research on organizational and environmental factors and conclude with more research recommendations.

MEASURES OF ORGANIZATION ACTIVITIES AND OUTPUTS

Police organizations, like the people in them, vary considerably. The ability to measure and understand this variation depends on the frequency with which information is collected, the "coverage" or the number and variety of agencies from which collection takes place, the quality of data, and the degree to which the research framework that interprets these data is meaningful and valid.

All of the activities or police outputs reviewed in this section are important to understating the operation of police organizations. Most are obtained directly from the agencies, either from surveys initiated by researchers or by federal data-gathering systems. In a few cases the data come from other organizations, including those in the justice system. In many instances, very few data exist to measure activities or outputs of police organizations, even though they may be a regular feature of police work.

Lethal Force

During a five-year period in the early 1990s, officers in the Washington, DC, Metropolitan Police Department shot and killed 57 people. During the same period, police officers in Chicago—which had five times the population and three times the number of officers—shot and killed 54 people (Leen et al., 1998). What factors explain this considerable variation in the use of lethal force by police in these two cities? A report by the *Washington Post* examined and dismissed several possible explanations, including the size of the population, the amount of violent crime, the number of homicides, the size of the police force, and the number of arrests for violent offenses (Leen et al., 1998). For instance, DC police averaged 2.3 fatal police shootings per 1,000 officers, compared with 1.5 in 26 other big city police departments and 1.7 in the nine U.S. cities with the highest homicide rates (Leen et al., 1998).

There is no more important piece of data regarding police behavior than that on the exercise of lethal force and, indeed, data are available nationally and have been collected systematically by the Federal Bureau of Investigation (FBI, in its Supplemental Homicide Reports module) since 1968. Yet these data are not published, in part because the FBI "cannot vouch for its accuracy" (Fyfe, 2002:18).

Data on police lethal force are also collected routinely by the National Center for Health Statistics in the *Vital Statistics of the United States* (Kania and Mackey, 1977). Sherman and Langworthy (1979) argue that estimates of justifiable homicide by police derived from vital statistics data deviate substantially from estimates derived from other data sources. They list six reasons for this finding, including vagueness in the instructions for completing standardized death certificates, inconsistencies in the decisions made by coroners and medical examiners, the close relationships between local police and medico-legal agencies, and logistical problems in coding, transporting, and entering data. Sherman and Langworthy (1979) offer mixed conclusions about the utility of vital statistics data for explaining variation in lethal force rates across cities. On one hand, they claim that the data should not be used to compare cities because such comparisons "are likely to be dangerously misleading" (p. 559). On the other hand, they find that the data may be useful for correlational analysis of the factors influencing variations in lethal force across cities (p. 559). Several studies have examined variations in lethal force over place and time.

The most accurate data on lethal force that identify jurisdictions have been obtained by newspapers threatening or actually litigating under the Freedom of Information Act (Fyfe, 2002). Yet these data are not systematically collected or available.

Nonlethal Force

The past decade has seen a pronounced increase in the level of research attention devoted to nonlethal force by police. While many individual police agencies track use of force by their officers, they have only recently begun to collect and assemble these data in a format useful for comparing police organizations. Thus, findings in this area must be subject to more review and research.

In 1992, Pate and Fridell (1993) conducted a national survey on police use of force. More than 1,100 agencies responded to the survey (response rate of 65.5 percent). Data from this study form the basis for much of what is known about use of force at the agency level and the kinds of relevant information that are collected by police organizations. Furthermore, data from this study continue to be used for scholarly inquiry in secondary analyses (e.g., Archbold and Maguire, 2002; Cao, Deng, and Barton, 2000; Cao and Huang, 2000). Pate and Fridell (1993) acknowledge that since some agencies do not require officers to report all use-of-force incidents, measures computed from these data may be imprecise. Their findings show that less severe forms of force are most prevalent, with handcuffs being used 490 times per 1,000 officers in 1991, bodily force being used 272 times, and weapons being unholstered approximately 130 times. Lethal force was used an average of 0.9 times per 1,000 officers in 1991, vehicle rammings 1 time, and dog bites 6.5 times.

While the Police-Public Contact Surveys (discussed in chapters 3 and 8) have been very useful and have provided important information on a variety of topics, their utility for exploring hypotheses about interagency variation in the use of force is limited because they do not contain agency or jurisdiction-level identifiers. They are unlikely to become the instruments through which researchers learn the most regarding police use of force. Another major data collection initiative, funded jointly by the Bureau of Justice Statistics and the National Institute of Justice in 1996 and 1997, sought to create a voluntary, anonymous national reporting center for police agencies to report their use of force data. Funding for the creation of a national data base was provided to the International Association of Chiefs of Police (IACP) in 1996 and 1997. In 1998, the IACP provided its own funding for the project, but the lack of outside support and low coverage convinced the organization to disband the project in 2001 (see Chapters 3 and 7 for further discussion of these data; Henriquez, 1999).

Arrest Rates

Arrest rates represent one of the most visible output measures of police agencies. They are collected consistently from most police agencies in the country through the Uniform Crime Reports (UCR). However, even this measure, which might appear on its face to be clear, has problems. Sherman (1980a, 1980b) found that the legal definition of arrest varied widely across agencies. He concluded that "differing arrest definitions make productivity comparisons between agencies impossible" (Sherman, 1980b:468). Sherman and Glick (1984) used a variety of research methods to study the quality of arrest statistics, including mail survey data from a sample of police agencies and state agencies responsible for compiling police data, brief site visits to 18 police agencies, and intensive case studies in four police agencies. Their findings suggest that state Uniform Crime Reporting agencies failed to ensure quality control of arrest data, and that in some cases they failed to understand the rules themselves. Furthermore, some police agencies neglected to include citations, summonses, and citizens' arrests.

Sherman's research on the quality of arrest statistics, which was completed in the early 1980s, has not been replicated; researchers do not know whether the findings apply nearly two decades later. The Justice Research and Statistics Association, a national nonprofit organization linking the directors of state statistical analysis centers, as well as other researchers and practitioners, serves as a professional vehicle for improving criminal justice data collected from states and localities. However, whether there has been any improvement in the quality of arrest statistics since Sherman's study is unknown.

Clearances

Like the arrest rate, the clearance rate is another measure of police output that is collected widely and frequently from police agencies around the nation. As discussed in Chapter 3, once reported, an offense is designated as founded and it may be cleared in two ways: by arrest or by exception (Federal Bureau of Investigation, 1980; Martin and Besharov, 1991).

Clearance rates vary over time and place, and this variation is important to understand. For instance, Riedel and Jarvis (1999) report that clearance rates for homicide have been falling almost linearly over the past four decades, dropping from 92 percent in 1960 to 66 percent in 1997 (p. 279 and p. 301). Presumably, a larger proportion of murderers are now walking the street than four decades ago. Understanding the factors that influence clearance rates is more than just an intellectual game; it is a fundamental question in the study of the police.

Nearly all clearance rate measures use reported crime as the denominator (Cordner, 1989). Some use arrests in the numerator (Decker, 1981), while others use arrests and exceptions (Cordner, 1989). Clearance rates are routinely used as a proxy for investigative effectiveness or success, yet clearance rates are beset with measurement problems (Alpert and Moore, 1993; Riedel and Jarvis, 1999). For instance, Cordner (1989:146) argues that both the numerator and denominator used in computing the clearance rate are "susceptible to manipulation and measurement error." Similarly, in their report on the future of the Uniform Crime Reporting program, Poggio and his colleagues (1985) list a number of problems with clearance rates that reduce their utility for measuring police performance. Liska, Chamlin, and Reed (1985) examined variation in "certainty of arrest" or "certainty of punishment," which they operationalized as the ratio of arrests to reported crimes. While not strictly a clearance rate (as operationalized by the FBI Uniform Crime Reports), it is conceptually similar and avoids the potential for "bureaucratic manipulation" by the police (p. 123). Despite these problems with the measurement of clearance rates, they are reported routinely by police departments and used routinely by researchers.

Citations

There are no national data on citations issued by police agencies. This situation may begin to change as police organizations continue to implement data collection systems related to racial profiling. Because there are no data sets, there is little knowledge about departmental variations in the issuance of citations to citizens, and consequently few empirically supported explanations for these differences.

Of the estimated 19.3 million drivers who were pulled over by police at least one time in 1999, about 54 percent received a traffic citation, about 26 percent received a warning, and only about 3 percent were arrested. Given the volume of citations issued by the police relative to other outcomes they produce, research and theory on what the police do should not neglect this fundamental task. Very little is known about interagency variations in the issuance of citations.

Traffic tickets are not the only kind of citation used by police agencies. Many jurisdictions now rely on citations in lieu of arrest for certain misdemeanors. For instance, many states authorize the use of citations for possession of small amounts of marijuana (Feeney, 1982:38). There are at least three general categories of citations (Feeney, 1982; Welsh, 1993). The names used to describe them vary widely across jurisdictions. The first, often referred to as a field citation, is like a traffic ticket and is issued in lieu of a custodial arrest. The second, known as a station citation, is issued after a custodial arrest has been made and is used in lieu of detention. The third, known as a jail citation, is used by sheriffs' deputies or other jailers to release detainees. The field citation is the only one of interest in this report, since it represents an alternative measure of police output that does not involve a custodial arrest. Since the police issue field citations with such frequency, understanding the factors responsible for interagency variation in their use seems to be an important component of explaining what police organizations do.

Civilian Complaints

Citizen complaints arise when a citizen takes action in response to an encounter with an officer that generates a record of the grievance. These data have been used as indirect indicators of the behavior of the organization, as seen through the eyes of aggrieved parties. At first glance, the nature and pattern of citizen complaints might appear to be a useful indicator of police misbehavior during interactions with citizens. After all, police officers who behave in a civil, professional manner are likely to generate fewer complaints than officers who behave in a rude, abrasive, unprofessional manner.

However, aggregated data on citizen complaints have many shortcomings. Chief among these is that the number of complaints may say more about a department's openness in seeking out, welcoming, and investigating feedback from the community than it does about police behavior on the streets (Adams, 1999; Walker, 1998, 2001). In addition, Walker (2001) provides numerous examples of police agencies failing to uphold their own complaint intake policies by thwarting citizens' efforts to file complaints. There is also doubtless substantial variation in the willingness of citizens to step forward and press complaints, linked to neighborhood, cultural and historical factors. If they reach the legal system by other channels, the willingness of municipalities to negotiate informal settlements of formal suits or complaints affects which ones become known to the public.

These factors cloud the interpretation of complaints and other complaint-related measures of police behavior, including the rate at which civil suits are filed against departments and civil rights complaints are made against them. As Adams (1999:10) notes, "because the legal process is highly selective in terms of which claims get litigated, lawsuits are a very unreliable measure of illegal use of force." National studies of civil suits (Archbold and Maguire, 2002; Pate and Fridell, 1993) have not found them a persuasive measure of police behavior. In two major surveys (Pate and Fridell, 1993; Worrall, 2001), complaint questions generated lower response rates than other items, suggesting that the data are not routinely collected and tallied by some agencies. Furthermore, even when agencies do provide numerical summaries, there are serious doubts among the academic community about the reliability and validity of the measures. Given the fundamental importance of police-citizen relationships, however, the topic is important enough to warrant considerable effort in building a reliable body of knowledge. One potentially fruitful avenue to explore is the use of citizen surveys that ask respondents about recent contacts with police. Because these surveys are independent of the department's complaint process, they can provide a reliable measure of citizens' grievances whether or not they were filed or processed.

NEGLECTED DIMENSIONS OF POLICE BEHAVIOR

Despite their many limitations, the measures reviewed thus far have provided researchers and evaluators with data to assess how police exercise their formal enforcement powers. However, these measures are clearly insufficient for tracking police organizations' progress in achieving new notions of the police mission that became popular in the late 20th century and are likely to continue well into the 21st century. Indeed, research over the last 40 years clearly shows that most police resources are expended on activities that do not result in formal enforcement, and that citizens care a great deal about when, where, and how these informal activities occur (Mastrofski, 1983; Whitaker et al., 1980) Research also suggests that they may have a significant influence on the crime control effectiveness of the police (see Chapter 7). The overwhelming emphasis on recording only certain formal enforcement activities in policing is analogous to a hospital's maintaining records only on the surgery its physicians perform, leaving unrecorded the many other important treatments administered by its staff.

As Chapter 3 indicates, police have been shown to rely on formal enforcement powers relatively rarely, and, just as importantly, new strategies such as community and problem-oriented policing call for police to engage in a much broader range of activities to accomplish desired outcomes. And even more recently, concerns about a more effective police response to the risks of terrorism have illuminated just how little systematic information there is about police policies and practices concerning the gathering, processing, and dissemination of information (Ericson and Haggerty, 1997).

Policy makers who want to measure police agencies' progress toward implementing practices consistent with these new directions need a new set of institutionalized measures that simply do not exist in any systematic form in agencies across the United States. At a minimum, the following types of indicators are needed to capture the wide range of approaches to police work with which local agencies are experimenting: applications of police authority other than formal enforcement of the criminal law, forms of police assistance, indicators of the quality of the policing process that citizens experience, measures of mobilizing and working with the community, measures of problem solving, and indicators of police as information brokers. Each of these categories is briefly discussed below.

Applications of Police Authority
That Do Not Invoke the Criminal Process

Research shows that police relatively rarely resort to their formal authority to arrest or cite someone in dealing with the myriad situations they handle. This is not only because the police, more often than not, choose leniency when the evidence would support formal enforcement, but also because they must often deal with situations in which formal enforcement action is not legally warranted but they feel compelled to do something to correct a situation or prevent matters from deteriorating. Thus, they seek citizen compliance and order maintenance by such methods as simply making their presence or interest known to potential troublemakers, stopping and questioning them, persuading, advising, commanding, or threatening them, or referring problems to other agencies. Broken-windows policing relies heavily on these informal methods of enforcement, as well as arrests and citations for minor offenses (Wilson and Kelling, 1982; Kelling and Sousa, 2001), yet police departments do not routinely record most of these actions, making it difficult to determine how and how thoroughly this approach has been implemented. Many departments do maintain records on certain field interrogations, which are stops of suspects that do not result in an arrest, and of traffic stops that do not result in a citation. However, the diligence with which these are recorded varies greatly and the comparability of record-keeping across agencies is unknown. The availability of useful cross-agency data may be changing, however, due to standardization imposed by vendors of records management systems in multiple agencies.

While the Uniform Crime Reports have done a relatively good job of indicating the formal aspects of police performance over time and across jurisdictions, there is no comparable body of data on the far more frequently employed informal methods by which police authority is exerted. The nation's accounting system for police authority leaves exertions of that authority unrecorded. Given the challenges of making the UCRs a reliable data source, the difficulties of developing a more comprehensive system for monitoring the informal exercise of police authority are truly daunting. Nonetheless, it might be possible to develop a uniform reporting system for certain aspects of police agencies' documentation of calls for service and field interrogations, one that would call for agencies to use a standardized system to note which informal, as well as formal, uses of authority were applied in each situation recorded by the agency. Such a system would enable police leaders and policy makers to develop a far more comprehensive picture of policing as most people in their communities are actually experiencing it. **The committee recommends that support be given to the Bureau of Justice Statistics to develop and pilot test in a variety of police departments a system to document informal applications of police authority.**

Police Assistance to Citizens

Police in the United States have long performed a wide range of services, most of which receive little attention in the analysis of organizational performance. During previous eras of reform, these activities were discredited as "not real police work," which detracted from the ability of police to fight crime (Fogelson, 1977; Walker, 1977). Yet currently popular community policing and problem-oriented policing reforms encourage police to engage in an even broader range of services as a means of more effective crime prevention, enhancing the quality of community life, and securing greater community support for and participation in police efforts.

Police are frequently called to exert their authority to protect one party from another (Mastrofski et al., 1996; Snipes, 2001) which is one kind of service, but they are also often asked to do things that could be performed by a private service provider, things that require no special police authority but are provided because of the availability of officers to respond in a timely fashion (Wilson, 1968). These range from pulling stranded cats out of trees, to providing crime prevention advice to neighborhood groups, to running midnight basketball leagues designed to keep youths from engaging in illegal and disruptive activities. Some departments engage in more of this activity than do others, and the existence of this natural variation creates opportunities to judge the effects of these efforts on a wide range of outcomes, such as crime, fear of crime, and police legitimacy.

For example, the public in one community might find it useful to compare its department's level of nonenforcement service delivery to that of other similar communities, just as consumers of privately delivered services find it useful to have such information on service providers. Such data, if available on a large number of police departments, would allow researchers to determine the contribution of nonenforcement service delivery to crime control and community satisfaction with the police. **The committee recommends development of measures that better document at the jurisdiction level the nature and extent of nonenforcement services delivered by police. This program of development should consider the variety of current measures available in U.S. police agencies, pilot test a system at several sites, and then propose a large, multiagency data collection system.**

Policing Processes

There is value in measuring various aspects of the *processes* of policing, not only because the quality of those processes appears to have consequences for valued outcomes (such as reducing law violations), but also because the public highly values certain aspects of police behavior in and of themselves (such as being reliable, attentive, responsive, competent, respectful, and fair) (Mastrofski, 1999). As Chapter 8 shows, whether and how police perform these processes is *at least* as important to citizens as police effectiveness in crime control.

We have noted some of the limitations of using complaints against the police and lawsuits to measure the quality of these processes. Another limitation is that complaints and lawsuits at best measure only bad performance and leave unattended acceptable or good performance. Chapter 8 recommends a way to generate useful information about these processes by conducting surveys of police "clients." Here we note that the character of those processes appears to be so important to securing police legitimacy and crime reduction that developing a national jurisdiction-level system of data collection on policing processes is essential to a comprehensive characterization of what police organizations do.

Mobilizing and Working with the Community

Community policing reformers have made it widely expected that police in the United States work closely with community groups to prevent crime and enhance the quality of life. As discussed elsewhere in this chapter, a number of survey projects have attempted to measure this kind of activity, one of which has been institutionalized in the Law Enforcement Management and Administrative Statistics (LEMAS) surveys periodically conducted in the nation's larger police agencies. The problem with existing survey data is that they offer weak measures of the scope and intensity with which such activities are undertaken, noting usually only whether an agency is currently engaging in such activities, but not how much police and community effort is exerted (Maguire and Mastrofski, 2000). For example, two departments may report that they work with community groups to prevent crime, but there is a tremendous difference between one that meets frequently with many community groups and one that meets occasionally with a few. The current inability to measure the dosage of such efforts greatly limits the ability of researchers to distinguish substantial differences among agencies in how and how much they engage in these activities. **The committee recommends that the Bureau of Justice Statistics develop measures that provide a more accurate indication of the extent to which community liaison and mobilization activities are engaged by individual police agencies.**

Problem Solving

The desirability of a problem-solving approach to policing has taken hold in many police agencies in the United States (Scott, 2000). A conference devoted to problem solving, sponsored annually by the Police Executive Research Forum, is attended by members of hundreds of departments from around the nation. Surveys of police agencies suggest that the popularity of this approach is widespread (Maguire and Mastrofski, 2000), yet it too suffers from the same measurement difficulties as does community liaison and mobilization. Some research suggests that great variation exists in the kinds of problems targeted for these methods, as well as in how problem solving is actually conducted. Some have distinguished weak problem-solving efforts from stronger ones. The extent of problem analysis, the search for effective solutions, evaluation, and follow-up are important aspects of the dosage issue for problem solving (Eck and Spelman, 1987). **The committee recommends that the Bureau of Justice Statistics develop measures that provide a more accurate indication of what problems and populations are targeted for problem-solving efforts, as well as the intensity and quality of those efforts.** Because problemsolving can occur at many levels and in many ways in a given police organization, a feasible measurement method will undoubtedly require sampling problem-solving efforts over a given time period in each surveyed department.

Police as Information Brokers

Some researchers have argued that by the late 20th century, the core police capacity had shifted from being purely that of coercion to that of information gathering, processing, analysis, and dissemination (Ericson and Haggerty, 1997). Certainly community and problem-oriented policing call for increased levels of this sort of activity, but the current domestic war on terrorism has heightened sensitivity to this responsibility for local law enforcement agencies. A later section of this chapter deals with the question of how the war on terrorism is affecting police structure and practices. Here we note the need to gather systematic data on what those structures and practices are.

As with any broker, learning certain things about the information gathering, processing, and dissemination will be an important foundation to assess how well police agencies are performing this function, specifically:

- nature of the information collected,
- how the information is gathered and what other organizations contribute to it,
- how the information is checked for accuracy, processed, archived, and retrieved within the police agency,
- how and to whom information is disseminated inside and outside the agency, and
- how information is used and how useful it is to the users.

Police deal in far too much information to gather data on the above elements for *all* types of information. Strategically focusing inquiry on police information brokering is necessary, and the committee recommends two areas that are especially timely: (a) information on criminal events and (b) intelligence on terrorist suspects and potential terrorist activities.

In the first case, police departments around the country are undergoing major changes in the technology of gathering, storing, mapping, and analyzing criminal events (Anselin et al., 2000). Advocates of such programs as CompStat claim that it is revolutionizing the management of police crime control and service delivery (Bratton, 1998; Silverman, 1999; McDonald, 2001), yet there is relatively little rigorous study of how, if at all, it is changing police organizations, and that which is available has produced intriguing findings. For example, a national survey of police agencies conducted in 1999 found that agencies that had implemented CompStat tended to place greater emphasis on empowering, rather than challenging, the traditional hierarchical paramilitary structure of municipal police organizations in the United States (Weisburd et al., 2003). **The committee recommends that the National Institute of Justice support a program of rigorous evaluation of new crime information technologies in local police agencies.** This program should go well beyond describing variation in technologies and whether they "work" in a technical sense; it should track the impact of changes on organizational structures and practices over time in selected departments and compare the impact of these technologies in a variety of departments. Such information will help police agencies establish which technologies, and which ways of organizing to cope with those technologies, will work best for them.

In studying local police agencies as information brokers on terrorism, data collection issues are complicated by the recentness of local agencies attending to this function, the high level of interagency coordination entailed, and the need to maintain the necessary security for these information systems. Such information networks will obviously extend to federal agencies and departments, such as the FBI and the Department of Homeland Security. Some of the data elements bulleted above will involve working with classified information, so special arrangements will need to be made to obtain researcher access to data, and the distribution of results will be challenging. Nonetheless, the importance of the terrorism intelligence function is too important to leave unexamined or reported only in classified documents not available to the wide range of policy makers with responsibilities for funding, planning, and developing terrorism intelligence systems involving local police agencies. The U.S. Department of Justice has already funded a small pilot project, run by the Police Executive Research Forum (PERF), exploring issues of federal-local coordination in dealing with information on terrorism. **The committee strongly encourages using the results of this effort to develop a long-term national program for tracking and evaluating the performance of local police departments' efforts in gathering and handling intelligence on terrorism.**

INFLUENCE OF POLICE ORGANIZATION

The ostensible function of an organization is to structure the activities of its members to accomplish goals. Policy makers and administrators attempt to manipulate various features of police organizations to accomplish such goals as crime control, legal compliance, and community contentedness. In this section we consider several features of police organizations thought to influence police *practices* that are presumed relevant to the accomplishment of these goals. We first consider the size of a police agency. Then we turn to structural features that have been frequent objects of policy manipulation: the degree to which decision making is centralized or decentralized, the degree of complexity (defined in various ways), and the extent to which policies are formalized. Finally, we consider CompStat, a currently popular omnibus reform package that combines several of these structural elements.

Police Agency Size

Proposition 1: The size of a police organization is a product of policy choices. Some claim that larger departments tend to yield more and better police activity, while others claim that large police departments enjoy no particular advantage and that they may often suffer disadvantages. The committee finds that the effects of police agency size are mixed and contingent on too many factors to conclude that police agencies of any size—small, medium, or large—are necessarily to be preferred.

As suggested in Chapter 3, police service delivery in the United States is fragmented among thousands of police agencies, most of which are very small, the median local police department had only 7 sworn officers in 2000 (Bureau of Justice Statistics, 2002). There are three major reasons for this: the tradition of local government service delivery in a federal system, the proliferation of small suburbs that limited the growth of large center cities, and the general lack of enthusiasm among police leaders for consolidation of departments (Reiss, 1992:64-65). Since the 1930s, "good government" reformers have advocated consolidating small departments in metropolitan areas to facilitate police professionalism, improve productivity, and enhance service quality (Walker, 1977:141-146). Several blueribbon commissions in the 1960s and 1970s endorsed this approach (U.S. Advisory Commission on Intergovernmental Relations, 1963; President's Crime Commission, 1967; Committee for Economic Development, 1972:31; National Advisory Commission, 1973), and progressive police leaders frequently asserted its benefits for police efficiency and effectiveness (Altshuler, 1970:38). Consolidation, when it has occurred, has occasionally taken the form of integrating numerous agencies into a single county police agency; more often it occurs when a small jurisdiction contracts with a larger one for police service, or when it disbands its police force and relies on the county sheriff or state police to provide services (Mastrofski, 1989:10-11; Reiss, 1992:66).

Running counter to the consolidation movement was a call from the "community control" reform movement to break up large police departments. It surfaced briefly in the late 1960s and early 1970s. Many police progressives of the time claimed that breaking up large police departments would threaten impartial law enforcement and return to the corruption and inefficiencies of machine-era policing (Mastrofski, 1981:44-45). Large departments could afford to implement the latest technological innovations, support a large supervisory hierarchy for quality control, hire and retain highly qualified people, and provide for more and better training (Wilson, 1968:284-299). The validity of these claims was questioned by some reformers and researchers, who argued that "bigger was not better," and that in fact, smaller departments might well serve their communities better (Ostrom, 1973, 1976; Ostrom et al., 1973). Smaller communities would rely less on organizational hierarchy and more on elected officials and citizens to oversee police actions, thereby enhancing productivity and efficiency. Furthermore, some argued that any gains to be had in the greater professionalism of larger police agencies were undermined by the costs imposed by heightened bureaucratization: greater alienation from the citizenry and less responsiveness to their needs and preferences, trends acknowledged by bigger-is-better advocates and that concerned them too (Schmandt, 1972; Murphy and Plate, 1977; Peterson and Pogrebin, 1977).

Despite the popularity of the consolidation movement among blue ribbon commissions and some big-city chiefs, it simply has not transformed the structure of the American police industry, which remains overwhelmingly populated by small agencies, while a major portion of the public is served by large agencies (Reaves and Goldberg, 1998). Of course, police agency consolidations do occur on a small scale, but they are rarely of spectacular proportion, such as merging many small and medium-sized agencies into a single county organization (Mastrofski, 1989:10). Consequently, most of what researchers know of the consequence of police agency size for police practice comes from comparisons of a cross-section of large and small departments at a given point in time. Much of this research focuses on outcomes, such as crime rates, citizen satisfaction, and cost-efficiency. However, some research has examined the implications of agency size for actual practice, and it is this literature that the committee reviewed.

Two major studies examined the consequences of police agency size for the ability of departments to mobilize police, that is, to put patrol officers on the street. Elinor Ostrom and colleagues examined patrol deployment of over 1,000 local departments providing patrol services in 1974-1975 in 80 metropolitan areas of the United States. More than half of the sample had no more than 10 full-time sworn officers, 45 had more than 150 (and only 10 of these employed more than 500 sworn). For municipal police (as well as other local police agencies) they found that the smaller the agency, the more officers per resident were on patrol. For example, they found that departments with only 5-10 sworn officers typically placed 4.2 per 10,000 residents on patrol at 10:00 p.m., while departments with more than 150 sworn officers managed only 2.3 per 10,000 (Ostrom et al., 1978:85-91). They found that smaller departments accomplished this by allocating a much higher percentage of their sworn force to patrol operations and much less to administration, auxiliary services, and other direct services. What that meant in practical terms was that the chief and supervisors often performed rank-and-file patrol duties as well as supervisory and administrative functions. In a follow-up, Langworthy and Hindelang (1983) compared the Ostrom et al. results to those of another data set comprised of a national sample of 69 larger departments (more than 134 sworn officers) surveyed in 1977. Langworthy found that the sample of larger departments showed a median level of patrol mobilization consistent with that found by Ostrom and colleagues. Additionally, he noted that, like the Ostrom data, his sample displayed considerable variability in both agency size and patrol mobilization. Examining the relationship of agency size to patrol mobilization among these larger departments, he found a weak *direct* relationship between agency size and number of officers on patrol per citizen. Thus, while the Ostrom study indicated that the consolidation of small agencies would yield a lower level of patrol mobilization, Langworthy's analysis suggested that breaking up the largest agencies into smaller ones would not necessarily yield higher levels of patrol mobilization.

Although citizens are certainly concerned with the *level* of police presence on the street, they are equally concerned with what the police *do* while on the street. The entertainment media undoubtedly encourage the public to perceive small and large departments in different ways by stereotyping them. For example, Dragnet and Adam 12 depicted big-city police as legalistic, technically sophisticated, and enforcement-oriented, while Andy of Mayberry showed small-town law enforcement as service-oriented, humanistic, and inclined to seek less coercive, informal solutions to problems. To what extent does research support these stereotypes?

Some of the research suggests that the relationship between police department size and actual practice is weak or nonexistent, but a fair amount of the available research does in fact tend to support the popular stereotypes (see Mastrofski, 1981:Ch. 3 for a review). On one hand, several studies have shown that, taking other influential factors into account, large departments tend to have higher arrest rates (per officer or per capita), to have officers who are more aggressive and less selective in using their formal law enforcement powers, and to resort to force more frequently (Brown, 1981; Mastrofski, 1981:Ch. 6). On the other hand, smaller agency size is associated with officers who are more familiar with individual citizens and neighborhood organizations, provide more assistance to neighborhoods, and more follow-up to citizens' crime reports (Parks, 1979, 1980; Whitaker, 1979). However, these studies, which compared police practice in large center-city neighborhoods with that in comparable neighborhoods in nearby small cities, also found some significant exceptions. For example, citizens were more likely to report incidents of police mistreatment in the smaller departments of two of the studies, but in general the differences found were not large. Studies that looked at middle-sized departments sometimes showed a curvilinear relationship. The mid-sized agencies outperformed both the large and small ones when the bases of comparison were citizens' perceptions and evaluations of police service in general, not associated with a particular event. Because the specific pattern of results varied with the study, one of the evaluators concluded that while the evidence did not always favor small departments, sometimes varying with the race or class makeup of the neighborhood, "Contrary to what most contemporary critics of American policing have argued, we have not found performance advantages for residential neighborhoods that received police services from large departments" (Parks, 1980:4-60).

There are some interesting exceptions to the tendencies just discussed. The impact of agency size on enforcement levels, as measured by arrest rates, has been shown to vary with the type of offense. For example, one study found that small middle-class suburbs showed higher arrest rates for breaches of the peace than did the nearby large county police force, but the reverse was true when agencies were compared on arrest rates for theft (Wilson, 1968:211-215). The researcher hypothesized that smaller agencies were more responsive to the priorities of the citizens in those communities who would find breaches of the peace quite troubling. Furthermore, the smaller departments had fewer alternatives to arrest. In contrast, larger departments would be more buffered from the preferences of the neighborhoods and also had more nonarrest alternatives available. However, regarding thefts, the issue is less one of community outrage than of rectifying the victims' losses. Here larger, specialized departments are presumed to have the advantage in solving crimes and catching thieves.

Another exception running counter to the popular images of small versus large departments is found in research on drunk-driving enforcement. Small departments have been shown to show a striking inclination to exercise more initiative and less discretion in enforcing drunk-driving laws than found in large departments (Mastrofski et al., 1987; Mastrofski and Ritti, 1990, 1992). A study of 735 municipal Pennsylvania agencies found that departments with 1-5 full-time sworn officers had a per-officer DUI arrest rate more than three times that of departments with more than 100 sworn officers (Mastrofski and Ritti, 1996). In general, drunk driving is at least as prevalent in jurisdictions served by large departments as those served by small ones. Researchers noted that small departments generally have a less intensive workload than larger ones, thereby giving officers more available time to initiate time-consuming DUI stops, and smaller communities may tend to see drunk-driving enforcement as a higher priority (Mastrofski et al., 1987). But they attributed much of the difference between small and large agencies to differing sets of opportunities available for these departments to demonstrate their law enforcement prowess. Large departments have many ways of demonstrating their law enforcement proficiency by developing specialist units to deal with serious crimes. Small departments had fewer serious crimes and much less resource availability to devote to the kinds of specialist structures that signify law enforcement competence (see Chapter 8 for a discussion of this approach to enhancing organizational legitimacy).

Finally, some studies of clearance rates provide a picture of American policing at odds with the big city and small town stereotypes. A study of national UCR data found mixed results when examining the effect of agency size on clearance rates for various offense categories (Cordner, 1989). In a national sample, agency size had a negative effect on the clearance rate, but in a supplemental sample of Maryland agencies, size had no effect. In the Maryland sample, agencies located in the Baltimore-Washington metropolitan area also had lower clearance rates, suggesting the likelihood of an urban-rural effect. The researcher concluded that the environment may have had a stronger influence on clearance rates than the organizational characteristics, which suggests that there are limits to what can be accomplished by manipulating agency size. A study of child sexual abuse cases found that large agencies had much lower clearance rates, although the researcher noted the susceptibility of these rates to earlier decisions to found cases or discard weak ones (Maguire, 2002c).

It is hazardous to offer specific policy recommendations from this relatively modest body of research on the impact of agency size on police practice, but several general lessons can be drawn. First, policy makers should not *assume* that consolidation of small police departments will yield greater productivity or changes in the quality of police practice. Many studies suggest that smaller agencies serve their jurisdictions as well or better than do larger agencies serving similar areas. Furthermore, one of the costs of achieving economies of scale by consolidation may be reduced responsiveness to some of the jurisdictions served. Indeed, a case study of the feasibility of small-department consolidation revealed that not one of five different service arrangement options served each jurisdiction equally well (Mastrofski, 1989). Similarly, breaking up large agencies into smaller ones (something that occurs very rarely), also carries no guarantees of improved performance. Finally, it appears that the consequences of agency size for enforcement productivity may depend on the type of offense under consideration. Independent of the extent to which the problem exists, large agencies appear more active in enforcing some kinds of laws than are small agencies, but the reverse is also true. Smaller agencies pay more attention to some offenses than do large agencies. This suggests the importance of taking into account what priorities for enforcement are communicated from a department's environment, and what mechanisms exist to channel pressures into or away from police agency policies and practice.

Decentralization of Decision-Making Authority

Proposition 2: Police reformers over the last three decades have supported decentralization of decision-making authority in the police agency as a powerful tool to accommodate to varying needs and priorities in the agency's jurisdiction. This began as a movement toward administrative decentralization in the late 1960s that has continued under the banner of community policing. The committee found very little research on the topic and is therefore unable to draw conclusions about the extent to which decentralized organizational structures do produce practices that meet the needs and demands that vary within the jurisdiction served.

Centralization is the extent to which the decisions in an organization are concentrated; decentralization is the extent to which they are distributed more evenly throughout the organization. Decentralization of police departments has had its advocates since the late 1960s (Mastrofski, 1981), and it has remained a staple of police reform in the 1990s under both community policing (Skogan and Hartnett, 1997) and CompStat (Bratton, 1998). Advocates of decentralization have argued for moving more decision-making authority down the chain of command—from headquarters to the precinct station, and from the precinct station to the first-line supervisors and officers on the street.

The justifications for decentralization have been several, but two stand out. One is that a decentralized structure is better able to deal with variations in the department's work environment. For example, where neighborhoods vary in culture, wealth, and demographic profile, they are also likely to vary in the sorts of crime and disorder problems they experience, and their service needs may differ too. Advocates of decentralization argue that those closest to the neighborhood are in a position to know more about its needs and the preferences of its residents than those further up the chain of command. It therefore makes sense to give lower ranking personnel greater authority to decide what problems should take priority and how to handle them. A second, related argument for decentralization is that true professionalism requires the delegation of authority to the professionals who must cope with the problem. Effective human services, especially those dealing with the diversity of problems that police must handle, require well-educated and well-trained professionals who must be given a substantial degree of leeway to exercise their judgment. Uniform rules and procedures issuing from headquarters will restrict the exercise of this professional discretion and result in reduced effectiveness.

How should decentralization affect police practices? Presumably, decentralized structures will promote greater variation in how police do their work, assuming that there is substantial variation in their work environment—say neighborhoods. But reformers expect more than variation in practice; they expect police practices to vary *appropriately* with the needs and demands of the environment. Thus, a neighborhood with high levels of street disorder would receive one kind of policing, while a neighborhood with low levels of crime and disorder would receive another. Of course, the specification of conditions might be more complex, also factoring in the neighborhood's capacity and willingness to act collectively in concert with the police to handle problems. Presumably, research on what is most effective under what circumstances would prescribe the appropriate approach, but the challenge here is to determine whether a decentralized structure is more likely to facilitate the selection and implementation of the best approach than a more centralized structure.

Research of the sort just described is generally not available, due largely to problems with measuring both decentralization and its effects on practice. It is difficult to measure the degree of centralization or decentralization because they are aggregate organizational properties. In other words, measuring the level of centralization in an organization would mean determining at what level a particular decision or set of decisions is made. This might be done by observation, but because that is very time-consuming, it is usually accomplished by asking one or a few informants in the organization where the locus of decision making is. The problem with this is that informants may have a biased or inaccurate view. Asking more people in the organization how much *they* participate in the decisions in question would yield a more robust, and undoubtedly more complex, picture of decentralization, but that consumes a lot of resources, which means that research of this sort is usually limited to case studies of a single organization.

One example of this is a long-running study of a community policing in Chicago, which has provided some evidence that greater decentralization has yielded more customizing of police strategies and tactics to the needs and preferences of neighborhood residents (Skogan and Hartnett, 1997). Cross-sectional research of large numbers of police organizations has relied heavily on using a single informant (the survey respondent designated to speak for the department) to characterize the degree of decentralization in the department by indicating the degree to which employees at various levels in the hierarchy are able to make important decisions. Computing composite centralization scores using this method, recent research has found that police organizations have, in fact, become more decentralized during the 1990s (Maguire et al., 2003). However, these researchers have not taken the next step, which is to correlate the degree of decentralization with measures of police practice.

The principal obstacle to measuring police practices relevant to decentralization is determining the criteria that establish what is the best police activity relevant to a given targeted population, such as a neighborhood. One way to deal with this might be to establish how much actual police practice (documented in agency records, officer surveys, or field observations) deviates from the preferences of neighborhood residents (determined from opinion surveys). If decentralization advocates are correct, then greater decentralization should yield patterns of police behavior in greater congruence with the neighborhood's expectations than more centralized decision making.

Organizational Complexity

Organizations are more or less complex in terms of how they structure the division of labor among members (Hall, 1991:50ff). The police organization can be more or less occupationally complex by adjusting the number of job specialists (e.g., detectives, crime analysts, juvenile officers, community policing officers). It can become more or less functionally complex by adjusting the number of divisions or units. It can be more or less vertically complex by manipulating the degree of hierarchy (e.g., levels of supervision and management). And it can increase spatial complexity by adding more geographic units or shifting job responsibilities from occupational specialty to spatial specialty (e.g., by assigning officers to permanent beats in which they "specialize" their activities).

Job Specialization

Proposition 3: Police organizations create job specialties and specialist units for a variety of reasons, including exerting greater control over the activities of personnel. The degree of job specialization appears to be increasing among American police agencies. However, there have been few studies of the effects of police job specialization of either form, and the results are mixed.

One of the hallmarks of the professional or advanced police organization has traditionally been increased job specialization. This occurs when certain police tasks become the responsibility of individuals who specialize in performing that task. This occupational specialization is assumed to benefit the agency by providing for increased training and experience in a particular type of work, for increased sharing of knowledge and communication among experts in a particular line of work, and for focusing the mission and monitoring the performance of those specialists, whether they operate independently or in a specialist unit. When organizations are divided into separate units that perform different functions (e.g., patrol, detectives, juvenile, crime analysis), they are said to be functionally differentiated. The general trend in policing for the 20th century has been to increase the degree of occupational and functional specialization in police departments, with civilians taking over many functions previously performed by sworn officers, and increasingly dividing and subdividing responsibilities among different organizational units, often at the cost of reducing the proportion of the organization devoted to the most generalist work, patrol (Reiss, 1992; Maguire, 2002b). Nonetheless, with the emergence of team policing as a reform ideal, a countermovement toward despecialization in policing took root in the late 1960s. For example, advocates found it desirable to return some of the follow-up investigative responsibilities that had devolved to criminal investigations specialists to the patrol officer. Although team policing quickly faded in the 1970s as a passing fad, the benefits of despecializing police became part of the mantra of community policing reform that emerged in the 1980s (Mastrofski, 1998:163).

The handful of studies on community policing specialization suggest that specialists do spend more time on community policing activities than generalist officers, and they may be less likely to engage problem citizens, but they do not appear to show appreciable differences in how they deal with problem citizens when they do engage them in face-to-face encounters. Given the dearth of research in this area, the committee recommends analyses that estimate the relative merits of assigning community policing work to specialists, generalists, or both.

Most studies measure functional differentiation by counting the number of special units or functional divisions in an organization. Reformers have called for police organizations to despecialize, placing more authority in the hands of generalist officers, and encouraging them to provide a broader range of services. Although there have been numerous studies on the causes and correlates of functional differentiation (Langworthy, 1986; Maguire, 2002a), there is limited research on its effects on police practice. One reason for this is that researchers often include specialization as one indicator in a composite score measuring overall bureaucratization. Many scholars who study complex organizations, both inside and outside policing, have argued that bureaucratization is not a viable concept—that studying its individual components, like functional differentiation, is far more meaningful.

Two recent studies have examined changes in the functional differentiation of police organizations. The first (Maguire, 1997) found conclusively that during the time when community policing was growing in popularity, functional differentiation was increasing. The second found conclusively that it is not decreasing, but was unable to determine due to data problems whether it is increasing (Maguire et al., 2003). Either way, changes in functional differentiation are not following the reform prescriptions. This is probably because specialization appeals powerfully to police and other policy makers as a solution to organizational problems. First, it is believed to be an effective means of concentrating expertise in an organizational unit, focusing the mission of that unit on the proper exercise of that expertise, and rewarding its members accordingly. Thus, police leaders believe it to be an effective mechanism to get the organization to respond to its directives, especially when the leadership wishes to launch a new and unfamiliar approach to policing. A second powerful attraction of functional specialization is that it can work to satisfy demands for doing something about a problem while isolating the effects of organizational change to the boundaries of a well-defined unit, leaving the remainder of the organization to operate with minimal disruption to organization routines (see Chapter 8 for a detailed discussion of the effects of specialization on police legitimacy).

Both of these reasons have probably caused police departments to sustain or even increase the level of functional specialization, even in a time when community policing reform rhetoric calls for despecialization. What this has meant in practical terms is that police leaders have been deciding whether to implement community policing through special squads or to give all officers equal responsibility. Perhaps the most popular approach is a hybrid, which creates one or more specialist units responsible for conducting community policing activities exclusively (or in some cases, conducting traditional police patrol duties exclusively), while still training and encouraging generalist patrol officers to engage in community policing as well (Skogan and Hartnett, 1997). Ideally, researchers would assess the overall impact of generalist, specialist, and hybrid approaches by measuring the effects in the aggregate on a wide range of police activities, including those falling into both the traditional and community policing categories. This has not been done, but a handful of studies have compared the practices of community policing specialists to generalists in the patrol division. This research, which may shed some light on the consequences of specialization, is summarized below.

One study, focusing on data from the Project on Policing Neighborhoods (POPN) for Indianapolis and St. Petersburg, compared community policing specialists (CPOs) and patrol generalists (beat officers) in two departments that used hybrid systems of specialization. In both cities, CPOs were freed from calls-for-service responsibilities so that they could devote more time to community policing activities. Patrol generalists, who were responsible for responding to calls for service, were expected to have their actions suffused with the department's community policing philosophy and to engage in community policing as time permitted. In both cities, community policing specialists spent less time dealing with the public face-to-face than did patrol generalists, and they tended to deal with problem citizens (those with elevated emotions) at a lower rate as well (Parks et al., 1999). In Indianapolis, the department where police leaders emphasized the need to deal with public disorders aggressively, CPOs were *less* likely to spend time on handling these problems than patrol generalists, even though the specialists were freed from answering calls for service so that they could spend more time on these problems. In both departments, CPOs did tend to spend more time on community outreach and problem solving than did generalists, although the difference was most pronounced in St. Petersburg, where these aspects of community policing were emphasized. Even here, however, CPOs were observed to spend on average only 17 percent of their time on problem solving, 4 percent attending community meetings, and 2 percent on casual chats with the public—leaving more than three-fourths of their work time to other, noncommunity policing activities. A subsequent multivariate analysis showed that when other factors were taken into account, the CPO specialists in Indianapolis spent no more time on problem solving than did beat officers, although the strong difference between specialists and generalists did remain in St. Petersburg (DeJong et al., 2001). Interestingly, St. Petersburg specialists were not assigned to a separate community policing unit, but rather were integrated into community policing teams, with the patrol generalists assigned to each neighborhood. Another study using the POPN data found that CPOs in these two jurisdictions were no more likely than beat officers to grant citizens' requests to control another person who was bothering them (Mastrofski et al., 2000).

A comparison of CPOs and beat officers in Cincinnati also used POPN observation protocols, but in this city there was a sharper distinction drawn between the responsibilities of beat officers (traditional preventive patrol and calls-for-service response) and CPOs (mostly community policing duties) (Novak et al., 1999). The study employed a multivariate analysis that controlled for the effects of situational influences, officer characteristics, and neighborhood characteristics. The analysis showed that the nature of the officer's job assignment had no effect on whether the officer would resort to an informal, order maintenance solution to a crime or dispute (p. 178), and no influence on the likelihood that the officer would resort to arrest (p. 203). In the exercise of these traditional forms of police discretion, police observed in this study were not affected by the nature of their functional job assignment.

The results of four studies in three police departments are insufficient to draw conclusions about the effects of functional specialization on police practice. When differences have been found, they have been measured in how and with whom officers spend their time, although even here, being assigned to a specialist unit is no guarantee that the officer will expend more time engaged in the activities designated for the job specialty than his or her generalist colleague. Where police discretion is measured in terms of a discrete decision about how to deal with a specific individual in a specific encounter, studies have found no appreciable difference in the exercise of discretion. This is as might be expected. Management may not wish for officers to exercise their discretion differently in disposing of particular persons causing problems, but managers may well expect to see differences in how officers choose to spend their time generally.

Hierarchical Differentiation

Proposition 4: In recent years, police reformers have regarded the many layers in the rank structure of the typical large or even middle-sized municipal police agency as responsible for organizational inefficiency and sluggishness. However, there is little information on the effects of the degree of hierarchical differentiation in police agencies, and what is available is mixed. The committee finds insufficient evidence to draw conclusions about the effects of hierarchy on police practices.

As with functional specialization, police organizations during the 20th century have tended to become increasingly differentiated vertically. Many police agencies have grown in size and functional complexity, and as they have done so, policy makers have discerned a need to assign a larger share of personnel to supervise, manage, and coordinate others as their primary job responsibility (Reiss, 1992). But emerging in the late 20th century was a popular organizational development movement to reduce the degree of hierarchy in public and private organizations (Mickelthwait and Wooldridge, 1996), a trend that became part of the popular community policing reform movement (Mastrofski, 1998:163). Cutting out entire levels in the supervisory hierarchy, or "delayering," became especially popular (Greene et al., 1994; Robinette, 1989; Weatheritt, 1993). Reformers blame the police hierarchy for many of the ills of modern policing. It is conventional wisdom in progressive policing circles that the police rank structure is responsible for a variety of problems, ranging from poor communication and low morale to sluggish and unresponsive organizations. Furthermore, the police rank structure is thought to be notoriously resistant to change. One popular article likened changing the police rank structure to "bending granite" (Guyot, 1979). As popular as this conventional wisdom about the problems of the police rank structure might be, it is backed up by virtually no research evidence.

The committee was able to identify only a handful of studies on the effect of the police rank structure. For example, in an examination of Illinois police departments, Crank (1990) found that departments with taller hierarchies made more arrests. King (1998) found that taller police departments had higher scores on a scale measuring "management oriented administrative innovations." Zhao (1996) found that hierarchy had no effect on the adoption of either the internal or external elements of community policing. Clearly, the research on the effects of the police hierarchy is insufficient to support the conventional wisdom about its dysfunctionality.

Although such research is rare in policing, King (2003) reviewed 18 studies on the effects of hierarchy in samples of nonpolice organizations. He found that rank structure impedes performance and internal group processes in small groups (of approximately five or less), but that in larger groups it has either no effect or a positive effect. Overall, King (2003) concluded that the evidence for the deleterious effects of rank structure in organizations of all types is weak: some studies find negative effects, some find no effects, and some find positive effects.

One thing that is clear, however, is that in spite of reform rhetoric, there was not a wholesale reduction in the depth of police hierarchies in the 1990s. Based on an analysis of longitudinal data collected throughout the 1990s, Maguire and his colleagues (2003) found that vertical differentiation has not changed significantly during the community policing era. Some agencies eliminated rank levels, a smaller number of agencies added them, and most maintained their existing number of rank levels. Overall, changes in rank structure were not statistically significant.

Future research could help to clarify the effects of the degree of hierarchy by exploring the possibility suggested by King's review of literature on nonpolice organizations—that the effects of hierarchy may depend on other organizational features or task environments. For example, when accountability up the chain of command is tightly coupled, an elaborated hierarchy may work to further the organization's objectives, such as reducing the incidence of inappropriate force by officers (Klockars, 1995). When higher ranks are not held closely accountable for the performance of their subordinates, the effects of management's policies may be quickly diffused.

Geo-Focused Policing

Proposition 5: Some police reformers have suggested that policing that is geographically focused on small neighborhood populations would facilitate greater officer familiarity with people in those neighborhoods and ultimately generate more service-oriented practice in those areas. The team policing movement of the late 1960s and 1970s embraced this view. The available research suggests that geo-focused structures may have facilitated greater police knowledge of the neighborhoods to which officers were assigned, but unless other organizational structures were implemented to reinforce the desired practices, the prospects of achieving those results were slim and the scope of the effects usually modest.

Police organizations devoted much of the 20th century to reducing the significance of geographic assignment to police work (Reiss, 1992). As increasing numbers of officers took specialist job assignments, the geographic territories for which they became responsible increased in size, often to include the entire jurisdiction because beat assignments were frequently changed. In the 19th and early 20th centuries, foot patrol was the common assignment of most officers; they were physically restricted to small beats in which they became "specialists" over the years that they worked that same area. But when the automobile, telephone, and portable two-way radio revolutionized policing, the geographic scope of an officer's assigned territory was no longer so limited. As officers finished an assignment, they could be sent to another anywhere in the city to minimize the response time, rather than waiting for the officer assigned to that beat to become free to answer the call. This made it harder to develop knowledge of and contact in particular geographic areas, a trend accelerated by the increasingly common practice of frequently rotating beat assignments precisely to prevent too much familiarity and corruption between the patrol officer and the residents (Mastrofski, 1981:Ch. 2).

By the late 1960s, team policing advocates began calling for a reversion to permanent beat assignments and limiting out-of-beat dispatches. These were promoted by such blueribbon commissions as the President's Crime Commission (1967) and the National Advisory Commission on Criminal Justice Standards and Goals (1973:113). Many expected that officers with permanent assignments would be more friendly toward neighborhood residents (Wilson, 1968:290-296; Myren, 1972:721-722; Rossi et al., 1974:150-165; Gay et al., 1977:17-19). Some believed that these officers would become more protective of their turf and hence more aggressive in crime control (Davis, 1978:136). Later, under community policing, reformers went beyond permanent beat assignment, advocating that departments relieve officers of some of the burden of responding to calls for service so that they could spend time getting to know residents on their assigned beat and work with them to solve problems (Mastrofski, 1998:163). Permanent beat assignments became a fixture of community policing (Kane, 2000), and by 1999, 94 percent of local police departments with 100 or more sworn officers reported giving patrol officers responsibility for fixed geographic areas, and 47 percent reported assigning cases to detectives on that basis (Reaves and Hart, 2000:xii). Of course, those figures do not reveal the extent to which departments were successful in keeping officers in their assigned geographic areas and how long they were assigned to the same area before receiving a new assignment. However, there are a few studies that do examine the effect of increasing geographic specialization on patrol officer behavior.

Most of the available evidence on the effects of geo-focused policing comes from evaluations of team policing and implementing stable beat assignments in the 1970s (see Mastrofski, 1981:75-79 for a review). Evaluations are based on three types of data: officer surveys of attitudes and self-reported behavior, citizen perceptions of police practice, and field observations of police practice. Although the nature and extent of effects vary with the particular measure, permanent beat assignments are more likely to result in officers who are more knowledgeable of or familiar with citizens in those areas, especially if the stable beat assignments are accompanied by a program that emphasizes the importance of obtaining community support (Boydstun and Sherry, 1975:66; Schwartz and Clarren,

1977:34-39; Mastrofski, 1983). With such programmatic direction, officers appear more positively inclined to be service-oriented, but without that kind of guidance, permanent beat assignments appear to give officers freer rein to follow their own preferences, which in one study meant more aggressive crime control methods (Bloch and Specht, 1973:67-75). Two studies that examined the effects of permanent beat assignments over time indicated that whatever positive officer attitudes toward the community might develop could deteriorate over time (Bloch and Specht, 1973; Schwartz and Clarren, 1977). Ironically, even though team policing tended to increase officers' sense that citizens supported them, when police practices were viewed through the lens offered by citizen surveys, most studies showed that team policing produced few significant changes (Gay et al., 1977; Fowler et al., 1979:127-139). Finally, a study based on systematic field observation of 42 urban neighborhoods assessed the impact of focusing officers' beat assignments on very small to very large geographic areas (measured as the population of the officer's assigned area over a year's time). Of the 11 police behaviors measured, the researcher found that only 3 were significantly affected by the size of the officer's patrol assignment area (Mastrofski, 1981:190). Smaller areas were associated with higher numbers of public relations contacts, more comforting behavior toward victims, and more citizens contacted for whom the officer showed some familiarity. Unaffected behaviors included the frequency of service-oriented encounters, residential security checks, suspect and traffic stops, various forms of assistance, the use of force in nonthreatening situations, arrests, and showing hostility to citizens.

One study has reported a more aggressive, crime-focused policing as a consequence of geographically focusing the patrol officer's work. Using an interrupted time-series design, a study of patrol in the Philadelphia Housing Authority found that officers who received permanent beat assignments did increase their level of (officer-initiated) field investigations after the implementation of permanent assignments, leading the researcher to conclude that geo-focused policing had produced a greater sense of officer responsibility for the assigned area (Kane, 2000). The greater methodological rigor of this quasi-experimental design compared with the cross-sectional regression analysis of the previous studies should be noted, but the comparability of a public housing area to a general police jurisdiction leaves open the question of the generalizability of these findings.

In general, this body of literature suggests that geo-focused policing can alter police behavior in ways that have been seen as desirable by team policing and later community-policing reformers, but without other organizational structures to channel police behavior in a particular way, officers do not tend to show distinct or predictable patterns of behavior.

Formalizing Police Policies

Proposition 6: One of the frequent recommendations to effect police organization change is to establish new policies by formally instituting rules or procedures that restrict the range of judgment or discretion allowed to police. Limited available evidence suggests that formalizing policy in this way, especially in the area of use of lethal force, can reduce the frequency that officers resort to force. However, instituting a formal policy alone may be an insufficient step to ensure the desired impact. Police leaders may need to implement other changes, such as training, and may need to implement the new formal policy in a larger context of strong political pressure that will reinforce the need for change as felt both inside and outside the department.

Formalization is the extent to which the organization imposes rules and procedures to govern the practices of its members (Hall, 1991:63-65). The more formalized an organization is, the less judgment or discretion its members are authorized to exercise. Formalization is often measured as the extent to which rules, procedures, and practices are written, thus associating formalization with standardization and documentation. Police agencies resort frequently to formalization as a strategy to govern the practice of their officers, so there should be ample opportunity to judge the impact of formalization on police practice.

Few studies of the formalization of police policy have examined the impact of formalization generally across a broad range of policy concerns, and in the few cases when they have done so, they have not attempted to isolate the effects of formalization from a variety of other bureaucratic features thought to be strongly associated with high levels of formalization (centralization, specialization, hierarchy) (Maguire et al., 2003:48-59). Most of the studies of police agency formalization have examined the impact of formalizing a particular policy or changing the nature of an already established formal policy. Such studies help to determine whether the rules and procedures of policing matter.

One policy that has received some research attention is the imposition of restrictive deadly force policies. For instance, Fyfe (1979) found that a restrictive shooting policy implemented in 1972 by New York City's police department produced a dramatic reduction in shootings of fleeing felons. In a later study, Fyfe (1982) attributed the difference in the number of shootings in Memphis and New York to the lack of internal agency controls and the absence of clear shooting guidelines in the former compared with the latter. In a review of his and four other studies, Fyfe concluded that "reductions in police shooting frequency and changes in police shooting patterns have followed implementation of restrictive administrative policies on deadly force and weapons use" (1988:181). In this same article, he presented evidence supporting this conclusion from three other large agencies.

Research has suggested that the *extent* of the effects of restrictive deadly force policies depends on other factors, some organizational and some environmental. Training, for example, is held as an amplifier of the effects of restrictive use policies (Fyfe, 1988). Another analysis of restrictive use policies in New York, Atlanta, and Kansas City attributed their success to their following on the heels of highly publicized "critical incidents," creating a political environment which enabled reform-minded chiefs to impose and sustain severe administrative and disciplinary changes (Sherman, 1983). This, the author noted, was similar to the effect of corruption scandals on implementing similarly severe policies to reduce corruption (Law Enforcement Assistance Administration, 1977) (see Chapter 7 for a discussion).

In general, research on other aspects of formalizing specific policies suggests that, by itself, formalizing policy will often not suffice to secure the desired change in police practice. This was found in case studies on handling public drunks and making pornography arrests (Aaronsen et al., 1984:408-436) and the implementation of domestic violence policies (Sherman, 1992:112).

CompStat and Strategic Problem Solving

Proposition 7: CompStat is a recent reform that many police leaders feel will revolutionize the management of police organizations. Very little objective empirical research has been done on CompStat or similar management strategies. What is available suggests that it has changed the work practices of middle managers responsible for districts or precincts. However, the research also suggests a number of forces at work that limit the effects of CompStat and may even work at cross purposes. Much more research on the implementation of CompStat is needed before conclusions can be drawn.

The previous discussion has focused on the impact of discrete structural features of police departments, but contemporary reform efforts often entail changing a number of features as a package of "organizational development." In recent years, police leaders in the United States have shown tremendous interest in adopting an innovation called CompStat, which surfaced in New York City in 1994. A 1999 national survey of departments with 100 or more sworn officers showed that a quarter of the sample reported implementing a CompStat-like program and another third of the sample was planning to do so (Weisburd et al., 2003). CompStat's originators promised to reduce crime by enabling police organizations to think and act strategically—putting resources where crime problems were emerging and doing so on a timely basis, before problems became insurmountable (McDonald, 2001; Bratton, 1998; Maple and Mitchell, 1999; Silverman, 1999).

An interesting feature of this reform is that the primary targets of change are the middle managers of the police organization, especially those charged with commanding the precincts and districts into which the territory of large urban departments are divided. They become the mechanism by which the police organization is made responsive to the leadership of top management, and they do so by taking responsibility for closely monitoring the state of crime in their assigned areas and identifying patterns in crime problems as they emerge, of devising and implementing solutions to those problems, and of following through to make sure that those solutions have worked. Top management and the rank and file in the precincts both have a role to play. The former is responsible for clarifying the organization's mission and holding middle managers accountable; the latter are responsible for following the direction provided by the middle managers.

CompStat programs around the nation go by many names, but they share the following elements (Weisburd et al., 2003):

- *Mission clarification.* A crime control mission that is clarified, simplified, and measurable, such as reducing crime by 10 percent in a given year.
- *Internal accountability.* Middle managers (district commanders and heads of specialist units) whose job assignments and career prospects depend on knowing what is going on with crime problems in their areas, discern patterns and likely causes of crime, devise effective solutions to those problems, act decisively to implement them, and follow through to make sure that they are successful.
- *Geographic organization of command.* An organization that commits most of its resources to the direction of commanders whose responsibilities are defined geographically, that is, districts or precincts.
- *Organizational flexibility.* A commitment to flexibility in allocating and deploying resources, so that they will be available when and where they will be most effectively applied to crime problems as they are identified.
- *Data-driven decision making.* The timely analysis of accurate data on crime, so that the organization can mobilize responses rapidly to those areas most needing attention, making heavy use of computerized data systems and crime mapping to identify and monitor hotspots.
- *Innovative tactics and strategies.* Customizing the police response to crime problems as they arise by carefully analyzing the underlying causes and selecting the responses with the best prospects for success rather than resorting to a standardized and uniform response; innovation is prized.

These features were made most visible in a periodic meeting in which top executives, required middle managers to discuss crime in their areas of responsibility, using computerized pin maps projected onto large overhead screens and lengthy printed reports detailing past and current crime patterns and agency activity. During these events, individuals commanders were held accountable, but all others present were expected to contribute information and ideas in a group problem-solving effort. The national survey showed that departments indicating that they had adopted a CompStat program showed distinctly different patterns in the policies and practices they described in the areas of mission clarification, internal accountability, and using data for decision making (Weisburd et al., 2003). However, they were indistinguishable from non-CompStat departments on the other features, suggesting that CompStat is not so much generating a new reform wave as riding one that was already begun.

The important issue for this chapter's purpose is whether and how the behavior of the police has changed as a consequence of CompStat. There are very few objective analyses of CompStat's impact on organizational practice. A case study of New York City's CompStat program, published a few years after the program was initiated, considered it a resounding success in all of the above areas (Silverman, 1999). A later field study of CompStat implemented in Lowell, Newark, and Minneapolis suggested a mixed result (Willis et al., 2003). Across the three sites, researchers found the most powerful and consistent pattern of effects was manifested in the behavior of district commanders. These middle managers keenly felt the pressure of their responsibility to know about crime in their districts and act quickly to intervene where spikes in crime statistics and hot spots emerged. Virtually all of these middle managers reported that CompStat had changed the way they spent their work time, devoting many hours to studying crime reports and crime maps to prepare for CompStat meetings. Before CompStat, they would have only occasionally referred to crime statistics, and seldom in a way so focused as individual hot spots. After CompStat, they were obsessed with data. Although some of their motivation clearly derived from a desire not to lose their prestigious job assignment by looking bad to top management, the most powerful motivation appeared to be not looking bad before the entire audience, especially their peers. And CompStat meetings increased the frequency with which middle managers consulted each other on their problems. This formal, routinized exchange of information replaced an informal, haphazard pattern of interaction.

Yet the field research also revealed a number of limitations and unintended consequences of CompStat at these three sites. First, the intense sense of accountability for results did not trickle down to the rank and file, who were largely ignorant of and unaffected by what went on at CompStat meetings. None of these departments routinely held *district-level* CompStat meetings, during which district commanders held *their* subordinates accountable, and the absence of these meetings may have limited the diffusion of CompStat's effects throughout the organization, an effect reported in New York City, where such meetings were held (Kelling and Sousa, 2001). Second, the data analysis employed tended (a) to react to short-term changes in crime patterns while avoiding analysis of broader long-term trends, (b) to focus on identifying the location of hot spots but not figuring out what to do about them, (c) to focus disproportionately on what was happening with individual cases rather than larger patterns, and (d) to be underused for evaluating the effects of police interventions. Third, although district commanders did enjoy a larger measure of authority delegated from headquarters, they remained constrained by civil service rules, union contracts, and local politics in where and how they could mobilize their personnel. Fourth, the pressure on middle managers to come to CompStat meetings with problems already identified and solutions already implemented tended to make irrelevant the suggestions of colleagues, who were also reluctant to offer radically different suggestions, since this would reflect badly on the commander who had already committed to a course of action. This preference for decisiveness over rumination mirrored the culture of the officer on the street, albeit at a higher level in the agency. Finally, resort to *innovative* strategies was the exception, not the rule; most responses involved the traditional responses of increasing levels of police surveillance and enforcement activities.

The researchers concluded that some of the limitations on CompStat derived from inadequate changes to fundamental structures needed to support a fuller implementation of CompStat, such as the absence of in-depth management training in data analysis and its uses and inadequate staffing of the crime analysis operation. They noted that, although CompStat programs promulgated a narrowing of the police mission to focus on crime control, none of the departments undertook a significant restructuring of their workload to eschew tasks not focused on crime control. Thus, in many respects, CompStat reforms appeared to have been transplanted onto traditional policing structures, rather than having replaced them. The researchers also suggested that CompStat has some built-in internal contradictions that cannot be overcome, such as the pressure for individual accountability versus the pressure for collaboration or the desire to give district commanders control of more resources versus the need for flexibility in moving resources from district to district as the need arises.

A national survey and a handful of case studies are not adequate to draw conclusions about the impact of CompStat on police practice in the United States. The above findings are at best suggestive. Future research on

CompStat should take special pains to track its impact on decision making at the district level. What are the mechanisms of accountability between the district commander and his or her subordinates? To what extent do they use the crime analysis tools and services of crime analysts to identify problems and devise solutions? How do management practices change when (a) CompStat meetings are routinely held at the district level? (b) middle managers are selected and trained to be adept in the use of data analysis, and (c) crime analysis units are given substantially larger staffs with the requisite expertise and resources to provide more cutting-edge support services?

INFLUENCE OF EXTERNAL FORCES

Police and police organizations are often targeted by outside individuals and groups who seek to influence the way policing is practiced. Sometimes the effects of outside forces are passive, meaning that there is no purposive effort to manipulate police practice, but there is an effect nonetheless. For example, the creation of a tourist attraction in a community alters who will be present and for what purposes, thereby changing the kinds of problems requiring police attention that will arise. In this section the committee considers some of the wide variety of external forces that may play on police. The section begins with a discussion of two types of external influences in which it is assumed that the police react to the demographic, social, and economic features of the community at both the neighborhood level and then at the city, metropolitan area, or regional levels. Subsequently the chapter turns to purposive efforts to shape policing, issuing from political oversight, interorganizational effects from other criminal justice and human service agencies, the state legislature, and the federal government.

Neighborhood Characteristics

Proposition 8: A common social science research hypothesis is that neighborhood factors directly influence both individual and organizational behavior, including that of the police and police agencies. The relatively small body of research that examines neighborhood effects on police practice shows with fairly high consistency that disadvantaged and higher crime neighborhoods are more likely to receive punitive or enforcement-oriented policing, other things being equal. However, the strength of these effects is small compared with the effects of situational factors, such as those characterized as legal concerns in the previous chapter.

The idea that police behavior is affected by neighborhood conditions in addition to legal, victim, offender, and situational factors has been discussed at length by Klinger (1997). In his ecological theory of police response, Klinger argues that officers learn through experience that crime, especially violent crime, is disproportionately found in areas characterized by socioeconomic disadvantage. In such areas, police officers are busier and lack the resources for attending to other service requests. Thus, officers must make triage decisions regarding which actions they will attend to and which they will disregard relative to other matters in their own beat or district. Through work group practices, behaviors that might be defined as deviant in some districts come to be regarded as normal in high-crime areas, and officers understanding of district deviance become unique in each neighborhood.

It has also been hypothesized that officers' experiences in high-crime neighborhoods tend to produce a higher level of cynicism and the view that higher proportions of victimizations are at least partially deserved. The fact that offenders are more likely to be victimized than nonoffenders means that officers also learn to regard certain events as expected; again, a greater proportion of deviance in these places is viewed as normal and pursued with less vigor. In addition, higher levels of dangerousness are anticipated in these areas, and consequently greater use of physical restraint, coercive authority, and arrests is more likely.

The ecological theory of police response suggests numerous hypotheses about behavior, and the broadest notion is that encounters will produce greater similarities in officer behavior within neighborhoods than between them. According to this theory, differences in police behavior should be found when one community (or district or beat) is compared with another, but relatively few differences should be found among officers working within these areas. To date, these hypotheses have not been tested with empirical data.

Nevertheless, a relatively small body of research has examined whether neighborhood characteristics are related to police practices and thus far suggests only weak links. Motivated by concerns about equity, this research has studied whether police respond in similar ways to incidents that occur in different kinds of communities. For example, do police devote the same level of attention to crimes in disadvantaged areas as they do to crimes in wealthier areas of the city? Are police more likely to arrest or use force against suspects in certain types of neighborhoods? Do the characteristics of suspects or victims matter in some places but not others? If certain types of communities are neglected by the police or, alternatively, receive overly aggressive policing, then fundamental concerns about justice are raised.

Research in this area typically has used observational data on police-citizen encounters to assess whether neighborhood conditions are independently related to officers' behaviors. Once situational, suspect, complainant, and officer characteristics are taken into account, if neighborhood factors are found to be significantly related to police behavior, it suggests that area conditions may be influencing police decision making. Similarly, data from these kinds of studies have also been used to examine whether suspect or complainant influences might have more subtle influences—for example, whether force is more likely to be used against minority suspects in certain types of neighborhoods. Much of the research on community influences has relied on data from the 1977 Police Services Study (PSS). Generally, this research has found that a variety of neighborhood characteristics are related to police behavior, although the direct effects are much smaller than the effects of legally relevant characteristics (Smith, 1984, 1986, 1987).

In analyses of police activity during unassigned time, Smith (1984, 1986) found that assistance was somewhat more common in areas of lower socioeconomic status and greater racial heterogeneity and less common in neighborhoods with greater proportions of single-parent families with children. However, police assistance was not significantly related to neighborhood levels of mobility, percentage nonwhite, income heterogeneity, turnover, or age composition. Proactive investigation was somewhat more common in areas with greater proportions of nonwhites, racial heterogeneity, and people over age 65, and somewhat less common in areas with more people living alone. The broader conclusion inferred from this mixed pattern of weak relationships was that officer-initiated encounters with citizens during discretionary time are relatively unrelated to neighborhood characteristics (1986:325).

In contrast, given a contact between an officer and a citizen, neighborhood factors were found to be significantly associated with the likelihood of arrest, the use of coercive authority, and the filing of official reports. Net of individual and situational factors, arrest was more likely if the encounter occurred in a neighborhood of lower socioeconomic status. For example, approximately 12 percent of interpersonal violence incidents resulted in arrest in low-poverty places, while nearly 45 percent of similar incidents in high-poverty areas led to arrest. However, rates of arrest also varied significantly according to race: white suspects were approximately three times more likely than black suspects to be arrested once controls for community and incident characteristics were considered. Accordingly, Smith suggests that this is primarily a reflection of the victim's status. He also found that police were less likely to arrest the suspect when the victim was black or female. Thus, in incidents of interpersonal violence, police decision making appeared to vary according to community context and victim characteristics. Similarly, coercive authority was used more often if the encounter was in a nonwhite or racially mixed neighborhood. Finally, community crime victimization rates and stability influenced official reporting. Police were less likely to file reports in high-crime areas, but more likely to file in unstable neighborhoods (Smith, 1986:330-332). In addition, Smith found that police were more likely to file reports for incidents occurring in black neighborhoods, and they were less likely to do so for black victims in predominantly black or white areas.

A popular conditional effect hypothesis is that black suspects are more likely to be arrested or treated with coercive authority if the encounter occurs in a predominantly white neighborhood. No such pattern was observed in the decision to arrest; however, there was a significant interaction between suspect's race and the racial mix of the community for the use of coercive authority. All else equal, police were more likely to use coercive authority against blacks in predominantly black areas than in white areas.

The extent to which these findings may be generalized to other types of places or to contemporary policing strategies is not altogether clear. The PSS data were collected over 25 years ago, prior to the implementation of community policing reforms and mandatory arrest policies in domestic violence incidents. In addition, the demands of observational research limited the sites to three metropolitan areas. Hence, the extent to which these findings could be generalized to places outside urban areas or of more recent history is unknown. While differences across neighborhoods motivate contextual hypotheses, the time and expense of directly observing police activity necessarily limit the number of research sites and (perhaps) the generalizability of the findings. Moreover, the contingent nature of many of the findings suggests that neighborhood influences are very complex, or perhaps very sensitive to model specification.

Findings based on the more recent Project on Policing Neighborhoods offer an assessment of neighborhood influences that better reflects contemporary patterns. Mastrofski et al. (2000) studied the extent to which police officers fulfilled citizens' requests for action, such as advising or warning the offender or arresting the offender. The factors that were considered include legal considerations, offender characteristics, victim-offender relationship, and need. These results showed that police were most likely to comply with a citizen's request for a particular action if there was evidence to support the charge, the citizen was credible, the action requested was not the most severe, and the citizen was not requesting action against someone with whom they had a very close relationship. The citizen's race and social status were not significantly related to outcome; however, younger police officers committed to community policing ideals were more likely to comply with requests. While community characteristics were not the focus of this research, it was noted that, despite differences between the two cities in poverty rates and race and family composition, there was very little variation in the predictors of these police behaviors across the two sites. Hence, this research suggests that at a broader level of definition, community factors are less important than legal and situational considerations.

Using POPN data, Mastrofski and colleagues (2002) also examined the effects of concentrated disadvantage in a neighborhood on the inclinations of officers to behave disrespectfully toward suspects. Their hierarchical analysis found that where concentrated disadvantage was high, there was a significantly greater likelihood that officers would behave disrespectfully toward suspects, taking into account a number of characteristics and behaviors of the suspect and the encounter.

Neighborhood differences have been uncovered in the POPN data in police use of physical restraints. Reisig and Parks (2000) examined the relationship between area levels of homicide, concentrated disadvantage, and physical restraint and found that officers are more likely to take such actions in communities with higher homicide rates and in areas with concentrated disadvantage. However, because this research was designed to investigate whether the use of restraints was the source of greater citizen dissatisfaction with the police in these areas, no multivariate assessments of restraint were provided. Thus, while it can be concluded that such activity is more common in disadvantaged neighborhoods, it is not clear whether this reflects police response to higher levels of danger or to some other community condition.

Influence of City and Metropolitan Area

Proposition 9: Some "conflict" social theorists argue that American police use their enforcement powers in ways that disproportionately benefit privileged social and economic groups by maintaining the status of those groups—using force against lower and marginalized social and economic groups. They argue that if their proposition is correct, then the coercive aspects of police work should be higher in cities or areas where there is greater inequality and racial diversity, other things being equal. The available research does tend to show that this relationship holds, but there are other theoretical interpretations for these results besides conflict theory. The same social groups that may experience disproportionate coercion from police may also experience disproportionate benefit, if those who are most susceptible to victimization also come from these disadvantaged and marginalized groups. Until researchers can estimate the full range of control and benefits distributed by police, there will not be an adequate test of this proposition.

A second research tradition of exogenous factors that influence police has examined how city or metropolitan-area characteristics are related to police activity. The general approach of this research has been to use census data and police department information to examine whether such factors as levels of poverty, economic inequality, minority population size, and segregation are correlated with arrest rates or use of force rates once levels of crime are taken into account. Much of this research has been prompted by conflict theory hypotheses, which assert that the police serve as agents of the privileged classes and that economic inequality is maintained by force or the threat of force by agents of the state (Jacobs, 1978a, 1978b; Jacobs and Britt, 1979; Williams and Drake, 1980; Liska et al., 1981, 1985; Loftin and McDowall, 1982; Liska and Chamlin, 1984). If this hypothesis is correct, then police use of arrest, force, or coercion should be higher in areas with greater economic inequality, controlling for violent crime rates.

Similar kinds of research have been prompted by the "racial threat" hypothesis, which asserts that once racial or cultural minorities reach a certain proportion of the population (e.g., 20-30 percent; Liska et al., 1985), they are perceived as a threat to the existing political and social order. According to this perspective, racial segregation is one way of reducing this threat, because problematic groups can be controlled more easily if they are spatially segregated. Thus according to this theory, controlling for crime rates, greater policing resources, and higher rates of arrest, force, and coercion should be found in metropolitan areas with higher levels of racial inequality. In addition, the percentage minority in a metropolitan area should have a weaker relationship with policing activities in places where segregation is greatest.

Empirical support for many of the above hypotheses has been obtained from analyses of city- or state-level data. For instance, Jacobs and Britt (1979) found that states with higher levels of income inequality tend to exhibit greater police use of lethal force than states with lower levels of income inequality. These models controlled for state differences in violent crime rates, police officers per capita, percentage black, percentage urban, population growth, and region of the country. In these analyses, violent crime rates and population growth rates were also significant.

Because most policing jurisdictions are not state-level agencies, the study of differences across metropolitan areas or cities offers more refined conclusions. Jackson and Carroll (1981), Jacobs (1978), Liska and Chamlin (1984), and Liska et al. (1981) found that the racial and economic characteristics of cities and metropolitan areas are related to police department size (resources dedicated to social control), controlling for reported crime rates. In other words, cities with greater proportions of blacks or nonwhites had more police officers per capita and thus a greater capacity for crime control. Similarly, earlier research demonstrated that fear of crime is higher in cities with greater proportions of nonwhites (controlling for crime rates) (Lizotte and Bordua, 1980; Liska et al., 1981).

In two of the most complete investigations of variation in arrest rates, Liska and colleagues studied how urban characteristics influenced police crime control activity (i.e., the ratio of arrests to number of reported crimes). Economic theories of crime control hypothesize that there should be a positive relationship between arrest rates and such factors as number of police per capita (Liska and Chamlin, 1984; Liska et al. 1985). This research found that income inequality, percentage nonwhite, and levels of segregation were significantly related to property and personal crime arrest rates, while police size was not.

Moreover, evidence about the role of segregation suggested that both the threat and a "benign-neglect" hypotheses were supported. In segregated cities with fewer nonwhites, arrest rates were lower, while in less segregated cities with greater proportions of nonwhites, arrest rates were significantly higher. Thus, these findings support conflict hypotheses by demonstrating that arrest rates are greater in cities in which minorities are more visible. They also challenge the simpler economic hypothesis. Arrest rates are related to policing resources, not because greater resources increase the likelihood of arrest, but because both resources and arrest rates are to a large extent influenced by the percentage nonwhite, the segregation patterns, and the economic inequality level of urban areas (Liska and Chamlin, 1984; Liska et al., 1985).

A recent study by Holmes (2000) investigated interagency variation in civil rights complaints. He obtained data from the Justice Department's Civil Rights Division on civil rights complaints against the police from 1985 to 1990. Testing a conflict theory explanation, Holmes (2000) found that "measures of the presence of threatening people (percent black, percent Hispanic [in the Southwest], and minority/majority income inequality) were related positively to average annual civil rights criminal complaints" (p. 343). Holmes's study is another in a long line of research evidence supporting conflict theory explanations for police organizational outcomes; as noted earlier, the committee recommends more research in this area.

There are a number of limitations to the research that attempts to test conflict theory applied to policing. First, the results are subject to alternative interpretations. Police arrests may be targeted *against* persons who live in areas where there are large numbers of low-income or minority residents, but the police may be doing much of their enforcement work at the request of low-income and minority persons who also reside in those same areas (Vold et al., 2002:243). Thus, it is not clear that it is the privileged classes who derive exclusive, or even the most, benefit from these practices. Second, because these studies use aggregate data, they are unable to specify precisely who (that is, which race or social class) receives police enforcement attention in an area. This is especially problematic where there is considerable variability in a geographic area of study, or where there is a high level of movement of people through the area who do not reside there. Finally, the studies do not consider the full range of services police provide, many of which may be viewed as a form of social control but nonetheless highly desired by those subject to them (handling disputes, for example).

Political Oversight: Local Elected Officials

Proposition 10: Whether and in what ways politics should influence policing have been topics of debate since Americans formed full-time police departments. Good or appropriate influence is often characterized as "accountability," while bad or inappropriate influence is termed "interference," "corruption," or just "politics." Making a judgment about the rightness of the influence belongs to the realm of political philosophy, but there are interesting theories available to account for the circumstances under which political influence of whatever sort is most or least likely to have an effect. Based mostly on a few case studies, the available evidence suggests that when local officials, such as the mayor, exercise influence over the department, they tend to do so most potently through executive appointment, job review, and threat of removal from office. However, to assess the relative strength of influence exerted by those with official responsibility for political oversight of police, researchers need to consider the relative strength of a wide range of alternative political influences as well, such as collective bargaining units, courts, and civil service commissions.

Depending on one's perspective (and assumptions about the character and motivations of elected officials), a demonstration that the preferences of mayors or other local officials have an impact on police programs and practices is either good news or bad news. A substantial portion of the literature on policing views the political environment as potentially corrupting of local law enforcement and, like the trend toward professionalism in policing, assumes that a dichotomy between politics and administration (in this case, police administration) is a good thing. Those holding to a classic overhead model of democracy assume that democratic accountability is possible only if police departments are responsive to the will and political preferences of the officials that the public has elected.

Political Principals and Their Agents

Cross-cutting this difference in normative perspective is the empirical question of the extent to which elected officials actually do (or even could) influence police programs and operations. This is a specific instance of the more general question of the extent to which there can be political control of the bureaucracy—a question that has yielded a very substantial research literature based on principal-agent theory. This theory, originally developed in economics to deal with contractual arrangements between buyers and sellers in a marketplace, has been extended to the question of political control of the bureaucracy. In the language of this theory, bureaucratic officials are the agents who are tasked with carrying out the preferred policies of political principals, such as legislators. However, because specialized administrators have information advantages compared with their principals, due to their expertise and to their more direct involvement in bureaucratic processes, and because there may be goal conflict between the agent and the principal, the principal is faced with a problem. Agents may well shirk their duty—that is, act contrary to the principal's preferences. Much of principal-agent theory is then focused on mechanisms for ensuring that agents follow their principals' preferences—such mechanisms as the appointment of agency leaders who share the political principal's goals, monitoring of bureaucratic activity, and bureaucratic design features that provide incentives.

The principal-agent problem is not necessarily solved simply because of the existence of these mechanisms. This point is well made by Guyot (1991) in her review of some of the key mechanisms that one might have assumed would be useful in maintaining the accountability of police departments to their political overseers. Appointing a new police chief, Guyot observes, is sometimes so fraught with multiple political considerations having nothing to do with substantive police policy issues that it becomes ineffective as a tool to ensure accountability (1991:237).

Elected officials control police department budgets, but this does not constitute a strong tool for accountability because (1) so much of the police department budget is in personnel, and both civil service and union rules constrain redirection of these resources; (2) the nature of the policing function means that the kind of program budgeting that would be needed to make budgetary changes toward policy redirection is not possible; and (3) the more general constraints on the budgeting process—that is, tight time lines and decision making in the absence of long-range planning—also limit the ability of political leaders to use budgetary decisions as a mechanism for controlling the policy direction of the police department. Once hired, a police chief exercises considerable control over police functions not covered by legal, including contractual, obligations.

Waterman and Meier (1998) have recently expanded principal-agent theory by noting that the principles of information asymmetry and goal conflict on which it is based should be treated as variables rather than constants. That is, in some situations, bureaucratic agents may have substantial information advantages over their political principals, but in other situations, both bureaucratic agents and their principals lack information, and in still other (admittedly rarer) situations, political principals may have the information advantage. Similarly, Waterman and Meier argue that in some circumstances, agents and principals may share goals rather than exhibiting goal conflict. Taken together, these considerations suggest several possible scenarios that must be incorporated into future research.

In addition, Waterman and Meier (1998) offer several important deductions that are particularly relevant to policing. First, they suggest that in the situation in which the principal and the agent both lack information yet have goal consensus—a situation they claim to be characteristic of less technical, morality-based matters, such as drunk driving and drug control—there will be a tendency for the political principal to "grab whatever ideas are floating around and adopt them. This permits the politician to take credit for combating the problem. Bureaucrats in these policy areas become advocates—or perhaps more harshly, cheerleaders—for the principal's proposed solutions" (p. 181). By contrast, in those rare situations in which there is goal consensus and the principal has the information advantage, presumably because they have access to big picture information that agents lack, the principal-agent problem is solved in favor of the principal's preferences, and agents have minimal discretion. This scenario is hypothesized to characterize the handling of such issues as nude dancing, enforcement of dog licensing laws, and parking on main streets in relatively small communities.

While they do not offer such pointed applications to policing, Waterman and Meier's other scenarios can be used to suggest still other hypotheses relevant to police policy and practice. For example, when there is goal consensus and the agent has information advantages over the principal, the classic model of a politics-administration dichotomy is said to arise, with the principal delegating maximal responsibility for administration to the agent, monitoring loosely through regular reports and intervening only in crises. This scenario may be hypothesized to characterize many of the core functions of policing, such as basic crime control. No work as yet systematically tests the hypotheses derived by (or derivable from) Waterman and Meier's research (1998).

Case Studies

Not surprisingly, most studies of the extent to which political officials influence policing are based on case studies or comparative case studies. This is because there are no systematic data bases available to measure relevant independent variables across a large, representative sample of jurisdictions. Such case studies do, however, have the advantage of allowing a richly textured treatment of political leaders' attempts to influence policing, as well as the capacity to use a historical approach to examine change in a single department (or a small number of departments) over time.

By and large, such studies tend to find that political officials have a limited influence on police policy and practice, or that the influence that political officials do have is pernicious. For example, in his case study of the politics of policing in Cedar City from 1960 to 1980, Scheingold (1991) emphasizes the police department's "formidable capacity to resist and divert" the forces pushing for change. Despite the mayor's aggressive use of appointment power in an attempt to redirect the department by bringing in a series of new police chiefs, the department lurched unevenly in a more progressive direction, influenced more by departmental reaction to scandal and the chief's ability to make use of federal funds for hardware acquisition than by mayoral initiatives. In this case, the limited ability of political officials to influence policing stemmed in part from the relatively low salience of street crime in the community.

In her case study of the Troy, NY, police department in the late 1970s to early 1980s, Guyot (1991) explicitly introduces normative criteria to distinguish political officials' involvements in policing that are acts of forcing accountability from those that are acts of political interference. She uncovers some instances in which elected officials "appropriately" used their powers to make (or at least try to make) the police department accountable to policy priorities. These include redirecting departmental attention to the problem of excessive use of force, an initiative to establish a police-community relations board, and the redirecting of priorities toward downtown safety. However, the bulk of the city council's actions with respect to the police were judged by her to be acts of interference, such as the institution of neighborhood safety centers, efforts to establish foot patrols downtown, and the introduction of team policing (1991:244-250). Guyot's results might be interpreted somewhat differently if the question is simply an empirical one of the extent to which police policy and practice are influenced by elected officials (regardless of the efficiency, effectiveness, fairness or propriety of that influence). Some of the acts that she judged to involve political interference would be categorized as examples of a lack of influence, because the attempt at interference was rebuffed by the department (i.e., the police chief's refusal to institute foot patrols); similarly, some acts she judged to involve accountability would have to be reclassified into examples of a lack of influence, again because the attempt at political control failed (i.e., the attempt to institute a civilian review board).

A number of studies suggest that mayors and other local elected officials do have an influence on police policies, and that they are more likely to affect policies than practices. In a study of the determinants of lethal force, Jacobs and O'Brien (1998) find that, while the rate of police killing of black citizens is positively related to both the size of and the recent growth in the city's black population, it is negatively affected by the presence of a black mayor. Chaney and Salzstein (1998), in the study referenced earlier, found that the existence of a local-level mandatory arrest ordinance had even greater impact than a state-level mandatory arrest law, thus suggesting that through the enactment of direct orders (here mandatory arrest in domestic disturbance situations), elected officials can influence the behavior of the police. However, Chaney and Salzstein also found that the presence of a female mayor did not significantly affect arrest patterns for domestic disturbances. And Salzstein (1989), using a cross-sectional design based on a national sample of police departments, found that the presence or absence of a black mayor did not affect police practice in handling public disorder incidents, such as vagrancy, loitering, public drunkenness, noise complaints, and the like.

These null findings can be interpreted as showing a disconnect between elected official preferences and police practice, but they included no actual measures of officials' policy preferences. Instead, these studies assumed that female mayors have preferences for arrests in domestic disturbance situations, and (perhaps with more validity) that black mayors prefer fewer police killings of black civilians. Salzstein (1989) acknowledges that, because the black community has mixed preferences with respect to police handling of public disorder incidents, minority mayors may not be attempting the sort of strong and consistent policy direction in this area that they do with respect to such matters as police use of force against minorities and the need for civilian review boards.

Empirical studies showing a connection between mayors or city council members and police policy seem to be more prevalent, encompassing effects on police policy ranging from the hiring of minority police officers to adoption of civilian review boards to police corruption. Salzstein (1989) found that the presence of a black mayor is a significant predictor of two police policy outcomes important to blacks: black representation among sworn officers and the adoption of civilian review of the police. That finding parallels an earlier finding of Browning, Marshall, and Tabb, in a comparative time-series study of 10 California cities from 1960 to 1979, which found that the extent to which racial minorities are "incorporated" in local elected office (i.e., either capture the mayoral office or are part of the dominant coalition of the city council) is a key predictor of the adoption of civilian review boards. In particular, they found that in both cities in which minority incorporation was strong, a civilian review board had been adopted by 1980; in all three cities in which minority incorporation was moderate, such a review board was considered but not approved; and in all five cities in which minority incorporation was weak, a civilian review board was not even considered (Browning, Marshall, and Tabb, 1984:153). Interestingly enough, the same Salzstein (1989) study that showed a connection between black mayors and both minority hiring and civilian review boards showed no evidence that black elected leadership was linked to the adoption of another policy outcome—community-oriented policing.

In addition to these studies, using systematic data to analyze variation across multiple cities, there are a number of case studies that demonstrate the impact of elected officials, and especially mayors, on police policy and practice. For instance, Greene (1999) offers a case study analysis of how Mayor Rudolph Giuliani was able to substantially alter police policy and practice in New York City by appointing Police Commissioner William Bratton, an individual whose zero tolerance approach emphasizing large-scale arrests of petty criminals and crackdowns on threats to public order meshed with the quality of life issues stressed by the mayor in his campaign.

Negative Influence

While studies such as these provide evidence that political officials influence police policy in a way that is consistent with notions of democratic accountability, there are also studies suggesting that political officials influence police policy in a much more negative fashion. In his systematic analysis of four police departments' experience with corruption scandals, Sherman (1978) makes clear that corruption can at times become the "policy" of some police departments and that political control by corrupt politicians makes this possible. By the same token, Sherman also makes clear that reform of corrupt police departments is initiated by political officials' replacement of corrupt police leadership with new leadership. Crucial decisions about new policies for internal control of corruption were largely left to the new police leadership rather than being made by external political leadership. Thus, political leaders exert indirect influence (through the appointment process) in policy development for reform of corruption.

Still other studies reflect elected officials' impact on both police policy and practice. In a time-series analysis of two police departments, Meehan (2000) showed the "degree to which gang problems are an artifact of political interests and their effect on police practices." Using a combination of data sources—transcripts and logs of telephone calls to the department 911 number; gang car patrol logs and taped officer responses to dispatch; field notes; newspaper accounts; and an aggregate data set of citizen calls for police service in the city over a six-year period—Meehan shows how the mayor's determination to show high-profile responsiveness to neighborhoods during an election year led the police chief to create and publicize a citywide program to curtail street gangs, including the institution of a special "gang car," and how this high-level policy led to the classification of dispatch calls as gang-related in an unusually high number of cases during the election year. In the two preceding nonelection years, police officials had indicated that gang-related problems were not a priority; in both those years and the subsequent nonelection year, the number of dispatch calls classified as gang-related was lower than in the election year. In short, while limited to a pair of case study communities, this research quite explicitly suggests something like the policing equivalent of what political scientists have called the "political business cycle," which involves the timing of tax reductions and government benefit increases so as to provide credit-claiming opportunities for politicians during election years.

Whether positive or negative, the nature and extent of political influence on police policy and practice appear to be contingent, not surprisingly, on the character of the political environment. That environment can change over time in a given jurisdiction, and it can vary at any given time among jurisdictions. A good example of this perspective is a comparative case study analysis of New York, Chicago, and Philadelphia in the 1960s and early 1970s (Ruchelman, 1974). This study considered the ability of mayors to shape police policy and practice in the face of the then growing strength of the police bureaucracy, defined largely in terms of organized power exercised through collective bargaining units. In New York and Philadelphia, political parties no longer exerted the kind of influence over municipal politics generally, and policing in particular, that they once had in the heyday of machine politics. In New York, the mayor faced a powerful police bureaucracy that won almost as many political contests as did the mayor. In Philadelphia, a powerful police commissioner, who enjoyed the support of the policemen's association, was able to coopt the mayor, who had limited power as a lame duck, as well as a greatly weakened party organization. However, in Chicago, where the mayor headed a still robust local Democratic party, the police department was very responsive to his bidding. Circumstances have changed in all three cities, so it is important to keep in mind that the nature and extent of mayoral influence in each city may also have changed. This study also suggests that a comprehensive analysis of contemporary political influences on police should extend beyond "principal agents" who have official responsibility for governance; other political actors, such as unions, civil service boards, and courts can exercise significant influence.

However, based on the limited evidence available, the oversight exercised by local government officials over the police seems to be most potent in the act of executive appointment and, correspondingly, job review and the threat of job loss, an argument made by James Q. Wilson (1968) in his comparison of policing styles in eight local jurisdictions in the 1960s.

Political Oversight: Citizen Review Boards

Proposition 11: When police departments face charges of police misconduct, there is often pressure to institute citizen review boards, which in various ways involve nonpolice in gathering and assessing facts about allegations, review of investigative documents, hearing appeals of complaint dispositions, and reviewing police policies and practices. Despite the popularity of citizen review boards, very little research is available to indicate the nature and extent of their effect on police practices. The committee recommends a program of evaluation research to determine the nature and extent of such influence on actual police practices.

Citizen oversight of the police, and particularly citizen participation in the review of complaints against police officers, is a common prescription for the ailment of police misconduct (Skolnick and Fyfe, 1993). Citizen involvement in complaint review takes many different forms in the United States. Some efforts have been made to reduce this complexity in order to describe the main features of citizen review. One such effort describes four models of citizen review:

• complaint review that provides for fact-finding investigations of complaints by persons who are not sworn police officers (i.e., external investigations), reports of which are reviewed by other civilian officials, who make recommendations about disposition to the police executive;
• complaint review that provides for investigations conducted by police personnel (internal investigations) with citizen input in the review of investigative reports, whereby citizens may monitor police handling of complaints;
• complaint review that provides for citizen involvement in an appellate capacity, with a board to which complainants may appeal if they are dissatisfied with the outcomes of their complaints; and
• complaint review that provides not only for citizen involvement in the review of police investigations of individual cases, but also for a citizen role in reviewing police policies and procedures and making recommendations for change (Walker, 2001:61-63; also see Kerstetter, 1985, and Perez, 1994).

Citizen involvement in complaint review is thought to have a number of salutary effects. It may improve the perceived receptivity of the complaint review system to complaints; the perceived efficacy of the complaint review system; the rate at which perceived misconduct is reported to authorities; the depth and thoroughness of complaint investigations; the satisfaction of complainants with their experiences with the complaint review system; the procedural fairness of complaint review, as it is judged by complainants; and police performance in interactions with citizens. Complaint review is therefore about much more than the accurate and fair disposition of individual allegations of police misconduct.

Little empirical evidence has been produced about the extent to which citizen review meets these expectations. Some evidence suggests that most citizens who believe that they have reason to complain do not complain. Walker and Graham (1998) analyzed data collected through a survey of

12,000 respondents in 3 metropolitan areas encompassing 24 jurisdictions in 1977. About 6 percent said that they had a reason to complain about an aspect of police service in the preceding 12 months, and of those, 36 percent had complained (half of those had reportedly called the police department). But the study could not examine whether the reporting rate was higher in jurisdictions that provided for greater citizen involvement in complaint review. The popularity of citizen review and optimism about its benefits far outstrip the empirical evidence that citizen review has salutary effects.

The committee recommends that a program of rigorous evaluation research consider a wide variety of citizen review boards, assessing their impact on a range of police practices (but especially those features that are frequent targets of citizens' complaints), controlling for the influence of other institutions that might also be responsible for overseeing police integrity (e.g., the police organization itself and the courts). A comprehensive evaluation would go beyond examining the effect of civilian review on complaints filed but would consider other data sources, such as citizen surveys of high-risk populations (e.g., arrestees and those interrogated during field stops) and direct field observation.

Interorganizational Effects: Other Criminal Justice and Human Service Agencies

Proposition 12: It is widely assumed that the police are part of a criminal justice system in which policies and practices in one part of the system reverberate in many others. Changes in prosecutorial practices in charging and plea negotiations, penal policies, and correctional release decisions all presumably have important implications for the police work environment, some intended and some not. The available research is too scant to make generalizations about the nature and extent of these influences.

Most examinations of criminal justice influence focus on prosaic, but nonetheless powerful, effects. In his 1969 book, *Traffic and the Police*, Gardiner explored interagency variations in traffic citations, finding substantial variation in citations for moving violations (as opposed to parking violations) in his two samples: a national sample of 508 police agencies and a sample of 180 Massachusetts cities and towns. He found that local court rules about the appearance of officers at traffic ticket hearings had an effect on ticketing rates. Those jurisdictions requiring officers to appear at the next available court hearing date had lower ticketing rates than those jurisdictions with more flexible courtroom procedures. This is one indication of an interorganizational effect on police outputs, an effect that Feeney (1982) was unable to detect in his analysis of the relationship between the use of field citations and court orders to reduce jail crowding.

Relying on data from 58 California counties, Welsh (1993) tested the hypothesis that court orders to reduce jail overcrowding would expand the use of citations and reduce the number of custodial arrests. While these changes occurred in some cases, Welsh was unable to find evidence of an aggregate change in police arrest and citation behaviors based on the court-ordered reductions in jail crowding.

The scant research on this important question suggests that interorganizational effects appear to depend on the particular link in question. For instance, in Gardiner's study, court acquittal rates for traffic offenses are not associated with police ticketing rates. But Van Dijk (1988) reports that in Holland a change in prosecution policies regarding bicycle theft reverberated through the system, subsequently changing police arresting and charging decisions and, later, victimization rates. Research in this genre needs to take into account the dynamic nature of systems, including feedback processes.

Intergovernmental Influences: State Legislation

State legislation is logically an obvious source of influence on police programs and operations, in the sense that it provides mandates for action (e.g., state laws requiring arrests in domestic violence incidents), opportunities or tools for action (e.g., state laws allowing for on-site revocation of licenses of drivers found to exceed legal blood alcohol levels), and constraints on action. That state legislation influences what local police do may therefore be so obvious that it has not motivated as much research as has other topics. However, there is some systematic, empirical research supporting the logical conclusion that state law influences what the police do.

For example, Chaney and Saltzstein (1998), in a cross-sectional analysis of a national sample of municipal police departments, examined the extent to which state and city laws requiring the arrest of perpetrators of domestic violence actually affected policing activity in that regard. They found that the existence of mandatory arrest laws do influence police arrest patterns, at least in those situations in which violence was threatened. Similarly, Haider-Markel (2001), in a study based on survey data from police departments and district attorneys, found that the existence of a state hate crime law influenced the perceived likelihood of police arrest in a hypothetical hate crime incident, as well as district attorney pursuit of such cases, although it did not influence the perceived likelihood that police officers on the scene would classify the crime as a hate crime.

The proposition that changes in the criminal justice system influence police behavior, sometimes in unintended and unanticipated ways, has not received sufficient research attention. For example, one of the most common assumptions in this regard is that laws passed that allow police to keep some portion of assets seized in drug arrests have served as an incentive for police to increase their attention in this area. Sollars, Benson, and Rasmussen (1994) found that local police in Florida "substantially increased arrests for drug offenses relative to arrests for property and violent crimes" in response to drug asset forfeiture laws. Blumenson and Nilsen (1998) argue broadly that the drug war has transformed the criminal justice, including law enforcement practice, and credit this change to forfeiture laws. Given the importance of this question, it is surprising how little research has addressed this issue.

There is clearly scope for a great deal of additional research on the impact of legislation on the activities of the police and other criminal justice agencies. When states change (and usually tighten) the rules surrounding drunk driving, domestic violence, child abuse, hate crime, gun carrying, and the like, the effects should reverberate through the system. Where there are data, multistate interrupted time-series and quasi-experimental research designs show great promise for estimating the effects of legal interventions on both the problems of interest and the efforts of the criminal justice system against them. And because there is likely to be variability in both the efforts and effectiveness of individual agencies within states, much more can be learned about the actual implementation of law at the operating level.

Intergovernmental Influences: Court Rulings

Proposition 13: The American system of government relies heavily on the judicial branch to oversee police practices, and many legal scholars and policy makers assume that most police dutifully follow court rulings when made. The available research suggests that police compliance with restrictive court rulings tends to be gradual and incomplete at first, but it increases over time. However, police often seek ways of getting around the requirements of the ruling, often in legal ways.

In the United States, the judiciary has a major responsibility for interpreting laws that specify how the police should practice certain aspects of policing. The most examined of these practices relate to police adherence to constitutional standards of due process in the areas of search and seizure, in-custody interrogation, and use of force. This literature is reviewed in detail in Chapter 7, so in this section we draw general implications from that review and refer the reader to Chapter 7 for details.

The body of empirical research on the impact of U.S. Supreme Court rulings suggests that when the Court issues a ruling that restricts or constrains police powers, the police reaction is *not* one of automatic compliance. At first a considerable degree of noncompliance may be expected, as was recorded in studies following the *Miranda* ruling, which required that the police advise suspects of their right not to self-incriminate and their right to an attorney. Researchers attributed police unfamiliarity with the requirements of the new ruling, but it is also likely that much of the noncompliance issued from reluctance to alter customary practices. Subsequent research, many years after the *Miranda* standards were established, has noted a high degree of compliance with *Miranda*, but the police attempt to subvert the protections it affords the suspect by offering perfunctory reading of the rights and attempting to persuade the suspect to waive his or her rights. Studies of applications for search warrants show a similar tendency to get around the standards for issuing a search warrant, which include shopping for a judge sympathetic to loose standards, distorting facts, and sometimes even lying. Studies of search and seizure vary considerably in their estimate of the degree of police compliance—due no doubt in part to differences in methods of collecting data—but there is reason to believe that police compliance is much higher when the police desire to seek a successful prosecution, but noncompliance with legal requirements is considerably less likely when the police purpose is to disrupt illicit practices or harass the suspect. This, of course, is a product of the restricted domain of effects that the exclusionary rule can have, since it is only relevant (if raised) when an arrest is made and the prosecutor files charges.

The available research suggests that it is safe to conclude that restrictive appellate court rulings will meet with various forms of resistance, subversion (both legal and illegal), and just the inertia of old habits dying hard. Resistance and noncompliance out of ignorance give way to more subtle manipulations of the rules as police become accustomed to the new way of doing things over time. Interestingly, researchers have not paid much attention to what happens when the courts loosen restrictions on police. Whether police eagerly take advantage of the loosened rules or whether they also tend to continue past practices is an unanswered question.

Intergovernmental Influences: Incentives and the Federal Government

There is a substantial, albeit largely descriptive, case study literature suggesting that intergovernmental incentives have a significant impact on both police programs and practices. The most obvious manifestation of this influence, of course, is when the federal government provides grants-in-aid to encourage particular programmatic initiatives. With respect to community policing, for example, there is at least some evidence that Community Oriented Policing Services (COPS) grants made a difference in the adoption of the community policing model (Moore et al., 2000).

Handling Protests

There is also empirical evidence of the federal government's influence on policing even when grants-in-aid are not involved. For example, McPhail, Schweingruber, and McCarthy (1998) have documented a major shift in how police agencies handle protests in the United States and link that shift to several different actions by the federal government—actions that substantially changed the incentive structure. Specifically, they document a shift from an "escalated force" policy of policing protests to a "negotiated management" policy. In contrast to an escalated force policy, a negotiated management policy emphasizes the First Amendment rights of protesters, tolerates a substantial amount of community disruption, entails substantial communication between police and protesters, aims to minimize both the extent and aggressiveness of arrest tactics, and involves a minimal use of force rather than the principle of using a dramatic show of force (1998: 52-54). The shift from an escalated force to a negotiated management policy of policing protest is attributed to three key federal actions: (1) the critical commentary on the escalated force policy produced by several presidential commissions investigating the riots of the 1960s, (2) a series of Supreme Court decisions establishing a settled body of "public forum law" that instructs police agencies on the need for maximal tolerance of First Amendment rights in spaces that have come to be traditionally used as places for expressive activity, and (3) the civil disturbance orientation course (or SEADOC) developed by the U.S. Army's Military Police School (1998: 54-63). In related research, McCarthy and colleagues (McCarthy, McPhail, and Crist, 1995) estimated that "as many as ten thousand police administrators, police officers, and other public officials may have gone through the SEADOC courses" (p. 62). In sum, through court decisions, presidential commissions, and training courses, the federal government changed the legal and informational contexts in ways that significantly altered the incentives of police departments with respect to the policing of protests.

Another facet of the federal influence on local policing may be the FBI National Academy, which receives nominations from departments across the country for potential attendees. A selected number participate in an 11-week training designed for upper and mid-level law enforcement officers, administered to law enforcement managers in four sessions each year at the FBI training academy complex in Quantico, Virginia. It was established in 1935, and since then has graduated more than 32,000 students. While most are from law enforcement agencies in the United States, more than 2,000 students from 128 foreign nations have graduated from the academy as well. A 1999 internal review of graduates showed that more than 5,700 were currently serving as agency heads, including nearly 4,900 local chiefs of police (Federal Bureau of Investigation, 2002). There is not a single other centralized source through which so many police executives in the United States pass. The FBI National Academy is an important source of innovation diffusion, both in the United States and abroad, about which virtually nothing systematic is known by social scientists (for basic descriptive statistics, see LaSante and Scheers, 1988).

Handling Terrorist Attacks

Proposition 14: The terrorist attacks of September 11, 2001, may have altered police structure, behavior, and policing style in the United States.

It takes only a cursory review of headlines to note that the events of September 11, 2001, altered expectations about policing in the United States. Now there are calls for police to respond to suspicious situations, uncover terrorist networks, and work with other agencies and jurisdictions in an unprecedented way. In the event of an attack, police would find themselves as first-line emergency responders, perhaps faced with biological or radiological hazards. However, little is known about the capability of especially local police to handle these weighty responsibilities.

The most important public study to date was conducted in 1992, by researchers from the RAND Corporation. They surveyed several hundred state and local law enforcement agencies about their level of preparation to deal with terrorist incidents (Riley and Hoffman, 1995). At the time, the respondents envisioned terrorism as encompassing both domestic and international groups. Although surveys were administered to samples drawn from three different kinds of agencies (state emergency planning agencies, state police agencies, and local police agencies), we restrict our discussion to the findings for local police agencies. Half of the sample was selected to represent all police agencies, while the remainder was selected because they were deemed "more likely to be targets of terrorism" (Riley and Hoffman, 1995:6). Therefore, as the authors acknowledge, the findings drawn from this study are clearly not generalizable to the population of police agencies in the United States. The response rates for the local police agencies were low; 53 percent for the stratified random sample and 46 percent for the targeted sample.

Preparedness and Response. Like any study of agency responses to terrorism, the RAND project began with their level of preparedness. One-third of those surveyed had identified terrorist groups within their jurisdiction. About a quarter of respondents had conducted an investigation or conducted surveillance on suspected terrorist groups in the past five years, though only 8 percent reported participating in a terrorism-related prosecution. Nearly 23 percent had conducted a threat assessment of potentially vulnerable targets. Just over 35 percent had a "special unit, section, group, or person that is specifically concerned with terrorism" (Riley and Hoffman, 1995:53). Nearly three-quarters of responding agencies indicated that at least one empoyee had received special training in antiterrorism or counter-terrorism. Almost a decade before the deadly attacks on the Pentagon and the World Trade Center on September 11, 2001, terrorism was clearly on the minds of some police agencies.

Relationships with Outside Agencies. The ongoing threat of terrorism, par-ticularly international terrorism, will require police to work in cooperation with other agencies at different levels of government. The RAND study found that, despite popular impressions about jurisdictional squabbles, the relationship between police and other investigative agencies appeared to be fairly good. The departments surveyed reported having the best relation-ship with other local agencies (91 percent were rated as "good" or "very good," followed by state agencies (81 percent) and the federal government (71 percent). In an effort to improve this state of affairs in the wake of September 11, FBI Director Robert Mueller created the Office of Law En-forcement Coordination and selected a retired police chief to head the of-fice. Follow-up evaluations could determine whether the FBI's efforts are having the intended effects.

Outlook for the Future. Prior to September 11, some viewed the likelihood of terrorist attacks in the United States as negligible (e.g., Crock, 2000). The nation's police, however, were less optimistic. In 1992, nearly half viewed it as "very" or "somewhat" likely that a major terrorist attack would take place in the United States during the next 10 years. Eerily, more than 72 percent viewed it as likely that terrorists would attack a domestic com-mercial airliner. However, only 1 percent of respondents viewed it as very likely that they would experience a terrorist attack in their own jurisdiction in the next 10 years, with another 26 percent viewing such an attack as somewhat likely. Finally, and tellingly, only 1 percent of respondents viewed their agencies as very well prepared for a terrorist incident; another 11 percent considered their agencies to be well prepared and 57 percent "some-what prepared."

Little systematic knowledge exists on local police preparedness for ter-rorist incidents in the wake of September 11. A recent book on disaster preparedness in general (Tierney, Lindell, and Perry, 2001) laments the lack of research on the role of police in disaster situations. They conclude that "almost nothing new has been learned about police and fire department disaster preparedness" (p. 51). In general, their review of research suggests that police agencies are ill-equipped to deal with large-scale disasters, whether natural or man-made. Wenger, Quarantelli, and Dynes (1989), on the basis of many years of research at the University of Delaware's Disaster Research Center, report that police agencies tend to plan for disasters in isolation from other community agencies and to think of disaster response procedures as being a simple linear extension of the procedures they ordinarily use. According to the authors, police departments "tend to devote few resources to emergency planning.... Larger departments are more likely to plan than smaller ones. When they do plan, police agencies tend to plan internally, in isolation from other community organizations; few have adopted an interorganizational approach to the disaster problem. The police appear to believe that disasters can be handled through the expansion of everyday emergency procedures—that is, they do not consider the qualitative (as opposed to the quantitative) difference between disasters and 'everyday' emergencies" (Wenger, Quarantelli, and Dynes, 1989:51).

Of course, the apparent tendency for police to plan in isolation is not unique. A recent report on chemical and biological terrorism by the National Research Council (1999:30) suggests the need for "an institutionalized linkage between the law enforcement and medical communities." The report suggests that the inclusion "of key medical personnel in anti-terrorist intelligence activity would no doubt be facilitated by their willingness to undergo training on the needs of the law enforcement community, especially procedures for proper preservation of evidence" (p. 30). They conclude that few local medical communities have effectively developed structural linkages with law enforcement. Local response teams should include a law enforcement officer whose responsibility is to "establish relationships with the local FBI office and other law enforcement agencies sufficient to ensure that the team has the maximum prior warning of potential nuclear, chemical, or biological incidents" (p. 31).

The role of local police in prevention and response to terrorism remains unclear. The police are just one element of a vast interorganizational network of agencies with an interest in terrorism. These networks are both horizontal and vertical. Horizontally, a variety of agencies performing different functions—medical, fire, civil defense, etc.—must all work together in cooperation with the police. Vertically, the response to terrorism takes place a many different levels, including local, county, state, federal, and international authorities. The proper role of police in these networks is still emerging.

Although many agencies play a role in the response to terrorism, at the local level, police agencies are now dealing with a host of expanded responsibilities. A post-9/11 survey of 192 cities by the U.S. Conference of Mayors found that the 45 percent of total spending on "unanticipated, additional security and readiness costs incurred between September 11 and December 31" was concentrated on the police, with fire, emergency medical services, public health, and other agencies also incurring expanded costs. Respondents estimated that 31 percent of additional costs in 2002 would be expended on the police. Anecdotes provided by survey respondents suggest that most police agencies have been experiencing a variety of increased burdens since September 11, including:

- Responding to suspicious packages in the wake of the anthrax scare.
- Providing extra security for buildings, critical infrastructure (such as water treatment plants), and events.
- Reassigning personnel to a variety of new assignments, such as regional task forces and special units.
- Creating new units and positions to respond to security concerns.
- Rapid expansion in hiring.
- New training needs.
- Assessing local security risks.
- Increased planning and policy development.
- Dealing with a shortage in staff due to the deployment of National Guard and military reserve units.

Only five of the 192 cities surveyed by the U.S. Conference of Mayors reported that their communities had not incurred additional costs for security in the wake of September 11.

Research Issues. Understanding how police agencies in the United States are preparing for and responding to the terrorist threat presents a special set of challenges for researchers. The 1992 RAND survey described earlier obtained a response rate much lower than is typical for establishment surveys of police agencies (see Maguire et al., 2003). The researchers suggest that the sensitivity of the topic probably had an influence on the response rate. The infrequency of actual terrorist incidents on American soil means that random samples of agencies would include few or even none that had experience in dealing with terrorism. Security concerns have probably made repetition of the RAND study even more difficult, for police agencies are nervous about sharing their preparation strategies, perhaps fearing this will increase their vulnerability (Pluchinsky, 2002). In the interest of national security, many federal and state agencies are now paying more attention to the need for protecting sensitive but unclassified information (Parker, Johnson, and Locy, 2002; Sammon, 2002). The burden is on the research community to ensure continued access to police agencies in a manner that accommodates these concerns.

One possible, if more subtle, effect of the attacks of September 11 could be the acceleration of an already existing organizational posture that some observers have dubbed "militarism." As early as 1970, Bittner noted that "the conception of the police as a quasi-military institution with a warlike mission plays an important part in the structuring of police work in modern American departments" (Bittner, 1970:52). The roots of militarism extend well back into the history of policing, and Klockars (1988) argued that the emergence of the military analogy served three important functions: (1) it conferred honor and respect on policing as an occupation, (2) its rhetorical focus on fighting a war on crime enabled police to attach a moral urgency to their work, and (3) it sought to adjust the relationship between police chiefs and local politicians to resemble more closely the relationship between military generals and national politicians.

Yet it is also the case that the level of militarism is distributed unequally, so that some police organizations are more militaristic than others (Kraska and Cubellis, 1997; Kraska and Kappeler, 1997), and the overall level of militarism in policing, both in the United States and abroad, is expanding (Kopel and Blackman, 1997; Weber, 1999; Kraska, 1996, 2001; McCulloch, 2001). Kraska and his colleagues have noted an increase in the number of agencies with police paramilitary units. About 89 percent of the large agencies they surveyed reported having such a unit, up from 59 percent in 1982 and 78 percent in 1990. Furthermore, this trend is now making its way into routine patrol operations and into small town police departments (Kraska and Cubellis, 1997; Kraska and Kappeler, 1997; Weber, 1999; McCulloch, 2001).

Police are not only relying increasingly on the "lethal artifacts" of the military, but also on a variety of advanced nonlethal technologies (Haggerty and Ericson, 1999). These include sophisticated communications and surveillance technologies designed for the battlefield, but adapted for law enforcement. Haggerty and Ericson note that the diffusion of military technologies to civilian law enforcement defies an unconscious trickle-down explanation. Rather, the diffusion is due to a conscious, direct effort on the part of "powerful military/corporate interests…to justify the 'dual-use' status of their technologies " (p. 248). This is one of many substantive areas in which private-market vendors appear to be influencing policing. Some suggest that the militarization of criminal justice agencies is a by-product of the emergence of the "criminal justice industrial complex," a term coined by Richard Quinney (1980) (Haggerty and Ericson, 2001; Kraska, 2001). Haggerty and Ericson (2001:54) describe Quinney's concern as with "the alliance being forged between the criminal justice establishment and corporations that require markets for technologies of social control."

The effects and extent of militarism must be examined much more closely, since the attacks of September 11 suggest that this trend will continue. Police organizations around the nation are struggling to prepare themselves for the possibility of future attacks, and some of these responses are likely to be paramilitaristic.

In light of the dearth of research in this area, **the committee recommends research on the organizational demands of responding to terrorism.** What has been done suggests that responding to terrorism places new demands on municipal police agencies. It requires them to coordinate their efforts with multiple levels of government; to plan in coordination with public health and medical organizations and with the military; and to learn to safeguard their own employees from new chemical and biological risks. They must continue to maintain open communication with the communities they serve and their commitment to lawful conduct, while they are faced with new information and intelligence needs. From the perspective of local departments, more research is needed on how to respond to these organizational challenges.

CONCLUSION

The oft-repeated theme of this chapter is that the available evidence is insufficient to draw conclusions and that more research is needed. The deficiencies in the research on organizational and environmental effects on police practice fall into four categories. One is simply the absence of studies entirely or of studies more rigorous than the case study. This can be said of virtually all of the propositions considered, but is an especially severe problem for those pertaining to the effects of decentralization, hierarchy, CompStat, oversight by local elected officials, citizen review boards, other criminal justice and human service agency practices, and terrorism since September 11, 2001. In these areas research offers *at most* interesting speculation about what might be happening.

A second deficiency is that even the research that goes beyond the case study design is overwhelmingly limited to cross-sectional comparisons that statistically control for the effects of other variables. Studies using quasi-experimental and experimental designs are quite rare. Consequently, it is difficult to have confidence that relationships shown in the data are attributable to causation.

A third problem is that much of the data currently collected on police practice have significant problems that limit their utility for applied and scholarly research. The areas of lethal and nonlethal force should be especially high priorities for improvement, since they generate so much concern among the public and are the cause for the more extreme legal measures taken to seek civil remedies for individuals, as well as to enjoin and alter police practices.

A fourth deficiency is that measures of organizational practice tend to be heavily biased in favor of measures of policing that are now regarded as traditional such as arrest, use of force, and case clearances. These are, of course, important aspects of what police do, but the data that are collected on a widespread, national basis neglect police practices that reflect the desires of many citizens, politicians, and the police. Police handle most disorders and minor crimes without invoking the criminal process, yet the Uniform Crime Reports, the principal national data resource, report only rates of arrest. Police provide an array of other services that often are poorly documented on the agency's records, not to mention their absence from a nationwide database. The same goes for problemsolving, mobilizing and working with the community, and gathering or brokering information functions that will be absolutely critical to the successful waging of a war on terrorism.

The committee judges that the federal government can and should play a key role in stimulating data collection and research that enables researchers to fill the many gaps discussed in this chapter. The ready availability of standardized data, collected in many agencies repeatedly over an extended period of time, provides the raw material needed to facilitate a proliferation of quality studies of the impact of police organization and environmental features. However, unlike the top-down approach used in the development of the Uniform Crime Reports, the committee recommends that the federal government begin with a bottom-up approach. Rather than impose new data systems on police agencies or try to persuade them to adopt them, the federal government should begin by supporting the development and testing of a variety of different data collection systems in various police departments around the nation.

This will have two benefits. First, it will stimulate competition, thus increasing the quality of results, and it will increase the likelihood of uncovering systems that will work for the broadest possible array of local departments. Second, such an approach is more likely to result in systems that local departments themselves can and will use for their own practical purposes. The ultimate goal, of course, is to have in place systems that large numbers of departments will commit to using over long time periods, but unlike the Uniform Crime Reports, it may be less important to promote comprehensive adoption than it is to ensure that adoption be sufficiently widespread that policy makers can evaluate the effects of organizational innovation and environmental influences over a wide range of conditions.

The committee judges none of the propositions considered in this chapter to have conclusive findings, but certain of them point in directions that have implications for public policy. First, it appears that simple recommendations about increasing or decreasing the size of the police organization to produce a particular pattern of behavior are unlikely to yield desirable results with a high degree of predictability. The effects of size appear to be contingent on many other factors, although current research is unable to specify what those conditions are. Second, when police organizations create new job specialties, such as community policing officer, how those officers spend their time may change in the direction anticipated by the department, but patterns in how the officers interact with the public do not appear to be different from those of generalist patrol officers. Third, when patrol officers' responsibilities are focused geographically by permanent beat assignments, they may increase their knowledge of the geographic area, but there do not appear to be clear changes in patterns of officer *behavior* unless they are reinforced with other structures, such as training, supervision, and incentives. Fourth, formalizing restrictive policies on the use of lethal force can reduce the frequency with which police use it, but the strongest effects may occur only when the policy change is stimulated by a crisis. Fifth, how police behave toward the public does appear to be conditioned by the character of the neighborhood, disadvantaged and high crime areas receiving more punitive policing than other areas. Similarly, at the level of city and metropolitan area, police deliver punishment to those communities that are more disadvantaged. Although these results are consistent with a conflict theory perspective, they are also consistent with the notion that the police are serving the disadvantaged persons in those areas. Finally, police appear to respond to restrictive court rulings initially by resisting them. However, over time they do acclimate to them, increasing the frequency of compliance. Yet they also find ways to get around the purpose of those rulings, suggesting that whatever the courts' expectations, police are not inclined to accept the goals of efforts to change their practices through litigation.

6

The Effectiveness of
Police Activities in Reducing Crime,
Disorder, and Fear

The public expects the police to accomplish many things, and the reduction of violent crime is often ranked among the most important. But public disorder, as characterized by public alcohol consumption, prostitution, vagrancy, and drug dealing, may loom larger in any given neighborhood than a concern for serious violence (Schneider, 1980). More recently, both researchers and police have come to view disorder and crime as linked to a community's level of fear about crime and its ability to prevent it (Skogan, 1990). In large part because of prominent public concern over these issues, considerable research has been conducted on the effectiveness of the police at reducing three public concerns: crime, disorder, and fear of crime. This body of research is the main concern of this chapter.

It is important to note at the outset that the committee recognizes that other mechanisms, both within and outside law enforcement, play a role in addressing these concerns. For instance, an offender might be successfully deterred from committing crime by criminal penalties; a community might diminish its own fear of crime by forming neighborhood patrols; an individual might simultaneously impose an effective criminal deterrent and reduce his or her fear by installing a home security system; and so on. Other social and economic forces may also have impact on crime and disorder. Criminologists and economists, for example, have long recognized that demographic changes, have important impacts on crime rates. These include shifts in age, family composition, household organization, poverty, and employment patterns (Becker and Landes, 1974; Yamada, 1985; Corman et al., 1987; Glaeser et al., 1996). Crime is importantly affected by drug use and availability, access to guns, and alcohol consumption. Private citizens can increase or decrease their risk of victimization by the precautions they choose to adopt and their daily routines and lifestyles. The police are but one part of the formal and informal mechanisms in place to reduce crime, disorder, and fear of crime, and there is no definitive evidence of the relative size of the role they play.

Moreover there are significant measures of police work that are not treated fully in this chapter. A vitally important concern since the inception of modern policing has been public acceptance of police use of authority as legitimate (Miller, 1977). We examine what is known about the specific relationship between legitimacy and outcome measures, but the broader problem of the legitimacy of police practices is examined in Chapters 7 and 8. Many other measures of police effectiveness have yet to receive sustained research attention. For example, there has been little or no research on the quality of police as first responders to emergency calls. Do the police provide appropriate medical attention? Do the police calm victims and provide solace? Do the police provide relevant, accurate, and useful information to victims and witnesses? Similarly, there has been little research on the services provided in police-initiated stops of citizens. Are citizens treated politely? Are the citizens informed as to the nature of the stop? How intrusive and inconvenient are the stops? And surprisingly, there is also little research on how the police contribute to criminal justice; are police actions just in both outcome and process? These and other understudied police activities warrant serious and sustained research.

In this chapter we review a large of body of research on police using a very specific criterion: How effective are police strategies at reducing crime, disorder, and fear of crime? We begin by discussing how the evidence was evaluated and assessed by the committee. What criteria did we use for distinguishing the value of studies for coming to conclusions about the effectiveness of police practices? How did we decide when the evidence was persuasive enough to draw more general statements about specific programs or strategies? We then turn to a series of propositions concerning specific police practices that can be drawn directly from the research literature. Our approach here is to identify what existing studies say about the effects of core police practices. Having summarized the research literature in this way, we conclude the chapter with a more general synthesis of the evidence reviewed. Are there more general conclusions that can be reached regarding what works in policing from the specific research we review? Are there suggestive patterns that can lead us to identify new and promising directions, even if the present research does not directly test these practices?

STRENGTH OF THE EVIDENCE

There is no hard rule for determining when studies provide more reliable or valid results, or any clear line to indicate when there is enough evidence to come to an unambiguous conclusion. Nonetheless, social scientists generally agree on some basic guidelines for assessing the strength of the evidence available. Perhaps the most widely agreed-on criterion relates to what is often referred to as internal validity (Sherman et al., 2002; Weisburd et al., 2001). Research designs that allow the researcher to make a stronger link between the interventions or programs examined and the outcomes observed are generally considered to provide more valid evidence than designs that provide for a more ambiguous connection between cause and effect. In formal terms, the former designs are considered to have higher internal validity. In reviewing studies, we used internal validity as a primary criterion for assessing the strength of the evidence provided.

It is generally agreed that randomized experiments, if successfully implemented and sustained, generally provide a higher level of internal validity than do nonexperimental studies (see, e.g., Boruch et al., 2000; Campbell and Boruch, 1975; Cook and Campbell, 1979; Farrington, 1983; Feder et al., 2000; Shadish et al., 2002; Weisburd, 2003). In randomized experiments, people or places are randomly assigned to treatment and control or comparison groups (Pocock, 1983). This means that all causes, except treatment, can be assumed to be randomly distributed among the groups. Accordingly, if an effect for an intervention is found, the researcher can conclude with confidence that the cause was the intervention itself and not some other confounding factor. In general in policing, seldom are there groups that can be called true control groups in a randomized study, since they generally receive some type of intervention. Policing experiments mostly compare a new or innovative program or strategy with traditional police practices.

Another class of studies, referred to here as quasi-experiments, typically allow for less confidence in making a link between the programs or strategies examined and the outcomes observed (Cook and Campbell, 1979). Quasi-experiments generally fall into three classes. In the first class, the experiment compares an "experimental" group with a control or comparison group, but the subjects of the study were not randomly assigned to the categories. This results in less confidence than true experimental approaches that the treatment was the actual cause if there is a difference in outcomes. It may have been, but the difference in outcome may be due to some preexisting difference between the treatment and the control groups that has not been taken into account by the researchers.

In the second class of quasi-experiments, a long series of observations is made before the treatment, and another long series of observations is made after the treatment. The established before-treatment trend allows research-ers to predict what might have happened without intervention. The differ-ence between what really happened after the treatment and the predicted outcome demonstrates the treatment effect. But these approaches are still subject to the criticism that other confounding factors not accounted for in the design may have caused the observed differences.

The third class of quasi-experiments combines the use of a control group with time-series data: this approach provides the strongest conclusions in quasi-experiment research. In theory, these designs are still likely to have a lower level of internal validity than randomized experimental studies. How-ever, some scholars argue that such quasi-experiments can sometimes pro-duce results of the same quality as randomized experiments (see, e.g., Shadish et al., 1993; Lipsey and Wilson, 1993). Others have found that even strongly designed quasi-experiments are still likely to produce less valid outcomes than well executed randomized experiments. In practice it is nec-essary to judge the persuasiveness of quasi-experiments on a case-by-case basis. (Weisburd, Lum and Petrosino, 2001).

Finally, studies that rely only on statistical controls—generally termed nonexperimental or observational designs—are often seen to represent the weakest level of confidence (Cook and Campbell, 1979; Sherman et al., 1997). In nonexperimental research, neither researchers nor policy makers intentionally vary treatments to test for outcomes. Rather, researchers ob-serve natural variation in outcomes and examine the relationships between that variation and police practices. For example, when trying to determine if police staffing levels influence crime, researchers might examine the rela-tionship between staffing levels and crime rates across cities. The difficulty with this approach is apparent: there can easily be other factors that influ-ence crime that are not accounted for. To address this concern, researchers attempt to control for these other factors statistically. One issue is that variation in the policy variable of interest (for example, police staffing lev-els) may be correlated with unknown or unmeasured variables that also influence the outcome (crime rates). The estimated effect of the policy vari-able will then be biased because it will be confounded by the effects of the unobserved variables (Kunz and Oxman, 1998). Under some circumstances this problem can be overcome by the use of instrumental-variables estima-tion technique, which exploits the availability of a variable (the instrument) that has a known effect on the policy variable, but no direct effect on the outcome variable (Angrist and Krueger, 2001). For example, Levitt's (1997) study of the effects of police hiring on crime rates takes advantage of the fact that municipal police hiring tends to follow the electoral cycle. Increases in the size of the police forces are disproportionately concentrated in may-oral and gubernatorial election years, but, he asserts, there is little reason to believe that the election-cycle has any direct effect on crime rates. The electoral cycle then serves as an "instrument" for police hiring. However, it is generally agreed that causes unknown or unmeasured by the researcher are likely to be a serious threat to the internal validity of these observational studies (Pedhazur, 1982; Kunz and Oxman, 1998; Feder and Boruch, 2000). Importantly, despite the limitations of such research, sometimes nonexperimental studies are the only investigation method possible in sensitive areas of crime and justice. Some scholars have argued that when the theory underlying a research problem is well developed and the quality of data are very high, it is possible to develop statistical models that provide highly valid results (Heckman and Smith, 1995). However, in the view of the committee, theories of police effectiveness and the data generally available for research on policing do not warrant such confidence.

In our evaluation, we rely strongly on these general assessments of the ability of research to make statements of high internal validity regarding the practices evaluated. However, we also recognize that other criteria are important in assessing the strength of research. While it is generally recognized that randomized experiments have higher internal validity than nonrandomized studies, a number of scholars have suggested that the results of randomized field experiments can be compromised by the difficulty of implementing such designs (Clarke and Cornish, 1972; Pawson and Tilly, 1997). In practice it can be difficult to sustain randomized trials in the field, and the integrity of randomized experiments must also be assessed on a case-by-case basis. Accordingly, in assessing the evidence, we also took into account the quality of both the measures identified and the implementation of the research design.

The external validity of a study refers to our ability to generalize from its findings to other settings, times and even conditions. Even if a researcher can make a very strong link between the practices examined in a study and their influence on crime, disorder, or fear, if one cannot generalize from that study to the more general problems and practices of policing, then the findings will not be very useful. Randomized field experiments may be problematic in this respect, since they are conducted under artificial circumstances, with the orders to the police and the data collection procedure dictated to some extent by the experimental design rather than by standard operating procedures. On the other hand, the process of instituting new procedures and management routines may mimic the reform measures that are being evaluated, if they are in turn to be implemented in practice. An experiment evaluating a particular intervention is often limited with respect to time and place. For these and other reasons our confidence with which an impact assessment's findings can be extrapolated to similar programs or from the program as tested to the program as implemented must be examined. Moreover, it is generally agreed by social scientists that caution should be used in drawing strong policy conclusions from a single study, no matter how well designed (Weisburd and Taxman, 2000; Manski, 2003). For these reasons we took into account additional factors related to our ability to generalize from study findings in drawing our conclusions. For example, when the committee found multiple studies with similar conclusions, we call them a "consistent" body of evidence. The strength of this consistent evidence was judged primarily on the quality of the majority of the studies. When there were contradictory findings among studies, we also assessed the quality of studies involved in order to be able to characterize the research. When we found a body of weakly designed studies with contradictory results, or strongly designed studies with contradictory results, we call that body of research conclusions "ambiguous." That is, when the strength of studies supporting opposite conclusions was judged comparable, no definite conclusion could be drawn. And when we found a group of strong studies contradicted by a group of weak studies, the committee favored the conclusions of the better quality studies, with appropriate qualifications.

It is also important to note that although the committee makes judgments about police effectiveness, the strength and scope of these judgments were limited by the extent and rigor of policing research more generally. For example, it is common in research in the social sciences today to compute standardized effect coefficients that allow assessment of the absolute size of the impacts of interventions and comparison of impact of interventions across studies (Wilson and Lipsey, 2001). Very few of the studies we reviewed included standardized effect sizes. Moreover, it was beyond the scope of the committee's work to independently construct these estimates, especially since the reporting of results was many times not detailed enough to allow independent and accurate computation of such statistics. The committee sought to gain a general assessment of the strength of the findings reported in each of these studies based on the evidence presented by the original investigators and the methods used.

It is also important to point out that evaluations of police tactics to reduce crime and disorder often involve comparisons of areas receiving varying levels of the tactic in question. Evaluations based on spatial comparisons must account for complex spatial dependencies. Two well-recognized spatial dependencies are displacement (Cornish and Clarke 1986) and diffusion of crime prevention benefits (Clarke and Weisburd 1994). Substantial progress has been made in consistently measuring these phenomena over the past two decades. However, many of the evaluations reviewed either did not describe findings regarding spatial displacement or diffusion, or it appeared that measurements of displacement and diffusion were not central to the overall evaluation.

Displacement and diffusion relate to spatial dependencies introduced by the police tactic. Of equal concern should be spatial dependencies that confound presumed causal relationships between tactics and outcomes. One set of confounders comes from the nested nature of crime: crime events are clustered at specific locations—for example, addresses or street blocks (Eck and Weisburd, 1995), and such locations tend to cluster in larger areas (Sherman, Gartin, and Buerger, 1989). While such nesting of events suggests the importance of taking into account the hierarchical nature of the effects of policing, police research has seldom taken such concerns into account (see Kelling and Sousa, 2001 for a recent attempt to develop hierarchical models for evaluating a police strategy). A related phenomena is the tendency for nearby locations to have correlated characteristics. Just as failure to account for temporal autocorrelation in time-series analysis can result in biased results, failure to account for spatial autocorrelation in nonexperimental and quasi-experimental evaluations of police tactics may also bias the results (Odland, 1988). Again, police research today has generally not addressed such potential biases.

Once again, we present our evaluation in the form of propositions. These propositions summarize what is known regarding police effectiveness in the areas that we have reviewed. They represent both recurring themes in policing and relatively recent but nevertheless influential changes in police practice or philosophy.

STANDARD MODEL OF POLICE PRACTICES

Proposition 1: The standard model of policing has relied on the uniform provision of police resources intended to prevent crime and disorder across a wide array of crimes and across all parts of the jurisdictions that police serve. Despite the continued reliance of many police agencies on these standard practices, the evidence the committee reviewed suggests that such approaches are generally not the most effective strategy for controlling crime and disorder or reducing fear of crime.

Over the past two decades, there has been increasing criticism of what has come to be considered the standard model of police practices (Goldstein, 1990; Visher and Weisburd, 1998). This model relies generally on a "one size fits all" application of reactive strategies to suppress crime, in contrast to more customized and proactive strategies. The standard model also emphasizes the role of arrests and the threat of punishment in achieving this objective, with less emphasis on other capabilities of the police. The standard model of policing has assumed that generic strategies for crime reduction can be applied throughout a jurisdiction, regardless of the level of crime, the nature of crime, or other possible variations. Because the model is focused on providing a generalized model of police service, it has often been criticized as focused more on the means of policing or the resources that police bring to bear (i.e., providing the generalized strategy throughout a jurisdiction) than on the effectiveness of policing in reducing crime, disorder, or fear (Goldstein, 1979). This model has also been criticized because of its almost sole reliance on the traditional law enforcement powers of police in preventing crime (Moore et al., 1992).

We identified five general types of strategies that have been prominent in the standard model of policing and have been the focus of systematic research over the last three decades:

1. Increasing the size of police agencies.
2. Random patrol across all parts of the community.
3. Rapid response to calls for service.
4. Generally applied follow-up investigations.
5. Generally applied intensive enforcement and arrest policies.

Increasing the Size of Police Agencies

There has long been a presumption among politicians and the public that more police will mean more safety in the community. However, research in this area is ambiguous and the evidence is often drawn from studies that use quasi-experimental or observational methods. Moreover, it is generally very difficult to identify what the added police actually did in such studies once they were brought into the community. This is particularly the case when a long time series is employed, because police organization, technology, and even their core missions may have changed dramatically over time and these may be confounded with re-sizings of police forces. In this sense, it is difficult to distinguish the circumstances under which the addition of police is likely to provide benefit.

Research on the number of police employed shows two different results with regard to crime (disorder has not been studied). Evidence from case studies in which police have suddenly left duty (e.g., police strikes) shows that the absence of police is likely to lead to an increase in crime (Sherman, 1997; Sherman and Eck, 2002). While these studies are generally not very strong in their design, their conclusions are consistent and appear persuasive. To completely abandon police service in the community would be likely to result in more crime. One can logically conclude from these case studies that there is an "absolute benefit" to the creation of police agencies or the introduction of police to areas that have not been policed previously.

Aside from this indirect evidence that the introduction of police in situations in which no police are found can reduce crime, does research support the idea that adding officers to an existing police force is effective? This might be called the marginal effectiveness of policing that is produced by increasing the relative number of police in an agency. The results here are ambiguous, and it is difficult to reach an overall conclusion. A series of studies involving comparisons of police agencies with more officers than others as well as studies of the effects of variation in police strength over time suggest that normal variation in police strength has no influence on crime (Van Tulder, 1992; Niskanen, 1994; Chamlin and Langworthy, 1996; Eck and Maguire, 2000). Nonetheless, two recent studies using sophisticated econometric methods conclude that marginal increases in the number of police are related to decreases in crime rates (Marvell and Moody, 1996; Levitt, 1997). The Levitt study is of particular interest. It attempts to overcome the statistical problem of reverse causation (that crime rates influence police hiring as well as the reverse) by employing an instrumental-variables estimation technique. Levitt documents the fact that police hiring is concentrated in mayoral and gubernatorial election years, and asserts that the election cycle is unlikely to affect crime rates directly. Using a large sample of municipalities over a number of years, he estimates the effect on crime rates of that portion of variability in police staffing that is associated with the election cycles. His estimates indicate that the effect is negative, suggesting that at the margin the police are effective in controlling crime. The committee views these latter studies as representing important efforts to advance statistical methods of analyzing the relationship between police strength and crime rates. However, while recognizing the elegance of the statistical designs employed, in our view these nonexperimental designs are still likely to be confounded with many unmeasured or indeed unknown causes of variability in crime rates.

For example, these studies generally do not take into account what the police do. In policing it is common for police agencies to increase and redeploy officer strength as they also change policing strategies. New York City in the 1990s is a recent example of this (McDonald, 2001). Changes in mayoral administrations presaged by the electoral cycles employed in some econometric studies can bring new police chiefs, new management policies, changes in deployment patterns, the adoption of new tactics and programs, and new commitments regarding levels of police service, all of which almost inevitably seem to require more police officers. As a result, shifts in their numbers can covary with unmeasured changes in what they actually do to attack crime. As we show later, there is also evidence that some policing strategies are more effective than others. Accordingly, it may be that the effects of police strength observed in such studies are confounded with the unmeasured impacts of the effects of changes in the strategies of policing. Such potential confounding makes it difficult to draw strong policy conclusions from these and other studies of the relationship between police strength and crime rates.

Random Patrol Across All Parts of the Community

Random preventive patrol across police jurisdictions has continued to be one of the most enduring of standard police practices. Despite the continued use of random preventive patrol by many police agencies, the evidence supporting this practice is very weak and the studies reviewed by the committee are more than a quarter-century old. Two studies, both using weaker quasi-experimental designs, suggest that random preventive patrol can have an impact on crime (Dahmann, 1975; Press, 1971). However, a much larger scale and more persuasive evaluation of preventive patrol in Kansas City found that the standard practice of preventive patrol does not reduce crime, disorder, or fear of crime (Kelling et al., 1974).

The Kansas City Preventive Patrol Experiment increased preventive patrol in five beat areas in the city, reduced it in five others, and left patrol at standard levels in still five others. The study found no significant differences among the three types of beats with regard to crime, disorder, or fear, leading the investigators to conclude that there is no evidence that preventive patrol significantly influences any of these core measures of the outcomes of policing. However, while this is a landmark study, the validity of its conclusions has been challenged because of methodological flaws that relate to the allocation of study beats, the measurement of crime and disorder, and the actual number of police cars on patrol (Minneapolis Medical Research Foundation, 1976; Larson and Cohn, 1985; Sherman and Weisburd, 1995). These problems illustrate the general difficulty of sustaining an experimental intervention in the field, especially as in this case where some police were required to change their routines in ways that they may have thought inappropriate.

Rapid Response to Calls for Service

A third component of the standard model of policing, rapid response to emergency calls for service, has also not been shown to reduce crime or even lead to increased chances of arrest in most situations. The crime reduction assumption behind rapid response is that if the police get to crime scenes rapidly they will apprehend offenders, thus providing a general deterrent against crime; there are no studies of the effects of this strategy on disorder or fear of crime. In principle, one can distinguish between absolute and marginal effects of rapid response, as is the case with adding police. There are no documented studies of the absolute effect of rapid response: that is, the shifting from a situation with rapid response to one of no response or long-delayed response.

The best evidence about the marginal effectiveness of rapid response comes from two studies conducted in the late 1970s (Kansas City Police Department, 1977; Spelman and Brown, 1981). Evidence from five cities examined in these two studies consistently shows that most crimes (about 75 percent at the time of the studies) are discovered some time after they have been committed. Accordingly, offenders in such cases have had plenty of time to escape. For the minority of crimes in which the offender and the victim have some type of contact, citizen delay in calling the police blunts whatever effect a marginal improvement in response time might provide. These studies show that, on average, citizens delayed calling the police for about five minutes, so a slight improvement in how fast the police arrive at the crime scene is unlikely to make much difference in the probability of apprehending the suspect. Contrary to the view that rapid response on the part of the police can increase police effectiveness, both of these studies point to the importance of creating change in the activities of citizens. The greatest benefit in terms of effectiveness is seen to come from increasing the speed at which citizens call the police.

There have been no direct studies of the effects of response time on crime rates. It is possible that a slight decline in police response time might be detectable by the average offender, and the average offender might, as a consequence, perceive an increase in apprehension risk sufficient to serve as a deterrent. This seems to be a remote possibility, however, given the fact that offenders often have limited or sometimes even invalid information on police activity.

It is important to distinguish between the effectiveness of rapid response as a general policy to reduce crime and the effectiveness of rapid response to clear emergencies in which offenders are present or citizens are injured. In the former, the question is whether crime for the jurisdiction is reduced, and the evidence suggests that this is unlikely. In the latter case, the question is whether improving rapid responses to crimes in which an offender is present or there are injuries results in more arrests and improved assistance to citizens in crisis. The committee found no studies shedding light on the effectiveness of focused rapid response.

Generally Applied Follow-Up Investigations

Studies consistently show that most property crimes and many violent crimes are unsolved (Greenwood et al., 1975; Eck, 1983; Brandl and Frank, 1994; Horvath et al., 2001). Another example of the standard model of policing assumes that general improvements in police investigations to improve the rate at which crimes are solved will prevent future crime. Once a serious crime has been reported to the police, and if officers who first respond to the incident have arrested no one, there is often a follow-up investigation. This model suggests that such investigations increase the risk of apprehension for offenders, thus providing a general deterrent (Eck, 1983). Alternatively, the capture and sanctioning of offenders stemming from investigations might reduce crime by imprisoning active offenders.

The research to date suggests otherwise. Most property crimes, such as burglaries, are not solved by investigations, probably due to the absence of clues and the large ratio of cases to investigators (Greenwood, Petersilia, and Chaiken, 1977; Eck, 1983). Contact crimes, such as robberies, have a greater chance of being solved, but eyewitness testimony often is insufficient to identify or charge a suspect (Skogan and Antunes, 1979).

Studies from the 1970s and 1980s consistently show that if clues pointing to specific suspects were not provided by citizens to the first responding officers, then follow-up investigators had great difficulty solving the case (Greenwood, Petersilia, and Chaiken, 1977; Eck, 1983). As with response time, there are no studies that directly link investigation efforts to crime reductions. Nonetheless, it is possible that follow-up investigations may be important for imparting a sense of justice to citizens, even if they have few or no crime reduction effects. This conjecture also has not been studied.

It is important to note that most of the studies of criminal investigations were conducted in the 1970s and early 1980s and that they examined only a limited number of crime types, usually burglary and robbery. Detailed empirical examinations of the investigation of homicide, larcenies, auto theft, rape, and arson have not been conducted. Furthermore, there is little evidence showing whether technological advances in investigation (computer data bases, automatic fingerprint systems, and DNA analysis, for example) have improved investigative performance. A recent mail survey of investigative practices in police agencies suggests that the impact of these advances is limited. Horvath et al. (2001:5) conclude that "in many fundamental respects, the police criminal investigation process has remained relatively unaffected by the significant changes that have occurred in policing, the crime problem and technology in the past thirty years." The limited amount of research covering a variety of crimes and taking into account recent technological changes makes it difficult to draw firm conclusions about current investigative effectiveness.

Generally Applied Intensive Enforcement and Arrests

Tough law enforcement strategies have long been a staple of police crime-fighting. We review three broad areas of intensive enforcement within the standard model: disorder policing, generalized field interrogations and traffic enforcement, and mandatory and preferred arrest policies in domestic violence.

Disorder Policing

The intensive model of enforcement applied broadly to incivilities and other types of disorder has been described recently as broken-windows policing (Kelling and Coles, 1996; Kelling and Sousa, 2001) or zero tolerance policing (Cordner, 1998; Dennis and Mallon, 1998; Bowling, 1999; Manning, 2001). These approaches share the premise of having the police enforce laws and ordinances against such minor offenses as littering, panhandling, prostitution, and other behaviors generally grouped under the terms "incivilities" or "public disorders." These approaches have drawn justification from academic research that suggests a strong link between less serious crime and disorder and more serious crime and decay in American communities (Wilson and Kelling, 1982; Skogan, 1990). While the link between disorder and more serious crime has recently been challenged (Taylor, 2001), even the critics of this approach recognize that disorder should be an important focus of community crime control.

There is a widespread perception among police policy makers and the public that enforcement strategies (primarily arrest) applied broadly against offenders committing minor offenses lead to reductions in serious crime. Research does not provide strong support for this proposition. Albert J. Reiss, Jr., carried out one of the earliest studies of disorder-focused policing in the central business district of Oakland, California (Reiss, 1985). Using foot and horse patrols, the police began to enforce order maintenance regulations, and general crime statistics suggested drops in a series of crimes from theft to rape and robbery. However, the Oakland study included many elements of problem-oriented policing and was not simply aggressive enforcement of minor offenses.

Studies reported by Skogan (1990, 1992) suggest mixed results for broadly based intensive enforcement strategies. Looking at programs in seven cities, Skogan (1992) found that intensive enforcement overall increased social disorder. However, intensive enforcement in one neighborhood in Newark, New Jersey, was found to decrease social disorder (Skogan, 1990). It is important to note that intensive enforcement in the Newark program included a number of different elements, from street sweeps to random checks to road blocks, and a central component was foot patrol, which is often seen as an essential element of community policing.

In the late 1990s, the role of intensive enforcement strategies in reducing crime became particularly contentious. Crime statistics in New York City, in particular, have been used as evidence for the effectiveness of this approach (Karmen, 2000; Harcourt, 2001). During the period when New York City implemented an aggressive disorder enforcement policy, there were strong drops in the crime rates. The overall rate of felony complaints, for example, fell some 44 percent between 1993 and 1997 (Greene, 1999). Homicides declined more than 60 percent in this same period, a result that led many policy makers and some scholars to see the New York approach to policing as the most dramatic and important innovation of the last decade (DiIulio, 1995; Kelling and Coles, 1996; Bratton, 1998a; Silverman, 1999).

In the committee's view, these data do not provide a valid test of the effectiveness of generalized intensive enforcement on crime. First, the general program of intensive enforcement was implemented in New York as part of a larger set of organizational changes. Those changes, implemented under the title of CompStat (Bratton, 1998a), led to a redefinition of the mission of the New York City Police Department, the structures of accountability used, and the methods for allocating police resources to control crime (Silverman, 1999; Weisburd et al. 2003). While CompStat is generally assumed to have facilitated the implementation of generalized intensive enforcement approaches, its impact on policing is not isolated to this policing strategy alone.

Second, a number of observers have noted that other factors unrelated to police activities may have played an important role in the observed drop in crime. For example, a group of studies have shown that the decline in New York City's crack epidemic may explain a good part of observed changes in crime (see Blumstein, 1995; Bowling, 1999). Others have argued that crime was already falling before the implementation of intensive enforcement activities in New York, suggesting that the trend of declining crime rates was not the result of police reform efforts after 1993 (Eck and Maguire, 2000; Joanes, 2001). Finally, studies show that the changes in the homicide rate in New York during that period are not dissimilar from those found in surrounding states and in other large cities that did not implement aggressive enforcement policies for disorder during the same period (Eck and Maguire, 2000; Karmen, 2000).

A recent study of New York precincts, however, indicates a strong relationship between the rate of arrests for minor crimes and crime rates in precincts in New York (Kelling and Sousa, 2001). Using a multilevel research design, the authors provide one of the first indications of a direct link between a generalized program of intensive enforcement and declines in more serious crime. While the study uses an innovative modeling approach to estimate this effect, limitations in the data available raise questions regarding the validity of the results (Blumstein, 2000; Fagan et al., 2003). Moreover, in a review of the strategies employed in the New York City program, Kelling and Souza suggest that disorder policing was often applied selectively at the precinct level, focusing on specific areas or problems. In the committee's view, accordingly, intensive enforcement in New York was not necessarily implemented as a generalized strategy, but rather as a focused and specific approach, which was one of the goals of the city's management accountability process. We deal with this approach to policing later in the chapter.

Field Interrogations and Traffic Enforcement

A small group of studies support the position that field interrogations and aggressive traffic enforcement can reduce crime. However, the number of studies available and the generally lower quality of the research designs used do not allow for the development of strong conclusions regarding such approaches.

The strongest study available for evaluating the effectiveness of field interrogations was conducted by the Police Foundation in San Diego, CA, in the 1970s (Boydstun, 1975). Field interrogations involve the identification of suspicious citizen behavior and police intervention to stop and question those identified. The goal of the interview is not necessarily to arrest those stopped, but it can include information gathering and making police presence and willingness to intervene known to potential offenders. In the San Diego study, researchers tested the effects of the introduction or suspension of police stops in one police district using a strong equivalent time-series design. The study found that when field interrogations were introduced, there was a decrease in disorder crime. When field interrogations were suspended, disorder crime increased (Boydstun, 1975). Whittaker et al. (1985) report similar findings in a nonexperimental study of crime in 60 neighborhoods in Tampa, FL; St. Louis, MO; and Rochester, NY.

Researchers have also investigated the effects of field interrogations by examining variations in the intensity of traffic enforcement. One early nonexperimental study, for example, by the Urban Institute (Wilson and Boland, 1979) found that cities with high levels of traffic citations had lower levels of robberies than those with lower levels. One problem with this study is that one cannot establish a direct causal link between crime levels and traffic tickets. In another study, Sampson and Cohen (1988) found that communities with higher numbers of arrests for driving under the influence of alcohol and disorderly conduct had lower rates of robbery. Again, the causal link between enforcement and crime is uncertain. In a more direct investigation of the relationship between traffic stops and crime, Weiss and Freels (1996) compared a treatment area in which traffic stops were increased with a matched control area. They found no significant differences in reported crime for the two areas.

Generalized Arrest Strategies Applied to Domestic Violence

Mandatory arrest in misdemeanor cases of domestic violence is now required by law in many states. Consistent with the standard model of policing, these laws apply to all cities in a state, in all areas of the cities, for all kinds of offenders and situations. Some research on mandatory arrest for domestic violence suggests that the effects of arrest vary by city (Schmidt and Sherman, 1993), while others find that effects vary by neighborhood and offender characteristics but not by city (Maxwell et al., 2001). These experiments, funded by the Department of Justice, replaced police officer discretion at the scene of the incident by assigning them, prior to arrival at the scene, to the randomized treatment of arrest, separation, or mediation.

Main effects analysis by Schmidt and Sherman (1993) of randomized experiments in six different cities compared repeat offending rates after arrest with no arrest when suspects were still present when police arrived. This analysis found deterrent effects of arrest in three cities and no effect of arrest in three other cities. In Minneapolis, MN (Berk and Sherman, 1984a, 1984b); Miami-Dade County, FL (Pate, Hamilton, and Annan, 1991); and Colorado Springs, CO (Berk et al., 1992), arrest was reported to have a deterrent effect across most measures of repeat offending. In Omaha, NE (Dunford et al., 1990); Charlotte, NC (Hirschel and Hutchinson, 1992); and Milwaukee, WI (Sherman et al., 1991), arrest had no effect on repeat offending across most measures. A seventh experiment in Omaha (Dunford et al., 1990) focused on suspects who leave the scene before police arrive, which includes about 40 percent of domestic violence incidents reported to police in big cities. That study found a deterrent effect of issuing an arrest warrant (but not finding or apprehending the suspect) in the same city in which in-custody arrest had no effect on repeat violence.

Other analyses of these data have attempted to determine the overall effect of arrest across these experiments. A more recent analysis aggregated selected cases across five of the randomized trials. Despite major cross-site differences in response rates to victim surveys, methods of recording official data, and deviations from the random assignment of cases, this review concluded that there is on average a small but significant deterrent effect (Maxwell, Garner, and Fagan, 2001).

COMMUNITY-ORIENTED POLICING

Proposition 2: Over the past two decades there has been a major investment on the part of the police and the public in community policing. Because community policing involves so many different tactics, its effect as a general strategy cannot be directly evaluated. Some community policing strategies appear to reduce crime, disorder, or fear of crime. Many others have not been found to be effective when evaluated.

Community policing is extremely difficult to define, and its definition has varied over time and among police agencies (Green and Mastrofski,

1988; Eck and Rosenbaum, 1994). However, one of the principal assumptions of community policing is that the police can draw from a much broader array of resources than is found in the traditional law enforcement powers of the police. For example, most scholars agree that community policing should entail greater community involvement in the definition of crime problems and in police activities to prevent and control crime (Skolnick and Bayley, 1986; Goldstein, 1990). Yet in terms of strategies and tactics this broad rubric includes as much as it excludes: police agencies responding to surveys have listed an enormous variety of programs (Bayley and Worden, 1996; Maguire et al., 1997). Some scholars argue that community policing also demands decentralization of police agencies, and greater emphasis on the autonomy and tasks of street-level police officers (Skolnick and Bayley, 1986). Problem-oriented policing is often considered one of the core elements of community policing, and accordingly some of our discussion below in Proposition 4 relates to programs that were initiated or developed in the context of a community policing initiative. We have for analytic purposes separated them in this report; however, we think it important to recognize the complex ways in which police strategies are implemented and developed.

Police practices associated with community policing have been particularly broad, and the strategies associated with community policing have sometimes changed over time. Foot patrol, for example, was considered an important element of community policing in the 1980s, but it has not been a core component of more recent community policing programs. Consequently, it is often difficult to determine if researchers studying community policing in different agencies at different times are studying the same phenomena. When this fact is coupled with variations in research design, measurement, and statistical analysis, it is very difficult to draw definitive conclusions regarding the crime control effectiveness of community policing.

In the view of the committee, community policing may be seen as reaction to the standard models of policing. It demands recognition of the community context of policing and suggests that the activities and strategies of the police must be fit to the special needs and circumstances of local communities (Weisburd and McElroy, 1988). Moreover, community policing departs from the standard models of policing on another important dimension. While the standard model of policing has relied primarily on the resources of the police and its traditional law enforcement powers, community policing suggests a reliance on a more community-based crime control that draws not only on the resources of the police but also on the resources of the public.

Community policing programs, such as neighborhood watch, general foot patrol, storefront offices, and community meetings have not been found to reduce crime, although storefront offices and community meetings may influence perceptions of disorder. Door to door visits, however, have been found to reduce both crime and disorder. In a review of the effectiveness of community policing initiatives, Sherman (1997) broke community policing down into distinct strategies and summarized the evidence about the crime reduction effects of each. He concludes that neither neighborhood watch nor community organizing more generally reduces crime. On average the studies reviewed do not show statistically significant crime reductions. However, poorer and more disadvantaged neighborhoods in which such programs would appear to be most needed appeared to benefit the least from them (Rosenbaum, 1989).

Other widely used strategies in community policing are based on improving the information exchange between the police and the public. Studies do not support the view that community meetings (Wycoff and Skogan, 1993), storefront offices (Skogan, 1990; Uchida et al., 1992), or newsletters (Pate et al., 1989), which are generally believed to increase such information exchange, reduce crime, though Skogan et al. (1995) found that such tactics reduce community perceptions of disorder. Door to door visits have been found to reduce both crime (see Sherman, 1997) and disorder (Skogan, 1992). However, simply providing information about crime to the public does not have crime prevention benefits (Sherman, 1997).

As noted above, foot patrol was an important component of early community policing efforts and it is a common policing tactic. In 1999, local police departments that routinely used foot patrol employed about three-fourths of all officers in the United States (BJS, 1999). An early uncontrolled evaluation of foot patrol in Flint, MI, concluded that foot patrol reduced reported crime (Trojanowicz, 1986). Bower and Hirsch (1987), however, found no discernable reduction in crime or disorder due to foot patrols in Boston, MA. A more rigorous evaluation of foot patrol in Newark, NJ, found that it did not reduce criminal victimizations (Police Foundation, 1981). Nonetheless, the same study found that foot patrol reduced residents' fear of crime.

There is also evidence that community policing lowers the community's level of fear when programs are focused on increasing community-police interaction. Community policing strategies are expected to influence fear of crime by making the police an easily accessible and more visible presence, or reducing the sense of physical, social, and psychological distance between ordinary citizens and police officers, or both (Wycoff and Skogan, 1986). The Police Foundation conducted many of the studies examining community policing strategies and fear of crime; these studies tend to have similar designs and are conducted in a small group of cities. The cities involved include Baltimore, MD (Pate and Annan, 1989); Houston, TX (Wycoff and Skogan, 1986); Newark, NJ (Pate and Skogan, 1985); and Madison, WI (Wycoff and Skogan 1993). The research designs usually involved a cross-sectional or panel study of survey data evaluating fear of crime among individuals in neighborhoods in which a particular policing strategy had been implemented, comparing these with neighborhoods not experiencing the innovation.

Although the results of the Police Foundation studies are mixed, two general patterns appear. First, studies show that policing strategies characterized by more direct involvement of police and citizens, such as citizen contract patrol, police community stations, and coordinated community policing, often have the predicted negative effect on fear of crime among individuals and on individual level of concern about crime in the neighborhood (Pate and Skogan, 1985; Wycoff and Skogan, 1986). Although these results were found in different studies and in different cities, they are not necessarily uniform across all groups. For example, Brown and Wycoff (1987) found that fear among black residents and renters was not reduced in view of the presence of citizen contact patrols or community stations.

An aspect of community policing that has only recently received systematic research attention concerns the influences of police officer behavior toward citizens, thus shaping the behavior of citizens. Citizen noncompliance with requests from police officers can be considered a form of disorder. Does officer demeanor influence citizen compliance? Based on systematic observations of police-citizen encounters in Richmond, VA, Mastrofski, Snipes, and Supina (1996) studied whether officer treatment of citizens influenced their compliance with officer requests. Controlling for other relevant situational characteristics, they found that when officers were disrespectful toward citizens, citizens were less likely to comply with their requests. In a related study, based on observations of police-citizen encounters in St. Petersburg, FL, and Indianapolis, IN, McCluskey, Mastrofski, and Parks (1999) also found that officers' disrespect resulted in less citizen compliance. However, in this larger study, the researchers found that officers who were respectful were more likely to obtain compliance with their requests, controlling for other factors about the situation.

FOCUSED POLICING EFFORTS

Proposition 3: There has been increasing interest over the past two decades in police practices that target very specific types of crimes, criminals, and crime places. In particular, policing crime hot spots has become a common police strategy for reducing crime and disorder problems. While there is only preliminary evidence suggesting the effectiveness of targeting specific types of offenders, a strong body of evidence suggests that taking a focused geographic approach to crime problems can increase the effectiveness of policing.

While the standard model of policing suggested that police activities should be spread in a highly uniform pattern across urban communities and applied uniformly across the individuals subject to police attention, a growing number of police practices focus on allocating police resources in a focused way. One of the most important changes in American policing over the last decade has been the emergence of a geographic focus to police efforts to control crime. A series of national surveys suggests that police in the United States are not only developing the technological capabilities to examine the geographic distribution of crime, but that they are also using those technologies to focus their efforts on very specific places where crime is most strongly concentrated (Weisburd, 2002). For example, a National Institute of Justice survey of police departments conducted in 1998 suggests that 36 percent of police agencies with more than 100 sworn officers have the capability to produce computerized maps of crime (Mamalian and LaVigne, 1999). In a more recent Police Foundation study, more than 7 in 10 departments with more than 100 sworn officers reported using crime-mapping to identify crime hot spots (Weisburd, Greenspan, and Mastrofski, 2001).

There has, in turn, been long-standing interest in the possible crime control benefits of targeting specific types of offenders in the criminal justice system (National Research Council, 1986). For example, it is often assumed that targeting the most active offenders will lead to significant crime reduction (Spelman, 1990; National Research Council, 1986). It has also been suggested that the social and economic characteristics of offenders may influence their responses to criminal justice sanctions.

We review research in four specific areas: (1) police crackdowns, (2) hot-spots policing, (3) focus on repeat offenders, and (4) mandatory arrest for domestic violence.

Police Crackdowns

While the focusing of police resources on specific areas is often seen as a part of a recent innovation in policing, there is a long history of police practices that target particularly troublesome locations or problems. Such tactics can be distinguished from more recent hot-spots policing approaches (described below) in that they were usually focused on one or a small number of targets and did not represent a more general strategy for dealing with crime problems.

Police crackdowns have been found to have short-term benefits in reducing crime and disorder. Reviewing 18 case studies, Sherman (1990) found strong evidence that crackdowns produce initial deterrence. This is not to say that research evidence is uniformly in support of this proposition. Some studies report contrary findings (see, e.g., Annan and Skogan, 1993;

Barber, 1969; Kleiman, 1988; Sviridorf et al., 1992). However, when crack-downs are tightly focused, evidence suggests that immediate crime preven-tion benefits are likely. This does not mean, however, that such crackdown strategies are likely to lead to long-term effects on crime or disorder. The case studies examined by Sherman suggest that the deterrent effects of crack-downs, even those that are extended, are likely to decay rapidly over time.

Sherman (1990) also reports that crackdowns did not lead to spatial displacement of crime to nearby areas in the majority of studies he reviewed. This absence of spatial displacement is consistent with more general re-views of the displacement research. Spatial displacement in response to tar-geted crime prevention efforts has not been found to be common, and when it occurs it is less than the overall crime reduction effect (Cornish and Clarke, 1986; Barr and Pease, 1990; Eck, 1993; Clarke and Weisburd, 1994; Hesseling, 1994).

Hot-Spots Policing

Although there is a long history of efforts to focus police patrols (Gay, Schell, and Schack, 1977; Wilson, 1967), the emergence of what is often termed hot-spots policing is generally traced to theoretical, empirical, and technological innovation in the 1980s and 1990s (Weisburd and Braga, 2003; Braga et al., 2001; Sherman and Weisburd, 1995). The theoretical underpinnings of this approach can be found in the development of prob-lem-oriented approaches to policing (Goldstein, 1990) and the more gen-eral situational crime prevention perspective that emerged in England (Clarke, 1992a), as well as in the routine activities approach to crime pat-terns (Cohen and Felson, 1979). In each of these approaches, the place where crime occurs is often a central factor (Eck and Weisburd, 1995; Har-ries, 1999; Weisburd, 2002). Because hot-spots policing programs often include elements of problem solving, we also discuss hot-spots programs in that context under Proposition 4 below. In this section we confine our dis-cussion to police effectiveness when using a specifically geographic focus.

The empirical grounding for the hot-spots approach was laid in a series of studies that documented the high concentration of crime in discrete places, like street corners, specific addresses, street blocks, or small clusters of addresses and street blocks (Pierce, Spaar, and Briggs, 1988; Sherman, Gartin, and Buerger, 1989. Weisburd, Maher, and Sherman, 1992; Weis-burd and Green, 1995a; Spelman, 1995; Swartz, 2000). These studies showed that crime is concentrated in specific places in the urban landscape and is not spread evenly in wide areas or neighborhoods. Indeed, it ap-peared that even in neighborhoods that were seen as crime prone, there were many places free of crime events as measured by official police data, and in areas considered to be "good" neighborhoods there were often crime hot spots (Weisburd and Green, 1994). The policy conclusion developed from this work was that the police could be more effective if they focused their resources on hot spots of crime (Sherman and Weisburd, 1995).

While the emergence of hot-spots approaches in American police agencies can be traced to theoretical and empirical contributions, it is unlikely that such strategies would have been widely implemented had there not been important innovation in the technologies available to the police. The development of desk crime-mapping programs made it practical for police agencies to begin to develop geographic understandings of crime in their cities (Weisburd and McKewen, 1998).

A series of randomized field trials shows that policing that is focused on hot spots can result in meaningful reductions in crime and disorder.[1] The first major application of a hot-spots approach in policing, the Repeat Call Policing (RECAP) experiment (Sherman, 1990; Buerger, 1994), did not lead to encouraging findings. In a randomized experiment involving 500 commercial and residential addresses with the highest frequency of citizen calls for service in Minneapolis, no significant differences were found between control and experimental locations. However, investigators reported a number of threats to the integrity of the study. In particular, the study intended to apply problem-solving strategies at each experimental location, but the large caseload for the unit responsible for implementing the study made it impossible to apply problem solving with sufficient depth (Buerger, Cohen, and Petrosino, 1995).

While this early application of the hot-spots approach did not provide promising results, six subsequent studies with strong experimental designs suggested that hot-spots policing was effective in responding to crime and disorder problems. The first of these, the Minneapolis Hot Spots Patrol Experiment (Sherman and Weisburd, 1995), used crime-mapping of crime calls to identify 110 general crime hot spots, roughly of street block length. These hot spots showed stability in crime trends over time and were not geographically contiguous with one another. The hot spots were then randomly assigned to experimental and control locations within statistical blocks (determined by crime activity level). Police patrol was doubled on average for the experimental sites over a 10-month period. The study found that the experimental compared with the control hot spots experienced statistically significant reductions in crime calls. These differences were of moderate size and were largest when disorder-related calls were examined. Systematic observations of crime and disorder also produced findings of significant reductions in the experimental compared with the control hot spots.

---

[1]This section draws strongly from a review of hot-spots policing conducted for the Campbell collaboration by Anthony A. Braga (2001).

In another randomized experiment, the Kansas City Crack House Raids Experiment (Sherman and Rogan, 1995a), crackdowns on drug locations were also found to lead to significant relative improvement in the experimental sites, although the effects (measured by citizen calls and offense reports) were modest and decayed in a short period. In yet another randomized trial, however, Eck and Wartell (1996) found that if the raids were immediately followed by police contacts with landlords, crime prevention benefits could be reinforced and would be sustained for long periods of time.

More general crime and disorder effects are reported in two randomized experiments that take a more tailored problem-oriented approach to hot-spots policing (see the next section for a more detailed discussion of problem-oriented policing approaches). In the Jersey City Problem Oriented Policing in Violent Crime Places study (Braga et al., 1999), strong and statistically significant differences were found for total crime calls and crime incidents between the experimental and the control sites. Importantly, all crime categories experienced reductions, and observational data revealed statistically significant declines in social disorder as well. In the Jersey City Drug Hot Spots Experiment (Weisburd and Green, 1995a), hot-spots-specific tactics were found to be more effective at reducing disorder at drug places than was generalized enforcement. However, in this drug hot-spots experiment, the tailored approaches to drug control had no significant impact on violent crime. Problem-solving interventions were implemented at the experimental sites in both of these experiments, although it is important to note that, in practice, aggressive disorder enforcement tactics were often the central strategy for the units assigned to carry out treatment. Green-Mazzerole and Rohl (1998) also found strong reductions in crime and disorder in an experimental evaluation of civil remedy interventions at drug-involved locations.

These experimental findings are supported by a small group of non-experimental research studies. For example, Hope (1994) compared total calls for service in three hot-spots locations in which problem solving was applied with addresses proximate to the treated locations as well as those on other blocks in surrounding areas. Problem solving in this study, as in the Jersey City studies, relied primarily on traditional enforcement tactics. Significant crime reductions were reported. The Kansas City Gun Project (Sherman and Rogan, 1995b) also suggests strong crime control benefits for hot-spots approaches. Using intensive enforcement in an 8 × 10 block area, including traffic stops and searches, researchers found a 65 percent increase in guns seized and a 49 percent decrease in gun crimes compared with a matched control area.

While there is strong evidence that focusing on hot spots reduces crime and disorder, research has not yet distinguished the types of strategies that lead to the strongest prevention benefits (Braga, 2001). The studies reviewed above suggest that the most generalized strategies, for example preventive patrol (Sherman and Weisburd, 1995) and drug raids (Sherman and Rogan, 1995a), are likely to have less impact than approaches that include more problem-solving elements, such as working with landlords (Eck and Wartell, 1996; Green-Mazzerole and Rohl, 1998). However, more work with a much larger number of studies is required to define the types of strategies that work best in what circumstances using hot-spots approaches.

Our review suggests that there is strong empirical support for the hot-spots policing approach. However, we have so far discussed only the effects of hot-spots strategies on the places that are the focus of police interventions. Such approaches would be much less useful if they simply displaced crime to other nearby places. While measurement of crime displacement is complex and a matter of debate (see, e.g., Weisburd and Green, 1995b), a number of studies reported above examined geographic displacement, often in terms of the areas immediately proximate to the treated areas. For example, in the Jersey City Drug Market Analysis Experiment (Weisburd and Green, 1995a), two block displacement areas around each experimental location were examined. No significant displacement of crime or disorder calls was found. Importantly, however, the investigators found that drug-related and public morals calls actually declined in the displacement areas. This "diffusion of crime control benefits" (Clarke and Weisburd, 1994) was also reported in the Problem Oriented Policing in Violent Crime Places experiment (Braga et al., 1999), the Beat Health study (Green-Mazzerole and Rohl, 1998), and the Kansas City Gun Project (Sherman and Rogan, 1995b). In each of these studies, no displacement of crime was reported, and some improvement in the surrounding areas was found. Only Hope (1994) reports direct displacement of crime, although this occurred only in the area immediate to the treated locations, and the displacement effect was much smaller overall than the crime prevention effect.

Focusing on Specific Types of Offenders

A number of scholars have suggested that policies directed at specific types of offenders will be more effective than generalized enforcement strategies described earlier under Proposition 1 (Farrington, Ohlin, and Wilson, 1986). "Types" of offender generally refers not to the specific offense, but to the social or demographic characteristics of the offender. This approach has not been directly examined with respect to police interventions, primarily because it raises significant questions regarding the fair application of police powers. Indeed, recent concern with police profiling of minority offenders in such areas as drug enforcement has raised significant constitutional questions and has led to strong community concern that the police not target specific individuals simply because of their racial or ethnic backgrounds (Harris, 2002, 1999, 1997). Of course, police have always profiled individuals who they believe are suspicious, and such profiling is a well-known part of police culture. Nonetheless, only recently has profiling become an important focus of police research.

One area in which the targeting of specific offenders has been studied by police scholars is in what are often termed "repeat offender" programs. Here, the criteria for focused police intervention are not related to the social or demographic characteristics of offenders, but rather to their criminal records. Police have demonstrated substantial ability to apprehend known repeat offenders. Randomized controlled trials in Washington, DC (Martin and Sherman, 1986), and in Phoenix, AZ (Abrahamse et al., 1991), of repeat offender units found that covert investigation of high-risk, previously convicted offenders has a high yield in arrests and incarceration per officer hour, relative to other investments of police resources. Thus, it appears that investigation effectiveness is enhanced to the degree that it focuses on a relatively few high-rate offenders rather than spreading resources over a large number of crimes with few clues. It is important to note, however, that these evaluations have examined the apprehension effectiveness of repeat offender programs. These are only indirect examinations of their effect on reducing crime, and conclusions about their crime reduction effectiveness rely on ancillary assumptions about the effectiveness of selective incarceration and incapacitation.

A recent and promising application of the repeat offender approach was developed in the Boston Ceasefire project. In this instance, the problem was the high level of firearm related killings of black youth. Extensive analysis led to a multiagency and community project designed to communicate directly to youth gangs that firearm violence would not be tolerated (Kennedy, Braga, and Piehl, 1997). This is sometimes referred to as the "pulling levers" strategy (Kennedy 1997). A time-series analysis of young adult and youth homicide indicated a 63 percent reduction in these killings as well as declines in other gun related events (Kennedy et al., 2001). Statistical controls were used to control for citywide violence trends, employment, and the number of youth in the population. Comparisons with other large cities during the same time were used to control for national trends. Although other cities have implemented similar pulling-levers projects, the results are descriptive rather than evaluative.

Another method for identifying and apprehending repeat offenders are "anti-fencing" or property sting operations. These typically involved undercover police posing as receivers of stolen goods (Pennell, 1979; Criminal Conspiracies Division, 1979; Weiner, Chelst and Hart, 1984). Did these programs apprehend repeat offenders? And did this result in reductions in property crime? Although a number of evaluations were conducted of these operations, most employed weak research designs, thus making it difficult to provide definitive answers to these questions. There seems to be a consensus among the evaluations that antifencing operations of this type do apprehend more older and criminally active offenders than are arrested in more traditional law enforcement practices (Criminal Conspiracies Division, 1979; Pennell, 1979; Weiner et al., 1983). However, as noted, the empirical support for this consensus is weak.

Evidence that the effect of arrest policies varies according to the social and demographic characteristics of offenders is drawn from nonexperimental reanalyses of the domestic violence experiments discussed earlier under Proposition 1. In Milwaukee, WI, and Omaha, NE (Sherman and Smith, 1992), as well as Miami-Dade County, FL (Pate, Hamilton, and Annan, 1991) and Colorado Springs, CO (Berk et al., 1992), arrest effects varied with the employment status of the suspect. In all four correlational tests for interaction in the randomized experiments, suspects who were employed at baseline (the time of random assignment) were more deterred by arrest than unemployed suspects. In three of the cities (Milwaukee, Omaha, and Miami-Dade), the unemployed suspects became substantially more likely to reoffend during the follow-up period if they were arrested than if they were merely warned. Marciniak (1994) found the same interaction effect across neighborhoods in Milwaukee, where arrest had deterrent effects in areas of low unemployment but increased repeat domestic violence in areas of medium to high unemployment.

However, Garner and Maxwell (2000), in an examination of victimization interviews, found that combining either employment or marriage with arrest did not reduce significantly the quantity of victimization any more than did arrest by itself. Therefore, these results call into question the validity of the stakes in conformity theses. They suggest that the results reported earlier using the official data may in large part reflect victims' willingness to report the incidents and the police officer's willingness to record the incident. In other words, victims may be less willing to call the police and, if they do call, the police may also be less willing to record the incident when the suspect is employed. They both may independently choose to do this because they both understand the negative consequences that arrest may have on continued employment.

Overall, these studies suggest that there may be an important interaction between the nature of offenders and the effects of police practices. Nonetheless, the committee notes that even if this relationship were to be confirmed directly through experimental research, it is unlikely that it would lead to significant policy changes in policing since larger constitutional questions remain. It is unlikely that any jurisdiction would be able to vary police arrest practices according to the social and demographic characteristics of individual citizens. Although it may be more acceptable to vary such practices across jurisdictions with differing types of populations, important questions regarding fairness and constitutionality are likely to arise. With these caveats in mind, findings in these studies do provide a more textured understanding of the effects of arrest policies.

PROBLEM-ORIENTED POLICING

Proposition 4: Problem-oriented policing emerged in the 1990s as a central police strategy for solving crime and disorder problems. There is a growing body of research evidence that problem-oriented policing is an effective approach.

As we have already noted, the standard model of policing came under increasing criticism in the 1970s and 1980s (see, e.g., Goldstein, 1979; Visher and Weisburd, 1998). Herman Goldstein proposed one response to the standard model in 1979, calling it "problem-oriented policing." Goldstein stated that police were focusing so much attention on internal management concerns and standard law enforcement that they had largely ignored the objectives, or ends, of policing. His proposal challenged the one size fits all approach of standard models of policing, replacing it with an approach focused on specific problems, and looked to the development of tailor-made police practices to address such problems. Importantly, his approach also demanded that the police focus more attention on the ends of policing. In the standard model, the necessity of providing a common type of service across broad areas or problems naturally led police to a concern with monitoring whether that service was actually being delivered. In this process, the goals of policing were often given a secondary place in police management. In the problem-oriented model, the results of policing are placed very much at the center of police efforts.

In the problem-oriented policing model, police are expected to undertake systematic analysis of community problems, engage in broad searches for effective solutions, and evaluate the results of their efforts. Problems are patterns of events that members of the public expect the police to address. Problems have both a behavioral and an environmental component (Eck and Clarke, 2003). The behavioral component describes how the motives of the parties involved (offenders, victims, and third parties) and the parties interact. The environmental component defines the type of place in which the problem is located. Consequently, problems are highly specific. In a problem-oriented approach, law enforcement is one of many possible means for reducing problems, and this tactic will vary in appropriateness, depending on the specific characteristics of each problem. Examples of problems include thefts from vehicles in downtown parking lots, aggressive panhandling in commercial areas, robberies of gas stations, speeding in residential neighborhoods, and club drug use at teen-oriented entertainment businesses.

We have already noted in Proposition 2 that there is often overlap between community-oriented and problem-oriented policing, in the sense that both approaches expand the police function beyond the traditional law enforcement powers of the police. In addition, we have also noted the overlap in Proposition 3 between focused policing and problem solving. Problem-oriented policing extends focused policing beyond geography or specific offenders to include the analysis of community problems. In this sense, problem-oriented policing includes elements of both trends in policing innovation that we reviewed above.

Problem-oriented policing was originally directed at department-wide analysis of persistent problems. Police agencies expanded the scope of problem-oriented policing to include beat-level problem-solving efforts by patrol officers and detectives as part of their normal duties (Cordner, 1986; Eck and Spelman, 1987). This aspect of problem-oriented policing has received the most attention in police research. Furthermore, various forms of beat-level problem solving have been incorporated into community policing programs.

Problem-oriented policing refers to the overall organizational direction of a police agency that focuses its efforts on addressing problems (Goldstein, 1990). In this context, a problem is a recurring set of related harmful events in a community that members of the public expect the police to address (Eck and Spelman, 1987; Goldstein, 1990). Problem solving per se refers to the actual handling of a specific problem. Problem solving can be employed by any agency on an ad hoc basis, whether that agency adopts a comprehensive organization-wide problem-oriented policing approach or not. Consequently, far more agencies employ problem solving than might be defined as problem-oriented.

In some ways, problem-oriented policing is untestable. The claim that policing should direct its attention to problems is a normative proposition. One could argue that policing should focus solely on emergency response, or should focus solely on law enforcement. No amount of evidence could test either of these assertions. If one accepts that the police should focus on problems, it is hard to argue against systematic and empirical analysis of problems before selecting the intervention that best fits the data. In essence, a problem-oriented approach calls for the application of the scientific method to policing. Nevertheless, it is important to answer two questions: Does the application of problem solving actually reduce problems? Is this application more effective than other police activities?

Research is consistently supportive of the capability of problem solving to reduce crime and disorder. However, as in other areas of our review, we raise the caution that many studies to date have used relatively weak research designs. There are a number of quasi-experiments going back to the mid-1980s that consistently demonstrate that problem solving can reduce violent and property crime (Eck and Spelman, 1987), firearm-related youth homicide (Kennedy et al., 2001), fear of crime (Cordner, 1986), and various forms of disorder, including prostitution and drug dealing (Eck and Spelman, 1987; Hope, 1994; Capowich and Roehl, 1994). For example, a quasi-experiment in Jersey City, NJ, public housing complexes (Mazerolle et al., 2000) found that police problem-solving activities caused measurable declines in reported violence and property crime, although the results varied across the six housing complexes studied. In another example, Clarke and Goldstein (2002) report a reduction in thefts of appliances from new home construction sites following careful analysis of this problem by the Charlotte-Mecklenburg, NC, Police Department and the implementation of changes in building practices by construction firms.

The two experimental evaluations of applications of problem solving in hot spots, reviewed above, also suggest its effectiveness in reducing crime and disorder. In a randomized trial with Jersey City violent crime hot spots, Braga et al. (1999) report reductions in property and violent crime in the treatment locations. While this study tested problem-oriented approaches, it is important to note that focused police attention was brought only to the experimental locations. Accordingly, it is difficult to distinguish between the effects of bringing focused attention to hot spots and that of such focused efforts being developed using a problem-oriented approach. In the Jersey City Drug Market Analysis Experiment (Weisburd and Green, 1995a), more direct support can be found for the application of problem-solving approaches as opposed to standard models of policing. In that study, a similar number of narcotics detectives was assigned to treatment and control hot spots. However, Weisburd and Green compared the effectiveness of unsystematic, arrest-oriented enforcement based on ad hoc target selection (the control group) with a treatment strategy involving analysis of assigned drug hot spots, followed by site-specific enforcement and collaboration with landlords and local government regulatory agencies, and concluding with monitoring and maintenance for up to a week following the intervention. Compared with the control drug hot spots, the treatment drug hot spots fared better with regard to disorder, but there were no significant differences between the two groups with regard to violent crime.

Evidence of the effectiveness of situational and opportunity-blocking strategies, while not necessarily police based, provides indirect evidence supporting the effectiveness of problem solving in reducing crime and disorder. Problem-oriented policing has been linked to routine activity, rational choice perspectives, and situational crime prevention (Eck and Spelman, 1987; Clarke, 1992b). Recent review of prevention programs designed to block crime and disorder opportunities in small places noted that most of the studies report reductions in target crime and disorder events (Eck, 1997; Poyner, 1981; Weisburd, 1996). Furthermore, many of these efforts were the results of police problem-solving efforts. We note that many of the studies reviewed employed relatively weak designs (Clarke, 1997; Eck, 1997; Weisburd, 1997).

One example of a methodologically strong investigation into the way in which the actions of the public can influence the effectiveness of police is research on the deterrent effects of Lojack, a hidden radio-transmitter device used for retrieving stolen vehicles (Ayers and Levitt, 1998). The authors found an association between increases in the fraction of Lojack-equipped vehicles—an unobservable victim precaution—and a substantial decline in auto theft, without any displacement of crime to other crime categories. They estimate the marginal social benefit of Lojack installation at 15 times greater than its social cost, concluding that Lojack affects auto theft even at low market penetration rates (p. 74). This is a quasi-experimental study with very high internal validity, used in a situation in which a randomized experiment would be impossible because the crime reduction benefits accrue to the metropolitan area, not the individual users of Lojack. Furthermore, it has a very high level of generalizability.

CONCLUSION

We have reviewed the literature of research on the effectiveness of police practices in controlling crime, disorder and fear in the context of four broad propositions:

Proposition 1: The standard model of policing has relied on the uniform provision of police resources intended to prevent crime and disorder across a wide array of crimes and across all parts of the jurisdictions that police serve. Despite the continued reliance of many police agencies on these standard practices, the evidence the committee reviewed suggests that such approaches are generally not the most effective strategy for controlling crime and disorder or reducing fear of crime.

Proposition 2: Over the past two decades there has been a major investment on the part of the police and the public in community policing. Because community policing involves so many different tactics, its effect as a general strategy cannot be directly evaluated. Some community policing strategies appear to reduce crime, disorder, or fear of crime. Many others have not been found to be effective when evaluated.

Proposition 3: There has been increasing interest over the past two decades in police practices that target very specific types of crimes, criminals, and crime places. In particular, policing crime hot spots has become a common police strategy for reducing crime and disorder problems. A strong body of evidence suggests that taking a focused geographic approach to crime problems can increase the effectiveness of policing. There is no consistent evidence regarding the targeting of specific types of offenders.

Proposition 4: Problem-oriented policing emerged in the 1990s as a central police strategy for solving crime and disorder problems. There is a growing body of research evidence that problem-oriented policing is an effective approach.

It is important to note that there is much about police practice and its effectiveness that is still unknown. While our review documents a substantial amount of research over the past four decades, it also illustrates the fact that many established police practices have not been carefully evaluated. Even in the case of programs that have received broad national attention, such as community-oriented policing, there is often little research evidence about what works and under what circumstances. One reason for the lack of evidence is the complexity and ambiguity of police strategies. But even in the case of approaches that are more clearly defined, such as problem-oriented policing, our review suggests a need for more carefully designed studies.

It is also important to state again, as noted at the beginning of this chapter, that a century of criminological research has documented the powerful impact of a long list of social and economic factors on crime. These include some of the most fundamental aspects of our society. Their influence extends far beyond crime, and they are mainly beyond the reach of the police. A thoroughgoing research agenda on crime and policing would endeavor to identify the role of the police among these factors, but that question lies beyond the scope of this report.

To draw useful lessons from 20 years of police effectiveness research the committee had to organize these strategies in a meaningful way. Figure 6-1 depicts the relationships of four somewhat overlapping policing strategies. The figure has two dimensions. The first dimension represents the content of the practices employed. Strategies that rely primarily on traditional law enforcement are low on this dimension. Strategies that expand the "toolbox" of policing (see Taylor, 2001), whether in partnerships with the community or through the use such strategies as civil remedies, are high on this dimension. The second dimension represents the extent of focus or targeting of police activities. Strategies that are focused on specific places or that are tailor made to respond to specific types of problems, are high on

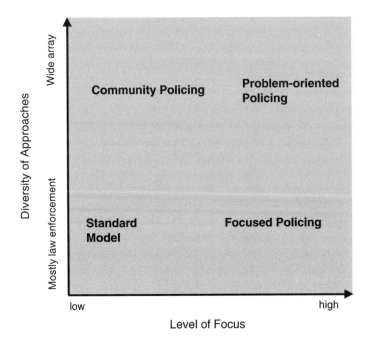

FIGURE 6-1 Dimensions of policing strategies.

this dimension. Strategies that are generalized and applied uniformly across places or offenders score low on this dimension. The four strategies are shown in their relative position. Although one can describe these strategies as clearly separable ideal types, in practice there are no clear boundaries among them. The committee has noted, for example, that community-oriented policing often incorporates elements of problem-oriented policing, and that problem-oriented policing and focused policing share important features.

The standard model provides a common set of services throughout a jurisdiction. Police agencies using the standard model employ a limited range of approaches, overwhelmingly oriented toward enforcement, and make relatively little use of institutions outside policing (with the notable exception of other parts of the criminal justice system). Community policing makes greater use of institutions outside policing, particularly community groups and private organizations. Although law enforcement powers still are an important tool of community-oriented policing agencies, such agencies can employ a greater range of tools to address crime and disorder. When community policing is employed without problem solving, it too provides a common set of services throughout a jurisdiction. The services provided by focused policing—generally incorporating hot spots and repeat offender strategies—vary considerably by geography or type of offender. Like the standard model, focused policing tends to rely almost exclusively on law enforcement. Unlike both the standard model and community policing, the application of police powers is tightly focused. Problem-oriented policing incorporates the precise resource targeting of focused policing with the diversity of approaches in community policing. So a problem-oriented policing agency selects from a wide variety of approaches to address very specific problems.

The committee used the framework depicted in Figure 6-1 to synthesize its findings. This synthesis is found in Table 6-1. It is the committee's judgment, based on our review, that the standard model of policing, represented in the lower left corner of the table, which draws on generally applied tactics and uses primarily the law enforcement powers of the police, has generally not been found to be effective either in reducing crime or disorder or

TABLE 6-1 Synthesis of the Committee's Findings on Police Effectiveness Research

Police Strategies That...	Are Unfocused	Are Focused
Apply a diverse array of approaches, including law enforcement sanctions.	**Little or no evidence of effectiveness** —Impersonal community policing, e.g., newsletters **Weak to moderate evidence** —Personal contacts in community policing —Respectful police-citizen contacts —Improving legitimacy of police —Foot patrols (fear reduction)	**Moderate evidence of effectiveness** —Problem-oriented policing **Strong evidence of effectiveness** —Problem solving in hot spots
Rely almost exclusively on law-enforcement sanctions.	**Little or no evidence of effectiveness** —Adding more police —General patrol —Rapid response —Follow-up investigations —Undifferentiated arrest for domestic violence	**Inconsistent or weak evidence of effectiveness** —Repeat offender investigations **Moderate to strong evidence of effectiveness** —Focused intensive enforcement —Hot-spots patrols

decreasing citizen fear. Whether the strategy examined was generalized preventive patrol, efforts to reduce response time to citizen calls, increases in numbers of police officers, or the introduction of generalized follow-up investigations or undifferentiated intensive enforcement activities, studies fail to show consistent or meaningful crime or disorder prevention benefits or evidence of reductions in citizen fear of crime. Given the widespread and continued use of the standard model of police practice in policing in the United States, these findings have significant policy implications.

In contrast to these findings, there is evidence of police effectiveness in each of the remaining cells of the table. In the cell that represents focused policing, we found promising evidence regarding the effects of arrest targeting specific types of people committing specific types of offenses. We found even stronger evidence regarding the use of traditional enforcement strategies that are targeted at specific places. Indeed, studies that focused police resources on crime hot spots provide the strongest collective evidence of police effectiveness that is now available. On the basis of a series of randomized experimental studies, we conclude that the practice described as hot-spots policing is effective in reducing crime and disorder and can achieve these reductions without significant displacement of crime control benefits. Indeed, the research evidence suggests that the diffusion of crime control benefits to areas surrounding treated hot spots is stronger than any displacement outcome.

The two remaining cells of the table indicate the promise of new directions for policing in the United States. The choice of police tactics is of course a normative concern that must be considered not only in relationship to what is effective but also to the effects it has on communities. The choice of police tactics must also be assessed in light of their economic cost to the community. In this context, it is often argued that the law enforcement powers of the police, found mostly in their power to arrest, are costly both in human and economic terms and should be limited when possible (Goldstein, 1979). While substantive research on the costs of police strategies is not presently available (for an exception, see Levitt, 1997), we discuss in the next chapter some of the normative concerns surrounding traditional law enforcement practices. Our findings suggest that other strategies beyond law enforcement can be effective in controlling crime and disorder and reducing fear.

It is particularly instructive that specific community policing strategies may be effective. Importantly, these strategies, while consistent with the standard model of policing in their application to a general class of problems, contrast strongly with that model in their reliance on nonenforcement-related approaches and community crime control. The evidence base here does not allow for definitive conclusions. Nonetheless, the research available suggests that when the police partner more generally with the public, levels of citizen fear will decline. Moreover, when the police are able to gain wider legitimacy among citizens and offenders, nonexperimental evidence suggests that the likelihood of offending will be reduced. These promising themes form a primary focus of discussion in Chapter 8.

There is greater and more consistent evidence, although it is based primarily on nonexperimental studies, that focused strategies drawing on a wide array of nonlaw enforcement tactics can also be effective in reducing crime and disorder. These strategies, found in the upper right of the table, may be classed more generally within the model of problem-oriented policing. While many problem-oriented policing programs employ traditional law enforcement practices, many also draw on a wider group of strategies and approaches. The research available suggests that such tools can be effective when they are combined with a tactical philosophy that emphasizes the tailoring of policing practices to the specific characteristics of the problems or places that are the focus of intervention.

Taken together, these research findings allow for strong policy recommendations for policing in the 21st century. Several decades of research have found weak or, at best, mixed evidence regarding the effectiveness of what we have defined as the "standard model" of policing. A large body of carefully conducted research has found much evidence of the effectiveness of what we have defined as the focused model of policing.

Many police innovations over the past two decades have sought to reduce crime and disorder and reduce fear by focusing on specific problems. Such approaches have great promise and should be the subject of more systematic investigation. There is very strong research evidence that the more focused and specific the strategies of the police, the more they are tailored to the problems they seek to address, the more effective police will be in controlling crime and disorder. This should be a guiding principle of developing strategies to reduce crime and disorder in the 21st century.

7

Lawful Policing

Learning whether the police have been successful in reducing crime and fear of crime is important to our normative evaluation of the police, as well as our scientific interests in understanding their behavior. There is an equally important set of criteria by which citizens make judgments about the police: their fairness and restraint. Concern about these issues arises primarily because the police are authorized to use force and authority in carrying out their mission. When the authority of the state is used, those who are subjected to it have a right to understand its use and to query whether it has been brought against them fairly and justly. We characterize this concern as the lawfulness of the police, as a companion to the concern about their crime control effectiveness. Lawfulness is closely linked to the concept of legitimacy, or the perceptions of citizens regarding police fairness. Legitimacy is the subject of Chapter 8.

The same tools that have enabled researchers to examine what police do, why they do it, and their crime control effectiveness can also be turned to the study of whether the police are fair and legitimate. Some of the earliest and most important pieces of police research were animated by concerns about fairness and lawfulness. Empirical methods were developed to discover the extent to which the police had discretion in how they behaved and how they used the discretion available to them. The achievement of those studies was to show that the world of policing was shot through with discretion, and that the choices the police made about how to use their discretion were only imperfectly guided by the legal standards that they ought to have been following. Concerns about whether the police behave fairly, whether they are racially biased, whether they are corrupt, whether they are brutal, whether they are aggressive or trigger-happy have continued to exist and to be investigated using the methods of the social sciences.

Our review of the social science evidence on police lawfulness focuses especially on research that examines police compliance with the U.S. Constitution, state and other laws, and with the policies of their departments. Concern about police use of force and the intrusive exercise of their authority leads political institutions to develop rules that bring police into compliance with such standards. The rules were adopted over time to promote the legitimacy of the police, as a rule-bound institution engaged in the even-handed pursuit of justice and as the protector of individual liberty. We summarize research on police compliance with rules and standards for interrogations, search and seizure, the use of excessive and deadly force, and corruption. Courts, legislatures, mayors, and city councils impose standards for conduct on police; the empirical question driving much of this work has been the extent to which they are followed—that extent serves as one measure of the legitimacy of police in a free society.

POLICE COMPLIANCE WITH THE LAW
AND THE CONSTITUTION

The legitimacy of police activity is closely tied to police compliance with legal standards. The goal of ensuring lawfulness in police conduct finds expression in rules guarding individuals' rights to liberty and property, freedom from unreasonable intrusions, and fair and equal treatment. The Fourteenth Amendment to the United States Constitution forbids deprivations of life, liberty, or property without due process of law. The "rule of law [means]...that the citizen should be free from arbitrary power" (LaFave, 1965:64). Through their power to enforce laws—or not—police are invested with a great deal of control over the liberty interests of individuals. Concern about these issues has led to sustained scholarly interest in both the question of how the police use their discretionary power and how best to control it.

In recent decades, concern about the exertion of arbitrary police power, as well as racial bias in the exercise of police power, has driven important developments in constitutional law. In *Brown* v. *Mississippi* (297 U.S. 278, 1935), the Supreme Court invalidated the defendant's conviction by a Mississippi court because the conviction rested almost entirely on a confession extracted through torture. In overturning Brown's conviction, the Supreme Court articulated a constitutional standard of fundamental fairness for the evaluation of police practices—with regard to practices pertaining to interrogation—to be applied to states via the Fourteenth Amendment. *Brown* v. *Mississippi* marked the first time the Supreme Court was willing to regulate police practices at the state level, and it set an important limitation on how the police can use their force and authority to generate evidence to be used at trial. The role of race in determining how Brown was treated also demonstrates how closely the articulation of constitutional criminal procedural rights in the United States has been tied to this country's history of racial discrimination (Klarman, 2000). The constitutional rules that prescribe the manner in which police are allowed to legitimately carry out their tasks have their genesis not only in the Court's concerns about how much state authority is appropriate to use in the pursuit of law enforcement objectives, but also in the Court's continuing concern with the fairness of policing—in particular, with its efforts to guard against racial discrimination.

Like *Brown*, later criminal procedure decisions—a muscular body of interconnected doctrines that govern the everyday machinery of law enforcement—also were influenced by the Court's interest both in restraining the state and rooting out institutional racism and other forms of bias (Kahan and Meares, 1998). In the law, rules of criminal procedure provide the state-level link between constitutional principles and the daily actions of participants in the criminal justice system. Historically, law enforcement was a key instrument of racial repression, in both the North and the South, before the civil rights revolution of the 1960s. Modern criminal procedure reflects the Supreme Court's contribution to eradicating it. The Court, beginning in the 1960s, erected a dense network of rules to delimit the permissible bounds of discretionary law enforcement authority. These decisions, while reflecting a concern for the effects of racism, make up a more general regime of criminal procedure that tells individual police officers when and how they can interact with criminal suspects on the street;[1] minutely regulate the nature of police interrogations of suspects in custody;[2] and spell out in detail the procedures that police must follow before they conduct searches or engage in related forms of surveillance (LaFave, 1996). These rules constrain, in both substance and form, the authority of police to maintain public order.[3] Although rarely couched as such, the unmistakable premise of these doctrines was the assumption that the historically empowered groups in communities could not be trusted to police their own police because of the distorting influence of racism.

---

[1]See, e.g., *California v. Hodari D.*, 499 U.S. 621, 638-39 (1991) (describing interlocking maze of doctrines governing "consensual encounters," "investigative stops," and "seizures of person").

[2]See, e.g., *Davis v. United States*, 512 U.S. 452, 458-62 (1992) (describing multiple "prophylactic" rules designed to conform interrogation to right to counsel).

[3]See, e.g., *Papachristou v. City of Jacksonville*, 405 U.S. 156 (1972); *Kolender v. Lawson*, 461 U.S. 352 (1983).

Of course, the articulation of rules does not automatically lead to legitimate policing. The rules of criminal procedure are not self-enforcing, nor are the laws regulating the honesty and ethical behavior of police officers. Even assuming that rules consistent with legitimate policing have been approved by the legislature or adopted by a court, it is necessary for individual officers to actually follow them. The next sections of this chapter review research on the extent to which police follow the rules that govern their behavior in four key areas: interrogations, use of deadly force, searches and seizures, and police corruption.

Police Interrogations

The Supreme Court began extensive regulation of local police practices in a case involving a clearly unlawful interrogation and racial bias. In a series of cases between 1936 and 1964, the Supreme Court reviewed the particular facts of cases in order to determine whether a confession was voluntary and in accord with the due process clause of the Fourteenth Amendment.[4] The difficulties inherent to administering a fact-based voluntariness test led the Court to develop the more easily administered, and perhaps more effective, method of controlling interrogation techniques in *Miranda* v. *Arizona* (372 U.S. 436, 1966).

Miranda holds that any confession obtained during custodial interrogation is compelled in violation of the right against self-incrimination unless a police officer has first given specific warnings to the person being questioned and unless that person specifically waives those rights. In the famous "Miranda warning," police are required to advise persons they question (1) that they have the right to remain silent, (2) that police are entitled to use any statement they make against them, (3) that they have a right to counsel, and (4) that counsel will be provided if they cannot afford one. Prior to the *Miranda* decision, the operating standard for confessions or otherwise incriminating statements elicited from a suspect in custody was "voluntariness." Only the Federal Bureau of Investigation (FBI) operated under specific instructions to issue a warning informing suspects in custody of their rights.

Miranda is no doubt the best-known criminal procedure decision in the United States. The positive obligation handed to law enforcement as the result of the decision provoked an immediate reaction, reflecting society's division over the police effectiveness issue (Dalton, 1984:62-63). There were complaints that Miranda requirements would undercut the ability of police to catch and convict criminals, and it was predicted that issuing Miranda

---

[4]See, e.g., *Fikes* v. *Alabama*, 352 U.S. 191 (1957).

warnings would unnecessarily hamstring police in their pursuit of criminals. Since that time, empirical studies have found that Miranda requirements only minimally curtailed the investigative function of police (Seeburger and Wettick, 1967; Wald et al., 1967; Zeitz et al., 1969; Black and
Reiss, 1967a, 1967b; Milner, 1971a; Schaefer, 1971). In a recent opinion in
another case involving police powers, the chief justice of the Supreme Court
acknowledged the status of *Miranda*, stating that the ruling "has become
embedded in routine police practice to the point where the warnings have
become part of our national culture."[5]

The question is, do police regularly adhere to its strictures? The bulk of
the studies of *Miranda* occurred shortly after the decision.[6] Research on the
ruling is of two types. A set of effect studies examine confession rates before
and after *Miranda* was decided, to see whether the warnings affected the
number of confessions obtained by police. The second stream of research
involves the direct observation of police behavior.

One of the earliest empirical assessments of police compliance comes
from the research project directed by Donald Black and Albert Reiss that
was already under way when the Supreme Court announced its decision
(Black and Reiss, 1967a, 1967b). Their findings belied the police contention that interrogation was necessary in obtaining evidence against a suspect. Especially in felonies, Black and Reiss noted that there typically was
alternate evidence against a suspect that police could rely on, including
physical evidence and other witness testimony (1967b:53). They also found,
following the Miranda decision, that when police officers initially encountered and arrested suspects, the required warning was rarely given (Black
and Reiss, 1967a:102-109).

The lack of compliance observed by Black and Reiss may have stemmed
from the fact that the decision had been handed down only recently. Subsequent studies found that police by and large did issue the Miranda warning,
albeit in an often perfunctory and superficial fashion (Wasby, 1970; Leiken,
1971; Baum, 1979).

Summaries of *Miranda* effect studies suggest that the warning as it is
actually delivered may have resulted in a reduction in confessions of be-

---

[5]*Dickerson* v. *United States*, 120 S. Ct.2326, 2336 (2000).

[6]*See* Neil A. Milner, The Court and Local Law Enforcement: The Impact of *Miranda* (1971);
David W. Neubauer, Criminal Justice in Middle America (1974); John Griffiths and Richard
Ayres, Faculty Note, *A* Postscript to the Miranda *Project, Interrogation of Draft Protesters*,
77 Yale L.J. 395 (1967); Lawrence S. Leiken, *Police Interrogation in Colorado: The Implementation of* Miranda, 47 Denv. L.J. 1 (1970); Richard Medalie et al., *Custodial Police Interrogation in Our Nation's Capital: The Attempt to Implement* Miranda, 66 Mich. L. Rev. 1347
(1968); Neil A. Milner, *Comparative Analysis of Patterns of Compliance*.

tween 4 and 16 percent.[7] Milner (1971a, 1971b), examining the use of *Miranda* in four Wisconsin cities, attributed some intercity variation he found to differences in police training and access to other sources of legal information across departments.

Miranda studies based on interviews with police or offenders or on official records cannot tell us directly whether police follow the Miranda requirements; for this, the best evidence is direct observation. Leo (1998) has compiled the best data on the topic. In an observational study of police detectives, Leo found that detectives provided Miranda warnings in all the cases in which they were legally required to do so, or in approximately 96 percent of the cases. In the remaining cases, the Miranda warning was not legally required because the suspect was not technically "in custody." Several other empirical studies also conclude that police overwhelmingly follow the guidelines set forth in *Miranda*.[8]

Leo also found that police seek to present the Miranda warnings in ways that encourage individuals to waive their constitutional rights. The only social, legal, or case-specific variable that was a significant predictor of the suspect's likelihood to invoke Miranda rights was the existence of a criminal record. After Miranda rights were invoked, 96 percent of suspects were returned to jail; in the remaining 4 percent of cases, detectives continued to question the suspects after informing them that information provided could not be used in a court of law against them.

Cassell and Hayman (1998) also observed the implementation of *Miranda*. They concluded that "evidence suggests that police have adjusted to *Miranda* by shifting to non-custodial 'interviews' to skirt *Miranda*'s re-

---

[7]Law & Soc'y Rev. 119 (1970); David W. Neubauer, *Confessions in Prairie City: Some Causes and Effects*, 65 J. Crim. L. & Criminology 103 (1974); Cyril D. Robinson, *Police and Prosecutor Practices and Attitudes Relating to Interrogation as Revealed by Pre- and Post-Miranda Questionnaires: A Construct of Police Capacity to Comply*, 3 Duke L.J. 425 (1968); Roger C. Schaefer, *Patrolman Perspectives on Miranda*, 1971 Law & Soc. Ord. 81; Richard Seeburger and R. Stanton Wettick, Jr., Miranda *in Pittsburgh —A Statistical Study*, 29 U. Pitt. L. Rev. 1 (1967); Otis Stephens et al., *Law Enforcement and the Supreme Court: Police Perceptions of the* Miranda *Requirements*, 29 Tenn. L. Rev. 407 (1972); Michael Wald et al., *Interrogations in New Haven: The Impact of* Miranda, 76 Yale L.J. 1519 (1967); James W. Witt, *Non-Coercive Interrogation and the Administration of Criminal Justice: The Impact of* Miranda *on Police Effectuality*, 64 J. Crim. L & Criminology 320 (1973); Evelle J. Younger, *Interrogation of Criminal Defendants—Some Views on Miranda* v. *Arizona*, 35 Fordham L. Rev. 255 (1966); Evelle J. Younger, *Results of a Survey Conducted in the District Attorney's Office of Los Angeles County Regarding the Effect of the* Miranda *Decision upon the Prosecution of Felony Cases*, Am. Crim. L. Q. 32 (1966).

[8]*See* Tracey L. Meares and Bernard E. Harcourt, *Transparent Adjudication and Social Science Research in Constitutional Criminal Procedure*, 90 J. Crim. L. & Criminology 733, 769, tbl. 11.

quirements" (p. 228). Although much of their evidence for the change in behavior is anecdotal, Cassell and Hayman do indicate that 70 percent of their observed interviews were custodial, while 30 percent were noncustodial. Whether this represents a change from pre-*Miranda* figures is unclear. Cassell and Hayman further argue that police were less successful in noncustodial interviews. The fact that police have begun to use them more despite their lower rate of success suggests to the authors that, "contrary to the view of some defenders of *Miranda*, . . . interrogating police officers believe the *Miranda* rules are harmful to their efforts" (p. 229-230). Another way of interpreting Cassell and Hayman's finding is that *Miranda* actually does provide individuals protection against state power.

Research in this area is dated, perhaps reflecting earlier findings that police were by and large complying with the letter of the law, and that it did not appear to have much effect on their effectiveness. Other custodial rights issues have not been investigated at all. Because the most compelling research in this area involves the direct observation of police behavior, including both by patrol officers and detectives, it is laborious and expensive to conduct. The resulting data typically represent only one jurisdiction, making it difficult to infer the effects of departmental policy and other management-level factors on the implementation of legal rules.

Excessive and Lethal Force

The potential for using force underlies many of the functions exercised by the police. In fact, one definition of the police is that it is the body lawfully authorized to exercise lethal force against citizens of the state, holding a virtual monopoly over this power. As a price for holding this monopoly, and because its use is inevitable, there are standards for the application of force by police. When force is appropriate to use, and how much and what kind of force may be used, are all defined both by constitutional rules and by statutes that create a liability for both police departments and individual police officers who misuse the force and authority entrusted to them. In addition, police administrators usually strive for economy in the use of force; good police work, in this view, is policing that employs only the force that is required in a particular situation, and not more. A key concern to policing in the 21st century is the proper use of force, since the real or perceived misuse of force can thoroughly and quickly undermine police legitimacy.

In the United States, use of lethal force has been a major source of conflict between minority groups and the police since the inception of the institution (Walker, 1977). Numerous studies have demonstrated that blacks are shot and killed by the police in numbers that are vastly disproportionate to the number of whites who are shot and killed. Between 1950 and 1960, one study found that blacks were killed by Chicago police at a rate of 16 per 100,000, compared with a rate of 2 per 100,000 for whites (Robin, 1963). From October 1966 to October 1974, the Memphis Police Department recorded approximately 225 instances of firearm discharges to attempt to stop fleeing felon suspects; 114 of those shot by police were suspected of nonviolent property crimes. Of the 114 shot, 96 were black. In a study of fleeing felons in Memphis between 1969 and 1974, one researcher found that police officers shot and killed 13 blacks and 1 white person (Fyfe, 1982). Many see such disparities in the exercise of force lying at the core of challenges to the legitimacy of policing in the United States in the 21st century.

The constitutional rule adopted by the Court to circumscribe the use of deadly force by police officers is a product of another case, *Tennessee* v. *Garner*. In 1985, the Supreme Court overturned that state's permissive fleeing felon rule, which allowed police officers to use "all the means necessary to effect an arrest," even of an unarmed fleeing felon, after notice of intention to arrest was given. Scholars have found that guidelines contained in *Garner* led to a few changes in state law. However, by 1990 only 4 of the approximately 30 states whose laws fell outside the *Garner* boundaries had changed their laws to bring them into compliance with Court guidelines.[9] Most of the remainder continued to legally authorize shootings of nonviolent fleeing felons (Fyfe and Walker, 1990). There were more changes in the administrative policies of departments governing police use of force (Skolnick and Fyfe, 1993). These rules in turn have been evaluated and appear to have had an effect on police shootings. Tennenbaum (1994) concluded that *Garner* reduced fatal police shootings in the United States by about 60 per year.

This is a difficult research area. There is no central repository of data on police use of force, and the data collected nationally by the FBI on the use of lethal force are deeply flawed. They are voluntarily submitted and they do not include injuries that fall short of death. The data that are submitted are known to be inaccurate, based on comparisons between them and other data sources (Fyfe, 2002). Gaining access to local records on this potentially explosive and politically sensitive topic is difficult, and agencies have much to lose by cooperating with researchers. As a result of these difficult circumstances, virtually every study of police use of force has been based on the records of one or a small number of local police departments.

---

[9]*See, e.g.,* Paul G. Cassell and Bret S. Hayman, *Police Interrogation in the 1990s: An Empirical Study of the Effects of* Miranda, *in* The Miranda Debate: Law, Justice, and Policing 222, 231 (Richard A. Leo and George C. Thomas III eds., 1998) ("Our data thus support the emerging consensus that police play by the *Miranda* rules.").

Furthermore, it makes a difference how the data are obtained. On one hand, studies conducted in agencies that voluntarily open their records to researchers appear to represent agencies that are most confident of their professionalism. In general, these studies show that racial minorities are subjects of police force at higher rates than for whites, but that shootings by police are fairly racially balanced (see, for example, Fyfe, 1981, and Blumberg, 1981). On the other hand, studies of agencies that are forced to open their records because of suits alleging use of excessive force, or Freedom of Information Act suits by media organizations, tend to find more racial disparity in the use of force, a great deal of disparity in the use of lethal force, and a higher rate of shootings of racial minorities that appear to be questionable (Fyfe, 2002). For example, Meyer (1980) found in Los Angeles that blacks were more often unarmed when they were shot, and Fyfe (1982) found that blacks in Memphis were more often shot in circumstances that were not as threatening to the officer. Official case files typically are the source of data on these incidents, and these documents present a version of events in which every incentive exists for the organization to present a favorable version of events, and much of the information is based on paperwork completed by the officer who used the force.

One of the few firm conclusions that can be drawn from this research is that rates of police use of force and lethal force are highly variable. Fyfe (2002) analyzed the results of a project conducted by the *Washington Post* that assembled data on fatal police shootings in 51 large municipal and county police and sheriff's departments during 1990-2000. Fatal shootings rates for county police departments varied by a factor of 14, while for city departments the ratio of shootings from top to bottom was 8 to 1; among sheriff's departments, it was almost 6 to 1. In a seven-city study by Milton et al. (1977), the top to bottom ratio was also 6 to 1. Another general and important conclusion from these analyses is that most police use of force is nonfatal. In one 6-agency study, only 18 percent of adult custody arrests involved the use of physical force or threats of physical force, and most of the force was confined to threats, the use of restraints, weaponless tactics, and control holds (Garner and Maxwell, 1999). A final conclusion is that, as noted above, there is usually racial disparity in the use of nonlethal force, and often considerable racial disparity in the use of lethal force.

Despite problems with the data, there is evidence of the positive effects of legal and administrative efforts to control police use of force. In a study of the use of force by the New York police department, Fyfe (1979) found that a policy change by that agency led to a precipitous drop in shootings by officers there. He also found that New York City police rarely shot unarmed people. Sparger and Giacopassi (1992) conducted a follow-up study in Memphis, the jurisdiction in which the *Garner* decision originated; they found a dramatic reduction in racial disparities in police shootings in the post-*Garner* period.

In a study in Philadelphia, Waegel (1984) used data collected from media reports by a nongovernmental organization, the Police Project of the Philadelphia Public Interest Law Center, to examine the effect of a 1973 state statute restricting use of force by police officers. He concluded that officers did not comply with the statute, and that compliance did not increase with time (p. 128): "With but one exception (1977), in every year the most frequent category of lethal force incidents involved an unarmed person who was fleeing after the commission of a felony (1970-1972) or an unarmed person who had not committed a violent felony (1974-1978)." However, in a later analysis, Skolnick and Fyfe (1993) concluded that administrative changes imposed by the city's mayor Frank Rizzo worked against the intent of the statute. In response to the state legislation, he rescinded the city's long-standing and more restrictive deadly force policy, thus effectively expanding the potential role for deadly force in the city. Later, when a new mayor reestablished the more restrictive deadly force policy, fatal shootings declined in Philadelphia by 67 percent in the following year (Fyfe, 1981). Skolnick and Fyfe (1993) were also critical of the use of media reports as a source of data for police shootings, finding that one-third were not reported in the press. (For more on this, see also Fyfe, 1988 and 1987).

The committee has deliberated on the problems inherent with data collection on police use of lethal force; we remain convinced that the obligation to collect such information outweighs its inherent difficulties. As we have already noted, an effort to collect these data has been undertaken by the International Association of the Chiefs of Police (IACP).

Like the development of the Uniform Crime Reports in the early part of the 20th century (Cross, 1917), implementing a voluntary data collection initiative on the use of force by police agencies is a challenging endeavor filled with complexity and the potential for error and subversion. While operationalizing concepts can be difficult in any large national study, the definitional problems in this area are readily apparent. The IACP defines police use of force as "the amount of force required by police to compel compliance by an unwilling subject" (Henriquez, 1999:20). This definition excludes excessive force, since excessive implies that the amount of force exceeds that required to compel compliance. If anything, it sounds like a definition for "reasonable" force, not use of force more generally. It also imposes a normative standard, forcing localities to define the amount of force required to compel compliance and then count those instances in which that level of force was used. A better definition would rely on the officers' overt forceful behaviors, whether justified or not, rather than on divergent local interpretations of how much force is necessary to compel compliance. Furthermore, the anonymous nature of the data collection means that there is no way to check the reliability or validity of the data. The voluntary nature of agency reporting also has several undesirable consequences, most notably that the resulting collection of data cannot be treated as a representative sample of police in the United States. Therefore the data cannot be used to draw inferences about police more generally. Furthermore, since there is no mechanism for ensuring consistent reporting by agencies, the data also cannot be used to calculate trends in police use of force (Henriquez, 1999).

Many of the problems with the IACP data will probably iron themselves out as police agencies continue to participate in the initiative and develop standards for reporting. Even if the data collection becomes routine, there is still one fundamental problem: the anonymous reporting system means that data from this study cannot be merged with data from other sources, such as the Uniform Crime Reports, the census, or other data sources. This limitation means that the range of potential explanatory variables will be limited; thus the data are not well suited for explaining differences among police organizations.

The development of measures useful for assessing interagency variations in use of force is still in its infancy. Although isolated studies have collected national data on police use of force, the only systematic effort to record police use of force nationally is still several years away from realizing its potential as a data source on policing. **The committee recommends legislation requiring police agencies to file annual reports to the public on the number of persons shot at, wounded, and killed by police officers in the line of duty.** As long as the only comprehensive national data set on police use of force continues to operate in a voluntary and anonymous fashion, it will fail to capture the data that are, arguably, the most important of all.

Seizures and Searches

The Fourth Amendment states that "the right of the people to be secure in their persons, houses, papers and effects, against unreasonable searches, shall not be violated, and no Warrants shall issue, but upon probable cause, supported by Oath or affirmation, and particularly describing the place to be searched, and the person or things to be seized." Searching citizens and their property is a basic law enforcement tool for solving crimes and building criminal cases against defendants. The framers of the U.S. Constitution recognized the state's legitimate interests to engage in searches, but they were so concerned about the risks of abuse that they enshrined their proscription of "unreasonable" searches and seizures in the Fourth Amendment, the first of several to address concerns about due process of law.

Although Americans have long been interested in the contribution their police make to reducing crime, they also expect the police to operate by the rules of law (Roberts and Stalans, 1997:Ch. 7). Since 1961, the Supreme Court has used the Fourth Amendment to establish rules regulating every-day police search and seizure practices. In *Mapp* v. *Ohio* (367 U.S. 643, 1961), the Supreme Court applied an exclusionary rule, which already governed federal prosecutions, to the states as well. The rule excluded the fruits of unlawful searches from consideration in court. The Court did so in order to deter unlawful police conduct and secure the guarantee of the Fourth Amendment against unreasonable searches and seizures, since there appeared to be no feasible alternative to controlling such behavior. The largest body of social science research on police compliance focuses on the effects of the exclusionary rule.

Immediately following *Mapp*, researchers began a series of studies concluding that, at least in some areas of the country, the exclusionary rule may have caused police officers to adhere more closely to the requirements of the Fourth Amendment (Goldstein, J Crim Law, 1967; Amsterdam, Minn Law Rev, 1974). Skolnick's (1966) study of Eastville and Westville police is one early example. Skolnick employed direct observation to identify common police search practices. The study notes that officers frequently skirted constitutional standards. It identifies an officer outlook that motivated and justified such actions: a focus on discovering and controlling crime and applying conventional morality to standards of police behavior in dealing with suspects. In this light, technicalities of constitutional law are viewed as unreasonable obstacles to reasonable police goals, and any normative pressure to conform to law is substantially mitigated. Other studies were mixed: some found that the exclusionary rule deterred misconduct (Canon, 1974; Wasby, 1976), some found little or no effect (Oaks, 1970), and some were inconclusive.[10]

A new wave of studies followed the Supreme Court's embrace of a cost/benefit approach to the exclusionary rule in *U.S.* v. *Calandra*.[11] These attempted to measure and balance the costs (excluded evidence) and the benefits (deterrence of police misconduct) of the exclusionary rule. Many focused exclusively on the social costs of the exclusionary rule ("lost convictions"), and they overwhelmingly concluded that those costs were marginal.[12]

---

[10]See Brief *amicus curiae* of the Florida Chapter of the National Bar Association in support of the Respondent-Appellee, *Tennessee* v. *Garner*, No. 83-1035, 3 (1984).

[11]Note, *Effect of Mapp* v. *Ohio on Police Search-and-Seizure Practices in Narcotics Cases*, 4 Colum. J. Law & Soc. Probs. 87 (1968).

[12]414 U.S. 338 (1974).

More recently, researchers have returned to examinations of actual police practices. Studies based on field observations provide the most reliable effect data (Cannon, 1991) but are relatively rare in the exclusionary rule literature. Older studies sponsored by the American Bar Foundation concluded that police officers knew the relevant constitutional standards and did their best to work around them when searching suspects.[13] In addition to being dated, these studies suffer from a reliance on interviews with the police rather than observations of behavior in the field.

In 1986, Orfield (1987) studied Chicago narcotics officers to determine how the exclusionary rule has influenced their behavior. Orfield conducted structured interviews with 26 narcotics officers. He found that the exclusionary rule had changed police, prosecutorial, and judicial procedures on the institutional level. At the individual level, Orfield found that the officers he interviewed generally adhered to the exclusionary rule and that the rule deterred constitutional violations—at least if the goal was to prosecute the offender, as opposed to confiscate contraband. LaFave (1965) and LaFave and Remington (1965) reported earlier that restrictions on searches and seizures were ineffective when their purpose was instead to disrupt illicit networks or assert police authority on the street.

Other studies based on interviews with police officers have been used to estimate the frequency of illegal police procedures (Canon, 1991; Krantz, 1979; Milner, 1971a; Wasby, 1976). This method has the advantage of offering interviewed officers an opportunity to speak confidentially about their work, which could encourage them to be frank regarding their practices. However, police surveys and interviews suffer from a variety of other limitations. Some officers may be unaware that certain search practices in which they engage are illegal (or legal), thus producing unreliable estimates of the rate of illegal search practice. In addition, officer recall of search practice may be faulty. Studies that give officers hypothetical scenarios to respond to may not reflect what they actually do on the job.

In a study of officers in the early 1990s, Gould and Mastrofski (2001) conducted field observations of 115 searches conducted by 44 lead officers.[14] They conclude that 29 percent of the searches were conducted unconstitutionally. This extrapolates to a rate of 6-7 illegal searches per 100 residents over a year's time. However, they report that only three violations were rated so egregious as to "shock the conscience" (p. 36). Importantly,

---

[13]See, e.g., Comptroller of the United States, *Impact of the Exclusionary Rule on Federal Criminal Prosecutions* (1979); Peter Nardulli, *The Societal Cost of the Exclusionary Rule: An Empirical Assessment*, 3 Am. B. Found. Res. J. 585 (1983).

[14]American Bar Foundation, Survey of the Administration of Justice (1957); L.P. Tiffany, D.M. McIntyre, and D.L. Rotenberg, Detection of Crime: Stopping and Questioning, Search and Seizure, Encouragement and Entrapment (1967).

this research includes data from searches that do not lead to arrest or a suppression motion. In fact, Gould and Mastrofski found that "only 7 percent of the suspects who were arrested or cited experienced an unconstitutional search, while 43 percent of those who were not arrested or cited experienced a violation of their constitutional right" (p. 36). Clearly, studies that limit their focus to lost convictions (which require first an arrest and then a suppression motion) can miss a significant number of unconstitutional searches. Gould and Mastrofski also found that "when constitutional violations occur, they are more likely to involve the frisk of a suspect's outer clothing than a full search of his person or possessions" (p. 38). Furthermore, the violations were generally not exceptionally invasive; the authors estimate that only two or three of the searches would "rise to the level of egregiousness required for civil liability" (p. 38). Finally, the data indicated that "illegal searches were highly concentrated in a few officers....[S]ix officers (14 percent of the officers in the sample) accounted for 22, or two-thirds, of the illegal searches" (p. 53). The design of the study did not enable them to determine the eventual fate of the 7 percent of cases in which they observed unconstitutional sanctioning.

Gould and Mastrofski had limited data on the background of the observed officers, so their analysis focused mostly on the features of the suspects and the situation. They found that the most powerful predictor affecting the probability of an unconstitutional search was whether the officers were explicitly looking for drugs and whether the search was a pat-down as opposed to a more intrusive search. They concluded that this pattern of effects suggested that the city's "war on drugs contributed to the rate of illegal searches. Notably, the study found no evidence that blacks were more likely than whites to receive an unconstitutional search. Interestingly, although a small number of officers accounted for a disproportionately large share of the unconstitutional searches, these officers did not conform to a "rotten apple" portrait. Instead these officers were strongly committed to community policing and to treating citizens with respect. Their searches, both legal and illegal, were performed in a respectful, even solicitous manner. The researchers found that the rate of illegal searches appeared to be high, but most police transgressions were relatively minor. Given that so few of the illegal searches were officially recorded, the exclusionary rule would prove irrelevant to preventing or correcting most violations.

The Supreme Court's *U.S.* v. *Leon* decision in 1984 permitted a "good faith" exception to the exclusionary rule for faulty warrant searches. One post-*Leon* study tracked hundreds of cases in seven cities throughout the legal process, from the beginning of the search warrant request to disposition and disposition of appeal (Sutton, 1986). The research drew on official records, firsthand observation of warrant reviews, and interviews with police and court decision makers. The study found that the search warrant process was rarely used, the process was perfunctory (with magistrates serving more as allies than independent judges committed to maintaining due process standards), and it was often subverted by circumventing the warrant requirement, ignoring it, or meeting it through fabrication or falsification of evidence. Another group of researchers did a pre-post study of search warrant practices in the same seven cities and found that they remain unchanged by *Leon*, thus adding to the body of research that finds little or no effect from appellate court rulings on police practices (Uchida and Bynum, 1991).

More recently, the New York Office of the Attorney General conducted a study of police stop and frisk practices in New York City.[15] The study analyzed 175,000 forms completed by police officers over a one-year period. Researchers compared patterns of stops with census data, crime statistics, and demographic information, yielding a quantitative portrait of stop and frisk practices.[16]

In analyzing this and other studies like it, it is important to note that the Supreme Court legitimated many stop and frisk practices in *Terry* v. *Ohio*.[17] In *Terry*, the Court interpreted the Fourth Amendment by balancing individual interests in liberty (privacy, property, and autonomy) against societal interests in safety (which include, of course, the stopped and searched person's interests). The Court departed from its then long-time insistence that police searches and seizures be justified by the level of particularized suspicion known as probable cause.[18] The Court instead determined, focusing on the reasonableness clause of the Fourth Amendment, that a protective pat-down of a stopped person's clothing that fell short of a full-blown search need be justified only by reasonable, articulable suspicion that criminal activity was afoot and that the person with whom the officer was dealing may be armed and dangerous.[19]

---

[15]See Jon B. Gould and Stephen D. Mastrofski, *Suspect Searches: Using Constitutional Standards to Assess Police Behavior* (unpublished manuscript on file with author).

[16]Civil Rights Bureau, Off. Of the Att'y Gen., *The New York City Police Department's "Stop & Frisk" Practice: A Report from the Office of the Attorney General* (December 1, 1999).

[17]The forms that provide the fodder for this analysis are known as UF-250s. According to the New York Police Department's Patrol Guide, a police officer who stops, questions, and frisks an individual on the basis of reasonable suspicion must complete a UF-250. In situations in which probable cause exists before stops are conducted, no form is completed. In situations that fall outside these four contexts, a police officer may fill out a form if he or she desires to do so. The pool of forms analyzed in the study contained about three quarters mandated reports and the rest voluntary. *Id.* at 91. The forms covered stops that occurred in 1998 and the first three months in 1999.

[18]392 U.S. 1 (1968).

[19]*Terry*, 392 U.S. at 27.

The study of the New York Attorney General's Office used the form submitted by police officers themselves to identify stops that clearly meet the constitutional standard of reasonable suspicion according to *Terry* and its progeny and those that did not. The data may be biased because they were drawn from police reports. Examining them, Fagan and Davies found that the facts as stated did not meet the reasonable suspicion standard of *Terry* in 14 percent of cases (Fagan and Davies, 2000).

The New York report also examined the disparate effect of stop and frisk practices. When classified by race, the percentage of wrongful stops—those that did not articulate reasonable suspicion—were about the same for blacks, Hispanics, and whites: 16, 14, and 17 percent, respectively. These differences were not statistically significant. The New York report used decennial census estimates to calculate the rate at which persons of different races were stopped, and concluded that the rate for blacks was much higher than that for whites. The report also used race-specific arrest totals to calculate crime-based stop rates (stops per arrest), and found that by this measure blacks were stopped at twice the rate of whites. However, Chapter 8 considers the methodological problems involved in using population counts and other measures of at-risk populations as a basis for examining patterns of racial profiling, concluding that these must be considered with caution.

In grappling with the issue of police compliance with constitutional or legal standards, it is crucial to understand the nature of the evidence, and stop and search procedures are no exception. Studies based on official records have limitations when they are used for estimating the frequency with which police violate constitutional protections regarding search and seizure. First, records that document searches can also be used to evaluate their performance, and the officers whose performance is to be evaluated are the very persons responsible for completing the documents. They are well aware of these downstream uses and may understandably craft their reports to cast their own performance in the most favorable light, perhaps by leaving out uncomplimentary material, being vague, or even falsifying records. Second, official records, whether police- or court-generated, are substantially incomplete. Many searches go undocumented by police because no arrest was made. A systematic field study of the police in the early 1990s reported that 39 percent of searches without warrant resulted in an arrest or citation that would produce an official document of the search, and only 9 percent of unconstitutional searchers were so documented (Gould and Mastrofski, 2001). Even when searches are reported, a thorough judicial review of the legality of that search depends on defense counsel's filing a suppression motion. Given the cursory review afforded to most criminal cases by defense counsel and the ubiquity of quick plea bargains in routine criminal cases, court documents constitute an unreliable means of assessing the constitutionality of police practices.

Police Corruption

Corruption is another way that police deviate from the law. Corruption is usually characterized as the abuse of authority for personal gain (Barker and Carter, 1986:3; Goldstein, 1975:5; Klockars et al., 2000:1; Lersch, 2000; Sherman, 1974:5).[20] It has also been described as "profit-motivated misconduct." Police corruption can take a variety of forms: gratuities (free meals, small gifts); bribes (not to enforce the law or enforce it selectively, to provide information about police activities and investigations, to provide false testimony, to secure a promotion or desired assignment within the department); and theft, burglary, and other misapplications of police power that benefit the officer (shakedowns of drug dealers, accepting payment from private citizens for harassing and arresting persons when there is no legal justification) (Walker, 1999:245-248). There is debate about whether some of these practices, such as the acceptance of gratuities, should be considered corruption.[21] There is also debate about whether off-duty offenses by officers, which could range from drug abuse and burglary to domestic violence, should be considered. As a result, studies vary somewhat in how corruption is defined and measured. We draw on a broad range of these studies in our review, which covers how much corruption there is, its causes, what is known about how to control it, integrity as an alternative measure, and corruption's effect on the legitimacy of police.

Measuring Corruption

It is difficult to measure police corruption reliably, because those who have the most knowledge about the corrupt acts are themselves usually implicated in those practices and have a vested interest in keeping these practices undetected (Klockars, 1999:208). Those who bribe police officers are quite unlikely to report it to authorities that might seek to put a stop to

---

[20]*Terry*, 392 U.S. at 30. Justice Warren's majority opinion said very little about stops that accompany or are antecedent to frisks, but Justice Harlan in concurrence emphasized that the frisk in the case depended on the reasonableness of the accompanying stop, and that the right to frisk must be automatic "if the reason for the stop is, as here, an articulable suspicion of a crime of violence." *Id.* at 33.

[21]Some analysts consider that corruption should also include abuses of authority that do not render a personal benefit but are in fact undertaken to further what the actor perceives as larger organizational or societal objectives that are widely embraced, such as reducing crime and delivering justice (Muir, 1977:271). Such forms of "noble cause" corruption as giving false testimony "to win the war on crime" have been noted at least as far back as the 1931 Wickersham Commission (Barker, 2002:12). While this is certainly worthy of study, we are guided here by Klockars' caveat not to cast the conceptual net regarding corruption too broadly, perhaps rendering it useless for purposes of understanding its causes.

such practices. Officers understandably do not report their own corrupt practices and, as with many other occupations, are reluctant to report the corrupt practices of their colleagues. Some argue that the problem is especially severe in policing because of a strongly developed informal code of not reporting their colleagues' misbehavior and even condoning it (Klockars et al., 2000:2; Stoddard, 1995). Some have suggested that the problem is not as severe now as it once was (Sherman, 1977). Citizens who know about corrupt practices are reluctant to report them to the authorities because their own illicit behavior may be revealed, or because they fear retaliation by the police or that the authorities will not believe their claims. And many citizens simply do not have knowledge of specific corrupt acts. Thus, the usual methods of collecting data on commonly measured legal offenses (official crime reports and surveys of victims or offenders) fail to capture most of the corrupt events.

This problem is compounded by the considerable variation that exists in mechanisms used to uncover, expose, and punish corruption. Communities in which police departments, other state and local government institutions, and the press are vigorous in pursuing corruption may well find it, while communities that are less energetic may not, regardless of how much is actually going on. That is, we lack a measure of corruption that is independent of the effectiveness of the policies and procedures we are trying to evaluate. We must acknowledge at the outset that the available scientific evidence on corruption is severely flawed as a result.

Those who look for national statistics on police corruption will not find them (General Accounting Office, 1998:10). Some police departments publish annual statistics on the status of complaints against the police and their disposition, and on rare occasion these will indicate the nature of the misconduct. Usually, however, this information is not made public in any detailed, systematic fashion.[22] The FBI's Public Corruption Unit maintains statistics on corruption cases in which it has jurisdiction. It reported that the number of officers convicted annually as a result of its investigations ranged between 83 and 150 during the 1993-1997 fiscal year period (General Accounting Office, 1998:11).

Most of what we know about police corruption is drawn from investigations that follow in the wake of scandals. Among the most widely known recent reports are those of the Knapp Commission report (City of New York, 1973), the Mollen Commission report (City of New York, 1994), and the Pennsylvania Crime Commission report (1974).

---

[22]One recent statistical analysis of police misconduct in New York City between 1975 and 1996 draws on information about a wide range of misconduct, including, but not limited to, corruption as we have defined it (Kane, 2002).

The Knapp Commission's report on New York City followed a corruption scandal that surfaced in 1970. The report created a typology of corrupt practice, distinguishing "grass-eaters," officers who accept gratuities and solicit small payments from legitimate and illegitimate enterprises, from "meat-eaters," those who aggressively and constantly exploit their position for substantial financial gain. The commission speculated that grass-eaters comprised the vast majority of corrupt officers and that meat-eaters were only a small portion of the entire force, but that was a measure of their faith rather than any data. The commission concluded that corruption was "an extensive, Department-wide phenomenon, indulged in to some degree by a sizable majority of those on the force and protected by a code of silence on the part of those who remained honest" (City of New York, 1973:61).

The pervasiveness of the corruption uncovered by the Knapp Commission stands in sharp contrast to the typical claim that corruption is limited to a few rotten apples (due to the moral deficiency of a few individuals) or at most, "rotten pockets" (a few small work groups in which corruption is widely practiced) (Sherman, 1974:7; Skogan, 1979). Although the rotten apple view is the usual conclusion of police leaders and boards of inquiry, independent researchers have often concurred with this assessment, such as with the River Cops in Miami in the late 1980s (Delattre, 1989); the New York City drug corruption scandal of the early 1990s that was investigated by the Mollen Commission (Barker, 2002); the Rampart scandal in Los Angeles; the Chicago drug scandal of the mid-1990s; and the Seattle incident of a detective stealing money from the home of a man killed in a police shootout (Barker, 2002).

An attempt at assessing the extent of corruption across cities was offered in the wake of the corruption scandals revealed by Knapp Commission investigation. Sherman (1978) examined New York and three other cities that were attempting to reform their police departments. He acknowledged the impossibility of gathering valid and reliable data on corruption events in these cities, but he argued that it was possible to classify the degree to which corruption was organized in each city—how much cooperation among police occurred in corrupt practices. His cross-department study employed a variety of indicators of the degree of organizational corruption: the level of active cooperation among two or more officers (based on investigative accounts); the level of passive cooperation among officers (e.g., failure to report corrupt activities of other officers, the number of officers working for a superior officer who accepts bribes for ordering subordinates not to enforce the law); and the level of citizen-police cooperation (e.g., the ratio of citizen-consenting types of corruption to the number of citizen-victimizing types of corruption). The study found that corruption was organized to a high degree before the scandals surfaced, even though a high level of organizational effort at corruption control existed in three of the four departments.

Most academic experts and observers of policing agree that most police officers are honest (General Accounting Office, 1998:11), but there is little evidence to evaluate this claim, or more important, to provide more precise estimates of the true nature and extent of corruption. Are police more likely to be corrupt than those in other occupations? There is no systematic evidence on this, although it seems likely that police corruption is more newsworthy than that in occupations not imbued with such authority and high expectations of rectitude. The public may regard such corruption as a greater threat to the social good and be more sensitized to it when it is publicized. Interestingly, however, the public tends to hold the police in fairly high esteem for honesty and integrity compared with other occupations to which they are routinely compared (Gallagher et al., 2001:63). National surveys repeatedly show the police receiving fewer negative ratings about their honesty and ethical standards than about two-thirds of the other occupations listed, including judges, funeral directors, governors, journalists, and lawyers (Bureau of Justice Statistics, 2001:114). In recent years, the level of negative ratings for lawyers has been about 30 percent higher than for police.

Causes of Corruption

The research literature is long on theory and short on evidence about what causes police corruption. The putative causes of corruption can be grouped into four categories: characteristics of individual officers, opportunities for corruption, characteristics of police organizations, and characteristics of the larger environment (Walker, 1999:250).

Characteristics of Individual Officers. One set of explanations focuses on the personal character of officers (Muir, 1977; Sherman, 1974). Refusing to accept applicants for police positions who have demonstrated serious moral lapses (e.g., committed crimes or abused drugs) is one way that departments act on the theory that officers themselves carry with them the seeds of their own success or failure regarding corruption. Studies do not provide a rigorous indication of how successful such selection strategies are in reducing corruption. However, in general, personality-based explanations are not popular among researchers. They note the poor performance of psychological screening tests in predicting and explaining past and future performance (Burbeck and Furnham, 1985:65; Daley, 1980; Malouff and Schutte, 1980; Talley and Hinz, 1990), and that such explanations fail to account for varying situations that influence officer behavior, or to take into account the effect of the police organization and environment (Dwyer et al., 1990). A perhaps more viable theory of corruption posits that officers who perceive a pathway for legitimate advancement in their career are less likely to pursue corrupt practices than those who perceive limited opportunities for career advancement (Sherman, 1974). Career opportunities serve as both an incentive for staying on track (to increase the prospects of success) and a deterrent to corruption (to avoid placing their career prospects at risk).

Opportunities for Corruption. Opportunities to act corruptly arise from exposure to the temptations of corruption and the capacity to conceal it. High discretion, low visibility jobs with stable work groups in areas (geographic or functional) with high levels of lucrative illicit trade provide the greatest opportunity for corruption. Although almost all police enjoy considerable discretion in their work, detectives enjoy a great deal of freedom about how they spend their work days, and they also work out of uniform, which reduces their visibility (General Accounting Office, 1998:11). When they operate in work groups with changing membership, they have the opportunity to acclimate new members to the norms of the group and to assess their willingness to tolerate the level of corruption the group finds acceptable. Narcotics detective units are thought to experience especially high levels of opportunity for corruption because they deal with preventing traffic in a commodity that commands very high sums of money and purveyors who are highly motivated to bribe police to engage in nonenforcement or selective enforcement (General Accounting Office, 1998; Manning and Redlinger, 1977). Sherman (1978:9) concluded from his four-city study that management strategies to eliminate opportunities for corruption available in the environment proved effective. This was done by reducing police responsibilities for enforcing certain laws that exposed them to corruption pressures (e.g., gambling), urging the public not to offer gifts to officers, and stricter enforcement of bribery laws against the public.

Characteristics of Police Organizations. Police organizations are thought to exert a considerable influence over the level of corruption in the department, through both formal means (policies, rules, and procedures) and informal means (the subculture norms and practices of police workers) (Klockars, 2003; Sherman, 1974, 1977). Many formal aspects of the organization are explicitly designed to limit corruption, by creating systems to define it (by establishing rules), detect it (internal affairs investigations of allegations, integrity tests), and punish it. Departments that had become more authoritarian and bureaucratized were found to have lower post-reform levels of corruption (Sherman, 1977). Specific management strategies associated with success at controlling corruption were high levels of personnel turnover; holding supervisors accountable for their subordinates' performance; closer surveillance of operations; and termination of policies that encouraged corruption (e.g., ending quotas for vice arrests, which encouraged perjury about hard-to-get evidence). Sherman (1978) also found that covert and proactive techniques (integrity tests that provide officers the opportunity to act corruptly) were more effective than standard investigations based only on formal complaints about past practices.

The tolerance of the police work group for corrupt practices constitutes an informal organizational characteristic of considerable theoretical importance for explaining high levels of corruption (Klockars, 2003; Pennsylvania Crime Commission, 1994; Sherman, 1974). On one hand, an accepting or tolerant attitude toward corruption among officers eases the transition to corrupt practices ("Everybody thinks it's ok"), and it minimizes the risk of disclosure by coworkers. On the other hand, when there is widespread intolerance of corruption among officers, those who are involved in it risk becoming an outcast and denied the protections of a loyal support group.

Characteristics of the Environment. Researchers have looked to a wide variety of environmental influences on corruption that affect individual officers and entire organizations. Perhaps the most obvious is the criminal law, which by defining what is criminal, regulates the demand for police corruption (Walker, 1999:250). By prohibiting the manufacture and sale of alcoholic beverages in the 1920s, the United States created a tremendously lucrative market for police corruption. Presumably, the pressure and rewards for police corruption recede when popular products and services are legalized and regulated.

While the criminal law is determined by relatively large political units (the states and the nation), other aspects of the environment relevant to corruption vary at the community level. Public standards about what constitutes intolerable corruption (and what does not) are believed to be an important influence on how local government generally and the police in particular are pressured and induced to behave (Goldstein, 1975; Klockars, 2003; Sherman, 1977). Communities in which a "public-regarding" ethos is dominant are hypothesized to have less corruption than those with a "private-regarding" ethos (Sherman, 1974:16). The former places highest priority on promoting the general community welfare; the latter focuses on promoting self-interest. Where public-regarding is the dominant perspective, "good government" reformers have attempted to keep politicians from meddling in police operations, and this presumably has made it less likely for police corruption to flow from elected officials. One might also hypothesize that where political competition is perpetually close (that is, no single party or political group dominates local politics), there is less likely to be police corruption. This should be especially the case when the local prosecutor is of a different party from the municipal chief executive. Under these circumstances, the prosecutor is more likely to see political merit in uncovering and prosecuting police corruption. In a somewhat different vein, higher levels of culture conflict (based on race, ethnicity, religion, lifestyle) are thought to facilitate police corruption, because culture conflict leads to divergence on the rightness of some laws, and this in turn creates pressure for uneven enforcement of those laws (Sherman, 1974:17).

Scandal itself is viewed as a powerful influence on the level of corruption. The existence of scandal relies on news media vigorously investigating the possibility of police corruption (Sherman, 1974:30). Scandal appears to reduce the degree to which corruption is organized, at least in the short run (Sherman, 1978:12). However, whether the benefits of this publicity will endure depends heavily on the reform policies that are subsequently implemented and whether those policies are sustained or allowed to deteriorate over time.

Recent scholarship in this field has returned to the individual level. There is a new focus on officer surveys, asking not about reports of their own offending, but rather measuring integrity via their attitudes, perceptions, and self-reports of how they would respond to situations in which integrity is an issue (Klockars et al., 2000). The idea is that in departments of high integrity, officers will know and support the rules governing police misconduct; they will know the disciplinary threats associated with various rule violations; they will assess the department's disciplinary practice as fair; and they will be willing to report misconduct. This allows researchers to describe "in a fairly precise way, the characteristics of a police agency's culture that encourage its employees to resist or tolerate certain types of police misconduct" (Klockars et al., 2000:10). Klockars and colleagues (2000) surveyed officers in 30 police departments in the United States and found that overall a majority would not report a colleague who engaged in the least serious misbehaviors (e.g., accepting free meals and discounts), but that they would report someone who engaged in behaviors judged to be at intermediate or high levels of seriousness (e.g., accepting kickbacks from an auto repair shop for referrals, turning in a lost wallet while keeping the cash from that wallet). Their study also found that police departments varied considerably in the climate of integrity.

Using integrity measurement as a means of indirectly addressing the corruption problem appears to show considerable promise. Surveys are relatively inexpensive and easy to administer; they are not nearly as threatening as the more intrusive forms of integrity testing that departments use to catch individual officers; and importantly, the method provides quantifiable indicators that do not rely on officers' self-reporting their own or their colleagues' misdeeds. Nonetheless, there are limitations to this method. Perhaps most importantly, and as its advocates acknowledge, what officers indicate on an attitude survey about a series of scenarios does not necessarily predict with a high degree of accuracy how the officers would actually behave if actually confronted with those situations. The strongest test of this survey methodology would be to examine officers' actual behaviors. For example, do officers who score high on integrity actually report officer misconduct at a higher rate than those who score low? Do agencies that score high on integrity actually show less tolerance of discovered misconduct than those that score low? For these and other reasons, it is not safe to assume that organizations that score high on integrity will necessarily score low on corruption (Klockars et al., 2000:10).

PROMOTING COMPLIANCE WITH LEGAL AND CONSTITUTIONAL RULES

It is one thing to write down a set of rules that describe the proper use of police force and authority; it is quite another to have those rules reliably guide the day-to-day conduct of the police on the street. Indeed, if there is one important thing that decades of research on the police have taught, it is that there are many powerful factors influencing the conduct of police beyond the laws and rules that are supposed to guide them. Nonetheless, it is important that society find effective means for guiding the conduct of the police, and a great deal of experience has accumulated with different ways of trying to do so. We present the evidence on this experience below.

This section first considers research on the efficacy of criminal and civil actions against the police in controlling police misconduct. Both lethal and excessive force claims are governed by civil suits grounded either in state tort law or federal civil rights laws or both, and excessive force claims also are circumscribed by criminal law. The section next considers the effects of federal civil actions against police departments for "pattern or practice" claims that they promote unlawful behavior. These cases were authorized by the same Violent Crime Control and Law Enforcement Act that supported the expansion of community policing. Administrative policies and procedures have also been adopted by policing agencies to address misconduct, including internal inspections and early warning personnel systems. This section also examines research on external accountability mechanisms, addressing what is known about controlling police corruption.

Criminal and Civil Liability

It is difficult to determine the effectiveness of criminal and civil liability in deterring police use of excessive force because data regarding the frequency and severity of excessive force incidents are weak. Among the myriad of obstacles to measuring excessive force is the fact that even official records regarding police abuse of force are rarely kept or are not available to the public (Human Rights Watch, 1998). In 1994, Congress mandated that the U.S. Department of Justice "acquire data about the use of excessive force" by police officers and "publish an annual summary of the data" (Bureau of Justice Statistics, 2001). However, even the Department of Justice has been unable to collect this information; in order to comply with the mandate, it has instead published statistics regarding the general use of force by police, acknowledging that "current indicators of excessive force...are all critically flawed." Notwithstanding this barrier, the data that are available indicate that criminal and civil liability for excessive force has little effect on police behavior. Administrative guidelines are an effective deterrent to the use of excessive force when they are consistently enforced by police management.

Criminal Law

Criminal prosecution represents one means of bringing to justice officers who have broken the law, either through corruption or excessive use of force. At the local level, prosecutors may bring criminal charges against police officers for excessive force under general state laws regarding assault, battery, murder, etc. Some states also have specific statutes that make excessive police force a separate crime. Federal and state grand juries also have the power to investigate and bring indictments against police officers for alleged criminal actions.

Most experts regard criminal prosecution as an extremely limited vehicle for achieving meaningful accountability. Obtaining the conviction of officers is extremely difficult, as judges and juries exhibit a high level of deference to the testimony of police officers. Also, criminal prosecution of individual officers or even small cadres of officers does not address systemic organizational problems that contribute to officer misconduct (Vera Institute, 1998).

It appears that comprehensive data regarding rates of prosecution, conviction, and sentencing are not compiled in most states. However, by all accounts, local criminal prosecution of officers for excessive force is extremely rare (Human Rights Watch, 1998; Adams, 1996 in Geller &Toch). In Los Angeles, the district attorney's office prosecuted only 43 excessive force cases between 1981 and 1991, less than 0.25 percent of alleged acts of excessive force (Levinson, 1994). In 1998, a district attorney in Atlanta reported to Human Rights Watch that he remembered only three excessive force cases from the past five years.[23] Researchers attribute this phenomenon to two sources. The first is reluctance on the part of prosecutors to

---

[23]U.S. Commission on Civil Rights, *supra* note 8 at 131, 133.

bring excessive force cases, due to lack of support by public officials, their need for good working relationships with the police, and the low probability of conviction as a result of evidentiary and witness credibility problems and jury identification with officers.[24] In addition, there are very few referrals from police internal affairs units, which review excessive force complaints before deciding whether to refer them to the district attorney's office.[25] Between 1986 and 1990, 98 percent of excessive force complaints were not referred for prosecution by the Los Angeles Police Department's internal affairs unit.[26]

Excessive police force is a federal crime under 18 U.S.C. § 242, which makes it criminal for an individual acting under color of law to deprive any person of his or her civil rights. Investigations of such violations are conducted by the FBI and then referred to the Civil Rights Division of the Department of Justice. In order for a police officer to be convicted under section 242, the prosecutor must prove that he or she had "specific intent" to deprive an individual of his or her civil rights.[27]

Federal prosecution and conviction for excessive police force is also extremely rare. Less than 1 percent of cases reported to the Department of Justice lead to prosecution.[28] In 1994, 96 percent of police misconduct cases recommended for prosecution by federal investigative agencies were not pursued by the Department of Justice.[29] Of the official misconduct cases prosecuted, the rate of conviction is unusually low compared with other types of cases brought by the Civil Rights Division, for which there is almost a 100 percent success rate. In 1994, 78 percent of federal police misconduct cases were successful; in 1996, only 64 percent were successful.[30] One reason cited for the low conviction rate is the specific intent requirement, which is considered a significant obstacle to conviction.[31] Finally, even when police officers are convicted, they usually receive light sentences. Although section 242 allows a maximum sentence of 10 years in prison and a fine when bodily injury is inflicted, most convicted officers spend little or no time incarcerated.[32]

---

[24]Skolnick and Fyfe, *supra* note 25 at 205.

[25]Patton, *supra* note 29 at 801.

[26]Chevigny, *supra* note 32 at 101.

[27]42 U.S. 14141 (1994).

[28]*Screws* v. *United States*, 325 U.S. 91 (1945).

[29]Human Rights Watch, *supra* note 1 at 94.

[30]Marshall Miller, "Police Brutality," *17 Yale L. & Pol'y Rev.* 149, 153 (1998).

[31]Human Rights Watch, *supra* note 1 at 99.

[32]See id. At 85; Cheh, *supra* note 5 at 247; United States Commission on Civil Rights, *supra* note 5 at 101.

Given these statistics, it is not surprising that most researchers have concluded that criminal sanctions are not a significant deterrent to excessive force by police officers. The risk of prosecution and conviction is so small that officers are likely to believe (correctly) that they can use excessive force without criminal consequences.[33]

Civil Liability

A second use of the courts involves civil suits by private individuals seeking damages for harm done by officers. In most states, victims of excessive police force can sue for damages under traditional theories of tort liability, such as assault or battery. The elements of proof and the legal standards for determining civil liability vary from state to state.[34] Injured persons may also bring civil suits against the police under federal law, specifically 42 U.S.C. § 1983. Municipalities can also be held liable for a police officer's misconduct if it occurred pursuant to policy or custom.[35] Suits grounded in federal civil rights laws seek to enforce constitutional standards and have been acknowledged by the court to be important supplements to the exclusionary rule.

On its face, section 1983 permits plaintiffs to recover not only monetary damages, but also equitable relief. However, the Supreme Court has severely restricted the availability of injunctions under section 1983, making it nearly impossible for plaintiffs to obtain injunctive relief from specific police practices or patterns of abuse.[36] There is some evidence of a significant increase in civil litigation, at least in certain major departments over the years (Newell, Pollock and Tweedy, ICMA, 1992). A number of civil rights and civil liberties activists have embraced civil litigation as a reform strategy, assuming that rising damage awards will force public officials to undertake significant reforms in the police department, especially if they bring cases challenging existing police practices. Attempts to evaluate the effect of civil litigation have found that it has often not produced the desired reforms (McCoy, 1984; Yale Law Journal, 1979).

Although civil suits alleging excessive force are difficult to win,[37] the amount paid in police misconduct cases has grown steadily over the past 30 years,[38] and many American cities are now paying massive amounts of

---

[33]Cheh, *supra* note 5 at 260

[34]*Montell v. Department of Social Services*, 436 U.S. 658 (1978)

[35]*See Rizzo v. Goode*, 423 U.S. 362 (1976); *City of Los Angeles v. Lyons*, 46 U.S. 95 (1983).

[36]*See* Rob Yale, "Searching for the Consequences of Police Brutality," 70 S. Cal. L. Rev. 1841 (1997).

[37]Jerome H. Skolnick and James J. Fyfe, *Above the Law* 202 (1993).

[38]The Christopher Commission, *supra* note 10 at 56.

money in settlements with and judgments for victims of police brutality. Between 1986 and 1990, Los Angeles paid over $20 million in 300 suits against police officers alleging excessive use of force.[39] Between 1994 and 1996, New York City juries awarded $70 million in claims alleging police misconduct, although some of these awards were overturned on appeal or were settled for lesser amounts to avoid appeal by the city.[40] These amounts do not include the costs of litigation and negotiating settlement.

Despite this financial burden, it is well recognized that civil suits offer little deterrence to excessive police force. With regard to individual police officers, there are two primary reasons for this lack of deterrent effect. First, legal fees, settlements, and judgments are paid for by the government. These awards are further limited by the immunity of local governments from punitive damages. In most, if not all, jurisdictions, individual police officers are protected by law from having to pay legal fees and damages in civil suits.[41] City attorneys are responsible for defending officers in misconduct cases; for the most part, the officer's only responsibility is to participate in depositions and trial testimony.[42] Thus civil suits provide no financial incentive to individual officers to cease using excessive force. Second, even successful excessive force suits do not lead to any sort of disciplinary action and have no effect on promotion in the vast majority of cases. In Los Angeles, civil suits are not recorded in police personnel files, and they are not considered by internal affairs unit in investigating complaints.[43] A 1992 investigation found that of 185 officers involved in 100 civil lawsuits in 22 states, only 8 were disciplined; 17 of the officers were actually promoted.[44]

The outcomes of civil suits are equally ineffective in influencing systemic change within police departments. Studies have shown that neither the Los Angeles nor the New York City police departments make institutional or policy changes in response to successful civil suits. The results of civil suits are not even monitored.[45] One reason for this is that damages in these suits are not significant in relation to total police budgets and, more importantly, are not even paid out from the police budget but out of general city funds.[46] More broadly, the minimal influence of civil suits on policy

[39]Matthew Purdy, "In New York, the Handcuffs are One-Size-Fits-All," *New York Times*, August 24, 1997, A1.

[40]*See, e.g.*, Cal Gov't Code § 825 (West 1993).

[41]Alison L. Patton, "The Endless Cycle of Abuse: Why 42 U.S.C. § 1983 is Ineffective in Deterring Police Brutality," 44 Hastings L.J. 753, 768 (1993).

[42]*Id.* at 784.

[43]Human Rights Watch, *supra* note 1 at 82, citing Rochelle Sharpe, "How Cops Beat the Rap," *Gannett News Service*, March 1992.

[44]Paul Chevigny, *Edge of the Knife* 102 (1995).

[45]*Id.*

[46]U.S. Commission on Civil Rights, *supra* note 8 at 131, 133.

and institutional change can be explained by the dominant viewpoint among public officials and police departments that civil damages are the cost of doing business rather than indicative of problematic patterns or practices.[47] In Los Angeles, the cost of civil suits is considered "a reasonable price for the presumed deterrent effect of the [police] department's most violent responses to lawbreaking."[48]

In an early study of this matter, LaFave collected data prior to *Mapp* v. *Ohio*'s restrictions on search and seizure (LaFave, 1965). He identified three potential pre-*Mapp* sanctions for unconstitutional arrests and searches in Kansas, Michigan, and Wisconsin: tort suits, criminal penalties, and administrative sanctions. Officers interviewed in the three relevant states expressed little concern about the threat of a tort action for false imprisonment following an improper arrest. In all three states such suits were infrequent and typically brought only when there was an allegation of extreme physical force and violence. Similarly, researchers could not find one instance of criminal prosecution against a police officer for an unconstitutional arrest. Finally, LaFave notes that department discipline for arrest was infrequently used, especially if the person arrested was guilty.

Although civil suits do not provide an effective deterrent to excessive force, there are rare instances in which a particular suit results in so much media attention that police departments are forced to respond.[49] It is also possible that a particularly large judgment in a small city or town will lead to reform because the financial consequences are more severe when the judgment is paid out from a small budget.[50] For the most part, however, the availability of recourse under state law and section 1983 to victims of excessive force has had no influence on police behavior.

Federal "Pattern and Practice" Actions

In 1994, Congress enacted the Violent Crime Control and Law Enforcement Act, under which the federal government has the power to conduct investigations and bring suit against any police department where there is "a pattern or practice of conduct by law enforcement officers…that deprives persons of rights, privileges, or immunities secured or protected by

---

[47]Skolnick and Fyfe, *supra* note 25 at 205.
[48]Patton, *supra* note 29 at 801.
[49]Chevigny, *supra* note 32 at 101.
[50]42 U.S. 14141 (1994).

the Constitution."[51] As of October 2001, the Department of Justice was in the process of investigating 13 agencies for a pattern and practice of police abuse. Six additional investigations resulted in settlement, four through consent decrees and four through settlement agreements.[52] The latest of these agreements, issued September 4, 2002, between the department and the police of Columbus, Ohio, came only after a civil complaint was filed.

Generally, reforms introduced as the result of these agreements include implementing agreed-on best practices, including reporting systems and early warning systems. Provisions regarding the use of force are included in all of the settlement agreements. Each consent decree creates a role for a court-appointed monitor who oversees compliance with the agreement. The police departments involved are required, among other things, to improve officer training regarding the use of force, to provide detailed reports of each incident of force, and to initiate internal investigations whenever a criminal or civil suit alleging misconduct is brought against an officer. A 2002 consent decree with the Cincinnati Police Department specifically limits the use of chokeholds, chemical sprays, canines, beanbag shotguns, and 40 mm foam rounds.[53]

For the most part, these settlement agreements are too recent to determine whether they have actually decreased the use of excessive force by police officers. However, the Vera Institute of Justice has been monitoring police activity in Pittsburgh, which entered the first of the settlement agreements with the Department of Justice in 1997. It reports that Pittsburgh police are largely in compliance with the consent decree.[54] In light of this report, this approach to deterring excessive force appears promising, although its effectiveness in implementing permanent reform remains to be seen.

---

[51]U.S. Department of Justice, Civil Rights Division, Special Litigation Section, "Frequently Asked Questions," http://www.usdoj.gov/crt/split/faq.htm (June 19, 2002). The settlements covered the following agencies: Pittsburgh Bureau of Police, PA (consent decree, 1997); Steubenville Police Department, OH (consent decree, 1997); New Jersey State Police (consent decree, 1999); Los Angeles Police Department, CA (consent decree, 2001); District of Columbia Metropolitan Police Department (settlement agreement, 2001); Highland Park Police Department, IL (settlement agreement, 2001). As of April 12, 2002, the Department of Justice has also entered into a consent decree with Cincinnati Police Department, Ohio; see http://www.usdoj.gov/crt/split (June 19, 2002).

[52]Memorandum of Agreement between the United States Department of Justice and the City of Cincinnati, Ohio and the Cincinnati Police Department, http://www.usdoj.gov/crt/split (June 21,2002).

[53]Vera Institute of Justice, "Pittsburgh's Experience with Police Monitoring," http://www.vera.org/project/ project1_1.asp?section_id=2&project_id=13 (June 14, 2002).

[54]The Christopher Commission, *supra* note 10 at 26.

Administrative Reform

Research indicates that clear administrative guidelines regarding the use of force, coupled with consistently imposed sanctions for misconduct, reduces the incidence of excessive force. Not surprisingly, written policies are not in themselves an effective deterrent to police misconduct. Since 1979, the Los Angeles Police Department has restricted the use of force to that which "is reasonable and necessary" once "other reasonable alternatives have been exhausted."[55] Clearly, this rule had little influence on the police officers involved in the beating of Rodney King in 1991. However, a written guideline can be sufficient in itself to encourage brutality. For example, the Los Angeles Police Department's official position for many years was that a chokehold is a nonlethal pain compliance technique, while virtually every other major police department considered the use of chokeholds to be a form of potentially lethal force. Perhaps as a consequence, the number of chokehold-related deaths in Los Angeles during the late 1970s was twice the combined total of the remaining 20 largest U.S. police departments.[56]

The effectiveness of administrative guidelines intended to deter excessive force depends on whether or not the performance measures and disciplinary actions implemented by police management provide any incentive to abide by the rules. Most police departments measure performance in quantitative terms, for example, how many tickets were given or how many drugs dealers were arrested.[57] As a result, police officers are not rewarded for the quality of their work. Skolnick and Fyfe compare this to measuring the performance of lawyers by the number of their cases without considering whether the cases were won or lost.[58] Furthermore, this approach encourages officers to ignore guidelines when doing so helps the bottom line. The disincentives provided by performance measures can be exacerbated by the failure of police departments to take disciplinary action when it becomes apparent that an officer has violated restrictions on the use of force. The Christopher Commission reported that there were a significant number of Los Angeles police officers who persistently ignored written guidelines regarding force, and, instead of being punished, they were often rewarded with positive evaluations and promotions.[59] When disciplinary actions were taken, the punishments were inappropriately lenient.[60] Independent com-

---

[55]Skolnick and Fyfe, *supra* note 25 at 42.
[56]*Id.* at 125.
[57]*Id.*
[58]*Id.* at iii-iv (foreword).
[59]*Id.* at 167.
[60]*See* Human Rights Watch, *supra* note 1 at 63-64.

missions in New York City and Boston also found many shortcomings in the way that internal affairs divisions handled complaints.[61]

The influence of police leadership over individual officers, whether through performance and disciplinary measures or through general tone-setting, may be substantial. In a study of the Indianapolis and St. Petersburg police departments, Terrill found that the official position of police administrators on the "style of policing practiced" was directly related to the amount of force used by officers. Police leadership in Indianapolis promoted a get-tough approach to policing, while St. Petersburg's approach was more toned down and emphasized a problem-solving model. As a result, police officers in Indianapolis were more likely to use higher levels of force than those in St. Petersburg.[62] Other researchers have also concluded that "whether through act or omission, the chief is the main architect of police officers' street behavior."[63]

It is not surprising, then, that there is wide consensus that police administrators are significantly more effective than the courts in deterring the use of excessive force. The more difficult question is why so many police departments have failed to provide incentives to individual officers to abide by use of force rules. One explanation is that there is public and political pressure on police leadership to get tough on crime rather than deter the use of excessive force. Only when there is a particularly outrageous and well-publicized incident of police brutality does public attention turn to the issue of excessive force. Over the past 15 years, there have been a number of police beatings that received significant media attention and resulted in public and political demands for reform. Civil rights attorneys believe that this increased scrutiny of police force has led to change: "Fifteen years ago, police officers would beat people up all the time. Today, there are more limits on police.... People are also more sensitized to the issue and won't tolerate as much violence."[64] Thus, to a certain extent, it appears that public and political pressure is the most effective deterrent to the use of excessive force.

Policies and Procedures

Internal accountability mechanisms have been developed at the initiative of police departments themselves, often in response to lawsuits or pres-

---

[61]William Terrill, *Police Coercion* 233 (2000).

[62]Skolnick and Fyfe, *supra* note 25 at 136.

[63]E.g., the 1989 beatings of alleged suspects in the Carol Stuart murder in Boston; the 1991 beating of Rodney King in Los Angeles; the 1997 beating and rape of Abner Louima in New York City.

[64]Patton, *supra* note 29 at 801 (quoting a civil rights attorney she interviewed).

sure from citizen groups concerned about police misconduct. In some departments, internal mechanisms have been imposed by the federal courts as a part of the settlement of civil suits brought by the U.S. Department of Justice, in addition to suits by private litigants in Pittsburgh, Los Angeles, and Cincinnati. Finally, the constitutional decisions discussed above have had the effect of invalidating both state statutes and the policies and procedures of many police departments; many internal policies and procedures take the form they do today in order to conform with those decisions.

Thus an important role of police departments' policies and procedural rules is to implement federal and state court rulings, along with state statutes and city ordinances. For example, the types of weapons that are made available to officers, the rules for their use, training in weapon use, reporting requirements when they are employed, and the procedures for reviewing the appropriateness of their use, all make up part of a police department's use of force policy, which must be aligned with state and federal statutory and constitutional requirements. Most of the research on police compliance with administrative policies therefore examines the implementation of constitutional guidelines in police agencies. It is at the administrative level that controlling police behavior becomes a "management problem." However, to date there has been little research on the effectiveness of managerial and organizational strategies to motivate officer compliance with department policies and procedures. In contrast to the private sector, relatively little has been attempted, much less evaluated, to evaluate the effect of varying pay and perquisites, for example. More has been written on the impediments to managing police, including the effect of police unions, police culture, and the law and order politics of many cities.

Administrative Rules

The principal mechanism for building and maintaining accountability involves administrative rulemaking by police departments. This approach involves attempting to control the exercise of police officer discretion in critical incidents through (1) written policies that structure and confine discretion, (2) the requirement that officers complete written reports about particular incidents, and (3) review by supervisory officers (Davis, 1975; Goldstein, 1977; Walker, 1993).

One significant application of this approach on which there has been some research involves police officer use of lethal force (Fyfe, 1979; Geller and Scott, 1992). As we have noted, beginning in the early 1970s police departments replaced the permissive fleeing felon rule with the more restrictive defense of life standard. Official policies also prohibited warning shots and other uses of firearms. Early studies found that administrative rules were successful in reducing the number of firearms discharges and the number of citizens shot and killed (Fyfe, 1979; Sparger and Giacopassi, 1992).

Research on administrative rulemaking has since been extended to other types of incidents involving the use of police authority. These include studies of the use of physical force (Walker, Alpert, and Kenney, 2001), high-speed pursuits (Alpert, 1997; Alpert and Dunham, 1990), domestic violence (Sherman 1992), the use of canines, and nonlethal technologies (e.g., pepper spray). There is limited evidence on the effectiveness of administrative controls in these areas, however. Controls over high-speed pursuits do appear to reduce the number of pursuits and consequently the number of injuries and fatalities (Alpert, 1997). Research on the use of physical force has been limited to investigating the prevalence of force incidents and the factors associated with its use (Bureau of Justice Statistics, 1999; Geller and Toch, 1995). The deterrent effect of mandatory arrest in domestic violence incidents has been investigated through a number of experiments, but there is limited evidence regarding officer compliance with domestic violence policies in nonexperimental conditions (Sherman, 1992).

Early warning systems represent a new internal accountability mechanism that has developed in recent years. In brief, an early warning system is a data-based management tool designed to identify officers who appear to have performance problems and to subject those officers to some administrative intervention, usually in the form of counseling or retraining (Walker, Alpert and Kenney, 2001). Early warning systems are an outgrowth of the development of administrative rule-making since the required reports principally use data on use of force and other actions to analyze officer performance.

Early warning systems have been growing rapidly and are recognized as one of the best practices in police accountability (Walker, Alpert, and Kenney, 2001). However, the evidence for the success of early warning systems is limited at this point. The only evaluation of early warning systems found that they were effective in reducing the use of force and citizen complaints among officers subject to intervention, but the study itself was limited by a number of methodological problems, including questions about the official data that were used (Walker, Alpert, and Kenney, 2001). Nevertheless, these systems embody the trend toward increased accountability of the police to the community—a trend that speaks directly to the importance of both perceived and objective legitimacy of the police.

Internal Inspections

Responsibility for enforcing internal standards of conduct lies with police department internal affairs units, or what are increasingly called professional standards units. Despite the fact that police management experts recognize that internal affairs units play a critical role, very little research has been conducted on these units. Little is known about the organization, management or staffing of these units. Nor is much known about the investigative procedures used or patterns of discipline. There is a sizeable anecdotal literature on the failure of these units to maintain accountability and integrity (Kerner Commission, 1968; Christopher Commission, 1991; Mollen Commission, 1994), but none of these reports or investigations rises to the level of a scientific study.

Police Data Collection

The advent of sophisticated information systems and a growing awareness of the power of gathering data for internal accountability processes, has encouraged police administrators to routinely collect more data on police operations and practices. Sometimes this is in response to external demands for closer police accountability. In the case of the debate over racial profiling, for example, the mandated collection of official data on traffic stops has emerged as the principal strategy on the part of civil rights groups for ending the practice, defined as a pattern of stopping black and Hispanic drivers on the basis of race or ethnicity rather than suspected criminal activity (Harris, 1997, 1999, 2002; Police Executive Research Forum, 2000; Ramirez, McDevitt, and Farrell, 2000).

As an accountability mechanism, traffic stop data collection operates on the same assumption as administrative rulemaking: that requiring officers to complete official reports on critical decisions will simultaneously put them on notice that their actions are being scrutinized and create a systematic data base that will permit determination of whether a pattern of illegal racial or ethnic discrimination exists.

This is an area in which there is rapid policy change. A growing number of states have enacted laws requiring law enforcement agencies to collect data on traffic stops. In addition, a large and growing number of agencies have undertaken data collection voluntarily. Many of these efforts have yielded publicly available data sets on traffic enforcement patterns (San Jose Police Department, 2001; San Diego Police Departtment, 2000). A great deal of controversy surrounds the proper benchmark for interpreting traffic stop data (Bland et al., 2000; General Accounting Office, 2000; Harris, 1997, 1999, 2002). For the purposes of litigation, this question has been addressed by the use of observational studies of traffic patterns on interstate highways conducted in Maryland and New Jersey (Harris, 2002). In these cases, the data were interpreted as supporting the contention that race discrimination existed in those instances.

More difficult is the question of determining the extent to which patterns in traffic enforcement that indicate racial or ethnic disparities represent patterns of illegal discrimination: the challenge is to develop an appropriate benchmark. Official reports to date generally find racial and ethnic disparities in traffic stops, searches, and arrests (San Jose Police Department, 2001). With respect to traffic stops, these studies use the resident population of the specific area in question as the benchmark. Walker (2001) argues that the resident population is not a valid benchmark because it does not represent the at-risk driving population, and that related benchmarks using estimates of the driving-age population by race and ethnicity are similarly flawed. Attempts to investigate possible discrimination in field stops of pedestrians with resident population data serving as the benchmark are similarly flawed because population data do not reflect either the overall pedestrian population or pedestrians who exhibit legitimate suspicious behavior. Walker proposes using an early warning system approach in which the activity levels of groups of officers with comparable assignments serve as a benchmark for individual performance. In a sense, this would mean measuring police officers against other police officers, as opposed to measuring the citizens stopped by police against some satisfactory benchmark. With respect to searches and arrests of people stopped by police, the population of drivers or pedestrians stopped serves as the appropriate benchmark, thereby facilitating the research effort.

Other strategies for eliminating racial profiling have been advanced, including exhortation, training, in-car video cameras, and various administrative controls, such as requiring officers to notify dispatchers about key features of stops (Fridell et al., 2001; Cohn, Lennon, and Wasserman, 1999). To date there are no studies investigating the effect of any of the proposed reforms designed to eliminate discrimination in traffic enforcement, although a General Accounting Office (2000) report on searches by the U.S. Customs Service suggests that administrative controls can simultaneously reduce racial disparities and increase the efficiency of enforcement efforts.

Controlling Corruption

With few exceptions, what is known about the effectiveness of various methods to control police corruption is based on the experiences of police leaders and the impressions and expertise of scholars. The U.S. General Accounting Office (1998:19-25) surveyed practitioners to identify strategies for preventing police corruption, especially that which is drug-related. They noted the importance of a commitment to integrity by top department leaders, holding managers accountable for corruption in their units, more rigorous hiring policies and more training for recruits, empowering independent auditors to oversee the handling of corruption allegations, and changing the police culture from protecting one's peers to protecting integrity. The study also reported the practitioners and experts' recommendations on detecting corruption more effectively. The practitioners surveyed stressed the importance of placing officers suspected of corruption under surveillance, turning corrupt officers to testify against others involved in corrupt practices, interviewing arrested drug dealers to get information on police corruption, employing proactive investigations (including integrity testing) in areas that have high concentrations of drug-related corruption complaints, and developing an early warning system of factors and behavior patterns that may indicate a corruption problem.

The above list is consistent with research-based recommendations, which have also included rewarding officers for good performance, pursuing federal prosecution, and working with the news media to mobilize public opinion to fight corruption and pressure elected officials to support effective policies (Walker, 1999:254-63). We note that the systematic evidence supporting these claims is almost nonexistent, due to the extreme difficulty of obtaining valid and reliable measures of police corruption.

EXTERNAL ACCOUNTABILITY MECHANISMS

The tradition of local accountability of police is sometimes extended by the creation of external bodies charged with overseeing police operations. The logic behind this strategy seems apparent: what police do is important, and they are one of the most visible parts of local government. Where there is dissatisfaction with police internal accountability mechanisms, citizen groups have demanded the creation of external mechanisms as well. In recent decades citizen dissatisfaction, reflecting an apparent loss of perceived legitimacy, has been primarily centered in the black community and has traditionally been labeled "the police-community relations problem" (Kerner Commission, 1968).

Citizen Oversight Bodies

The principal demand for external accountability by civil rights groups has been for the creation of citizen oversight agencies, commonly termed civilian review boards (Walker, 2001). Specifically, citizen groups have demanded that an external oversight agency be given responsibility for receiving, investigating, and disposing of citizen complaints against agencies. This demand reflects the belief that police internal affairs units, in varying degrees, discourage complaints, fail to investigate complaints thoroughly and fairly, and fail to discipline officers who are found to have committed misconduct. The police and their supporters generally deny that excessive force is a problem and argue that police departments are better equipped to investigate complaints than are people who are not sworn officers.

External citizen oversight agencies have been growing steadily since the late 1970s. By 2001 these were slightly more than 100 such agencies. Police departments in nearly 90 percent of the big cities are subject to some form of oversight regarding complaints. Citizen oversight also exists with respect to a number of medium-sized and small police departments, along with some county sheriff's departments. These figures are based on the broadest definition of external oversight and include any procedure in which there is some citizen input into the review process, however limited, by persons who are not sworn police officers. Virtually all of these agencies are authorized by local ordinance (Walker, 2001). Because of the bargaining that takes place in the legislative process that created them, citizen oversight agencies take a number of different forms. Walker (2001) classifies them by four different models of oversight: under this scheme, only Class I systems have original jurisdiction with regard to the investigation of complaints. Other institutional arrangements include boards that play an auditing or monitoring function with regard to police-run investigations.

There is very limited evidence regarding the effectiveness of citizen oversight agencies. As already noted, considerable anecdotal evidence exists regarding the shortcomings of internal affairs units (Kerner, 1968; U.S. Commission on Civil Rights, 1981), but no comparative studies indicating that external citizen oversight agencies are more effective than internal affairs units. This kind of evaluation of internal accountability mechanisms poses a number of difficulties (Brereton, 2000; Walker, 2001). The published literature generally fails to take into account the multiple goals of oversight agencies; these include, but are not limited to, conducting thorough and fair investigations of citizen complaints and building citizen confidence in the complaint process. Comparative studies of their effectiveness are also difficult because local external and internal units or boards tend to handle very different kinds of cases and hear different types of allegations (Hudson, 1972, Walker, 2001).

Blue Ribbon Commissions

A traditional approach to pressing for greater accountability has been through the formation of authoritative commissions that investigate police problems and issue reports with recommendations for reform (Walker 1985). At the national level, the most important examples include the 1931 Wickersham Commission (National Commission on Law Observance and Enforcement, 1931), the President's Crime Commission (1967), the National Advisory Commission on Civil Disorders (the Kerner Commission) of 1968 and the American Bar Association Standards for Urban Police Function (1973). There have also been numerous state and local commissions created in the wake of local legitimacy crises; the 1922 Cleveland Crime

Survey initiated this trend. Other notable commissions include the Christopher Commission, formed in response to events associated with the Rodney King incident in Los Angeles, which published its findings in 1991; and both the Knapp Commission and the Mollen Commission, created in response to allegations of widespread corruption in the New York City Police Department.

Blue ribbon commissions have played an important role in setting general standards for the police and in that respect guiding reform efforts across the country. In some cities, reform-minded police chiefs have been able to use the legitimacy crisis engendered by the investigations conducted by commissions to effect needed changes in their departments (Murphy and Plate, 1977). The major weakness of this approach to reform is that blue ribbon commissions are temporary agencies that disband following publication of a final report. Consequently, there has been no mechanism to ensure implementation of their recommendations (Walker 1985). For example, there has been controversy over the implementation of the Christopher Commission report in Los Angeles (Christopher Commission, 1991; Bobb et al., 1996). Walker (2001) argues that the role of blue ribbon commissions has been superseded by the auditor model of citizen oversight, which involves a permanent body that has the capacity to oversee and report on the implementation of recommended reforms (San Jose Independent Auditor, 1993-present; Special Counsel, Los Angeles County Sheriff's Department, 1993-present). Currently, New York City has the only permanent external corruption control agency in the nation, the New York City Commission to Combat Police Corruption.

Not enough is known about the extent of police lawfulness, or police compliance with legal and other rules, nor can the mechanisms that best promote police lawfulness be identified. The committee recommends renewed research on the lawfulness of police and a coordinated research emphasis on the effectiveness of organizational mechanisms that foster police rectitude.

8

Police Fairness:
Legitimacy as the
Consent of the Public

Research has examined the legitimacy of policing as well as its lawfulness. By legitimacy we mean the judgments that ordinary citizens make about the rightfulness of police conduct and the organizations that employ and supervise them. Unlike police lawfulness, which is defined in large measure by legal and administrative standards and can be observed in part in the field, legitimacy lies in the hearts and minds of the public. Perceptions of legitimacy are, by definition, subjective. They can be affected by many factors, and may not mirror the activities of the police as they are measured in other ways. However, legitimacy in the eyes of the public is one of the important outputs of policing, and attention to it is warranted on a number of grounds.

First, the more legitimacy the police have among their different audiences, the more effective they can be in achieving their goals. If citizens trust the police, they will be willing to invest more authority in the police and spend more taxpayer dollars on them. If citizens trust the police, they will call them when they need help and help them identify offenders; crimes that are investigated as a result are more likely to be solved than if citizens are reluctant to call. If those stopped by the police think they have been stopped legitimately, they are more likely to cooperate than if they think they have been unfairly rousted. Perhaps most important, if the police are seen as legitimate, at least one of the threats that might concern citizens—that they could be mistreated by the police as well as by criminals—can be set aside.

Second, police fairness is an end in itself. In a democracy where citizens are policed by consent, the exercise of state power must be seen as an expression of the community and not an action against it. This does not mean that police are engaged in a popularity contest. Our review of research concludes that legitimacy grows out of how police treat victims, witnesses, bystanders, people reporting crime, and those who commit crime. When they adhere to the rules, maintain their neutrality, and treat people with dignity and respect, police legitimacy increases. Perceptions regarding police fairness are created and sustained by the process of policing itself.

This chapter examines the process by which police organizations attempt to garner legitimacy through efforts to make their operations more responsive to the felt needs of citizens. This path involves organizational change. Legitimacy can be gained through the adoption of programs, policies, and procedures that are viewed by the community and civic leaders as effective and desirable. It can also be gained by hiring personnel and allocating departmental resources in ways that are viewed as equitable. In each case, departments acquire legitimacy by organizing themselves in ways that are acceptable and seem responsive to professional and public standards.

Research on fairness and legitimacy draws on the findings of surveys and experimental research. Surveys are used to gather information on what people think about the police and to collect self-reports of the experiences of individuals. Because these surveys are often national in scope and some have been carried out for a number of years, they can also point to trends in legitimacy over time and for major subgroups in the population. Studies utilizing experimental designs look at the effects of a variety of factors on people's assessments of police legitimacy, and consider whether the factors that influence legitimacy have similar effects among different groups in the population.

Research on legitimacy has focused on several audiences. One is simply the general public, who can be understood as comparing what they know about police performance with some conception of how they would *like* the police to behave. If citizens were generally knowledgeable about and committed to the many rules that regulate police conduct, this standard would be identical to the standards discussed in Chapter 7. While the public may not be knowledgeable of these rules in great detail, surveys have long confirmed that people want the police to behave in accord with simple principles of justice.

A second audience whose views are important consists of those who call the police for assistance. This group most closely approximates the customer base of the police (but see Moore, 2002, for a discussion of the limitations of this assumption). They are the ones who ask for and benefit from service by the police. An important goal of policing, and one of the important ways in which they gain legitimacy, is by meeting the expectations of those who call them for assistance: those who have been victims of crimes, those who are afraid, and those who need emergency assistance of one kind or another.

A third audience consists of those who are stopped, cited, or arrested by the police. These people, unlike those who call the police, did not choose to have their particular encounter and do not necessarily expect to benefit from it. In general, people who call, flag down, or approach the police are more satisfied with what happened—and with policing generally—than are those who are pulled off the road or stopped by patrol officers while walking on foot. For example, in a review of the literature Decker (1981) dubbed them voluntary and involuntary contacts. He concluded that voluntary contacts, those initiated by citizens, are more positive in substance than involuntary, police-initiated contacts. He reasoned that police play a supportive role in citizen-initiated contacts, while police-initiated contacts are likely to be of a more suspicious, inquisitorial and adversarial nature. These differences have been observed in many studies. For example, Southgate and Ekblom (1984) found that, in Britain, being involved in field interrogations and vehicular stops generated three times as much public "annoyance" (as they measured it) as other kinds of encounters with police.

However, studies have shown that even those involuntarily stopped by the police notice the difference between being fairly and respectfully treated on one hand, and abused on the other. They hope to be treated in a way that respects their rights and their dignity as well as their safety, and it is valuable as an end in itself that even those who are ticketed or even arrested feel that they are treated fairly and with dignity (Coupe and Griffiths, 1999; Reisig and Chandek, 2001). Moreover, it serves an instrumental purpose: research indicates those who feel fairly treated are more likely to comply with the demands of the police (Tyler, 1997; Tyler and Huo, 2002).

These three groups overlap considerably. In a given year, the largest will be those who have paid only intermittent attention to the police and have formed a generalized view of how they conduct themselves. Among them will be a smaller group of citizens who called for help or experienced a police "service encounter," as well as a still smaller group who have been stopped, cited, or arrested and therefore experienced what Moore (1992) dubbed an "obligation encounter." As a result, there are a variety of perspectives from which people form their opinions of the police. It is important to evaluate the police from these three vantage points, since citizens will use all three kinds of experiences in deciding whether the police are legitimate or not.

Race is one important dimension along which people in all three of these groups divide in their opinion of the police. Surveys routinely reveal that when the subject is the police, Americans divide sharply along racial lines when they describe their feelings and experiences. The importance and consistency of this result warrants special attention.

LEGITIMACY AND POLICING

A core function of the police is to bring the behavior of citizens into line with the law. This is true both in personal encounters between members of the public and the police, during which officers make decisions about what is appropriate conduct that people need to accept and follow, and in the case of people's everyday compliance with the law in the absence of legal supervision. The need for legal authorities to secure ready compliance with both specific instructions and voluntary obedience in everyday life has been widely noted by legal scholars and social scientists: "The lawgiver must be able to anticipate that the citizenry as a whole will...generally observe the body of rules he has promulgated" (Fuller, 1971:201). This is the case because the effective exercise of legal authority requires compliance from "the bulk of [citizens] most of the time," (Easton, 1975:185). Decisions by police officers mean very little if people generally ignore them, and laws lack importance if they do not affect public behavior in a routine way (Tyler, 1990).

It is widely assumed that the ability of democratic legal systems to function depends on gaining voluntary compliance with the law (Parsons, 1967; Engstrom and Giles, 1972; Scheingold, 1974; Easton, 1975; Sarat, 1977). Whether such voluntary compliance is, in fact, necessary for social regulation, it is unquestionably true that legal authorities benefit when the public is generally motivated to follow the law. If many or most of the people in a society voluntarily follow the rules, police are able to direct their coercive efforts against a smaller subset of community members who do not hold supportive internal values.

Three major factors help explain why people voluntarily obey the law: when it is instrumental, when they believe in the moral rightfulness of the substantive law, and when they believe in the legitimacy of the process of making and evoking the law. The police play an important role in the first and third of these compliance processes.

Instrumental Motives

One perspective on social regulation builds on human motivations that are instrumental or "rational" in character. In this view, individuals minimize their personal costs and maximize their rewards. This conception underlies deterrence, sanctioning, or social control models of social regulation (Nagin, 1998). These all emphasize the ability of legal authorities and institutions to shape people's behavior by threatening to deliver or by actually delivering negative sanctions for rule-breaking. To implement deterrence strategies, police officers in the United States carry guns and clubs and can threaten citizens with physical injury, incapacitation, or financial penalties. Their goal is to establish their authority and "the uniform, badge, truncheon, and arms all may play a role in asserting authority" in the effort to "gain control of the situation" (Reiss, 1971:46). The police seek to control the individual's behavior "by manipulating an individual's calculus regarding whether 'crime pays' in the particular instance" (Meares, 1998). Judges similarly shape people's acceptance of their decisions by threatening fines or even jail time for failure to comply.

Research suggests that the ability to threaten or deliver sanctions is generally effective in shaping people's law-related behavior. In particular, a number of studies on deterrence suggest that people are less likely to engage in illegal behaviors when they think that they might be caught and punished for wrongdoing. This core premise of deterrence models is supported by many, but not all, studies examining the factors that shape people's law related behavior (Paternoster et al., 1983; Paternoster and Iovanni, 1986; Paternoster, 1987, 1989; Tyler, 1990; Nagin and Paternoster, 1991; Nagin, 1998).

Studies of deterrence also point to several factors that limit the likely effectiveness of deterrence models of social regulation. Perhaps the key factor limiting the value of deterrence strategies is the consistent finding that deterrence effects, when they are found, are small in magnitude. For example, in a review of studies of deterrence in the area of drug use, MacCoun (1993) finds that around 5 percent of the measured variance in drug use behavior can be explained by variations in indicators of the expected likelihood or severity of punishment. This suggests that much of the variance in law-related behavior flows from other factors besides risk estimates.

A further possible limitation of deterrence strategies is that, while deterrence effects can potentially be influenced by either estimates of the likelihood of being caught and punished for wrongdoing (certainty of punishment), or by estimates of the likely cost of being caught (severity of punishment), studies suggest that both factors are not equally effective. A difficulty for policy is that the factor that most strongly influences people's behavior is the certainty of punishment (Paternoster and Iovanni, 1986; Paternoster, 1987, 1989; Nagin and Paternoster, 1991), which is also the part of the deterrence equation that is most difficult to effectively change. To influence behavior, risk estimates need to be high enough to exceed some threshold of being psychologically meaningful (Teevan, 1975; Ross, 1982). For most crimes in the United States, the objective risk of being caught and punished is quite low. There are a number of methods for estimating these probabilities, and results vary. For burglary, the apprehension rate has been found to be as low as 4 percent; for homicide, apprehension rates have approached 80 percent in many cities, before they recently began to fall (see Skogan and Antunes, in Bayley, 1998).

In addition, the effectiveness of "instrumental means of producing compliance always depend[s] on resource limits" (Meares and Harcourt, 2000: 401). The question is how much society is willing to invest in crime control, and how much power legal authorities will be allowed to have to intrude into people's lives. Resources need to be deployed in strategic and effective ways. Sherman (1998), for example, notes that in the United States police resources are typically expended more in response to political pressures than to actual crime threats, with the consequence that the ability of the police to deter crime is less than optimal. Based on his analysis, Ross (1992) argues that it is difficult to implement deterrence approaches in the context of the political realities of democratic societies.

Thus the problem faced by those responsible for the everyday enforcement of law in democratic societies is that deterrent effects are apparently modest, certainty of punishment is low under many circumstances, and there are political constraints on resource allocation. As a consequence, deterrence strategies alone are unlikely to be a sufficient basis for an effective system of social regulation. Deterrence can form the foundation of efforts to maintain the legal order, but it cannot be a complete strategy for gaining compliance (Ayres and Braithwaite, 1992). An effective strategy for ensuring public compliance with legal authorities requires additional reasons for obeying the law (Tyler, 1990, 2003; Sherman, 1993, 1998, 2001).

Substantive Morality

The second motivation to comply with legal authorities involves the moral or ethical values that shape people's feelings about how it is appropriate to behave. If their personal values are consistent with the law their cooperation will be to a large extent voluntarily, and people will be "self-regulatory." Morality or ethics are both concerned with feelings about what is right or wrong. The degree to which people view law as consistent with their own values is clearly one factor shaping their law-related behavior, independent of issues of legitimacy (see Robinson and Darley, 1995; Tyler, 1990; Tyler and Darley, 2000; Sunshine and Tyler, 2003). To the extent that people are following laws because of their ethical values, society need not devote resources to agents of social control like the police. Tyler (2001a) refers to a society in which people are internally motivated to obey the law as "a law-abiding society."

However, morality or ethics are social and cultural phenomena. While personal values can facilitate compliance with the law, they can also undermine it. On one hand, a person may refrain from stealing because they think it is wrong to do so, irrespective of whether the law forbids it. On the other hand, a person may defy and undermine laws allowing abortion or promoting integration, because those laws contradict personal values. Unlike legitimacy, personal values can either promote or undermine the rule of law (see Tyler and Darley, 2000).

Belief in Legitimacy

This chapter focuses on legitimacy, rather than the morality of the law. It does so because legitimacy is a characteristic of legal authorities and can therefore be created or undermined by their behavior. Legitimacy is the property that a rule or an authority has when others feel obligated to voluntarily defer to that rule or authority. In other words, a legitimate authority is one that is regarded by people as entitled to have its decisions and rules accepted and followed by others (French and Raven, 1959; Merelman, 1966).

The roots of the modern discussion of legitimacy are usually traced to Max Weber's discussion of authority and the social dynamics of authority (Weber, 1968). Weber argued that the ability to issue commands that will be obeyed does not rest solely on the possession and ability to use power. He described an additional aspect to authority—legitimacy, or the quality possessed by an authority, a law, or an institution that leads others to feel obligated to obey its decisions and directives. Legitimacy, in this sense, is a characteristic of public institutions, yet it is conferred on institutions by the people.

A similar view of responsibility and obligation to others is articulated by other social observers. As Hoffman notes: "The legacy of both Sigmund Freud and Emile Durkheim is the agreement among social scientists that most people do not go through life viewing society's moral norms as external, coercively imposed pressures to which they must submit. Though the norms are initially external to the individual and often in conflict with [a person's] desires, the norms eventually become part of [a person's] internal motive system and guide [a person's] behavior even in the absence of external authority. Control by others is thus replaced by self control [through a process labeled internalization]" (Hoffman, 1977:85).

As with Weber, the key issue addressed by Durkheim and Freud is the personal taking on of obligations and responsibilities that become self-regulating, so that people feel individually responsible for deferring to society, social rules, and authorities. In this report we follow Weber in focusing on the internalization of the obligation to obey authorities, as opposed to the internalization of the responsibility to follow principles of personal values. This particular feeling of responsibility includes a willingness to suspend personal considerations of self-interest and to ignore personal values because an individual thinks that an authority or a rule is entitled to determine appropriate behavior in a given situation or situations.[1]

---

[1]Kelman and Hamilton (1989) refer to legitimacy as "authorization," to reflect the idea that a person authorizes an authority to determine appropriate behavior in some situation and then feels obligated to follow the directives or rules that the authority establishes. As they indicate, the authorization of actions by authorities "seem[s] to carry automatic justification for them. Behaviorally, authorization obviates the necessity of making judgments or choices. Not only do normal moral principles become inoperative, but—particularly when the actions are explicitly ordered—a different type of morality, linked to the duty to obey superior orders, tends to take over" (Kelman and Hamilton, 1989:16).

CREATING LEGITIMACY

While legitimacy can be a general feeling of obligation or responsibility to obey that encourages deference in any situation, it is also something that is created by individual police officers in an encounter with members of the public (Reiss, 1971). Recognizing this, police officers focus not only on displays of force, but also establishing their legitimate right to intervene in a particular situation (Reiss, 1971:46). Police interventions into people's lives are viewed by the people affected as more legitimate when there is some additional reason for the intervention beyond the officer's personal judgment, such as a complaint from another citizen. When the subject or observer of the intervention perceives legitimacy as low, the police are more likely to resort to physical force, thereby introducing the risk of injury to both the arrested person and the officer (Reiss, 1971:60). Interestingly, Reiss found that 73 percent of injuries to officers occur when the officers are interfered with, and interference most typically comes from people other than the parties involved in the immediate situation—for example, bystanders and family members. Reiss observed: "when such persons question the legitimacy of police intervention and a police officer reacts to control their behavior, more serious conflict may ensue as each party attempts to gain control of the situation. This results more often in injury to the officer" (Reiss, 1971:60).

In addition to being created in a particular type of situation, legitimacy is also created by individual police officers. When a police officer responds to a call or stops someone on the street, what happens affects general feelings that people have regarding the extent to which authorities are legitimate and are entitled to be obeyed. In turn, to the degree that community residents see police officers as legitimate, the task of particular police officers is made easier. Tyler and Huo (2001) found that people who view legal authorities as legitimate are generally more willing to defer to the directives of specific police officers. The behavior of the officer in a particular situation can, in turn, influence this more generalized legitimacy of the police.

The cyclical nature of this pattern brings out one of the potential virtues of community policing, in which community residents develop a long-term relationship with particular police officers. It gives those officers an opportunity to build support for their role, thereby carving out an individual and potentially positive relationship with community members. Tyler and Darley (2000) found that the effects of the particular actions of police officers are greater than the effects of general legitimacy. That is, whatever generalized view of legitimacy people have, it is overwhelmed by their reactions to the actions of the particular police officers with whom they are dealing. Particular police officers can therefore either build on whatever legitimacy they bring into the situation, or they can rapidly undermine it.

While legal scholars are concerned about police focus on statutory and court-determined rules of conduct and professional standards, many social scientists focus on the effects of police actions on the beliefs and actions of the public. This perspective assumes that police behavior should in substantial part be evaluated against the public's ethical and moral standards. An example of such an approach is provided by Slobogin (1991; Slobogin and Schumacher, 1993), who evaluates the intrusiveness of law enforcement searches and seizures using ratings derived from public opinion. He argues that standards of acceptable police behavior should be crafted with reference to the role of police activity itself and the subsequent ways in which that activity shapes views of legitimacy of the police, the courts, and the law. Perhaps most important, studies find that people evaluate the actions of authorities against prevailing standards of ethical behavior (Leventhal, 1980; Tyler, Boeckmann, Smith, and Huo, 1997; Tyler and Smith, 1997).

The central goal for empirical research on legitimacy has been to test when and how the process of people conferring legitimacy on the police actually occurs, and how this in turn explains their response to the law and directives of legal authorities. Researchers have measured legitimacy in a variety of ways. In the case of laws and legal authorities, studies have often used an index of the perceived obligation to obey them. Typical items from such a scale, in this case drawn from Tyler (1990), include: "People should obey the law even if it goes against what they think is right" (82 percent yes); "I always try to follow the law, even if I think it is wrong" (82 percent yes); and "If a person is doing something, and a police officer tells them to stop, they should stop even if they feel that what they are doing is legal" (84 percent yes).

The perceived obligation to obey is the most direct extension of the concept of legitimacy. Building on studies by political scientists and the conceptual framework of Easton (Easton and Dennis, 1969), legitimacy has also been measured in terms of support, allegiance, institutional trust, and confidence. Drawing on this literature, Tyler (1990) measured legitimacy by asking people's agreement to items like: "I have a great deal of respect for the Chicago police" and "I feel that I should support the Chicago police."

More recently, legitimacy has been conceptualized as cynicism about the law (Silbey and Ewick, 1998). This analysis considers the degree to which people feel that the law and legal authorities represent their interests, as opposed to the interests of a select group. On the basis of this conceptual model, Tyler and colleagues (2000, 2002) operationalized cynicism using several items, including: "The law represents the values of the people in power, rather than the values of people like me," "People in power use the law to try to control people like me," and "The law does not protect my interests."

Race and Legitimacy

Research on race and police legitimacy has yielded consistent and important results. When asked about the police, surveys reveal large differences among people of different races in the United States. Black Americans almost universally report the most negative views of the police (for a rare exception, see Frank et al., 1996). Whites are less inclined than are blacks to believe that police discriminate against minorities. Blacks are more likely to think that police racism is common and that police treat them more harshly than they do whites (Weitzer, 2000). Whites, blacks, and Hispanics often are in close agreement about the effectiveness of police in preventing crime, but they stand far apart on questions about how police respect and help people and treat them fairly (Roberts and Stalans, 1997). When asked hypothetical questions about police use of force under various circumstances, blacks are more likely than whites to disapprove of police use of violence (Tuch and Weitzer, 1997; Roberts and Stalans, 1997). They are also less likely to report having confidence that police can protect them from violent crime (Tuch and Weitzer, 1997). Whites have substantially more confidence in police than they do in the Supreme Court (in a 1994 national survey the difference was 13 percentage points), while blacks have about equal confidence in police and the Supreme Court (Roberts and Stalans, 1997). In a 1994 study, 52 percent of whites, but only 39 percent of blacks, would go beyond the Supreme Court (in *Tennessee v. Garner*) by endorsing police use of lethal force to stop a person suspected of burglary (Cullen et al., 1996).

People of different races also vary in reports of their own experiences with the police. Summarizing this research, Tuch and Weitzer (1997:646) note that "blacks are more likely than whites to report having involuntary, uncivil, or adversarial contacts with police; to be stopped, questioned and/or searched without due cause; and to personally experience verbal or physical abuse." In other surveys, blacks are also more likely to report in surveys that police have been discourteous to them (Roberts and Stalans, 1997) and that they have observed police wrongdoing (Flanagan and Vaughn, 1996).

These differences were documented most recently in a large national survey conducted by the Census Bureau for the Bureau of Justice Statistics (BJS) (Langan et al., 2001). After screening respondents to determine who among them had direct experiences with the police during the previous year, interviewers asked follow-up questions about those experiences. In the BJS survey, blacks were more likely to report being stopped by the police, and they were more likely to be stopped repeatedly. They were less likely than whites to think they were stopped for a legitimate reason, and they were more likely to be ticketed, arrested, and handcuffed. They were much more likely than were whites to report that the police used physical force during those encounters, and they were even more likely to report that the force was excessive. Blacks were twice as likely as whites to report that police did not behave properly, and when they were searched they were less likely to believe that the search was legitimate. Hispanic respondents generally fell in between whites and blacks on these measures. These consistent results speak to need for police to work to gain legitimacy among minority groups.

Procedural Justice and Legitimacy

Another striking finding has resulted from research on police fairness: empirical studies suggest that the key to developing and maintaining the legitimacy of law and of legal authorities and to obtaining public cooperation lies in citizens' evaluations of the *procedures* through which legal rules are created and implemented. Studies of personal encounters with police officers and judges consistently suggest that people's attitudes, feelings, and behaviors are influenced by their sense of what is right and wrong, just or unjust (Tyler et al., 1997; Tyler and Smith, 1997).

Despite claims that people are interested only in outcomes that favor themselves, the dominate finding of studies exploring people's post-experience feelings and behaviors is that they are most strongly influenced by the degree to which they experience procedural justice—an evaluation of the fairness of the manner in which their problem or dispute was handled. This is especially true when people are dealing with third-party authorities, whether they are police officers, judges, managers, political leaders, or any other type of authority (Lind and Tyler, 1988; Tyler et al., 1997; Tyler and Smith, 1997; Tyler, 2001). The argument underlying the procedural justice literature is that people will defer to decisions because those decisions are made through fair processes. This procedural justice effect is believed to be distinct from the influence of concerns about either outcome favorability or outcome fairness. As such, it provides a way for acceptable decisions to be made in situations in which people cannot be given what they want or feel they deserve.

Thibaut and Walker conducted what is considered the original research on procedural justice (Thibaut and Walker, 1975). Their hypothesis was that people would be willing to accept outcomes because they were fairly decided on—that is, because of the justice of the decision-making procedures used. They performed the first systematic experiments that demonstrated that people's assessments of the fairness of third-party decision-making procedures shape their satisfaction with their outcomes. Their finding has been confirmed in subsequent laboratory studies of procedural justice (Lind and Tyler, 1988; Tyler et al., 1997).

Subsequent studies found that, when third-party decisions are fairly made, people are more willing to voluntarily accept them (MacCoun et al.,

1988; Kitzman and Emery, 1993; Lind et al., 1993; Wissler, 1995). What is striking about these studies is that procedural justice effects are found in studies of real disputes in real settings, confirming the experimental findings of Thibaut and Walker.

Procedural justice judgments are found to have an especially important role in shaping adherence to agreements over time. This is important in light of the reminder of Mastrofski, Snipes, and Supina (1996) that citizens can acquiesce at the scene yet later renege. Pruitt and his colleagues study the factors that lead those involved in disputes to adhere to mediation agreements that end disputes. They find that procedural fairness judgments about the initial mediation session are a central determinant of whether people are adhering to the mediation agreement six months later (Pruitt et al., 1993). A study by Paternoster et al. (1997) also finds that procedural justice encourages long-term obedience to the law. They examined the long-term behavior of people who dealt with the police who came to their home on a domestic violence call. In such cases the problem was typically that a man was abusing his spouse or significant other. When at the home, the police could threaten the man and even arrest and take him into custody. Their study found that a strong predictor of future rule-breaking was whether the man involved experienced his treatment by the police as fair. If he did, he was less likely to break the law in the future.

Clearly, procedural justice influences the feelings and actions of citizens engaged in specific encounters with the police. But this does not indicate whether procedural justice matters when people are making general evaluations of the police as an institution—that is, does it shape trust and confidence in the police?

The four studies of the police and the courts reviewed by Tyler (2001) explore the factors underlying public trust and confidence. These studies examined the general population, rather than focusing on people with personal experiences. The results suggest that people consider both performance in controlling crime and procedural fairness when evaluating the police and the courts in general. Significantly, the major factor is consistently found to be the fairness of the manner in which the police and the courts are believed to treat citizens. For example, in a study of Oakland, California, residents living in high-crime areas, it was found that the primary factor shaping overall evaluations of the police was the quality of their treatment of community residents (which explained 26 percent of the unique variance in evaluations), with a secondary influence of performance evaluations (which explained 5 percent of the unique variance).

Sunshine and Tyler (2003) examined trust and confidence in the New York Police Department among residents of New York City, contrasting evaluations of crime control activities to judgments about the fairness of the police. The researchers considered both procedural fairness (whether the police make their decisions fairly and treat people in fair ways) and distributive fairness (whether the police treat all citizens equally). These fairness judgments were then compared with assessments of how effectively the police were controlling crime. They found that public evaluations of the police were primarily influenced by procedural justice judgments. A second factor was effectiveness in controlling crime, followed by distributive fairness. The study further found that views about the legitimacy of the police, compliance with the law, and willingness to help the police control crime were all shaped by procedural justice judgments.

These findings suggest that procedural justice is not just an issue to people during personal experiences with police officers. Perceived fairness plays a role for evaluations of the police in general, and this is true across racial and ethnic categories. The argument that legitimacy is rooted in the fair exercise of authority is not a new one, or one that applies only to policing. It has been extended to other criminal justice institutions as well. Consider the case of prisons, institutions that people often think of as highly coercive. Even in prisons, authorities seek and benefit from cooperation with prisoners. Studies of prisons suggest that the fair administration of prison rules facilitates such cooperation (Sparks, Bottoms, and Hay, 1996). Similarly, discussions of the U.S. Supreme Court emphasize that the legitimacy of the Court is linked to public views about the fairness of its decision-making procedures. Murphy and Tanenhaus (1969) noted that the Court has retained a substantial reservoir of public support even when it makes unpopular decisions. They attribute this continued support for the legitimacy of the Court's role as an interpreter of the Constitution to the public belief that Court decisions are principled applications of legal rules, and not political in character. This point has been emphasized by members of the Court itself, when arguing that it must present an image of principled decision making to retain public support (Tyler and Mitchell, 1994). In addition, evidence from the private sector also supports the procedural justice argument. Selznick's classic examination of industrial settings makes a similar point about workplace rules, commenting that "there is a demand that the rules be legitimate, not only in emanating from established authority, but also in the manner of their formulation, in the way they are applied, and in their fidelity to agreed-upon institutional purposes. The idea spreads that the obligation to obey has some relation to the quality of the rules and the integrity of their administration" (Selznick, 1969:29). This argument has received widespread support in studies of employee behavior in workplaces (see Tyler and Blader, 2000).

Dimensions of Fairness

Given that procedural justice increases compliance, then understanding how citizens who are the objects or observers of police power determine fairness becomes an important task. Studies have identified a wide variety of issues that influence the degree to which people evaluate a procedure's fairness. Furthermore, it has been found that the importance of procedural criteria varies depending on the setting. Studies consistently point to several elements as key to people's procedural justice judgments.

Participation is one key element. People are more satisfied with procedures that allow them to participate by explaining their situation and communicating their views about situations to authorities. Interestingly, being able to control the outcome is not central to feeling that one is participating. Rather, what people want is to feel that their input has been solicited and considered by decision makers.

A second key element is neutrality. People think that unbiased authorities that use objective indicators to make decisions, as opposed to personal views, act more fairly. Evidence of evenhandedness and objectivity therefore enhances perceived fairness.

Third, people value being treated with dignity and respect by the police and other legal authorities. The quality of interpersonal treatment is consistently found to be a distinct element of fairness, separate from the quality of the decision-making process. Above and beyond the resolution of their problem, people value being treated with dignity and having their rights acknowledged.

Finally, people feel that procedures are fairer when they trust the motives of decision makers. If, for example, people believe that authorities care about their well-being and are considering their needs and concerns, they view procedures as fairer. Authorities can encourage people to view them as trustworthy by explaining their decisions and accounting for their conduct in ways that make clear their concern about giving attention to people's needs.

Consequences of Legitimacy for Policing

Tyler and Huo (2001, 2002) demonstrate that legitimacy changes the basis on which people decide whether or not to cooperate with legal authorities. They contrast two reasons for deferring to the decisions made by police officers. The first is that the decisions are viewed as desirable. The second is that the police officers involved are seen as exercising their authority in fair ways. Tyler and Huo found that the procedural justice of police actions had an important role in shaping people's willingness to consent and cooperate with the police. The opposite corollary has also been found to be true: Paternoster et al. (1997), as well as Tyler (1997, 1990) and Tyler and Smith (1997) reported that people who experience disrespectful behavior from police are less inclined to cooperate with them. Disrespect may also stimulate resistance, thus making it harder for the authorities to fulfill their official responsibilities (Chevigny, 1969:Ch. 3; Mastrofski et al., 1996; White et al., 1991). Repeated disrespect may ultimately undermine the legitimacy of the state and contribute to civil disorder (Gurr, 1970: 26; Kakalik and Wildhorn, 1968:305).

Since the police are often in situations in which they cannot provide people with outcomes that they view as fair or favorable, the police benefit if people defer to their decisions because those decisions are fairly made. One important implication of these findings is that the police should engage in process-oriented policing, in which they are attentive to the way that they treat citizens.

Public compliance with police cannot be taken for granted. As Mastrofski, Snipes, and Supina (1996:272) suggest, "although deference to legal authorities is the norm, disobedience occurs with sufficient frequency that skill in handling the rebellious, the disgruntled, and the hard to manage—or those potentially so—has become the street officer's performance litmus test." These researchers found an overall noncompliance rate of 22 percent; 19 percent of the time when the police told a person to leave another person alone; 33 percent of the time when the police told a person to cease some form of disorder; and 18 percent of the time when the police told a person to cease illegal behavior. A replication of this study in Indianapolis, Indiana, and St. Petersburg, Florida, found an overall noncompliance rate of 20 percent; 14 percent of the time when the police told people to leave another person alone; 25 percent of the time when the police told a person to cease some form of disorder; and 21 percent of the time when the police told a person to cease illegal behavior (McCluskey, Mastrofski, and Parks, 1999). Similarly, Sherman (1993) highlights the problem of defiance and the need to minimize resistance to the directives of the police.

Another important consequence of legitimacy that can be examined is everyday compliance with the law. Much of people's law-related behavior occurs outside the immediate presence of legal authorities, although the possibility of sanctions may always exist in the background.

Tyler (1990) examined the influence of views about the general legitimacy of the law on citizen's everyday compliance and found that legitimacy had a significant influence on the degree to which people obeyed the law. He also found that influence was distinct from and greater than the effects of increases in the estimated likelihood of being caught and punished for wrongdoing. Separate subgroup analyses of whites and nonwhites indicate that legitimacy shapes compliance. Hence, legitimacy is a motivation shaping whether both white and minority residents comply with the law.

The suggestion that the maintenance of internal values in community residents is important to effective policing has also been made by research on restorative policing (see Braithwaite, 1999; Strang and Braithwaite, 2000, 2001; Sherman, Strang, and Woods, 2001). The core argument of this literature is that the police and courts should behave in ways that "restore" victims and communities to their well-being before the crime, thereby restoring offenders to law-abiding behavior. The goal of restorative policing is to reconnect offenders to an awareness of their own social values and social relationships that will discourage them from lawbreaking behavior in the future. They will recognize that their behavior violates values they believe in, that define appropriate conduct, and it damages social relationships with friends, family and the community that they value.

The value of this model, which consists of police-led meetings between victims, offenders, and their families and friends, is being tested in a set of field experiments being conducted in Canberra, Australia. Those studies explore the long-term effects of restorative justice experiments on law-abiding behavior. While data on long-term behavior are still being collected, results already available suggest that people who experience restorative justice conferences express greater respect for the law and view the police as more legitimate than do those whose cases are processed via traditional court procedures (Sherman, 2001b). The increased legitimacy that restorative justice creates does not always reduce repeat offending, but four randomized experiments conducted by the Australian federal police suggest important dimensions of this idea.

The Canberra research examined four kinds of offenders: adults charged with drinking while driving, juveniles charged with shoplifting from large stores, juveniles charged with property offenses affecting personal (not corporate) victims, and offenders up to age 30 charged with violent crimes. The results suggest that restorative justice works best when the offender's moral guilt may be greatest. While there was no difference in repeat offending between cases handled by restorative justice and those handled by conventional prosecution for either juvenile shoplifting or property crimes against persons, restorative justice produced a 38 percent relative reduction in repeat offending among violent offenders. This success was a sharp contrast to drinking and driving cases, in which restorative justice was associated with a slight increase in repeat offending (Sherman, Strang, and Woods, 2001).

The lack of any victim in the conferences on drinking and driving, compared with the emotionally powerful statements of victims of violent crime, suggests that the emotional impact of restorative conferences may be the major factor in determining their success in producing compliance. This research also found powerful benefits for victims who attend a conference, even if there is no effect on repeat offending (Strang, 2002). These benefits may ultimately include increased compliance with the law by the victims, whose own sense of the legitimacy of the police was increased by restorative policing. Further research testing of restorative policing is currently under way by the University of Pennsylvania and Australian University in partnership with Scotland Yard in London and the Northumbrian Police in the

Newcastle area (Sherman et al., 2001), focusing on serious adult crimes, such as robbery and burglary.

Many of the ideas outlined here are not only implications of a procedural justice or restorative justice approach to policing. They are also part of community approaches to policing. Community policing emphasizes police efforts to proactively work with neighborhood residents to solve local problems. Studies suggest that people value having the police talk to citizens and cooperating with citizens to solve community problems. They support more bike and pedestrian patrols because they "like to perceive the police as friends and helpers and they would support endeavors to improve the work of the police force much in the sense of what community and problem oriented policing propose" (Weitekamp, Kerner, and Meier, 1996: 16). Similarly a study of public complaints about the police showed that the two primary reasons for complaining were "rude, arrogant, unfriendly, over-casual treatment (38 percent)" and "unreasonable, unfair behavior (46 percent)" (Skogan, 1994).

One final implication of procedural justice policing must be noted. The social science perspective on legitimacy focuses on the conditions under which people will defer to authorities, rather than on the conditions under which people *ought* to defer to authorities.

Some might argue that there are groups in American society that are objectively disadvantaged, who therefore have no moral or normative obligation to cooperate with legal authorities. This issue is not addressed in social science studies of legitimacy. It should be noted that psychological research strongly supports the suggestion that disadvantaged people often view as legitimate political, legal, economic, and social arrangements in which they experience objective deprivation (Tyler and McGraw, 1986; Tyler and Smith, 1997; Tyler et al., 1997), an irony that Karl Marx famously dubbed "false consciousness." For example, Tyler et al. (1997: Ch. 6) point to the lack of differences in views about the legitimacy of the legal system found between white and minority or between rich and poor community residents interviewed in a study of Chicago residents. However, when people were asked about their personal experience with legal authorities, minorities and the poor were more likely to report experiencing injustice. Such personally experienced injustice did not translate to lower legitimacy.

The tendency to legitimize the status quo, seeing "what is" as "what ought to be" is found not only in people's reactions to legal and political authorities, but also in reactions to the economic system, particularly in people's attributions of responsibility for economic success and failure (Hochschild, 1989; Kluegel and Smith, 1986; Major, 1994). People tend to uncritically accept meritocratic explanations for inequality (Tyler and McGraw, 1986; Jost and Banaji, 1994), a tendency that justifies the status quo. Because of the potential disjuncture between objective and subjective views of society and social authorities, it is important to distinguish the study of the behavioral effects of subjective views about the legitimacy of the law and the police from the study of the objective quality and equity of policing activities across communities. It is possible for people to feel that the law is legitimate even under conditions in which they are objectively disadvantaged. Hence, the study of subjective legitimacy must be distinguished from concerns about structural inequality or the injustice of the distribution of opportunities, resources, and services across individuals and communities.

BUILDING LEGITIMACY THROUGH ORGANIZATIONAL REFORM

As noted earlier, police organizations can enhance their legitimacy by demonstrating that they produce desired outcomes (e.g., reducing crime and disorder), and that an even more powerful source of legitimacy is tapped when police fulfill public expectations about the processes of policing (e.g., treating people with fairness). There is another route to police legitimacy as well: adaptation and reform, which involves organizational change. Legitimacy can be gained through the adoption of programs, policies, and procedures that are viewed by the community and civic leaders as desirable. It can also be gained by hiring personnel and allocating departmental resources in ways that the community views as equitable. In each case, departments acquire legitimacy by organizing themselves in ways that are acceptable and seem responsive to professional and public standards.

Adopting Units and Programs

How do particular organization structures come to be widely accepted as desirable or superior? One route is professional validation. Decisions by policy makers and police administrators about programs and policies can be driven by professional norms regarding what is technically effective at producing the outcomes of policing. To the extent they can afford it, they base their decisions on the best evidence, following a path that one observer has termed "evidence-based policing" (Sherman, 1998), coined after the popular "evidence-based medicine" slogan that has been popular in the field of medicine. Police agency accreditation, which usually involves a great deal of organizational adaptation to meet professional standards, speeds this process. When their operations fall under scrutiny, adopting agencies can point in defense to the practices of other departments, publications by professional associations, and best practices reports distributed by federal agencies and research institutes. This route for gaining legitimacy can also take advantage of developing knowledge about what works in policing, by adapting in response to new findings.

The committee examined what is known about the police structures and strategies that are most effective in producing technical performance. If police organizations adopt structures because they are technically superior, key decision makers should place a high value on evidence of technical performance and base their decisions accordingly. There is some reason to believe that police agencies are increasingly paying attention to scientific evidence about what works (Weisburd et al., 2001).

A popular historical perspective following this line is that the professional model of police organizations became popular by the 1950s because police organizations found it more successful in coping with crime. It was discredited by the 1970s in the face of large increases in crime and disorder and disaffection with policing processes. Consequently, the professional model lost favor as a way to organize police forces, and by the 1990s it was supplanted with another—the community policing model (Fogelson, 1977; Kelling and Moore, 1988). According to this model of organizational adaptation, police organization structures are formed and modified to maximize technical effectiveness and efficiency in such things as safety from crime.

The rapid diffusion of versions of New York City's CompStat process reflects this drive to appear to be organized in a technically effective way. Only five years after it was implemented in 1994, 58 percent of departments with 100 or more sworn officers reported that they had either implemented a CompStat-like program or were planning to do so. Interestingly, however, there have been no rigorous evaluations of the effect of the program on crime, and one study casts doubt on the claims of CompStat's crime control effectiveness (Eck and Maguire, 2000; but see Kelling and Sousa, 2001). Police organizations have sought and claimed cutting-edge status by adopting CompStat (Weisbund et al., 2003).

A second route to building legitimacy through organizational adaptation focuses not on the technical merits of a proposed change, but rather on the cultural and political forces that create pressures to accept certain structures as superior, perhaps even in the absence of evidence of their technical effectiveness. These organizational changes build on the beliefs of elected officials, agency heads, the press, union leaders, blue ribbon commissions, professional associations, and other interest groups. Adopting programs and policies that resonate with their values sustains and builds police legitimacy. The literature on policing suggests that the adoption of police policies, procedures, and programs are driven by political and cultural forces at work in society.

One example is the adoption of mandatory arrest policies for misdemeanor domestic assault (Sherman, 1992). The findings of the Minneapolis study supported a policy position that was gaining increasing national momentum as interest groups intensely lobbied police and lawmakers for change. New arrest policies were also motivated by police vulnerability to civil suits, as in *Thurman v. Connecticut* (1984), in which police were found negligent in a domestic violence case and the victim was awarded $2.6 million as a result. Interestingly, subsequent replications of the Minneapolis study produced more complex results—namely, that mandatory arrest may not always reduce domestic assault and may even contribute to subsequent increases under some circumstances. These findings, which now represent the best evidence on the matter, have had very little policy effect, perhaps because there is no political or cultural mandate to undo the new status quo.

The adoption of police organizational structures in response to public demands is a recurring theme of police reform in America. Civilian review of citizen complaints against the police may or may not be an effective bulwark against police misbehavior (proponents and opponents argue both positions), but departments facing a crisis in public confidence due to allegations of excessive force will certainly find themselves under pressure to adopt a civilian complaint review system. Civilian oversight has become popular despite the absence of evidence about its effectiveness in preventing or correcting any of a variety of the forms of police malpractice for which it is targeted (Walker, 2001). Chiefs and mayors may find it useful because it conforms to popular expectations about how the police department should be organized to respond to citizen complaints.

Creating special units to deal with specific problems is an especially useful way to deal with threats to the department's legitimacy, especially in locales where interest groups actively press police to tend to particular issues. In any city police department, leaders face a multitude of demands for new and different services but have limited resources with which to respond. Creating a relatively small but highly focused specialist unit to cope with a given problem may do little to reduce that problem, but it does a great deal to alleviate pressure from the community without disrupting many organizational routines. For example, small specialist squads of traffic officers can provide community groups alarmed about drunk driving with a tangible victory in their effort to get a department to be responsive to their concerns, and the creation of that unit allows the much larger patrol division to continue operations more or less as usual (Mastrofski and Ritti, 1992, 1996). This does not mean that special units that are created in response to external demands are necessarily ineffective. On the contrary, a study of the effects of police training in handling drunk drivers showed that in some departments, more training in handling drunk-driving problems was a powerful predictor of officers making more drunk-driving arrests (Mastrofski and Ritti, 1996). But special programs can also be a "presentational" strategy (Manning, 1977) designed to give evidence to external constituents that a department was doing something significant in response to a problem.

Other special squads have been put under this analytic microscope. Researchers have found that, in some communities, special gang units were formed by police in order to heighten the public's sense of threat from gangs, in the hope of gaining resources in return (Zatz, 1987; McCorkle and Miethe, 1998). On other occasions, gang units have been created in response to external pressure. Katz (2001) found that the gang unit he studied was created at a time when there was no particular threat from gangs; rather, the unit was a result of "pressures placed on the police department from various powerful elements within the community, and that once created, the gang unit's response to the community's gang problem was largely driven by its need to achieve and maintain legitimacy among various [influential people] in their environment" (p. 65). The gang unit's actual function was largely ceremonial. Most of its effort went into maintaining good relations with important officials, organizations, and units in the department that could ensure that the unit survived and prospered. Building these alliances took precedence over law enforcement activities.

Observers of community policing have also noted its resonance with community leaders and residents, as well as the remarkable speed in which it has spread during the last two decades. In the mid-1980s, community policing had little visibility among police or police researchers, but, by 1993, 98 percent of a national sample of the nation's local law enforcement chief executives agreed that "the concept of community policing is something that law enforcement agencies should pursue" (Wycoff, 1994). Nearly as many considered it a highly effective way to provide police service, and almost three-fourths felt that every aspect of law enforcement would benefit from community policing. National surveys have confirmed that in the wake of federal financial support for community policing that began in 1994, large numbers of departments report implementing or planning to implement specific policies, programs, and procedures associated with it (Maguire and Mastrofski, 2000; Maguire and Uchida, 2000).

A content analysis of several years of *Police Chief*, a monthly publication of the International Association of Chiefs of Police, and *Law Enforcement News*, a biweekly professional newspaper, shows that the vast majority of articles making detailed comments on community policing were completely or mostly positive about community policing (Ritti and Mastrofski, 2002). Most praised community policing or assumed its benefits. The handful that included negative comments typically focused on challenges to implementing it, not whether community policing itself was worthwhile. A content analysis of major daily newspapers in 26 cities around the nation also showed an overwhelmingly positive picture of community policing presented to the public (Mastrofski and Ritti, 1999). Several observers have argued that the rapid growth in popularity of community policing reflects the political environment facing police departments and not its technical merits (Manning, 1984; Klockars, 1988; Mastrofski and Uchida, 1993; Crank, 1994; Skogan and Hartnett, 1997; Mastrofski, 1998; Mastrofski and Ritti, 2000).

An unanswered question is how much legitimacy is conferred on police organizations by adapting to their political environment. How much public acceptance is produced? Some evidence of the legitimating effectiveness of community policing can be found in case studies of individual cities. Based on surveys over time of city residents, the effects are mixed (compare the positive findings of Skogan and Hartnett, 1997, with the negative findings by McEwen, 2000). The ability of police organizations to weather crises is another indicator of their legitimacy. What happens following outbreaks of police corruption or brutality? If the structures that are in place to respond are judged to work, they sustain the organization's legitimacy. Another indicator of the legitimating benefits of a program or policy is its popularity among "new broom" police leaders for dealing with the problems that led to the departure of their predecessor. As the market for top police executives has become increasingly national in scope, competition for the chief's job has become more intense. These "up-and-comers" are highly invested in divining what will be popular with hiring agencies. Learning from those who make the decision about who to hire as chief would also provide insight into the degree of legitimacy various organization structures are providing police agencies in the United States.

Ensuring Fairness in Hiring

Another path for building legitimacy is police hiring. Police have always been under pressure to adjust their hiring patterns to reflect the changing social and political complexion of the communities they serve. At least since the 1960s, nationwide complaints about police hiring practices have focused on race. In the 1970s, this was joined by a new emphasis on equality of hiring by gender.

The Law Enforcement Management and Administrative Survey (LEMAS) surveys show a steady but slow increase in the percentage of full-time officers who are Hispanic and black. During the decade between 1987 and 1997, the percentage of sworn officers who were Hispanic rose from 4.8 to 7.8 percent, and the percentage of black officers rose from 9.5 to 11.7 percent (Reaves and Goldberg, 2000). The percentage of officers of Asian and Pacific Islander and American Indian and Alaskan Native origin grew much faster but overall accounted for only 2.1 percent by 1997 (Reaves and Goldberg, 2000). Newer numbers available since the 1999 LEMAS survey did not ask about the race or gender composition of departments. In 1997, blacks and Hispanics were found in the largest proportions in cities with a population in the range of 500,000 to 1 million. In these departments, blacks constituted almost one-quarter of the force, and Hispanics another16 percent (Reaves and Goldberg, 2000).

Women constituted 10 percent of all full-time officers in 1997, a figure up from 7.5 percent a decade earlier. Like racial minorities, women were most heavily represented in larger cities, those over 250,000 in population (Reaves and Goldberg, 2000).

Despite these gains, women and racial and ethnic minorities are consistently less well represented in supervisory ranks than they are at the rank and file level. A 1998 study found that women represented 15 percent of sworn officers at the line level, 10 percent at the supervisory level, and 8 percent in top command positions (National Center for Women and Policing, 1998:8). The major exception to this rule is at the rank of chief executive, in which blacks are heavily represented as chiefs in large city departments. Appointments to the rank of chief are discretionary and not subject to the formal procedures that govern promotion to the ranks of sergeant and above.

There is mixed evidence regarding the factors that explain the increase in the number of racial and ethnic minority and female officers. Much of the increases are due to informal social and political pressure on police departments. Changes in the local population, particularly the increase in the Hispanic population, also have some effect. The increase in the number of female officers is undoubtedly due to changing patterns of work force participation by women and the entry of women into many occupations that were previously predominantly male. An estimated 40 percent of police departments serving cities with populations greater than 100,000 had a formal affirmative action plan in place, including both court-ordered and voluntary plans (Zhao and Lovrich, 1998). Martin (1990:50) found a positive correlation between the existence of an affirmative action plan and the percentage of women in selected departments. Zhao and Lovrich (1998), in contrast, found that the percentage of blacks in the local community was the only factor associated with increases in black officers.

It is most useful to examine police employment practices on an agency-by-agency basis. This is particularly important with respect to racial and ethnic minorities, since the black and Hispanic populations are very unevenly distributed across the country (Brewer and Suchan, 2001). Aggregate data mask significant variations among police departments with respect to minority hiring (Walker and Turner, 1992). Another reason for focusing on individual agencies is that many authorities, including the law enforcement accreditation standards, argue that in the interest of building legitimacy the composition of a police department should reflect the community served (Commission on Accreditation for Law Enforcement Agencies, 1999:31.2.1). A number of police departments currently meet or nearly meet this standard with respect to black and Hispanic officers. Many others, however, lag far beyond this standard (Walker and Turner, 1992). Interestingly, there is anecdotal evidence that recruitment efforts by local police departments make a significant difference in racial and ethnic minority employment.

The employment of women officers lags far beyond the employment of racial and ethnic minorities. A total of 60 percent of all women were in the labor force in 2000, yet only a few law enforcement agencies have more than 20 percent female officers and most have only about 13 percent (Bureau of Justice Statistics, 1999; National Center for Women and Policing, 1998).

Ensuring Fairness in Resource Allocation

Most of the research on policing summarized in this report has examined fairness and lawfulness in the way the police treat individual citizens they may encounter, customers who call them, and persons they apprehend. But these concepts apply to decisions made at the organizational as well as the individual level. One important kind of equity lies in the distribution of police services at the neighborhood level.

In this instance, legitimacy is to be found in fairness and lawfulness in the distribution of those services. Evidence of bias in their allocation would signal that police policy makers should pay more attention to "equity planning" issues, by considering the equity effect (Sanchez, 1998) of their decisions about where to locate police stations, draw beat boundaries, allocate personnel, and prioritize rapid response to calls for service.

Much of this research has been conducted by political scientists, reflecting their interest in who gets what from government. They typically compare quantitative measures of service levels for different areas, ranging from blocks or census tracts to officially designated agency service areas. Serve rates are calculated using appropriate denominators (usually population), and the resulting figures are correlated with measures of the social, economic, and political composition of the areas. Almost all of these studies control for measures of service need and other factors that presumably should affect the resource allocation decisions of municipal service bureaucracies. Some take into account how much people pay in taxes to examine the link between what they pay and what they get. All of these studies use multivariate statistical models to parcel out the relative effect of contrasting clusters of explanatory variables. One goal of this research has been to identify bias in the distribution of services, especially after controlling for measures of service need.

Bias has been found in the distribution of services by race, income and location, including distance from the downtown. Many studies of municipal service delivery have also found "unpatterned" inequality (e.g., uncorrelated with race and class measures), and often they conclude that service needs, professional standards, and other factors reflecting bureaucratic rationality largely determine the spatial allocation of government resources.

In the policing field, the service measures have included area-level expenditure estimates (Cingranelli, 1981; Sanger, 1981), the number of police officers assigned (Illinois Advisory Committee to the U.S. Civil Rights Commission, 1991; Weicher, 1971; Lineberry, 1977; Nardulli and Stonecash, 1981), police response time (Mladenka and Hill, 1978), and the time spent on calls. In these studies, service need has been measured by crime rates or calls for service. Other measures of agency and bureaucratic factors have included the availability of resources at the time a crime occurred and dispatchers' prioritizing of the urgency of calls (Nardulli and Stonecash, 1981; Mladenka and Hill, 1978).

In the main, this research has found that crime rates and other measures of service need dominate the distribution of police service. For example, Cingranelli (1981) found that service need was three times as important as any other factor in determining the distribution of police resources among Boston neighborhoods. The correlation there between the crime rate and the allocation of police expenditures across areas was .92. Predominately black areas reported higher levels of crime, so policing levels were highest where they were concentrated, but there was a smaller residual statistical bias in favor of positioning more officers in predominately white areas that were more commercial in character. He also found evidence of political factors, measured by voter turnout and support for the incumbent mayor. Like some other investigators, Sanger (1981) found a U-shaped relationship between area income and protection, with the areas of the lowest and the highest incomes of New York City experiencing (by this measure) the most protection, although most likely for different reasons. Boyle and Jacobs (1982) report that New York City police expenditures were higher in poorer neighborhoods, but also in areas that were paying a great deal in taxes. Another New York City study found that, in comparison to other kinds of city expenditures, policing was quite insulated from political pressures and was responsive mostly to measures of need (Lee, 1994). Research in many other cities (including Worden, 1980) has pointed to relative racial and income equality in the distribution of police services, once crime and other need factors are taken into account. In Houston, response times were slightly faster in poor and minority areas, but the distribution of police resources was virtually equal once crime rates were taken into account (Mladenka and Hill, 1978). In a smaller city, Coulter (1980) found the explicit department policy was equality for all of its districts.

Most of this research is quite dated, as is the literature on urban services delivery generally. This may be significant, since the demographics and politics of U.S. cities and their suburban rings during the latter half of the 20th century have changed. One of the few longitudinal studies of a municipal service (parks, in Chicago) found that over 22 years there was ". . . a fundamental redistribution of resources between black and white wards. In fact, the worst-category in the city is [now] white rather than black" (Mladenka, 1989:581). Especially in a time of plummeting crime rates, it may be time to readdress these questions, with a special focus on how resource allocation decisions are actually made.

The authors in the field also readily acknowledge the limitations of their measures. For example, Mladenka and Hill (1978:114) noted: "we have little idea of the relationship between police activity levels and the benefits conferred, it cannot be assumed that the distribution of activities is the same as the distribution of benefits." It is instructive that, 25 years later, there are still few solid findings to report. In another study, Bloch (1974) observed that having a well-motivated and well-trained police force may be more important than their sheer numbers, but he had only numbers to analyze. Another limitation is that the findings appear to be very city-specific, which is understandable if local political calculations play a significant role in shaping the allocation of the benefits bestowed by government. For example, Bolotin and Cingranelli (1983) report that, because blacks in Boston strongly supported the incumbent mayor Kevin White, they received even more police in response; there, political factors worked in their favor.

Some studies have pointed to more subtle variations in service quality than is typically assessed in the research. For example, Nardulli and Stonecash (1981) report that while officers responding at the moment to reports of violent victimization were fairly evenhanded in their work, there was evidence that later follow-up investigations were more quickly dismissive of crime in the black community. They also found racial bias in ticketing, once the decision to stop someone had been made. Rossi, Berk, and Eidson (1974) found that white policemen in 15 cities were generally biased in their view of blacks, but presented no evidence that this affected how they actually did their work.

Although the existing body of research on the equality of service distributions is quite dated, this may change. Research of this type will be facilitated by the widespread use of geographic information system (GIS) technology, which prioritizes attaching geographical locators to virtually every piece of municipal data. **The committee recommends expanding the scope of outcome measures used in this research to encompass significant aspects of service delivery.** To date, most research has been on what has been termed "outputs" (or activity levels), rather than on "outcomes" (their consequences) for individuals and neighborhoods. Mladenka (1989) and others have called for more research on service "quality," and they anticipate uncovering more variation and possible bias in measures of it.

A final limitation of this research is that the data and their analysis are inevitably tied to municipal boundaries. Because policing in the United States is so highly localized, the relevant bureaucratic decisions that are under investigation are local as well. Research has been confined to cities in part because legal guarantees of equal protection in the allocation of government benefits apply only within jurisdictions and generally not among them (Lineberry, 1974). Discovering evidence of the illegitimate distribution of benefits has been one motivation for these studies (Ostrom, 1983; Rich, 1979). None of this research has broached the larger issue of the balance of the central-city versus suburban distribution of public safety resources, nor equity in the outcomes of policing in those widely varying places. But as Rich (1978) points out, in important ways the metropolitan area has superseded the central city as the relevant unit for most aspects of life—except for policing and a few other municipal services. **The committee recommends that research on police service delivery be expanded to include the metropolitan area as the relevant domain of concern.**

Responding to the Challenge of Racial Profiling

The final issue raised here is the role of research in one of the paramount legitimacy issues of the day: racial profiling. Because police must make many discretionary decisions in the course of their day, it is not surprising that some of these judgments could be influenced by racial, ethnic, or gender stereotypes. While police have long exercised this kind of discretion, two developments during the 1980s granted officers even more latitude in making judgments on whom to stop, whom to search, and whom to arrest.

First, the public responded to escalating violence associated with drug trafficking by endorsing aggressive law enforcement policies. The U.S. Drug Enforcement Agency (DEA), the federal office charged with enforcing the nation's drug laws, developed a new strategy to intercept the distribution of illegal drugs: drug courier profiling (Webb, 1999). The DEA and, to some extent, the U.S. Department of Transportation, trained local and state law enforcement officers to identify the characteristics of an illegal drug courier in a program called Operation Pipeline (American Civil Liberties Union, 1999). The list of identifying characteristics of a drug courier is long, occasionally puzzling, and contradictory. Many lawyers and activists have quoted extensively from the list in legal briefs or in speeches as a way of demonstrating that almost anyone who the police wanted to stop, they could stop. Whatever the actual content of the training conducted by these federal agencies—and 48 states participated in this training—the result was that race or ethnicity became, in the minds of many officers, a possible indicator of illegal activity. As a consequence of this official effort to stymie the dissemination of illegal drugs, police proactively stopped or searched citizens, even when no criminal activity was evident. This expansion of police power echoed the aggressive policing of the 1950s that liberally and proactively applied police power to urban communities in hopes of deterring criminal activity (Goldstein, 2000:27).

The second development legitimized, in a legal sense, the first. Key decisions from the U.S. Supreme Court sanctioned this increased police discretion. In *Ohio* v. *Robinette* (1996), the court rejected the argument that police were required to inform citizens of their right to refuse a request to search either their person or their vehicle. Once consent to a search is given, police have broad powers to proceed; if consent is not granted, police must demonstrate probable cause for a search. Thus many citizens have consented to searches and been surprised how long law enforcement could legally detain them and intrusively probe their person or their car.

In the same session, the Supreme Court also handed down the *Whren* v. *United States* decision, which held that police could conduct traffic stops to investigate their suspicions even if those suspicions had nothing to do with the traffic offense for which a citizen was being stopped. This has become known as "pretextual traffic stops," or using traffic violations as a nominal reason to stop a car for investigation when in fact the real motivation for the stop lay elsewhere. In some instances, the traffic violations used as a pretext have been so minor that police would not, under normal circumstances, stop any other car for the same violation.

Along with these developments, complaints of racial profiling surfaced, and many were articulated by law-abiding, prominent black Americans who had nevertheless been stopped by police and were subjected to, at times, humiliating treatment. Henry Louis Gates, Jr., chronicled some of these complaints in 1995, adding that "there's a moving violation that many blacks know as D.W.B.: Driving While Black" (Gates, 1995). Soon after, law professor David A. Harris used this term as the title for his book examining racial profiling. Gradually and by process of accretion, stories describing incidents of racial profiling prompted a general discussion of the issue.

Initially some in the law enforcement community responded to charges of racial profiling by admitting that they considered race as one among many probabilistic factors of criminal activity by police (see Kennedy, 2001, for some examples). Some defended this practice by citing statistics that demonstrated that black males made up a disproportionate number of suspects arrested, convicted, and sentenced nationwide. However, many who challenged racial profiling countered that these statistics proved only that the criminal justice system in this country targeted black males. More recently the terms of the debate have shifted. Many police agencies now define racial profiling as the decision to stop or search a person *exclusively* because of race, usually denying that they engage in such practices. Yet there is a general public belief that racial profiling is in fact common practice. The Gallup News Service reported the results of a nationwide poll in 1999: a substantial majority of blacks believed racial profiling to be "widespread" (77 percent), and so did a majority (56 percent) of whites (Gallup Poll News Service, 1999).

Legal developments have spurred data collection in this area. As noted earlier, the Violent Crime Control and Law Enforcement Act of 1994 authorizes the attorney general to investigate any "pattern or practice of conduct by law enforcement officers...that deprives persons of rights, privileges, or immunities secured or protected by the Constitution or laws of the United States." The consent decrees that have resulted from the threat of litigation have required the collection of data on departmental practices, and these data are unusually extensive.

While police use of force has been the most common area of research, the consent decree governing operations of the New Jersey State Police require the collection of data on stops made by police, and a court ruled that these data revealed a significant disparity between white and black motorists.[2] Documents discovered as the result of Department of Justice litigation also demonstrated that the New Jersey State Police believed themselves to be engaged in racial profiling on the New Jersey Turnpike. This, coupled with the data gathered to support the consent decree, bolstered the public's perception that racial profiling did indeed occur. Combined with the efforts of advocacy groups, this has led to an explosion of data collection efforts and racial profiling policies across the country.

In general, the policy response has included affirmations that prohibit racial profiling; diversity of training for officers; a mandate to collect data in some fashion; and new mechanisms for filing complaints by people who believe they have been unjustly stopped by police. It is noteworthy that some police agencies began voluntarily to collect data or implement other features of this response to racial profiling. At this writing, 24 states and the District of Columbia have taken some action on racial profiling, either through an executive order of the governor or, more frequently, by passing legislation. Currently there are 16 bills pending in various states, and 11 of these have been introduced in states that do not have any previous policy response to racial profiling.

---

[2]*United States* v. *New Jersey*, No. 99-5970 (MLC), (D.N.J. Dec. 30, 1999).

Data Collection and Research Efforts

The fact that various strategies have been adopted to monitor racial profiling invites closer attention to the viability and effectiveness of these approaches. In particular, the committee has special interest in efforts underway to collect data on the prevalence of racial profiling, and the research designed to promote best practices in that data collection effort.

On a basic level, the same problems that dog other kinds of data collection also plague efforts to gather information on racial profiling. These problems include unintentional and intentional errors committed by the police or by the civilian in the recording of racial or ethnic information (see, for example, Bland et al., 2000). Simplified reporting systems have been promoted by some police agencies as a way to reduce unintentional misreporting. In particular, efforts have been made to trim the amount of paperwork required of officers who must collect data. For example, the San Jose Police Department in California, which has voluntarily been collecting data since June 1999, has developed a mobile data terminal to record information, but the letter codes developed for the system can also be relayed verbally via the police radio. Whether the information is input directly into the terminal or transmitted on the radio, a San Jose police officer does not have to file a written report as part of this data collection. Montgomery County, Maryland, police utilize special Palm Pilots" that record information input by the officer for their data collection efforts. Once returned to the police station at the end of an officer's shift, the chip is removed from the device, and the relevant information is automatically printed on forms. This practice simplifies racial profiling data collection, reducing error, and the labor-saving device also reduces time spent on other kinds of paperwork-related traffic stops.

Despite these innovations, which clearly have beneficial application beyond racial profiling data collection, concerns persist both inside and outside the law enforcement community. Many argue that police will not be able to and should not be expected to record accurately the race of persons they stop and search, for often it is not obvious. In addition, the United Kingdom's efforts to collect data on race or ethnicity of those stopped have revealed that self-reporting by those who are stopped is deeply flawed (Bland et al., 2000). Misreporting and false reporting are concerns in any kind of police field data collection.

In addition, the range of encounters for which data collection is required varies significantly; state and local statutes differ in what they require police to record or collect. Some jurisdictions record all traffic stops, some record only stops that result in a citation of some kind, and still others record traffic stops that result in a police search. Thus, efforts to make general assessments regarding the prevalence of racial profiling based on these varied data are immediately hampered. In addition, since inconsistent data collection results from disagreement over exactly what ought to be measured, resolution of this issue will not be simple.

Given these concerns, data collection efforts currently under way by police may not reliably answer the question of whether or not a department is engaging in racial profiling. Another problem besetting racial profiling data collection is methodological, and it is sometimes called the "denominator" or "benchmarking" problem. Imagine that police stop only blacks driving on one particular street during one night. That might seem to be racial profiling. But imagine again that the street is in the middle of an overwhelmingly black neighborhood; the fact that police stopped only blacks might not, when it is placed in context, be the effect of bias. Therefore, in addition to the number of stops made, a sense of context or a benchmark is needed. This sets up a numerator—the number of stops made by police as classified by race or ethnicity—and a denominator—the typical pool of traffic (pedestrian or motor) in the area sorted by race or ethnicity. Thus far police have been collecting and supplying information on the numerator.[3] Even if all of the problems with establishing this numerator were eliminated (problems such as misreporting or inconsistencies in the universe of concern), interpreting that numerator reliably would require a denominator to measure it against.

There is still more complexity to proper measurement of racial profiling. The most accurate denominator, or benchmark, is not the typical traffic on the street, but the pool of traffic offenders. The best analysis would measure offending rates for the groups and areas under examination and use those as denominators in assessments of profiling patterns. In the case of traffic, this might involve observational studies of samples of the driving population. Calculating correct denominators for profiling studies is expensive, requiring elaborate data collection and skilled modeling; it is not a process that can realistically occur in every community. Moreover, the denominator is a moving target; a community cannot, for example, establish a denominator once and apply it at all times and in all places. Traffic patterns, to say nothing of crime patterns, shift. Given these problems, constructing a denominator has become just as controversial as deciding on the proper numerator.

Several criminal justice researchers have conducted important efforts to grapple with this denominator problem. The first such attempt by John Lamberth, was used in court to establish that the New Jersey State Police engaged in racial profiling (*New Jersey* v. *Soto*, 734 A.2d 350, Superior Court of New Jersey, 1996). Lamberth testified that blacks constituted 13.5

---

[3]Some police, such as the San Jose Police Department, do establish a benchmark to measure their data collection against. San Jose measures stops against local residential populations (U.S. Department of Justice, 2000).

percent of drivers on one southern stretch of the New Jersey Turnpike, and 15 percent of drivers speeding. Yet black drivers represented 35 percent of those drivers stopped and 73.2 percent of those arrested. Lamberth used a stopwatch and timed cars across a known distance to determine the speed of passing traffic. His work pioneered empirical data collection for assessing the prevalence of racial profiling, and his methodology refined the denominator category to more accurately determine offense rates across racial and ethnic categories. However, one major problem with this study is that the stops were not necessarily for speeding (General Accounting Office, 2000).

To further explore the issue of appropriate benchmarking, in 2000 the National Institute of Justice funded a data collection effort led by Matt Zingraff of North Carolina State University. This comprehensive study examined whether the North Carolina Highway Patrol officers stop minorities on the road at higher rates than whites, which factors motivate highway stops, and how ethnic minorities respond to police stops. The research team endeavored to answer these questions by integrating data collected from three separate sources: a survey of drivers, official police records, and their own data collection on 14 separate stretches of North Carolina highway. While the survey and the police records included information on local police, the independent data collection, used in the construction of the denominator, was aimed exclusively at the North Carolina State Highway Patrol, and therefore it was to that police agency that the researchers confined their results. In order to create an appropriate denominator, the research team drove five miles over the speed limit on defined stretches at defined intervals during the day. They carried a stopwatch in the car and used it to determine the miles-per-hour of every car that passed them. They also recorded the characteristics of the driver in that car. Before using this "modified carousel method," the researchers tested the accuracy of using the stopwatch to determine miles-per-hour at a racetrack, and they confirmed that the method worked well.

The advantage of this methodology is considerable: researchers were not only able to establish an offender denominator—the rate at which different race and ethnic groups sped on the highway—they were able to distinguish among different classes of offender denominators. When it comes to highway speeding, rating the severity of the offense is critical. Highway patrol officers may not stop drivers who speed at 62 mph on a regular basis, but they may consistently stop drivers who speed at 82 mph. Zingraff et al. determined that young white males accounted for the majority of drivers in the most severe speeding offense category, and they also constituted most of the drivers pulled over by the North Carolina State Highway Patrol. The researchers found that black drivers were pulled over at a rate slightly higher than the offense denominators would indicate, but that the increase was not statistically significant. One caveat to their results: the time intervals that the researchers measured speeding on the highway all occurred during the day, for the simple reason that researchers could not reliably discern race/ethnic/gender characteristics at night.

Zingraff et al. (2000) mentioned several items in their study that, while not related to their results, raise new questions about data collection itself. First, in their telephone surveys, they found that blacks self-reported a much higher rate of stops by local (and not state highway) police. Second, their review of local police records indicated that there was indeed a high number of stops of blacks made by local police. Since the researchers were concerned only with the state highway patrol, and in particular with the crime of speeding, they did not use this information to formulate their results. Nevertheless, these items remain important. The crime of speeding is most often detected by use of radar; usually a decision to act is made by police even before they have had visual contact with a driver. Reliance on radar limits police discretion on this issue. It would follow, then, that intentional or even cognitive bias would remain low.

How does one establish a denominator for other traffic and moving violations? Local police may stop cars for speeding, but it is clear that they also stop drivers for a host of other reasons as well: tag violations, running a red light, missing license plates, aggressive driving, not wearing a seatbelt, and so on. Researchers standing on a corner could not reliably detect all of these infractions on every car that passed, thus undermining the establishment of a denominator. A similar problem confronts research on pedestrian stop and search procedures. Benchmarking discretion—and considerable discretion is used by local police in traffic and pedestrian situations—is the challenge. Without the right denominator, there will be no way to judge the numerator results that are being produced by police right now.

The energy and resources currently devoted to analysis of racial profiling demand that requisite attention be paid to the development of interpretative frameworks that allow for sound judgment. The committee concludes that current efforts to collect data on public encounters with police that are intended to inform judgments on whether police agencies engage in racial profiling are not very effective. The committee finds that current efforts to collect data on public encounters with police that are intended to inform judgments on whether police agencies engage in racial profiling are not very effective. **The committee recommends further research on the collection and analysis of systematic data on the lawfulness of police activities.**

Other Approaches to Accountability

Apart from mandates to collect some form of data, other noteworthy features of state racial profiling bills include measures designed to increase police accountability to the public. In Colorado, for instance, police officers who stop motorists but do not issue tickets must hand out business cards to the driver that state the officer's name and a number to call if the driver feels that he or she was pulled over only because of race. A slightly different procedure operates in Minnesota, where police officers must verbally relate their name, badge number, and agency that they work for to any motorist that they stop. Some states, such as Kentucky, have started a telephone hotline for motorists to call to report allegations of racial profiling. All of these procedures add a new dimension of accountability of the police to the community, advancing an already prominent trend in urban policing. In order to gauge the effectiveness of these and other accountability measures, **the committee recommends research on the collection of data on police lawfulness generally.** A number of programs have emerged for collecting data on officer performance for the purpose of identifying problem behavior and providing a basis for corrective action. Some early intervention or early warning programs collect data on a broad range of officer performance measures. They have been adopted voluntarily by many law enforcement agencies and have been imposed by consent decrees in other agencies. Rigorous evaluations are required to determine if these programs effectively produce police accountability.

Federal Response to Racial Profiling

The federal government has addressed the problem of racial profiling in several ways. First, an executive memorandum issued by President Clinton prohibits federal law enforcement agencies from engaging in racial profiling and mandates that those agencies collect data. President George W. Bush has endorsed data collection on this issue and called for the elimination of racial profiling and Attorney General John Ashcroft has publicly endorsed this mission.

Second, Congress has initiated, through the U.S. General Accounting Office, research inquiries into this issue (General Accounting Office, 2000a). One influential recent study, released in March 2000 (General Accounting Office, 2000b), examined U.S. Customs Service's targeting of airline passengers and found that black women were stopped and searched in disproportion to their offense rates.[4] During this period of racial targeting, successful apprehension of drug couriers occurred at such a low rate that a randomized search of passengers yielded better results. The Customs Ser-

---

[4]U.S. General Accounting Office, "U.S. Customs Service: Better Targeting of Airline Passengers for Personal Searches Could Produce Better Results," *GGD-00-38* March 17, 2000.

vice agreed to new training and procedures, including more rigorous review of complaints filed against the agency.

Finally, the 107th Congress introduced several bills on racial profiling. In the House, H.R. 965 and H.R. 1907 would have required states to ban racial profiling or risk losing up to 10 percent of federal highway funds. H.R. 2074 and its companion bill, S. 989, would have required states to adopt racial profiling policies in order to receive federal grants. H.R. 1907 defined racial profiling as the consideration of race "to any degree or in any fashion" by an officer when deciding whom to stop or search, except when race is part of a specific description of an offender who committed a crime. Data collection was not a feature of this bill (H.R. 965 is the same bill without any language that defines racial profiling). S. 989, sponsored by Senator Russell Feingold in the Senate, and the identical H.R. 2074, sponsored by Representative John Conyers in the House, went into considerably more detail. These bills defined racial profiling in the same way as H.R. 1907, but also required "collection of data on routine investigative activities sufficient to determine if law enforcement agents are engaged in racial profiling and submission of that data to the Attorney General" (S. 989). The attorney general would have been required to develop an appropriate benchmark for police agencies to use in collecting data; in addition, the attorney general would be required to report annually on the results of this data collection effort to Congress. Police agencies that do not comply with the provisions of this bill would lose funding from any or all of the following grant programs: the Edward Byrne Memorial State and Local Law Enforcement Assistance Programs; the Cops on the Beat program under Part Q of Title I of the Omnibus Crime Control and Safe Streets; and the Local Law Enforcement Block Grant program of the Department of Justice. It remains to be seen whether either of these bills, which did not pass the 107th Congress, will be reintroduced and, if so, whether either garner more support.

Resolving the Issue of Racial Profiling

There is a divergence between the law enforcement community and the general public on whether or not racial profiling is a widespread phenomenon. In part this difference reflects just how one defines racial profiling, since the public definition is more expansive than what has thus far been proffered by law enforcement. While general agreement exists that race should not be used as the basis for stopping or searching a citizen, debate still surrounds the use of race as one among other factors that can be legitimately used by police in making a decision to stop or search.

The difficulty in establishing benchmarks for collecting data on racial profiling should neither undermine current efforts under way in gathering such data nor serve to discredit the utility of data themselves for public policy purposes. Instead, it should encourage redoubled attention to the limitations of data collection and to the important roles of police training and accountability measures in effecting change in law enforcement. Perhaps most important is the need for guided discretion among police officers.

The terrorist attacks of September 11, 2001, represent one important and still largely unknown factor in this debate and in policing in general. A Gallup poll from November 29, 2001, found that 60 percent of respondents favored steps the government had taken to carry out a war on terror, including detainment of immigrants and others singled out for attention because of their country of origin. Anecdotes and editorials provide some qualitative evidence that many people also support the use of race and ethnicity at airports as a factor in considering who should be subjected to increased scrutiny. How much this trend will influence everyday urban policing and how long it will last remain important but unanswered questions.

CONCLUSION

Research on public opinion documents the profound gulf between the races in American's views of the legitimacy of the police. The committee calls for more research on the experiences of crime victims, persons stopped by the police, and the public, focusing on practices in policing that support or undermine public confidence in the institution. To support this, the committee recommends conducting a regular national survey to gauge the extent and nature of police-citizen contacts, including items that speak to public assessments of the quality of police service in their community.

Current efforts to collect data on public encounters with police that are intended to inform judgments on whether police agencies engage in racial profiling are not very effective. We call for more research on the collection of reliable and valid encounter data under field conditions that then can be analyzed in ways that point unambiguously to policy recommendations and personnel decisions.

The committee also recommends research on mechanisms for ensuring lawfulness. A number of programs have emerged for collecting data on officer performance for the purpose of identifying problem behavior and providing a basis for corrective action. Some early intervention or early warning programs collect data on a broad range of officer performance measures. They have been adopted voluntarily by many law enforcement agencies and have been imposed by consent decrees in other agencies. Rigorous evaluations are required to determine if these programs effectively produce police accountability.

9

The Future of Policing Research

The future of policing research will depend heavily on federal policy decisions. Will police be able to reduce violence, including the growing threat of global terrorism? Will police be able to enhance democracy, by ensuring fair and equal treatment of all people in a diverse society? The answers to these questions may depend on how much, and how well, research can address them. Police research depends heavily on public funding, and, given severe constraints on state and local budgets, such funding seems possible only at the federal level.

Since the Safe Streets Act of 1968, federally sponsored research on police has contributed to the substantial accumulation of knowledge that is reviewed in this report. Federal interventions of a variety of kinds have helped make American policing far more receptive to the use of scientific research in the advancement of their mission. They have created a demand for even more knowledge about what works and what doesn't to prevent crime and promote fairness and justice. Policing stands in first place among all criminal justice agencies in the use of the tools of social science, including surveys, sophisticated statistical analysis and mapping, systematic observation, quasi-experiments, and randomized controlled trials. Neither prosecutors nor prisons nor courts can match the intensity with which police have embraced social science.

However, the test of success of any program of police research is not the methods it uses, but what it accomplishes. This report includes a number of specific research and policy recommendations that reflect what we have learned via a variety of methodologies. Also reflecting the field as a whole, they represent a mix of operational and theoretical concerns.

ENHANCING CRIME CONTROL EFFECTIVENESS

Among the central questions in police research are how the police can prevent crime and injury, how they can more effectively foster desistance once it has developed, and how they can minimize the damaged caused to victims, their families, and the community. The committee concludes that there is strong evidence supporting the effectiveness of focused and specific policing strategies. The more strategies are tailored to the problems they seek to address, the more effective police will be in controlling crime and disorder. Crime control strategizing should consider the specific locations, crimes, criminals, and facilitating community factors that are linked to crime hot spots. The strategies themselves should be diverse and carefully targeted.

The committee's review of research also suggests that police should look beyond reactive law enforcement strategies in their search for ways to reduce crime, disorder, and fear of crime. Criminologists have long recognized that rates of crime and fear are affected by many powerful social forces. Although the role of the police among these forces is not entirely clear, community factors doubtlessly weigh more heavily in the long run. The police should seek ways to engage the broader community in the task of securing safety. Such approaches have promise and should be the subject of more systematic investigation.

ENHANCING THE LAWFULNESS OF POLICE ACTIONS

When the authority of the state is evoked, the public has a right to understand its use and to query whether it has been used fairly and justly. However, not enough is known about the extent of police lawfulness or their compliance with legal and other rules, nor can the mechanisms that promote police lawfulness be identified. Modern police research had its origin in the study of police lawfulness in the exercise of their discretion. The committee recommends renewed research on this topic, as well as a coordinated research emphasis on the effectiveness of organizational mechanisms that foster police rectitude.

To advance this, the committee recommends legislation requiring police agencies to file annual reports to the public on the number of persons shot at, wounded, and killed by police officers in the line of duty. The committee also recommends an emphasis on measuring citizen views of the quality of police service, through support for the Bureau of Justice statistics to develop and pilot test in a variety of police departments a system to document the nature and extent of police-citizen encounters and informal applications of police authority.

ENHANCING THE LEGITIMACY OF POLICING

By legitimacy we mean the judgments that ordinary citizens make about the rightfulness of police conduct and the organizations that employ and supervise them. The report reviews what is known about the factors that help build trust and confidence in the police. However, given the regular recurrence of allegations of racial injustice by the police and the inconclusive nature of the available findings, the committee judges it a high research priority to establish the nature and extent to which race and ethnicity affect police practice, independent of other legal and extralegal considerations. The committee recommends the launching of a periodic national survey to gauge public assessments of the quality of police service in their community. The committee recommends expanding data collection to encompass a wider range of policing outcomes, to enable the monitoring of the quality of police service and not just its quantity. The committee also recommends that research on police service delivery be expanded to include the metropolitan areas of cities as a relevant domain of concern.

IMPROVING PERSONNEL PRACTICES

In the end, policing policies are implemented by the men and women serving in the field, and, as a service organization, the police depend heavily on the quality of their recruitment and training practices. In the case of recruitment, a prominent point of discussion in policing circles is educational requirements for aspiring officers. However, the committee finds the available evidence inadequate to make recommendations regarding the desirability of higher education for improving police practice and strongly recommends rigorous research on the effects of higher education on job performance. The committee also recommends more research on police training, including the following questions: What should training be? What methods work best? Who makes the most effective instructors? At what point should an officer receive training of a given type? What is the appropriate duration/intensity?

FOSTERING INNOVATION

In its report the committee describes many innovative ideas that have influenced American policing but notes that important features of the policing industry may serve to retard their adoption. The committee recommends a special study of innovation processes in policing, one that includes factors that can be influenced by federal and state governments. To monitor the status of policing, the committee recommends that the Bureau of Justice Statistics continue to conduct an enhanced, yearly version of its current

Law Enforcement Management and Administrative Statistics Survey. To support this and other organizational research, the committee recommends that the Bureau of Justice Statistics' Agency Directory Survey be improved and updated on a regular basis, and that it conduct a special study of the validity of responses to surveys and experiment with methods to ensure accurate reporting of agency characteristics.

The committee further recommends that the National Institute of Justice support a program of rigorous evaluation of new crime information technologies in local police agencies. To better understand the nature of the policing industry, the committee recommends a special study of the dimensions of the private security industry, and that the Current Population Survey be used to secure an estimate of the size and characteristics of the labor force in this sector.

ASSESSING PROBLEM-ORIENTED AND COMMUNITY POLICING

Problem-oriented and community policing, two recent innovations in policing, receive special scrutiny in this report. To better understand their nature and extent, the committee recommends that the Bureau of Justice Statistics develop measures that provide a more accurate indication of the extent to which community liaison and mobilization activities, as well as other community oriented programs, are adopted by police agencies. The committee also recommends development of measures that better document at the jurisdiction level the nature and extent of nonenforcement services delivered by police. This program of development should consider the variety of current measures available to U.S. police agencies, pilot test a system at several sites, and then propose a large, multiagency data collection system.

RESPONDING TO TERRORISM

The committee recommends research on the organizational demands of responding to terrorism. The committee strongly encourages using the results of recent research on terrorism to develop a long-term national program for tracking and evaluating the performance of local police departments' efforts in gathering an handling intelligence on terrorism.

ORGANIZING RESEARCH

Federal support for police research has been highly variable from year to year, posing great obstacles to the institutionalization of research as a central element of American policing. Given the importance of the goals of police research, the committee recommends that careful attention be given to the extent and stability of research funding. Research conducted in police agencies could be coordinated with other studies of crime causation and patterning, extending basic criminological research as well.

Police chiefs, communities, police officers and crime victims all need answers to the research questions posed here—and to many others. What has been accomplished so far demonstrates that many police departments are willing hosts for researchers and consumers of their findings. What can be accomplished in the future depends heavily on the organization and financing of police research, for in the work of the police, there has rarely been any doubt that evidence matters.

References

CHAPTER 2

Bayley, D.H., and H. Mendelson
  1969   *Minorities and the Police.* New York, NY: Free Press.
Bayley, D.H., and E. Bittner
  1984   Learning the skills of policing. *Law and Contemporary Problems* 47:35-59.
Bayley, D.H., and J. Garofalo
  1987   Patrol officer effectiveness in managing conflict during police-citizen encounters. Pp. 81-88 in *Report to the Governor, Volume III.* Albany, NY: New York State Commission on Criminal Justice and the Use of Force.
  1989   Management of violence by police patrol officers. *Criminology* 27:1-25.
Biderman, A.D., and L. Johnson, J. McIntyre, and A. Weir
  1967   *Report on a Pilot Study in the District of Columbia on Victimization and Attitudes Toward Law Enforcement.* (President's Commission on Law Enforcement and the Administration of Justice. Studies in Crime and Law Enforcement in Metropolitan Areas, Field Surveys I.) Washington, DC: U.S. Government Printing Office.
Bittner, E.
  1970   *The Functions of the Police in Modern Society: A Review of Background Factors, Current Practices, and Possible Role Models.* Rockville, MD: National Institute of Mental Health.
Bittner, E., and R.G. Rumbaut
  1979   Changing conceptions of the police role: A sociological review. Pp. 239-288 in M. Tonry and M. Morris, eds., *Crime and Justice, Volume 1.* Chicago, IL: University of Chicago Press.
Black, D., and A.J. Reiss
  1967a Interrogation and the criminal process. *Annals of the American Academy of Political and Social Science* 374:47-57.
  1967b Patterns of behavior in citizen and police transactions. Pp. 1-139 in *Studies of Crime and Law Enforcement in Major Metropolitan Areas, Field Surveys III, Volume 2.* Washington, DC: U.S. Government Printing Office.

Brown, M.K.
  1981   *Working the Street: Police Discretion and the Dilemmas of Reform.* New York,
          NY: Russell Sage Foundation.
Bureau of Justice Statistics
  1998   *Criminal Victimization and Perceptions of Community Safety in Twelve Cities.*
          Washington, DC: U.S. Government Printing Office.
Bynum, T.W., and R.E. Worden
  1996   *Police Drug Crackdowns: An Evaluation of Implementation and Effects.* Washing-
          ton, DC: National Institute of Justice.
Chermak, S.M., and E.C. Riksheim
  1993   Causes of police behavior revisited. *Journal of Criminal Justice* 21:353- 382.
Davis, K.C.
  1969   *Discretionary Justice: A Preliminary Inquiry.* Baton Rouge, LA: Louisiana State
          University Press.
DeJong, C., S.D. Mastrofski, and R.B. Parks
  2001   Patrol officers and problem-solving: An application of expectancy theory. *Justice
          Quarterly* 18:31-61.
Dunworth, T.
  2000   *National Evaluation of the Youth Firearms Violence Initiative.* Washington, DC:
          U.S. Department of Justice.
Eck, J.E.
  1983   *Solving Crimes: The Investigation of Burglary and Robbery.* Washington, DC: Po-
          lice Executive Research Forum.
Eck, J.E., and E.R. Maguire
  2000   Have changes in policing reduced violent crime? An assessment of the evidence. In
          A. Blumstein and T. Wallman, eds., *The Crime Drop in America.* New York, NY:
          Cambridge University Press.
Flanagan, T., and D.R. Longmire, eds.
  1966   *Americans View Crime and Justice.* Thousand Oaks, CA: Sage.
Fosdick, R.B.
  1920   *American Police Systems.* Montclair, NJ: Patterson Smith.
Fridell, L., R. Lunney, D. Diamond, and B. Kubu
  2001   *Racially Biased Policing: A Principled Response.* Washington, DC: Police Executive
          Research Forum.
Goldstein, H.
  1979   Improving policing: A problem oriented approach in crime. *Crime and Delinquency*
          25:236-258.
Green-Mazerolle, L.
  1999   *Controlling Drug and Disorder Problems: Oakland's Beat Health Program.* Wash-
          ington, DC: National Institute of Justice.
Greenwood, P., J. Petersilia, and J. Chaiken
  1977   *The Criminal Investigation Process.* Lexington, MA: D.C. Heath.
Jacob, H.
  1971   Black and white perceptions of justice in the city. *Law and Society Review* 6:69-90.
Kelling, G.L., T. Pate, D. Dieckman, and C.E. Brown
  1974   *The Kansas City Preventive Patrol Experiment: Technical Report.* Washington, DC:
          Police Foundation.
Kerner Commission
  1968   *National Advisory Commission on Civil Disorder.* Washington, DC: U.S. Govern-
          ment Printing Office.

Lafave, W.R
    1965   *Arrest: The Decision to Take a Suspect into Custody.* Boston, MA: Little, Brown and Co.
Levitt, S.D.
    1997   Using election cycles in police hiring to estimate the effect of police on crime. *Public Policy* 23:523-545.
Lewis, J.H., and G.L. Kelling
    1979   The police foundation: Research and reform. Pp. 254-270 in J. Knutsson, E. Kuhlhorn, and A. Reiss, eds., *Police and the Social Order.* Stockholm, Sweden: National Swedish Council for Crime Prevention.
Loftin, C., and D. McDowall
    1982   The police, crime, and economic theory: An assessment. *American Sociological Review* 47:393-401.
Manning, P.K.
    1977   *Police Work.* Cambridge, MA: MIT Press.
Marvell, T.B., and C.E. Moody
    1996   Specification problems, police levels and crime rates. *Criminology* 24:55-72.
Mastrofski, S.D., A.J. Reiss, R.B. Parks, and R.E. Worden
    1998   *Community Policing in Action: Lessons from an Observational Study.* Washington, DC: U.S. Department of Justice.
Mastrofski, S.D., J.B. Snipes, R.B. Parks, and C.D. Maxwell
    2000   The helping hand of the law: Police control of citizens on request. *Criminology* 38:307-342.
McCluskey, J.D., S.D. Mastrofski, and R.B. Parks
    1999   To acquiesce or rebel: Predicting citizen compliance with police requests. *Police Quarterly* 2:389-416.
Muir, W.K., Jr.
    1977   *Police: Streetcorner Politicians.* Chicago, IL: Chicago University Press.
Mulhausen, D.
    2002   *Research Challenges Claims of COPS Effectiveness.* (Center for Data Analysis Report #02-02.) Washington, DC: Heritage Foundation.
National Research Council
    1993   *Understanding and Preventing Violence: Panel on the Understanding and Control of Violent Behavior.* A.J. Reiss and J.A. Roth, eds. Washington, DC: National Academy Press.
Parks, R., S. Mastrofski, M.K. Gray, and C. DeJong
    1999   How officers spend their time with the community. *Justice Quarterly* 16:483-518.
President's Commission on Law Enforcement and the Administration of Justice
    1967   *Task Force Report: The Police.* Washington, DC: U.S. Government Printing Office.
Reiner, R.
    1994   Policing and the police. Pp. 705-772 in M. Maguire, R. Morgan, and R. Reiner, eds., *The Oxford Handbook of Criminology.* London, England, and New York, NY: Oxford University Press.
Reiss, A., Jr.
    1971   *Police and the Public.* New Haven, CT: Yale University Press.
    1979   Systematic social observation in police research. In J. Knutsson, E. Kuhlhorn, and A. Reiss, eds., *Police and the Social Order.* Stockholm, Sweden: National Swedish Council for Crime Prevention.
Rosenbaum, D.P., ed.
    1994   *The Challenge of Community Policing.* Thousand Oaks, CA: Sage.

Roth, J., J. Ryan, and C.S. Koper
    2000   *National Evaluation of the COPS Program—Title I of the 1994 Crime Act.* Washington, DC: The Urban Institute.
Samuels, J.
    2000   Remarks to Committee to Review Research on Police Policy and Practices Meeting, June 27, National Academy of Sciences, Washington, DC. Washington, DC: Public Access Records Office, National Academy of Sciences.
Sherman, L.S.
    1983   Patrol strategies for police. In J.Q. Wilson, ed., *Crime and Public Policy.* San Francisco, CA: ICS Press/Transaction Books.
Sherman, L.W.
    1973   Sociology and social reform of the American police 1950-1973. *Journal of Police Science and Administration.*
    1992   *Policing Domestic Violence: Experiments and Dilemmas.* New York, NY: Free Press.
Sherman, L.W., D. Gottfredson, D. MacKenzie, J. Eck, P. Reuter, and S. Bushway
    1997   *Preventing Crime: What Works, What Doesn't, and What's Promising.* College Park, MD: University of Maryland.
    1998   *Preventing Crime: What Works, What Doesn't, What's Promising.* (Research in Brief.) Washington, DC: National Institute of Justice.
Skolnick, J.H.
    1966   *Justice Without Trial.* New York, NY: John Wiley and Sons, Inc.
Skolnick, J.H., and J.J. Fyfe
    1993   *Above the Law: Police and the Excessive Use of Force.* New York, NY: Free Press.
Smith, B.
    1949   *Police Systems in the United States.* New York, NY: Harper and Row.
Smith, P.E., and R.O. Hawkins
    1973   Victimization, types of citizen-police contacts and attitudes toward the police. *Law and Society Review* 8:135-152.
Terrill, W.
    1997   *Police Coercion: Application of the Force Continuum.* New York, NY: LFB Publishing.
Toch, H., and W.A. Geller, ed.
    1996   *Police Violence.* New Haven, CT: Yale University Press.
Travis, J.
    1995   *Criminal Justice Research and Public Policy in the United States.* Presentation to the Ninth United Nations Congress on the Prevention of Crime and Treatment of Offenders, Cairo, Egypt, May 2.
Trojanowicz, R.
    1986   Evaluating a neighborhood foot patrol program: The Flint Michigan Project. In D. Rosenbaum, ed., *Community Crime Prevention: Does it Work.* Thousand Oaks, CA: Sage.
Van Maanen, J.
    1974   Working the street: A developmental view of police behavior. In H. Jacob, ed., *The Potential for Reform in Criminal Justice.* Thousand Oaks, CA: Sage.
Walker, S.
    2001   *Police Accountability: The Role of Citizen Oversight.* Belmont, CA: Wadsworth.
Weisburd, D.
    2000   *Police Attitudes Toward Abuse of Authority: Findings from a National Survey.* Washington, DC: National Institute of Justice.

Weisburd, D., and L. Green
  1995   Policing drug hot spots: The Jersey City drug market analysis experiment. *Justice Quarterly* 12:711-735.
Westley, W.
  1953   Violence and the police. *The American Journal of Sociology* 59:34-41.
Wilson, J.Q.
  1968   *Varieties of Police Behavior: The Management of Law and Order in Eight Communities.* Cambridge, MA: Harvard University Press.
  1977   *Investigators: Managing the FBI and Narcotics Agencies.* New York, NY: Basic Books, Inc.
Wilson, J.Q., and G. Kelling
  1982   Broken windows: The police and neighborhood safety. *Atlantic Monthly* 249:29-38.
Zhao, J., and Q. Thurman
  2001   A National Evaluation of the Effect of COPs Grants on Crime from 1994 to 1999. Unpublished study.

CHAPTER 3

Adams, B.
  1995   *Evaluation of Police Training Conducted Under the Family Violence Prevention and Services Act.* Washington, DC: Urban Institute.
Alpert, G.P., and R.G. Dunham
  1999   The force factor: Measuring and assessing police use of force and suspect resistance. Pp. 45-60 in *Use of Force: Overview of National and Local Data.* Washington, DC: U.S. Department of Justice.
American Bar Foundation
  1957   *Survey of the Administration of Justice.* Washington, DC: American Bar Foundation.
Avakame, E.F., and J.J. Fyfe
  2001   A differential police treatment of male-on-female spousal violence: Some more evidence on the leniency thesis. *Violence Against Women* 7:22-45.
Avakame, E.F., J.J. Fyfe, and C. McCoy
  1999   Did you call the police? What did they do? An empirical assessment of Black's theory of mobilization of law. *Justice Quarterly* (December):765-792.
Bard, M.
  1970   The role of law enforcement in the helping system. *North Carolina Journal of Mental Health* 4:3-15.
Bayley, D.H.
  1986   The tactical choices of police patrol officers. *Journal of Criminal Justice* 14:329-348.
  1994   *Police for the Future.* New York, NY: Oxford University Press.
  1998   *What Works in Policing?* New York, NY: Oxford University Press.
Bayley, D.H., and J. Garofalo
  1987   Patrol officer effectiveness in managing conflict during police-citizen encounters. Pp. B1-B88 in *Report to the Governor, Volume III.* Albany, NY: New York State Commission on Criminal Justice and the Use of Force.
  1989   Management of violence by police patrol officers. *Criminology* 27:1-25.
Bayley, D., and D. Shearing
  2001   *The New Structure of Policing: Description, Conceptualization and Research Agenda.* Washington, DC: U.S. Department of Justice, National Institute of Justice.

Bayley, D.H., and R.E. Worden
   1998   *Police Overtime: An Examination of Key Issues*. (National Institute of Justice Research in Brief.) Washington, DC: U.S. Department of Justice.
Bittner, E.
   1970   *The Functions of the Police in Modern Society: A Review of Background Factors, Current Practices, and Possible Role Models*. Bethesda, MD: National Institute of Mental Health.
Black, D.
   1976   Social organization of arrest. Pp. 1087-1111 in W.B. Sanders and H.C. Daudistel, eds., *Criminal Justice Process: A Reader*. Westport, CT: Praeger Publishers.
   1980   *The Manners and Customs of the Police*. New York, NY: Academic Press.
Bloch, P.B., and D. Anderson
   1974   *Policewomen on Patrol*. Washington, DC: Police Foundation.
Braga, A., D.L. Weisburd, E.J. Waring, L. Green-Mazerolle, W. Spelman, and F. Gajewski
   1999   Problem-oriented policing in violent crime places: A randomized controlled experiment. *Criminology* 37:541-580.
Brandl, S.G.
   1993   Impact of case characteristics on detectives' decision making. *Justice Quarterly* 10:395-414.
Brandl, S.G., and J. Frank
   1994   The relationship between evidence, detective effort, and the disposition of burglary and robbery investigations. *American Journal of Police* 13:149-168.
Bromley, M.L., and B.A. Reaves
   1998   Comparing campus and municipal police: The human resource dimension. *Policing, An International Journal of Police Strategies and Management* 21:534-546.
Brown, J.M., and P.A. Langan
   2001   *Policing and Homicide, 1976-1998: Justifiable Homicide by Police Officers Murdered by Felons*. Washington, DC: U.S. Department of Justice.
Bureau of Justice Statistics
   1998   *Census of State and Local Enforcement Agencies, 1996*. Available: http://www.ojp. usdoj.gov/bjs/pub/pdf/cslea96 [June 25, 2002].
   1999   *American Indians and Crime*. Available: http://www.ojp.usdoj.gov/bjs/pub/pdf/ aic.pdf [June 25, 2002].
   2000   *Law Enforcement Management and Administrative Statistics, 1999: Data or Individual, State, and Local Agencies with 100 or More Officers*. Washington, DC: U.S. Department of Justice.
Bynum, T.S., G.W. Cordner, and J.R. Greene
   1982   Victim offense characteristics: Impact on police investigative decision making. *Criminology* 20:301-318.
Carter, D.L.
   1986   Hispanic police officers' perception of discrimination. *Police Studies* 9:204-210.
Carter, D.L., A.D. Sapp, and D. Stephens
   1983   *State of Police Education; Policy Direction for the 21st Century*. Washington, DC: Police Executive Research Forum.
Clarke, R.V.
   1997   *Situational Crime Prevention: Successful Case Studies* (92nd edition). New York, NY: Harrow & Heston.
Commission on Accreditation for Law Enforcement Agencies
   1994   *Standards for Law Enforcement Agencies, 3rd Edition*. Fairfax, VA: Commission on Accreditation for Law Enforcement Agencies.

Crank, J.P., and R. Langworthy
  1992 Institutional perspective of policing. *Journal of Criminal Law and Criminology* 83:338-363.
Cumming, E., J. Cumming, and L. Edell
  1965 Policemen as philosophers, guide, and friend. *Social Problems* 12:276-286.
Damanpour, F.
  1991 Organizational innovation: A meta-analysis of the effects of determinants and moderators. *Academy of Management Journal* 34:555-590.
Davis, R.C., C. Ortiz, N.J. Henderson, J. Miller, and M.K. Massie
  2002 *Turning Necessity into Virtue: Pittsburgh's Experience with a Federal Consent Decree.* New York, NY: Vera Institute.
Donner, F.
  1990 *Protectors of Privilege: Red Squads and Police Repression in Urban America.* Berkeley, CA: University of California Press.
Dulaney, W.M.
  1996 *Black Police in America.* Bloomington, IN: Indiana University Press.
Eck, J.E.
  1983a *Solving Crimes: The Investigation of Burglary and Robbery.* Washington, DC: Police Executive Research Forum.
  1983b *Investigations Management Conference Participants Manuals.* Washington, DC: Police Executive Research Forum.
  2002 Preventing crime at places. Pp. 241-294 in L.W. Sherman et al., eds., *Evidence-Based Crime Prevention.* New York, NY: Routledge.
  2003 Police problems: The complexity of problem theory, research and evaluation. In J. Knuttsen, ed., *Problem-Oriented Policing: From Innovation to Mainstream, Crime Prevention Studies 15.* Monsey, NY: Criminal Justice Press.
Eck, J.E., and D. Rosenbaum
  1994 The new police order: Effectiveness, equity and efficiency in community policing. Pp. 2-23 in D. Rosenbaum, ed., *Community Policing: Testing the Promises.* Thousand Oaks, CA: Sage.
Eck, J.E., and W. Spelman
  1987 *Problem Solving: Problem-Oriented Policing in Newport News.* Washington, DC: Police Executive Research Forum.
Ericson, R.V.
  1981 *Making Crime: A Study of Detective Work.* Scarborough, Canada: Butterworth.
Ericson, R.V., and K.D. Haggerty
  1997 *Policing the Risk Society.* Toronto: University of Toronto Press.
Federal Bureau of Investigation
  2001 *Crime in the United States 2000.* (Unified Crime Reports.) Washington, DC: U.S. Department of Justice.
Feinman, C.
  1986 Police problems on the Navajo reservation. *Police Studies* 9:194-198.
Fogelson, R.M.
  1977 *Big City Police.* Cambridge, MA: Harvard University Press.
Forst, B., and P.K. Manning
  1999 *Privatization of Policing: Two Views.* Washington, DC: Georgetown University Press.
Fridell, L., R. Lunney, D. Diamond, and B. Kubu
  2001 *Racially Biased Policing: A Principled Response.* Washington, DC: Police Executive Research Forum.

Friedrich, R.J.
  1980   Police use of force—individuals, situations, and organizations. *Annals of the American Academy of Political and Social Science* 452:82-97.
Fyfe, J.J.
  1978   *Shots Fired: An Examination of New York City Police Firearms Discharges.* Microfilms International, Ann Arbor, MI. Dissertation, State University of New York, Albany.
  1979   Administrative interventions on police shooting discretion: An empirical examination. *Journal of Criminal Justice* 7:309-323.
  1981   Who shoots? A look at officer race and police shooting. *Journal of Police Science and Administration* 9:367-382.
  1983   *Police Personnel Practices, Baseline Data Reports* (Volume 15, No. 1.) Washington, DC: International City Management Association.
Fyfe, J.J., D.A. Klinger, and J.M. Flavin
  1997   Differential police response to male on female spousal violence. *Criminology* 35:455-474.
Gardiner, J.A.
  1969   *Traffic and the Police: Variations in Law Enforcement Policy.* Cambridge, MA: Harvard University Press.
Garner, J.H., and C.D. Maxwell
  1999   Measuring the amount of force used by and against the police in six jurisdictions. Pp. 25-44 in *Use of Force by Police: Overview of National and Local Data.* Washington, DC: National Institute of Justice.
Garner, J.H., J. Buchanan, T. Schade, and J. Hepburn
  1996   *Understanding the Use of Force By and Against the Police.* Washington, DC: National Institute of Justice.
Garofalo, J., and S. Martin
  1992   *Bias Motivated Crimes, Their Characteristics, and Law Enforcement Response.* Carbondale, IL: Southern Illinois University.
Geller, W.A., and M. Scott
  1992   *Deadly Force: What We Know; A Practitioner's Desk Reference on Police-Involved Shootings.* Washington, DC: Police Executive Research Forum.
Geller, W.A., and H. Toch, eds.
  1995   *And Justice for All: Understanding and Controlling Police Abuse of Force.* Washington, DC: Police Executive Forum.
General Accounting Office
  1996   *Federal Fugitives: More Timely Entry on National Wanted Person File Needed.* Washington, DC: General Accounting Office.
  2000a   *Racial Profiling: Limited Data Available on Motorists Stops.* Washington, DC: General Accounting Office.
  2000b   *U.S. Customs Services: Better Targeting of Airline Passengers for Personal Searches Could Produce Better Results.* Washington, DC: General Accounting Office.
Goldstein, H.
  1977   *Policing a Free Society.* Cambridge, MA: Balinger Publishing Company.
  1979   Improving policing: A problem oriented approach in crime. *Crime and Delinquency* 25:236-258.
  1990   *Problem-Oriented Policing.* New York, NY: McGraw-Hill.
Goldstein, J.
  1960   Police discretion not to invoke criminal process: Low visibility decisions in the administration of justice. *Yale Law Journal* 60:543-594.

Green, L.
  1995   Policing places with drug problems: The multi-agency response team approach. Pp. 199-216 in J.E. Eck and D. Weisburd, eds., *Crime and Place: Crime Prevention Studies 4*. Monsey, NY: Criminal Justice Press.
Greenberg, D.B., and B. Hantz
  1975   *Supercops: Play it to a Bust*. New York, NY: Hawthorne Books.
Greene, J.R.
  2000   Community policing in America: Changing the nature, structure, and function of the police. Pp. 299-370 in J. Horney, ed., *Policies, Processes, and Decisions of the Criminal Justice System: Criminal Justice, Volume 3*. Washington, DC: U.S. Department of Justice.
Greenwood, P., J. Petersilia, and J. Chaiken
  1977   *The Criminal Investigation Process*. Lexington, MA: D.C. Heath.
Harris, D.A.
  2002   Racial profiling revisited: "Just common sense" in the fight against terror. *Criminal Justice* 17:36-59.
Hickman, M.J., and B. Reaves
  2001   *Community Policing in Local Police Departments, 1997 and 1999*. Washington, DC: U.S. Department of Justice.
International Association of Chiefs of Police
  1973   *Juvenile Justice Administration*. Washington, DC: International Association of Chiefs of Police.
Jeffries, E.S., J. Frank, B.W. Smith, K.J. Novak, and L.F. Travis III
  1998   An examination of the productivity and perceived effectiveness of drug task forces. *Police Quarterly* 11:85-107.
Kakalik, J.S., and S. Wildhorn
  1977   *The Private Police: Security and Danger*. Santa Monica, CA: Rand Corporation.
Kapur, S.
  1995   Technical diffusion with social learning. *Journal of Industrial Economics* 43:173-196.
Karmen, A.
  2000   *New York Murder Mystery: The True Story Behind the Crime Crash of the 1990s*. New York, NY: New York University Press.
Katz, C.
  2001   *Establishment of a Police Gang Unit: An Examination of Rational and Institutional Considerations*. Washington, DC: U.S. Department of Justice.
Kelling, G.L., T. Pate, D. Dieckman, and C.E. Brown
  1974   *The Kansas City Preventive Patrol Experiment: A Technical Report*. Washington, DC: Police Foundation.
Kerner Commission
  1968   *National Advisory Commission on Civil Disorder*. Washington, DC: U.S. Government Printing Office.
King, W.R.
  1998   Innovativeness in American Municipal Police Organizations. Doctoral dissertation, University of Cincinnati.
Kleck, G.
  1991   *Point Blank: Guns and Violence in America*. Hawthorne, NY: Aldine de Gruyter Publishing Company.
Klinger, D.A.
  1995   Policing spousal assault. *Journal of Research in Crime and Delinquency* 32:308-324.

1996   Quantifying law in police-citizen encounters. *Journal of Quantitative Criminology* 12:391-415.

Klinger, D.A., and G.S. Bridges
   1995   Measurement error in calls-for-service as an indicator of crime. *Criminology* 35:705-726.

Klinger, D.A., and K. Hubbs
   2000   Citizen injuries from law enforcement impact munitions: Evidence from the field. *Wound Ballistics Review* 4:9-13.

Klockars, C.B., and W.E. Harver
   1993   *Production and Consumption of Research in Police Agencies in the United States.* Washington, DC: National Institute of Justice.

Klockars, C.B., S.K. Ivkovich, W.E. Harver, and M.R. Haberfeld
   2000   *Measurement of Police Integrity.* (Research in Brief). Washington, DC: National Institute of Justice.

Knapp, W.
   1973   *The Knapp Commission Report on Police Corruption.* New York, NY: George Braziller.

Lafave, W.R.
   1962   *The Administration of Criminal Justice in the United States: A Monograph on the Decision to Take a Suspect into Custody.* Chicago, IL: American Bar Foundation.
   1965   *Arrest: The Decision to Take a Suspect into Custody.* Boston, MA: Little, Brown and Co.

Lafree, G., B.F. Reskin, and C.A. Visher
   1983   Juror's response to victim's behavior and legal issues in sexual assault trials. *Social Problems* 32:389-407.

Langan, P.A., L.A. Greenfeld, S.K. Smith, M.R. Durose, and D.J. Levin
   2001   *Contacts Between Police and the Public.* Washington, DC: Bureau of Justice Statistics. Also available: http://www.ojp.usdoj.gov/bjs/pub/pdf/cpp99.pdf [January 2003].

Law Enforcement Assistance Administration
   1973   *LEAA Activities July 1, 1972 to June 30, 1973.* Washington, DC: U.S. Department of Justice.

Leinen, S.
   1993   *Gay Cops.* New Brunswick, NJ: Rutgers University Press.

Lempert, R.
   1984   From the editor. *Law and Society Review* 18:v.
   1989   Humility is a virtue: On the publication of policy-relevant research. *Law and Society Review* 23:145-161.

Loving, N.
   1980   *Responding to Spouse Abuse and Wife Beating—A Guide for Police.* Washington, DC: Police Executive Research Forum.

Luna, E.
   1998   Growth and development of tribal police: Challenges and issues for tribal sovereignty. *Journal of Contemporary Criminal Justice* 14:75-86.

Manning, P.K.
   1992   Information technologies and the police. Pp. 349-398 in M. Tonry and M. Norval, eds., *Modern Policing.* Chicago, IL: University of Chicago Press.

Martin, S.E.
   1980   *Breaking and Entering-Policewomen on Patrol.* Berkeley, CA: University of California Press.
   1990   *On the Move: The Status of Women in Policing.* Washington, DC: Police Foundation.

Martin, S.E., and L.W. Sherman
  1986   *Catching Career Criminals: The Washington DC Repeat Offender Project.* Washington, DC: Police Foundation.

Marx, G.T.
  1988   *Undercover: Police Surveillance in America.* Berkeley, CA: University of California Press.

Mastrofski, S.D.
  1990   Prospects of change in police patrol: A decade in review. *American Journal of Police* 9:1-79.

Mastrofski, S.D., J.B. Snipes, and A.E. Supina
  1996   Compliance on demand: The public's response to specific police requests. *Journal of Research in Crime and Delinquency* 33:269-305.

Mastrofski, S.D., A.J. Reiss, R.B. Parks, and R.E. Worden
  1998   *Community Policing in Action: Lessons from an Observational Study.* Washington, DC: U.S. Department of Justice.

Maxwell, C.D., J.D. Garner, and J.A. Fagan
  2001   *The Effects of Arrest on Intimate Partner Violence: New Evidence from the Spouse Assault Replication Program.* (NCJ Research in Brief 188199.) Washington, DC: U.S. Department of Justice.

Mazerolle, L.G., J. Ready, W. Terrill, and E. Waring
  2000   Problem-oriented policing in public housing: The Jersey City evaluation. *Justice Quarterly* 17:129-158.

McDonald, P.P.
  2001   *Managing Police Operations: Implementing the New York Crime Control Model, CompStat.* Belmont, CA: Wadsworth.

McEwen, J.T., E.F. Connors, and M.I. Cohen
  1986   *Evaluation of the Differential Police Response Field Test.* Washington, DC: U.S. Department of Justice.

McLaughlin, V.
  1992   *Police and the Use of Force: The Savannah Study.* Westport, CT: Praeger Publishers.

McPhail, C., D. Schweingruber, and B. McCarthy
  1998   Policing of Protests in the United States, 1960-1995. Pp. 49-69 in D. della Porta and H. Reiter, eds., *The Control of Mass Demonstrations in Western Democracy.* Minneapolis, MN: University of Minnesota Press.

Meisel, J.B., and S.L. Levin
  1985   Intermarket differences in the early diffusion of an innovation. *Southern Economic Journal* 51:672-680.

Mijares, T.C., R.M. McCarthy, and D.B. Perkins
  2000   *Management of Police Specialized Tactical Units.* Springfield, IL: Charles C. Thomas.

Milton, C.H., J.W. Halleck, J. Lardner, and G.L. Abrecht
  1977   *Police Use of Deadly Force.* Washington, DC: Police Foundation.

Monkkonen, E.H.
  1981   *Police in Urban America, 1860 to 1920.* Cambridge, MA: Cambridge University Press.

Moore, M.H., M. Sparrow, and W. Spelman
  1996   Innovations in policing: From production lines to job shops. Chapter 12 in A.A. Altshuler and R.D. Behn, eds., *Innovation in American Government: Challenges, Opportunities, and Dilemmas.* Washington, DC: Brookings Institution Press.

Moore, M.H., W. Spelman, and R. Young
  1992   Innovations in Policing: A Test of Three Different Methodologies for Identifying Important Innovations in a Substantive Field. Unpublished Paper. Cambridge, MA: Harvard University, Kennedy School of Government.
Mullen, K.
  1996   The Computerization of Law Enforcement: A Diffusion of Innovation Study. Doctoral Dissertation, State University of New York at Albany.
National Center for Women and Policing
  1998   *Equality Denied: The Status of Women and Policing, 1998.* Available: http//www.womenandpolicing.org [November 15, 2002].
Ostrom, E., G. Whitaker, and R. Parks
  1978   Policing: Is there a system? In J. May and A. Wildavsky, eds., *The Policy Cycle.* New York, NY: Russell Sage Foundation.
Parks, R., S. Mastrofski, M.K. Gray, and C. DeJong
  1999   How officers spend their time with the community. *Justice Quarterly* 16:483-518.
Powell, W.W., and P. DiMaggio
  1991   *The New Institutionalism in Organizational Analysis.* Chicago, IL: University of Chicago Press.
President's Commission on Law Enforcement and the Administration of Justice
  1967   *Task Force Report: The Police.* Washington, DC: President's Commission on Law Enforcement and the Administration of Justice.
Puro, S., R. Goldman, and W.C. Smith
  1997   Police decertification: Changing patterns among the states, 1985-1995. *Policing* 20:481-496.
Ramirez, D., J. McDevitt, and A. Farrell
  2000a *A Resource Guide on Racial Profiling Data Collection Systems. Promising Practices and Lessons Learned.* Washington, DC: U.S. Department of Justice.
  2000b *Problem Oriented Policing: Reflections on the First 20 Years: A Summary Report.* Washington, DC: U.S. Office of Community Oriented Policing.
Rampart Independent Review Panel
  2000   Report of the Rampart Independent Review Panel: A Report to the Los Angeles Board of Police Commissioners concerning the operations, policies, and procedures of the Los Angeles Police Department in the Wake of the Rampart Scandal. Available: http://www.ci.la.ca.us/oig/rirprpt.pdf [November 1, 2003].
Reaves, B.A., and A.L. Goldberg, eds.
  2000   *Local Police Departments, 1997.* Washington, DC: U.S. Department of Justice.
Reaves, B.A., and T.C. Hart
  2000   *Law Enforcement Management and Administrative Statistics, 1999: Data for Individual State and Local Agencies with 100 or more Officers.* Washington, DC: U.S. Department of Justice.
Reiss, A.J., Jr.
  1971   *The Police and the Public.* New Haven, CT: Yale University Press.
Robin, G.
  1963   Justifiable homicides by the police. *Journal of Criminal Law, Criminology, and Political Science* 54:225-231.
Rogers, E.M.
  1983   *Diffusion of Innovations, 3rd Edition.* New York, NY: Free Press.
Rosenbaum, D.
  1989   Community crime prevention: A review and synthesis of the literature. *Justice Quarterly* 5:323-395.

Rosenbaum, D.P., ed.
    1994   *The Challenge of Community Policing*. Thousand Oaks, CA: Sage.
Roth, J., J. Ryan, and C.S. Koper
    2000   *National Evaluation of the COPS Program—Title I of the 1994 Crime Act*. Washington, DC: The Urban Institute.
Sandler, G.B., and E. Mintz
    1974   Police organizations: Their changing internal and external relationships. *Journal of Police Science and Administration* 2:458-463.
Scheirer, M.A.
    1990   The life cycle of an innovation: Adoption versus discontinuation of the fluoride mouth rinse program in schools. *Journal of Health and Social Behavior* 31:203-215.
Schultz, D.M.
    1995   *From Social Worker to Crimefighter: Women in United States Municipal Policing*. Westport, CT: Praeger Publishers.
Scott, E.J.
    1981   *Calls for Service-Citizen Demand and Initial Police Response*. Washington, DC: U.S. Department of Justice.
Seaskate, Inc.
    1998   *The Evolution and Development of Police Technology*. Washington, DC: The National Committee on Criminal Justice Technology.
Sherman, L.W.
    1978a   *Controlling Police Corruption: The Effects of Reform Policies, Summary Report*. Washington, DC: U.S. Department of Justice.
    1978b   How police solve crimes. In N. Johnston and L.D. Savitz, eds., *Justice and Corrections*. Washington, DC: U.S. Department of Justice.
    1992   The influence of criminology on criminal law: Evaluating arrests for misdemeanor domestic violence. *Journal of Criminal Law and Criminology* 83:1-45.
Sherman, L.W., and J. Eck
    2002   Policing for crime prevention. Pp. 295-329 in L.W. Sherman, D.L. MacKenzie, and D.P. Farrington, eds., *Evidence-Based Crime Prevention*. New York, NY: Routledge.
Sherman, L.W., P.R. Gartin, and M.E. Buerger
    1989   Hot spots of predatory crime: Routine activities and the criminology of place. *Criminology* 27:27-55.
Sherman, L.W., J. Schmidt, and D.P. Rogan
    1992   *Policing Domestic Violence*. New York, NY: Free Press.
Sherman, L.W., D. Gottfredson, D. MacKenzie, J. Eck, P. Reuter, and S. Bushway
    1997   *Preventing Crime: What Works, What Doesn't, and What's Promising*. College Park, MD: University of Maryland.
Silverman, E.B.
    1999   *NYPD Battles Crime: Innovative Strategies in Policing*. Boston, MA: Northeastern University Press.
Skogan, W.
    1985   Making better use of victims and witnesses. Pp. 332-339 in W.A. Geller, ed., *From Police Leadership in America*. Westport, CT: Praeger Publishers.
Skogan, W., and S.M. Hartnett
    1997   *Community Policing: Chicago Style*. New York, NY: Oxford University Press.
Skolnick, J.H., and J.J. Fyfe
    1993   *Above the Law: Police and the Excessive Use of Force*. New York, NY: Free Press.
Sparrow, M.K., M.H. Moore, and D.M. Kennedy
    1990   *Beyond 911: A New Era for Policing*. New York, NY: Basic Books.

Teplin, L.
   1986   *Keeping the Peace: The Parameters of Police Discretion in Relation to the Mentally Disordered.* Washington, DC: U.S. Department of Justice.
Terrill, T.
   2001   *Police Coercion: Application of the Force Continuum.* New York, NY: LFB Scholarly Publishing, LLC.
U.S. Attorney General
   1997   *Annual Report of the Attorney General of the U.S.* Available: http://www.usdoj.gov/ag/annualreports/ar97 [June 21, 2002].
U.S. Census Bureau
   1997   *Public Education Finances, Volume 4, Government Finances.* Available: http://www.Census.gov/prod/gc/97/gc974-1.pdf [September 1, 2003].
   1999   *Population, 1999.* Suitland, MD: U.S. Census Bureau.
Wakeling, S., M. Jorgensen, and S.N. Michaelson
   1999   *Policing on American Indian Reservations: A Report to the National Institute of Justice.* Cambridge, MA: Harvard University Press.
Walker, S.
   1977   *A Critical History Reform: The Emergence of Professionalism.* Lexington, MA: Heath and Company.
   1985   Setting the standards: The impact of "blue-ribbon" commissions on the police. Pp. 354-370 in W. Geller, ed., *Police Leadership in America: Crisis and Opportunity.* New York, NY: Praeger Publishers.
   1993   *Taming the System: The Control of Discretion in Criminal Justice, 1950-1990.* New York, NY: Oxford University Press.
   1998   *Popular Justice: A History of American Criminal Justice, 2nd Edition.* New York, NY: Oxford University Press.
   2001   *Police Accountability: The Role of Citizen Oversight.* Belmont, CA: Wadsworth Publishing Company.
Walker, S., and K.B. Turner
   1992   *A Decade of Modest Progress: Employment of Black and Hispanic Police Officers, 1983-1992.* Washington, DC: Equal Opportunity Employment Commission.
Walker, S., G.P. Alpert, and D.J. Kenney
   2001   *Early Warning Systems: Responding to the Problem Police Officer.* Washington, DC: U.S. Department of Justice.
Walker, S., C. Spohn, and M. Delone
   2000   *Color of Justice: Race, Ethnicity and Crime in America, Second Edition.* Belmont, CA: Wadsworth Publishing Company.
Weisburd, D.
   2002   From criminals to criminal contexts: Reorienting criminal justice research and policy. *Advances in Criminological Theory* 10:197-216.
Weisburd, D., S.D. Mastrofski, A.M. McNally, R. Greenspan, and J.J. Willis
   2003   Reforming to preserve: Compstat and strategic problem-solving in American policing. *Criminology and Public Policy* 3:421-455.
Weiss, A.
   1997   The communication of innovation in American policing. *Policing* 20:292-310.
   1998   *Informal Information Sharing Among Police Agencies, NIJ Research Preview.* Washington, DC: National Institute of Justice.
   2001   Police Innovation and Communication Networks. Paper prepared for the National Research Council Committee to Review Research on Police Policy and Practice, July, Washington, DC.

Wellford, C., and J. Cronin
  2000   Clearing up homicide clearance rates. *NIJ Journal* (April):3-7.
Wilson, J.Q.
  1968   *Varieties of Police Behavior: The Management of Law and Order in Eight Commu-
         nities.* Cambridge, MA: Harvard University Press.
Wilson, J.Q., and B. Boland
  1980   *The Effect of the Police on Crime.* Washington, DC: U.S. Department of Justice.
Wilson, J.Q., and G.L. Kelling
  1982   *Broken windows: The police and neighborhood safety. Atlantic Monthly* 249:29-
         38.
Worden, R.E.
  1989   Situational and attitudinal explanations of police behavior: A theoretical reappraisal
         and empirical assessment. *Law & Society Review* 23:667-711.
  1996   The causes of police brutality: Theory and evidence on police use of force. Pp. 23-51
         in W.A. Geller and H. Toch, eds., *Police Violence: Understanding and Controlling
         Police Abuse of Force.* New Haven, CT: Yale University Press.
Worden, R.E., and A.A. Pollitz
  1984   Police arrests in domestic disturbances: A further look. *Law and Society Review*
         18:105-119.
Zhao, J.
  1996   *Why Police Organizations Change: A Study of Community-Oriented Policing.*
         Washington, DC: Police Executive Research Forum.
Zhao, J., N.P. Lovich, and Q. Thurman
  1999   The status of community policing in American cities. *Policing, An International
         Journal of Police Strategies and Management* 22:74-92.

CHAPTER 4

Ajzen, I., and M. Fishbein
  1977   Attitude-behavior relations: A theoretical analysis and review of empirical
         research. *Psychological Bulletin* 84:888-918.
Alex, N.
  1969   *Black in Blue: A Study of the Negro Policeman.* New York, NY: Appleton-Century-
         Crofts.
Alpert, G.P.
  1989   Police use of deadly force: The Miami experience. Pp. 480-495 in R. Dunham and
         G. Alpert, eds., *Critical Issues in Policing: Contemporary Readings.* Prospect
         Heights, IL: Waveland Press.
Anderson, E.
  1990   *Streetwise: Race, Class, and Change in an Urban Community.* Chicago, IL: Univer-
         sity of Chicago Press.
  1999   *Code of the Street: Decency, Violence, and the Moral Life of the Inner City.* New
         York, NY: W.W. Norton and Company.
Balch, R.W.
  1972   Police personality: Fact or fiction. *Journal of Criminal Law, Criminology and Police
         Science* 63:106-119.
Baro, A.L., and D. Burlingame
  1999   Law enforcement and higher education: Is there an impasse? *Journal of Criminal
         Justice Education* (Spring):57-73.

Bayley, D.H.
  1986   The tactical choices of police patrol officers. *Journal of Criminal Justice* 14:329-348.
Bayley, D.H., and E. Bittner
  1984   Learning the skills of policing. *Law and Contemporary Problems* 47:35-59.
Bayley, D.H., and J. Garofalo
  1989   Management of violence by police patrol officers. *Criminology* 27:1-25.
Berk, S.F., and D.R. Loseke
  1981   Handling family violence: Situational determinants of police arrest in domestic disturbances. *Law & Society Review* 15:317-346.
Berman, J.S.
  1987   *Police Administration and Progressive Reform: Theodore Roosevelt as Police Commissioner of New York.* Westport, CT: Greenwood Publishing Group.
Bernard, T.J., and R.S. Engel
  2001   Conceptualizing criminal justice theory. *Justice Quarterly* 18:30.
Bittner, E.
  1967   Police discretion in emergency apprehension of mentally ill persons. *Social Problems* 14:278-292.
  1970   *The Functions of the Police in Modern Society: A Review of Background Factors, Current Practices, and Possible Role Models.* Bethesda, MD: National Institute of Mental Health.
  1974   Florence Nightingale in pursuit of Willie Sutton: A theory of the police. Pp. 17-44 in H. Jacob, ed., *The Potential for Reform of Criminal Justice.* Thousand Oaks, CA: Sage.
Black, D.
  1971   The social organization of arrest. *Stanford Law Review* 23:1087-1111.
  1976   Social organization of arrest. In W.B. Sanders and H.C. Daudistel, eds., *Criminal Justice Process: A Reader.* Westport, CT: Praeger Publishers.
  1980   *The Manners and Customs of the Police.* New York, NY: Academic Press.
Black, D., and A.J. Reiss, Jr.
  1967   Patterns of behavior in police and citizen transactions. Pp. 1-139 in *Studies of Crime and Law Enforcement in Major Metropolitan Areas, Volume 2.* Washington, DC: U.S. Government Printing Office.
  1970   Police control of juveniles. *American Sociological Review* 35:63–77.
Bloch, P.B., and D. Anderson
  1974   *Policewomen on Patrol.* Washington, DC: Police Foundation.
Blumberg, M.
  1982   Use of Firearms by Police Officers: The Impact of Individuals, Communities and Race. Dissertation, State University of New York at Albany.
Boydstun, J.E., and M.E. Sherry
  1975   *San Diego Community Profile Final Report.* Washington, DC: Police Foundation.
Bradford, D., and J.E. Pynes
  1999   Police academy training: Why hasn't it kept up with practice? *Police Quarterly* 2:283-301.
Brandl, S.G.
  1993   Impact of case characteristics on detectives' decision making. *Justice Quarterly* 10:395-414.
Brehm, J., and S. Gates
  1993   Donut shops and speed traps: Evaluating models of supervision on police behavior. *American Journal of Political Science* 37:555-582.

Broderick, J.J.
   1977   *Police in a Time of Change*. Morristown, NJ: General Learning Press.
Brown, M.K.
   1981   *Working the Street: Police Discretion and the Dilemmas of Reform*. New York, NY: Russell Sage Foundation.
Buckley, L.B.
   1991   Attitudes toward higher education among mid-career police officers. *Canadian Police College Journal* 15:257-273.
Buerger, M.E.
   1998   Police training as pentecost: Using tools singularly ill-suited to the purpose of reform. *Police Quarterly* 1:27-63.
Bureau of Justice Statistics
   2002   *Police Departments in Large Cities, 1990-2000*. Washington, DC: Office of Justice Programs.
Bynum, T.S., G.W. Cordner, and J.R. Greene
   1982   Victim offense characteristics: Impact on police investigative decision making. *Criminology* 20:301-318.
Carter, D.L., and A.D. Sapp
   1990   Evolution of higher education in law enforcement: Preliminary findings from a national study. *Journal of Criminal Justice Education* 1:59-85.
Cascio, W.F.
   1977   Formal education and police officer performance. *Journal of Police Science and Administration* 5:89-96.
Decker, S.H., and R.L. Smith
   1981   Police minority recruitment: A note on its effectiveness in improving black evaluations of the police. *Journal of Criminal Justice* 8:387-393.
Dejong, C.
   2000   Gender Differences in Officer Attitude and Behavior: Providing Comfort to Citizens. Unpublished report. East Lansing, MI: Michigan State University.
Dejong, C., S. Mastrofski, and R.B. Parks
   2001   Patrol officers and problem solving: An application of expectancy theory. *Justice Quarterly* 18:31-61.
Donohue, J., and S. Levitt
   2001   The impact of race on policing, arrest patterns, and crime. *Journal of Law and Economics* 44:367-394.
Douthit, N.
   1975   August Vollmer, Berkeley's first chief of police and the emergence of police professionalism. *California Historical Quarterly* 54:101-124.
Engel, R.S.
   2000   Effects of supervisory styles on patrol officer behavior. *Police Quarterly* 3:262-293.
Engel, R.S., and E. Silver
   2001   Policing mentally disordered suspects: A reexamination of the criminalization hypothesis. *Criminology* 39:225-252.
Engel, R.S., J. Sobol, and R.E. Worden
   2000   Further exploration of the demeanor hypothesis: The interaction effects of suspects' characteristics and demeanor on police behavior. *Justice Quarterly* 17:235-258.
Feinman, C.
   1994   *Women in the Criminal Justice System, Third Edition*. Westport, CT: Praeger Publishers.
Ferraro, K.J.
   1989   Policing woman battering. *Social Problems* 36:61-74.

Finckenauer, J.O.
    1975   Higher education and police discretion. *Journal of Police Science and Administration* 3:450-457.
Finn, M.A., and L.J. Stalans
    1997   Influence of gender and mental state on police decisions in domestic assault cases. *Criminal Justice and Behavior* 24:157-176.
Fogelson, R.M.
    1977   *Big City Police.* Cambridge, MA: Harvard University Press.
Frank, J.
    1996   *Street-Level Policing in Cincinnati: The Content of Community and Traditional Policing and the Perceptions of Policing Audiences.* Washington, DC: National Institute of Justice.
Frank, J., and L.F. Travis
    1998   *Suburban and Small Town Policing: An Observational Study.* Washington, DC: National Institute of Justice.
Frank, J., S.G. Brandl, F.T. Cullen, and A. Stichman
    1996   Reassessing the impact of race on citizen's attitudes toward the police: A research note. *Justice Quarterly* 13:321-334.
Frenkel-Brunswick, E., D.J. Levinson, and T.W. Adorno
    1993   *The Authoritarian Personality (Studies in Prejudice).* New York, NY: W.W. Norton and Company.
Friedrich, R.J.
    1977   The Impact of Organizational, Individual, and Situational Factors on Police Behavior. Ann Arbor, MI: University of Michigan, Doctoral Dissertation.
    1980   Police use of force: Individuals, situations, and organizations. *Annals of the American Academy of Political and Social Science* 452:82-97.
Fyfe, J.J.
    1980   Geographic correlates of police shooting: A microanalysis. *Journal of Research in Crime and Delinquency* 17:101-113.
    1981a   Race and extreme police-citizen violence. Pp. 89-108 in R.L. McNeely and C.E. Pope, eds., *Race, Crime, and Criminal Justice.* Thousand Oaks, CA: Sage.
    1981b   Who shoots? A look at officer race and police shooting, *Journal of Police Science and Administration* 9:367-382.
    1982   Blind justice: Police shootings in Memphis. *Journal of Criminal Law and Criminology* 73:707-722.
    1995   Training police to minimize excessive use of force. In H. Toch and W. Geller, eds., *And Justice for All.* Washington, DC: Police Executive Research Forum.
Fyfe, J.J., D.A. Klinger, and J.M. Flavin
    1997   Differential police response to male on female spousal violence. *Criminology* 35:455-474.
Gallagher, C., E.R. Maguire, S.D. Mastrofski, and M.D. Reisig
    2001   Psychological screening of law enforcement officers: A case for job relatedness. *Journal of Police Science and Administration* 17:176-182.
Garner, J.H., C.D. Maxwell, and C.G. Heraux
    2002   Characteristics associated with the prevalence and severity of force used by the police. *Justice Quarterly* 19:705-746.
Garner, J.H., T. Schade, J. Hepburn, and J. Buchanan
    1995   Measuring the continuum of force used by and against the police. *Criminal Justice Review* 20:146-168.
Geller, W.A., and K.J. Karales
    1981   Shootings of and by Chicago police: Uncommon crises. Part I: Shootings by Chicago police. *Journal of Criminal Law and Criminology* 72:1813-1866.

Geller, W.A., and H. Toch, eds.
1995   *And Justice for All: Understanding and Controlling Police Abuse of Force.* Washington, DC: Police Executive Forum.

Goldstein, H.
1990   *Problem-Oriented Policing.* New York, NY: McGraw-Hill.

Haar, R.N.
1997   Patterns of interaction in a police patrol bureau: Race and gender barriers to integration. *Justice Quarterly* 14:53-85.
2001   The making of a community policing officer: The impact of basic training and occupational socialization on police recruits. *Police Quarterly* 4:402-433.

Hayeslip, D.W., Jr.
1989   Higher education and police performance revisited: The evidence examined through meta-analysis. *American Journal of Police* 8:49-62.

Heeren, T., R. Hingson, and A.R. Myers
1989   Discretionary leniency in police enforcement of laws against drinking and driving: Two examples from the state of Maine, USA. *Journal of Criminal Justice* 17:179-186.

Herbert, S.
1998   Police subculture reconsidered. *Criminology* 36:343-369.

Hirsh, H., F. Schmidt, and J. Hunter
1986   Estimation of employment validities by less experienced judges. *Personnel Psychology* 39:337-344.

Hogg, A., and C. Wilson
1995   *Is the Psychological Screening of Police Applicants a Realistic Goal? The Successes and Failures of Psychological Screening.* (Report Series 124.) Payneham, South Australia: National Police Research Unit.

Hudzik, J.H.
1978   College education for police-problems in measuring component and extraneous variables. *Journal of Criminal Justice* 6:69-81.

Jacobs, D., and J. Cohen
1978   Impact of racial integration on the police. *Journal of Police Science and Administration* 6:68-183.

Jones, D.A., and J. Belknap
1999   Police responses to battering in a progressive pro-arrest jurisdiction. *Justice Quarterly* 16:249-273.

Kavanagh, J.
1994   The Occurrence of Force in Arrest Encounters. Unpublished doctoral dissertation, Rutgers University, Newark, NJ.

Kelling, G.L.
1999   *Broken Windows and Police Discretion.* (NCJ #178259.) Washington, DC: National Institute of Justice.

Kelling, G.L., and C. Coles
1996   *Fixing Broken Windows: Restoring Order and Reducing Crime in Our Communities.* New York, NY: Free Press.

Kenney, D.J., and S. Watson
1990   Intelligence and the selection of recruits. *American Journal of Police* 10:39-63.

Kerner Commission
1968   *National Advisory Commission on Civil Disorder.* Washington, DC: U.S. Government Printing Office.

Klinger, D.A.
1994   Demeanor or crime? Why "hostile" citizens are more likely to be arrested. *Criminology* 32:475-493.

1995   The micro-structure of nonlethal force: Baseline data from an observational study. *Criminal Justice Review* 20:169-186.

1996   Quantifying law in police-citizen encounters. *Journal of Quantitative Criminology* 12:391-415.

1997   Negotiating order in patrol work: An ecological theory of police response to deviance. *Criminology* 35:277-306.

LaFave, W.R.
1965   *Arrest: The Decision to Take a Suspect into Custody.* Boston, MA: Little, Brown and Co.

Lafree, G.
1998   *Losing Legitimacy: Street Crime and the Decline of Institutions in America.* Boulder, CO: Westview Press.

LaGrange, T.
2000   Distinguishing Between the Criminal and the Crazy: Decisions to Arrest in Police Encounters with the Mentally Disordered. Paper presented at the American Society of Criminology, San Francisco, CA.

Langworthy, R.
1987   Police cynicism: What we know from the Niederhoffer scale. *Journal of Criminal Justice* 15:17-35.

Lasley, J.R.
1994   The impact of the Rodney King incident on citizen attitudes toward police. *Policing and Society* 3:245-255.

Lefkowitz, J.
1975   Psychological attributes of policemen: A review of research and opinion. *Journal of Social Issues* 31:3-26.

Leinen, S.
1984   *Black Police, White Society.* New York, NY: Columbia University Press.

Lundman, R.J.
1974   Routine police arrest practices: A commonwealth perspective. *Social Problems* 22:127-141.

1994   Demeanor or crime? The midwest city police-citizen encounters study. *Criminology* 32:631-656.

1996   Demeanor and arrest: Additional evidence from previously unpublished data. *Journal of Research in Crime and Delinquency* 33:306-323.

1998   City police and drunk driving: Baseline data. *Justice Quarterly* 15:527-546.

Lundman, R.J., R.E. Sykes, and J.P. Clark
1978   Police control of juveniles: A replication. *Journal of Research in Crime and Delinquency* 15:74-91.

Manning, P.K.
1994   Dynamics and Tensions in Police Occupational Culture. Unpublished manuscript, Michigan State University.

Martin, S.E.
1990   *On the Move: The Status of Women in Policing.* Washington, DC: Police Foundation.

Mastrofski, S.D.
1983   Control in the police organization. *The Journal of Criminal Law and Criminology* 74:1133-1137.

1990   Prospects of change in police patrol: A decade in review. *American Journal of Police* 9:1-79.

1998   Community policing and police organization structure. Pp. 161-189 in J.P. Brodeur, ed., *How to Recognize Good Policing: Problems and Issues.* Thousand Oaks, CA: Sage.

Mastrofski, S.D., and R. Parks
   1990   Improving observational studies of police. *Criminology* 28:475-496.
Mastrofski, S.D., and R.R. Ritti
   1996   Police training and the effects of organization on drunk driving enforcement. *Justice Quarterly* 13:291-320.
Mastrofski, S.D., R.B. Parks, C. DeJong, and R.E. Worden
   1998   Policing and Race: A Research Perspective. Paper presented at the 12th Congress of International Criminology, Seoul, Korea.
Mastrofski, S.D., M.D. Reisig, and J.D. McCluskey
   2002a   Police disrespect toward the public: An encounter-based analysis. *Criminology* 40:519-551.
Mastrofski, S.D., R.R. Ritti, and J. Snipes
   1994   Expectancy theory and police productivity in DUI enforcement. *Law & Society Review* 28:113-148.
Mastrofski, S.D., J.B. Snipes, and A.E. Supina
   1996   Compliance on demand: The public response to specific police requests. *Journal of Research in Crime and Delinquency* 3:269-305.
Mastrofski, S.D., R.E. Worden, and J.B. Snipes
   1995   Law enforcement in a time of community policing. *Criminology* 33:539-563.
Mastrofski, S.D., J.J. Willis, and J.B. Snipes
   2002b   Styles of patrol in a community-policing context. Pp. 81-111 in M. Morash and J. K. Ford, eds., *The Move to Community Policing. Making Change Happen.* Thousand Oaks, CA: Sage.
Mastrofski, S., J.B. Snipes, R.B. Parks, and C.D. Maxwell
   2000   The helping hand of the law: Police control of citizens on request. *Criminology* 38:307-342.
McEwen, T.
   1997   Community Policing Training Survey: Draft Report. Unpublished manuscript, Institute for Law and Justice, Alexandria, VA.
McNamara, J.H.
   1967   Uncertainties in police work: The relevance of police recruits' backgrounds and training. In D.J. Bordua, ed., *The Police: Six Sociological Essays.* New York, NY: John Wiley and Sons, Inc.
Menzies, R.J.
   1987   Psychiatrists in blue: Police apprehension of mental disorder and dangerousness. *Criminology* 25:429-453.
Meyer, M.W.
   1980   Police shootings of minorities: The case of Los Angeles. *Annals of the American Academy of Political and Social Science* 452:98-110.
Milton, C.H., J.W. Halleck, J. Lardner, and G. Abrecht
   1977   *Police Use of Deadly Force.* Washington, DC: Police Foundation.
Moore, M., and D.W. Stephens
   1991   *Beyond Command and Control: The Strategic Management of Police Departments.* Washington, DC: Police Executive Research Forum.
Muir, W.K., Jr.
   1977   *Police: Streetcorner Politicians.* Chicago, IL: University of Chicago Press.
National Research Council
   2001   *Juvenile Crime, Juvenile Justice.* J. McCord, C. Spatz Widom and N. Crowell, eds. Committee on Law and Justice and Board on Children, Youth and Families, Division of Behavioral and Social Sciences and Education. Washington, DC: National Academy Press.

Niederhoffer, A.
  1967   Cynicism questionnaire. In S.L. Brodsky and H.O. Smitherman, eds., *Handbook of Scales for Research in Crime and Delinquency*. New York, NY: Plenum.

Novak, K., J. Hartman, A. Holsinger, and M. Turner
  1999   The effects of aggressive policing of disorder on serious crime. *Policing: An International Journal of Police Strategies and Management* 22:171-190.

Paoline, E.A., III, S.M. Myers, and R.E. Worden
  2000   Police culture, individualism, and community policing: Evidence from two police departments. *Justice Quarterly* 17:575-605.

Police Executive Research Forum
  1989   *State of Police Education: Policy Direction for the 21st Century*. Washington, DC: Police Executive Research Forum.

Poole, E.D., and R.M. Regoli
  1979   Examination of the effects of professionalism on cynicism among police. *Social Science Journal* 6:59-66.

Regoli, R.M.
  1975   Police cynicism reconsidered—An analysis of smallest place analysis. *Criminology* 13:168-192.
  1976   Empirical assessment of Niederhoffer's police cynicism scale. *Journal of Criminal Justice* 4(3):231-241.

Reiss, A.J., Jr.
  1968   Police brutality: Answers to key questions. *Transaction* 5:10-19.
  1971   *The Police and the Public*. New Haven, CT: Yale University Press.
  1985   *Policing a City's Central District: The Oakland Story*. Washington, DC: National Institute of Justice.

Reuss-Ianni, E.
  1983   *Two Cultures of Policing: Street Cops and Management Cops*. New Brunswick, NJ: Transaction Publishers.

Riksheim, E.C., and S.M. Chermak
  1993   Causes of police behavior revisited. *Journal of Criminal Justice* 21:353-382.

Rosenbaum, D.P.
  1987   Coping with victimization: The effects of police intervention on victims' psychological readjustment. *Crime and Delinquency* 33:502-519.

Rossi, P.
  1974   Seriousness of crimes—Normative structure and individual differences. *American Sociological Review* 39:224-237.

Rubinstein, J.
  1973   *City Police*. New York, NY: Farrar, Straus and Giroux.

Schuman, H., and M.P. Johnson
  1976   Attitudes and behavior. *Annual Review of Sociology* 2:161-207.

Scrivner, E.M.
  1994   *Controlling Police Use of Excessive Force: The Role of the Police Psychologist*. Washington, DC: National Institute of Justice.

Sherman, L.W.
  1980   Causes of police behavior: The current state of quantitative research. *Journal of Research in Crime and Delinquency* 17:69-100.
  1992   *Policing Domestic Violence: Experiments and Dilemmas*. New York, NY: Free Press.

Sherman, L.W., and M. Blumberg
  1981   Higher education and police use of deadly force. *Journal of Criminal Justice* 9:317-331.

Shernock, S.K.
   1992   Effects of college education on professional attitudes among police. *Journal of Criminal Justice Education* 3:71-92.
Skolnick, J.H.
   1966   *Justice Without Trial*. New York, NY: John Wiley and Sons, Inc.
Smith, D.A.
   1986   The neighborhood context of police behavior. Pp. 313-342 in A. Reiss and M. Tonry, eds., *Crime and Justice: A Review of Research*. Chicago, IL: University of Chicago Press.
Smith, D.A., and E. Ostrom
   1974   *Effects of Training and Education on Police Attitudes and Performance*. Thousand Oaks, CA: Sage.
Smith, D.A., and J.R. Klein
   1983   *Police Agency Characteristics and Arrest Decisions*. Thousand Oaks, CA: Sage.
Smith, D.A., and C.A. Visher
   1981   Street-level justice: Situational determinants of police arrest decisions. *Social Problems* 29:167-177.
Smith, D.A., C. Visher, and L.A. Davidson
   1984   Equity and discretionary justice: The influence of race on police arrest decisions. *Journal of Criminal Law and Criminology* 75:234-249.
Smith, N., and C. Flanagan
   2000   *Effective Detective: Identifying the Skills of an Effective SIO*. London, England: Great Britain Home Office.
Snipes, J.B.
   2001   Police Response to Citizen Requests for Assistance: An Assessment of Deservedness, Workload, Social Status, and Officer Predisposition Perspectives. Ph.D. Dissertation, University of Albany, State University of New York.
Snipes, J.B., and S. Mastrofski
   1990   An empirical test of Muir's typology of police officers. *American Journal of Criminal Justice* 14:268-296.
Spano, R.
   2002   Potential Sources of Observer Bias in Observational Studies of Police. Unpublished Ph.D. dissertation. University of Albany, State University of New York.
Sparrow, M.K., M.H. Moore, and D.M. Kennedy
   1990   *Beyond 911: A New Era for Policing*. New York, NY: Basic Books.
Steadman, H.J.
   1986   Psychiatric evaluations of police referrals in a general hospital emergency room. *International Journal of Law and Psychiatry* 8:39-47.
Stewart, A.L., and K. Maddren
   1997   Police officers' judgment of blame in family violence: The impact of gender and alcohol. *Sex Roles* 37:921-934.
Sykes, R.E., and E.E. Brent
   1980   The regulation of interaction by police: A systems view of taking charge. *Criminology* 18:182-197.
Sykes, R.E., J.C. Fox, and J.P. Clark
   1974   A socio-legal theory of police discretion. In A. Niederhoffer and A.S. Blumberg, eds., *The Ambivalent Force: Perspectives on the Police, 2nd edition*. Hinsdale, IL: Dryden Press.
Teplin, L.
   1984   Managing disorder: Police handling of the mentally ill. Pp. 157-175 in L.A. Teplin, ed., *Mental Health and Criminal Justice*. Thousand Oaks, CA: Sage.

1986 *Keeping the Peace: The Parameters of Police Discretion in Relation to the Mentally Disordered.* Washington, DC: U.S. Department of Justice.

1994 Psychiatric and substance abuse disorders among male urban jail detainees. *American Journal of Public Health* 84:290-293.

Teplin, L.A., K.M. Abram, and G.M. McClelland

1996 Prevalence of psychiatric disorders among incarcerated women: I. Pretrial jail detainees. *Archives of General Psychiatry* 53:505-512.

Terrill, T.

2001 *Police Coercion: Application of the Force Continuum.* New York, NY: LFB Scholarly Publishing, LLC.

Terrill, W., and S. Mastrofski

2002 Reassessing situational and officer based determinants of police coercion. *Justice Quarterly* 19:215-248.

Terry, R.M.

1967 The screening of juvenile offenders. *Journal of Criminal Law, Criminology and Police Science* 58:173-181.

Triplett, R.

1996 The growing threat of gangs and juvenile offenders. Pp. 137-150 in T.J. Flanagan and D.R. Longmire, eds., *Americans View Crime and Justice.* Thousand Oaks, CA: Sage.

Van Maanen, J.

1974 Working the street: A developmental view of police behavior. Pp. 83-130 in H. Jacob, ed., *The Potential for Reform of Criminal Justice.* Thousand Oaks, CA: Sage.

1978 The asshole. In P.K. Manning and J. Van Maanen, eds., *Policing: A View from the Street.* Santa Monica, CA: Goodyear.

Visher, C.A.

1983 Gender, police arrest decisions, and notions of Chivalry. *Criminology* 21:5-28.

Walker, S.

1977 *A Critical History of Police Reform.* Lexington, MA: Lexington Books.

1985 Racial-minority and female employment in police: The implications of glacial change. *Crime and Delinquency* 31:555-572.

1998 *The Police in America: An Introduction, 3rd Edition.* Columbus, OH: McGraw-Hill.

Weiner, N.

1974 Effect of education on police attitudes. *Journal of Criminal Justice* 2:317-328.

Weinstein, A.G.

1972 Predicting behavior from attitudes. *Public Opinion Quarterly* 36:355-360.

Weirman, C.L.

1978 Variances of ability measurement scores obtained by college and non-college educated troopers. *Police Chief* 45:34-36.

Weisburd, D., and R. Greenspan, E.E. Hamilton, H. Williams, and K.A. Bryant

2000 *Police Attitudes Toward Abuse of Authority: Findings From a National Study.* Washington, DC: National Institute of Justice.

Westley, W.A.

1953 Violence and the police. *American Journal of Sociology* 59:34-41.

1970 *Violence and the Police: A Sociological Study of Law, Custom, and Morality.* Cambridge, MA: MIT Press.

White, W.

1972 Perspective on police professionalization. *Law and Society Review* 6:61-85.

Wilson, J.Q.

1968 *Varieties of Police Behavior: The Management of Law and Order in Eight Communities.* Cambridge, MA: Harvard University Press.

Wilson, J.Q., and G. Kelling
   1982   Broken windows: The police and neighborhood safety. *Atlantic Monthly* 249:29-38.
Wilson, O.W.
   1963   *Police Administration*. New York, NY: McGraw-Hill.
Wood, R.L., M. Davis, and A. Rouse
   2003   Diving into quicksand: Program implementation and police subcultures, In W.G. Skogan, ed., *Community Policing: Can It Work?* Belmont, CA: Wadsworth Publishing Company.
Worden, A.P.
   1993   Attitudes of women and men in policing: Testing conventional and contemporary wisdom. *Criminology* 31:203-242.
Worden, R.E.
   1989   Situational and attitudinal explanations of police behavior: A theoretical reappraisal and empirical assessment. *Law & Society Review* 23:667-711.
   1995a The "causes" of police brutality: Theory and evidence on police use of force. In W.A. Geller and H. Toch, eds., *And Justice for All: Understanding and Controlling Police Abuse of Force*. Washington, DC: Police Executive Research Forum.
   1995b Police officers' belief systems: A framework for analysis. *American Journal of Police* 14:49-81.
Worden, R.E., and A.A. Pollitz
   1984   Police arrests in domestic disturbances: A further look. *Law & Society Review* 18:105-119.
Worden, R.E., and S.M. Myers
   1999   *Police Encounters with Juvenile Suspects*. (Report to the National Institute of Justice.) Albany, NY: Hindelang Criminal Justice Research Center, University of Albany.
   2000   *Police Encounters with Juvenile Suspects*. (Report to the National Institute of Justice.) Albany, NY: University of Albany.
Worden, R.E., and R.L. Shepard
   1996   Demeanor, crime, and police behavior: A reexamination of police services study data. *Criminology* 34:83-105.
Worden, R.E., R.L. Shepard, and S.D. Mastrofski
   1996   On the meaning and measurement of suspects' demeanor toward the police: A comment on demeanor and arrest. *Journal of Research in Crime and Delinquency* 33:324-332.
Zhao, J., N.P. Lovich, and Q. Thurman
   1999   The status of community policing in American cities. *Policing, An International Journal of Police Strategies and Management* 22:74-92.

CHAPTER 5

Aaronsen, D., C. Dienes, and M. Musheno
   1984   *Public Policy and Police Discretion*. New York, NY: Clark Boardman.
Adams, K.
   1999   What we know about police use of force. In *Use of Force by Police: Overview of National and Local Data*. Washington, DC: Office of Justice Programs.
Alpert, G.P., and M.H. Moore
   1993   Measuring police performance in the new paradigm of policing. In *Performance Measures for the Criminal Justice System*. (Princeton University Study Group on Criminal Justice Performance Measures, NCJ 143505.) Washington, DC: U.S. Department of Justice, Bureau of Justice Statistics.

Altshuler, A.A.
 1970 *Community Control*. New York, NY: Bobbs-Merrill Co.
Anselin, L., J. Cohen, D. Cook, W. Gorr, and G. Tita
 2000 Spatial analyses of crime. Pp. 213-262 in D. Duffee, D. McDowall, L. Green Mazerolle, and S.D. Mastrofski, eds., *Measurement and Analysis of Crime and Justice*. Washington, DC: National Institute of Justice.
Archbold, C., and E.R. Maguire
 2002 Studying civil suits against the police: A serendipitous finding of sample selection bias. *Police Quarterly* 5(2):222-249.
Bayley, D.H.
 2002 Foreword. In E. Maguire, ed., *Organizational Structure in American Police Agencies: Context, Complexity and Control*. Albany, NY: SUNY Press.
Bittner, E.
 1970 *The Functions of the Police in Modern Society: A Review of Background Factors, Current Practices, and Possible Role Models*. Bethesda, MD: National Institute of Mental Health.
Bloch, P.B., and D.I. Specht
 1973 *Evaluation of Operation Neighborhood*. Washington, DC: Urban Institute.
Blumenson, E., and E. Nilsen
 1998 Policing for profit: The drug war's hidden economic agenda. *University of Chicago Law Review* 65:35-114.
Boydstun, J.E., and M.E. Sherry
 1975 *San Diego Community Profile Final Report*. Washington, DC: Police Foundation.
Bratton, W.
 1998 Crime is down in New York City: Blame the police. In W.J. Bratton et al., eds., *Zero Tolerance: Policing a Free Society*. London, England: Institute of Economic Affairs Health and Welfare Unit.
Brown, M.K.
 1981 *Working the Street: Police Discretion and the Dilemmas of Reform*. New York, NY: Russell Sage Foundation.
Browning, R.P., D.R. Marshall, and D.H. Tabb
 1984 *Protest Is Not Enough: The Struggle of Blacks and Hispanics for Quality in Urban Politics*. Berkeley, CA: University of California.
Bureau of Justice Statistics
 2002 *Police Departments in Large Cities, 1990-2000*. Washington, DC: Office of Justice Programs.
Cao, L., and B. Huang
 2000 Determinants of citizen complaints against police abuse of power. *Journal of Criminal Justice* 28:203-213.
Cao, L., X. Deng, and S. Barton
 2000 Test of Lundman's organizational product thesis with data on citizen complaints. *Policing* 23:356-373.
Chaney, C.K., and G.H. Salzstein
 1998 Democratic control and bureaucratic responsiveness: The police and domestic violence. *American Journal of Political Science* 42:745-768.
Committee for Economic Development
 1972 *Reducing Crime and Assuring Justice*. New York, NY: Committee for Economic Development.
Cordner, G.W.
 1989 Police agency size and investigative effectiveness. *Journal of Criminal Justice* 17:145-155.

Crank, J.P.
  1990   The influence of environmental and organizational factors on police style in urban
          and rural environments. *Journal of Research in Crime and Delinquency* 27:166-
          189.
Crock, S.
  2000   The terrorist threat in America is . . . overblown? *Business Week*, December 7.
Davis, E.M.
  1978   *Staff One: A Perspective on Effective Police Management.* Englewood Cliffs, NJ:
          Prentice-Hall, Inc.
Decker, S.
  1981   Citizen attitudes toward the police: A review of past findings and suggestions for
          future policy. *Journal of Police Science and Administration* 9:80-87.
DeJong, C., S.D. Mastrofski, and R.B. Parks
  2001   Patrol officers and problem-solving: An application of expectancy theory. *Justice
          Quarterly* 18:31-61.
Eck, J.E., and W. Spelman
  1987   *Problem Solving: Problem Oriented Policing in Newport News.* Washington, DC:
          Police Executive Research Forum.
Ericson, R.V., and K.D. Haggerty
  1997   *Policing the Risk Society.* Toronto: University of Toronto Press.
Federal Bureau of Investigation
  1980   *Uniform Crime Reporting Program Data: Offenses Known and Clearances by Ar-
          rest, 1980* [Codebook]. Ann Arbor, MI: Inter-university Consortium for Political
          and Social Research.
  2002   *FBI National Academy.* Available: http://www.fbi.gov/hq/td/academy/na/na2.htm
          [June 30, 2002].
Feeney, F.
  1982   *Police and Pretrial Release.* New York, NY: Lexington Books.
Fogelson, R.M.
  1977   *Big City Police.* Cambridge, MA: Harvard University Press.
Fowler, F.J., Jr., M.E. McCalla, and T.W. Mangione
  1979   *Reducing Residential Crime and Fear: The Hartford Neighborhood Crime Preven-
          tion Program.* Washington, DC: U.S. Government Printing Office.
Fyfe, J.J.
  1979   Administrative interventions on police shooting discretion: An empirical examina-
          tion. *Journal of Criminal Justice* 7:309-323.
  1982   Blind justice: Police shootings in Memphis. *Journal of Criminal Law and Criminol-
          ogy* 73:707-722.
  1988   Police use of deadly force: Research and reform. *Justice Quarterly* 5:165-205.
  2002   *Too Many Missing Cases: Holes in Our Knowledge about Police Use of Force.*
          Washington, DC: U.S. Department of Justice.
Gardiner, J.A.
  1969   *Traffic and the Police: Variations in Law Enforcement Policy.* Cambridge, MA:
          Harvard University Press.
Gay, W.G., J.P. Woodward, H.D. Talmadge, J.P. O'Neil, and C.J. Tucker
  1977   *Values in Team Policing: A Review of the Literature.* (National Institute of Law
          Enforcement and Criminal Justice, Law Enforcement Assistance Administration.)
          Washington, DC: U.S. Government Printing Office.
Greene, J.
  1999   Zero tolerance: A case study of police policies and practices in New York City.
          Crime and Delinquency 45:171-187.

Greene, J.R., W.T. Bergman, and E.J. McLaughlin
   1994   Implementing community policing: Cultural and structural change in police organi-
          zations. Pp. 92-109 in D.P. Rosenbaum, ed., *The Challenge of Community Policing:
          Testing the Promises*. Thousand Oaks, CA: Sage.
Guyot, D.
   1979   Bending granite: Attempts to change the rank structure of American police depart-
          ments. *Journal of Police Science and Administration* 7:253-284.
   1991   *Policing as Though People Matter*. Philadelphia, PA: Temple University Press.
Haggerty, K., and R. Ericson
   1999   The militarization of policing in the information age. *The Journal of Military and
          Political Sociology* 27:233-245.
   2001   The military technostructures of policing. Pp. 43-64 in P. Kraska, ed., *Militarizing
          the American Criminal Justice System: The Changing Roles of the Armed Forces
          and the Police*. Boston, MA: Northeastern University Press.
Haider-Markel, D.P.
   2001   Implementing controversial policy: Results from a national survey of law enforce-
          ment department activity on hate crimes. *Justice Research and Policy* 3:29-61.
Hall, R.H.
   1991   *Organizations: Structures, Processes, and Outcomes*. Englewood Cliffs, NJ: Prentice-
          Hall, Inc.
Henriquez, M.A.
   1999   IACP national database project on police use of force. In *Use of Force by Police:
          Overview of National and Local Data*. Washington, DC: Office of Justice
          Programs.
Holmes, M.D.
   2000   Minority threat and police brutality: Determinants of civil rights criminal complaints
          in U.S. municipalities. *Criminology* 38:343-365.
Jackson, P.I., and L. Carroll
   1981   Race and the war on crime: The sociopolitical determinants of municipal police
          expenditures in 90 non-Southern U.S. cities. *American Sociological Review* 46:290-
          305.
Jacobs, A.
   1978a Impact of racial integration on the police. *Journal of Police Science and Administra-
          tion* 6:168-183.
   1978b Some observations regarding crime control. *Indiana Law Review* 11:403-429.
Jacobs, D.
   1978   Inequality and the legal order: An ecological test of the conflict model. *Social Prob-
          lems* 25:515-525.
Jacobs, D., and D. Britt
   1979   Inequality and police use of deadly force: An empirical assessment of a conflict
          hypothesis. *Social Problems* 26:404-412.
Jacobs, D., and R.M. O'Brien
   1998   The determinants of deadly force: A structural analysis of police violence. *American
          Journal of Sociology* 103:837-862.
Kane, R.J.
   2000   Permanent beat assignments in association with community policing: Assessing the
          impact on police officers' field activity. *Justice Quarterly* 17:259-280.
Kania, R.E., and W.C. Mackey
   1977   Police violence as a function of community characteristics. *Criminology* 15:27-48.
Kelling, G., and W.H. Sousa, Jr.
   2001   *Do Police Matter? An Analysis of the Impact of New York City's Police Reforms*.
          (Civic Report 22). New York, NY: Manhattan Institute for Policy Research.

Kerstetter, W.A.
1985   Who disciplines the police? Who should? In W.A. Geller, ed., *Leadership in America: Crisis and Opportunity.* New York, NY: Praeger Publishers.

King, W.R.
1998   Innovativeness in American Municipal Police Organizations. Doctoral dissertation, University of Cincinnati.
2003   Bending granite revisited: The command rank structure of American police organizations. *Policing, An International Journal of Police Strategies and Management* 26(2).

Klinger, D.A.
1997   Negotiating order in patrol work: An ecological theory of police response to deviance. *Criminology* 35:277-306.

Klockars, C.B.
1988   The rhetoric of community policing. Pp. 239-258 in J.R. Greene and S.D. Mastrofski, eds., *Community Policing: Rhetoric or Reality.* New York, NY: Praeger Publishers.
1995   A theory of excessive force and its control. In W.A. Geller and H. Toch, eds., *And Justice for All: Understanding and Controlling Police Abuse of Force.* Washington, DC: Police Executive Research Forum.

Kopel, D., and P. Blackman
1997   Can soldiers be peace officers? The Waco disaster and the militarization of American law enforcement period. *Akron Law Review* 30:619-659.

Kraska, P.B.
1996   Enjoying militarism: Political/personal dilemmas in studying U.S. police paramilitary units. *Justice Quarterly* 13:405-429.

Kraska, P.B., ed.
2001   *Militarizing the American Criminal Justice System: The Changing Roles of the Armed Forces and the Police.* Boston, MA: Northeastern University Press.

Kraska, P.B., and L.J. Cubellis
1997   Militarizing Mayberry and beyond: Making sense of American paramilitary policing. *Justice Quarterly* 14:607-629.

Kraska, P.B., and V.E. Kappeler
1997   Militarizing American police: The rise and normalization of paramilitary units. *Social Problems* 44:1-18.

Langworthy, R.
1986   Police shooting and criminal homicide: The temporal relationship. *Journal of Quantitative Criminology* 2:377-388.

Langworthy, R.H., and M.J. Hindelang
1983   Effects of police agency size on the use of police employees: A reexamination of Ostrom, Parks, and Whitaker. *Police Studies* 5:11-19.

LaSante, A.B., and N.J. Scheers
1988   FBI National Academy: Attendance trends from 1976-1987. *FBI Law Enforcement Bulletin* 57:12-17.

Law Enforcement Assistance Administration
1977   *Controlling Police Corruption, Scandal, and Organizational Reform.* Washington, DC: Ford Foundation.

Leen, J., J. Craven, D. Jackson, and S. Horwitz
1998   District police lead nation in shootings: Lack of training supervision implicated as key factors. *Washington Post*, November 15. P. A01.

Liska, A., and M. Chamlin
1984   Social structure and crime control among macro-social units. *American Journal of Sociology* 90:383-395.

Liska, A.E., M.B. Chamlin, and M.D. Reed
  1985 Testing the economic production and conflict models of crime control. *Social Forces* 64:119-138.
Liska, A., J. Lawrence, and M. Benson
  1981 Perspectives on the legal order: The capacity for social control. *American Journal of Sociology* 87:413-426.
Lizotte, A., and D. Bordua
  1980 Firearms ownership for sport and protection. *American Sociological Review* 45:229-243.
Loftin, C., and D. McDowall
  1982 Police, crime, and economic theory—An assessment. *American Sociological Review* 47:393-401.
Maguire, E.R.
  1997 Structural change in large municipal police organizations during the community policing era. *Justice Quarterly* 14:701-730.
  2002a Multiwave establishment surveys of police organizations. *Justice Research and Policy* 4(Special Issue):Ch 4.
  2002b *Organizational Structure in American Police Agencies: Context, Complexity, and Control.* Albany, NY: SUNY Press.
  2002c *Police Organizational Structure and Child Sexual Abuse Case Attrition.* Paper under review.
Maguire, E., and S.D. Mastrofski
  2000 Patterns of community policing in the United States. *Police Quarterly* 3:4-45.
Maguire, E.R., Y. Shin, J. Zhao, and K. Hassell
  2003 Structural Change in Large Police Agencies during the 1990s. Prepared for a Special Issue of *Policing, An International Journal of Police Strategies and Management* 26.
Maple, J., and C. Mitchell
  1999 *The Crime Fighter: Putting the Bad Guys Out of Business.* New York, NY: Doubleday.
Martin, S.E., and D.J. Besharov
  1991 *Police and Child Abuse: New Policies for Expanded Responsibilities.* (NIJ Issues and Practices Series.) Washington, DC: National Institute of Justice.
Mastrofski, S.D.
  1981 Reforming Police: The Impact of Patrol Assignment Patterns on Officer Behavior in Urban Residential Neighborhoods. Ph.D. dissertation, University of North Carolina, Chapel Hill.
  1983 Control in the police organization. *The Journal of Criminal Law and Criminology* 74:1133-1137.
  1989 Police agency consolidations: Lessons from a case study. In J.J. Fyfe, ed., *Police Practice in the 90s: Key Management Issues.* Washington, DC: International City Management Association.
  1998 Community policing and police organization structure. Pp. 161-189 in J.P. Brodeur, ed., *How to Recognize Good Policing: Problems and Issues.* Thousand Oaks, CA: Sage.
  1999 *Policing for People.* Washington, DC: U.S. Department of Justice.
Mastrofski, S.D., and R. Ritti
  1990 *More Effective DUI Enforcement in Pennsylvania: Final Report.* (Report to the Pennsylvania Department of Transportation.) University Park, PA: Pennsylvania State University.
  1992 You can lead a horse to water . . .: A case study of a police department's response to stricter drunk-driving laws. *Justice Quarterly* 9:465-491.

1996   Police training and the effects of organization on drunk-driving enforcement. *Justice Quarterly* 13:291-320.
2000   Making sense of community policing: A theory-based analysis. *Police Practice and Research: An International Journal* 1:183-210.

Mastrofski, S.D., M.D. Reisig, and J.D. McCluskey
2002   Police disrespect toward the public: An encounter-based analysis. *Criminology* 40:519-551.

Mastrofski, S.D., R. Ritti, and D. Hoffmaster
1987   Organizational determinants of police discretion: The case of drinking-driving. *Journal of Criminal Justice* 15:387-402.

Mastrofski, S.D., J.B. Snipes, and A.E. Supina
1996   Compliance on demand: The public response to specific police requests. *Journal of Research in Crime and Delinquency* 3:269-305.

Mastrofski, S.D., J.B. Snipes, R.B. Parks, and C.D. Maxwell
2000   The helping hand of the law: Police control of citizens on request. *Criminology* 38:307-342.

McCarthy, J., C. McPhail, and J. Crist
1995   *The Emergence and Diffusion of Public Order Management Systems: Protest Cycles and Police Responses.* Presentation to the Conference on Cross-National Influences and Social Movement Research, Mont Pelerin, Switzerland, June 16-18.

McCulloch, J.
2001   *Blue Army: Paramilitary Policing in Australia.* Carlton South, Victoria, Australia: Melbourne University Press.

McDonald, P.P.
2001   *Managing Police Operations: Implementing the New York Crime Control Model, CompStat.* Belmont, CA: Wadsworth Publishing Company.

McPhail, C., D. Schweingruber, and B. McCarthy
1998   Policing of protests in the United States, 1960-1995. In D. della Porta and H. Reiter, eds., *The Control of Mass Demonstrations in Western Democracy.* Minneapolis, MN: University of Minnesota Press.

Meehan, A.J.
2000   Transformation of the oral tradition of the police subculture through the introduction of information technology. *Sociology of Crime, Law, and Deviance* 2:107-132.

Micklethwait, J., and A. Wooldridge
1996   *The Witch Doctors: Making Sense of the Management Gurus.* Portsmouth, NH: Heinemann.

Moore, M.H., D. Thacher, F.X. Hartmann, C. Coles, and P. Sheingold
2000   COPS grants, leadership, and transitions to community policing. Pp. 247-274 in J. Roth et al., *National Evaluation of the COPS Program.* Washington, DC: National Institute of Justice.

Murphy, P., and T. Plate
1977   *Commissioner: A View from the Top.* New York, NY: Simon and Schuster.

Myren, R.A.
1972   Decentralization and citizen participation in criminal justice systems. *Public Administration Review* (October):718-738.

National Advisory Commission on Criminal Justice Standards and Goals
1973   *A National Strategy to Reduce Crime.* Washington, DC: Law Enforcement Assistance Administration.

National Research Council
1999   *Chemical and Biological Terrorism: Research and Development to Improve Civilian Medical Response.* Washington, DC: National Academy Press.

Novak, K., J. Hartman, A. Holsinger, and M. Turner
  1999   The effects of aggressive policing of disorder on serious crime. *Policing: An International Journal of Police Strategies and Management* 22:171-190.
Ostrom, E.
  1973   Does local community control of police make a difference?—Some preliminary findings. *American Journal of Political Science* 17:48-76.
  1976   Size and performance in a federal system. *Publius* (Spring):33-73.
Ostrom, E., R.B. Parks, and G.P. Whitaker
  1973   Do we really want to consolidate urban police forces? A reappraisal of some old assertions. *Public Administration Review* (September/October):423-432.
Ostrom, E., G. Whitaker, and R. Parks
  1978   Policing: Is there a system? In J. May and A. Wildavsky, eds., *The Policy Cycle.* New York, NY: Russell Sage Foundation.
Parker, L., K. Johnson, and T. Locy
  2002   Post-9/11: Government stingy with information. *USA Today*, May 15.
Parks, R.B.
  1979   *Assessing the Influence of Organization on Performance—A Study of Police Services in Residential Neighborhoods.* Washington, DC: U.S. Department of Justice.
  1980   *Victim's Satisfaction with Police—The Response Factor Police Services Study Technical Report.* Washington, DC: U.S. Department of Justice.
Parks, R.B., S. Mastrofski, M.K. Gray, C. DeJong
  1999   How officers spend their time with the community. *Justice Quarterly* 16:483-518.
Pate, A.M., and L.A. Fridell
  1993   *Police Use of Force: Official Reports, Citizen Complaints, and Legal Consequences, Volumes I and II.* Washington, DC: Police Foundation.
Perez, D.W.
  1994   *Common Sense About Police Review.* Philadelphia, PA: Temple University Press.
Peterson, J., and M. Pogrebin
  1977   Team policing: A modern approach to decentralization of police decision making. *Abstracts on Police Science* 5:1-13.
Pluchinsky, D.
  2002   They heard it here, and that's the trouble. *Washington Post*, Sunday, June 16, B03.
Poggio, E.C., S.D. Kennedy, J.M. Chaiken, and K.E. Carlson
  1985   *Blueprint for the Future of the Uniform Crime Reporting Program: Final Report of the UCR Study.* Washington, DC: U.S. Department of Justice.
President's Commission
  1967   *Task Force Report: The Police.* Washington, DC: President's Commission on Law Enforcement and Administration of Justice and U.S. Government Printing Office.
Quinney, R.
  1980   *Providence: The Reconstruction of Social and Moral Order.* New York, NY: Longman, Inc.
Reaves, B.A., and A.L. Goldberg
  1998   *Census of State and Local Law Enforcement Agencies, 1996.* Washington, DC: U.S. Department of Justice.
Reaves, B.A., and T.C. Hart
  2000   *Law Enforcement Management and Administrative Statistics, 1999: Data for Individual State and Local Agencies with 100 or More Officers.* Washington, DC: U.S. Department of Justice.
Reisig, M.D., and R.B. Parks
  2000   Experience, quality of life, and neighborhood context: A hierarchical analysis of satisfaction with police. *Justice Quarterly* 17:607-630.

Reiss, A.J., Jr.
  1992   Police organization in the twentieth century. Pp. 51-98 in M. Tonry and N. Morris, eds., *Modern Policing*. Chicago, IL: University of Chicago Press.
Riedel, M., and J. Jarvis
  1999   The decline of arrest clearances for criminal homicide: Causes, correlates and third parties. *Criminal Justice Policy Review* 9:279-306.
Riley, K.J., and B. Hoffman
  1995   *Domestic Terrorism: A National Assessment of State and Local Preparedness*. Santa Monica, CA: Rand Corporation.
Robinette, H.M.
  1989   Operational streamlining. *FBI Law Enforcement Bulletin* 58:7-11.
Rossi, P., R.A. Berk, and B.K. Edison
  1974   *Roots of Urban Discontent*. New York, NY: John Wiley and Sons, Inc.
Ruchelman, L.
  1974   *Police Politics: A Comparative Study of Three Cities*. Cambridge, MA: Ballinger Publishing Company.
Saltzstein, G.H.
  1989   Black mayors and police policies. *The Journal of Politics* 51:525-544.
Sammon, B.
  2002   Web sites told to delete data. *Washington Times*, March 21.
Scheingold, S.A.
  1991   *Politics of Street Crime: Criminal Process and Cultural Obsession*. Philadelphia, PA: Temple University Press.
Schmandt, H.J.
  1972   Municipal decentralization: An overview. *Public Administration Review* (October):571-588.
Schwartz, A.I., and S.N. Clarren
  1977   *The Cincinnati Team Policing Experiment: A Summary Report*. Washington, DC: Police Foundation.
Scott, M.
  2000   *Problem-Oriented Policing: Reflections on the First 20 Years*. Washington, DC: Office of Community Oriented Policing Services.
Sherman, L.S.
  1983   Patrol strategies for police. Pp. 145-163 in J.Q. Wilson, ed., *Crime and Public Policy*. San Francisco, CA: ICS Press/Transaction Books.
Sherman, L.W.
  1978   *Controlling Police Corruption: The Effects of Reform Policies, Summary Report*. Washington, DC: U.S. Department of Justice.
  1980a Enforcement workshop: Defining arrest, practical consequences of agency differences (Part 1). *Criminal Law Bulletin* 16:376-380.
  1980b Enforcement workshop: Defining arrest, practical consequences of agency differences (Part 2). *Criminal Law Bulletin* 16:468-471.
  1992   *Policing Domestic Violence: Experiments and Dilemmas*. New York, NY: Free Press.
Sherman, L.W., and B.D. Glick
  1984   The quality of arrest statistics. *Police Foundation Reports* 2:1-8.
Sherman, L.W., and R.H. Langworthy
  1979   Measuring homicide by police officers. *Journal of Criminal Law and Criminology* 70:546-560.
Silverman, E.B.
  1999   *NYPD Battles Crime: Innovative Strategies in Policing*. Boston, MA: Northeastern University Press.

Skogan, W.G., and S.M. Hartnett
1997 *Community Policing, Chicago Style.* New York, NY: Oxford University Press.
Skolnick, J.H., and J.J. Fyfe
1993 *Above the Law: Police and the Excessive Use of Force.* New York, NY: Free Press.
Smith, D.A.
1984 The organizational context of legal control. *Criminology* 22:19-38.
1986 The neighborhood context of police behavior. Pp. 313-342 in A. Reiss and M. Tonry, eds., *Crime and Justice: A Review of Research.* Chicago, IL: University of Chicago Press.
1987 Police response to interpersonal violence: Defining the parameters of legal control. *Social Forces* 65:767-782.
Snipes, J.B.
2001 Police Response to Citizen Requests for Assistance: An Assessment of Deservedness, Workload, Social Status, and Officer Predisposition Perspectives. Ph.D. Dissertation, University of Albany, State University of New York.
Sollars, D.L., B.L. Benson, and D.W. Rasmussen
1994 Drug enforcement and the deterrence of property crime among local jurisdictions. *Public Finance Quarterly* 22:22-45.
Tierney, K.J., M.K. Lindell, and R.W. Perry
2001 *Facing the Unexpected: Disaster Preparedness and Response in the United States.* Washington, DC: Joseph Henry Press.
U.S. Advisory Commission on Intergovernmental Relations
1963 *Performance of Urban Functions: Local and Area-wide.* Washington, DC: U.S. Government Printing Office.
Van Dijk, J.J.M.
1988 *Changing Victim Policy: The United Nations Victim Declaration and Recent Developments in Europe.* Report on Expert Group Meeting. Helsinki, Finland: HEUNI.
Vold, G.B., T.J. Bernard, and J.B. Snipes
2002 *Theoretical Criminology, 5th Edition.* New York, NY: Oxford University Press.
Walker, S.
1977 *A Critical History Reform: The Emergence of Professionalism.* Lexington, MA: Heath and Company.
1998 Achieving police accountability. Research brief, The Center on Crime. *Communities and Culture* 3(September):1-16.
2001 *Police Accountability: The Role of Citizen Oversight.* Belmont, CA: Wadsworth Publishing Company.
Walker, S., and N. Graham
1998 Citizen complaints in response to police misconduct: The results of a victimization survey. *Police Quarterly* 1:65-89.
Waterman, R.W., and K.J. Meier
1998 Principal-agent models: An expansion? *Journal of Public Administration Research and Theory* 8:173-202.
Weatheritt, M.
1993 Getting more from less: Thinking about the use of police resources. In A.N. Doob, ed., *Thinking About Police Resources.* Toronto, Canada: University of Toronto, Centre of Criminology.
Weber, D.C.
1999 *Warrior Cops: The Ominous Growth of Paramilitarism in American Police Departments.* Washington, DC: Cato Institute.
Weisburd, D., S.D. Mastrofski, A.M. McNally, R. Greenspan, and J.J. Willis
2003 Reforming to preserve: Compstat and strategic problem-solving in American policing. *Criminology and Public Policy* 3:421-455.

Welsh, W.N.
   1993   Changes in arrest policies as a result of court orders against county jails. *Justice Quarterly* 10:89-120.

Wenger, D., E.L. Quarantelli, and R.R. Dynes
   1989   *Disaster Analysis: Police and Fire Departments.* Newark, DE: University of Delaware, Disaster Research Center.

Whitaker, G.P.
   1979   *Police in Society.* London, England: Methuen and Company.

Whitaker, G.P., S. Mastrofski, E. Ostrom, R.B. Parks, and S.L. Percy
   1980   *Basic Issues in Police Performance.* Washington, DC: U.S. Department of Justice.

Williams, K.R., and S. Drake
   1980   Social structure, crime and criminalization: An empirical examination of the conflict perspective. *Sociological Quarterly* 21:563-575.

Willis, J.J., S.D. Mastrofski, and D. Weisburd
   2003   *Compstat and Organizational Change: Intensive Site Visit Report.* (Report to the National Institute of Justice.) Washington, DC: Police Foundation.

Wilson, J.Q.
   1968   *Varieties of Police Behavior: The Management of Law and Order in Eight Communities.* Cambridge, MA: Harvard University Press.

Wilson, J.Q., and G. Kelling
   1982   Broken windows: The police and neighborhood safety. *Atlantic Monthly* 249:29-38.

Worrall, J.L.
   2001   *Civil Lawsuits, Citizen Complaints, and Policing Innovations.* New York, NY: LFB Scholarly Publishing, LLC

Zhao, J.
   1996   *Why Police Organizations Change: A Study of Community-Oriented Policing.* Washington, DC: Police Executive Research Forum.

CHAPTER 6

Abrahamse, A.F., P.A. Ebener, and P.W. Greenwood
   1991   An experimental evaluation of the Phoenix repeat offender program. *Justice Quarterly* 8:141-168.

Angrist, J.D., and A.B. Krueger
   2001   Instrumental variables and the search for identification: From supply and demand to natural experiments. *Journal of Economic Perspectives* 15(Fall):69-86.

Annan, S., and W. Skogan
   1993   *Drug Enforcement in Public Housing: Signs of Success in Denver.* Washington, DC: Police Foundation.

Ayers, I., and S.D. Levitt
   1998   Measuring the positive externalities from unobservable victim precaution: An empirical analysis of Lojack. *Quarterly Journal of Economics* 43:113.

Barber, R.
   1969   Prostitution and the increasing number of convictions for rape in Queensland. *Australian and New Zealand Journal of Criminology* 2:169-174.

Barr, R., and K. Pease
   1990   Crime placement, displacement and deflection. Pp. 277-318 in M. Tonry and N. Morris, eds., *Crime and Justice: A Review of Research.* Chicago, IL: University of Chicago Press.

Bayley, D.H., and R. Worden
  1996   *Federal Funding of Police Overtime: A Utilization Study.* Washington, DC: U.S. Department of Justice.
Becker, G.S., and W.M. Landes
  1974   *Essays in the Economics of Crime and Punishment.* New York, NY: Columbia University Press.
Berk, R.A., and L.W. Sherman
  1984a   *Specific Deterrent Effects of Arrest for Domestic Assault in Minneapolis.* Washington, DC: National Institute of Justice.
  1984b   Specific deterrent effects of arrest for domestic assault. *American Sociological Review* 49:261-272.
Berk, R.A., A. Campbell, R. Klap, and B. Western
  1992   Bayesian analysis of the Colorado Springs spouse abuse experiment. *Journal of Criminal Law and Criminology* 83:170-200.
Blumstein, A.
  1995   Youth violence, guns and the illicit gun industry. *Journal of Criminal Law and Criminology* 86:10-36.
  2000   Disaggregating the violence trends. In A. Blumstein and J. Wallman, eds., *The Crime Drop in America.* Boston, MA: Cambridge University Press.
Boruch, R., B. Snyder, and D. DeMoya
  2000   Importance of randomized field trials. *Crime and Delinquency* 46:156-180.
Bower, W., and J. Hirsch
  1987   The impact of foot patrol staffing on crime and disorder in Boston: An unmet promise. *American Journal of Policing* 6:17-44.
Bowling, B.
  1999   The rise and fall of New York murder. *British Journal of Criminology* 39:531-554.
Boydstun, J.
  1975   *The San Diego Field Interrogation Experiment.* Washington, DC: Police Foundation
Braga, A.A., D.M. Kennedy, E.J. Waring, and A.M. Piehl
  2001   Problem-oriented policing, deterrence, and youth violence: An evaluation of Boston's operation ceasefire. *Journal of Research in Crime and Delinquency* 38:195-225.
Braga, A.A., D.L. Weisburd, E.J. Waring, L.G. Mazerolle, W. Spelman, and F. Gajewski
  1999   Problem-oriented policing in violent crime places: A randomized controlled experiment. *Criminology* 37:541-580.
Brandl, S.G., and J. Frank
  1994   The relationship between evidence, detective effort, and the disposition of burglary and robbery investigations. *American Journal of Police* 13:149-168.
Bratton, W.
  1998a   Crime is down in New York City: Blame the police. Pp. 29-43 in N. Dennis, ed., *Zero Tolerance: Policing a Free Society.* London, England: Institute of Economic Affairs Health and Welfare Unit.
  1998b   *Turnaround: How America's Top Cop Reversed the Crime Epidemic.* New York, NY: Random House.
Brown, L., and M. Wycoff
  1987   Policing Houston: Reducing fear and improving service. *Crime and Delinquency* 33:71-89.
Buerger, M.E.
  1994   The problems of problem-solving: Resistance, interdependencies, and conflicting interests. *American Journal of Police* 13:1-36.

Buerger, M.E., E.G. Cohn, and A.J. Petrosino
  1995 Defining the "hot spots of crime": Operationalizing theoretical concepts for field research. Pp. 237-257 in J. Eck and D. Weisburg, eds., *Crime and Place: Crime Prevention Studies 4*. Monsey, NY: Criminal Justice Press.
Bureau of Justice Statistics
  1999 *Law Enforcement Management and Administrative Statistics, 1997: Data for Individual State and Local Agencies with 100 or More Officers*. Washington, DC: U.S. Department of Justice.
Campbell, D.T., and R.F. Boruch
  1975 Making the case for randomized assignment to treatments by considering the alternatives: Six ways in which quasi-experimental evaluations in compensatory education tend to underestimate effects. Pp. 195-296 in C.A. Bennett and A.A. Lumsdaine, eds., *Evaluation and Experiment: Some Critical Issues in Assessing Social Programs*. New York, NY: Academic Press.
Capowich, G.E., and J.A. Roehl
  1994 Problem-oriented policing: Actions and effectiveness in San Diego. Pp. 127-146 in D.P. Rosenbaum, ed., *Community Policing: Testing the Promises*. Thousand Oaks, CA: Sage.
Chamlin, M.B., and R.H. Langworthy
  1996 Police, crime, and economic theory: A replication and extension. *American Journal of Criminal Justice* 20:165-182.
Clarke, R.V.
  1992a Situational crime prevention: Theory and practice. *British Journal of Criminology* 20:136-147.
  1992b *Situational Crime Prevention: Successful Case Studies*. Albany, NY: Harrow and Heston.
  1997 *Situational Crime Prevention: Successful Case Studies* (92nd edition). New York, NY: Harrow and Heston.
Clarke, R.V., and D.B. Cornish
  1972 *Controlled Trial in Institutional Research—Paradigm or Pitfall for Penal Evaluators*. London, England: Her Majesty's Stationary Office.
Clarke, R.V., and H. Goldstein
  2002 Reducing theft at construction sites: Lessons from a problem-oriented project. Pp. 89-130 in N. Tilley, ed., *Analysis for Crime Prevention, Crime Prevention Studies 13*. Monsey, NY: Criminal Justice Press.
Clarke, R.V., and D. Weisburd
  1994 Diffusion of crime control benefits: Observations on the reverse of displacement. *Crime Prevention Studies* 2:165-184.
Cohen, L.E., and M. Felson
  1979 Social change and crime rate trends: A routine activity approach. *American Sociological Review* 44:588-608.
Cook, T.D., and D.T. Campbell
  1979 *Quasi-Experimentation: Design and Analysis Issues for Field Settings*. Chicago, IL: Rand McNally.
Cordner, G.W.
  1986 Fear of crime and the police: An evaluation of a fear-reduction strategy. *Journal of Police Science and Administration* 14:223-233.
  1998 Problem-oriented policing vs. zero-tolerance. Pp. 303-314 in T. O'Connor, S. and A.C. Grant, eds., *Problem-Oriented Policing*. Washington, DC: Police Executive Research Forum.

Corman, H., T. Joyce, and N. Loftvich
   1987   Crime, deterrence and the business cycle in New York City: A VAR approach. *The Review of Economics and Statistics* 69:695-700.
Cornish, D., and R.V. Clarke
   1986   Situational prevention, displacement of crime and rational choice theory. Pp. 1-16 in K. Heal and G. Laycock, eds., *Situational Crime Prevention: From Theory into Practice*. London, England: Her Majesty's Stationery Office.
Criminal Conspiracies Division
   1979   *What Happened: An Examination of Recently Terminated Anti-Fencing Operations: A Special Report to the Administrator*. Washington, DC: Law Enforcement Assistance Administration, U.S. Department of Justice.
Dahmann, J.S.
   1975   *Examination of Police Patrol Effectiveness*. McLean, VA: Mitre Corporation.
Dennis, N., and R. Mallon
   1998   Confident policing in Hartlepool. Pp. 62-87 in N. Dennis, ed., *Zero Tolerance: Policing a Free Society*. London, England: Institute of Economic Affairs Health and Welfare Unit.
Dilulio, J.J.
   1995   Arresting ideas: Tougher law enforcement is driving down urban crime. *Policy Review* 7:12-16.
Dunford, F.W., D. Huizanga, and D.S. Elliot
   1990   Role of arrest in domestic assault: The Omaha police experiment. *Criminology* 28:183-206.
Eck, J.E.
   1983   *Solving Crimes: The Investigation of Burglary and Robbery*. Washington, DC: Police Executive Research Forum.
   1993   The threat of crime displacement. *Criminal Justice Abstracts* 25:527-546.
   1997   Preventing crime at places. Pp. 7-1, 7-62 in L.W. Sherman, D. Gottfredson, D. MacKenzie, J. Eck, P. Reuter, and S. Bushway, eds., *Preventing Crime: What Works, What Doesn't, What's Promising—A Report to the Attorney General of the United States*. Washington, DC: United States Department of Justice, Office of Justice Programs.
Eck, J.E., and R.V. Clarke
   2003   Classifying common police problems: A routine activity approach. Pp. 7-40 in M.J. Smith and D.B. Cornish, eds., *Theory for Practice in Situational Crime Prevention. Crime Prevention Studies 16*. Monsey, NY: Criminal Justice Press.
Eck, J.E., and E. Maguire
   2000   Have changes in policing reduced violent crime? An assessment of the evidence. Pp. 207-265 in A. Blumstein and J. Wallman, eds., *The Crime Drop in America*. New York, NY: Cambridge University Press.
Eck, J.E., and D. Rosenbaum
   1994   The new police order: Effectiveness, equity and efficiency in community policing. Pp. 3-26 in D. Rosenbaum, ed., *Community Policing: Testing the Promises*. Thousand Oaks, CA: Sage.
Eck, J.E., and W. Spelman
   1987   *Problem Solving: Problem Oriented Policing in Newport News*. Washington, DC: Police Executive Research Forum.
Eck, J.E., and J. Wartell
   1996   *Reducing Crime and Drug Dealing by Improving Place Management: A Randomized Experiment*. (Report to the San Diego Police Department.) Washington, DC: Crime Control Institute.

Eck, J.E., and D. Weisburd
  1995 Crime places in crime theory. Pp. 1-33 in J.E. Eck and D. Weisburd, eds., *Crime and Place: Crime Prevention Studies 4*. Monsey, NY: Criminal Justice Press.
Fagan, J., F.E. Zimring, and J. Kim
  2003 Declining homicide in New York: A tale of two trends. *Journal of Criminal Law and Criminology* 88:1277-1347.
Farrington, D.
  1983 Randomized experiments on crime and justice. Pp. 257-308 in M. Tonry and N. Morris, ed., *Crime and Justice—An Annual Review of Research, Volume 4*. Chicago, IL: University of Chicago Press.
Farrington, D., L. Ohlin, and J.Q. Wilson
  1986 *Understanding and Controlling Crime Towards a New Research Strategy*. New York, NY: Springer-Verlag.
Feder, L., and R. Boruch
  2000 Need for experiments in criminal justice settings. *Crime and Delinquency* 46:291-294.
Feder, L., A. Jolin, and W. Feyerherm
  2000 Lessons from two randomized experiments in criminal justice settings. *Crime and Delinquency* 46:380-400.
Garner, J.H., and C.D. Maxwell
  2000 What are the lessons of the police arrest studies? *Journal of Aggression, Maltreatment and Trauma* 4:83-114.
Gay, W.G., T.H. Schell, and S. Schack
  1977 *Prescriptive Package: Improving Patrol Productivity, Volume I Routine Patrol*. Washington, DC: Office of Technology Transfer, Law Enforcement Assistance Administration.
Glaeser, E.L., B. Sacerdote, and J.A. Scheinkman
  1996 Crime and social interactions. *The Quarterly Journal of Economics* 111:507-548.
Goldstein, H.
  1979 Improving policing: A problem-oriented approach. *Crime and Delinquency* 24:236-258.
  1990 *Problem-Oriented Policing*. New York, NY: McGraw-Hill.
Green-Mazzerole, L., and J. Roehl, eds.
  1998 *Civil Remedies and Crime Prevention: Crime Prevention Studies, Volume 9*. Monsey, NY: Criminal Justice Press.
Greene, J.
  1999 Zero tolerance: A case study of police policies and practices in New York City. *Crime and Delinquency* 45:171-187.
Greene, J.R., and S.D. Mastrofski
  1988 *Community Policing*. Westport, CT: Praeger Publishers.
Greenwood, P., J. Petersilia, and J. Chaiken
  1977 *The Criminal Investigation Process*. Lexington, MA: D.C. Heath.
Greenwood, P.W., J.M. Chaiken, M. Petersilia, and L. Prusoff
  1975 *Criminal Investigation Process, Volume III: Observations and Analysis*. Santa Monica, CA: Rand Corporation.
Harcourt, B.E.
  2001 *Illusion of Order: The False Promise of Broken Windows Policing*. Cambridge, MA: Harvard University Press.
Harries, K.
  1999 *Mapping Crime: Principle and Practice*. Washington, DC: National Institute of Justice.

Harris, D.A.
  1997   Driving while black and all other traffic offenses: The Supreme Court and pretextual
          traffic stops. *Journal of Criminal Law and Criminology* 87:544.
  1999   Stories, the statistics, and the law: Why "driving while black" matters. *Minnesota
          Law Review* 84:265-325.
  2002   Racial profiling revisited: "Just common sense" in the fight against terror. *Criminal
          Justice* 17:36-59.
Heckman, J.J, and J.A. Smith
  1995   Assessing the case for social experiments. *Journal of Economic Perspectives* 9:85-
          110.
Hesseling, R.B.P.
  1994   Displacement: A review of the empirical literature. Pp. 197-230 in R.V. Clarke, ed.,
          Crime Prevention Studies 3. Monsey, NY: Criminal Justice Press.
Hirschel, J.D., and I.W. Hutchison, III
  1992   Female spouse abuse and the police response: The Charlotte, North Carolina ex-
          periment. *Journal of Criminal Law and Criminology* 83:73-119.
Hope, T.
  1994   Problem-oriented policing and drug market locations: Three case studies. Pp. 5-31
          in R.V. Clarke, ed., *Crime Prevention Studies 2*. Monsey, NY: Criminal Justice
          Press.
Horvath, F., R.T. Meesig, and Y.H. Lee
  2001   *A National Survey of Police Policies and Practices Regarding the Criminal Investi-
          gation Process: Twenty-five Years after RAND*. East Lansing, MI: Michigan State
          University Press.
Joanes, A.
  2001   Does the New York City Police Department deserve credit for the decline in New
          York City's homicide rates? A cross-city comparison of policing strategies and ho-
          micide rates. *Columbia Journal of Law and Social Problems* 33:265-311.
Kansas City Police Department
  1977   *Response Time Analysis*. Kansas City, MO: Kansas City Police Department.
Karmen, A.
  2000   *New York Murder Mystery: The True Story Behind the Crime Crash of the 1990s*.
          New York, NY: New York University Press.
Kelling, G., and C. Coles
  1996   *Fixing Broken Windows: Restoring Order and Reducing Crime in Our Communi-
          ties*. New York, NY: Free Press.
Kelling, G., and W.H. Sousa, Jr.
  2001   *Do Police Matter? An Analysis of the Impact of New York City's Police Reforms
          Civic Report 22*. New York, NY: Manhattan Institute for Policy Research.
Kelling, G., T. Pate, D. Dieckman, and C.E. Brown
  1974   *The Kansas City Preventive Patrol Experiment: Technical Report*. Washington, DC:
          Police Foundation.
Kennedy, D.M.
  1997   Pulling levers: Chronic offenders, high-crime settings, and a theory of prevention.
          Valparaiso University Law Review 31:449-484.
Kennedy, D.M., A.A. Braga, and A.M. Piehl
  1997   (Un)Known universe: Mapping gangs and gang violence in Boston. Pp. 219-262 in
          D. Weisburd and T. McEwen, eds., *From Crime Mapping and Crime Preventions*.
          Monsey, NY: Criminal Justice Press.
Kennedy, D.M., A.A. Braga, A.M. Piehl, and E.J. Waring
  2001   *Reducing Gun Violence: The Boston Gun Project's Operation Ceasefire*. Washing-
          ton, DC: U.S. Department of Justice.

Kleiman, M.
  1988   Crackdowns: The effects of intensive enforcement on retail heroin dealing. Pp. 3-34
         in M. Chaiken, ed., *Street-Level Drug Enforcement: Examining the Issues.* Wash-
         ington, DC: National Institute of Justice.
Kunz, R., and A. Oxman
  1998   The unpredictability paradox: Review of empirical comparisons of randomized and
         non-randomized clinical trials. *British Medical Journal* 317:1185-1190.
Larson, R., and M. Cohn
  1985   *Synthesizing and Extending the Results of Police Patrols.* Washington, DC: U.S.
         Government Printing Office.
Levitt, S.D.
  1997   Using election cycles in police hiring to estimate the effect of police on crime. *Public
         Policy* 23:523-545.
Lipsey, M.W., and D.B. Wilson
  1993   The efficacy of psychological, educational, and behavioral treatment: Confirmation
         from meta-analysis. *American Psychologist* 48:1181-1209.
Maguire, E.R., J.B. Kuhns, C.D. Uchida, and S.M. Cox
  1997   Patterns of community policing in nonurban America. *Journal of Research in Crime
         and Delinquency* 34:368-394.
Mamalian, C., and N. LaVigne
  1999   *The Use of Computerized Crime Mapping by Law Enforcement: Survey Results.*
         Washington, DC: National Institute of Justice.
Manning, P.K.
  2001   Theorizing policing: The drama and myth of crime control in the NYPD. *Theoreti-
         cal Criminology* 5:315-344.
Manski, C.
  2003   Credible research practices to inform drug law enforcement. *Criminology and Pub-
         lic Policy* 2:543-556.
Marciniak, E.M.
  1994   Community Policing of Domestic Violence: Neighborhood Difference in the Effect
         of Arrest. Unpublished doctoral dissertation, University of Maryland, College Park.
Martin, S., and L. Sherman
  1986   Selective apprehension: A police strategy for repeat offenders. *Criminology* 24:55-
         72.
Marvell, T.B., and C.E. Moody
  1996   Specification problems, police levels, and crime rates. *Criminology* 34:609-646.
Mastrofski, S.D., J.B. Snipes, and A.E. Supina
  1996   Compliance on demand: The public response to specific police requests. *Journal of
         Research in Crime and Delinquency* 3:269-305.
Maxwell, C.D., J.D. Garner, and J.A. Fagan
  2001   *The Effects of Arrest on Intimate Partner Violence: New Evidence from the Spouse
         Assault Replication Program.* (NCJ Research in Brief 188199.) Washington, DC:
         U.S. Department of Justice.
Mazerolle, L.G., J. Ready, W. Terrill, and E. Waring
  2000   Problem-oriented policing in public housing: The Jersey City evaluation. *Justice
         Quarterly* 17:29-158.
McCluskey, J.D., S.D. Mastrofski, and R.B. Parks
  1999   To acquiesce or rebel: Predicting citizen compliance with police requests. *Police
         Quarterly* 2:389-416.
McDonald, P.P.
  2001   *Managing Police Operations: Implementing the New York Crime Control Model,
         CompStat.* Belmont, CA: Wadsworth Publishing Company.

Miller, W.R.
  1977   *Cops and Bobbies: Police Authority in New York and London, 1830-1870.* Chicago, IL: University of Chicago Press.

Minneapolis Medical Research Foundation, Inc.
  1976   Critiques and commentaries on evaluation research activities—Russell Sage reports. *Evaluation* 3:115-138.

Moore, M.H., W. Spelman, and R. Young
  1992   Innovations in Policing: A Test of Three Different Methodologies for Identifying Important Innovations in a Substantive Field. Unpublished paper, Cambridge, MA: Harvard University, Kennedy School of Government.

National Research Council
  1986   *Criminal Careers and "Career Criminals," Volume I.* Report of the Panel on Research on Criminal Careers, A. Blumstein, J. Cohen, J.A. Roth, and C.A. Visher, eds. Washington, DC: National Academy Press.

Niskanen, W.A.
  1994   *Crime, Police, and Root Causes.* Washington, DC: Cato Institute.

Odland, J.
  1988   *Spatial Autocorrelation.* New York, NY: Russell Sage Foundation.

Pate, A., and S. Annan
  1989   *The Baltimore Community Policing Experiment: Technical Report.* Washington, DC: Police Foundation.

Pate, A., E.E. Hamilton, and S. Annan
  1991   *Metro-Dade Spouse Abuse Replication Project: Draft Final Report.* Washington, DC: National Institute of Justice

Pate, A., M. Wycoff, W. Skogan, and L. Sherman
  1989   *Reducing Fear of Crime in Houston and Newark: A Summary Report.* Washington, DC: Police Foundation.

Pate, A.M., and W. Skogan
  1985   *Coordinated Community Policing: The Newark Experience. Technical Report.* Washington, DC: Police Foundation.

Pawson, R., and N. Tilley
  1997   *Realistic Evaluation.* Thousand Oaks, CA: Sage.

Pedhazur, E.J.
  1982   *Multiple Regression in Behavioral Research, Second Edition.* New York, NY: Holt, Rinehart, and Winston.

Pennell, S.
  1979   Fencing activity and police strategy. *Police Chief* 46:71-75.

Pierce, G., S. Spaar, and L. Briggs
  1988   The Character of Police Work: Strategic and Tactical Implications. Unpublished paper, Northeastern University, Center for Applied Social Research.

Pocock, S.J.
  1983   *Clinical Trials: A Practical Approach.* Chichester, England: John Wiley and Sons, Inc.

Police Foundation
  1981   *The Newark Foot Patrol Experiment.* Washington, DC: Police Foundation.

Poyner, B.
  1981   Crime prevention and the environment—Street attacks in city centres. *Police Research Bulletin* 37:10-18.

Press, S.J.
  1971   *Some Effects of an Increase in Police Manpower in the 20th Precinct of New York City* (R-704-NYC). New York, NY: Rand Corporation.

Reiss, A.J., Jr.
  1985   *Policing a City's Central District: The Oakland Story.* Washington, DC: National
         Institute of Justice.
Rosenbaum, D.
  1989   Community crime prevention: A review and synthesis of the literature. *Justice Quar-
         terly* 5:323-395.
Sampson, R.J., and J. Cohen
  1988   Deterrent effects of the police on crime: A replication and theoretical extension.
         Law & Society Review 22:163-189.
Schmidt, J.D., and L.W. Sherman
  1993   Does arrest deter domestic violence? *American Behavioral Scientist* 36:601-609.
Schneider, J.
  1980   *Detroit and the Problem of Order, 1830-1888.* Lincoln, NE: University of Nebraska
         Press.
Shadish, W.R., D. Heinsman, and K. Ragsdale
  1993   *Randomized versus Quasi-Experiments: Do They Give the Same Results?* Dallas,
         TX: American Evaluation Association.
Shadish, W.R., Jr., T.D.Cook, and D.T. Campbell
  2002   *Experimental and Quasi-Experimental Designs for Generalized Casual Inference.*
         Boston, MA: Houghton Mifflin.
Sherman, L.W.
  1990   Police crackdowns: Initial and residual deterrence. Pp. 1-48 in M. Tonry and N.
         Morris, eds., *Crime and Justice: A Review of Research, Vol. 12.* Chicago, IL: Uni-
         versity of Chicago Press.
  1997   Policing for prevention. Pp. 8-1, 8-58 in L.W. Sherman, D. Gottfredson, D.
         MacKenzie, J. Eck, P. Reuter, and S. Bushway, eds., *Preventing Crime: What Works,
         What Doesn't, What's Promising, A Report to the Attorney General of the United
         States.* Washington, DC: U.S. Department of Justice, Office of Justice Programs.
Sherman, L.W., and J. Eck
  2002   Policing for crime prevention. Pp. 295-329 in L.W. Sherman, D.L. MacKenzie, and
         D.P. Farrington, eds., *Evidence-Based Crime Prevention.* New York, NY: Routledge.
Sherman, L.W., and D. Rogan
  1995a Deterrent effects of police raids on crack houses: A randomized, controlled, experi-
         ment. *Justice Quarterly* 12:755-781.
  1995b Effects of gun seizures on gun violence: "Hot spots" patrol in Kansas City. *Justice
         Quarterly* 12:673-693.
Sherman, L.W., and D.A. Smith
  1992   Crime, punishment, and stake in conformity: Legal and informal control of domes-
         tic violence. *American Sociological Review* 57:680-690.
Sherman, L.W., and D. Weisburd
  1995   General deterrent effects of police patrol in crime "hot spots:" A randomized, con-
         trolled trial. *Justice Quarterly* 12:625-648.
Sherman, L.W., P.R. Gartin, and M.E. Buerger
  1989   Hot spots of predatory crime: Routine activities and the criminology of place. *Crimi-
         nology* 27:27-55.
Sherman, L.W., D. Gottfredson, D. MacKenzie, J. Eck, P. Reuter, and S. Bushway
  1997   *Preventing Crime: What Works, What Doesn't, and What's Promising, A Report to
         the Attorney General of the United States.* Washington, DC: U.S. Department of
         Justice, Office of Justice Programs.

Sherman, L.W., J.D. Schmidt, D.P. Rogan, P.R. Gartin, E.G. Cohn, D.J. Collins, and A.R. Bacich
  1991   From initial deterrrence to long-term escalation: Short-custody arrest for poverty ghetto domestic violence. *Criminology* 29:821-850.
Silverman, E.
  1999   *NYPD Battles Crime: Innovative Strategies in Policing.* Boston, MA: Northeastern University Press.
Skogan, W.G.
  1990   *Disorder and Decline: Crime and the Spiral of Decay in American Cities.* New York, NY: Free Press.
  1992   *Impact of Policing on Social Disorder: Summary of Findings.* Washington, DC: U.S. Department of Justice, Office of Justice Programs.
Skogan, W.G., and G.E. Antunes
  1979   Information, apprehension, and deterrence: Exploring the limits of police productivity. *Journal of Criminal Justice* 7:217-241.
Skogan, W.G., S. Hartnett, J. DuBois, J. Lovig, L. Higgins, S.F. Bennett, P.J. Lavrakas, A. Lurigio, R. Block, and D. Rosenbaum
  1995   *Community Policing Chicago Style: Year Two.* Chicago, IL: Illinois Criminal Justice Information Authority.
Skolnick, S.H., and D.H. Bayley
  1986   *The New Blue Line: Police Innovation in Six American Cities.* New York, NY: Free Press.
Spelman, W.
  1990   *Repeat Offenders.* Washington, DC: Police Executive Research Forum.
  1995   Criminal careers of public places. Pp. 115-144 in J.E. Eck and D. Weisburd, eds., *Crime and Place: Crime Prevention Studies 4.* Monsey, NY: Criminal Justice Press.
Spelman, W., and D.K. Brown
  1981   *Calling the Police: A Replication of the Citizen Reporting Component of the Kansas City Response Time Analysis.* Washington, DC: Police Executive Research Forum.
Sviridoff, M., S. Sadd, R. Curtis, R. Grinc, and M.E. Smith.
  1992   *The Neighborhood Effects of Street-Level Drug Enforcement: Tactical Narcotics Teams in New York.* New York, NY: Vera Institute of Justice.
Swartz, C.
  2000   The spatial analysis of crime: What social scientists have learned. Pp. 33-46 in V. Goldsmith, P.G. McGuire, J.H. Mollenkopf, and T.A. Ross, eds., *Analyzing Crime Patterns: Frontiers of Practice.* Thousand Oaks, CA: Sage.
Taylor, R.B.
  2001   *Breaking Away from Broken Windows: Baltimore Neighborhoods and the Nationwide Fight Against Crime, Grime, Fear, and Decline.* Washington, DC: U.S. Department of Justice.
Trojanowicz, R.
  1986   Evaluating a neighborhood foot patrol program: The Flint, Michigan project. Pp. 157-178 in D. Rosenbaum, ed., *Community Crime Prevention: Does It Work?* Thousand Oaks, CA: Sage.
Uchida, C., B. Forst, and S.O. Annan
  1992   *Modern Policing and the Control of Illegal Drugs: Testing New Strategies in Two American Cities.* Research Report. Washington, DC: National Institute of Justice.
Van Tulder, F.
  1992   Crime, detection rate, and the police: A macro approach. *Journal of Quantitative Criminology* 8:113-131.

Visher, C., and D. Weisburd
  1998 Identifying what works: Recent trends in crime prevention strategies. *Crime, Law and Social Change* 28:223-242.
Weiner, K., K. Chelst, and W. Hart
  1984 Stinging the Detroit criminal: A total system perspective. *Journal of Criminal Justice* 12:289-302.
Weiner, K.A., C.K. Stephens., and D.L. Besachuk
  1983 Making inroads into property crime: An analysis of the Detroit anti-fencing program. *Journal of Police Science and Administration* 11:311-327.
Weisburd, D.
  1996 *Reorienting Crime Prevention Research and Policy: From the Causes of Criminality to the Context of Crime.* Washington, DC: U.S. Government Printing Office.
  2002 From criminals to criminal contexts: Reorienting criminal justice research and policy. *Advances in Criminological Theory* 10:197-216.
  2003 Ethical practice and evaluation of interventions in crime and justice: The moral imperative for randomized trials. *Evaluation Review* 27:336-354.
Weisburd, D., and A. Braga
  2003 Hot spots policing. Pp. 337-355 in H. Kurry and J. Obergerfeld Fuchs, eds., *Crime Prevention: New Approaches.* Mainz, Germany: Weisser Ring.
Weisburd, D., and L. Green
  1994 Defining the drug market. Pp. 61-76 in D.L. MacKenzie and C.D. Uchida, eds., *Drugs and the Criminal Justice System: Evaluating Public Policy Initiatives.* Thousand Oaks, CA: Sage.
  1995a Policing drug hot spots: The Jersey City drug market analysis experiment. *Justice Quarterly* 12:711-735.
  1995b Assessing immediate spatial displacement: Insights from the Minneapolis hot spot experiment. Pp. 349-361 in J. Eck and D. Weisburd, eds., *Crime and Place: Crime Prevention Studies 4.* Monsey, NY: Crininal Justice Press.
Weisburd, D., and J.E. McElroy
  1988 Enacting the CPO (Community Patrol Officer) role: Findings from the New York City pilot program in community policing. Pp. 89-102 in J.R. Greene and S.D. Mastrofski, eds., *Community Policing: Rhetoric or Reality.* New York, NY: Praeger Publishers.
Weisburd, D., and T. McKewen, eds.
  1998 *Crime Mapping and Crime Prevention.* Monsey, NY: Criminal Justice Press.
Weisburd, D., and F. Taxman.
  2000 Developing a multi-center randomized trial in trial in criminology: The case of HIDTA. *Journal of Quantitative Criminology* 16:315-339.
Weisburd, D., R. Greenspan, and S. Mastrofski
  2001 *Compstat and Organizational Change: Preliminary Findings from a National Study.* Washington, DC: U.S. Department of Justice.
Weisburd, D., C.M. Lum, and A. Petrosino
  2001 Does research design affect study outcomes in criminal justice? Pp. 50-70 in D.P. Farrington and B.C. Welsh, eds., *Annals of the American Academy of Political and Social Science.* Thousand Oaks, CA: Sage.
Weisburd, D., L. Maher, and L. Sherman
  1992 Contrasting crime general and crime specific theory: The case of hot spots of crime. *Advances in Criminological Theory* 4:45-70.
Weisburd, D., S. Mastrofski, A.M. McNally, R. Greenspan, and J. Willis
  2003 Reforming to preserve: Compstat and strategic problem solving in American policing. *Criminology and Public Policy* 3:425-456.

Weiss, A., and S. Freels
  1996   Effects of aggressive policing: The Dayton traffic enforcement experiment. *American Journal of Police* 15:45-64.
Whitaker, G., C. Phillips, P. Haas, and R. Worden
  1985   Aggressive policing and the deterrence of crime. *Law and Policy* 7:395-416.
Wilson, D.B., and M.W. Lipsey
  2001   The role of method in treatment effectiveness research: Evidence from meta-analysis. *Psychological Methods* 6:413-429.
Wilson, J.Q., and B. Boland
  1978   Effect of the police on crime. *Law & Society Review* 12:367-390.
Wilson, J.Q., and G. Kelling
  1982   Broken windows: The police and neighborhood safety. *Atlantic Monthly* 249:29-38.
Wilson, O.W.
  1967   *Crime Prevention—Whose Responsibility?* Washington, DC: Thompson Books.
Wycoff, M.A., and W.G. Skogan
  1986   Storefront police offices: The Houston field test. Pp. 179-199 in D.P. Rosenbaum ed., *Community Crime Prevention: Does It Work?* Thousand Oaks, CA: Sage.
  1993   *Community Policing in Madison: Quality from the Inside, Out.* (Technical Report.) Washington, DC: Police Foundation.
Yamada, T.
  1985   *The Crime Rate and the Condition of the Labor Market.* Cambridge, MA: National Bureau of Economic Research.

CHAPTER 7

Adams, K.
  1996   Measuring the prevalence of police abuse of force. Pp. 52-93 in W. Geller and H. Toch, eds., *Police Violence: Understanding and Controlling Police Abuse of Force.* New Haven, CT: Yale University Press.
Alpert, G.
  1997   *Police Pursuit: Policies and Training* Washington, DC: National Institute of Justice.
Alpert, G.P., and R.J. Dunham
  1990   *Police Pursuit Driving: Controlling Responses to Emergency Situations.* Westport, CT: Greenwood Press.
American Bar Association
  1973   *Urban Police Function, Standards Relating to Supplement—Approved Draft.* Washington, DC: American Bar Association.
Amsterdam, A.G.
  1974   Perspectives on the Fourth Amendment. *Minnesota Law Review* 58:349-403.
Barker, T.
  2002   Ethical police behavior. Pp. 1-25 in K.M. Lersch, ed., *Policing and Misconduct.* Upper Saddle River, NJ: Prentice-Hall Inc., Criminal Justice and Police Training.
Barker, T., and D.L. Carter
  1986   *Police Deviance.* Cincinnati, OH: Pilgrimage.
Baum, L.
  1979   Impact of court decisions on police practices. In F.A. Meyer and R. Baker, eds., *Determinants of Law Enforcement Policies.* Lanham, MD: Lexington Books.
Black, D., and A.J. Reiss
  1967a   Interrogation and the criminal process. *Annals of the American Academy of Political and Social Science* 374:47-57.

1967b Patterns of behavior in citizen and police transactions. Pp. 1-139 in *Studies of Crime and Law Enforcement in Major Metropolitan Areas, Field Surveys III, Volume 2, Presidents Commission on Law Enforcement and the Administration of Justice.* Washington, DC: U.S. Government Printing Office.

Bland, N., J. Miller, and P. Quinton
2000 *Upping the PACE? An Evaluation of the Recommendations of the Stephen Lawrence Inquiry on Stops and Searches.* London, England: Great Britian Home Office.

Blumberg, M.
1982 Use of Firearms by Police Officers—The Impact of Individuals, Communities and Race. Dissertation, State University of New York at Albany.

Bobb, M.J., M.H. Epstein, and N.H. Miller
1996 *Five Years Later, A Report to the LA Police Commission on the Police Department's Implementation of Independent Commission Recommendations.* Los Angeles, CA: Special Counsel, Los Angeles Police Commission.

Brereton, D.
2000 Evaluating the performance of external oversight bodies. Pp. 105-124 in A. Goldsmith and C. Lewis, eds., *Civilian Oversight of Policing: Governance, Democracy and Human Rights.* New York, NY: Hart Publishing Company.

Burbeck, E., and A. Furnham
1985 Police officer selection. A critical review of the literature. *Journal of Policing Science Administration* 13:58-69.

Bureau of Justice Statistics
1999 *Law Enforcement Management and Administrative Statistics, 1997: Data for Individual State and Local Agencies with 100 or More Officers.* Washington, DC: U.S. Department of Justice.
2001 *Contact Between the Police and the Public: Findings from the National Survey.* (P.A. Langan, L.A. Greenfeld, S.K. Smith, M.R. Durose, and D.J. Levin.) Washington, DC: U.S. Department of Justice.

Canon, B.C.
1974 Is the exclusionary rule in failing health? Some new data and a plea against a precipitous conclusion. *Kentucky Law Journal* 62:681.
1991 Courts and policy: Compliance, implementation, and impact. In J.B. Gates and C.A. Johnson, eds., *American Courts: A Critical Assessment.* Washington, DC: Congressional Quarterly Press.

Cassel, P.G., and B.S. Hayman
1998 Police interrogation in the 1990s: An empirical study of the effects of Miranda. In *The Miranda Debate: Law, Justice, and Policing.* Boston, MA: Northeastern University Press.

Christopher Commission
1991 *Report of the Independent Commission on the Los Angeles Police Department.* Los Angeles, CA. (Popular title: *The Christopher Report.* Government Documents [Desk] HV7595.L7E3 1991.)

City of New York, Mayor's Commission to Investigate Allegations of Police Corruption
1973 *The Knapp Report on Police Corruption.* New York, NY: George Braziller.
1994 *Mollen Commission Report* (Appendix). New York, NY: City of New York, Mayor's Commission to Investigate Allegations of Police Corruption.

Cohn, J., J. Lennon, and R. Wasserman
1999 *Eliminating Racial Profiling: A Third Way Approach.* Washington, DC: Progressive Policy Institute.

Cross, W.T.
1917 Statistics of crime: Report of the Committee of the American Prison Association. *Journal of the American Institute of Criminal Law and Criminology* 16.

Daley, R.E.
  1980   The relationship of personality variables to suitability for police work. *DAI* 44:1551-1569.
Dalton, T.C.
  1984   *The State Politics of Congressional and Judicial Reform: Implementing Criminal Records Policy.* Dissertation. Ann Arbor, MI: University Microfilms International.
Davis, J.
  1975   *Police Discretion.* St. Paul, MN: West Publishing Company.
Delattre, E.J.
  1989   *Characters and Cops: Ethics in Policing.* Washington, DC: American Enterprise Institute.
Dwyer, W.O., E.P. Prien, and J.L. Bernard
  1990   Psychological screening of law enforcement officers: A case for job relatedness. *Journal of Police Science and Administration* 17:176-182.
Fagan, J., and G. Davies
  2000   Street stops and broken windows: Terry, race and disorder in the New York City. *Fordham Urban Law Journal* 28:457-482.
Fridell, L., R. Lunney, D. Diamond, and B. Kubu
  2001   *Racially Biased Policing: A Principled Response.* Washington, DC: Police Executive Research Forum.
Fyfe, J.J.
  1979   Administrative interventions on police shooting discretion: An empirical examination. *Journal of Criminal Justice* 7:309-323.
  1981   Observations on police deadly force. *Crime and Delinquency* 27:376-389.
  1982   Blind justice: Police shootings in Memphis. *Journal of Criminal Law and Criminology* 73:707-722.
  1987   Police shooting: Environment and license. In J.E. Scott and T. Hirschi, eds., *Controversial Issues in Crime and Justice.* Thousand Oaks, CA: Sage.
  1988   Police use of deadly force: Research and reform. *Justice Quarterly* 5:165-205.
  2002   *Too Many Missing Cases: Holes in Our Knowledge about Police Use of Force.* Washington, DC: U.S. Department of Justice.
Fyfe, J.J., and J.T. Walker
  1990   Garner plus five years: An examination of Supreme Court intervention in police discretion and legislative prerogatives. *American Journal of Criminal Justice* (Spring)14(2):167-188.
Gallagher, C., E.R. Maguire, S.D. Mastrofski, and M.D. Reisig
  2001   Psychological screening of law enforcement officers: A case for job relatedness. *Journal of Police Science and Administration* 17:76-182.
Garner, J.H., and C.D. Maxwell
  1999   *Use of Force by Police: Overview of National and Local Data.* Washington, DC: U.S. Department of Justice.
Geller, W.A., and M. Scott
  1992   *Deadly Force: What We Know: A Practitioner's Desk Reference on Police-Involved Shootings.* Washington, DC: Police Executive Research Forum.
Geller, W.A., and H. Toch, eds.
  1995   *And Justice for All: Understanding and Controlling Police Abuse of Force.* Washington, DC: Police Executive Forum.
General Accounting Office
  1998   *Law Enforcement: Information on Drug-Related Police Corruption.* Washington, DC: General Accounting Office.
  2000   *Racial Profiling: Limited Data Available on Motorists Stops.* Washington, DC: General Accounting Office.

Goldstein, H.
  1967 Administrative problems controlling police authority. *Journal of Criminal Law, Criminology, and Police Science* 58:160-172.
  1975 *Police Corruption: Perspective on Its Nature and Control.* Washington, DC: Police Foundation.
  1977 *Policing a Free Society.* Cambridge, MA: Balinger Publishing Company.
Gould, J., and S.D. Mastrofski
  2001 The Constitutionality of Police Searches. Paper delivered at the annual meeting of the Midwest Political Science Association, Chicago, IL.
Harris, D.A.
  1997 Driving while black and all other traffic offenses: The Supreme Court and pretextual traffic stops. *Journal of Criminal Law and Criminology* 87:544-582.
  1999 Stories, the statistics, and the law: Why "driving while black" matters. *Minnesota Law Review* 84:265-325.
  2002 Racial profiling revisited: "Just common sense" in the fight against terror. *Criminal Justice* 17:36-59.
Henriquez, M.A.
  1999 IACP national database project on police use of force. In *Use of Force by Police: Overview of National and Local Data.* Washington, DC: Office of Justice Programs.
Hudson, J.
  1972 Organizational aspects of internal and external review of the police. *Journal of Criminal Law, Criminology, and Police Science* 63:427-433.
Human Rights Watch
  1998 *Shielded from Justice: Police Brutality and Accountability in the United States.* New York, NY: Human Rights Watch.
Kahan, D.M., and T.L. Meares
  1998 The coming crisis of criminal procedure. *Georgetown Law Journal* 86:1153.
Kerner Commission
  1968 *National Advisory Commission on Civil Disorder.* Washington, DC: U.S. Government Printing Office.
Klarman, M.J.
  2000 The racial origins of criminal procedure. *Michigan Law Review* 99:99.
Klockars, C.B.
  1999 Some really cheap ways of measuring what really matters. Pp. 195-214 in R.H. Langworthy, ed., *Measuring What Matters: Proceedings from the Policing Research Institute Meetings.* Washington, DC: National Institute of Justice.
  2003 The virtues of integrity. In M. Amir and S. Einstein, eds., *The Uncertainty Series, Corruption, Policing, Security, and Democracy, Volume 4.* Huntsville, TX: Office of International Criminal Justice.
Klockars, C.B., J. Garner, and C. Maxwell
  2000 *The Measurement of Police Integrity.* Washington, DC: U.S. Department of Justice.
Klockars, C.B., S.K. Ivkovich, W.E. Harver, and M.R. Haberfeld
  2000 *The Measurement of Police Integrity.* (Research in Brief.) Washington, DC: National Institute of Justice.
Krantz, S.
  1979 *Police Policymaking: The Boston Experience.* Lexington, MA: Lexington Books.
Lafave, W.
  1965 *Arrest—The Decision to Take a Suspect into Custody.* Boston: MA: Little, Brown and Co.
  1996 Computers, urinals, and the Fourth Amendment: Confessions of a patron saint. *Michigan Law Review* 94:2553.

Lafave, W., and F.J. Remington
    1965   Controlling the police: The judge's role in making and reviewing law enforcement decisions. *Michigan Law Review* 63:987-1005.
Leiken, L.S.
    1971   Police interrogation in Colorado: The implementation of Miranda. *Denver Law Journal* 1:15-16.
Leo, R.A.
    1998   The impact of Miranda revisited. In R.A. Leo and G.C. Thomas, eds., *The Miranda Debate: Law, Justice, and Policing.* Boston, MA: Northeastern University Press.
Lersch, K.M.
    2000   Drug related police corruption: The Miami experience. Pp.132-144 in M.J. Palmiotto, ed., *Police Misconduct.* Upper Saddle River, NJ: Prentice-Hall, Inc.
Levinson, L.
    1994   The future of state federal civil rights prosecutions: The lessons of the Rodney King trial. *UCLA Law Review* 41:509-535.
Malouff, J., and N.S. Schutte
    1980   Using biographical information to hire the best new police officers. *Journal of Police Science and Administration* 14:256-267.
Manning, P.K., and L.J. Redlinger
    1977   Invitational edges of corruption: Some consequences of narcotics law enforcement. Pp. 279-310 in P. Rock, ed., *Drugs and Politics.* Rutgers, NJ: Transaction, Inc.
McCoy, C.
    1984   Lawsuits against police: What impact do they really have? *Criminal Law Bulletin* 20:49-56.
Meyer, M.W.
    1980   Police shootings at minorities: The case of Los Angeles. *Annals of the American Academy of Political and Social Science Philadelphia* 452:98-110.
Milner, N.A.
    1971a   *Court and Local Law Enforcement: The Impact of Miranda.* Thousand Oaks, CA: Sage.
    1971b   Supreme Court effectiveness and the police organization. *Law and Contemporary Problems* 36:467-487.
Milton, C.H., J.W. Halleck, J. Lardner, and G.L. Abrecht
    1977   *Police Use of Deadly Force.* Washington, DC: Police Foundation.
Mollen Commission
    1994   *Commission to Investigate Allegations of Police Corruption and the Anti-Corruption Procedures of the Police Department,* July 7.
Muir, W.K.
    1977   *Police: Street Corner Politicians.* Chicago, IL: University of Chicago Press.
Murphy, P., and T. Plate
    1977   *Commissioner: A View from the Top.* New York, NY: Simon and Schuster.
National Commission on Law Observance and Enforcement
    1931   *Report on Lawlessness in Law Enforcement.* Washington, DC: U.S. Government Printing Office.
Newell, C., J. Pollock, and J. Tweedy
    1992   *Financial Aspects of Police Liability.* (Baseline data report, Vol. 24, No. 2.) Washington, DC: International City/County Management Association.
Oaks, D.H.
    1970   Studying the exclusionary rule in search and seizure. *University of Chicago Law School Review* 37:665.

Orfield, M.
1987 The exclusionary rule and deterrence: An empirical study of Chicago Narcotics Officers. *University of Chicago Law School Review* 54:1016.

Pennsylvania Crime Commission
1974 *Report on Police Corruption*. Saint Davids, PA: Pennsylvania Crime Commission.
1994 *The Investigation into the Conduct of Lackawanna County District Attorney*. Conshohocken, PA: Commonwealth of Pennsylvania.

Police Executive Research Forum
2000 *Racially Biased Policing: A Principled Response*. Washington, DC: Police Executive Research Forum.

President's Commission on Law Enforcement and Administration of Justice
1967 *Task Force Report: The Police*. Washington, DC: U.S. Government Printing Office.

Ramirez, D., J. McDevitt, and A. Farrell
2000 *A Resource Guide on Racial Profiling Data Collection Systems: Promising Practices and Lessons Learned*. Washington, DC: Bureau of Justice Assistance.

Roberts, J.V., and L.J. Stalans
1997 *Public Opinion, Crime, and Criminal Justice*. Boulder, CO: Westview Press.

Robin, G.
1963 Justifiable homicide by the police. *Journal of Criminal Law, Criminology, and Police Science* 54:225-231.

San Diego Police Department
2000 *Vehicle Stop Study: Mid-Year Report*. San Diego, CA: San Diego Police Department.

San Jose Police Department
2001 *San Jose Police Department Vehicle Stop Demographic Study*. Available: http://www.sjpd.org/sjpd%20vehicle%20stop%20annual%20rpt.pdf.

Schaefer, R.C.
1971 Patrolman perspectives on Miranda. *Law and Social Order* 81.

Seeberger, R., and R.S. Wettick
1967 Miranda in Pittsburgh. A statistical study. *University of Pittsburgh Law Review* 29:1.

Sherman, L.W.
1974 *Police Corruption: A Sociological Perspective*. Garden City, NY: Archor Books.
1977 Police corruption control: Environmental context vs. organizational policy. In D.H. Bayley, ed., *Police and Society*. Thousand Oaks, CA: Sage.
1978 *Controlling Police Corruption: The Effects of Reform Policies, Summary Report*. Washington, DC: U.S. Department of Justice.
1992 Influence of criminology on criminal law: Evaluating arrests for misdemeanor domestic violence. *Journal of Criminal Law and Criminology* 83:1-45.

Skogan, W.G.
1979 On the take: From petty crooks to presidents. *Social Forces* 57:1416-1417.

Skolnick, J.H.
1966 *Justice Without Trial*. New York, NY: John Wiley and Sons, Inc.

Skolnick, J.H., and J.J. Fyfe
1993 *Above the Law: Police and the Excessive Use of Force*. New York, NY: Free Press.

Sparger, J.R., and D.J. Giacopassi
1992 Memphis revisited: A reexamination of police shootings after the Garner decision. *Police Quarterly* 9:211-225.

Stoddard, E.R.
1995 Informal code of police deviancy: A group approach to blue-coat crime. Pp. 185-206 in V.E. Kappeler, ed., *Police and Society*. Prospect Heights, IL: Waveland Press.

Sutton, P.
  1986   Fourth amendment in action: An empirical view of the search warrant process. *Criminal Law Bulletin* 22:405-429.
Talley, J.E., and L.D. Hinz
  1990   *Performance Prediction of Public Safety and Law Enforcement Personnel: A Study in Race and Gender Differences and MMPI Subscales.* Springfield, IL: Charles C Thomas.
Tennenbaum, A.
  1994   The influence of the Garner decision on police use of deadly force. *Journal of Criminal Law and Criminology* 85:241-260.
Uchida, C.D., and T.S. Bynum
  1991   Search warrants, motions to suppress, and "lost cases": The effects of the exclusionary rule in seven jurisdictions. *Journal of Criminal Law and Criminology* 81:1034-1066.
U.S. Commission on Civil Rights
  1981   *Who Is Guarding the Guardians? A Report on Police Practices.* Washington, DC: U.S. Government Printing Office.
Waegel, W.B.
  1984   Use of lethal force by police: The effect of statutory change. *Crime and Delinquency* 30:121-140.
Wald, M.S., R. Ayres, R. Hess, M. Schantz, and C. Whitebread
  1967   Interrogations in New Haven: The impact of Miranda. *Yale Law Review* 76:1519.
Walker, S.
  1977   *A Critical History Reform: The Emergence of Professionalism.* Lexington, MA: Heath and Company.
  1985   Racial-minority and female employment in police: The implications of "glacial" change. *Crime and Delinquency* 31:555-572.
  1993   *Taming the System: The Control of Discretion in Criminal Justice, 1950-1990.* New York, NY, and London, England: Oxford University Press.
  1999   *The Police in America. An Introduction, 3rd edition.* Boston, MA: McGraw-Hill.
  2001   Searching for the denominator: Problems with police traffic stop data and an early warning system solution. *Justice Research and Policy* 3:63-95.
Walker, S., G.P. Alpert, and D.J. Kenney
  2001   *Early Warning Systems: Responding to the Problem Police Officer.* Washington, DC: U.S. Department of Justice.
Wasby, S.L.
  1970   *The Impact of the United States Supreme Court: Some Perspectives.* Homewood, IL: Dorsey.
  1976   *Small Town Police and the Supreme Court: Hearing the Word.* Lexington, MA: Lexington Books.
Yale Law Journal
  1979   Suing the police in federal court. *Yale Law Journal* 88:781-824.
Zeitz, L., R.J. Medalie, and P. Alexander
  1969   Anomie, powerlessness, and police interrogation. *Journal of Criminal Law-Criminology-and-Police Science* 60:314-322.

CHAPTER 8

American Civil Liberties Union
  1999   *Driving While Black: Racial Profiling on our Nation's Highways.* Washington, DC: American Civil Liberties Union.

Ayres, I., and J. Braithwaite
  1992 *Responsive Regulation: Transcending the Deregulation Debate:* New York, NY: Oxford University Press.
Bayley, D.
  1998 *What Works in Policing?* New York, NY: Oxford University Press.
Bland, N., J. Miller, and P. Quinton
  2000 *Upping the PACE? An Evaluation of the Recommendations of the Stephen Lawrence Inquiry on Stops and Searches.* London, England: Great Britain Home Office.
Bloch, P.B.
  1974 *Equality in the Distribution of Police Services.* Washington, DC: Urban Institute.
Bolotin, F.N., and D.L. Cingranelli
  1983 Equity and urban policy: The underclass hypothesis revisited. *Journal of Politics* 45:209-219.
Boyle, J., and D. Jacobs
  1982 The intracity distribution of services: A multivariate analysis. *American Political Science Review* 76:371-379.
Braithwaite, J.
  1999 Restorative justice: Assessing optimistic and pessimistic accounts. Pp. 1-27 in M. Tonry, ed., *Crime and Justice: A Review of Research*, Vol. 25. Chicago, IL: University of Chicago Press.
Brewer, C.A., and T.A. Suchan
  2001 *Mapping Census 2000: The Geography of U.S. Diversity.* Washington, DC: U.S. Department of Commerce.
Bureau of Justice Statistics
  1999 *Law Enforcement Management and Administrative Statistics, 1997: Data for Individual State and Local Agencies with 100 or More Officers.* Washington, DC: U.S. Department of Justice.
Chevigny, P.
  1969 *Police Power: Police Abuses in New York City.* New York, NY: Random House.
Cingranelli, D.L.
  1981 Race, politics and elites: Testing alternative models of municipal service distribution. *American Political Science Review* 25.
Commission on Accreditation for Law Enforcement Agencies
  1999 *Standards for Law Enforcement Agencies, 4th edition.* Fairfax, VA: Commission on Accreditation for Law Enforcement Agencies.
Coulter, P.
  1980 Measuring the inequality of urban public services: A methodological discussion with applications. *Policy Studies Journal* (Spring):683-698.
Coupe, T., and M. Griffiths
  1999 The influence of police actions on victim satisfaction in burglary investigations? *International Journal of the Sociology of Law* 27:413-431.
Crank, J.P.
  1994 Watchman and community: Myth and institutionalization in policing. *Law and Society Review* 28:325-351.
Cullen, F.T., L. Cao, J. Frank, R.H. Langworthy, S.L. Browning, R. Kopache, and T.J. Stevenson
  1996 "Stop or I'll shoot": Racial differences in support for police use of deadly force. *American Behavioral Scientist* 39:449-460.
Decker, S.
  1981 Citizen attitudes toward the police: A review of past findings and suggestions for future policy. *Journal of Police Science and Administration* 9:80-87.

Easton, D.
1975   A reassessment of the concept of political support. *British Journal of Political Science* 5:435-457.

Easton, D., and J. Dennis
1969   *Children in the Political System: Origins of Political Legitimacy.* New York, NY: McGraw-Hill.

Eck, J.E., and E.R. Maguire
2000   Have changes in policing reduced violent crime? An assessment of the evidence. In A. Blumstein and T. Wallman, eds., *The Crime Drop in America.* New York, NY: Cambridge University Press.

Engstrom, R., and M.W. Giles
1972   Expectations and images: A note on diffuse support for legal institutions. *Law and Society Review* 6:631-636.

Flanagan, T.J., and M.S. Vaughn
1996   Public opinion about police abuse of force. In W. Geller and H. Tochs, eds., *Police Violence.* New Haven, CT: Yale University Press.

Fogelson, R.M.
1977   *Big City Police.* Cambridge, MA: Harvard University Press.

Frank, J., S.G. Brandl, F.T. Cullen, and A. Stichman
1996   Reassessing the impact of race on citizen's attitudes toward the police: A research note. *Justice Quarterly* 13:321-334.

French, J.R.P., and B. Raven
1959   The bases of social power. In D. Cartwright, ed., *Studies in Social Power.* Ann Arbor, MI: Institute for Social Research.

Fuller, L.L.
1971   *Principles of Social Order: Selected Essays of Lon L. Fuller.* Durham, NC: Duke University Press.

Gallup Poll News Service
1999   Available: http://www.gallup.com/poll/specialReports/pollSummaries/sr010711.asp [September 23, 2002].

Gates, H.L.
1995   Thirteen ways of looking at a black man. *New Yorker* (October):59.

General Accounting Office
2000a   *Racial Profiling: Limited Data Available on Motorists Stops.* Washington, DC: General Accounting Office.
2000b   *U.S. Customs Service: Better Targeting of Airline Passengers for Personal Searches Could Produce Better Results.* (Report #GGD-00-38, March 17). Washington, DC: General Accounting Office. Also available: http://www.gao.gov/archive/2000/gg00038.pdf [January 2003].

Goldstein, H.
2000   Improving policing: A problem-oriented approach. In W.M. Oliver, ed., *Community Policing: Classical Readings.* Upper Saddle River, NJ: Prentice-Hall, Inc.

Gurr, T.R.
1970   Sources of rebellion in Western societies: Some quantitative evidence. *Annals of the American Academy of Political and Social Science Philadelphia* 391:128-144.

Hochschild, J.L.
1989   Equal opportunity and the estranged poor. *Annals of the American Academy of Political and Social Science* 501:143-155.

Hoffman, M.L.
1977   Moral internalization: Current theory and research. In L. Berkowitz, ed., *Advances in Experimental Social Psychology.* New York, NY: Academic Press.

Illinois Advisory Committee to the U.S. Commission on Civil Rights
  1993   *Police Protection of the African-American Community in Chicago.* Washington,
          DC: U.S. Commission on Civil Rights.
Jost, J.T., and M.R. Banaji
  1994   The role of stereotyping in system-justification and the production of false con-
          sciousness. *British Journal of Social Psychology* 33:1-27.
Kakalik, J.S., and S. Wildhorn
  1968   *National Advisory Commission on Civil Disorder.* Washington, DC: U.S. Govern-
          ment Printing Office.
Katz, C.
  2001   *Establishment of a Police Gang Unit: An Examination of Rational and Institutional
          Considerations.* Washington, DC: U.S. Department of Justice.
Kelling, G.L., and M.H. Moore
  1988   From political to reform to community: The evolving strategy of police. Pp. 3-25 in
          J.R. Greene and S.D. Mastrofski, eds., *Community Policing: Rhetoric or Reality.*
          Westport, CT: Praeger Publishers.
Kelling, G.L., and W.H. Sousa, Jr.
  2001   *Do Police Matter?: An Analysis of the Impact of New York City's Police Reforms.*
          Civic Report 22. New York, NY: Manhattan Institute.
Kennedy, R.
  2001   Racial trends in the administration of criminal justice. In N.J. Smelser, W.J. Wilson,
          and F. Mitchell, eds., *America Becoming: Racial Trends and Their Consequences,
          Volume II.* Washington, DC: National Academy Press.
Kitzman, K.M., and R.E. Emery
  1993   Procedural justice and parents' satisfaction in a field study of child custody dispute
          resolution. *Law and Human Behavior* 17:553-567.
Klockars, C.B.
  1988   Rhetoric of community policing. Pp. 239-258 in J.R. Greene and S.D. Mastrofski,
          eds., *Community Policing: Rhetoric or Reality*: Westport, CT: Praeger Publishers.
Klockars, C.B., J. Garner, and C. Maxwell
  2001   Early warning systems as risk management for police. Pp. 219-230 in K.M. Lersch,
          ed., *Policing and Misconduct.* Washington, DC: U.S. Department of Justice.
Kluegel, J., and E. Smith
  1986   *Beliefs about Inequality: Americans' View of What Is and What Ought to Be.* New
          York, NY: Aldine De Gruyter.
Langan, P.A., L.A. Greenfeld, S.K. Smith, M.R. Durose, and D.J. Levin
  2001   *Contacts Between Police and the Public.* Washington, DC: Bureau of Justice
          Statistics.
Lee, S.J.
  1994   Policy types, bureaucracy and urban policies: Integrating models of urban service
          delivery. *Policy Studies Journal* 22:87-108.
Leventhal, G.S.
  1980   What should be done with equity theory? New approaches to the study of fairness
          in social relationships. Pp. 27-53 in K.J. Gergen, M.S. Greenbers, and R.H. Willis,
          eds., *Social Exchange: Advances in Theory and Research.* New York, NY: Plenum
          Press.
Lind, E.A., and T.R. Tyler
  1988   *Social Psychology of Procedural Justice.* New York, NY: Plenum Press.
Lind, E.A., C.T. Kulik, M. Ambrose, and M.V. de Vera Park
  1993   Individual and corporate dispute reduction: Using procedural fairness as a decision
          heuristic. *Administrative Science Quarterly* 38:224-251.

Lineberry, R.L.
  1974   Mandating urban equality: The distribution of municipal public services. *University of Texas Law Review* 53:26-59.
  1977   *Equality and Urban Policy: The Distribution of Municipal Public Services*. Thousand Oaks, CA: Sage.

MacCoun, R.J.
  1993   Drugs and the law: A psychological analysis of drug prohibition. *Psychological Bulletin* 113:497-512.

MacCoun, R.J., E.A. Lind, D.R. Hensler, D.L. Bryant, and P.A. Ebener
  1988   *Alternative Adjudication: An Evaluation of the New Jersey Automobile Arbitration Program*. Santa Monica, CA: Rand Corporation.

Maguire, E., and S.D. Mastrofski
  2000   Patterns of community policing in the United States. *Police Quarterly* 3:4-45.

Maguire, E.R., and C.D. Uchida
  2000   Measurement and explanation in the comparative study of police organizations. In D. Duffee, ed., *Measurement and Analysis of Crime and Justice*. Washington, DC: National Institute of Justice.

Major, B.
  1994   From social inequality to personal entitlement: The role of social comparisons, legitimacy appraisals, and group memberships. *Advances in Experimental Social Psychology* 26:293-355.

Manning, P.K.
  1977   *Police Work*. Cambridge, MA: MIT Press.
  1984   Community policing. *American Journal of Police* 3:205-227.

Martin, S.E.
  1990   *On the Move: The Status of Women in Policing*. Washington, DC: Police Foundation.

Mastrofski, S.D.
  1998   Community policing and police organization structure. Pp. 161-189 in J.P. Brodeur, ed., *How to Recognize Good Policing: Problems and Issues*. Thousand Oaks, CA: Sage.

Mastrofski, S.D., and R.R. Ritti
  1992   You can lead a horse to water . . .: A case study of a police department's response to stricter drunk-driving laws. *Justice Quarterly* 9:465-491.
  1996   Police training and the effects of organization on drunk driving enforcement. *Justice Quarterly* 13:291-320.
  1999   *Patterns of Community Policing: A View from Newspapers in the United States*. COPS Working Paper 2. Washington, DC: Office of Community Oriented Policing Services. Also available: http://www.usdoj.gov/cops/pdf/cp_resources/mastroski/wp_1_001.pdf.
  2000   Making sense of community policing: A theory-based analysis. *Police Practice and Research: An International Journal* 1:183-210.

Mastrofski, S.D., and C.D. Uchida
  1993   Transforming the police. *Journal of Research in Crime and Delinquency* 30:330-358.

Mastrofski, S.D., J.B Snipes, and A.E. Supina
  1996   Compliance on demand: The public's response to specific police requests. *Journal of Research in Crime and Delinquency* 33:269-305.

McCluskey, J.D., S.D. Mastrofski, and R.B. Parks
  1999   To acquiesce or rebel: Predicting citizen compliance with police requests. *Police Quarterly* 2:389-416.

McCorkle, R.C., and T.D. Miethe
  1998   The political and organizational response to gangs: An examination of a "moral panic" in Nevada. *Justice Quarterly* 15:41-64.
McEwen, T.
  2000   *Evaluation of Community Policing in Tempe, Arizona, Final Report.* (NCJ #183423.) Washington, DC: National Institute of Justice.
Meares, T.L.
  1998   Social organization and drug law enforcement. *American Criminal Law Review* 35:Rev 19.
Meares, T.L., and B.E. Harcourt
  2000   Transparent adjudication and social science research in constitutional criminal procedure. *Journal of Criminal Law and Criminology* 90:733-769.
Merelman, R.M.
  1966   Learning and legitimacy. *American Political Science Review* 60:548-561.
Mladenka, K.R.
  1989   The distribution of an urban public service: The changing role of race and politics. *Urban Affairs Quarterly* 24:556-583.
Mladenka, K.R., and K.Q. Hill
  1978   The distribution of urban police services. *Journal of Politics* 40:13-133.
Moore, M.H.
  1992   Problem-solving and community policing. Pp. 99-158 in M. Tonry and N. Morris, eds., *Modern Policing, Volume 15.* Chicago, IL: University of Chicago Press.
  2002   *Recognizing Value in Public Policing.* Washington, DC: Police Executive Research Forum.
Murphy, W.F., and J. Tanenhaus
  1969   Public opinion and the United States Supreme Court. *Frontiers of Judicial Research* 273:276-277.
Nagin, D.S.
  1998   Criminal deterrence research at the outset of the twenty-first century. *Crime and Justice: A Review of Research* 23:1-42.
Nagin, D.S., and R. Paternoster
  1991   The preventive effects of the perceived risk of arrest: Testing an expanded conception of deterrence. *Criminology* 29:561-587.
Nardulli, P.F., and J.M. Stonecash
  1981   *Politics, Professionalism, and Urban Services—The Police.* Boston, MA: Oelgeschlager, Gunn and Hain.
National Center for Women and Policing
  1998   *Equality Denied: The Status of Women and Policing, 1998.* Available: http// www.womenandpolicing.org [November 15, 2002].
Ostrom, E.
  1983   Equity in police services. In G.P. Whitaker and C.D. Phillips, eds., *Evaluating Performance of Criminal Justice Agencies.* Thousand Oaks, CA: Sage.
Parsons, T.
  1967   *Sociological Theory and Modern Society.* New York, NY: Free Press.
Paternoster, R.
  1987   The deterrent effect of the perceived certainty and severity of punishment: A review of the evidence and issues. *Justice Quarterly* 4:173-217.
  1989   Absolute and restrictive deterrence in a panel of youth: Explaining the onset, persistence/desistance, and frequency of delinquent offending. *Social Problems* 36:289-309.

Paternoster, R., and L. Iovanni
  1986   The deterrent effect of perceived severity: A reexamination. *Social Forces* 64:751-777.
Paternoster, R., R. Bachman, R. Brame, and L.W. Sherman
  1997   Do fair procedures matter? The effect of procedural justice on spouse assault. *Law and Society Review* 31:163-204.
Paternoster, R., L.E. Saltzman, G.P. Waldo, and T.G. Chiricos
  1983   Estimating perceptual stability and deterrent effects: The role of perceived legal punishment in the inhibition of criminal involvement. *Journal of Criminal Law and Criminology* 74:270-297.
Police Foundation
  1981   *The Newark Foot Patrol Experiment.* Washington, DC: Police Foundation.
Pruitt, D.G., R.S. Pierce, N.B. McGillicuddy, G.L. Welton, and L.M. Castrianno
  1993   Long-term success in mediation. *Law and Human Behavior* 17:313-330.
Reaves, B.A., and A.L. Goldberg
  2000   *Local Police Departments, 1997.* Washington, DC: U.S. Department of Justice.
Reisig, M.D., and M.S. Chandek
  2001   The effects of expectancy disconfirmation on outcome satisfaction in police-citizen encounters. *Policing: An International Journal of Police Strategies and Management* 21:88-99.
Reiss, A.J., Jr.
  1971   *Police and the Public.* New Haven, CT: Yale University Press.
Rich, R.
  1978   Voluntary action and public services: Introduction to the special issue. *Journal of Voluntary Research* 7:11.
  1979   Neglected issues in the study of urban service distributions: Research agenda. *Urban Studies* 16:14.
Ritti, R.R., and S.D. Mastrofski
  2002   *The Institutionalization of Community Policing: A Study of the Presentation of the Concept in Two Law Enforcement Journals.* Manassas, VA: George Mason University.
Roberts, J.V., and L.J. Stalans
  1997   *Public Opinion, Crime, and Criminal Justice.* Boulder, CO: Westview Press.
Robinson, P.H., and J.M. Darley
  1995   Justice, liability, and blame: Community views and the criminal law. In *New Directions in Social Psychology.* Boulder, CO: Westview Press.
Ross, H.L.
  1982   *Deterring the Drinking Driver: Legal Policy and Social Control.* Lexington, MA: Lexington Books.
  1992   The law and drunk driving. *Law and Society Review* 26:219-230.
Rossi, P., R.A. Berk, and B.K. Eidson
  1974   *Roots of Urban Discontent.* New York, NY: John Wiley and Sons, Inc.
Sanchez, T.W.
  1998   Equity analysis of capital improvement plans using GIS: Des Moines urbanized area. *Journal of Urban Planning and Development* 124(1):33-43.
Sanger, M.B.
  1981   Are academic models of urban service distributions relevant to public policy?: Lessons from New York. *Policy Studies Journal* 97:1011-1020.
Sarat, A.
  1977   Studying American legal culture: An assessment of survey evidence. *Law & Society Review* 11:427.

Scheingold, S.
   1974   *The Politics of Rights, Lawyers, Public Policy, and Political Change.* New Haven, CT: Yale University Press.
Selznick, P.
   1969   *Law, Societies, and Industrial Justice.* New York, NY: Russell Sage Foundation.
Sherman, L.W.
   1992   Influence of criminology on criminal law: Evaluating arrests for misdemeanor domestic violence. *Journal of Criminal Law and Criminology* 83:1-45.
   1993   Defiance, deviance and irrelevance: A theory of the criminal sanction. *Journal of Research in Crime and Delinquency* 30:445-473.
   1998   *Evidence-Based Policing.* Washington, DC: Police Foundation.
   2001a Trust and confidence in criminal justice. *Journal of the National Institute of Justice* 248:23-31.
   2001b Consent of the governed: Police, democracy, and diversity. Pp. 17-33 in M. Amir and S. Einstein, eds., *Policing, Security and Democracy: Theory and Practices.* Huntsville, TX: Office of International Criminal Justice.
Sherman, L.W., H. Strang, and D.J. Woods
   2001   *Recidivism Patterns in the Canberra Reintegrative Shaming Experiments (RISE).* Canberra, Australia: Centre for Restorative Justice, Research School of Social Sciences, Australian National University.
Silbey, S.S., and P. Ewick
   1998   *The Common Place of Law: Stories of Popular Legal Consciousness.* Chicago, IL: University of Chicago Press.
Skogan, W.G.
   1994   *Contacts Between Police and Public: Findings from the 1992 British Crime Survey.* (Home Office Research Study 134.) London, England: Her Majesty's Stationery Office.
Skogan, W.G., and G.E. Antunes
   1979   Information, apprehension, and deterrence: Exploring the limits of police productivity. *Journal of Criminal Justice* 7:217-241.
Skogan, W.G., and S.M. Hartnett
   1997   *Community Policing, Chicago Style.* New York, NY: Oxford University Press.
Slobogin, C.
   1991   The world without a Fourth Amendment. *UCLA Law Review* 39:1-107.
Slobogin, C., and J.E. Schumacher
   1993   Rating the intrusiveness of law enforcement searches and seizures. *Law Enforcement Searches and Seizures* 17:183-200.
Southgate, P., and P. Ekblom
   1984   *Contacts Between Police and Public.* (Home Office Research Study No. 77.) London, England: Her Majesty's Stationery Office.
Sparks, R., A.E. Bottoms, and W. Hay
   1996   *Prisons and the Problem of Order.* Oxford, England: Oxford University Press.
Sunshine, J., and T.R. Tyler
   2003   The role of procedural justice and legitimacy in shaping public support for policing. *Law and Society Review* 37:555-589.
Strang, H.
   2002   *Repair or Revenge? Victims and Restorative Justice.* Oxford, England: Oxford University Press.
Strang, H., and J. Braithwaite
   2001   *Restorative Justice and Civil Society.* Cambridge, England: Cambridge University Press.

Strang, H., and J. Braithwaite, eds.
2000 *Restorative Justice: Philosophy to Practice*. Aldershot, England: Ashgate.
Teevan, J.J.
1975 Subjective perception of deterrence. *Journal of Research in Crime and Delinquency* 13:155-164.
Thibaut, J., and L. Walker
1975 *Procedural Justice: A Psychological Analysis*. Hillsdale, NJ: Erlbaum.
Tuch, S.A., and R. Weitzer
1997 Racial differences in attitudes toward the police. *Public Opinion Quarterly* 61:642-663.
Tyler, T.
1990 *Why People Obey the Law*. New Haven, CT: Yale University Press.
1997 Procedural fairness and compliance with the law. *Swiss Journal of Economics and Statistics* 133:219-240.
2001 Public trust and confidence in legal authorities: What do majority and minority group members want from the law and legal institutions? *Behavioral Sciences and the Law* 19:215-235.
2003 Procedural justice, legitimacy, and the effective rule of law. In M. Tonry, ed., *Crime and Justice*. Chicago, IL: University of Chicago Press.
Tyler, T.R., and S.L. Blader
2000 *Cooperation in Groups: Procedural Justice, Social Identity, and Behavioral Engagement*. Philadelphia, PA: Psychology Press.
Tyler, T.R., and J.M. Darley
2000 Building a law-abiding society: Taking public views about morality and the legitimacy of legal authorities into account when formulating substantive law. *Hofstra Law Review* 28:707-739.
Tyler, T.R., and Y.J. Huo
2002 *Trust in the Law: Encouraging Public Cooperation with the Police and Courts*. New York, NY: Russell Sage Foundation.
Tyler, T.R., and K.M. McGraw
1986 Ideology and the interpretation of personal experience: Procedural justice and political quiescence. *Journal of Social Issues* 42:115-128.
Tyler, T.R., and G. Mitchell
1994 Legitimacy and the empowerment of discretionary legal authority: The United States Supreme Court and abortion rights. *Duke Law Journal* 43:703-802.
Tyler, T.R., and H.J. Smith
1997 Social justice and social movements. In D. Gilbert, S. Fiske, and G. Lindzey, eds., *Handbook of Social Psychology* (4th ed.). New York, NY: McGraw-Hill.
Tyler, T.R., R.J. Boeckmann, H.J. Smith, and Y.J. Huo
1997 *Social Justice in a Diverse Society*. Boulder, CO: Westview Press.
Tyler, T.R., E.A. Lind, and Y.J. Huo
2000 Cultural values and authority relations: The psychology of conflict resolution across cultures. *Psychology, Public Policy, and Law* 6(4):1138-1163.
Walker, S.
2001 *Police Accountability: The Role of Citizen Oversight*. Belmont, CA: Wadsworth Publishing Company.
Walker, S., and K.B. Turner
1992 *A Decade of Modest Progress: Employment of Black and Hispanic Police Officers, 1983-1992*. Washington, DC: Equal Opportunity Employment Commission.

Webb, G.
1999   Driving while black: Police stops motorists to check for drugs. *Esquire* (April):126.
Weber, M.
1968   *Economy and Society*. Berkeley, CA: University of California Press.
Weicher, J.
1971   The allocation of police protection by income class. *Urban Studies* 207-220.
Weisburd, D., C.M. Lum, and A. Petrosino
2001   Does research design affect study outcomes in criminal justice? In David P. Farrington and B.C. Welsh, eds., *Annals of the American Academy of Political and Social Science* 578:50-70.
Weisburd, D., S.D. Mastrofski, A.M. McNally, R. Greenspan, and J.J. Willis
2003   Reforming to preserve: Compstat and strategic problem-solving in American policing. *Criminology and Public Policy* 3.
Weitekamp, E.G.M., H.J. Kerner, and U. Meier
1996   *Problem Solving Policing*. Paper presented at the International Conference and Workshop on Problem-Solving Policing as Crime Prevention.
Weitzer, R.
2000   White, black, or blue cops?: Race and citizens' assessments of police officers. *Journal of Criminal Justice* 28:313-324.
White, M.F., T.C. Cox, and J. Basehart
1991   Theoretical considerations of officer profanity and obscenity in formal contacts with citizens. In T. Barker and D.L. Carter, eds., *Police Deviance*. Cincinnati, OH: Anderson Publishing Company.
Wissler, R.L.
1995   Mediation and adjudication in the small claims court: The effects of process and case characteristics. *Law and Society Review* 29:323-358.
Worden, R.E.
1980   Equity and the Distribution of Urban Public Services: Bureaucratic Decision Rules, Street-Level Bureaucrats, and the Distribution of Police Services. Unpublished M.S. Thesis, Department of Political Science, University of North Carolina.
Wycoff, M.A.
1994   Community Policing Strategies. Unpublished report. Washington, DC: Police Foundation.
Zatz, M.S.
1987   Chicano youth gangs and crime: The creation of a moral panic. *Contemporary Crises* 11:129-158.
Zhao, J., and N. Lovrich
1998   Determinants of minority employment in American municipal police agencies: The representation of African American officers. *Journal of Criminal Justice* 26:267-277.
Zingraff, M.T., H. Marcinda Mason, W.R. Smith, D. Tomaskovic-Devey, P. Warren, H.L. McMurray, and C.R. Fenlon
2000   *Evaluating North Carolina State Highway Patrol Data: Citations, Warnings, and Searches in 1998*. Raleigh, NC: North Carolina Department of Crime Control and Public Safety.

Appendix

Biographical Sketches

WESLEY G. SKOGAN *(Chair)* is professor of political science at Northwestern University and a member of the research faculty of Northwestern's Institute for Policy Research—positions he has held for almost two decades. He is the sole or principal author of six books whose subjects reflect his eclectic research interests in law and politics, including community policing, crime in urban America, crime victims and victim services, and how communities and neighborhoods cope with crime. His book, *Disorder and Decline: Crime and the Spiral of Decay in American Cities* won the 1991 distinguished scholar award of the American Sociological Association. Most of his current research focuses on citizens as producers and consumers of law. He has conducted surveys for Great Britain's Home Office on contacts between the police and the public in England and Wales; as well as surveys on drug enforcement in public housing in Washington, DC; problem-solving policing and racial conflict in the United States; crime and the racial fears of white Americans; community participation in community policing; and reactions to crime in cross-national perspective. He was a member of the National Research Council's Committee on Law and Justice. He has a Ph.D. in political science from Northwestern University

DAVID H. BAYLEY is distinguished professor in the School of Criminal Justice at the University at Albany, State University of New York. He was dean of the School of Criminal Justice from 1995 to 1999. A specialist in international criminal justice, with particular interest in policing, he has done extensive research in India, Japan, Australia, Canada, Britain, Singapore, and the United States. His work has focused on strategies of policing, police reform, accountability, and the tactics of patrol officers in discretionary law enforcement situations. Recently he served as a consultant to the U.S. government and the United Nations on police reform in Bosnia. His most recent books are *What Works in Policing* (1998) and *Police for the Future* (1994). He has an M.A. from Oxford University and a Ph.D. from Princeton University.

LAWRENCE D. BOBO is the Norman Tishman and Charles M. Diker professor of sociology and African and African American studies at Harvard University. He is also acting chair of Harvard's Department of African and African American Studies and acting director of the W.E.B. Du Bois Institute. He served on the National Research Council's Panel on Poverty and Family Assistance, and also on the board of overseers for the National Opinion Research Center's General Social Survey. He chaired the 1991 national conference of the American Association for Public Opinion Research. His research interests include racial attitudes and relations, social psychology, public opinion, and political behavior. He is an author or editor of several books on these topics, most recently *Prejudice in Politics: Public Opinion, Group Position, and Wisconsin Treaty Rights Conflict*. He is founding co-editor of the *Du Bois Review: Social Science Research on Race*. He is currently writing a book on the 2000 presidential election and a second on race and crime in American public opinion. He has M.A. and Ph.D. degrees in sociology from the University of Michigan.

RUTH M. DAVIS is president and chief executive officer of the Pymatuning Group, Inc., in Alexandria, Virginia, which specializes in industrial modernization strategies and technology development. She is chairman of the Aerospace Corporation and vice-chairman of the Betac Corporation. She serves on the boards of 12 corporations and private organizations and was a member of the board of regents of the National Library of Medicine from 1989 to 1992. She has served as assistant secretary of energy for resource applications, and deputy undersecretary of defense for research and advanced technology. She has taught at Harvard University and at the University of Pennsylvania, and she currently serves on the University of Pennsylvania's board of overseers of the School of Engineering and Applied Science. She also serves on a number of advisory committees to the federal government, the National Research Council, and the National Academy of Engineering. She was elected to the National Academy of Engineering in 1976. She advises and provides management coordination services to the Law Enforcement Technology Transfer Program, a joint effort of the Department of Justice and the Department of Defense. She has a Ph.D. in mathematics from the University of Maryland.

JOHN E. ECK is associate professor in the Division of Criminal Justice at the University of Cincinnati, where he teaches graduate courses on research methods, police effectiveness, and criminal justice policy and undergraduate classes on police administration. His research focuses on the prevention of crime at places, the analysis and mapping of crime hot spots, drug dealing and trafficking control, criminal investigations, and police problem-solving strategies. He is a former director of research for the Police Executive Research Forum, where he helped pioneer the development and testing of problem-oriented policing. He has served as a consultant to the Office of Community Oriented Policing Services, the National Institute of Justice, the Police Foundation, the Police Executive Research Forum, the Royal Canadian Mounted Police, and the London Metropolitan Police. He has a Ph.D. in criminology from the University of Maryland.

KATHLEEN FRYDL (*Study Director*), who served as a program officer of the Committee on Law and Justice, is an assistant professor of history at the University of California, Berkeley. She has a Ph.D. in American history from the University of Chicago (2000); her dissertation was on the World War II Servicemen's Readjustment Act (the GI Bill).

DAVID A. KLINGER is associate professor of criminology at the University of Missouri, St. Louis. His research interests include a broad array of issues in the field of crime and justice, with an emphasis on the organization and actions of the modern police. He has published scholarly manuscripts that address arrest practices, the use of force, and how features of communities affect the actions of patrol officers. He recently completed a federally funded research project on officer-involved shootings and is completing another federally funded study, which examines police special weapons and tactics (SWAT) teams. In 1997 he was the recipient of the American Society of Criminology's inaugural Ruth Caven young scholar award for outstanding early career contributions to the discipline of criminology. He has an M.A. in justice from American University and a Ph.D. in sociology from the University of Washington. Prior to pursuing his graduate degrees, he worked as a patrol officer for the Los Angeles and Redmond, Washington, Police Departments.

JANET LAURITSEN is professor of criminology and criminal justice at the University of Missouri-St. Louis and a fellow of the National Consortium on Violence Research at Carnegie Mellon University. She recently completed a visiting fellowship at the Bureau of Justice Statistics in Washington, DC. Her areas of interest are causes and consequences of victimization, the social context of crime, and quantitative research methods. Her current research focuses on disentangling the effects of individual, family, and community factors on the risk of violent victimization in the United States. Work in progress describes how the risk of violence is related to race, ethnicity, gender, family structure, and community disadvantage. She has published widely in the areas of violence, neighborhood disadvantage and crime, juvenile violence, and research methods. She currently serves on the editorial advisory board of the *Journal of Quantitative Criminology*. She has a Ph.D. in sociology from the University of Illinois at Urbana.

TRACEY MACLIN is professor of law at Boston University. His teaching and research interests include criminal procedure, constitutional law, and constitutional theory He has written numerous amicus curiae briefs on issues related to the constitutional right to be free from unreasonable searches and seizures, including for two cases argued before the U.S. Supreme Court. In addition to his teaching responsibilities at the School of Law, he has held visiting professorships at the law schools of Harvard and Cornell universities. He has also served as counsel of record for the American Civil Liberties Union and the National Association of Criminal Defense Lawyers in a number of U.S. Supreme Court cases. He is currently president of the board of directors of the Civil Liberties Union of Massachusetts. In 1999 he presented a review of the Supreme Court's 1998-1999 term at the Federal Judicial Center and "Driving While Black? A Study in Search and Seizure" at a meeting of the National Bar Association. Before teaching law, he clerked for Chief Judge Boyce F. Martin, Jr., of the U.S. Court of Appeals for the Sixth Circuit and practiced with the law firm of Cahill, Gordon and Reindel in New York. He a J.D. from Columbia University.

STEPHEN D. MASTROFSKI is the director of the Administration of Justice Program, director of the Center for Justice Leadership and Management, and professor of public and international affairs at George Mason University. He previously held positions on the faculty of the School of Criminal Justice at Michigan State University and the Administration of Justice Department at the Pennsylvania State University, and was a visiting fellow at the U.S. Department of Justice. His research interests include police reform and organizational change, measuring the performance of police organizations, testing theories of officer behavior, and field methods in criminological research. He and several colleagues recently conducted the Project on Policing Neighborhoods, a study on community policing at the street level, based on nearly 7,000 hours of systematic observation of patrol officers. He is widely published on the topic of policing, including police organizations, operations, and performance; communities and the police; and police innovation and reform. He has a Ph.D. in political science from the University of North Carolina, Chapel Hill.

TRACEY L. MEARES is professor of law at the University of Chicago and a research fellow at the American Bar Foundation. She is also a faculty member of the University of Chicago Center for the Study of Race, Politics and Culture and an executive committee member of the Northwestern/University of Chicago Joint Center for Poverty Research. Previously she served as an honors program trial attorney in the Antitrust Division of the U.S. Department of Justice and prior to that clerked for Judge Harlington Wood, Jr., of the U.S. Court of Appeals for the Seventh Circuit. Her teaching and research interests center on criminal procedure and criminal law policy, with a particular emphasis on empirical investigation of these subjects. She has a J.D. from the University of Chicago Law School.

MARK H. MOORE is the Daniel and Florence Guggenheim professor of criminal justice policy and management at the John F. Kennedy School of Government and director of the Hauser Center for Nonprofit Institutions at Harvard University. Founding Chair of the Kennedy School's Committee on Executive Programs, he served in that role for more than a decade. He is the faculty chair of the School's Program in Criminal Justice Policy and Management. He is a member of the National Research Council's Committee on Law and Justice and served as chair of the Committee on Lethal School Violence. His research interests are in public management and leadership, criminal justice policy and management, and the intersection of the two. In the area of public management, he has recently published *Creating Public Value: Strategic Management in Government*. In the area of criminal justice policy, he has written two books: *Buy and Bust: The Effective Regulation of an Illicit Market in Heroin* and *Dangerous Offenders: The Elusive Targets of Justice*. In the intersection of public management and criminal justice, he has written (with others) *From Children to Citizens: The Mandate for Juvenile Justice* and *Beyond 911: A New Era for Policing*. He has M.P.P. and Ph.D. degrees in public policy from Harvard University.

RALPH PATTERSON (*Senior Project Assistant*) is responsible for handling administrative matters and logistics for various studies under the auspices of the Committee on Law and Justice. Previously he worked for the Competitive Enterprise Institute in Washington, DC, on projects involving environment and health and safety issues. He has a B.A. in history from American University.

RUTH D. PETERSON is professor of sociology and director of the Criminal Justice Research Center at Ohio State University, where she has been on the faculty since 1985. She is also a fellow of the National Consortium of Violence Research, where she coordinates the Race and Ethnicity Research Program Area. She has conducted research on legal decision making and sentencing, crime and deterrence, and, most recently, patterns of urban crime. She is widely published in the areas of capital punishment, race, gender, and socioeconomic disadvantage. Her current research focuses on the linkages among racial residential segregation, concentrated social disadvantage and race-specific crime, and the social context of prosecutorial and court decisions. She has a Ph.D. in sociology from the University of Wisconsin-Madison.

ELAINE B. SHARP is professor of political science at the University of Kansas. Previously she was chair of the department and director of the Institute for Public Policy and Business Research at the University of Kansas. Her research interests include urban public policy and urban governance issues and, at the national level, processes of social policy formation. She has investigated variation in city governments' responses to volatile morality issues, such as abortion clinic protests, gay rights proposals, needle exchange programs, pornography, sexually explicit enterprises, and hate crimes. She was president of the American Political Science Association's organized sections on urban politics and on public policy. She has a Ph.D. in political science from the University of North Carolina, Chapel Hill.

LAWRENCE W. SHERMAN is director of the Jerry Lee Center of Criminology, chair of the Graduate Group in Criminology, and the Albert M. Greenfield professor of human relations in the Department of Sociology at the University of Pennsylvania. He previously served as distinguished university professor and chair of the Department of Criminology and Criminal Justice at the University of Maryland, as Seth Boyden distinguished visiting professor at Rutgers University, and as assistant and associate professor of criminal justice at the State University of New York at Albany. Since beginning his career as a civilian research analyst in the New York City Police Department as an Alfred P. Sloan urban fellow in 1971, he has collaborated with more than 30 police agencies around the world, evaluating policies designed to prevent crime, reduce domestic violence, get illegal guns off the streets, prevent police corruption, close down crack houses, and help victims of crime. He is the author or coauthor of four books and hundreds of articles on these topics. He is currently collaborating with the Australian Federal Police on an evaluation of victim-centered restorative justice programs for juvenile violence and crime. In 2002, he served as president of the American Society of Criminology. He has an M.A. from the University of Chicago, a diploma in criminology from Cambridge University, and a Ph.D. in Sociology from Yale University.

SAMUEL WALKER is Isaacson professor of criminal justice at the University of Nebraska at Omaha. He is the author of 11 books on policing, criminal justice policy, and civil liberties, including *Police Accountability*.

His current research involves police accountability, focusing primarily on citizen oversight of the police and police early warning systems. He has served as a consultant to the Civil Rights Division of the U.S. Justice Department and assisted in their investigations of the New Jersey State Police and the Metropolitan Police Department of Washington, DC. In June 2001, he received the distinguished alumni award from the College of Humanities of Ohio State University. He has a Ph.D. in American history from Ohio State University.

DAVID WEISBURD is professor of of criminology at the Hebrew University Law School in Jerusalem and professor of criminology and criminal justice at the University of Maryland, College Park. He is also a senior fellow at the Police Foundation and chair of its research advisory committee. He has held academic or research positions at Yale Law School, the Vera Institute of Justice, and Rutgers University, and as director of the Center for Crime Prevention Studies. He has broad experience in research and statistics in criminal justice. He has served as a principal investigator for a number of federally supported research studies, including the Minneapolis Hot Spots Experiment and the Drug Market Analysis Program in Jersey City. He has also served as a scientific and statistical adviser to local, national, and international organizations, including the National Institute of Justice, the Institute of Law and Justice, the Office of National Drug Control Policy, the New Jersey Administrative Office of the Courts, the British Home Office Research Unit, and the Israeli Ministry of Police. He is author of a number of books on such topics as violent crime, white-collar crime, policing, criminal justice statistics, and social deviance. He has M.Phil. and Ph.D. degrees in sociology from Yale University.

ROBERT WORDEN is associate professor of criminal justice at the University at Albany, State University of New York. He is also a gubernatorial appointee to the New York State Law Enforcement Accreditation Council. Most of his research has focused on the police or drug control policy, and it includes basic and applied studies on the accountability and responsiveness of criminal justice institutions to the public. This includes basic research—concerned with explaining the behavior of criminal justice actors in terms of political, organizational, and social influences—and applied research—concerned with the implementation and outcomes of criminal justice policies and programs. He is currently engaged in a number of projects that examine the delivery of police services in Albany. He is also the site director of the Capital District Arrestee Drug Abuse Monitoring (ADAM) project, and he directs the research for Project Safe Neighborhoods in the Northern District of New York. His most recent publications examine police officers' attitudes, behavior, and supervisory influences and police use of force. He has a Ph.D. from the University of North Carolina, Chapel Hill.

Index

A

Academy of Criminal Justice Sciences, 22
Accreditation, 102, 308–309
Activities of policing
   in community policing, 32, 85–88, 233
   conceptualization of, 57
   crackdowns, 236–237
   for crime prevention, 73
   disorder policing, 228–230
   exercise of authority, 63–69
   field interrogations, 231
   in focused policing, 235–236
   informal enforcement measures, 162–164
   information collection and processing,
     75–77, 166–168
   innovative approaches, 94–95
   investigations, 73–75
   legal constraints to, 253–254
   maintaining order, 69–71
   organizational measures and outputs,
     157–162
   in problem-oriented policing, 92–93, 243
   public interaction in, 58, 62–63
   random preventive patrols, 5, 17, 226
   for reducing fear in community, 86
   research needs, 214–215, 218
   service activities, 71, 164–165, 191
   specialized services, 77–78, 176–179,
     215–216, 310–311
   standard model, 94, 223–224
   terrorist incident prevention and
     response, 209–214
   time allocation for, 71
   uniformed patrol, 57–62
   See also specific activity
Aggressive preventive patrol, 60, 61
Allocation of police resources, 71, 314–317
American Bar Association, 22, 29
American Indian police departments, 50
American Police Systems, 21
American Society of Criminology, 22
Americans with Disabilities Act, 54
Arrests
   agency size as factor in rate of, 172
   citizen characteristics as factor in, 116–
     128
   deterrent effectiveness of, offender
     characteristics and, 242
   domestic violence intervention, 64–65,
     231–232, 309–310
   gender differences as factor in, 151, 152
   as goal of policing, 93
   illegal search leading to, 264–265
   legal definition, 159
   neighborhood characteristics and
     likelihood of, 191–192
   officer attitudes as factor in, 135, 136
   officer discretion, 64, 70
   organizational data on, 159
   percentage of investigations resulting in,
     74

police behavior in urban environments,
190–195
political factors in police practice and
policy, 199–200
at protest demonstrations, 65–66
racial factors in, 64, 122–126, 149–150,
191–192, 316
situational determinants of police
behavior, 115–117
state legislation and, 205
in traffic stops, 72, 160–161
vs. taking into custody, 70
See also Case clearance
Auditing organizations, 102
Auto theft, 246

B

Beat Health Study, 240
Behavior of police. *See* Determinants of
police behavior; Lawfulness of police
behavior
Bicycle patrol, 58
Boston Ceasefire project, 241
Brown v. *Mississippi*, 253–254
Bureau of Alcohol, Tobacco and Firearms,
76, 77
Bureau of Justice Assistance, 103
Bureau of Justice Statistics, 9, 107, 166,
328, 329–330

C

Case clearance
effectiveness of follow-up investigations,
227–228
organizational data, 160
rate, 74
size of police agency and, 172–173
Challenge of Crime in a Free Society, The, 20
Citation issuance, 160–161
Citizen oversight of police, 6, 19, 55, 202–
204, 288–289, 310
Citizen policing, 56–57, 89
Civil liberties, 57, 195
data collection on police practice, 319
excessive force lawsuits, 278–280
Miranda rights, 207, 255–258
policing of protest demonstrations, 65–
66, 70–71, 208

proactive policing and, 61–62, 75
search and seizure protections, 262–263
Civil Rights Act, 54, 81
Civilian review boards. *See* Citizen oversight
of police
Commission on Accreditation for Law
Enforcement Agencies, 102
Communication systems. *See* Dispatch
system
Community characteristics, 155–156
crime risk, 217–218
organization of police agency and, 174–
175
police behavior and, 189–193, 216
police corruption risk and, 273
See also Urban areas
Community Oriented Policing Program, 25
Community Oriented Policing Services
(COPS), 30–33, 103, 105, 207
Community police specialists, 178–179
Community policing
activities, 32, 85–88, 233
adoption and diffusion, 104–105, 106,
311–312
benefits, 61
characteristics, 5, 18, 84, 85, 233, 248–
249
community relations and, 61, 62, 88,
89–90, 91–92, 235, 298, 307
conceptual basis, 24
COPS effectiveness, 31–32
degree of innovation in, 84–85, 94–95
educational attainment of officers and
performance in, 140
effectiveness, 7, 33–34, 232–235, 246,
250–251
federal support for, 1, 11, 105–106, 207
gender differences in officer behavior in,
151–152
legitimating effects of, 312
officer attitudes in performance of, 32
organizational structure of policing for,
88–89, 173–174, 309
police culture and, 132
proactive policing and, 61–62, 87–88
problem-oriented policing and, 90–92, 93
recruitment and training of officers for,
105–106, 143, 144
relations with other government agencies
in, 89–90
research recommendations, 9, 33–34,
166, 330

research trends, 14, 24, 25
role of patrol officers in, 60
specialization in police agencies for, 78, 177, 178–179
Community Profile Development project, 142–143
Complainant behavior and characteristics
delay in calling police, 227
demeanor toward police, 119
as factor in police behavior, 116, 119, 120–121, 122, 192
gender, 122
perceptions of police legitimacy, 292
race, 123–124
social class, 120–121
Complaints about police behavior, 161–162
CompStat, 16, 76, 167, 174, 230, 309
adoption trends, 185
effects on policing practice, 185, 186–188
management structure and function, 186–187, 188
program features, 186–187
rationale, 185–186
research needs, 188–189
Computer-aided dispatch, 58
Conflict theory, 193–195, 216
COPS. *See* Community Oriented Policing Services
Corruption, 6, 7, 18
causes, 271–275
definition, 268
environmental risk factors, 273–275
forms of, 268
government commissions to investigate, 289–290
measurement, 268–271
officer characteristics predisposing to, 271–272
opportunity for, 272
organizational environment and, 272–273
political factors in police behavior and policy, 201
strategies for preventing, 287–288
in vice units, 74–75, 78
Cost of policing, 51
federal spending, 53–54, 105
County police force, 49–50
Court decisions, 99–100
influence on police behavior and policies, 54, 206–207, 216, 253–255, 260–261, 263–267, 273, 279–280
on interrogation practice, 253–258
racial equality concerns, 253–254
sanctioning police discretion in stop and search procedures, 318
on search and seizure procedure, 262–263
traffic enforcement and, 204–205
Crime control and prevention
activities of, 73
case clearance rate and, 227–228
characteristics of effective policing, 95–96
citizen requests for police service, 58–59, 60
citizen rights and, 61–62, 75
community policing perspective, 85–88
conceptualization, 72
disorder policing, 228–230
effectiveness of problem-oriented policing, 244–246
fairness in policing and, 1
federal law enforcement agencies, 50
focus on previous offenders, 236, 240–243
focused model, 4–5, 17–18
geo-focused policing, 181–183, 216
individual-level intervention, 87, 88
information technology for, 76
models of social regulation, 294–297
nonenforcement activities in, 164
nonpolice factors, 217–218
nonpolice participants, 56–57
opportunities for improving police capacity, 3
origins of suspect profiling, 317–318
patrol officer activities, 59–61, 71
police crackdown effectiveness, 236–237
in problem-oriented policing, 91
public expectations for policing, 1, 12
random patrol strategy, 226
recommendations for improving, 7, 328
research methodology, 4
research spending, 30
research trends and topics, 23–24
restorative policing rationale and effects, 305–307
situational approach, 87–88
size of police agency and, 224–225
standard model, 4, 17, 223–224
traffic enforcement and, 231
youth firearms violence prevention, 32

Crime-mapping, 100–101, 236, 238
Crime rate
    community characteristics and, 217–218
    declines in 1990s, 25, 229–230
    local distribution of police resources
        and, 315
    structure of police industry and, 25
Culture, police, 16, 18
    community policing and, 132
    gender issues, 80
    officer behavior and, 6, 16, 130–133

D

DARE program, 87
Data collection for research
    on community liaison and mobilization
        activities, 165–166
    on corruption, 268–271
    federal support for, 1, 11, 76–77, 215
    on informal activities of policing, 17,
        214–215
    on information technologies and
        practices, 167, 168
    on nonenforcement activities, 164–165
    on officer behavior, 8
    on organizational structure and
        functioning, 9, 214–215
    on policing processes, 165
    on public assessments of policing, 8, 292
    on racial profiling, 286–287, 319–323,
        324, 325–326
    recommendations, 262, 328, 329
    on search and seizure procedures, 267
    on use of force by police, 7–8, 67, 259–
        260, 261–262
Department of Justice, 1–2, 21, 30, 53, 105,
    277
Detective work. See Follow-up
    investigations
Determinants of police behavior, 215–216
    citizen behavior and characteristics, 116–
        128, 192
    citizen review boards, 202–204
    in community policing, 32
    court decisions and government
        regulation, 54, 206–207, 216, 253–
        255, 256–258, 260–261, 263–267,
        273, 279–280
    diversity of police force, 147–148

    ecological theory of, 190
    environmental factors, 155–156
    federal standards, 54, 207–214
    importance of research in, 109–110
    legal liability concerns, 275–280
    legally relevant factors, 3, 7, 15–16,
        115–117, 152–153
    local government controls, 54
    neighborhood characteristics, 189–193,
        216
    organizational factors, 4, 16, 110, 155,
        156, 171–172, 174–175, 215–216,
        282–288
    police culture, 6, 16, 130–133
    police leadership, 283
    political environment, 156, 196–202
    recruitment and training, 141–147, 153–
        154
    research methodology, 3, 15–16, 111–
        113
    research needs, 152–154
    research trends, 22–23
    state government standards, 54–55, 205–
        206
    urban context, 193–195, 216
    See also Environmental influences on
        police behavior; Officer
        characteristics; Situational factors in
        policing
Deterrence model of social regulation, 294–
    296
Disaster response, 75
Discretion of individual officers, 14–15, 57
    arrest decisions, 64, 70
    domestic violence intervention, 64–65
    formalization of police policies and,
        184–185
    in geo-focused policing, 182–183
    public perception of policing and, 2–3,
        15
    racist practices, 254
    research, 22–23, 24
    specialization and, 179
Dispatch system, 58–59, 60
Domestic violence, 64–65, 122, 200, 231–
    232, 285, 309–310
Drug crimes and drug law enforcement,
    206, 239, 240, 265, 317–318
Drug Enforcement Agency, 317
Drunk-driving enforcement, 172, 310
Due process, 253, 262

E

Early warning systems, 285
Ecological theory, 190
Educational attainment of officers, 79, 138, 139–141, 329
Effectiveness of policing
  assessment of, 7
  case clearance rate, 74, 160
  community policing, 7, 33–34, 232–235, 246, 250–251
  comparison of strategies, 247–251
  COPS investments and, 31–32
  crackdowns, 236–237
  disorder policing, 228–230
  drop in 1990s crime rate and, 25
  fairness in policing and, 2, 19
  federally mandated research, 1–2, 11
  field interrogations, 231
  focused model of policing, 235–243, 246–247, 250, 251
  follow-up investigations, 227–228
  geo-focused policing, 181–183
  hot-spots policing, 238–240
  innovation and, 95–96
  intensive enforcement strategies, 228–232
  models of crime control, 4–5, 17–18
  models of social regulation, 294–297
  perceived legitimacy of police and, 291, 293–294, 304–306
  potential effects of government sponsorship of research in, 34–35
  proactive patrol methods, 60–61
  problem-oriented policing, 33–34, 91, 243, 244–246, 251
  racial differences in public perception, 300
  random preventive patrols, 5, 17, 226
  recommendations for improving, 7, 328
  research methodologies, 218–223
  research needs, 247
  research trends and topics, 13–14, 23–24, 25
  response time and, 226–227
  size of agency and, 168–173, 215
  size of police agency and, 224–225
  specialization and, 78
  standard model, 223–224, 246, 247, 248, 249–250
  structural factors, 2, 52

  suspect characteristics and, 242–243
  understudied police activities, 218
  youth firearms violence prevention, 32
  See also Crime control and prevention
Environmental influences on police behavior, 155–156
  corruption risk, 273–275
  neighborhood characteristics, 189–193, 216
  scope of, 189
  size of community and police agency, 5, 17, 49, 168–173
  See also Community characteristics
Evidence-based policing, 308

F

Fairness in policing
  citizens' legal behavior related to perception of, 6, 19
  effectiveness of policing and, 2, 19
  federal enforcement, 53
  public perception, 5–6, 15, 19, 115
  research recommendations, 7–8, 314–317
  research trends, 13–14
  in resource allocation, 314–317
  See also Legitimacy of police; Racial profiling
Family intervention, 87
Federal Bureau of Investigation National Academy, 208–209
Federal government action, 1–2, 11, 30–34
  capacity to influence structure of policing, 53
  community policing initiatives, 25, 105–106
  data collection, 1, 11, 76–77, 215
  as driver of innovation, 103, 327
  to eliminate racial profiling, 324–325
  employment standards, 54
  influence on police behavior and policies, 54, 207–214
  local context of policing and, 2, 14
  police procedure standards, 54
  prosecution of excessive force cases, 277, 280–281
  recommendations for, 10
  research spending, 30, 31, 53–54
  spending on law enforcement, 53–54

Federal law enforcement, 50
Firearm violence, 32
    intensive enforcement strategy, 239, 241
Focused model of policing, 4–5, 17–18, 249
    effectiveness, 235–243, 246–247, 250,
        251
    recommendations, 7
    trends, 236
Follow-up investigations, 5, 17, 73–75
    effectiveness, 227–228
    opportunities for improving crime
        control, 15
    technological advances, 228
Foot patrols, 233, 234
Ford Foundation, 29–30, 100
Foreign police practices, 12, 53
Fourteenth Amendment, 253
Fourth Amendment, 262, 263, 266
Functions of the Police in Modern Society,
    The, 23

G

Gang crime, 201, 311
Gay and lesbian officers, 82
Gender
    citizen characteristics as determinants of
        police behavior, 121–122
    female officers, 79–80
    officer's, performance and, 147–148,
        151–152, 154
    as outcome factor in police-citizen
        interactions, 16
    political factors in police policy, 200
    recruitment trends, 132, 147, 312–313
Geo-focused policing, 181–182, 216, 236
    See also Focused model of policing
Guns. *See* Firearm violence

H

High-speed pursuits, 285
Hot-spots policing, 5, 17–19, 61, 100–101
    effectiveness, 238–240
    rationale, 237–238
    See also CompStat; Focused model of
        policing

I

Impact munitions, 69
Information management in police work
    activities in, 75–77, 83–84, 166–168
    CompStat program, 185–186, 187, 188
    for hot-spots policing, 5
    innovation in, 76
    for internal accountability analysis, 286–
        287
    problem identification in problem-
        oriented policing, 92–93
    for racial profiling assessment, 319–323,
        325–326
    recommendations for research on, 167,
        168
Innovation in policing
    adopting units and programs to foster
        legitimacy, 308–312
    adoption and diffusion of, 96, 97–99,
        102–103, 104–105
    CompStat as, 185, 188
    as continuous process, 95
    effectiveness of policing and, 95–96
    federal role, 103, 327
    identifying, 94, 98
    in information processing, 76
    local governance as source of, 101
    organizational structure of policing and,
        2, 47–48, 98, 106
    police receptiveness to, 6–7
    process of origination, 97–98, 99–103
    professional organizations as source of,
        101–102
    recent efforts, 82–83, 94
    research goals, 12
    research needs, 96, 99
    research recommendations, 9, 106–108,
        329–330
    as social learning process, 102–103
    strategic, 84–85
    technological, 83–84
    through court order, 99–100
    through federal action, 103
    through research, 100
    See also Community policing; Problem-
        oriented policing
Intelligence testing, 138
Internal affairs investigations, 285–286
International Association of Chiefs of
    Police, 101, 159, 261, 262

Interrogations, 6, 54
  effectiveness, 231
  effects of legal regulation on police
    practice, 253–254
  legal rights of citizens in, 256–258
  non-custodial interviews, 257–258
  police compliance with regulations on,
    256–258

J

Jersey City Drug Hot Spots Experiment, 239
Jersey City Drug Market Analysis
  Experiment, 240, 245
Jersey City Problem Oriented Policing in
  Violent Crime Places, 239
Justice Research and Statistics Association,
  159
Justice Without Trial, 22–23

K

Kansas City Crack House Raids
  Experiment, 239
Kansas City Gun Project, 239, 240
Kansas City Preventive Patrol Experiment,
  27–28, 100
Knapp Commission, 269–270

L

Law Enforcement Assistance
  Administration, 30
Law Enforcement Management and
  Administrative Statistics, 9, 107,
  165–166, 329–330
Lawfulness of police behavior, 5–6
  citizen complaint data, 161–162
  definition, 18, 252, 291
  external oversight, 288–290
  influence of law on, 54, 206–207, 216,
    253–255, 256–258, 260–261, 263–
    267, 273, 279–280
  internal affairs investigations, 285–286
  legal liability of individual officer, 275–
    280
  public perception of, 5–6, 19, 115
  recommendations for improving, 7–8,
    290, 328

regulatory trends, 253–255
  research needs, 7, 18–19, 290
  research recommendations, 323, 324,
    326, 328
  research trends, 13–14, 252–253
  state government oversight, 54–55
  strategies for promoting, 18–19, 275–
    290
  in use of force, 258–262
Leadership, police
  governance structure of police agencies,
    51–52
  influence on officer behavior, 283
  lawfulness of police behavior and, 6
  limitations of current research, 4
Legislation
  to eliminate racial profiling, 325
  federal, 1, 11, 54
  recommendations for, 7
  See also specific legislation
Legitimacy of police, 5–6, 218
  citizen behavior and, 304–308
  community policing effects, 312
  consequences of, 304–308
  definition, 18, 252, 291
  determinants of public perception, 15,
    291–292, 303–304
  disadvantaged citizens' perceptions of,
    307–308
  effectiveness of policing and, 291, 293–
    294, 304–306
  local control of police and, 51
  model of self-regulation, 296–297
  organizational role in establishing, 292,
    308–312
  perception of procedural justice and,
    301–303
  personnel practices and, 312–314
  proactive policing and, 61–62
  public perspectives, 292–293
  racial context, 300–301
  recommendations for improving, 8, 329
  research methods, 292, 299
  research needs, 326
  sources of, 298–299
  See also Fairness in policing; Public
    opinion and understanding
Lethal force, 66–67
  circumstances, 66–67, 260
  department and government policy, 67,
    259

formalized police policies on, 184–185, 216, 284–285
frequency of shootings, 66, 67, 259–261
organizational data, 157–158
organizational differences, 157
political factors in police behavior and policy, 199–200
racial context, 123, 259–260
See also Use of force by police
Local policing, 51
fairness in allocation of resources, 314–317
local government oversight, 55
organizational structure, 49–50
size of police force, 169, 170
Locally Initiated Research Project, 33
Lojack, 246

M

Mapp v. *Ohio,* 263, 280
Mayors, 196, 198–202, 261
Media portrayals, 47, 171
Mentally disordered citizens, 126–128
Militarist stance, 212–213
Minneapolis Domestic Violence Experiment, 100
Minneapolis Hot Spots Patrol Experiment, 238
Minneapolis Spouse Assault Project, 25
Miranda rights, 207, 255–258
Moral behavior, 296
Municipal police force, 49, 52
distribution of police resources, 316
size and structure, 170
See also Urban areas

N

National Crime Information Center, 76–77
National Evaluation of Youth Firearms Violence Initiative, 32
National Instant Criminal Background Check System, 77
National Institute of Justice, 1, 11, 23, 30–33, 53–54, 103, 112–113, 167
recommendations for, 10, 330
National Science Foundation, 30, 112
National Sheriffs Association, 101

O

Observational studies, 27, 63, 220–221
police behavior research, 111–113
Occupational Safety and Health Administration, 56
Office of Justice Programs, 53, 54
Officer characteristics
attitudes and beliefs, 135–136, 144–145, 153, 190
attitudes toward community policing, 32
authoritarian personality, 129–130
corruption risk, 271–272
cynicism, 133–134, 190
demographic trends, 79
early warning systems, 285
educational attainment, 79, 138, 139–141, 329
female officers, 79–80, 147–148, 151–152, 154
gay and lesbian officers, 82
integrity, 274–275
job satisfaction, 134
knowledge and skills, 137–139
limitations of current research, 3–4, 16
minority officers, 79, 81–82
performance assessments, 8, 76, 282–283
race, 147–150, 154
research base, 129
scope of, 110
search and seizure practices and, 265
training experiences, 141–147
Ohio v. *Robinette,* 318
Omnibus Crime Control and Safe Streets Act (1968), 1, 11
Operation Pipeline, 317
Organizational structure and functioning, 14–15
change processes, 9, 14
citizen oversight, 202–204
community liaison and mobilization activities, 165–166
for community policing, 85, 88–89, 309
complexity, 176–181
CompStat features and effects, 185–189
coordination among components, 52–53
corruption risk, 272–273
current state, 2, 48–51, 170–171
decentralization, 2, 14, 52–53, 88–89, 173–175

as determinant of police behavior, 4, 16, 110, 155, 156, 171–172, 215–216, 282–288
distribution of employees, 58
effect of civil lawsuits against police, 279–280
effectiveness of training programs influenced by, 144
in establishing legitimacy, 292, 308–312
external oversight, 288–290
federal capacity to influence, 53
formalization of police policies, 184–185
geo-focused policing, 181–183
governance, 51–52
hierarchical differentiation, 179–181
information collection and processing activities, 166–168
innovation and, 47–48, 98, 106
innovation in, 83
interaction with other governmental agencies, 204–205, 210, 211
job specialization, 77–78, 176–179
level of government and, 49–50
measures and indicators of, 156–162
militarism in, 212–213
nonenforcement service delivery, 164–165
number of agencies, 48, 50
number of employees, 48, 50
political context, 196–202
populations served, 48–49
for problem-oriented policing, 244
problems of fragmentation, 52–53
research needs, 214–216
research recommendations, 9
research trends and topics, 4, 23
self-assessment for legal compliance, 286–287
significance of, in achieving goals of policing, 168
size of agency, 5, 17, 49, 168–173, 215
state government influence, 54–55, 205–206
terrorist incident preparedness, 209–214
traditional model, 93–94
use of force policies, 282–283
See also Leadership, police
Overtime pay, 51

P

Peacekeeping mission of police, 69–71
Personality traits of officers
authoritarian, 129–130
corruption risk, 271–272
Police Executive Research Forum, 29–30, 101
Police Foundation, 29, 100
Police Project of the Philadelphia Public Interest Law Center, 261
Police-Public Contact Surveys, 159
Police Services Study, 112, 127, 191, 192
Police Systems in the United States, 21
Political context of policing, 4, 16–17, 52
commissions to investigate police behavior, 289–290
as determinant of police behavior, 156, 196–202
local distribution of police resources and, 315
police corruption risk and, 273–274
police hiring patterns, 225
race factors in police-citizen interaction and, 125
Pregnancy Discrimination Act, 54
President's Commission on Law Enforcement and the Administration of Justice, 20, 21, 29, 35, 112
Prevention. See Crime control and prevention
Principal-agent theory, 196–198
Private security industry, 55–56
research recommendations, 107
Problem-oriented policing
adoption and diffusion, 104
characteristics, 5, 18, 84, 90–91, 243–244, 249
community policing and, 90–92, 93
conceptual basis, 91, 243
crime prevention strategies, 87
degree of innovation in, 84–85, 94–95
effectiveness, 33–34, 243, 244–246, 251
problem identification, 92–93, 243–244
research recommendations, 9, 33–34, 166, 330
research trends, 14
role of patrol officers, 60
Problem Oriented Policing in Violent Crime Places, 240

Procedural justice, 301–303, 307
Processes of policing, 165
Professional organizations, 101–102
Professional standards units, 285–286
Project on Policing Neighborhoods in
    Indianapolis and St. Petersburg, 32,
    112–113, 124, 127, 178–179, 192,
    193
Protest demonstrations, 65–66, 70–71, 208–
    209
Public education, 73
    in community policing, 89
Public opinion and understanding
    community policing conceptualization
        of, 86
    community policing effects on fear of
        crime, 234–235
    complaints filed against police, 161–162,
        195
    determinants of, 47, 299
    discretionary authority of individual
        officers and, 2–3, 15
    expectations for police performance, 1,
        12, 217, 292
    lawfulness of police behavior, 5–6, 19,
        115
    models of social regulation, 294–297
    of organizational structure of police
        agencies, 171
    police corruption risk and, 273
    police-public interactions, 62
    of racial profiling, 319, 325, 326
    research recommendations, 8, 107–108,
        326, 328, 329
    research trends and topics, 18, 23
    size of police agency and, 171
    See also Legitimacy of police

Q

Quasi-experimental research, 27–28, 219–
    220

R

Race and ethnicity
    arrest behavior of police and, 64, 191–
        192, 316
    legal regulation of police procedure,
        253–254
    local distribution of police resources
        and, 314–315
    officer's, 147–150
    as outcome factor in police-citizen
        interactions, 16, 64, 122–126, 148–
        150, 191–192
    perception of police fairness, 2–3, 8, 15,
        300–301
    police force composition, 79, 81–82
    political factors in police behavior and
        policy, 199, 200
    proactive policing and, 61
    racial threat hypothesis, 194
    recruitment trends, 132, 147, 312–314
    research recommendations, 125–126
    research trends, 22, 25
    search and seizure practices and, 265,
        267
    use of force by police and, 25, 123, 260,
        300–301
    use of lethal force by police and, 66,
        123, 259–260
Racial profiling, 3, 6, 18, 25, 72, 124, 240–
    241, 318–320
    accountability measures, 323–324
    data collection on police practice, 319–
        323, 324, 325–326
    federal response, 324–325
    origins of, 317–318
    police agency self-assessments, 286–287
    public perception, 319
    research recommendations, 323, 326
    research trends, 13, 15
    strategies for eliminating, 287
Random patrols, 5, 17, 226
Randomized experiments, 219, 221
Recruitment and training of officers, 139
    civil disturbance management training,
        208
    for community policing, 105–106, 143,
        144
    demographic trends, 79, 132, 147, 312–
        314
    as determinant of officer performance,
        141–147, 153–154
    early warning systems, 285
    educational attainment considerations,
        139–141, 329
    Federal Bureau of Investigation National
        Academy, 208–209
    federal role, 54

female officers, 79–81
innovative approaches, 83
limitations of current research, 3–4, 14–15, 16
minority employees, 79, 81–82
organizational environment and, 144
political context, 225
predictors of training success, 138
reform strategy, 128–129
research needs, 146
research recommendations, 8, 147, 329
screening for corruption risk, 271–272
specialization, 77–78, 176–179
state government role, 54–55
trends, 142
use of force and, 63–64
Repeat Call Policing, 238
Repeat offenders, 236, 240–243
Research
advocacy and, 24
on antiterrorist efforts, 9–10, 330
benefits of, 35
on citizen review boards, 204
on community policing, 9, 14, 24, 25, 33–34, 330
on CompStat program, 188–189
on crime control effectiveness, 4–5, 19, 23–24
on crime prevention, 30
on determinants of police behavior, 3, 15–16, 22–23, 111–113, 152–154
on discretionary authority of individual officers, 22–23, 24
on distribution of police resources, 316–317
on effectiveness of policing, 218–223, 247–251
evaluating research quality, 25, 29, 33
on extent of community liaison activities, 166
on fairness of police behavior, 7–8, 13–14, 19, 252–253
federal mandates for, 1–2, 11–12, 30
funding of, 10, 29–30, 31, 34, 53–54
future prospects, 19, 327
generalizability, 221–222
goals, 1–2, 11–12, 30–31, 34–35
on hierarchical structuring, 180
on information technologies and practices, 167, 168
on innovation in policing, 9, 12, 96, 99, 106–108, 329–330

on lawfulness of police behavior, 6, 7–8, 18–19, 290, 326, 328
methodologies, 14, 27–29, 34, 67, 111–113, 219–223
national coordination of, 10, 330–331
on nonenforcement service activities in policing, 165
on officer characteristics, 3–4
on officer training, 146–147
on organizational factors, 4, 23, 175, 214–216
outcome evaluations, 34–35
on personnel practices, 8, 16, 329
on police-public interaction, 62–63
police receptiveness to, 6–7, 13, 24, 35
potential effects of government sponsorship, 34–35
on problem-oriented policing, 9, 33–34, 166, 330
on public experiences and perceptions, 8, 18, 23, 107–108, 292, 299, 328, 329
on race factors, 125–126
scale of, 21–22, 34
scholarly journals on policing, 21–22
scope of subject matter, 22–27, 36–46
on social class variables, 121
as source of innovation, 100
on specialization, 177, 178
terrorist incident preparedness, 212–214
on traffic enforcement, 3, 15
trends in, 13–14, 20–27, 34–35
on use of force by police, 7–8, 13, 24–25, 67
See also Data collection for research
Response time, 5, 17, 226–227
Restorative policing, 305–307

S

Safe Streets Act, 327
SARA, 91
School policing, 50–51
SEADOC, 208
Searches and seizures, 6, 54
data collection, 267
legal environment, 262–263, 280
police compliance with law, 207, 263–267
pretextual, 318
racial context, 265, 267
stop and frisk procedures, 266–267

suspect profiling and, 317–318
in traffic stops, 72
warrant practices, 265–266
Self-defense, 56
Serious Habitual Offender/Drug Involved
Program, 87
Service activities in policing, 71, 164–165
neighborhood factors in delivery of, 191
research recommendations, 165
Sheriff's departments, 49–50
Situational factors in policing
arrest decisions, 64
circumstances of unlawful searches, 265
complainant behavior and
characteristics, 119
crime prevention strategies in community
policing, 87–88
legal factors, 115–117
neighborhood *vs.* city-level factors, 4,
16–17
research goals, 115
scope of, 3, 15, 110, 114
significance of, in determining police
behavior, 114
suspect behavior and characteristics,
116–128
use of lethal force by police, 66–67, 260
Size of police force, 5, 168–173, 215
adoption of innovation and, 104
community policing movement, 169–170
consolidation movement, 169, 170, 173
current profile, 49, 169
effectiveness and, 171–173, 224–225
patrol mobilization and, 170–171
public perception, 171
Social class, 120–121
local distribution of police resources
and, 315
neighborhood characteristics, 189–191
police behavior in urban environments,
193–195
Specialization in policing, 77–78, 176–179,
215–216, 310–311
terrorist incident response, 209–210
State government, 54–55, 205–206
commissions to investigate police
behavior, 289–290
State law enforcement, 50
Sting operations, 241–242
Stun guns, 69
Suburban areas, 317

Suspect characteristics, 3, 16
age, 116–117
demeanor toward police, 117–120, 124
as determinant of police behavior, 116–
128
effectiveness of arrest policies related to,
242–243
employment, 242
gender, 121–122
mental capacity, 126–128
national data collection, 76–77
perceptions of police legitimacy, 292–
293
race, 64, 122–126
social class, 120–121
SWAT teams, 77–78
Systematic social observation, 27

T

Tailored responses to crime and disorder, 5,
18, 95–96
Team policing, 176–177, 181, 182–183
Tennessee v. *Garner,* 67, 259
Terrorist threat, 75, 156, 326
coordination of policing against, 52–53
information collection and processing
activities, 166–168
interorganizational coordination in
response to, 210, 211
local context of policing and, 2
police preparedness, 209–214
research needs, 212–214
research recommendations, 9–10, 330
Terry v. *Ohio,* 266, 267
Thurman v. *Connecticut,* 310
Traffic enforcement, 3, 15, 72
citations issued, 160–161
court outcomes and, 204–205
data sources, 160–161
drunk-driving enforcement, 172, 310
effects on general crime rate, 231
outcomes of traffic stops, 72
percentage of police-public interactions
in, 62
pretextual traffic stops, 318
as proactive strategy, 60–61
race as factor in arrest decision, 123
racial profiling in, 72, 124, 286–287
Transportation system policing, 50–51

U

Undercover work, 75
Uniform Crime Reports, 159, 160, 163–164, 215
Uniformed patrols, 57–62, 63
  community policing approach, 88
  distribution of activities, 71
  female officers, 79–80
  foot patrols, 233, 234
  geo-focused policing, 181–182, 216
  as percentage of local force, 170–171
  random preventive patrol, 5, 17, 226
Unions, police, 55
United Kingdom, 53
Urban areas, 193–195, 216
  distribution of police resources, 316, 317
  See also Municipal police force
Urban Institute, 31–32, 103, 104
U.S. v. *Calandra,* 263
U.S. v. *Leon,* 265–266
Use of force by police, 6
  circumstances and outcomes, 67–68
  civil liability of officers for, 275–276, 278–280
  community policing conceptualization, 86–87
  complainant characteristics as factor in, 119
  criminal liability of officers for, 275–278
  data collection, 7–8, 67, 259–260, 261–262
  definition, 261–262
  federal standards, 277, 280–281
  by female officers, 151–152
  frequency, 64, 67–69
  influence of administrative policies, 282–285
  in managing protest demonstrations, 208
  neighborhood characteristics and, 192, 193
  nonlethal technologies, 69
  officer attitudes and, 135
  officer educational attainment and, 140–141
  officer training, 63–64
  organizational data, 158–159
  police compliance with law in, 259, 260–261

  predisposing personality, 130
  racial context, 25, 123, 192, 260, 300–301
  in range of police responses, 63–64
  research recommendations, 7–8, 262, 328
  research trends, 13, 24–25
  situational determinants of police behavior, 115
  suspect characteristics as factor in, 118–119
  techniques, 68–69
  See also Lethal force

V

Victim characteristics, 122
Violence and the Police, 21
Violence and violent crime
  demographic features, 49
  domestic conflict, 64–65
  research spending on crime prevention per life lost, 30
  youth firearms violence prevention, 32
  See also Use of force by police
Violent Crime Control and Law Enforcement Act (1994), 1, 11, 30–34, 53, 75, 104, 105, 280–281

W

Warrant searches, 265–266
  See also Searches and seizures
Whren v. United States, 318

Y

Youth
  as factor in decision to arrest, 116–117
  firearms violence prevention, 32
  preventive interventions in community policing, 87, 88

Z

Zero tolerance policing, 60, 61, 228–230